FIFTH EDITION

Know Your Merchandise

FOR RETAILERS AND CONSUMERS

ISABEL B. WINGATE, Ph.D.
Formerly of the Institute of Retail Management
New York University

KAREN R. GILLESPIE, Ed.D.
Business Education Program
New York University

Contributor

MARY E. BARRY, Ed.D.
Department of Consumer Affairs
School of Home Economics
Auburn University

GREGG DIVISION
McGraw-Hill Book Company

New York   Atlanta   Dallas   St. Louis   San Francisco   Auckland   Bogotá
Guatemala   Hamburg   Johannesburg   Lisbon   London   Madrid   Mexico
Montreal   New Delhi   Panama   Paris   San Juan   São Paulo   Singapore
Sydney   Tokyo   Toronto

Sponsoring Editors: **Mary McGarry and Sylvia L. Weber**
Editing Supervisor: **Lucy Ferriss**
Design and Art Supervisor: **Meri Shardin**
Production Supervisor: **Priscilla Taguer**

Text Designer: **Blackbirch Graphics**
Cover Designers: **Meri Shardin and Renée Kilbride**
Cover Photographer: **Walter Paul Bebirian Photography**
Photo Editor: **Mary Ann Drury**

Library of Congress Cataloging in Publication Data
Wingate, Isabel Barnum.
  Know your merchandise.
  Includes index.
  1. Consumer education. 2. Distributive education.
I. Gillespie, Karen R. II. Barry, Mary. III. Title.
TX335.W5 1984   640.73   83-18742
ISBN 0-07-071016-3

 2 3 4 5 6 7 8 9 0 DOCDOC 8 9 1 0 9 8 7 6 5 4

ISBN 0-07-071016-3

Preface

Know *Your Merchandise: For Retailers and Consumers,* Fifth Edition, meets the expressed interest of the many loyal users of previous editions. Marketing and distribution, home economics, and consumer education courses will all be enriched by the use of this current, detailed, and extensively illustrated text. Consumers and retailers will also find the book a valuable reference source.

The text concentrates on fashion and home furnishings merchandise. Products made from textiles and nontextiles, or a combination of those materials, are thoroughly analyzed, explained, and depicted. Important new articles of wearing apparel and home goods have been added, and everything throughout the book has been updated.

ORGANIZATION OF THE TEXT

The text is divided into five units containing clusters of product knowledge. The first unit gives a broad background applicable to most merchandise, but with special emphasis on men's, women's, and children's apparel and accessories, and on furniture and home accessories. Chapter 1 covers the retailer's and consumer's need for knowledge of fashion and quality in products. Chapter 2 on color (including a color wheel in full color), Chapter 3 on line and design, and Chapter 4 on the historical development of products and designs complete this unit.

Unit 2, divided into eight chapters, is devoted to natural and manmade textile fibers and fabrics, focusing on their construction and qualities. Unit 3, containing four chapters, presents information on plastics, leather, lumber, and metals. Unit 4, with eight chapters, covers men's, women's, and children's inner and outer apparel items. Chapters on furs; jewelry; shoes; such accessories as handbags, belts, gloves, luggage, umbrellas, millinery, and men's hats; and cosmetics are included. Extensive, illustrated terminology sections provide easy reference.

Unit 5 has eleven chapters on home goods. Ceramics, glass, silver and other metal wares, lamps, clocks, mirrors, wallcoverings, paints, carpets, and hard and resilient floor coverings, housewares, domestics, curtains, draperies, upholstery fabrics, and furniture are all detailed and extensively illustrated.

Throughout the text, laws that apply to the advertising and labeling of all these various products are discussed.

The material in the text has been flexibly arranged for a variety of courses. It may be used for one all-inclusive year's course on merchandise. It may be used, if desired, for four specialized courses: a course on textiles, a course on nontextiles, a course on fashion, and a course on home furnishings. The *Instructor's Manual and Key* details the specific chapter numbers to be used for each grouping, whether for a full year, a semester, or a quarter course.

THE TEXT AS A GLOSSARY

Many instructors who had previously used the text suggested the addition of a glossary for quick reference. Since 75 to 200 new terms are introduced in each chapter, a usable glossary would occupy half the length of the text. Therefore, glossary terms have been put into boldface type in the text. All terms are carefully indexed alphabetically to aid speedy location.

TEACHING AIDS

At the end of each chapter is a complete set of student activities. The first is a set of ten discussion-provoking questions titled "Do You Know Your Merchandise?" The second activity is a problem called "Putting Your Merchandise Knowledge to Work." Most of these problems can be done after careful reading of the text. The final activity is a "Project" that requires some outside research or activity on the part of the student.

A separate *Instructor's Manual and Key* contains behavioral objectives for each chapter in the book and teaching suggestions to make each class session an exciting learning experience. The manual also includes unit bibliographies that offer additional reading suggestions. Finally, objective tests to be used at the ends of chapters or units, or as mid-term or final examinations, are included.

ACKNOWLEDGMENTS

Many people offered valuable assistance in the preparation of this major revision. Included in this group are the instructors who responded to questionnaires and indicated their desire to see the addition and expansion of certain topics and the elimination of others.

We are also grateful to the many instructors who made important suggestions regarding course content, instruction level, organization, and emphasis of value factors. Plaudits also go to the industry people who read and critiqued each chapter for accuracy, up-to-date information, and completeness. These reviewers are acknowledged by name on the next page.

Special thanks are extended to Dr. Mary E. Barry for her contributions to Unit 4.

Isabel B. Wingate
Karen R. Gillespie

Special Acknowledgments

Nancy Bailey, Bailey's in the Village, New York, N.Y.
Bonnie Benhayon, National Paint & Coatings Assn., Washington, D.C.
Adriana Scalamandre Bitter, Scalamandre Silks, New York, N.Y.
Marvin G. Britton, Corning Glass Works, Corning, N.Y.
James H. Casey, National Association of Glove Manufacturers, Gloversville, N.Y.
Bert Champion, Millinery Institute, New York, N.Y.
A. J. Davis, International Institute of Synthetic Rubber Producers, Houston, Tex.
Lloyd Dinkins, National Cotton Council, Memphis, Tenn.
Donald Doctorow, China Glass & Giftware Association, Clifton, N.J.
Sheldon Edelman, Belt Association, New York, N.Y.
Fashion Institute of Technology, New York, N.Y.
    Silvi Forrest
    Shep Goldman
    Jack Hyde
    Ed Morris
Footwear Council, New York, N.Y.
    Harold Gessner
    Andrea Rosen
R. C. Freeman, The Wool Bureau, Woodbury, N.Y.
Ellen R. Goldstein, National Handbag Association, New York, N.Y.
Raymond Gooley, Seth Thomas Clocks, Thomaston, Conn.
Richard P. Hall, Wallcovering Information Bureau, Springfield, N.J.
Wanda Hartman, Memphis State University, Memphis, Tenn.
Robert A. Holcombe, Chevy Chase, Md.
Houston Community College, Houston, Tex.
    Susan Burgess
    Anthony Lyons
Robert M. Johnston, Sterling Silversmiths Guild of America, Baltimore, Md.
Sandi Kabins, International Academy of Merchandising and Design, Chicago, Ill.
Jeffrey Keeffe, *Metals Week*, New York, N.Y.
Roland McBride, *Modern Plastics*, New York, N.Y.

James E. Mack, National Association of Mirror Manufacturers, Potomac, Md.
Theresa Mastrianni, The Berkley School, White Plains, N.Y.
James Morrissey, American Textile Manufacturers Institute, Washington, D.C.
National Home Fashions League, Dallas, Tex.
J. C. Penney Company, New York, N.Y.

Curtis Allen	John Costa	Thomas Keating	Robert Relay
Ward Becht	Pearl Fitzgerald	Anthony Kirsimagi	Martin Schuler
Fred Brown	Charles Gage	Martin Kowalski	Richard Ward
James Browne	Jack Gallagher	Joseph Mattera	Dale Wright

Harold Perl, County College of Morris, Dover, N.J.
William Rapp, East Meadow, N.Y.
Fischer Rhymes, Man-Made Fiber Products Association, Washington, D.C.
James A. Sanders, Evansville High School, Evansville, Ind.
Morton R. Sarett, Jewelry Industry Council, New York, N.Y.
Robert Story, Uncle Sam Umbrella Shops, New York, N.Y.
Jerome Wagner, American Fur Industry, Inc., New York, N.Y.
Dolores Ware, Color Association of the United States, New York, N.Y.

Picture Credits

Our thanks to the following for the photographs and illustrations that appear in this book:

Abraham & Straus: 10. Alexander's: 257. The American Can Co.: 178. American Fur Industry: 253. American Plywood Assn.: 180. American Textile Manufacturers' Institute: 77, 104, 125. Assn. of Home Appliance Manufacturers: 375. Armitron Corp.: 312. Avtex Fibers, Inc.: 126. Badische Corp.: 80. Belgian Linen Assn.: 109. Ben Kahn: 257. Boussac of France, Inc.: (426). Celanese Corp.: 10, 75. CIBA–GEIGY Corp.: 98. Cork Products Co., Inc.: (426). Country Floors, Inc.: (426). E.I. DuPont De Nemours & Co.: 97, 131, 137. Eastman Chemical Products, Inc.: 145, 148. Emba Mink Breeders Assn.: 250. The Firestone Tire & Rubber Co.: 150. Fostoria Glass Co.: 347. Franco et al., *The World of Cosmetology*, Gregg/McGraw-Hill, 1980, pp. 81, 126: 317, 324. Frank O. Gehry & Associates, Inc.: 441. The General Tire & Rubber Co.: 144, 426. The Goodyear Tire & Rubber Co.: 150. The Gorham Co.: 356, 359. Hercules, Inc.: 409. J. P. Stevens & Co., Inc.: 89. Lazare Kaplan & Sons: 303. Leather Industries of America: 157. Linens Domestics & Bath Products: 453. Man-Made Fiber Producers Assn.: 123. Masonite Corp.: 426. Mathesen, *Apparel and Accessories*, Gregg/McGraw-Hill, 1978, p. 89: 233. McGraw-Hill Book Co., School Division: Color plate. *Modern Plastics Encyclopedia*: 143. Mohasco Industries: 408. National Shoe Retailers Assn.: 271. NYT Pictures: 306. Oneida Ltd.: 355. PPG Industries: 135. Revere Copper & Brass Inc.: 369. The Sanforized Co.: 106. Sawyer of Napa: 161. Sekai Bunka Photo: 114. The Simmons Co.: 446. The Singer Co.: 433. Sona of India: 413. Steelways: 150. Steuben Glass: 348. Textile Museum, Washington, D.C.: 116. USDA: 96. U.S. Dept. of the Interior: 331. *Woodworking & Furniture Digest*: 440. The Wool Bureau, Inc.: 121. Workbench, Inc.: 443.

Contents

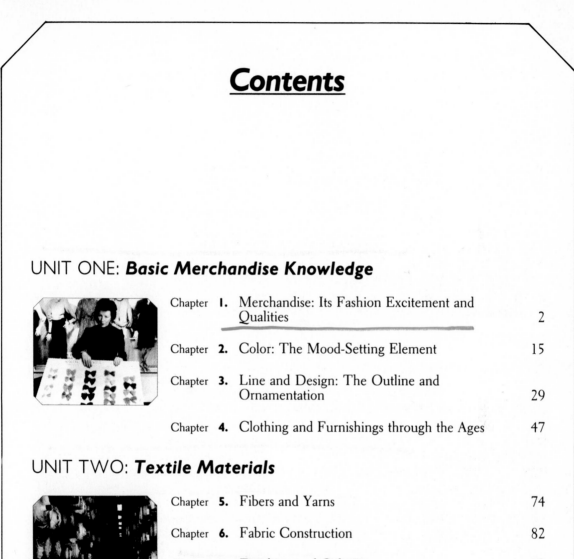

UNIT THREE: *Nontextile Materials*

UNIT FOUR: *Apparel and Accessories*

UNIT FIVE: *Homefurnishings*

UNIT ONE

Basic Merchandise Knowledge

Merchandise: Its Fashion Excitement and Qualities

Virtually every person in the United States is bombarded with pictures and messages about merchandise. These appear through the media of television, radio, newspapers, magazines, catalogs, bus and train advertisements, billboard posters, displays in store windows and on sidewalks, and in places of amusement.

Since every advertisement claims that the merchandise it is promoting is best, the problem of how to choose confronts everyone who uses, wears, or consumes products. Therefore, study about how to buy smart, which is the focus of this book, is desirable. If you are a customer, you will learn how to get value and satisfaction from your purchases. If you are a retailer, you will discover what determines quality and how to select products and to present them in an effective way to your customers.

Individual interests and tastes, changing lifestyles, innovations caused by new technology, expressions of national and local pride, needs and desires of people, and the commerce of local, national, and world markets are all involved in the buying and selling of goods. The raw materials that become parts of many products come from the four corners of the earth. Laboratories constantly experiment to find new materials, substitutes for scarce materials, new combinations, and new uses for products. Merchandise represents fashion, status, comfort, pleasure, prestige, warmth, safety, pride, beauty, satisfaction, and many other values for those who buy it, sell it, and use it.

The facts and information you gain from this book will aid you all your life, whether you purchase goods for yourself, family, or friends or, as a retailer, for resale to others. Regardless of your motives, you will find your life enriched by knowing your merchandise.

THE CYCLE OF MERCHANDISE DISTRIBUTION

The paths that goods take from producer to consumer are known as the **cycle of merchandise distribution**. See Figure 1–1. Goods get their start from the land, sea, or air. The vast **extractive industries** drill for oil and gas, dig for coal, metals, and other minerals, or extract raw materials from the ocean's depths. Water is sometimes obtained by digging, but it also comes from rain and melting snow or from lakes, rivers, and oceans. The land's surface provides forests where trees, bushes, grasses, and edible plants and fruits are found. The **farming industry** is responsible for raising most of the foodstuffs that we eat. Some animals live in the wild, but others are domesticated. Many of the latter are raised under controlled conditions to ensure that the quality, size, color, and texture of their fur or scales are uniform. Various animals supply meats, milk and

2

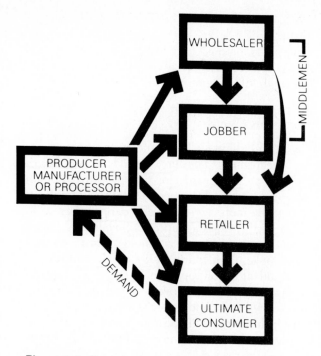

Figure 1-1. *The cycle of merchandise distribution, generated by consumer demand, ends with consumer use.*

its by-products, as well as fibers, furs, feathers, and leathers.

These **natural substances** obtained from extraction, lumber and farm industries, and the wild comprise a large part of our goods. Another supplier is the **chemical industry,** which, through the marvels of laboratory experiments, supplies us with a wide range of synthetic and imitation products.

Substances from all these sources go to the **manufacturers** and **processors** — those firms that use both the raw materials of nature and the synthetic and imitation products from the chemical industries — to be converted into foodstuffs, clothing, home goods, and all the other articles needed and wanted by consumers.

Manufacturers may be large or small, and they may work directly from raw materials or take partially fabricated products, such as cloth, leather, or fur, and turn them into garments or other

goods. The manufacturers and processors in turn sell their goods directly or through wholesalers and jobbers (middlemen) to the **retailers** who, in turn, sell them to the individual **customers.**

Consumers are the ultimate users of all these goods. Thus all people, whether or not they make the actual purchases as customers, are consumers. Consumers are the ones who make the demands that set the entire cycle of merchandise distribution in motion. This is a never-ending process of raw material exploration, product development, retailing, and consuming.

THE IMPORTANCE OF FASHION

Fashion touches every product, but it is an especially powerful influence in the apparel, accessories, and homefurnishings fields. Knowing the terminology of fashion is vital to understanding its impact. **Fashion** means the popularity and acceptance for a sustained period of time of an idea, a concept, a look, a product, or an entire group of products. Whatever is accepted by many people for a considerable period of time is said to be "in fashion."

Fashions in foods have made potatoes and bread less in demand and fruits and green vegetables more in demand. Fashions in eating have made fast-food shops popular. Fashions in clothing have allowed men to discard warm jackets and ties for streetwear in summer months. Fashions in home decoration have led customers to seek modular units (sectionals) to replace traditional sofas.

Fads, in contrast to fashions, enjoy popularity for a limited period of time. Almost instantaneously they create a demand that sends retailers scrambling to obtain the items, and just as quickly they fade from popularity. Bonnie and Clyde styles of the midseventies, the bubble umbrella of 1973, and Martian headbands[1] of 1982 are examples of items that have been widely accepted and then suffered a quick demise.

Style refers to the unique shape or form of any product. It may refer to specialized types of expression, such as taste in music and ethnic food preferences. But the term is generally used to mean the outline or distinctive look of a product. Platform shoes, turtleneck sweaters, gooseneck lamps, Afro hair arrangements, muu-muus, knickers, bean-bag chairs, and bow ties are examples of styles that have been fashionable in the past and that may return to fashion again.

A **classic** is a particular style that remains in modest demand continuously. Men's white shirts with barrel cuffs are classics that sustain a certain demand year in and year out.

Staples are items of merchandise so basic to customer demand that the retailer who carries those items must stock them at all times. Every classification of merchandise contains one or more staples, such as T-shirts, black cocktail dresses, hardware components, cast-iron frying pans, white muslin sheets, and neck-hugging pearl necklaces.

Fashion Trends

A **fashion trend** is the direction in which a particular fashion is moving. Fashion forecasters chart these directions and derive the trend from them. Thus whether skirts are getting longer or shorter and whether more leather is demanded in clothing articles are fashion trends. Consumers, retailers, and manufacturers are all concerned with fashion trends so that they will know what to demand, create, buy, sell, and use. For manufacturers and retailers, misinterpreting a fashion trend can be financially disastrous.

An article may remain in fashion, but its contours or details may change frequently. Change in the style of blue jeans is one of the most dramatic examples of this. Although a pair of jeans bought today looks quite different from one bought over 20 years ago when the fashion first started, the jeans themselves are still an important fashion item. Men, women, teenagers, and children have all succumbed to the fashion for jeans. They have been worn at various times as loose or hip-hugging, tight-legged or baggy, flared-leg or fitted, faded or rich blue, torn edged or neatly hemmed, with embroidery or plain stitching, and, most recently, as designer jeans with the designer's name prominently displayed on the right back pocket. Jeans have been one of the most phenomenal fashions of recent times, and they have represented a variety of fashion trends throughout this time period.

Fashion Cycles

When a fashion evolves it moves through periods of acceptance. The first period is **inception,** when the avant garde for that particular fashion first accepts it. The second is **popularization,** when the more aggressive and daring invest in it. The third is **mass acceptance,** when it is copied by the mass producers and bought in quantity by the public. The fourth period is **decline,** when demand drops off, and the final period is **abandonment,** when leftovers are found on the markdown racks and as-is counters. This is called the **fashion cycle.** It occurs rapidly for fads and more slowly for fashions. Classics rarely reach the last two stages, and staples have little or no cyclic selling activity at all. See Figure 1–2.

While one fashion is going into mass production, decline, and abandonment, another item or look is capturing the attention of the avant garde. A fashion cycle for that newer item thus begins.

Desires for new fashions may be triggered in a variety of ways. A First Lady's penchant for a particular color; a princess's hairstyle; the opening of trade with a country, such as China; the exposition of rare artifacts, such as those from Tutankhamen's tomb, which were displayed in major museums around the country in 1979; a new movie or television star, such as E.T., are examples of the ways fashions or fads begin. The wealthy, once considered fashions' leaders, have less impact today than do groups from SoHo in New York, country-western music festivals, the jazz world, or the movie and television industry.

Fashion Forecasting

To develop and nurture a new style to fashion maturity costs a great deal of money. Since the majority of newly created styles fail to be accepted, some way of forecasting consumer appeal

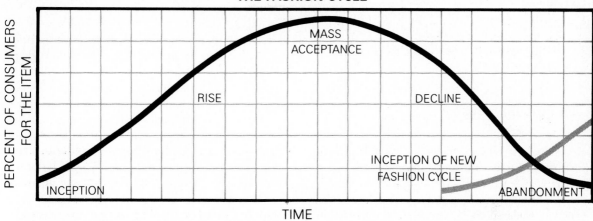

Figure 1-2. *The fashion cycle: Periods of consumer acceptance and abandonment vary among fads and fashions. Classics rarely reach the stages of decline and abandonment.*

and what consumers are likely to accept is important. Although no method has been developed that is wholly reliable, the following have considerable merit.

Consensus. The people and elements that compose the fashion world, such as designers, manufacturers, retailers, editors of fashion and home goods publications, and specialized fashion research agencies, continually exchange information. When agreement is reached that a certain trend is taking place in material, design, decoration, or color, the group judgment, or consensus, is likely to be accurate.

A special attempt is made to coordinate the forecast for each type of article so that, for example, the customer who buys a dress in a certain color will find outer apparel that will harmonize. To some extent, these forecasts determine which colors the manufacturer will use, so customers may find little else from which to choose. However, the customer, if dissatisfied, can simply refrain from buying and thus express that dissatisfaction.

Initial Acceptance. Another method of forecasting is for the central buyer of a chain of apparel or homefurnishings stores to place a few units of a new style in many of these store outlets before the beginning of the season. The buyer can then determine public response during the first few days these items are on sale. This is easily done with the use of a central computer that analyzes sales in different store units. A particular style may not show outstanding movement in any one store in the group. When the sales for all the units are accumulated, however, they may be sufficiently large to indicate that the style is about to achieve broad acceptance and that it is worthy of an immediate reorder.

Consumer Research. A method that has proven successful but that is costly to undertake is research studies of a cross section of fashion-conscious customers. These people are approached, either while shopping or as they leave the store, and are asked to describe the fashion details, including colors and designs, of the products they intend to buy during the coming season. With a large enough sample, these forecasts prove quite accurate.

Intuition. Some fashion designers and store buyers have an unusual ability to sense from observation, travel, and previous experience what customers will want in the season to come. Even though these people do no formal research, they frequently are able to create or select items that become fashionable.

The Fashion Industry

Fashion affects everything people do, think, wear, and use. However, when one refers to the **fashion industry,** the word "fashion" is limited to clothing and accessories items for men, women, and children. This is a vast worldwide industry. Once considered to be centered in France and the United States, the fashion industry today spans all of Europe and many parts of Asia and is rapidly being extended to many third-world countries. The industry incorporates the work of famous designers and those who are daring to create new and novel looks.

The Homefurnishings Industry

Another major industry whose products are discussed in this book produces and distributes merchandise used in the home, including furniture, chinaware, glassware, silverware, rugs, carpets, and home accessories. Styles in these products change more slowly and customer investments are generally made for longer periods of time than for fashion apparel.

VALUE COMPONENTS IN MERCHANDISE

For any item of merchandise, certain basic elements determine quality. These are design, materials, construction, finish, and, often, decoration. Fine-quality products incorporate the best under each of these categories, whereas poor-quality products are deficient in one or more of these components. Each element, however, influences the desirability, function, and quality of the finished product.

Design

Before any product can be made, a plan must be devised for that item. The **designer** is the innovative person employed to create that plan, which is known as a **design.** How carefully that design is made and how knowledgeable, famous, and inspired the designer is at the particular time are factors that will affect the desirability of the finished design and the cost of the final item. In making the plan the designer considers the materials available, the trends for that particular product, the socioeconomic factors that will affect its use, the purpose of the finished product, and possible applications. The design may be presented as a detailed drawing or as a three-dimensional model made from inexpensive materials. Once the design has been approved and accepted, the next stages in the creation of a product take place.

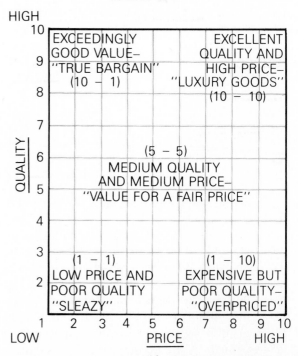

VALUE GRID

Figure l-3. *Both price and quality influence consumers' perceptions of the value of any finished product.*

Materials

Choosing the materials to be used for the product is as exacting as the creation of the plan

fine the materials and design for the article are, if construction is faulty, the finished item will not give good service.

Finish

The surface appearance of a product shows its **finish.** This may be achieved at least in part before the materials are assembled, but there are always last-minute procedures to make an item salable. Finishing may be as simple as polishing a spot where a **sprue** was removed (a sprue is a connector for products such as metals or plastics that are in liquid form before they are shaped). Finishes may place a shine, a matte (dull), or a textured (bumpy) surface on a product. Chemical finishes can leave a permanent shine or color or make a product hold its shape or be fire- or water-repellent. Well-finished products are more costly, appear more attractive, and retain that attractiveness longer.

Decoration

The ornamentation of a product may be inherent in the shape or the materials or may be applied ...rately. A handsome brocaded fabric, for ex-...le, provides its own decoration in the weave ...e cloth. Many articles, however, depend on ...d decoration for their beauty and desirability. ...elry, silverware, chinaware, and glassware are ...les that frequently have ornamentation to en-...their appearance and increase their salabil-...For example, an undecorated china plate ...sell for about $20. That same china plate ...elaborate, hand-applied gold and enamel ...ration may be worth as much as $500. Dec-...on, when artistically hand done, adds sub-...ially to the beauty and value of a product.

...hus all merchandise goes through design, ...rial selection, construction, and finishing ...esses. Some items also have added decora-...to make them more salable.

...RCHANDISE VALUES: ...TS AND BENEFITS

Using Facts

A product, such as a child's pair of shoes, may be described factually as follows.

- *Style or design*: blucher oxford
- *Materials*: calf leather upper with bend-leather sole
- *Construction*: Goodyear welt
- *Finish*: brown-dyed, smooth finish
- *Decoration*: brass eyelets with leather lacing

Turning Facts Into Benefits

Such factual information about a product, however, is rarely helpful to a customer. The customer is concerned with different features when buying a pair of shoes, such as comfort, appearance, durability, ease of getting the shoes on and off, ease of care, shape retention, and color. The facts stated above can be interpreted into customer-benefit language as follows.

- *Style or design:* a fashionable blucher oxford that is easy to put on, to remove, and to adjust across the instep for total foot comfort.
- *Materials:* the fine-quality leathers used in the uppers and sole will ensure long wear, continuous fine appearance, breathing comfort to keep feet cool, and a nonslippery sole for safety on wet surfaces.
- *Construction:* the Goodyear welt will ensure a smooth inside layer on which the sole of the foot rests, ease of resoling when needed, and a well-made shoe that will retain its shape through countless wearings.
- *Finish:* the brown-dyed, smooth-textured finish is easy to keep shiny with occasional waxing.
- *Decoration:* the brass eyelets add a contrasting color and make it easy to slip the leather laces into or out of the eyelets.

Selling Points, Buying Benefits

Whether you are a retailer who is advertising, labeling, or selling merchandise directly to customers or a customer who is seeking to buy goods, you are subjected to the technical language of merchandise. For every product category, there are special names given to the designs, materials, construction, finish, and decoration. These names are discussed in the ensuing chapters.

Unless the technical terms are understood, they do not help the advertisers, labelers, or salespeople to sell the goods or aid the customers in buying them. The terms need to be translated into lay language and interpreted to explain the advantages customers seek in their purchases. Customers are not as interested in the ways in which goods are made as they are in the benefits the goods offer to them. In addition to their interest in fashionable products customers are looking for products that will offer the following benefits.

Prestige. **Prestige** involves the power to command admiration. People get prestige from owning lovely jewelry, exquisite furnishings, or

antiques or from wearing the newest fashion that attracts the attention of associates.

Pride of Ownership. **Pride** means delight over the things you possess. Most people get pride from owning homes, cars, boats, fine furs, clothing, jewelry, and home goods.

Attractiveness. **Attractiveness** involves factors such as aesthetic appeal, beauty, loveliness, handsome looks, charm, and gracefulness. For most items of wearing apparel, for accessories, and for most homefurnishings attractiveness is an important quality.

Becomingness. No matter how attractive a product is, the way it looks on the wearer, or how well it goes with other clothing or accessories, or the way it harmonizes with other home furnishings is a dominant consideration in any purchase. **Becomingness,** that is, being in accord with the wearer's overall appearance or with other surrounding goods, often determines whether or not a person will buy a particular product. A handsome lamp may be totally out of place in a home with no pieces that harmonize with its outline, color, or style. Thus other qualities of merchandise desirability fade into insignificance if an article is not becoming.

Suitability. Being **suitable** means meeting your needs or wishes or being appropriate for the occasion or situation. Merchandise is bought mainly to fill this requirement. You often buy an item because nothing else that you own is right for that particular event or use.

Versatility. Merchandise that is adaptable for more than one use is said to be **versatile.** Sofa beds that are used as seating pieces in the daytime and as sleeping areas at night and coats with zip-out linings are examples of versatile products.

Durability. Holding up well, known as **durability,** is especially important when buying children's clothing and shoes, homefurnishings, work clothing, and heirlooms such as fine jewelry.

Correct Fit. Articles for which **size** is a factor, either to fit a person or a particular area in the home or office, must **fit correctly** for comfort, attractive appearance, and usefulness.

Stability. Products that do not change shape in use, keep their original look for a reasonable time, and continue to fit well are said to be **stable.** Suits that keep their shape when worn, sofas and mattresses that remain firm after some use, and shoes that hold their shape are examples of products that are stable.

Shrink- or Warp-Resistance. Closely allied to fit and stability is shrink- or warp-resistance. All washable articles need to be **shrink resistant** or else the customer must be advised to buy larger sizes to provide for shrinkage. **Warping,** or getting out of shape, may affect woods, as well as metals and some plastics that are used near heat. Construction or finishes that retard warping and directions for handling to avoid distortion of the product are helpful.

Colorfastness. Color, one of the most important factors in the selection of merchandise, may or may not be permanent. When colors fade, they are said to be **fugitive.** Most customers seek merchandise with colors that are permanent, or **colorfast** to washing and exposure to sunlight and air. Occasionally merchandise, such as imported madras shirts, some blue jeans, and saddle leather articles, feature the fact that the colors will change in use and handling. In these instances, fugitive colors become customer benefits.

Safety Ensurance. Although most products made from fabric, wood, leather, paper, rubber, and plastic will burn in the presence of open flames, they are reasonably safe. Other products are built to ensure **safety,** for example, rubber bath mats that prevent slippage, fans with protective shields that prevent fingers from reaching the blades, and fire- and open-flame-resistant mattresses and upholstered furniture.

Comfort. "Pride must be pinched," was a saying that applied to people who sacrificed comfort to wear the latest look in pointed toes, high heels, tightly cinched waists, or high celluloid collars. The modern consumer is rarely willing to undergo torture to have the "right" look. People today seek furniture that provides sitting and sleeping comfort, homes insulated against excessive heat and cold, and garments that do not bind or restrict movement.

Healthfulness. Some consumer goods are designed to be healthful, or at least not harmful. For example, open-mesh shoes for air circulation, dyes on infants' shoes that are not harmful when the shoes are chewed on, and paint that contains no lead are available. Some products, however, are used in ways or cause reactions not envisioned by the retailer and manufacturer. Toys with removable small parts have been swallowed by children, toy airplane glues have been inhaled, hairsprays have ignited in the presence of a flame, and hair dyes have caused allergic reactions. Even foods occasionally contain harmful residues from chemical sprays. There are government laws and rulings that help to protect consumers. A partial list is given later in this chapter. Manufacturers also put warning labels on articles to alert people to incorrect usage of the products.

Environmental Pollution. Poisoning of our water and the atmosphere has become an urgent concern. Wastes from both chemical-producing plants and an expanded population are being blamed. Accordingly, consumer goods that tend to reduce environmental pollution are being produced. Examples include cars that emit few harmful fumes, heaters that burn fuel cleanly, and articles that can be easily disposed of because they are **biodegradable** (will disintegrate when exposed to air, water, and soil) or can be recycled.

Ease of Use and Care. Customers seek products that stay clean or shiny and hold their shapes with a minimum amount of hard work

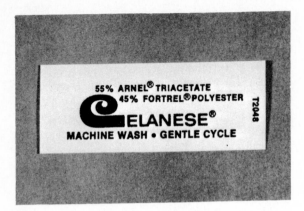

Figure 1-4. *Easy care of garments is an important buying benefit.*

and expense. For example, drip-dry no-iron shirts, curtains, and sheets eliminate the need to iron such items. Washable wallpaper eliminates costly cleaning processes. The ease with which items may be cared for is an important buying benefit. See Figure 1-4.

Reasonable Price. The price of any article is particularly important to people who seek to get good value for their money. **Value** for a customer involves two factors: quality and price. If the customer considers the price low for the quality of goods, the product is viewed as a **bargain**. If the price is low but the quality is poor, the product is regarded as **sleazy**. If the price of the goods is modest and the quality satisfactory, the product is viewed as **value for a fair price.** If the price of the goods is high and the quality excellent, the product is usually viewed as a **luxury** purchase — but one that will hold up well over time. If the price is high but the quality mediocre, the product is viewed as being **overpriced**. Value categories were shown on the value grid in Figure 1-3 on page 6.

PROTECTING THE CONSUMER

Since the early 1900s the government has been increasingly involved in protecting consumers and customers from injury and deceitful selling practices, including the misleading labeling of products. A recent movement connected with the government's efforts to safeguard buyers and users of products and services is known as **consumerism**. It is a general term for demands by consumers on their own behalf, whether such actions are in behalf of individuals or of members of an organization.

Federal Rulings and Regulations to Protect the Consumer

Consumerism has led to many laws and regulations to provide consumer product and credit protection. Several of these are listed below.

1. Federal Trade Commission Act of 1914. Restricts unfair methods of competition, including false and misleading selling and advertising.
2. Food, Drug, and Cosmetic Act of 1938. Excludes from the market food, drugs, and cosmetics that are of questionable value or that have not yet been proven safe. Requires that warnings be affixed to a product to tell users that it may not be safe when used as intended. Subsequent rules pertaining to cosmetics were issued between 1949 and 1976 by the Food and Drug Administration (FDA).
3. Wheeler-Lea Act of 1938. Extends the Federal Trade Commission coverage to include deceptive acts and practices and makes it (rather than the Food and Drug Administration) responsible for the advertising of foods, drugs, and cosmetics.
4. Wool Products Labeling Acts of 1939. Requires labeling of fiber content and of percentages of kinds of wool and other animal fibers.
5. Fur Products Labeling Act of 1951 with amendments through 1980. Protects against misnaming, mishandling, and misleading advertising of fur products.
6. Flammable Fabrics Act of 1953, amended in 1967. Prohibits the sale of many textile products that fail to pass standards of non-flammability.

7. Textile Fiber Products Identification Act (TFPIA) of 1959, amended in 1981. Requires that the generic names of the fibers included in the article and their relative importance be revealed in labels and in advertising.

8. Hazardous Substance Act of 1961. Requires the revealing of hazardous substances in products used in the home.

9. Household Furniture Trade Practice Rules, effective March 18, 1964. Requires that statements made about furniture be truthful.

10. Cigarette Labeling and Advertising Act of 1965. Requires warning labels on packages and in advertising.

11. Fair Packaging and Labeling Act of 1966, for packaged foods, requires that labels reveal weight or volume of contents, weight of single serving, limited air space, and no misleading designations. Separate regulations are set for nonfoods.

12. Consumer Products Safety Act of 1967. Sets up a commission to regulate toys and other products that may have a hazard in use. Bans products found to be dangerous.

13. Truth in Lending Act of 1969. Requires that the annual rate of credit charges be revealed, as well as all the details of the credit agreement.

14. Endangered Species Conservation Act of 1969. Updated in 1973 and 1977. Controls and monitors import and export of imperiled species of animals.

15. National Credit Control Act of 1969. Authorizes President to control retail credit, including credit card use.

16. Poison Prevention Packaging Act of 1970. Requires "childproof" packaging for hazardous household products, which means that the products must be packaged in containers that children under 5 years of age cannot open.

17. Federal Trade Commission's Trade Regulation Rule on Care Labeling of 1972. Requires that information on the care of the specific items be provided on the labels of many products.

18. Magnuson-Moss Warranty Act, effective in 1975. Requires guarantees be clear and dependable. Amendments in 1983 require specific instructions concerning cleaning, bleaching, and ironing. Labels must be on most garments, and those that are exempt must have hang tags.

19. Consumer Goods Pricing Act of 1975. Eliminates "fair trade" in interstate commerce. Manufacturers and distributors barred from setting retail prices at which their products must be resold. (Consumers can sue for damages under the Clayton Act.)

20. Substances Control Act of 1976. Requires testing and use restrictions on certain chemicals to protect human health and environment.

21. Amendments to Clean Air Act 1977 and to National Highway Traffic Safety Administration regulations 1972. Intended to reduce car exhaust (noxious emission) and to introduce safety features in cars.

In addition to these national laws and rulings, there are many state and local regulations that govern the distribution of consumer goods. Notable among these is the regulation that packaged goods must reveal not only the retail price of the package but also the price per unit of weight or other comparable unit of measurement of the contents. This information facilitates comparison with the prices of competing brands and sizes.

Some regulations protect manufacturers from misleading statements of other manufacturers. For example, even though consumers have little interest in the generic classes of textile fibers used for consumer goods, information on these fibers must, by law, be supplied to them by a label or tag attached to the product.

Where a Customer Can Go for Added Assistance

When a customer is dissatisfied with merchandise because of failure to perform, poor construction, hazardous features, and so on, there are a number of places to turn. The first is the store or mail-order distributor from whom the purchase

Figure 1-5. *Consumer goods for personal wear can be classified as durable or nondurable and as textile, nontextile, or combination. Apparel is considered a nondurable product.*

was made. This may lead to the manufacturer's nearest representative. If these contacts bring no satisfaction, the customer should contact the local better business bureau or the consumer service office in his or her community, county, or state. Other helpful agencies are the action or hot line departments of the media and small claims court, in which proceedings are informal and no lawyer is required. Federal agencies are the Consumer Products Safety Commission for hazards in general merchandise, the Food and Drug Administration (FDA) in regard to food pollution, and the Federal Trade Commission (FTC) for problems involving mail-order services, direct-to-the-home selling, warranties, labels on clothing, use of credit cards, and the activities of credit-reporting bureaus.

CLASSES OF CONSUMER GOODS

About 60 percent of consumer income is spent on goods for the person, the home, and means of transportation. These goods are classified in various ways. For census purposes they are grouped as durable and nondurable goods. **Durable goods** include products that last for a long time, such as automotive equipment, furniture, appliances, hardware, and building materials. **Nondurable goods** include products that are consumed immediately or fairly rapidly, such as food and drink, apparel, drugs and cosmetics, and gasoline. **General merchandise** covers nearly everything sold in a typical large store, such as apparel, cosmetics, homefurnishings, sporting goods, jewelry, luggage, toys and games, tobacco products, and garden equipment.

Consumer goods are also classified as textiles, nontextiles, and foods. **Textiles** are products made of natural fibers, such as cotton and wool, and of manmade fibers, such as rayon and polyester. These fibers can be woven, knitted, felted, braided, entangled, laced, netted, or bonded into cloth. Textiles are used for clothing and many homefurnishings. **Nontextiles** include all other consumer products, except foods. They are made from metal, rubber, plastics, paper, china, glass, wood, leather, and fur. Some stores, such as

hardware and stationery shops, primarily handle nontextile products. Other stores, such as some grocery stores and delicatessens, may carry only food. Many stores carry goods in all categories. A number of products, classified as **combinations**, combine both textiles and nontextiles. Among these are upholstered furniture, fabric-lined leather or plastic handbags and shoes, and cars with upholstered interiors.

METRIC SIZING AND MEASUREMENTS

The United States uses a system of sizing and weights and measurements that is used by only about 5 percent of the world's population. The remaining 95 percent use the metric system, which originated in France and was adopted there in 1799. Great Britain, West Germany, U.S.S.R., China, Japan, and other countries have converted to the metric system. In 1975, the United States signed the Metric Conversion Act into law. However, no timetable was set for the adoption of the metric system. Therefore, changes in sizes of containers, in signs, and in weights and measurements have occurred slowly and have varied according to industry. In this text, we give the standard systems or sizing and measurements currently used. Both metric and nonmetric sizes have been listed where appropriate.

NOTE

1. Ron Alexander, "A New Fad Invades: Martian Antennae," *The New York Times*, June 7, 1982, p. B11.

DO YOU KNOW YOUR MERCHANDISE?

1. Explain why all customers are consumers but not all consumers are customers.

2. Trace the cycle of merchandise distribution. What role does the consumer play in this cycle?

3. Why is fashion of importance to most customers? Define fashion, fad, style, classic, staple, fashion trend, fashion cycle.

4. Explain the difference between selling points and buying benefits.

5. Why are fact features not all that customers need to know in selecting goods? How can facts be made useful in selling goods?

6. Explain what the relationship is between price and value when buying a product.

7. In what ways does the government help to protect the consumer?

8. What sources of information does the customer have in order to aid in the proper selection of merchandise?

9. How do durable goods differ from nondurable goods?

10. What is meant by textiles? By nontextiles? By combination merchandise?

2

Color: The Mood-Setting Element

Light and color are eternally wedded elements. Without light, you cannot see color, and without color, light would reveal a drab world, such as seen in black-and-white movies. Whatever you can see is made more appealing, more impressive, and more desirable with color.

Color evokes reactions that are expressed in a variety of ways. The following are examples of how the word "color" is used to express ideas.

- Our thoughts are colored by that fact.
- That person has lived a colorful life.
- The story that person told was very colorful.

Color has fashion and psychological appeal and even makes things appear familiar. White oleomargarine, for example, had to be colored yellow to resemble butter before it could be successfully marketed, even though the taste of the white and the yellow varieties was identical.

Color appeals to people emotionally. Different colors have traditional meanings, affect the way we look, and reflect our moods. Color itself has many variations. One color changes appearance when placed next to other colors or when seen under different light. Color forecasters, color stylists, psychologists, chemical experts, and dyers all play a role in the determination of colors to be used for merchandise.

TYPES OF COLOR

Two kinds of color exist. They are those made by light and those made by coloring agents, such as pigments and dyes.

Colors Made by Light

Radiant, or energy-emitting, sources for color are the sun's rays, flames, lightning, electricity, laser beams and arcs, light bulbs, and neon gas. What you see from these light sources is dependent upon the wavelength of each band emitted. Radiant light from the sun emits wavelengths that yield invisible as well as visible light rays.[1] The white light from the visible ray area is composed of rainbow colors. These are seen when droplets of water split the sunlight into its component parts to yield an arched rainbow across the sky or when a glass, triangular-shaped prism bends light to reflect these various colors.

How the eye views color is not totally understood. The eye is believed to see only three light colors: red, blue, and green. They may be combined to give yellow, orange, and violet. This is quite different from the combining of pigment colors to be discussed later.

Your eyes, like cameras, absorb color and register it with your brain. As light diminishes, how-

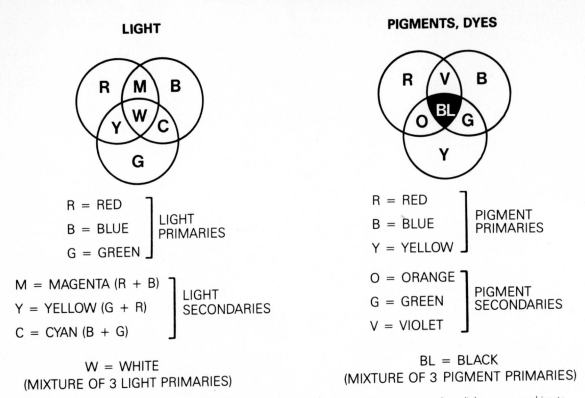

LIGHT

PIGMENTS, DYES

R = RED
B = BLUE
G = GREEN
   ] LIGHT PRIMARIES

M = MAGENTA (R + B)
Y = YELLOW (G + R)
C = CYAN (B + G)
   ] LIGHT SECONDARIES

W = WHITE
(MIXTURE OF 3 LIGHT PRIMARIES)

R = RED
B = BLUE
Y = YELLOW
   ] PIGMENT PRIMARIES

O = ORANGE
G = GREEN
V = VIOLET
   ] PIGMENT SECONDARIES

BL = BLACK
(MIXTURE OF 3 PIGMENT PRIMARIES)

Figure 2-1. *Light sources create different primary and secondary colors than do pigments or dyes; light waves combine to create white, while pigments combine to create black.*

ever, certain colors are no longer visible. Violet colors fade out first, then the reds, the blues, the oranges, and the greens. The last colors to remain visible under dim light are the yellow-greens. When the light waves diminish totally, your eyes see only black. Black is the absence of color through light.[2]

Colors Made by Pigments and Dyes

Dye and pigment colors perform quite differently from light colors. Mixing rainbow colors together in the form of light makes white light. Mixing rainbow colors together in the form of pigments and dyes makes black. White may indicate the absence of any pigment or it may be a pigment, such as zinc oxide.

Pigments, dyes, and stains come from a variety of natural and synthetic sources. Originally, all colors were produced from leaves and barks of trees, flowers, berries, fish, and metal oxides. For example, royal purple came from the juice of a small Mediterranean shellfish. Blue came from the leaves of a special tree, until indigo, from a plant, and woad, an herb, were discovered around the year 1300. Very early, alchemists discovered that dyes for ceramic and glass products could be made from metallic and mineral sources. Cobalt formed a rich blue, iron or chromium supplied green, copper or gold made ruby red and selenium formed yellow.

In 1856, an English chemist, Sir William Perkins, discovered that he could make mauve (a delicate violet color) from coal tar. German chemists discovered that alizarin, also made from coal tar, would produce red-orange. Colorfast fabric dyes, known as **vat dyes,** are also obtained from anthracene, a coal-tar product.

Today, most colors are created in laboratories from various chemicals. Most colors used on nonedible products are at least fade-resistant. Chemical dyes (coal-tar derivatives) used by the food industry are all approved by the FDA for safety.

THE LANGUAGE OF COLOR

If you have ever tried to match colors, you know the difficulty of doing so. Thousands of colors exist, and a simple addition or subtraction of a minute amount of a chemical in the dye bath can create many more variations.

To help sort out this vast array of colors, there exists a commonly understood color language. Colors are classified as being chromatic or achromatic. They are also classified by hue, intensity, and value.

Chromatic and Achromatic

The Greek word for color is **chroma.** Therefore, the rainbow colors referred to earlier are **chromatic** colors. By combining those rainbow colors in a variety of ways, many additional chromatic colors may be derived.

Achromatic means without color. It includes black and white and its intermediary, gray. Black, white, and gray may be used alone or with one another. They are also used to supply accents or background or to modify the chromatic colors.

Hue

Hue is synonymous with color. By naming the hue, we identify the color to which we are referring. Thus, red, green, blue, yellow, orange, violet are all hues.

Intensity

How brilliant, luminous, or saturated a color is determines its **intensity,** or chroma. Pure color is the most intense. When it is modified by the addition of other colors or by white or black, it loses some of its intensity. Intense colors are dramatic but tiring if you have to look at them for a prolonged period.

Value

How pale or how dark a color is determines its **value.** Any color with white added becomes paler and is known as a **tint** of that color. The same color with black added becomes darker and is known as a **shade** of that color.

Pale tints are known as **pastels.** Pink, for example, a mixture of red and white, is a tint of red. Shades or darker colors, include burgundy, a mixture of red and black, and brown, a mixture of orange and black.

Color Systems and Standards

Because of the many chromatic and achromatic differences and such an array of hues, intensities,

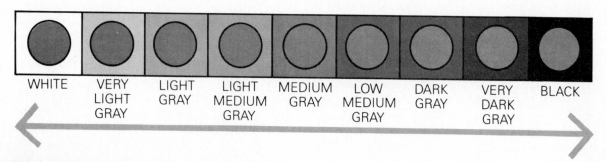

WHITE | VERY LIGHT GRAY | LIGHT GRAY | LIGHT MEDIUM GRAY | MEDIUM GRAY | LOW MEDIUM GRAY | DARK GRAY | VERY DARK GRAY | BLACK

Figure 2-2. *Achromatic tones range from white to black, with varying shades of gray in between. The medium gray dot appears darker toward the white and paler toward the black.*

and values, a method to help manufacturers and retailers identify exact colors is necessary. Many agencies, as well as the U.S. government, provide information on color.

The **Color Association of the United States** is a firm that registers colors and records exact formulas for those colors. It also keeps samples in airtight vaults to protect them from any color changes so as to ensure exact color matching. This firm, for example, records for manufacturers the exact red, white, and blue mixtures needed for the U.S. flag. It also issues color forecasts to its members.

The **Ostwald system** named for Wilhelm Ostwald (1853–1932), a German chemist, is popularly used throughout Europe and the United States. Ostwald prepared colors and placed them on a triangular form, thereby showing that a pure color changed to its many tints and shades by the addition of white or black. His basic theory comprised 24 different hues, and each hue was modified to reveal 28 different tints and shades.[3] These 672 different variations plus 8 achromatic tones totaled 680 representations.

The **Munsell system,** named for Albert H. Munsell (1859–1918), also plots an orderly sequence of color and uses the qualities of hue, intensity (chroma), and value to differentiate each change. He gave white to gray to black gradations in 11 steps. Munsell uses 10 basic hues with 10 intermediary hues within each group for a total of 100 hues. Within each hue, up to 10 gradations from pale to dark may be used.[4]

Designations of each variation of color by letter and number allow easy color identification and specification. This is a popularly used system in the United States.

The **Prang system** is credited to Louis Prang (1824–1909), a color and art specialist. He did research on the spectrum and devised a method to set standards and to define colors. The plan that he created is one of the most used systems for understanding colors and their relationships to one another. He developed the color wheel (described in detail below).

The Inter-Society Color Council (ISCC) in collaboration with the National Bureau of Standards (NBS) created the **ISCC-NBS color description system** that uses words to describe colors. ISCC and NBS published a dictionary of color names using the Munsell color charts as a key. The terms include hue names preceded by modifiers, such as pale blue, moderate blue, and strong blue.[5]

In addition to these systems and standards, paint companies, textile mills, fiber companies, carpet companies, magazines, and other organizations interested in color provide color charts and forecasts about color.

THE COLOR WHEEL

To identify pigment colors and dyes, colors are divided into groupings known as primary, secondary, tertiary, and quaternary. These groupings represent the order in which the individual colors (hues) are derived. The **color wheel** enables you to see colors in juxtaposition to one another and to analyze color combinations easily. (See the color plate following page 22.)

Primary Colors

Primary colors are independent and cannot be formed by combining other colors. They are the basic colors from which all others are produced. Red, yellow, and blue are the primary colors. To develop the color wheel, the primary colors are first placed in the form of a triangle with equal sides.

Secondary Colors

Colors made directly from mixing two primary colors are called **secondary colors.** Red mixed with yellow yields orange; yellow mixed with blue yields green; and red mixed with blue yields violet. Thus, orange, green, and violet are the secondary colors. The secondary colors can be arranged on an upside-down triangle that has equal sides, with purple at the bottom apex, orange between yellow and red, and green between yellow and blue. Superimposing this inverted triangle over the primary colors' triangle yields the foundation of the color wheel.

Tertiary Colors

Colors produced by combining one primary and one secondary color are called **tertiary colors.** For example, yellow mixed with green produces yellow-green, red mixed with orange produces red-orange, blue mixed with violet produces blue-violet. The primary, secondary, and tertiary colors make up the basic color wheel, which consists of 12 colors.

Quaternary Colors

Less frequently seen on color wheels are the colors made by mixing tertiary colors with either primary or secondary colors. For example, a red-violet may have more violet or red tonal qualities; an orange may be more red or more yellow. These combinations are known as **quaternary colors,** or fourth-step colors. These raise the total number of colors on the wheel to 24.

Addition of Achromatic Colors

For tints and shades of these color wheel hues, each color is given a range from white to black. Thus, pale pink shades to deeper pink, to red, to dark red, and finally to burgundy.

CHARACTERISTICS OF COLORS

People have observable reactions to colors. Colors evoke a feeling of warmth or of coolness, and colors advance or recede. People also have various emotional reactions to the different colors.

Cool Colors

Blue is considered to be the coolest color on the color wheel. Achromatic white is equally cool. Combining blue with white gives the iciest look possible. You sense the coolness that blue mixed with white conveys when you think of a pale blue sky or a pale blue sea.

Similarly, pale green reminiscent of celery, lettuce, or dewy grass gives the feeling of coolness. A room with pale green walls makes you feel cool even on a warm, sunny day. Green mixed with more yellow gains a little warmth. The tint of yellow-green, however, is still cool and relaxing.

Warm Colors

Research has confirmed that colors not only appear warm or cool to the eye, but they actually make a temperature difference depending on the color of clothing being worn or of containers used to store things. Over a period of several months, two gasoline containers stood side by side. Each was filled with an identical amount of gasoline. The white-painted tank had a loss of 1.4 percent of its contents. The otherwise identical red-painted tank had a loss of 3.54 percent of its contents, over two and one-half times as much.[6]

Red is considered to be the warmest color, rivaled only by achromatic black. Orange is next, followed by yellow, red-violet, and violet. Thus when red is used, people perceive their environment as warm.

Adding white to these warm colors progressively makes them appear and feel cooler. Pink (red plus white) is a frothy and cool-looking color — reminding people of strawberry sodas and refreshing watermelon. Pale yellow, pale orange, and pale red-violet are also cool-looking colors.

Adding black to these warm colors progressively makes them appear and feel warmer. Thus, brown (orange, red-orange, or yellow-orange plus black), burgundy, and deep violet are all warm-appearing colors.

Even otherwise cool-appearing colors gain warmth in darker shades. Also, pure intense colors are warmer-appearing than their tints. Royal blue (an intense electric blue), navy blue, midnight blue, dark green, and vivid turquoise and aqua (blue-green colors) all appear warmer than their paler counterparts.

Advancing and Receding Colors

In addition to giving the impression of being warm or cool, some colors appear to advance while others appear to recede. Generally, warm colors appear to advance and cool colors appear to recede. Thus, a wall painted red or orange will appear to come forward, while the same wall painted pale blue will appear to be farther away. Dimensions increase as colors get warmer, brighter, and purer. They decrease as colors get cooler, darker, and grayer. Therefore, a person dressed in all white appears larger than the same person dressed in an identical style in all black.

Emotional Reactions to Color

Color stylists, psychologists, and others who work with color are familiar with the emotional reactions people have to color. As more experiments are made with color, more knowledge is gained about its power.

Afterimages

Afterimage is a phenomenon that most people have experienced after staring intently at a vividly colored spot or an object and then looking at a neutral, white, or black color. Afterimages, or visual after-sensations, produce color contrasts. They are caused by first exciting the retina of the eye and then causing fatigue of that retina when the stimulus is removed.[7]

Thus, if you stare at a white dot on a black surface and then look at a black surface, a blacker dot will appear. Staring at a black dot on a white

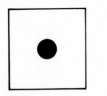

Figure 2-3. *Stare at each of these images and then focus on another black or white surface. See the afterimage?*

surface and then looking at another white surface will show an even whiter dot. See Figure 2-3. Similarly, staring at a small red dot will result in a green afterimage. Staring at a green dot produces a red afterimage. Blue yields an orange afterimage, while orange yields a blue afterimage. Yellow and violet yield afterimages of each other.

Summary Characteristics

The first standard color reference card was issued in 1915 to simplify color work by standardizing colors. Colors, designated by numbers, have been added from time to time. Names have been given to the colors to help to define them, but the colors are ordered by number. The Color Association has 192 colors on its chart. The table on page 22 describes 81 of those colors plus black, which has no reference number. Colors are arranged from pale tints to dark shades under each category.

Red. Red is the color that, for most people, evokes the greatest reaction. It is associated with blood and fire. Intense red keeps people awake and restless. Restaurants with red walls and red-padded furniture have a faster turnover of patrons than restaurants with paler or cooler-colored walls. Popular sayings in reference to red include the following.

- Feeling in the pink
- Having red-letter days
- Being a scarlet woman
- Seeing red
- Rolling out the red carpet (honoring someone)
- Seeing the world through rose-colored glasses

Orange. Since red is a component of orange, this color is also stimulating and exciting. Because it is a warm, advancing color, it attracts attention. Orange is associated with sunsets and autumn colors.

Yellow. Yellow, which is associated with the sun and warmth, springtime, a candle's flicker, and gold, is a cheerful, festive color. It is the most visible color from a distance. When the yellow color is intense, objects appear larger than any other colored objects of the same size.

Sayings associated with yellow are quite different from its other associations.

- Producing yellow journalism (unscrupulously sensational)
- Having a yellow streak
- Yellowing with age

Green. Green is known as nature's color because it is so profusely spread across the land. Green is restful and tranquil. Rooms painted in green are conducive to study, serenity, and reflection. Green is a cool, receding color that harmonizes with all other colors. But green also has some unpleasant associations. Popular sayings in reference to green include the following.

- Green with jealousy or envy
- Greenhorns
- Having a green thumb (being good at growing plants)

Blue. Blue is a cool, calming color and is restful and conservative. It symbolizes restraint, peace, and tranquility. Popular sayings in reference to blue include the following.

- Being a true-blue friend
- Being a blue blood
- Making a blue-chip investment (one of the finest)

Violet. Violet, known also as purple, has long been associated with royalty. Thus it has represented elegance, drama, splendor, opulence, and a regal appearance. It also evokes feelings of sorrow, affliction, and mystery. In general, violet is fairly warm in appearance except in its paler blue-violet tints. It is also a color that advances but not as much as red, orange, or yellow. Popular sayings in reference to violet (purple) include the following.

- Writing purple prose
- Being born to the purple
- Being purple with rage

Black. Black serves as a dramatic accent when used with white or other colors. It is also sophisticated in appearance. But black is also associated with funerals, depression, and nighttime.

When worn, black is slenderizing, but it attracts heat and therefore is quite warm. Black is hard to see unless it is placed against white or another light or bright color. Several sayings refer to black.

- Being blackballed
- Being in a black mood
- Feeling that a black shadow or cloud hangs over you

White. White represents innocence, purity, hope, peace, and surrender. It repels heat and is second only to yellow for visibility. Some sayings refer to white.

- Showing a white flag (surrendering)
- Having lily-white hands
- Being white with fury

Neutrals. Colors that are neither one thing nor the other, are quiet in tone, or are in a middle position are known as **neutrals.** The best known and truest neutral is **gray,** the achromatic midway between white and black. Popular sayings in reference to neutral gray are the following.

- What a gray day (gloomy)
- In a gray mood (unhappy)
- A gray area of the law (unclear)

Theoretically, when colors opposite each other on the color wheel are mixed together in the proper proportion, they yield gray. However, because of the difficulty in balancing the two colors, a true gray is difficult to achieve in this way. Instead, blue-grays, yellow-grays, green-grays, and red-grays emerge from such mixtures.

Tints of brown, which is a shade of red-orange, orange, and yellow-orange, are also considered to be neutrals. These tints are known by names such as tan, ecru, cream, eggshell, and off-white.

Table 2-1 EXAMPLES OF COLOR NAMES AND COLOR GRADATIONS

Neutral—White to Black

Bleached white (80001) Whiter than white

Pearl gray (80093) Pale gray-tinged neutral

Silver (80139) Pale gray like silver metal

Steel (80141) Slightly darker gray than silver

Smoke (80099) Dark gray like chimney smoke

Black (no number) Dark like a starless night

Pale Tan to Dark Brown

Natural (80008) Pale tan-tinted white

Champagne (80169) Pale tan like champagne wine

Sand (80124) Tannish gray like sand on the beach

Nude (80127) Rich pale tan

Ecru (80187) Medium tan

Beige (80188) Slightly deeper toned than ecru

Tan (80152) Rich medium-toned tan like fine leather

Toast brown (80128) Deep-toned light brown

Sandalwood (80177) Rich medium brown

Khaki (80162) Grayed tan for army uniforms

Light olive drab (80089) Medium-toned slightly grayed brown

Cocoa (80092) Pale chocolate brown

Spice brown (80129) Dark rich brown

Tobacco (80179) Very dark brown

Red

Flesh pink (80013) Pale pink tone of fair skin

Rose pink (80017) Deep rich pink

Old rose (80086) Grayed, medium-pink color

Schiaparelli pink (80049) Sharp, bright, candy-cane pink

Cherry (80051) Deeper, slightly bluish-pink

American beauty (80053) Deep rich red named for the American Beauty rose

Apple red (80107) Bright fire-engine red

Old Glory red (80108) Deep, bright red like the stripes in the U.S. flag

Strawberry (80183) A purplish red like ripe strawberries

Garnet (80083) Black-toned red like garnet stone

Maroon (80084) Slightly darker red than garnet

Burgundy (80186) Deep, blackish-red

Blue

Baby blue (80010) Off-white with a blue tint

Sky blue (80011) Like clear sky on a summer day

Dust blue (80043) Medium-toned gray-blue

Royal blue (80173) Deep-toned, rich, bright blue like lapis lazuli stone

Old Glory blue (80075) Similar to the dark blue ground used in the U.S. flag

Navy (80174) Dark, black-blue

Violet

Lavender (80055) Pale gray lilac tone

Lilac (80058) Slightly deeper than lavender named for the lilac flower

Violet (80057) Pale reddish-lilac with a slightly deeper tone

Periwinkle (80073) Medium-toned bluish-lavender

Cornflower (80074) Slightly deeper bluish-lavender than periwinkle

Looking at Color

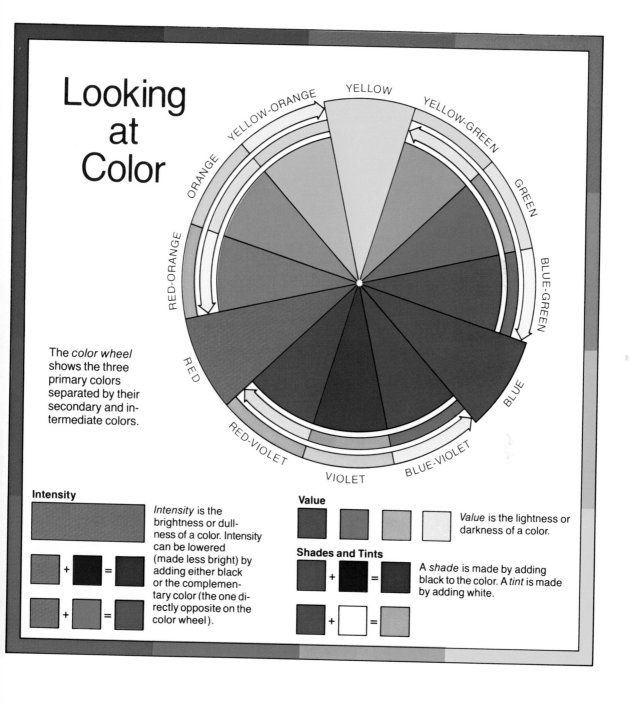

YELLOW

YELLOW-ORANGE

YELLOW-GREEN

ORANGE

GREEN

RED-ORANGE

BLUE-GREEN

RED

BLUE

RED-VIOLET

BLUE-VIOLET

VIOLET

The *color wheel* shows the three primary colors separated by their secondary and intermediate colors.

Intensity

Intensity is the brightness or dullness of a color. Intensity can be lowered (made less bright) by adding either black or the complementary color (the one directly opposite on the color wheel).

Value

Value is the lightness or darkness of a color.

Shades and Tints

A *shade* is made by adding black to the color. A *tint* is made by adding white.

Pansy (80059) Rich, pale purple-toned color

Purple (80060) Deeper toned than pansy, a rich, vibrant mixture of red and blue

Yellow

Ivory (80003) Warm white with yellow tint

Eggshell (80004) Slightly warmer than ivory

Chamois (80006) Pale orange-yellow color of chamois leather

Maize (80007) Color of rich golden corn

Lemon yellow (80090) Sharp bright yellow like lemon peel

Old gold (80109) Grayed yellow, like well-worn gold coins

Orange

Peach (80136) Pale-toned pink-orange

Tea rose (80025) Pale flesh-toned petals with warm yellow tinge

Coral (80091) Subtle, medium-toned orange-pink

Apricot (80037) Slightly darker than tea rose

Salmon pink (80026) Slightly darker than tea rose

Orange (80069) Solid mixture, like orange peel

Salmon (80039) Bright orange-pink, resembling the meat of the salmon fish

Tangerine (80040) Red-orange like ripe tangerines

Paprika (80041) Bright orange-red like the spice

Pimento (80042) Darker orange-red than paprika

Flame red (80030) Bright-toned like a candle flame

Geranium (80079) Bright yellow-tinted red, deeper than flame red

Scarlet (80080) Brighter, deeper orange-red than geranium

Burnt orange (80112) Rich-appearing, dark, grayed orange

Terra cotta (80113) Dark, rich grayed orange like the pottery

Henna (80114) Deeper-toned grayed orange than terra cotta

Green

Nile green (80031) Pale, whitish, grayed green; often called *Celadon* for the pale green porcelains of this color

Pistache (80033) Rich, pale green like the meat of pistachio nuts

Jade green (80118) Medium grayed green resembling the jadeite stone

Emerald (80063) Clear, bright, yellow-green like the emerald stone

Irish green (80120) Bright deep green color of shamrocks

Hunter green (80064) Dark shade of green

Evergreen (80036) Dark, rich, blackish-green like pine trees in the forest

Bottle green (80066) Blackish-green, darker than evergreen

Olive (80144) Dark yellowish-gray-green

Green-Blue

Forget-me-not (80012) Pale greenish-blue

Turquoise (80020) Pale tone between green and blue like the turquoise stone

Aqua (80133) Medium-toned greenish-blue like sea water

Peacock (80023) Deep rich green-blue

Electric blue (80104) Deep-toned, slightly grayed greenish-blue

Teal (80135) Deep-toned greenish-blue

This table was adapted from *The Standard Color Reference of America*, Tenth Edition, 1981, published by the Color Association of the United States.

The neutrals take on the characteristics of the color they most resemble. For example, pale stone-gray resembles white, while dark slate-gray resembles black. Neutrals are popularly used alone or in combination with other colors.

COLOR HARMONIES

What color goes with what other color? That is one of the most pervasive questions asked by customers. How colors are used alone or in combination to offer interesting, eye-appealing looks in apparel, accessories, home goods, packaging, signs, and building interiors and exteriors is both a science and an art. Arranging colors together attractively is known as **color harmony.**

People who have special ability and training in arranging colors are **color stylists.** For home interiors, they are called **interior decorators** or, when more specialized, **interior designers.** Color stylists are employed to select colors for cosmetics, fabrics, wallpaper, and other products. They also choose the colors for a garment or an outfit with its accessories, a room, a packaging material, an automobile, or even an entire home, hotel, or office building.

The color stylist has many color harmonies from which to choose. These may be further altered with the variety of tints and shades of each color, as well as with achromatic colors and neutral gray.

Commonly used color harmonies include monochromatic, analogous, triadic, complementary, split complementary, double complementary, tetrad, and asymmetric.

Monochromatic. **Mono** means one. Therefore, a color harmony that uses only a single color is **monochromatic.** Green, for example, may be used as the only color in a room. Tints and shades of the green may be used, but only the one color, green, is present. Because black, white, and gray are achromatic, they may also be used to make the monochromatic color scheme. Thus, a man's tie with a green stripe on a black background would be an example of a mono-

chromatic color harmony. A person dressed in blue jeans with a pale blue shirt and navy blue and white shoes would have a monochromatic color scheme.

Analogous. Any two or more colors adjacent to each other on the color wheel make an **analogous** color harmony. Red, red-orange, orange, and yellow-orange form an example of an analogous color harmony. This is one of the most used color harmonies for home decorating.

Triadic. **Triad** means a group of three. Any three colors spaced equally on the color wheel make a **triadic** color scheme. The primary colors (red, yellow, and blue) make a triadic color harmony. The secondary colors (orange, green, and violet) or any tertiary colors that are equidistant from each other on the color wheel also make triadic harmonies. These color combinations are rather dramatic in effect. They are usually used in small areas or where considerable excitement in color is desirable, such as in children's rooms or on toys.

Complementary. **Complement** means to complete. Those colors opposite each other on the color wheel that do not contain any part of the color that makes up the other one are **complementary.** For example, yellow, a primary color, has as its complement violet, which is made by mixing the other two primaries, red and blue. Similarly, orange, which is composed of red and yellow, has as its complement blue, which contains no red or yellow. Green, a blend of yellow and blue, has red as its complement. Blue-violet, a tertiary color, has yellow-orange as its complement. When exact parts of complementary colors are mixed together, they neutralize each other and produce gray.

Complementary colors that are intense have a vibrating effect when placed next to each other. Thus, sign painters, packagers, and others who want to attract attention often make use of these color harmonies. A straight line on a color wheel joins complementary colors.

SCHEMATIC SHOWING HARMONIES

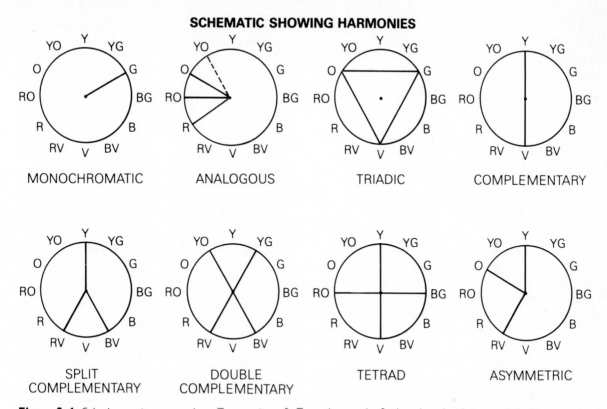

Figure 2-4. *Color harmonies are used to offer a variety of effects that can be further altered with tints and shades.*

Split Complementary. The vibrating effect of complementary colors can be softened by the use of **split complementary colors,** which are the colors from the color wheel on either side of the complementary color. Yellow would be used with blue-violet and red-violet; green would be used with red-violet and red-orange; and yellow-orange would be used with violet and blue. On the color wheel, such a harmony forms a Y shape (see Figure 2–4).

Double Complementary. Using the split complementaries from the spread part of the Y together with their respective complements to make an X form on the color wheel yields the **double complementary** color scheme. Thus, yellow-orange and yellow-green would be combined with red-violet and blue-violet. Each of the double complementary colors skips only one color in forming the narrow X on the wheel.

Tetrad. Tetrad is a four-color scheme that is interpreted in the form of a widespread cross on the color wheel. A tetrad scheme uses two complementary harmonies that are equidistant from each other on the color wheel. An example would be yellow and violet combined with red-orange and blue-green.

Asymmetric. Asymmetric two- or three-color harmony resembles analogous harmony since it uses colors from just one section of the color wheel. It differs from analogous harmony in that it skips one or two colors to form its harmonious arrangement. Thus, yellow, orange, and red-violet would make an asymmetric harmony.

USING COLOR

Even with a knowledge of colors and color harmonies, color stylists need to use judgment in putting colors together. They must consider amounts of color to use, how colors look at a distance, and how lighting and texture affect color.

Amounts of Color to Use

Selection of colors and color harmonies is only part of the task of making things look attractive together. How much of a color is used is another factor that affects a product's appearance. A dress made up of a complementary color scheme that uses one-half orange and one-half blue may be unattractive, but an orange dress with a touch of blue may be quite smart-looking. Similarly, a man's green tie with a small red motif may be handsome, whereas a tie with equal amounts of red and green may seem garish. Just knowing color harmony, therefore, is not enough. Mixing the colors in proper amounts makes designs and color schemes more interesting and more appealing.

In addition to the amount of each color that is used, the color stylist often varies the colors by using tints and shades, which alters the relationship of one color to another. For example, with a green suit a pale pink shirt may be eye-catching, whereas a red shirt may be too vivid.

Effect of Distance on Color

Colors can change dramatically when seen close up as opposed to being seen from several feet away. A small red-and-white check pattern will blur or blend to a pink from a short distance. Black-and-white checks, unless substantial in size, will appear to be gray from just a few feet away. When complementary colors, such as yellow and violet, are used together as checks, they appear to be gray from a short distance.

Intense colors also lose some of their intensity when seen from a distance. The makeup used by an actor or actress may look quite garish close up but may appear natural looking from a distance.

Effect of Lighting on Color

Lighting has a marked effect on color. Colors under artificial lighting in stores often appear one way, but in the daylight they may appear quite different. Because lighting can change color so dramatically, its effect should be known. Yellow lighting may intensify yellow colors, make blue colors appear somewhat gray or greenish, make orange colors somewhat lighter, turn red colors slightly orange, and make purple colors appear black or gray. Red lighting may make red colors look paler, cause blue colors to look purplish, and make green colors grayish. Many stores use special fluorescent lights that impart a healthy look to customers' faces but do little to change the color of merchandise.

COLOR IN FASHION APPAREL

Colors as well as silhouettes are changed frequently in fashionable wearing apparel and accessories. For any one season colors may be pale and subdued, jewel bright, or accented with inky black. New combinations of color or solids may be shown. During some seasons colors change only subtly from those of a year earlier. Other times, more dramatic changes take place.

Should you mix colors, match colors, wear one-color outfits, or wear multicolored outfits? Are multicolored stripes, dots, plaids, or checks in fashion? Are the new colors harmonious with those in the customer's closet? In addition to those questions, customers are interested in the way colors flatter them.

Men, once wearers of only the most subdued colors, have become peacocks in color selection. Shirts and ties are the usual places men express their interest in color, but clothes worn on the beaches, golf courses, and other recreational places have become a riot of color as men have adopted colored trousers, shorts, T-shirts, and bright umbrellas. Children and teenagers love color, and their clothes express not only what is fashionable but also their particular group's current color choice.

COLOR IN HOMEFURNISHINGS

Color sets the mood and drama for rooms. Although colors change yearly for homefurnishings' manufacturers, the color changes are more subtle than in the clothing industry. Some colors retain their fashionability for several years.

Careful thought must go into choosing colors in the home.

- Colors for walls, flooring, ceiling, furniture and accessories must be harmonious.
- Furnishings are not bought as often as clothing and therefore must serve for a longer period of time.
- Colors must look good both in daylight and under artificial light.
- Furniture may be rearranged or covered with slipcovers during different seasons. The furniture must harmonize with other colors in their new surroundings.
- Since people spend many hours in homes, the colors should be pleasing to the eye for a prolonged period of time.

In home decorating, the most common color schemes, while not always observed, are darker colors for the floor, medium colors for the walls, and paler colors for the ceiling. The ceiling and walls are often used for light reflection. Therefore, the paler these are, the more light that will be reflected throughout the room. Light-colored floors may also be used to reflect light. The furniture wood to be used, the floor covering, the draperies and curtains, the wall decorations, and other accessories must be considered in the overall color scheme.

Selection of homefurnishings should be made with the lighting available in the room in mind. Is the room sunny? Is it in shadows? If the room is sunny during the day, cool greens and blues will make the room seem more comfortable and relaxing. A shaded room may be given an appearance of warmth and a sunny effect by the use of yellow, orange, or red tones.

Another important consideration in planning a room is the use of artificial lighting at night. If the room will be used more often after sundown, colors should be chosen for their effect under artificial lighting.

NOTES

1. Faber Birren, *Selling Color to People*, University Books, New York, 1956, pp. 200–205.
2. *Color Is How You Light It*, Sylvania Electric Products, Inc., n.d., pp. 16–17.
3. Walter C. Granville, "Color Organization in the Ostwald System," *American Ink Maker*, June and August, 1948, reprint.
4. *Consumer Color Charts*, Munsell Color Co., Inc., Baltimore, Md., 1964, pp. 3, 16.
5. Birren, *Selling Color*, pp. 207–208.
6. Birren, *Selling Color*, pp. 68–69.
7. Maitland Graves, *Color Fundamentals*, McGraw-Hill Book Co., New York, 1952, p. 124.

DO YOU KNOW YOUR MERCHANDISE?

1. Explain what role light plays in reference to color.
2. How do colors obtained from light and colors obtained from pigments differ?
3. Define chromatic, achromatic, hue, intensity, value, tints, and shades.
4. Why are different color systems used?
5. Explain how the color wheel is created.
6. Why are red, yellow, and blue known as the primary colors in the pigment system?
7. Explain what the secondary colors are and how they are made. Explain what is meant by tertiary and quaternary colors and give some examples of each.
8. What are the unique characteristics of colors? Give examples of two or more of these characteristics.
9. What is meant by color harmony? Explain the meaning of the following harmonies: monochromatic, triadic, and tetrad.
10. Explain the effects of different colors of light on colored products. Why would a cosmetics store use special fluorescent lights?

PUTTING YOUR MERCHANDISE KNOWLEDGE TO WORK

Take a fashion count of colors worn by your classmates in one of your classes. Consider the color of their shoes, pants or skirts, shirts or blouses, handbags or briefcases, and accessories. What colors were most popular? What color harmonies did you observe? If such counts were done for an entire school, of what value might they be to a nearby retailer of those goods?

PROJECT

In one edition of a Sunday newspaper analyze newspaper advertisements for merchandise. What color names were listed? Group those colors by their primary and secondary color groupings, including achromatic. Which colors were most commonly mentioned? Were any color harmonies listed? What conclusions can you draw from this project?

3

Line and Design: The Outline and Ornamentation

When sufficient light is available, color is usually the first element of any item that is visible. After the color has registered, the outline, or shape, of the product emerges. This shape gives coherence to the item and makes it a product that is unique and different from any but identical items.

As with color, lines may be pleasing or displeasing to the viewer. Lines affect the way an article looks. Color and line make items or wearers look more slender or more rotund, taller or shorter, more masculine or more feminine, more restful or more agitated. The two elements of color and line have enormous importance to all merchandise. Lines by themselves or combined with color are joined to form designs, which are discussed later.

LINE

The most basic, elemental form of any object is the **line.** A line is a mark that may be drawn in sand or on paper, painted on any surface, or scratched into metal or stone. Lines may be used to form the outer contour of an object, or they may be used to develop the design that decorates an object. Lines may be short or long; thick, thin, or tapered; single or multiple; straight or curved; vertical, horizontal, or diagonal.

Lines are everywhere. They form the outlines of every object you see from the tiniest microscopic germ to the moon, stars, and planets in the universe. The designer uses lines to create common as well as rare objects. Lines are used by designers to create the forms of things such as homes, cars, computers, furniture, clothing, and accessories. Lines are also the elements for written communication. They form the letters of an alphabet and the symbols of calligraphy and hieroglyphics.

The Shape of Lines and Their Effect upon Us

Lines affect you because they carry your eyes along their length. In doing this, they appear to have vitality and movement. Horizontal, vertical, diagonal, and curvilinear lines all have their own characteristics.

Horizontal Lines. Lines that run crosswise are **horizontal lines.** These are relaxing and restful lines that usually do not jar or disturb the viewer. These lines are associated with a sleeping position, a symbol of inactivity. Moldings in rooms are horizontal and are parallel to ceilings. Furniture with horizontal planes, such as the backs of sofas and the tops of tables and chests, is comfortable to live with and to see daily. Horizontal lines may make an object look wider than it is. Therefore, a stout person with clothing that forms horizontal lines, such as a belt or a jacket bottom, may appear to be shorter and stouter than is actually the case.

Vertical Lines. Lines that run up and down are **vertical lines.** These lines are associated with a standing position, giving the appearance of power and strength. They are usually considered to lend importance to merchandise. Draperies, tall lamps, front closings on coats and suit jackets, and lengthwise stripes on clothing or homefurnishings are examples of vertical lines. A room with vertical lines appears higher than the same room with primarily horizontal lines. Vertical lines when worn by a very stout person, however, may be distorted and not give the desired tall effect.

Diagonal Lines. Straight lines that run at an angle, such as the sides of a triangle are **diagonal lines.** They are the lines associated with a person who is striding or walking. Furniture with peaked tops, triangularly formed lamps, clothes with an off-the-shoulder look or with diagonal stripes all create the effect of diagonal excitement. A few such lines add interest to a room or to clothes, but an excess of this effect may be jarring to the viewer.

Curvilinear Lines. Lines that undulate or are slightly bent are **curvilinear lines.** They appear soft and pleasant and are easy to look at. If curvilinear lines run crosswise, they seem even more restful and harmonious. Thus rounded backs on chairs, sofas, or chests and rounded tables and edges on furniture are pleasant to view daily. Round collars, round necklines on dresses, and slightly wavy patterns are all pleasant and restful to wear and to see. If curvilinear lines are deep and narrow, they take on the character of vertical lines. When curvilinear lines are combined with diagonal lines, they appear agitated and disturbed, like waves dashing against rocks in an angry sea.

DESIGN

The designer uses lines and space between lines to create order and rhythm that have appeal for different people under varying circumstances. By combining, isolating, and ordering various elements from nature or your imagination, **designs** may be formed. These may express picturelike representations, may suggest the original, may simply be influenced by the original, or may be entirely fanciful.

Everything that is created has a design, or plan. Whether or not the design is appealing to others, it represents a unification of elements that portrays what the designer wants to communicate to viewers or users. The designs may be realistic or naturalistic, stylized or conventionalized, geometric, or abstract.

Realistic or Naturalistic

Designs that follow the original element, whether human, animal, plant, or mineral, so they are

Figure 3-1. Above, a geometric flower shape; below, realistic flowers and leaves.

immediately recognizable and appear to be almost photographic are called **realistic** or **naturalistic**. Realistic or naturalistic designs are found on paper, canvas, other fabrics, in carvings on wood and metal objects, on chinaware, or wherever the designer wants to duplicate nature.

Some designers create such realistic-appearing designs that from a short distance the design appears to be the actual material or object. When the design is this realistic, it is known as *trompe l'oeil* in French or *quadrature*, meaning fool the eye, in Italian. Such realism is used only when unusual effects are sought.

Stylized or Conventionalized

When the designer finds duplicating nature is either too difficult or not desirable, the design may be changed, that is, **stylized** or **conventionalized**. The design may be made to conform to a given space, to be easier to represent, or to give a different appearance. For example, flowers that droop slightly in nature may be straightened and arranged more formally or articles may be simplified to achieve desired effects. This imparted change may make the finished objects more appealing, more dramatic, or more suitable for their intended use.

Geometric

Lines are used to make forms such as rectangles, triangles, stars, and circles that are known as **geometrics**. Horizontal and vertical lines may intersect to form crosses, checks, or plaids. Many vertical and horizontal lines of equal thickness that intersect at equal distances from one another form a checkered pattern. Horizontal and vertical lines of different thicknesses that intersect at different distances form plaids.

Calligraphy, writing or penmanship (especially Chinese, Japanese, and Islamic), forms a type of geometric design that is so attractive it is often used as decorative art. Chinese and Japanese paintings and fabrics sometimes consist solely of designs from their written language.

Abstract

When nature has been so distorted that it is almost unrecognizable or when nonobjective shapes have been used that do not resemble anything in nature, the design is said to be **abstract**. Abstract art is designed to evoke feelings and reactions that may be more intense than those achieved by realistic or conventionalized forms.

ELEMENTS OF DESIGN

Regardless of their size, designs form a composition. A room, or a single picture, or a tablesetting, or a person's outfit including the accessories may each represent a composition. A **composition** refers to a grouping of different parts of a work to give it order. The elements that make up a composition are color, line, space, shape, texture, pattern, and light. Not all are needed in every composition, but most will be represented in the majority of compositions.

Color. Color as a part of a design was discussed in Chapter 2. Color often plays an important part in designs.

Line. Line not only has direction and flat or curvilinear form, as discussed earlier, but it is also a component of space and of what occurs within that space. For example, lines shape the outline of a suit, including the lapel and pocket details, or the outline of a sofa or bench. Whatever is depicted is shown through lines. In addition, the effect of space is changed by the lines that surround it and that appear within it.

Space. Space has many meanings. People call the outdoors "space." When astronauts circle the world, people refer to them as being in "outer space." Space itself has no confines, but people put up walls and fences to encompass some of that space. A given item occupies space. People constantly refer to the amount of space they have in which to work, study, move, sleep, eat, entertain, and travel.

What you do within the confines of a given space determines how that space looks, how ample it appears, and how well it serves your needs and desires. Objects within space operate like color, appearing to enlarge or diminish the size of the space. Larger objects may make the space appear smaller, while smaller objects may make it appear larger. Vertical objects often make space appear higher, while horizontal objects may make it appear shorter. Thus, what the designer does within the space changes the apparent size of that space.

Shape. The outline, or contours, of an article formed by lines are its **shape.** You identify an object by its shape. The shapes of different peoples' eyes, noses, lips, and facial contours allow you to identify one from the other even though those shapes are quite similar.

When new or different shapes are introduced in a product, customers are sometimes confused by the new shape. After seeing it for a while, their eyes adjust to that shape and it often becomes an accepted one. Then it may be replaced by yet another shape. Thus, tail fins on automobiles grew enormously with each model year during the 1950s but receded and disappeared during the 1970s.

Texture. **Texture** usually applies to the feel of a product. However, your eyes also translate the appearance of a substance regardless of its actual feel. Thus, a product with a photographed alligator grain will appear to have a bumpy surface even though it is very smooth to the touch. Similarly, plastics with wood grain will appear to have a grainy texture even though they are smooth. Truly textured materials have light and shadow playing on the surface in addition to the feel or sensory experience the user has of them. Texture adds character to an article.

Pattern or Ornamentation. When the surface of an object is given added decorative appeal, a **pattern** or **ornamentation** has been applied. Furniture may have carvings, inlays, or painted surfaces. Chinaware may have embossed designs, moldings, gold encrustation, hand-painted designs, or decalcomanias (colored transfer prints) as decoration. Wallpaper, fabrics, leathers, woods, and plastics may be covered with printed designs and colors. Articles may be sparsely or heavily ornamented.

Light. Without light you would see none of the other elements of design. **Light** is both natural and artificial. Natural light ranges from brilliant sunshine to the dark skies. When daylight is not sufficient for seeing, artificial light may be used. The effects of lighting are further discussed in Chapter 29.

PRINCIPLES OF DESIGN

Although a design may be created that does not incorporate all the elements of design, most do include a majority of those elements. In order to make pleasing combinations the elements of design must follow a plan that enables them to form an attractive whole. This plan is based on the **principles of design.** These principles incorporate the scale of the articles in relation to the space in which they are used, the proportions of the articles to each other, the way the articles are balanced in use, the rhythm that results from their placement, the emphasis necessary to help the viewer focus on the most important area, and the overall harmony that results when viewing the total design.

Scale

Scale refers to the relative size of items, particularly in relation to a constant such as the human body. Clothing, for example, must be made to the scale of a person's figure. Furniture must be a suitable size for the intended user. If you have tried on a suit that is too large or sat in a chair that is too deep, you know that the scale of those articles differed from the scale you sought. Designers must observe the relative size of the people or objects for whom or with which their creations will be used.

Proportion

Proportion, which is closely related to scale, refers mainly to items or decorations within a given space. For example, the furniture for an adult may be proportional, one piece to the other, but be the wrong scale for a small child. Your sense of proportion helps you to judge when articles or representations appear to be right for each other. Thus, you may be disturbed by a very large chair in a small room, a very large bow on a child's dress, or a very large lamp on a small, spindly table.

Balance

You see the effects of balance everywhere. A large tree trunk supports the smaller spreading branches and leaves; a long stem holds spreading flower petals. When toe dancers stand on one toe, the ability to balance the rest of their bodies enables them to stay upright.

Balance may be achieved by weight or support, as well as by an arrangement of objects that allows them to appear equally distributed when you look at them. Balance may be achieved through the placement of shapes, textures, and sizes, by the tones of light and dark, and by colors. Balance may be symmetrical or asymmetrical.

Symmetrical or Formal Balance. The most obvious and easy to achieve balance is known as **symmetrical,** or **formal,** balance. This is a bilateral, or two-sided, balance that presents a mirror image of each side. Thus, a wall with a table in the center and a matching chair on each side of the table has symmetrical balance. A man's suit with lapels, pockets on each side, and a center closing has formal balance. Store displays with a product in the middle and identical but different sized products on either side have achieved this type of balance.

Another form of symmetrical balance that has a center from which forms emanate is known as **radial balance.** A tire with center hub cap and spokes is an example of radial balance.

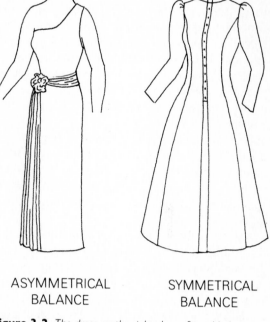

ASYMMETRICAL BALANCE   SYMMETRICAL BALANCE

Figure 3-2. *The dress on the right shows formal balance, while the shoulder and waist details give the dress on the left informal balance.*

Formal balance is easy to achieve and therefore commonly used. However, it is a rather static, passive, uninteresting type of balance that can become tiresome if overdone. A room with four walls each having formal balance would appear less exciting that the same room with only one wall having formal balance.

Asymmetrical or Informal Balance. When objects do not form mirror images on each side but still appear balanced to the viewer, an **optical** or **informal** or **asymmetrical** balance has been achieved. This is more difficult to arrange than formal balance, but it also adds interest and vitality to any arrangement.

The basic premise upon which asymmetrical balance is based may be understood by visualizing a teeter-totter such as children use in a playground. If two children of equal weight are placed on either end, formal balance is achieved because each sits the same distance from the center point on which the teeter-totter rests.

However, if the children are of unequal weight, the smaller child must sit farther from the center and the larger child must move nearer to the center to achieve balance. Similarly, on a mantelpiece, if two vases of unequal size were to be displayed, the smaller would need to be placed farther from the center and the larger nearer the center to achieve optical or asymmetrical balance.

Nature provides many examples of asymmetrical balance. Examples are windblown trees, flowers that face the sun, minerals that are found in odd shapes, and a landscape bounded by mountains on one side and the seashore on the other.

Asymmetrical balance is used in clothing and furnishings. Dresses and bathing suits may have one shoulder bared, jackets may button on the side, and a wall may have a piano or desk on one side and bookcases on the other. These and countless other examples of asymmetrical balance are seen daily.

Elements That Affect Balance. Not only shape is used to achieve balance. **Tonal values** also may be used, such as balancing lighter tones with darker tones. On a light- or medium-toned background, darker tones have more visual weight than lighter ones. In this situation a small dark object may be equal in visual weight to a larger light-toned object. On the other hand, if the background is dark, a small light-toned object will have more apparent weight than a larger dark object.

Texture also affects balance. Rough textures usually appear to be heavier than smooth textures. Thus, a room with a large floor space of smooth material may appear to balance a few pieces of wooden furniture. A small embroidered design may be effectively set on background of a smooth fabric.

Color, discussed in Chapter 2, also affects balance. Small amounts of brilliant colors may appear to be balanced when combined with large amounts of more neutral colors. An all-beige room with small accents of throw pillows and

Figure 3-3. *Rhythm may be achieved through patterns of shapes, colors, tonal values, sizes, or textures. Note the repeated motifs in the bedspread, china vases, plant, and decorative plates.*

vases of brilliant turquoise can appear quite dramatic and well balanced. A neutral colored dress accented with dramatically colored jewelry may give the wearer a balanced appearance.

Rhythm

Music and dance are familiar sources of rhythm. The beating of drums, as well as the repetition of the notes and rests, sets the rhythm in music. The movements of the dancers also create rhythm. In decoration, **rhythm** is achieved visually by repetition. The repetition may be of forms, colors, tonal values, or textures. It may be alternated (dot-dash-dot-dash); progressive (small dot, medium-sized dot, larger dot); or contrasting (small versus large, dark versus light). Polka dots, for example, have rhythm with the repetition of the dots throughout the cloth. A room that has a round table with round-shaped dishes on it has rhythm.

Rhythm gives a sense of movement. Things are not static but have a sense of excitement. Continuity of the design, form, or color produces rhythm in an article or in a setting.

Emphasis

Within every composition, your eye is usually attracted to one element that is dominant. This domination is referred to as **emphasis**. Emphasis may be achieved by size, position, shape, color, light, texture, or arrangement. The element toward which your eye is directed is the **focal point,** or point of emphasis, within a room or a composition. On a person, bows, necklaces, neckties, a hairdo, or other wearing apparel may become the focus of attention. In a room, a picture, a lamp, a wall hanging, a piece of furniture, or a special ornament may become the focus of attention.

Painters help direct the eye of the viewer to the area of most importance. Dancers pose in a manner that directs the viewer to the featured dancer. Compositions that are well-developed help to concentrate the eye of the viewer on the most important area.

Harmony

People instinctively look for harmony in things. The creator of any composition, ensemble, or assemblage of articles for a room hopes to create an overall **harmony.** This comes from the proper placement and unification of the various sizes, shapes, colors, and light arrangements of the various parts.

Components not in harmony with one another make for a discordant experience. For example, you would experience a lack of harmony in seeing a man attired formally with tuxedo, white shirt, and black bow tie, but wearing outsize soiled tennis shoes. A room with all modern, light-colored and pale-colored furniture would lack harmony if an ornate, Victorian-type picture dominated one wall.

To avoid monotony in objects or compositions, the harmony should provide some variety. Thus, a room with all round-shaped furniture and round decorations would have unity but not variety. Having some furniture with angular shapes and some wall decorations in square or rectangular shapes would add variety without destroying the overall harmony of the room.

FAMILIAR DESIGNS OR COMPONENTS OF DESIGN

The elements and principles of design have been used by artisans through the ages in the creation of patterns that appear and reappear on products. In different countries and at different times forms have been developed that have come to be admired and used by designers in other areas of the world. These forms have been given names that identify them. Their use gives character to the objects on which they are found. To help you to recognize these forms, they have been grouped either by the type of design they represent or by the country in which they were initially developed.

Geometric Designs

Combinations of lines that form angles or arcs make up hundreds of designs. **Geometric forms** are those forms that relate to surfaces, lines, angles, curves, and solids. In geometry, **solid** is the term for a three-dimensional figure that has

GEOMETRIC DESIGNS

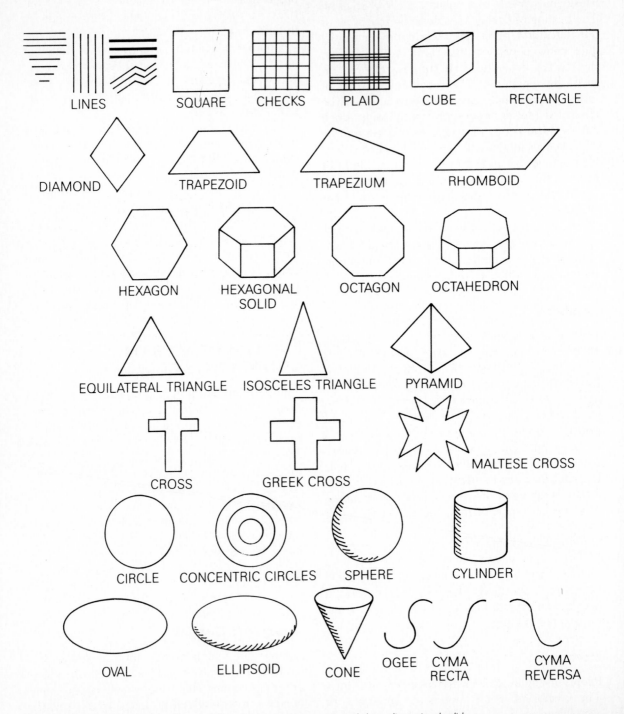

Figure 3-4. *Geometric forms relate to surfaces, lines, angles, curves, and three-dimensional solids.*

depth, as well as width and height of two-dimensional, or planar, figure.

Geometric forms include the following.

Lines: Straight lines alone or in groupings may form designs. By making the lines thicker or thinner and by arranging them in some order, many different designs may emerge.

Square: When four equal-length lines are joined at right angles (90 degrees) to one another, a square is formed. They may vary in size from tiny squares used in the checks on gingham cloth to vast squares that occupy a major portion of a wall. Some plaid designs are made by varying the thickness of the lines that intersect one another and by varying the placement of those lines.

Cube: Squares joined together to form six different sides form a solid cube.

Rectangle: The most common shape used for rooms, doors, and windows is the rectangle. It is composed of four lines like the square, but one pair of parallel lines is shorter than the other pair. Some plaids are composed of rectangles rather than squares.

Quadrilateral: Any four-sided figure is a quadrilateral. It may be square or have sides of unequal length.

Diamond: A diamond is a plane figure formed by four equal-length straight lines. When joined, these lines form two acute angles (less than 90 degrees) and two obtuse angles (more than 90 degrees).

Trapezoid: A trapezoid is a quadrilateral in which only two sides are parallel.

Trapezium: A trapezium is a quadrilateral in which no sides are parallel.

Rhomboid: A rhomboid is a parallelogram (figure with two pairs of sides parallel to each other) with oblique (either acute or obtuse) angles joining the adjacent sides.

Hexagon: A hexagon is a six-sided plane figure with six angles.

Hexagonal: A hexagonal is a solid six-sided figure.

Octagon: An octagon is a plane figure with eight sides.

Octahedron: An octahedron is a solid figure with an eight-plane surface.

Triangle: A triangle is a plane figure bounded by three lines and containing three angles.

　Equilateral triangle: An equilateral triangle has all three sides equal in length.

　Isosceles triangle: An isosceles triangle is a three-sided figure with only two sides equal in length.

Pyramid: A pyramid is a triangular-shaped conelike solid with triangular-shaped sides that rise to join each other at the apex. It may be composed of four or more triangles (including the base).

Cross: Many variations of the cross exist. Basically, it is a T-shaped figure.

　Greek cross: Two lines that intersect in the middle form a Greek cross.

　Maltese cross: Four-arms with V-shaped ends form a Maltese cross.

　Swastika: A greek cross with the end of each arm bent in the same direction forms a swastika.

Circle: A circle is a curved line in which every point is equidistant from the center. **Rondels** are designs formed primarily from circles.

Concentric circles: Various sized circles one inside the other but all with a common center form concentric circles.

Sphere or ball: A sphere is a solid round object or globe.

Cylinder: A cylinder is a three-dimensional shape with parallel sides and circular ends.

Oval or ellipse: An oval or ellipse is an off-center ball shape that is formed like a flattened circle.

Ellipsoid: An ellipsoid is a solid ellipse or oval shape.

Cone: A cone is a solid circular figure that tapers to a point or apex.

Ogee: An ogee is an S-shaped form, used especially for moldings and shapings on furniture.

　Cyma recta: The S-shaped ogee is called a **cyma recta.**

　Cyma reversa: The reverse S-shaped ogee is called a **cyma reversa.**

Egyptian Design

The ancient Egyptians primarily used objects from nature with which they were familiar. From 4,500 B.C. to A.D. 640 they fashioned many of the most impressive monuments and designs that have ever been created. These have been reproduced and adapted through time.

Animal feet, paws, and forms: These were used commonly in artistic decoration and as parts of furniture.

Griffin: In ancient and medieval legends, this creature had the head and wings of an eagle and the body of a lion. It is also called a **griffon** and a **gryphon.**

EGYPTIAN MOTIFS

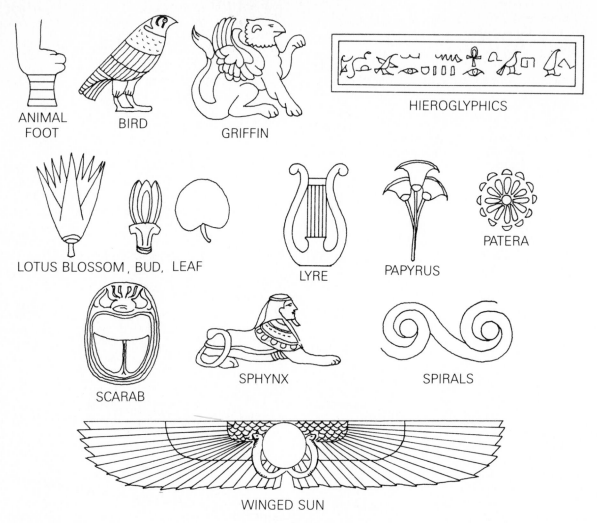

ANIMAL FOOT   BIRD   GRIFFIN   HIEROGLYPHICS

LOTUS BLOSSOM, BUD, LEAF   LYRE   PAPYRUS   PATERA

SCARAB   SPHYNX   SPIRALS

WINGED SUN

Figure 3-5. *Egyptian designs, created thousands of years ago, have been reproduced and adapted through time.*

Hieroglyphics: Hieroglyphics is a type of writing used in ancient Egypt in the form of pictographs. These were conventionalized pictures used to represent meanings.

Human form: Pictures of men and women attired in the scant clothing worn in ancient Egypt were used as decoration on most of the buildings and furniture.

Lotus: The lotus plant, which is a water lily with large shield-shaped leaves, is the national emblem of Egypt. The bud, the opening flower, the opened flower, and the leaf are all used in carved decorations and paintings.

Lyre: A lyre is a stringed musical instrument noted for its graceful, symmetrical shape. It was used as decoration in ancient Egypt and adapted extensively during the eighteenth century as a design on furniture.

Papyrus: Papyrus, a sedge or grasslike plant with a tall stem, grew in the marshes or swamps of ancient

Egypt. It was the hieroglyphic symbol for lower Egypt and a common motif in art. Tall columns often had papyrus leaves on the capital at their top.

Patera: Patera are flower petals in a formal pattern set in round or oval-shaped designs.

Scarab: A scarab is a beetle held sacred by ancient Egyptians. The image of the beetle was cut from a stone or gem. It was often engraved on its underside and worn as a charm.

Sphinx: A sphinx is a mythical monster, half-human and half-lion, with a human head and an ánimal body. It was used as an ornament for furniture and buildings.

Spirals: Spirals are border patterns of continuous wavelike circular forms.

Vulture: The vulture is a symbol of protection in Egypt. The vulture with outspread wings was familiarly used in drawings, as decoration on buildings, and on jewelry.

Winged Sun: A disk surrounded by wings, representing the god Horus of Edfu, was used over doorways in temples as protection.

Chinese Design

China has contributed to the enrichment of design since before 1200 b.c. to the present. Only a few of its symbolic designs are listed here. The term **chinoiserie,** referring to Chinese-type decoration, means especially products made since the eighteenth century that have embodied some of the Chinese design characteristics. The Chinese used both natural and mythical forms, as well as concepts of happiness and long life, as the basis of many of their designs.

Bat: A conventionalized form of the bat is emblematic of happiness and long life.

CHINESE MOTIFS

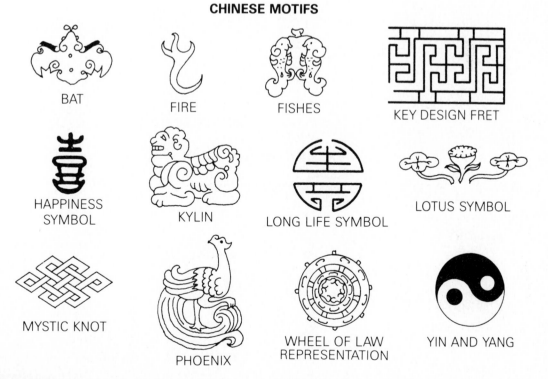

Figure 3-6. *The Chinese used natural and mythical forms, as well as mental concepts, for their symbolic designs.*

Dragon: The dragon is a mythical animal regarded by the Chinese as having a good influence. Dragons were shown on land, in the clouds, and in the sea. Five-clawed dragons were the symbol of the emperor.

Fire: One of the important elements affecting life, fire is depicted by flamelike designs.

Fishes: Pairs of fishes are among the auspicious signs from the footprint of Buddha signifying harmony and connubial bliss.

Happiness Symbol: Adapted from the calligraphy symbol for happiness, this balanced design is shown in several forms.

Key Design: A continuous border design used on furniture and furnishings. The design forms a fretwork pattern made of interlocking lines.

Knot of Everlasting Happiness or Mystic Knot: A small fret design with no beginning or end. This is a Buddhist symbol originally derived from India.

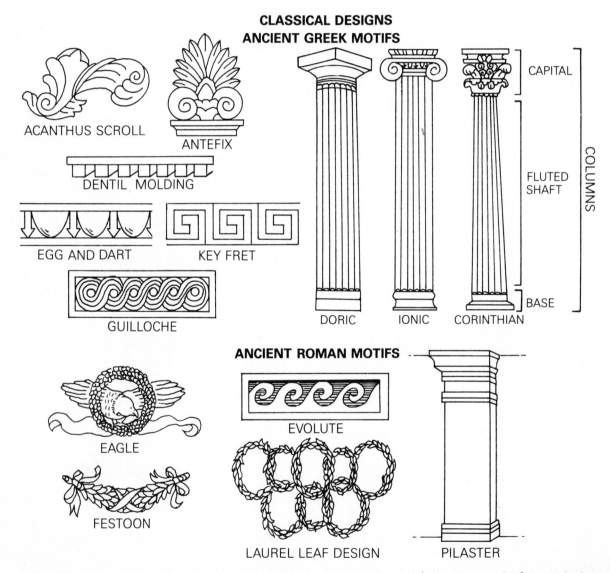

CLASSICAL DESIGNS
ANCIENT GREEK MOTIFS

ACANTHUS SCROLL

ANTEFIX

DENTIL MOLDING

EGG AND DART

KEY FRET

GUILLOCHE

CAPITAL

FLUTED SHAFT

BASE

COLUMNS

DORIC   IONIC   CORINTHIAN

ANCIENT ROMAN MOTIFS

EAGLE

FESTOON

EVOLUTE

LAUREL LEAF DESIGN

PILASTER

Figure 3-7. *Greek and Roman classical designs especially influenced architecture but also left their stamp on other forms used today.*

Kylin: A kylin is a mythological horselike beast with a head of a dragon and the back of a tortoise. It portends the birth of an eminent sage.

Long Life: The calligraphy symbol for long life has many forms that are used as decoration.

Lotus: The Chinese arranged the lotus in a symmetrical form. Its design carries auspicious wishes and was esteemed by both the Buddhists and the Taoists.

Phoenix: The phoenix is a mythological bird believed to have a good influence in times of peace and prosperity. It was the symbol of the empress.

Swastika: The swastika, used in many countries, came to China from India through Buddhism. It was believed to have come from heaven and represented an accumulation of lucky signs possessing 10,000 efficacies. It was used singly or as a fretwork pattern.

Wheel of Law: The wheel of law is an auspicious sign from the footprint of Buddha that is symbolic of the crushing effect of Buddha's teachings upon delusions and superstitions.

Yin and Yang: Yin and yang is the symbol for the egg showing the yolk and white and representing the positive and negative principles of universal life. The white part, yang, symbolizes heaven, sun, light, male. The dark part, yin, symbolizes the earth, moon, darkness, and female. Through their interaction, the yin and yang produce the elements — fire, water, air, and earth.

Classical Design — Ancient Greek

The Grecian architects and designers from approximately 2,000 B.C. until A.D. 1 used creative designs extensively. Many of the art forms they devised are still used in designs and decoration today. Greek architecture was particularly famous. Some of the most famous types of design motifs are listed below.

Acanthus Leaf: The leaf from the acanthus plant, a perennial shrub native to the tropics, was large and had a noticeable spine. It was stylized and used as a motif in architecture particularly.

Animal Forms: These were used in decoration both in shaping articles and as motifs inside border designs.

Antefix: Used at the summit of Greek temples, this was a stylized single palmetto leaf. The ornament is based on radiating leaves.

Anthemion: Also called a **palmetto,** this is a radiating, fan-shaped design suggestive of the honeysuckle found growing in warm climates. It was widely used on buildings and in decorative motifs as a border design.

Arabesques: Arabesques are scroll and leaf patterns with stems rising from a root and branching into spiral forms. The Greeks combined these with plant and animal forms into vertical patterns.

Architectural Orders: Especially famous were the Greek architectural orders that included the base or pedestal, columns, capitals, or decorative tops, and entablatures, or beams atop the columns, used in their famous buildings. The three capitals used were the Doric (used on the Parthenon), the Ionic, and less frequently, the Corinthian.

   Doric: The Doric is a plain capital that is sturdy appearing but graceful.

   Ionic: The Ionic capital has a volute scroll at the top and an egg and dart border between.

   Corinthian: The Corinthian capital has acanthus leaves bending out to form an elaborate design.

Atlantes: The word "Atlantes" is the plural of "Atlas." These were sculpted male figures serving as supports in buildings.

Caryatid: A Caryatid is a sculptured female figure serving as an ornamental support in place of a column in buildings.

Chimera: In Greek mythology, this animal was part lion, part goat, and part dragon.

Dentils: Dentils are teethlike squares used in moldings. They were initially used on Doric orders but are now used as decoration on mantels, furniture, and moldings.

Egg and Dart: The egg, or ovoid form, together with a separating dart, tongue, or anchor were designs used for moldings. The Greeks used these for borders and with Ionic capitals. The alternating egg and dart form an attractive raised design.

Fluting: Carvings that run the length of a column on the Greek orders are flutings. These carvings are concave and give an attractive molded appearance to the column. They are commonly used on furniture legs.

Fret: An interlocking design, usually carved in low relief on a solid ground is a fret. It is composed of geometric patterns.

Greek Key: A Greek key is a wavelike design made from geometric forms. It makes a fretwork pattern and is used to trim borders of furniture, carpets, other accessories and fabrics.

Guilloche: A guilloche is a border of interlacing

spirals enclosing circles or ornamented centers. It was carved into stone or wood.

Reeding: Reedings are carvings used on columns and furniture. The carvings run the length of the article. Reeding, as a design, comes from the appearance of a bunch of rushes or reeds tied together. They have a convex form in contrast to the concave form of fluted designs.

Rinceau: A rinceau is a continuous ornament of intertwined leaves and stems in a spiral or wavy form. It is the horizontal form of an arabesque.

Volute: A volute is a spiral scroll based on plants with leaves curling inward. The most notable example is on the Ionic capital.

Classical Design — Roman

Roman decorating, from the founding of Rome in 753 B.C. until its period of supreme power in the Mediterranean in A.D. 315, is included under classical styles. The Romans conquered other countries and absorbed their arts and adapted them to the Roman needs and culture. The Romans developed cement, an easier medium to work with than stone. They used variations of the Greek orders for their columns. They also used many figures, heads, and busts of famous Romans.

Some of the Roman designs they added to the classical Greek ones include the following.

Acanthus Leaf: This decorative leaf was even more stylized by the Romans than it had been by the Greeks.

Acanthus Scroll: A side view shows a gracefully arched form of the acanthus leaf

Amorini (cupids): Cupids both at rest and in active poses were used extensively as Roman decoration.

Corinthian Capital: The Roman Corinthian capital incorporated scrolls with the acanthus leaves to make an even more elaborate capital than the Greeks had used.

Doric Capital: The Doric capital of the Romans was slightly smaller and had more circular lines than that of the Greeks.

Eagle: The eagle was used by the Romans as a symbol of the power of their emperors. They portrayed the eagle with outspread wings and covered it with a wreath and ribbon.

Evolute: An evolute is a spiral wave pattern used for borders of furniture and furnishings. It is also called a **Vitruvian scroll,** after Vitruvius, the Roman authority on architecture at the time of Augustus.

Festoon: A festoon is a rope or garland of flowers and leaves that are painted, carved, or applied as separate ornament on furniture, walls, mantels, or accessory items.

Imbrication: An imbrication is a fish scale decoration used on the surface of stone, wood, or metal as ornamentation.

Laurel Leaf: A band of laurel leaves was used as a symbol for glory by the ancient Greeks and Romans. It was also used as a victory motif by the Etruscans.

Pilaster: The pilaster, which resembles a column, but is actually a flat projection with a base and capital, is a decorative feature introduced by the Romans. Pilasters are used at doorways, on walls to divide the surface into vertical parts, and as decoration on furniture.

Gothic Design

The late medieval period was characterized by the Gothic style. Gothic was the dominant structural and aesthetic mode in England and throughout Europe from 1140 until 1500. Gothic architecture is characterized by the strength of its various parts and the illusion that it soars into space. Stained glass became popular at this time, and great colorful windows added impressive design character to the gray stone buildings, as well as representing biblical stories. Most of the famous cathedrals of the world have the Gothic design as part of their architecture. Sculpture during this period became distinct from buildings and was shown more realistically. Some of the characteristic Gothic motifs are still adapted for furniture and accessories.

Chevron: A chevron is a continuous band of V-shaped carvings that was sometimes used as ornamentation on buildings and furniture.

Clovers: Whether three-leafed (**trefoil**), four-leafed (**quatrefoil**), or five-leaved (**cinquefoil**), the clover

GOTHIC MOTIFS

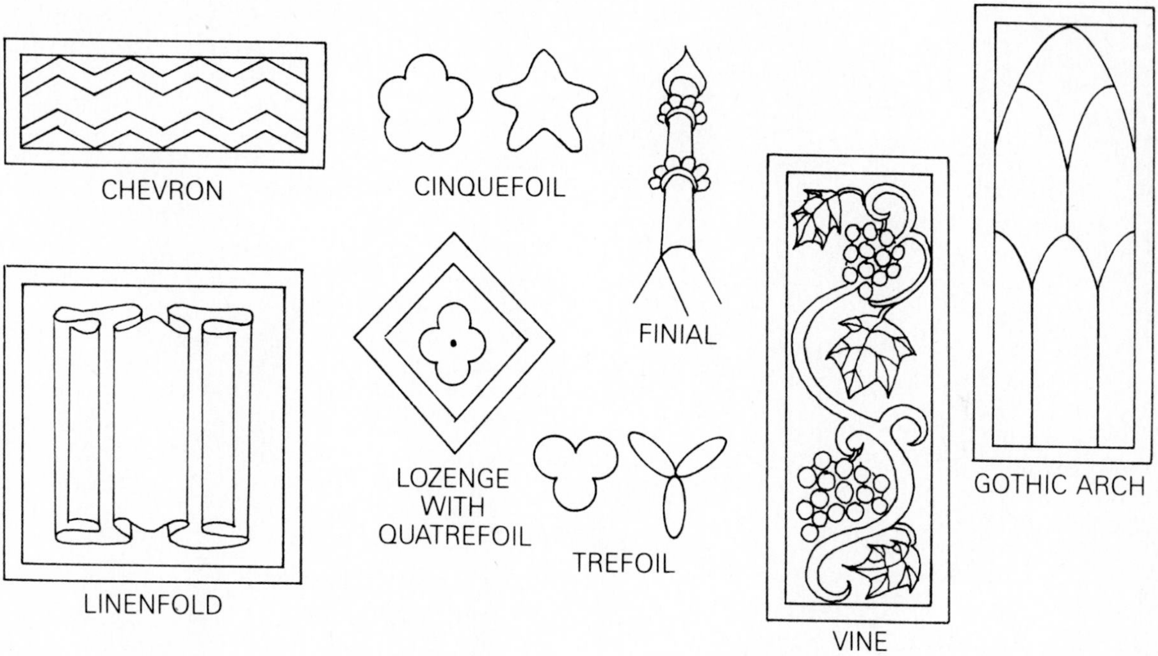

Figure 3-8. *Gothic design is most evident in stained glass, archways, and carved motifs.*

was used extensively in carvings and cut-out designs in both stone and wood. The trefoil was the Gothic symbol for the Holy Trinity.

Finial: A finial is a decorative ornament used at the top of pediments or to finish any end whether pointing upward or, as a **pendant,** downward on stone or wood. At first the finial was just a rounded ornament, but it then became more and more decorative.

Gothic Arch: A Gothic arch is slanted and pointed. It often has other Gothic arches within its framework. It is used on Gothic buildings and on furniture.

Linenfold: Linenfold is a carved design resembling the folded linen fabrics used in church services.

Lozenge: A lozenge is a diamond-shaped motif often used to enclose flower forms.

Tracery: The stone sections into which windows were fitted in design form became the inspiration for carving in wood. Tracery, or decorative carved openwork, imitates these stone dividers on furniture. Tracery was used on chests, chair backs, and wood paneling.

Vine Motif. Branches and leaves were used to form borders and decorative elements.

Designs Since the Eleventh Century

Since the eleventh century designs have been reformulated from those already discussed. These newer designs originated in various countries. Through trade and communication between people of different nationalities, the designs originating in one country have been adopted in other countries. Some designs that have been created since the eleventh century or greatly changed from traditional designs are discussed below.

Acorn: The seed of the oak tree has a distinctive shape that has been particularly useful as a turned ornament used either as a finial or as a pendant.

OTHER IMPORTANT DESIGNS

ACORN

FAN

FLEUR DE LYS

GADROON

LATTICE

PRINCE OF WALES FEATHERS

RIBBON

SWAG

SHELL

TUDOR ROSE

Figure 3-9. *Most designs since the eleventh century have been reformulated from earlier designs. Those shown here originated in various countries and were adopted by others.*

American Eagle: The eagle became the national emblem of the United States in 1782. As such, the eagle has particular meaning as a decorative motif.

Cartouche: A cartouche is a conventionalized shield or ovoid form used as an ornament. It may be enclosed with wreaths, garlands, or scrolls. It is used on exterior and interior architecture and on furniture and accessories.

Diaper Pattern: This term was adapted from the town d'Ypre in West Flanders, Belgium, where this type of design first came into prominence. These diamond-shaped forms are used in regular repeats. It is used to decorate wallcoverings, floor coverings, fabrics, and some furniture.

Fan: A fan is a radiating design used as a carved motif on furniture, as the shape for accessories, and as a printed pattern on fabrics.

Flame Pattern: A flame pattern is a deep zig-zag design. It is often in color and is used on fabrics to give the effect of colorful bursts of fire.

Fleur-de-Lys: A fleur-de-lys is a conventionalized iris flower. Some Gothic furniture had this design. It became famous, however, when used by the kings of France as a decorative motif symbolizing royalty. Every medium may have such a design carved, stitched, painted, or embossed on its surface.

Gadroon: Elongated ovoid forms, called gadroons, may be carved on wood or stone or molded into metal to make an attractive border design. The term comes from the word "goder" meaning to pucker.

Lattice: Lattice is a crisscross or fretwork pattern of interlaced strips. The pattern is used on backs of chairs, fronts of chests, screens, and other open spaces such as windows.

Lozenge: This hitherto flat diamond-shape design was given a raised, bas-relief look. It is used as a carved motif on furniture and as a cut design on glassware.

Lyre: With ornate leaf decoration on its arched sides and base, the lyre became a popular motif in eighteenth-century furniture and accessories.

Paisley: Made initially in the town of Paisley, Scotland, this colorful printed design, in the shape of an amoeba, was adapted from Persian motifs. It is used in various sizes on wallcoverings and fabrics for the home and for personal use. It may also be embossed on silverware or used to decorate dinnerware.

Pineapple: The conical shape of the fruit is well adapted to use as a carved ornament. Many finials use the pineapple shape for decoration.

Prince of Wales Feathers: Three long, curved ostrich feathers were used as ornamental design, especially during the eighteenth century in England. These feathers stood upright. They were carved to form the decorative splats on chair backs and were used as printed motifs on wallcoverings.

Ribband or Ribbon Motif: Interlaced ribbons were used in wood carvings particularly during the eighteenth century.

Rose: Although all flowers have their own particular beauty and all have been used for design by some artisan at one period or another, no flower has been as consistently a design inspiration as the rose. Both natural and conventionalized forms of the rose are used for designs. It is found in carvings, moldings, prints, inlays, engravings, paintings, and stampings on fabric, metal, paper, stone, plastics, and wood.

Shell: Shell shapes are used either as part of an ornamental design or alone. They may be seen as the ceiling form of an entry way, on the knee or back of a chair, on the handle of silverware, on the rim of dinnerware, or scattered over fabrics. The cockleshell, or scallop shell, is a fluted motif. It was an integral part of the rococo style of decoration in the seventeenth and eighteenth centuries.

Swag: Swag is a design of cloth, flowers, or other foliage draped in a looped effect.

Thistle: A thistle is a prickly plant with a seed pod at the top of the stem that opens to produce a downy crownlike spray. It is used as a motif for finials.

Tudor Rose: The conventional five-petal rose is designed with an inset of a second five-petal rose to form its center. The Tudor rose is used for carvings on English Renaissance furniture and accessories. It symbolized the marriage of the red rose (Henry VII of Lancaster) to the white rose (Elizabeth of York).

Unicorn: A unicorn is a one-horned equine (horse-like) mythological beast. It was considered to be a beautiful animal. Symbolizing innocence, purity, and good fortune, it has religious implications.

DO YOU KNOW YOUR MERCHANDISE?

1. Explain the effect of the following lines on the viewer: horizontal, vertical, diagonal, curvilinear.

2. Explain how an object would differ if portrayed realistically, stylized or conventionalized, or as an abstract.
3. Name five different elements of design and explain the role of each.
4. Explain what is meant by principles of design. Give examples of five different principles.
5. Name and describe five different geometric designs.
6. Explain griffin, hieroglyphics, lotus, papyrus, winged sun.
7. What are some of the characteristics that are unique in Chinese design in contrast to that of the other countries' designs discussed in this chapter.
8. Describe the Greek designs anthemion, Doric column, Ionic column, Atlantes, caryatid, and guilloche.
9. Describe the Roman designs amorini, evolute, imbrication, laurel leaf, and pilaster.
10. What features particularly differentiate Gothic designs from the classical Greek and Roman designs? Give examples of five different Gothic designs.

PUTTING YOUR MERCHANDISE KNOWLEDGE TO WORK

Assume the department store in which you are working is going to have a promotion of items from England in all of its merchandise departments. You are on the committee to select typical designs, both modern and traditional, for the buyers to find in the marketplace. Which designs would you recommend they seek? What merchandise items would appropriately use each of the designs you recommend?

PROJECT

Find examples of at least ten of the designs discussed in this chapter in current advertisements and pictures of merchandise. Bring these to class to show to other class members.

4

Clothing and Furnishings Through the Ages

Little remains of the clothing and furnishings of the poor people of earlier times. Their homes, furnishings, and clothing were made from inexpensive and plentiful materials. The items were used until they were worn out or were remade into new articles. The wealthy people, nobility, heads of church and state, and merchants, however, commissioned designers and craftspeople to create exquisite objects for their wear, comfort, and enjoyment. Therefore, most of their clothing and furniture of the past that we copy comes from the records and examples of the things they used.

People of each age modify the products from the preceding age. They find new materials, constructions, and styles to fit their current needs and desires.

HISTORIC PERIODS AND STYLES

Furniture and clothing styles are identified by broad time periods. The periods may be named for a country that contributed trend-setting products, influential monarchs, noted designers who created distinctive articles, or a historic event. Table 4–1 on page 48 shows the important design periods that have influenced U.S. clothing and furnishings.

Although specific dates are cited in the text for each major period or style, furniture, clothing, and accessories did not suddenly go out of fashion. They were usually phased into the following era. Thus, some people and households kept clothing and furnishings of earlier styles as new items were introduced, much as you do today when you purchase new outfits or home goods.

General Terms for Homefurnishings and Clothing Eras

Styles of furniture and homefurnishings that are popularly seen today are grouped into two major categories.

Traditional: mainly eighteenth-century French and English, early American, colonial, and provincial styles. Many of these styles were adopted from ancient times. Many home goods products are in traditional styles.

Contemporary: Mainly current styles inspired by creations from the nineteenth and twentieth centuries. Contemporary items are found in both home goods and clothing.

Some decorative motifs for clothing, accessories, and home goods reflect more ancient periods. For example, exhibits of ancient Chinese furniture and clothing have inspired demand for such items.

Table 4-1 DESIGN PERIODS AND STYLES

Influential Oriental Styles		Ancient Periods	
Chinese	3500 B.C.–A.D. 1912	Egyptian	4000–10 B.C.
		Tutankhamen	1361–1352 B.C.
Japanese	1500 B.C.–A.D. 1868	Greek	500–146 B.C.
		Roman	453 B.C.–A.D. 455
		Pompeii	1 B.C.– A.D. 79
		Herculaneum	

Middle Ages (Môyen Age)

Romanesque	A.D. 1000–1200
Gothic	A.D. 1200–1400
France	
England	
Germany	
Italy	
Spain	

Renaissance (A.D. 1400–1600) and Baroque (A.D. 1600–1700)

Italian	1400–1643	American	1620–1727
		Early Colonial	
French	1500–1775		
Louis XIII	1610–1643		
Louis XIV	1643–1715		
Provincial	1650–1700		

Home Goods Antiques, Reproductions, and Adaptations

Imported **antiques** are those objects that were made before 1830 when machine work began to be used more than handwork. Antique articles made in the United States are 100 or more years old. Objects that have lasted all those years often represent some of the most artistically attractive and finest made and constructed items from those earlier periods. Antiques can be very expensive.

Reproductions are articles made today as nearly like the originals as possible. Dimensions, surface appearance, and quality are all captured from the original. Even use marks and dents are reproduced. Good reproductions are very costly to make and to buy.

Adaptations are items that do not attempt to reproduce the quality, dimensions, or construction of earlier pieces. They merely have the general surface appearance of items from the past. Adaptations may be made of less costly materials and differ in size, ornamentation, and construction from the original. They are considerably less expensive and may be less attractive than reproductions.

Creators, Copiers, and Assemblers

Certain terms are associated with the people who create clothes, home goods, and homes.

Designers are creative artists who have the sensitivity and ability to interpret trends and develop products that may be made into usable,

English	1485-1702	Jacobean	1603-1649	
Tudor (Henry VII, Henry VIII, Elizabeth I)	1485-1603	Commonwealth	1649-1660	
		Carolean	1660-1688	
		William and Mary	1689-1702	

Eighteenth and Nineteenth Century Periods and Styles

French	1715-1814	Shaker	1774-1860	
Louis XV	1715-1744	Victorian		1830-1901
Regency	1715-1723	Eastlake	1868-1895	
Rococo	1730-1744			
Provincial	1700-1800	*English*		1702-1901
Louis XVI		Queen Anne	1702-1714	
(Neoclassic)	1744-1793	Early Georgian	1714-1727	
Directoire	1795-1799	Middle Georgian	1727-1760	
Consulate	1799-1804	Chippendale	1708-1779	
Empire	1804-1814	Late Georgian	1760-1820	
		Hepplewhite	1770-1786	
		Adam brothers	1728-1792	
		Sheraton	1751-1806	
American		Regency	1793-1830	
Late Colonial	1727-1820	Victorian	1830-1901	
American Empire	1790-1830			
Duncan Phyfe	1790-1830	*German*		1790-1850
Federal	1795-1830	Biedermeier		

Twentieth Century Periods and Styles

Mission	1895-1910	Bauhaus	1919-1933
Art nouveau	1890-1925	Scandinavian modern	Present
Art deco	1920-1945	Contemporary	Present

marketable forms. Any manufactured product has stemmed initially from a design or plan. In France, the clothing designer is known as a **couturier** (male) or **couturière** (female).

A **stylist** is a person who uses current events, world happenings, travel, and cultural events to determine the effect that consumers are seeking. They choose materials, color, shape, and texture that will appeal to and be marketable to the consumer segment to which they are directing their attention.

A **fashion coordinator** or **director** is a creative person who has the ability to assemble products that look good together. This person brings fabrics, other materials, designs, and finished articles into harmony with one another. Coordinators may assemble items for one product, an entire wardrobe, an advertisement, a fash-

ion show, or a window display to promote the products. They work for manufacturers or retailers. **Homefurnishings coordinators** assemble items to present vignettes and room settings for manufacturers or retailers.

Architects, who have specialized education, plan buildings and rooms within buildings. Occasionally, they design the furniture and create the decoration for the rooms.

Interior designers are skilled, specially educated, creative people who work closely with architects in planning rooms. They are qualified to plan, design, and execute interiors and to supervise people who make a room artistic and usable. Interior designers may commission artisans to make built-in furniture or to change or move walls. They may draw designs for the decor of a room and select the furniture and furnishings.

Interior decorators are people with a wide range of talents. They may perform just one service, such as selecting the colors for a wall, or may help to plan all the furniture and furnishings for a room and then hunt for these products in the marketplace. They usually have special training.

STYLES FROM ANTIQUITY

China, Egypt, Greece, and the Roman Empire are the countries whose ancient art and furnishings have most affected our modern-day products. Byzantium, Islamic countries, India, and Japan have also influenced our concepts of beauty and artistic form.

The Far East — China and Japan

Chinese artisans have excelled in work with metal, pottery, wood, carving, statuettes, paintings, silk weaving, and calligraphy. The Chinese made rice paper, developed printing and were the first to create vitrified (nonporous) chinaware.

Chinese periods are marked by dynasties, which began in 2205 B.C. with the legendary Hsai dynasty (2205–1523 B.C.) and continued until A.D. 1912, when the republican form of government came into being.

Although China had an ancient civilization that created many fine products, Chinese influence on European furniture and furnishings had little impact until the eighteenth century. Trade with China was very restricted in earlier times. Not until the time of the T'ang dynasty (A.D. 618–907) was trade with the West opened. After that, items such as the Chinese coromandel screens made from colorful lacquer panels, Chinese motifs, and fretwork, were adopted. By the eighteenth century, **chinoiserie** — the adaptation of Chinese styles and artistic ideas by European artists and artisans — occurred.

Chinese and Japanese customs, and therefore clothing and household articles, differed from those in the West. But as their delicate paintings, their calligraphy, their bamboo furniture, and their use of silk cloth became known, these items were adopted by the West. The furniture shapes and motifs were kept, but the dimensions were altered. Chinese Mandarin costumes, from richly decorated fabrics with exquisite embroidery and jeweled ornamentation, to sashes that were tied around the waist or hips to hold the loose garments in place and wide sleeves, became features of men's and women's clothing. The Japanese costume for men and women was the **kimono,** a loose-fitting garment with wide sleeves. Women wore an **obi,** a wide sash with a flat butterfly bow or a complicated flat knot at the back. Men's kimonos were of darker material with shorter sleeves and a wide sash wound around the waist and tied at the back in a loose bow.

Ancient Egypt

Tombs of the Egyptian pharaohs have preserved many artifacts from ancient Egypt. In addition to artifacts, the incised decorations that depict the lives of the nobles and artisans portray the clothing they wore and the types of chairs, stools, beds, and other articles of furniture they used.

Legs and feet of furniture were plain or were shaped in the form of hind and forefeet and forelegs of animals. These in turn were mounted on blocks. In some cases animals forms were extensively used to shape the entire furniture item. Magnificent chests were encrusted with stones, gold, and silver. The lotus, papyrus, vines and leaves, scrolls, patera, and special emblems such as the winged sun, winged serpent, and scarab were used as ornamentation.

Clothing was simple and made of cotton, linen, and wool. The warm climate permitted people to wear loose, comfortable clothes. From the cloth used to wrap the mummies, which have been so well preserved, we know that the Egyptians were able to spin gossamer-thin threads and to weave sheer, lightweight cloth.

Men wore loin cloths, short loosely wrapped skirts of white linen that hung to their knees, or longer and wider skirts with gathers at the front that made the skirt stand out as a triangular pro-

ANCIENT CULTURES

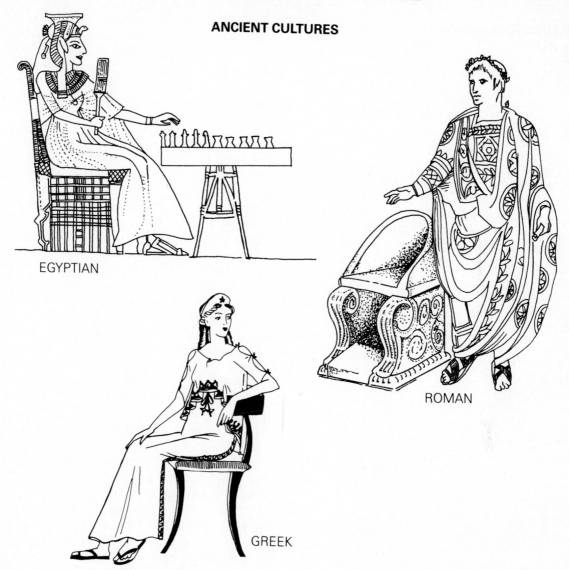

EGYPTIAN

ROMAN

GREEK

Figure 4-I. *Note the animal-shaped legs of the Egyptian chair; the classic Greek klismos chair; and the Roman stone-carved chair. Ancient dress was simple and elegant.*

jection.[1] Embroidered borders were often used on clothing.

Women wore simple, narrow garments that reached to their ankles. These were held in place by two straps over the shoulders. At a later time, the left shoulder was covered by the dress. In some cases, a semitransparent outer dress covered an opaque underdress.

Both men and women wore artificial wigs of straight hair arranged in tiny braids over shaved heads. Fans were popular, and cosmetics were used extensively by women to ornament their eyes, brows, lips, and fingernails. People also wore elaborate headdresses and necklaces. Bare feet were common, but some people did wear sandals.[2]

Classical Decoration — Greek and Roman

The ancient Greeks had a highly developed civilization from the fifth century B.C. until 146 B.C. when their civilization was absorbed by the Romans. The Greeks had already produced magnificent buildings and ornamented articles for home use and personal wear. When Greece was conquered by the Romans, the great concepts and art that had so dominated the Greek culture were absorbed with slight modifications. Thus, classical Greek and Roman art forms have much in common, and together this era is known as the **classical period.** Adaptations from classical Greek and Roman art are called **neoclassic.**

Greek. The furniture in the ancient Greek household was sparse. Chairs were thought of as thrones and were generally reserved for those in high office. Some Greek chairs were of the **klismos** type with curved top splat and legs that bent gracefully outward. They also used straight-legged chairs that often had animal forelegs and hind legs set on blocks. Because of their desire for portability, ancient Greeks had folding stools, chests that could be carried, and straw mats for beds.

Ornamentation included stylized acanthus leaves, fluting, reeding, palmette leaves, honeysuckle flowers (anthemion), antefix, and garlands and wreaths of laurel leaves. Arabesques, atlantes, caryatids, egg and dart, Greek fret, guilloche, rinceaus, and volute were other decorative motifs.

Men in Greece wore garments that reached to their knees or to their insteps. Capelike coverings that were fastened on each shoulder by a clasp were popular. Some were belted. Some long wraps covered one arm with the end of the garment thrown over the left shoulder.

Women wore long, draped dresses that were clasped over the shoulder or upper arm to form a type of sleeve. These dresses were often tied with a cord at the waist so that the soft material fell like pleats in the front of the garment. Lengths of decorative cloth were used to drape over the hips with one end thrown over the shoulder.

Both men and women wore sandals made of leather. Men's sandals often laced over the foot and up the leg. Peacock feather fans, wigs, bonnets, and jewelry were commonly worn by women. Cotton, wool, and linen were spun and woven into cloth.

Roman. The main rooms in Roman homes were large but sparsely furnished. Often, they had built-in cupboards and wardrobes. Metal safes were used to protect their valuables.[3] The Roman house had an atrium or courtyard and a central fountain. Poor people often lived in apartment-type buildings.

The furniture included chairs, stools, beds, and couches. The Romans used a dining couch rather than chairs at the table. Beds and couches were numerous and were covered with cushions. Elaborate inlays of tortoiseshell, ivory, bronze, and silver were found on luxurious furniture. Mirrors were made of polished metal, tapestries hung on the walls, large candlesticks provided light, and artwork was displayed on easels. For decoration, the acanthus leaf and scroll, amorini, atlantes, caryatids, sphinx, eagles, evolutes, festoons, laurel leaves, and pilasters were commonly used.

Men and women in ancient Rome wore the toga, which was a 2 1/2 by 6-yard-long woolen garment. It was put on by laying one end against the chest, carrying it over the left shoulder, wrapping it around the back, and placing it under the right arm and then over the left shoulder to tie in the back, leaving the right arm free. The toga was worn over a tunic. Both of these articles of clothing were often embroidered with gold thread.

Women wore an undertunic and over it a straight linen or wool robe that reached to the instep. It either hung straight or was bloused over a belt or girdle. Short, set-in sleeves completed the costume.

Both men and women wore sandles; later socklike boots were created. **Buskins,** boots with lacings from the toe portion to its top, were particularly popular for men.

THE MIDDLE AGES

Following the fall of the Roman Empire in A.D. 476 was a period later labeled as the Middle Ages because it occurred between the classical period and the Renaissance of the fifteenth century. Renaissance scholars also called this time the Dark Ages to describe what they considered to be the dormant state of its culture. The twentieth-century view of the Middle Ages, or Medieval times, is that it is a distinct historical period with a civilization and culture worthy of study, not just an interim.

The Middle Ages was an age of faith. With the widespread adoption of Christianity, religion became the focus of intellectual and artistic activity. Heathen temples were destroyed and churches were constructed. They served not only as places of worship but also as schools and centers of social and political life.

Because wood was a major construction material in early medieval times, many buildings were destroyed by fire. Much of what survived from the Middle Ages and influenced later styles dates from the Romanesque (about 1000–1200) and Gothic (about 1200–1400) eras.

Romanesque

Decorative objects in the Romanesque period continued to use many of the styles that were in vogue during the fall of the Roman Empire. Decoration was stiff and not very refined, and plant and animal forms were used. The simplified forms of the sculpture that embellished the churches could be seen by worshippers from a distance. Ornamentation depended upon Christian scripture combined with Roman motifs. The use of stone allowed many Romanesque churches to survive, but because the builders did not know how to support this heavy material, the buildings tended to be massive and dark, with small windows. Arches were rounded and columns adapted from Roman architecture were used.

Costumes began to change during this period. Roman men adopted the knee-length trousers worn by the Gauls from the North, and they shortened their togas. Elaborate silk and satin fabrics brought from the East were used, and kimono sleeves were introduced. Women wore their hair long and flowing but partially concealed by a veil.

Gothic

The Gothic period reflects the growing power of the Christian religion throughout Europe. The Crusades that sent the nobility and their attendants to recapture the Holy Land from the Muslims began in 1095 and continued until 1272. These Crusaders brought much of the art and culture of the Muslim countries back to France, Italy, Spain, Germany, and England.

Gothic churches made use of a pointed arch, which directed the weight of the stone downward. The arches within a Gothic building varied in width but were of the same height to give uniformity and beauty. Flying buttresses, stone projections perpendicular to the walls, gave additional support. These structural improvements allowed large-windowed churches to be built to lofty heights without the danger that the buildings would collapse under their own weight. Colorful stained glass windows showing scenes from the Bible are typical of Gothic churches.

The clover, whether three leafed (trefoil), four leafed (quatrefoil), or five leafed (cinquefoil), was used as decoration. Animals, statues of saints and other religious personages, gargoyles (unusually shaped animal forms), and geometric forms including chevrons, zigzags, and dentils were used. Tracery, linenfold, finials, and pendants were frequent ornamentations.

Interiors of buildings were hung with rich-looking tapestries. England commonly built its mansions with great halls over which a gallery was built to hold musicians who supplied the entertainment during meals.

Furniture was sparse, but giant fireplaces kept the room warm during the cold weather. Chests, trestle tables, benches, and stools were used. Sometimes small rugs were placed on the floor.

Large beds were carved; they had canopies from which curtains were hung that could be drawn together to protect the sleeper from the cold air. Oak and walnut were the commonly used woods.

Clothing during this period underwent considerable change. Men's clothing sometimes included short trousers worn over tights under close-fitting coats. Leather belts were used. Sleeves were elaborate and decorative. Men wore hip-length stockings or tights and soft leather shoes. The toes of the shoes were elongated so that sometimes it was necessary for a chain to be attached just below the knee to hold them up. Hoods on capes were used to cover men's heads. Feathers appeared for men to wear. For war, men wore metal protection in the form of armor.

By the fourteenth century, women had adopted the corseted gown, a snug-fitting bodice that has a full, long skirt trailing from it. Small caps or nets with sheer veils that hung to the shoulder were worn over their heads. A long, conical-shaped head covering was also worn.

Clothing had richly embroidered and elaborate woven designs. Velvet and silk from France were new fabrics.

RENAISSANCE

The Renaissance (1400–1600), which means rebirth, resulted in a time of great development in the arts. It began with a revival of classical art and architecture and went on to incorporate many creative design concepts. This was a period when individualism began to assert itself. Homes became smaller and more personal. People became more courteous, enjoyed intellectual companionship, writing, music, arts, and crafts.

Protestantism grew in reaction to the power of the Roman Catholic church. Although the church continued to be an important patron of the arts, people turned their attention to the world around them. In painting even religious subjects were often presented in contemporary terms.

In the late sixteenth to early seventeenth centuries, the classical forms that had been revived during the early Renaissance became more ornate, and the baroque style, roughly identified with the seventeenth century, emerged. Baroque designs are characterized by powerful curving lines and dramatic contrasts of highlights and

ITALIAN RENAISSANCE CLOTHING AND FURNITURE

Figure 4-2. *Renaissance styles like the sgabello chair shown here, began in Italy and spread throughout Europe.*

shadows. These features appear in tableware, furniture, and clothing as well as in painting, sculpture, and architecture.

The Italian Renaissance

In Italy, where the classical Roman artifacts were at hand, the Renaissance style first appeared. Trade and international politics helped to export the new Italian style to other European lands, and its influence continued through the baroque period.

Floors were tiled with brick, marble, and terrazzo (crushed marble mixed with cement). Fireplaces were decorated with classical motifs, and mantels were built above fireplaces. Statues were placed in niches in the walls. Cupids, elaborate silk fabrics, ornate curved forms of headboards of beds, arabesques, and pilasters were all combined to make a riot of sumptuous-appearing decoration.

Furniture became more usable and was placed in the room for comfort and social interaction. Walnut became the popular wood. Chests, credenzas (cabinets with doors and drawers), sgabellos (a wooded chair that began as a three-legged stool with a superimposed tall back and a narrow seat, with or without a drawer under the seat), armchairs, Savonarola-type chairs (with X-shaped legs) and beds with massive paneled headboards and footboards or four-poster beds with testers overhead that were richly ornamented were built. Refectory tables (long, narrow tables with heavy stretchers close to the floor), as well as small tables were used. Writing desks, wardrobes, and hanging shelves made their appearance. Inlay, marquetry, and leather and fabric coverings on chairs that were secured with nailheads all contributed to the abundance of opulent decoration.

Clothing also changed during this period. Men wore shirts, tunics, or doublets (short, skirted garments) and tights. A jerkin or jacket was sometimes worn over the doublet. Voluminous cloaks that draped about the figure were fashionable. Short puffed trunks over tights were worn. These were later supplanted by knee breeches. The long pointed toes on shoes and boots were even more fashionable than in the previous era. Berets were worn by men over short to shoulder-length hair. Mustaches and beards were common.

Women wore richly brocaded silks and velvets ornamented with pearls and gold thread. Furs were used to decorate gowns and cloaks. Dresses had snug, short-waisted bodices and sleeves that were long and tight. These were later puffed and slashed to reveal sheer lingerie underneath. Ruffs (elaborate frilly neck coverings) were adopted later in the period. Stockings were held up by garters, and shoes were made with low wedgelike heels. Belts and girdles that trimmed dresses were jeweled and held a money pouch. Wigs were worn or hair was covered with ribbons or caps. Ornate necklaces and earrings added luster to the costume.

The Baroque Period in France

Louis XIII (1610–1643) assumed the throne in France in 1619. However, Cardinal Richelieu became the spiritual adviser to the court and was responsible for ruling France from 1622 until 1642. At this time, France began its artistic triumphs that flowered to their greatest heights under the rule of Louis XIV.

The Court of Louis XIV. Louis XIV became the monarch in 1643, at the age of 5, and ruled until 1715. Money from the burgeoning Americas allowed him to become an extravagant ruler. He built the palace and gardens at Versailles and set the fashions for the Western world. The baroque style that had begun in Italy was carried to heights of splendor and magnificence in France.

Louis XIV established weaving factories, such as the Gobelins where tapestries were made and the Savonnerie where carpets were designed and woven. Old marble quarries were opened. The famous furniture designer, Andre Charles Boulle

Figure 4-3. *The baroque style was carried to heights of splendor during Louis XIV's reign in France.*

(1642–1732) created many of his masterpieces during this time.

Curved veneer surfaces, small salons and boudoirs, and ormolu (decorative metal) mounts were used on furniture; porcelain flowers were made; and furniture was upholstered for comfort.

Clothing at this time became as ornate as furniture and furnishings. Men wore ruffles and plumes, lace-trimmed short breeches, and stockings with leather shoes that had heels. Tricorne hats, fitted coats, lace or fabric cravats, and brocaded coats with buttons down the front and covered by a cape for further ornamentation were popular. Powdered wigs became the vogue.

Women used lace, ribbons, and tassels for trimming brocaded fabrics. Bodices fit tightly, and voluminous layers of skirts swept to the floor. Mules and midhigh heels became fashionable footwear. Enormous headdresses were coiffed and curled to give women added height.

Early French Provincial. Far from the center of the French court, life was simpler and less opulent. Some of the less grand styles of furniture that had been created during the reign of Louis XIII were adopted and modified by the people in the provinces. Since they were slower to adopt new styles, they kept their furniture and furnishings longer. Extremes were tempered; furniture had less ornate carving and was sturdily but attractively made. Early provincial furniture also showed considerable Gothic influence, which suited the life of the people.

Low cabinets with open shelves had racks and guardrails for the display of dinnerware. Armoires (large cabinets) with elaborately carved doors were used as wardrobes. Benches, settees, and chairs had simple turned legs and rush seats. Cane-back chairs were made. Beds were often enclosed in small rooms with shutters that permitted ventilation. Pewter and colorful pottery were used on the table.

Clothing also was simpler for people in the provinces. Women's dresses had long, bulging sleeves, tightly fitted bodices, large collars, and flowing wide-pleated skirts. A belt cord secured the high-waisted dresses. Wool, cotton, taffeta, and satin with shirred ribbon decoration were the materials that were used. Hair was dressed with curls and pulled back into a bun surrounded with ribbon bows. Braids were worn. Women's shoes were made of fabric and leather; small heels were popular.

Men wore slashed doublets. Their fitted breeches had decorations such as buttons and bows. Velvet, wool, linen, and cotton were the commonly used fabrics. Beaver hats had ostrich plumes. Boots with deep folds at the top covered the hose.

England

Seven different monarchs ruled in England from 1485 to 1702. Each contributed to the style of clothing and homefurnishings, which generally became more ornate.

England, being surrounded by water, was more remote from European influences than the countries that were contiguous to each other. Therefore, the Renaissance styles did not have the influence in England that they had on the Continent. Throughout the reigns of Henry VII (1485–1509) and Henry VIII (1509–1547), Gothic styles continued to be dominant.

By the time of Elizabeth's reign (1558–1603), England was becoming a world power. America had been colonized and the Puritan movement in England had begun. Shakespeare and Ben Jonson contributed to the enormous popularity of the English theater. The Jacobean period continued, with only minor modifications, the styles dominant during the reign of the Tudors (Henry VII, Henry VIII, Elizabeth I).

The major changes in furniture from that of the Gothic era were primarily in detail. Some romayne work (carvings with ornamental forms of human heads in circular medallions), scrolls, and dolphins were added to popular Tudor roses and the chevrons. Walnut began to supplant oak as the favored wood.

The furniture was large and heavy with huge, bulbous-shaped turnings and low, square stretchers. Large cupboards, chests, wardrobes, desk boxes, stools, tables, and beds with heavy canopies were used. Cradles were constructed for babies.[4]

The wainscot chair, a heavy-looking seat with a high wooden back that was decorated with carving or inlay, was often used.

Clothing reflected more of the Continental influence than did furniture. Sumptuous silks, elaborate brocades, velvets, and cloth of gold were imported. Jewelry was massive and colorful. Queen Elizabeth used her vast and elegant wardrobe as a display of power. Both men and women wore stand-up ruffs that were stiffened or wired to hold their shape. Women's clothes kept getting more elaborate. The bodice of the gown was fitted to a deep V in front and the skirt puffed out below it. Square or V-shaped necklines showed off magnificent and ornate jewelry. Long sleeves ended in a ruching of embroidered fabric. Elaborate brocades, velvets, and heavy silks were worn. Slippers for women had high heels, and the pump was worn for the first time. Silk hosiery also made its appearance during this period.

Men wore linen shirts with separate stomachers, handsome ornately decorated coverings that extended from the chest to the waist and laced or tied to the long tights. A close-fitting, short-sleeved doublet revealed the stomacher and the sleeves of the linen shirt. Men's long cloaks were shortened and were referred to as petticotes. Collars of capes became high standing. Trunks were very short, full, and padded. Stockings were elaborately gartered about the knee. Some men wore black wigs. Boots with flaring cuffs were also in fashion.

American Colonies

Early homes in America (1620–1727) usually had one large room with a fireplace that served for heating and cooking. Divisions of homes into more than one room occurred by the latter part of the early colonial period.

Furniture, which served basic needs, was made by hand from local woods. Stools, benches, tables on trestles, and cabinets for storage were found in all the early homes. Other pieces of furniture were crude copies of Jacobean, Carolean, and William and Mary styles. Ladder-back chairs with rush or wooden seats, wainscot chairs, Jacobean-style cupboards with huge bulbous turnings, butterfly tables, and large chests of drawers were handcrafted. The table chair served as a table and as a high-backed chair. It had a large back that tilted onto the arms to form a square or oblong top. Banister- and fiddle-back chairs and caned seats were also seen in homes. The chest-on-chest and lowboy were used for

ENGLISH RENAISSANCE AND AMERICAN COLONIAL

JACOBEAN WAINSCOT CHAIR

ENGLISH COSTUMES OF THE 1560s

COLONIAL LADDERBACK ROCKER, 1740

PURITAN COSTUMES

Figure 4-4. *English Renaissance styles included an abundance of detail, luxurious clothes, and ornamentation.*

storage. The local woods used included maple, pine, chestnut, cherry, and oak.

In general, the Puritan ethic dictated simplicity in both furniture and clothing. The clothing of the colonists was adapted from the styles in the countries from which the different groups had emigrated. Thus Spanish, Dutch, French, and English clothes were copied from the styles predominant in those countries.

Initially, the clothes were somewhat simpler than those worn in Europe. However, as people became more affluent, the clothing styles more nearly emulated those of the European nobility who were so admired.

In the northern Colonies, costumes resembled those worn at the time of Charles II. The long, collarless coat with linen neckcloth was worn with a waistcoat. Men's shoes were durable with leather heels.

Women's gowns consisted of a close bodice and full skirt looped back, sometimes over a petticoat. They wore white aprons, broad neckerchiefs, and turned back cuffs. Women's wraps were large capes. Many of them carried small round muffs. Women's shoes were durable leather with wooden heels.

EIGHTEENTH AND NINETEENTH CENTURY PERIODS AND STYLES

Furniture designed during the eighteenth and nineteenth centuries is usually referred to in the United States as traditional furniture. Many stores feature imitations of furniture made in this era.

French

The major styles that dominated traditional French furniture during the eighteenth and nineteenth centuries were influenced by Louis XV, Louis XVI, and Napoleon and the Directoire, Empire, and Provincial eras.

The Reign of Louis XV. Upon the death of Louis XIV, Louis XV (1715–1774) assumed the throne. He was greatly influenced by the Comtesse du Barry and Madame de Pompadour, who had enormous dominance over the styles of clothing and furnishings during Louis XV's reign. They adopted a simpler style of furniture than the baroque style of Louis XIV. The newer, lighter (in both weight and color), less opulent decor featured the famous **rococo style.** This was named for the rocks (*rocailles*) and shells (*coquilles*) often featured in its flowing asymmetrical curves. Pastoral scenes were commonly portrayed during this period. The curved cabriole leg (resembling a knee) was used for desks and chairs. Elaborate lacquered designs, gilt trimming, and decorative woods enhanced by marquetry panels were used. Chairs were upholstered for comfort, and walls were lavishly covered with ornamental tapestries.

Clothing worn by the French (as well as their customs and manners) during this and following periods influenced what was worn and how people behaved in other parts of the Western world. During the Louis XV period, men's coats, which extended to the knees, were fitted on top and full below the waist. Knee-length breeches were worn, and shoes often had buckles across the instep. The tricorne hat was adopted and was worn over a prim-looking side-curled wig that had a pigtail held with a bow at the nape of the neck.

Women's clothes usually had tight bodices and very full skirts that extended to the floor. Capes with hoods or small tricorne-shaped hats were worn in cold weather. Hair was powdered; for formal occasions, a tall wigged headdress was worn.

The Reign of Louis XVI. The taste in furniture of Louis XVI (1774–1793) and his Austrian wife, Marie Antoinette, was influenced by the excavations of Pompeii and Herculaneum, cities in the south of Italy that had been perfectly preserved when they were buried in volcanic ash from Mt. Vesuvius in A.D. 79. After 1748, when these cities were discovered and excavated, a revival of interest in Greco–Roman classical motifs was spurred. Furniture featured acanthus leaves,

SEVENTEENTH AND EIGHTEENTH CENTURY FRENCH DESIGNS

DIRECTOIRE

EMPIRE

LOUIS XVI CHAIR

MARIE ANTOINETTE

Figure 4-5. *Note the tightly fitted coats and bodices of the Louis XV and Louis XVI period, as well as the full skirt and elaborate designs. Empire style was simpler and more classical.*

egg and dart forms, arrows, lyres, and urns. Delicate-appearing furniture had slightly tapered legs that were fluted and grooved. Fabrics in neutral and pastel shades were used, and mirrors and paintings were hung on the walls.

Clothes for men during Louis XVI's reign became less full in the coat skirt but otherwise resembled those worn during Louis XV's reign.

Women's styles were set by Marie Antoinette. Tight-bodiced gowns were low cut. Skirts were elaborately ruffled or poufed. Some dresses had back panels that trailed on the floor. Fanciful hats trimmed with ostrich feathers sat atop coiffed wigs. Shoes were ornately embroidered and set with stones. Some walking shoes had buckles over the instep. Capelike cloaks were three-quarter length and often fur trimmed.

Directoire. Although the Directoire lasted for only a few years, (1795–1799) it dramatically changed the appearance of furniture, clothing, and decorations. This period reflected the interests of the people who dominated the French Revolution, which had begun in 1789. The revolutionaries favored simple, slender, straight-lined furniture adorned with arrows, wreaths, triangles, and other forms symbolic of freedom. The classical motifs were reintroduced into the simpler-appearing articles for the home and personal adornment.

Clothing for men was less elaborate. Knee breeches and ankle-length pantaloons were popular. Slippers or calf-height boots were worn. Waistcoats became longer and more slender. Felt bicorne hats with cockades were worn over natural hair cut just below the ears.

Women's clothes also became simpler. Smaller, less lavishly trimmed hats were worn over natural hair. Skirts were slimmer, and clothing had much less ornament. Some women adopted Roman-style clothing with its simple, classic lines. Slippers were cut low and ornamental clocks on stockings were revealed when skirts were slightly raised for walking.

Empire. In the period 1804–1815, the empire style reflected Napoleon's dominance of France.

The classic, symmetrical forms were revived in furniture and furnishings. Furniture became somewhat more bulky and was majestically ornamented with carvings and metal mounts. Arrows, wreaths, swords, shields, and other military motifs, as well as Napoleon's own initials surrounded by laurel leaves, were familiar designs. Mahogany was the popular wood used to make pedestal-based tables, boat-shaped beds, and stiff, straight-backed chairs.

At the turn of the eighteenth century tight-fitting, light-colored, full-length trousers were replacing knee breeches for men. Waistcoats were made in cutaway style and revealed vests made of elaborate cloth. Bulky cravats were wound around the neck revealing high-standing collars. Hussar or Hessian boots with high fronts and peaked backs that fit snugly or cuffed boots were frequently worn. Step-ins and pumps with instep straps were worn with street clothes. Hats were high with narrow, side-curled brims. Hair was no longer hidden under wigs but was cut short to reveal the ears.

Women frequently wore tunics over white sheaths. Classic designs were often embroidered onto cloth. Small neck ruffs, called Betsies, were sometimes worn. Spencers, short jackets with tight sleeves, were worn in dark colors over white dresses. Cashmere shawls were popular for warmth.

Women also abandoned wigs. Their hair was cut so that it framed the face and even revealed the ears. Bonnets of various sizes with simple-to-elaborate trim were worn. Slippers were low heeled and were worn with or without straps.

French Provincial. Far from the royal court, the simpler provincial style continued to evolve during the eighteenth and nineteenth centuries. The furniture was comfortable, sturdy, utilitarian, and pleasing to the eye. Curves on furniture backs and bottoms of chests were restrained. The craftspeople in each province expressed their own ideas and used native, natural woods and fittings of brass or polished steel. Fabrics were dyed with local dyestuffs and were usually dull red, blue, and mauve. Toile de Jouy prints and

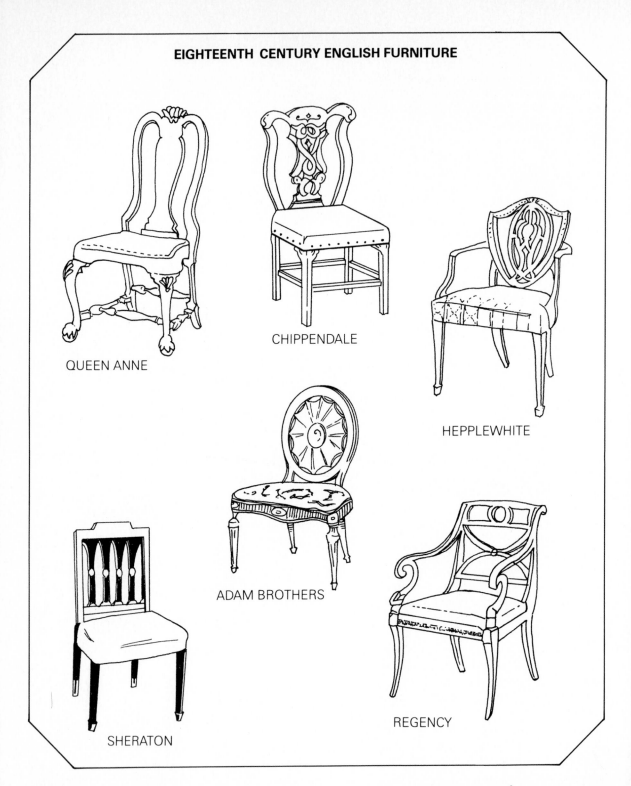

EIGHTEENTH CENTURY ENGLISH FURNITURE

QUEEN ANNE

CHIPPENDALE

HEPPLEWHITE

ADAM BROTHERS

SHERATON

REGENCY

Figure 4-6. *The eighteenth and nineteenth century in England saw many new designs and renovations in furniture.*

damasks were used, and handmade needlepoint was popular. Flocked wallpaper was invented to imitate more costly wall coverings. Pewter and crude pottery were used for decorative and utilitarian serving plates and mugs. The entire effect was rustic and simple.

Clothing in the provinces was adapted from the styles worn in the urban centers.

English

Furniture of the **Queen Anne** (1702–1714) period was known for its grace, symmetry, and beauty. Dominating motifs were cabriole legs, shell carvings, and pad or animal feet on chair and table legs. Curved top rails on chairs with fiddle-back shaped center splats were commonly seen. Wings on upholstered chairs that helped to avert drafts were also popular. Veneer patterns in mahogany and walnut were used. Decorative ornaments began to be kept in specially designed china cabinets.

Clothing changed little during this period, except that the petticoat for women had two flounces and an underpetticoat of canvas stiffened with crosswise strips, hoops, or whalebone.

Georgian (1714–1820) is the term that designates the furniture and furnishings created during the reigns of the kings who followed Queen Anne: George I (1714–1727), George II (1727–1760), and George III (1760–1820).

More important than the reigning monarch's tastes, however, were the noted cabinet makers and architects who created articles of lasting beauty and design. Like the French creators, they were affected by the excavations at Pompeii and Herculaneum.

Thomas Chippendale (1740–1779), master craftsman, was noted for his sturdy-appearing furniture adapted from English, Chinese, and French designs. He principally used mahogany. The legs on furniture items were slender or cabriole with club or claw-and-ball feet or were straight with grooved or carved decoration. On the cabriole legs, carvings were usually in the form of acanthus leaves. He used Chinese motifs

as frets on chair backs and pagoda shapes as the top rails on chairs or testers for beds. His yoke-shaped chair backs were decorated with pierced splats in a ribband form, or had ladder backs, or formed a fretwork. The bow-shaped camel-back tops of upholstered chair and sofa backs were exemplary of his style. His book, *The Gentleman and Cabinet-Maker's Director*, established him as an authority on furniture designs.

George Hepplewhite (1750–1768), noted for delicacy of line and proportion, designed slender, graceful furniture using mahogany and satinwood. The shield-back chairs, interlaced-heart chair backs, and serpentine-front sideboards are typical of his furniture. Straight and tapered chair legs, some with spade feet, Prince of Wales feathers for back splats, and wheat ears were also features used on the furniture he designed. His book, *The Cabinet-Maker and Upholsterer's Guide*, published after his death, served to make his furniture popular.

Thomas Sheraton (1750–1806), author of *The Cabinet-Maker and Upholsterer's Drawing Book*, also had enormous influence on the furniture designed during this period. He was the noted exponent of the straight line. He designed delicate-appearing but sturdily constructed furniture with side and back rails steadying slender legs. Mahogany and satinwood were commonly used and were occasionally combined with other rare woods. Small, delicate carvings, hand paintings of wreaths and scrolls, and brass rails ornamented his pieces. Chair backs had delicately carved posts, some with lyre-shaped splats or with splats showing delicate urn shapes. The furniture legs were square or tapered and often ornamented with reeding or fluting.

The Adam brothers — Robert, James, and William (1760–1792) — were noted for their designs and their architecture. Robert, the most famous of the brothers, studied art and architecture in Italy in 1754, making detailed drawings of famous palaces.

Adam furniture, created to harmonize with the architecture of the houses they planned, is characterized by classic, delicate forms. Inspired by the discoveries at Pompeii and Herculaneum, they used swags, urns, ribbands, and other classical motifs to decorate walls, ceilings, and furniture. They revived inlays and preferred satinwood, which was lighter in color, to mahogany. They particularly favored oval-shaped chair backs. Dainty, tapering legs on furniture with spade or block feet and finely detailed ornaments identify their furniture. Some Wedgwood plaques were used for insets in furniture, and marble was often used for table tops. Ceilings, walls, floors, furniture, and decoration were color and style coordinated in the homes they designed.

The **Regency Period,** 1793–1820 marked the time when George III was ill and the regent was George, Prince of Wales, who would later become George IV. During this period, the Pompeiian and Herculaneum influence declined and the Roman, Egyptian, and earlier Greek styles increasingly served as inspiration for furnishings. Small tables of all kinds were popular. They were often inlaid with brass or ebony and ornamented with brass mounts and galleries. Dining tables had pedestals for comfort and could be extended with leaves. Side chairs had square backs often with a top splat that was caned or pierced and legs that arched out to resemble the ancient Greek klismos chair. Seats were padded for comfort. Small upholstered sofas and love seats were fashionable. Colors were darker than they had been under the influence of the Adam brothers. The latter part of this era merged into the Victorian styles that are described below.

During the eighteenth century, clothes for men and women changed dramatically. For men, the English riding coat, created in 1725, developed into the cutaway that is today used for formal attire. Somber tones were in fashion. Knee breeches were lengthened to become trousers, which were in light colors and often held under the instep by straps. Men carried walking sticks, and cravats grew in size to give a bulky look at the collar front. Hats for men became tall and round, wigs were abandoned, and side whiskers were fashionable. Shoes were trim and neat and the straight-shaft Wellington boots were worn.

Women's clothes also became simpler. Some skirts began under the bosom and were full and long. Others lost their trains and moved up to ankle length. Women wore neck ruffs of lace. During the latter part of the eighteenth century, shawls were worn in place of coats. By the beginning of the nineteenth century, a capelike garment was worn. Muffs were carried out-of-doors. Pantalets with frills on them showed below some ankle-length gowns. Women wore fewer wigs. Hats were bonnet or cap shaped. Later, hat brims became enormous and were lavishly trimmed with ribbons, flowers, and feathers. Shoes were laced across the instep. Gloves were worn, and women often carried parasols.

American

Throughout the eighteenth and nineteenth centuries American design inspiration came mostly from Europe. A few American designers did, however, create lasting impressions with their expertise.

As a design period, **late colonial** (1725–1790) was a time of English adaptations. Mahogany, walnut, and fine fruitwoods were used, and American craftsmen produced furniture to grace the homes of the wealthy. The designs of Chippendale, Sheraton, Hepplewhite, and the Adam brothers were extensively copied. Ladder-back and Windsor chairs were widely adapted for American use. Other popular items were bookcases, highboys, four-poster and tester beds, bureaus, desks, and settees.

The **American federal and empire** (1780–1830) period, following the American Revolution, signaled the time for Americans to reject English designs and turn to the French for inspiration. Duncan Phyfe (1790–1850) was the noted American designer at this time. He took his inspiration from both English and French furniture. He chiefly used mahogany, and his favorite motif was the lyre. Legs on his tables and chairs were turned, carved, reeded, or fluted. They were often arched in the manner of the Greek klismos chair. Brass decoration graced chair backs and table bases. Pedestal-based tables

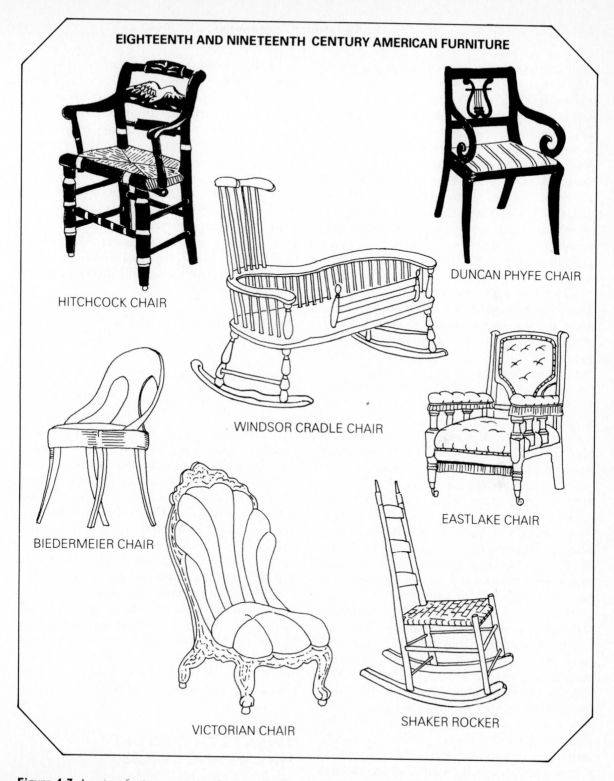

EIGHTEENTH AND NINETEENTH CENTURY AMERICAN FURNITURE

HITCHCOCK CHAIR

DUNCAN PHYFE CHAIR

WINDSOR CRADLE CHAIR

BIEDERMEIER CHAIR

EASTLAKE CHAIR

VICTORIAN CHAIR

SHAKER ROCKER

Figure 4-7. *American furniture was originally inspired by English designs, but in the period following the American Revolution, designers like Duncan Phyfe began to adapt French motifs.*

with curule feet tipped with brass are also typical of his style.

After the War of 1812, the bald eagle was a popular symbol that was used in home and furnishing decorations.

Another furniture manufacturer, Lambert Hitchcock (1795–1852), created the famous Hitchcock chair. It had colorfully stenciled fruit and flower designs on curved horizontal top and center back rails. The black-painted chair usually had a rush or cane seat and turned legs supported by sturdy turned stretchers.

Biedermeier (1815–1848) furniture, first created in Germany, had many of the same characteristics as French furniture. The style was named for two comic-paper characters; Biedermann and Bummelmeier, who satirized the middle class. The style came to denote stodgy but comfortable furniture.[5] Fruitwoods, walnut, maple, birch, and beech were used. Chairs had rounded backs and were decorated with lyres, plumes, and wreaths. American Biedermeier, adapted from the German, was thickened and made in light maple burl. Often bands of black lacquer were used to make a striking contrast against the light-colored woods.

Victorian furniture was made in England and in the United States during Queen Victoria's reign (1837–1901). The furniture was massive, ornate, and clumsy looking and had many curves and elaborate carvings. It used a conglomeration of Greek, Gothic, Venetian, and Egyptian motifs. Richly colored velvet, damask, and horsehair-covered and tufted upholsteries were used on massive chairs and sofas. Walls were covered with ornate wallpaper with pictures and ornaments superimposed upon them. The entire effect was one of overdecoration and confusion. John Belter (1844–1863), a master craftsman in America, was especially noted for his richly carved furniture with openwork designs.

A noted English designer of this period was Friar Charles Locke Eastlake (1793–1865), who made artistic furniture that was a mixture of Gothic and Tudor.[6] He used machine methods to produce assorted pieces of cherrywood furniture embellished with hardware and tile panels.

Clothes during the Victorian era went through many changes. Before the U.S. Civil War, women wore tightly laced bodices and huge skirts that were kept in place by many-layered crinolines or wire-hoop supports. Fancy bonnets that tied under the chin were worn. After the Civil War, skirts were less full. Toward the end of the nineteenth century, bustles were worn at the back of the skirt. Small hats were lavishly trimmed with feathers, flowers, or lace.

Men wore tight trousers with shortened waistcoats. Small, stiff collars had ascot, four-in-hand, or bow ties. Men's hats had lower crowns in rounded or square shapes and small, straight or side-upturned brims.

Street shoes for men and women extended over the ankles and buttoned in front or on the side.

Shaker Furniture

The Shakers, who flourished in the first half of the nineteenth century, had a passion for cleanliness, economy, and practicality. In their furniture and furnishings, form was fused with function. The furniture was austere and well made. Ladder-back chairs were hung on pegs when not in use. Trestle tables were made of wide, well-polished planks of wood. Beds with low headboards and footboards were utilitarian. Chests stood alongside beds to hold bed clothing. Rocking chairs, small tables, and chests of drawers were sturdily built from maple and pine woods.[7]

Clothes reflected this same austerity. Women wore wide skirts covered with an apron in front. Large white collars covered the upper part of the sleeve and the front of the dress. Close-fitting bonnets shaded their eyes and fabric hung over the dress collar at the back. Men wore white shirts, vests, and slim-fitted trousers.

TWENTIETH CENTURY PERIODS AND STYLES

By the twentieth century, communication was so speedy that as soon as a style was accepted in

NINETEENTH CENTURY CLOTHING STYLES

1840s

1860s

1890s

Figure 4-8. *Clothing styles underwent many changes in nineteenth century America.*

Europe, it could be manufactured in other countries. The movements discussed below have been important and have affected furniture and clothing throughout the Western world.

Mission Furniture

Mission-design furniture (1895–1910) began in England where William Morris helped artists to revitalize furniture crafts. Their ideas of functionalism became creditable during the early twentieth century. William Morris became famous because of his heavy oak chair with broad flat arms, cushioned seat and back, and substantial legs.

In the United States, mission furniture was also associated with the Spanish missions that were established in California. There, too, furniture was stolid and substantial.

Art Nouveau

As a reaction to the overornamentation of the Victorian era and the mechanistic appearance of furniture made by machines, art nouveau (1890–1925) was born in Belgium and swiftly adopted throughout Europe and the United States. Art nouveau was famous for its asymmetrical design, its flowing curves, its natural-colored woods, its pastel colors, and its extensive use of

WOMEN'S CLOTHING STYLES 1900-1950

EARLY 1900s

1910s

1920s

1930s

1940s

1950s

Figure 4-9. *Styles changed rapidly as communication became more speedy in the twentieth century.*

natural, especially floral, motifs. It was used in graphic and decorative arts, posters, lamps, and jewelry. Louis Comfort Tiffany (1848–1933) was devoted to creating art works in this style in the United States. His famous glass for windows, tableware, and lamps was sought wherever art nouveau was in demand. Charles R. Mackintosh (1868–1928) was a Scottish furniture designer whose creations reflected the art nouveau style.

During the art nouveau period clothes were drastically changed to meet the needs of the time. Men wore three piece suits and felt and straw hats. Women shortened their dresses slightly, removed the bustles, cut their hair, and gave up tight bodices. Silk stockings became fashionable, shoes were cut low with high heels, and fabrics were draped to have an easy-care look. Hats became smaller and less ornate. Women carried handbags.

Art Deco

Art nouveau was a reaction to the Victorian styles, and art deco (1925–1945) was a reaction to the asymmetrical forms of art nouveau in the earlier 1900s. This style began in Paris in 1925 at the Exposition Internationale des Arts Decoratifs et Industriels Modernes. It was a neoclassic, highly eclectic style. It borrowed from cubism, American Indians, Aztecs, and ancient Egyptians. "Palm-tree patterned slipcovers, torchier floor lamps, tubular chrome furniture, and mirrored coffee tables were the latest style and everything from bracelets to radios was made of Bakelite [a black plastic]."[8] Art deco represented the "flapper age," when women wore straight-lined short dresses, silk stockings, strap pumps, and headbands, often with feather trim. Men wore suits with tight pants, straw skimmers, and oxfords or step-in shoes. Soiled corduroy trousers with bright-colored shirts were typical campus wear.

When it was first introduced, the terms "modern" and "modernistic" were used for some art deco furniture. Some of the original pieces were heavy and angular and appeared awkward. Later refinements in furniture made the style more acceptable.

Contemporary Furniture

One of the nineteenth century designers who has had an important influence on our twentieth century popular furniture was Michael Thonet (1796–1871). In 1840 in Germany he created the bentwood process of making chair backs, arms, and legs. He also shaped many-layered veneers into arched forms to fit the curves of a seated person.

Begun in Germany in the early 1900s, the **Bauhaus** movement has been one of the most pervasive in modern furniture and architecture. Following World War I, Walter Gropius (1883–1969) consolidated an arts and craft school and an art academy to create a center for industrial design known as the Bauhaus. By 1925, famous artists, designers, and architects had become part of this movement. With the rise of Naziism, Gropius came to the United States where he continued to espouse his concepts. Marcel Breuer and Ludwig Mies Van der Rohe were two noted creators who contributed to this movement. Geometric forms and shapes appropriate to the materials used, simplicity, and utility were the characteristics of Bauhaus furniture.

Frank Lloyd Wright (1869–1959), architect of the Guggenheim Museum in New York and of many other famous buildings throughout the country, also designed functional furniture to fit into his creatively designed homes and buildings. Many of his pieces were designed as a unit system that permitted furniture to make one total architectural composition when it was placed against a wall or in the center of a room. He believed in total coordination of furniture and furnishings with the architecture of the room.

Eero Saarinen (1910–1961) was a creative designer born in Finland. He was famous for his molded plastic pedestal-based chairs and tables that made use of modern materials.

Charles Eames (1907–   ), born in the United States, created the molded plywood seat and back chairs attached to metal rods. His furniture, which was unusually comfortable, was made using new technology, materials, and equipment.

Swedish and Danish modern is the name given to graceful, lightweight furniture created by designers in Scandinavian countries. Bleached or natural-colored woods, an emphasis on flowing unbroken lines, and a minimum of ornamentation are characteristic of this furniture. Natural leather, corduroy, and crash cotton and linen fabrics are used for upholstery on the light-weight frames.

NOTES

1. Mary Evans, *Costume Throughout the Ages*, J.B. Lippincott, Philadelphia, 1930, p. 4.
2. R. Turner Wilcox, *The Mode in Costume*, Charles Scribner's Sons, New York, 1958, pp. 1,8.
3. George Savage, *A Concise History of Interior Decoration*, Grosset & Dunlap, New York, 1967, p. 11.
4. Sherrill Whiton, *Elements of Interior Design and Decoration*, J.B. Lippincott, Philadelphia, 1963, p. 243.
5. Joseph Aronson, *The Encyclopedia of Furniture*, Crown Publishers, New York, 1938, p. 18.
6. Rita Wellman, *Victoria Royal*, Charles Scribner's Sons, New York, 1939, p. 83.
7. "Shaker Crafts Revived," *Interior Design*, January 1967, p. 137.
8. Alexandra Anderson, "Right at Home in Art Deco Setting," *The New York Times*, March 27, 1980.

TWENTIETH CENTURY FURNITURE

ART NOVEAU SETTEE BY GAILLARD

MISSION CHAIR BY STICKLEY

BREUER CHAIR

BARCELONA CHAIR
BY MIES VAN DER ROHE

BENTWOOD CHAIR
BY THONET

EAMES CHAIRS

Figure 4-10. *Modern furniture reflects themes of simplicity, utility, coordination, and grace.*

DO YOU KNOW YOUR MERCHANDISE?

1. In reference to design periods, explain the meaning of the terms traditional and contemporary.
2. Differentiate among antiques, reproductions, adaptations. Which is most costly? Why?
3. Explain the main functions of a stylist, fashion coordinator, homefurnishings coordinator, interior designer, and interior decorator.
4. Why is the study of clothing and furnishings from antiquity desirable for the retailer? For the customer?
5. Explain why similarities exist in ancient Greek and Roman furnishings and design.
6. What was the inspiration for the Gothic period? Name and explain three features that differentiate the clothing and homefurnishings during this period from those of the Greek and Roman periods.
7. What is meant by Renaissance? What were some outstanding features of clothing and furnishings during this era?
8. Why are furniture styles more commonly copied from the eighteenth and nineteenth centuries than from earlier periods? Why are clothing styles not copied as frequently as furniture and furnishing styles?
9. Explain what features Empire, American Empire, Biedermeier, and Duncan Phyfe furniture share? Why do those styles share those common features?
10. What is meant by the statement, "Form follows function"? How does it apply to contemporary furniture and clothing?

PUTTING YOUR MERCHANDISE KNOWLEDGE TO WORK

Assume that you work in a costume house that provides clothing, accessories, and furnishings for plays. Students in a local college are putting on a 1920s play. What styles would you suggest they use for the furniture and clothing?

PROJECT

Select advertisements from daily newspapers that illustrate the following items.

1. Antiques
2. Reproductions
3. Adaptations
4. Clothing that uses design inspiration from any eras studied
5. Furniture that uses design inspiration from any eras studied

Be prepared to show the class your examples and to explain what each represents.

UNIT TWO

Textile Materials

5

Fibers and Yarns

A young woman walked into a clothing store and asked to see an all-wool sweater. Her only requirement was the fiber. She was not interested in the style, the color, or the size. The customer must have been aware of the qualities wool would contribute to her needs. This tendency for customers to express their requirements in terms of fiber content is a very common and important one. Thus, the basic unit from which a textile fabric is made must be thoroughly understood by the retail salesperson in order to meet customers' requirements.

Although the kind and quality of fiber used in a fabric are extremely important, other factors also play a critical role in determining if a fabric is suitable for a certain end use. These include the **yarn,** which is a continuous strand of textile fibers; the **fabric construction,** such as woven or knitted; and the **finish,** which includes the processes performed on the fabric after the fabric is made. Each of these factors may be likened to a link in a chain. Taken as a whole, the chain is a finished textile fabric, with each link an integral part. The short, unprocessed fibers (the first link) must be made into continuous strands to form yarn (the second link). The yarns are then woven, knitted, or manufactured by some other process into fabric (the third link). But all fabrics cannot be sold as they come from the loom or knitting machine. They must undergo a further processing called finishing (the fourth link). The

finishes are varied and include coloring, bleaching, stiffening or softening the fabric.

This chapter discusses the first two links in the textile fabric chain — fibers and yarns. Chapter 6 discusses the third link — the construction of fabrics, and Chapter 7 discusses the fourth link — finishing.

FIBERS

A **fiber** is a fine, flexible, and threadlike filament whose length far exceeds its diameter. It is found in many agricultural plants and is manufactured synthetically. The two basic groups are the **natural fibers,** such as cotton, wool, linen, and silk, and the **manmade fibers,** such as nylon, polyester, rayon, acetate, and acrylic. Within these groups are various types of fibers that produce yarns for a wide variety of fabrics for apparel,

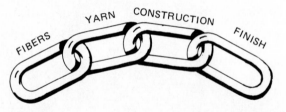

Figure 5-1. The chain of products and processes that make a finished textile fabric.

home, and industrial use. One kind of fiber may be used alone in a product such as in a nylon robe or two or more fibers may be combined in a blend such as in a polyester/cotton shirt.

Descriptions of fiber content are strictly prescribed by the Textile Fiber Products Identification Act (TFPIA), which went into effect on March 3, 1960, and was amended in February 1981. Under this law most textile merchandise must carry a label that includes the following information.

- The **generic,** or family, names of fibers contained in the fabric in amounts of 5 percent or more in order of their prominence. Fibers contained in amounts of less than 5 percent should be designated "other fibers."
- The percentage by weight in order of importance of each fiber that is used in the merchandise.
- The product manufacturer's name or registered identification number.
- The country of origin of imported fabrics.

A more recent rule, the Federal Trade Commission's (FTC) Trade Regulation Rule on Care Labeling, is also designed to aid the consumer by requiring that most apparel carry a permanently attached label giving care and maintenance instructions. As of July 3, 1972, instructions for apparel fabric sold by the yard at retail have been available for the consumer.

Natural Fibers

Silk, wool, cotton, and linen are the principal natural fibers. They fall into three classes — animal, vegetable, and mineral.

Animal Fibers. Certain animals provide substances out of which fibers are made. These substances may be part of the animal's protective outer coat or may be produced by the animal as in the case of silk. Silk, wool, and hair are the most important animal fibers.

Silk. Silk is the product of the tiny silkworm, which can spin a cocoon containing more than

Figure 5-2. *By law, most textile merchandise must carry a label like the one above, clearly identifying its fiber content.*

1,000 yards of continuous silk filament. Silk fiber is one of the strongest, for its size, and most easily processed of all textile fibers. It dyes easily into beautiful colors and, when made into fabrics, has a luster and a **hand** (feel) all its own.

Wool and Hair. Wool and hair are composed chiefly of a protein substance called **keratin.** They are both protective coverings for animals — wool protects sheep, and hair fibers protect a variety of animals such as the Angora goat (angora wool), Cashmere goat (cashmere wool), and camel (camel's hair). Wool, which in its raw state is yellowish white, brown, or black, is known for its warmth, resilience, and characteristic hand. Hair fibers, which are classed as specialty fibers, possess varying qualities of fineness, hand, and luster. Hair fibers are often blended with wool to produce special textures.

Vegetable Fibers.   Cotton, flax, hemp, jute, ramie, kapok, straw, and grass are examples of vegetable fibers. Cotton is the most popular worldwide textile fiber.

Cotton.   **Cotton** is a fiber produced from the cotton plant, which ranges from 2 to 20 feet in height, depending on the variety. The white or yellow-white cotton fiber, which is composed chiefly of **cellulose,** a solid, inert substance, is contained in the cotton boll.

Because of its versatility, cotton can be made into the sheerest of fabrics such as voile or heavy industrial fabrics such as tarpaulin. It is a strong, durable fiber that dyes easily and is comfortable to wear because of its ability to absorb moisture.

Flax.   The fiber obtained from the outside of the woody core of the flax plant is called **flax.** After it is made into yarn and constructed into cloth the fabric is called **linen.**

Like cotton, flax is composed chiefly of cellulose. Flax fiber possesses many of the desirable features of cotton. In addition, it is more absorbent, stronger, and quite resistant to attack by bacteria and mildew. Fabrics made from flax have a crisper, firmer hand than those made from cotton.

Minor Vegetable Fibers.   In addition to cotton and flax there are a number of other plant fibers. They are used mostly for cordage and other industrial purposes. Among them are **hemp, jute,** and **ramie.** These along with flax are called **bast fibers,** and are found in the inner layer of the bark of certain plants. Other vegetable fibers are **sisal,** from the leaves of a tropical plant, and **coir** from the outer husks of the coconut. In addition, grasses, straws, and rushes occur in fibrous form

and are suitable for weaving into items such as hats.

Mineral Fibers.   Aluminum foil may be cut into strips and used as decorative yarn, although it is not found in fibrous form in nature. It may be coated to look like gold. Gold and silver are too expensive to be practical for use as decorative yarns.

Asbestos is the chief mineral found in a fibrous state. It is obtained from rocks found primarily in Quebec, Canada, and is well known for its ability to resist fire. Although it is not resilient enough to be spun into yarn and woven into a fabric, it can be mixed with cotton to be used in a fabric such as a theater curtain. It may also be mixed with manmade fibers to make ironing board covers and stove pads.

It has recently been discovered that airborne and waterborne asbestos fibers ingested into the body can cause serious disease, including cancer.

Manmade Fibers

With the advent of manmade fibers in the twentieth century, people no longer have to rely only on the fibers nature provides and can manufacture fibers that exhibit special qualities and characteristics for specific end uses.

Most manmade fibers are formed by **extruding** (forcing) a syrupy chemical fluid similar to the consistency of molasses through tiny holes in a thimblelike device called a **spinneret** and then hardening it into continuous fibers.

There are two classes of manmade fibers: cellulosic and noncellulosic. Each of these classes is broken down into groupings that have a family, or generic, name. Most of these names have been assigned to the grouping by the FTC under the TFPIA.

Cellulosic Fibers.   Two of the natural fibers, cotton and linen, are **cellulosic** in that they consist largely of cellulose from the cell wall of

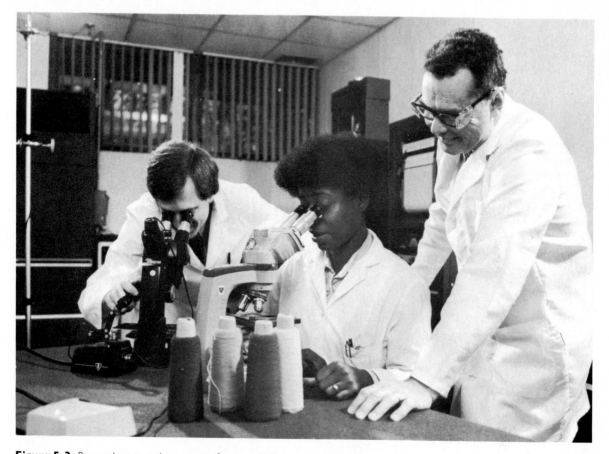

Figure 5-3. *Researchers test the content of manmade fibers.*

plants. Two manmade fibers, rayon and acetate, are made largely from wood chips and **cotton linters** (the short hairs covering cotton seeds), and are therefore cellulosic.

Noncellulosic Fibers.   Many of the **noncellulosic** fibers are made by chemically combining raw elements, such as oxygen, nitrogen, and carbon derived mostly from petroleum and natural gas, into new substances from which fibers can be extruded. Familiar generic names of these fibers are nylon, acrylic, polyester, and spandex.

Other noncellulosic fibers are manufactured from nonfibrous materials, such as glass from molten glass marbles and natural and synthetic

rubber. These and other noncellulosics are discussed in Chapter 12.

YARN

Before a fabric can be made, the relatively short fibers must be spun into continuous strands of yarn. These short fibers, called **staple fibers,** include cotton, wool, flax, and manmade fibers that have been cut into desired lengths to produce a fuzzy effect. Manmade fibers emerge from the spinneret in continuous strands that are twisted into filament yarns. If the fibers are not cut up, they do not have to be spun.

Probably the easiest way to understand how a strand of short fibers is twisted into yarn is to try to do it yourself. Take a bit of absorbent cotton and pull out the fibers into a very thin, filmy sheet. Keep pulling gently until it is like a ribbon. Now, alternately pull and twist the ribbon until a yarn is formed. If you don't follow these steps carefully, the yarn may break or, if twisted too tightly, be very uneven.

Figure 5-4. *Industrial yarn-spinning equipment yields the most uniform thicknesses of yarn.*

The Twist of the Yarn

If you have just tried to make a cotton yarn, you have found that the tighter you twisted the yarn, the stronger the yarn became. Similarly, a fabric made of tightly twisted, evenly spun yarn will tend to be stronger than one made of loosely twisted, irregularly spun yarn. A salesperson should know that fabrics made from loosely spun novelty yarns, although they have style value, are usually not as durable as fabrics made from more even, tightly twisted yarn. However, a yarn can be given too much twist and be uneven.

A yarn that is twisted so tightly that it begins to knot is called a **crepe yarn.** In hosiery, crepe yarns dull the luster of the fabric and decrease its tendency to snag. In dress fabrics, such as flat crepe, the crepe yarn is woven crosswise in the fabric, producing a crinkled surface.

The Ply of the Yarn

The cotton yarn you have made is called a **single yarn** because it is composed of one strand of twisted fibers. Break it in half and notice the force required. Now twist the two broken pieces of yarn together. This yarn is called a **two-ply yarn.** If you try to break this yarn, you will need at least twice as much strength as you needed to break the single yarn. In addition, a ply yarn is usually stronger than a single yarn of the same diameter. Combinations of three or four yarns twisted together are called **three-ply** and **four-ply** yarns, respectively.

Fabric appearance and texture can be affected by twisting together two different kinds of yarn, a single cotton and a single wool yarn, for example, to form a two-ply yarn. A variation in the twist of the single yarn used in a ply yarn will also change the fabric's looks and texture.

The Size of the Yarn

Yarns used to make fabric or sewing thread are given numbers that indicate their fineness or coarseness. The number tells you the **count of the yarn.** For cotton fabric or sewing thread the count is determined by the fact that 840 yards of yarn can be spun from 1 pound of cotton fiber. If 840 yards are spun from 1 pound of cotton, that yarn is called number 1; if 1,680 yards are spun, it is number 2; if 8,400 yards are spun, it is number 10. The letter s after the number indicates single yarn, as differentiated from ply yarn. For example, a number 10s cotton would be a single yarn that is 10 times as fine as that of a number 1 or 5 times as fine as a number 2. In cotton the finer the yarn, the higher the count. The same principle holds true for cotton sewing thread.

The count of the yarn is also measured for wool and short-fibered, or spun, yarns of silk and rayon, acetate, and other manmade fibers. In these yarns, too, the higher the count, the finer the yarn, although the method of figuring is not the same for all. The same principle is used for linen, except instead of "count" the term "lea" is used.

In numbering the size of longer-fibered filament yarns, such as silk and manmade fibers, the terminology is different and the principle of numbering is reversed. The term "denier" is used instead of "count." In order to determine denier, 450 meters of yarn are weighed on a scale. If the yarn weighs exactly 5 centigrams, the yarn is number 1 denier; if it weighs 10 centigrams, it is number 2 denier; and so on. A number 2 denier yarn is coarser than a number 1 denier. Thus, the higher the number, the coarser the yarn.

Denier may be important to the salesperson selling nylon hosiery because some customers may buy stockings according to denier. If a customer wants a pair of sheer stockings, she may ask for 15 denier; coarser stockings are 30 denier.

The Color of the Yarn

The method of coloring the yarn is an important selling point for the salesperson as well as a significant buying point for the customer. Four important methods of coloring yarn are yarn dyeing, fiber and solution dyeing, warp printing, and space dyeing.

Yarn Dyeing. Yarn dyeing means that the yarns are first dyed separately and then woven into fabric, for example, a checked gingham. The advantage of yarn dyeing is that dye usually penetrates to the center of the yarn and colors it thoroughly, producing a deep, rich color that is permanent. This is less true of linen yarns, however, because of their varying thicknesses.

Fiber Dyeing and Solution Dyeing. Sometimes fibers are **fiber dyed,** that is, they are dyed before they are spun into yarn. The dye penetrates to the core and is thus more colorfast. In the case of manmade filaments and yarns, the dye is sometimes mixed into the chemical solution before it is extruded into filaments. This is called **solution dyeing.**

Warp Printing. Printing the warp (lengthwise) yarns of a fabric to create a design before the fabric is woven is called **warp printing.** This creates a pattern with a hazy outline when the crosswise yarns are woven in. Warp prints are sometimes used for taffetas for formal wear or draperies.

Space Dyeing. By dyeing both the crosswise and the lengthwise yarns separately and in spaced patterns, called **space dyeing,** colorful designs emerge when the fabric is woven. This produces an effect similar to warp printing. However if the crosswise and lengthwise yarns are unraveled from the fabric you can see that each has different colors on it.

Novelty Yarns

The following **novelty yarns** are often used in fabrics to create a variety of pleasing and unusual textural effects that cannot be produced with conventional yarns.

Boucle Yarn: A bumpy, often knotted yarn made by plying single yarns of different sizes and amounts of twist.

Crimp Yarn: A permanently waved or crimped manmade yarn that looks like wool.

Figure 5-5. For this heavy bouclé, acrylic yarns are wrapped around a cotton core.

Thick and Thin Yarn: A manmade yarn that is alternately thick and thin. It is produced by extruding the liquid solution through the spinneret at different speeds, resulting in strands with varied diameters, which are then combed.

Slub and Nub Yarns: Yarns with soft, thick, untwisted lengths that alternate regularly with thin places. Shantung is an example. The enlarged places on the yarn are called **nubs** if rounded and **slubs** if soft and elongated.

Plastic-Coated Yarns: A natural or manmade yarn that has been coated with plastic for protection. Coating reduces friction and keeps metal (tinsel) yarns from tarnishing. Plastic-coated yarns will not absorb water and thus are suitable for rainwear.

Metallic Yarns: A decorative, shiny yarn made by twisting a strip of metal around cotton, silk, or rayon.

Textured Yarns: A permanently crimped, coiled, looped or curled manmade filament yarn. The treatment changes the yarn's appearance and improves its wearing comfort and wrinkle resistance. Crepeset is a trade name of a textured yarn.

Blended Yarns

A **blended yarn,** or simply a **blend,** is a yarn that contains two or more different kinds of fibers that are mixed together. In textiles you can blend almost any fibers together to make a yarn.

When fibers are blended in appropriate proportions, each fiber brings its desirable characteristics to the blend. For example, a 65 percent polyester and 35 percent cotton blend has been found to be a good fabric for men's shirts. The polyester adds strength, sheds water, dries quickly, and resists wrinkling. Cotton absorbs perspiration, keeps the wearer comfortable and washes easily. The blended material irons more easily than an all-cotton material.

Blending can increase the uses of a fabric; give it a different hand, appearance, and style appeal; and lower its cost. But fibers can also have disadvantages for a specific use. The textile technologist must not only select the right fibers for a specific use but must also use them in the right proportions to achieve optimum fabric performance.

DO YOU KNOW YOUR MERCHANDISE?

1. What facts in addition to fiber content are needed to estimate a fabric's suitability for a given use?
2. What information about the fabric must a manufacturer include on the label under the TFPIA and the FTC care-labeling rule?
3. Define natural fibers and list the three classes of them. Give examples of each.
4. Define manmade fibers and list the two major classes of them. Give examples of each.
5. What is a yarn?
6. What is a two-ply yarn? How does the use of ply yarns affect the fabric?
7. Define count of the yarn. How is count determined for cotton yarn?
8. Explain the differences between count and denier.
9. Name and describe four types of novelty yarns.
10. What is a blended yarn? What are its advantages?

PUTTING YOUR MERCHANDISE KNOWLEDGE TO WORK

Using some absorbent cotton, make a tightly twisted single yarn, a two-ply yarn, and a novelty yarn. Take the same amount of cotton that you used for the single yarn and divide it into two halves of approximately equal amounts. Twist each half into a finer single yarn that is just as long as the yarn you have already spun. Now you have two yarns of equal length that together contain the same amount of cotton as in the yarn you first twisted. Twist these two yarns together to form a two-ply yarn. Compare its strength with that of the single yarn of the same length.

PROJECT

Visit the sportswear department of a department store. Look through a rack of clothing, observing the labels. On the basis of your observations, do all the labels comply with the TFPIA and the FTC care-labeling rule?

6

Fabric Construction

About the time of the American Revolution and extending into the nineteenth century, the great industrial revolution took place in England. It soon spread to the entire Western world, including the United States. An agricultural society with home spinning and weaving was turned into an industrial society in which women were leaving the farms to work in the factories. This radical change was spearheaded by the textile industry. The inventions of mechanical methods to spin yarn and of the power loom to construct cloth caused a massive increase in foreign trade in the United States.

In the early days most of the cloth marketed was constructed by the weaving process. Today many other methods are used to achieve the third link in the chain referred to in Chapter 5. These are knitting, lace making, and nonwoven methods that bind fibers together without first constructing yarns. There are also special combination constructions, especially **tufting,** used to make rugs and certain curtain and upholstery fabrics. These will be explained in later chapters.

THE WEAVING PROCESS

The interlacing of two sets of yarn, usually at right angles, is called **weaving.** If you sell home-sewing fabrics in a store or make your own clothes, you may have heard the terms "warp" and "filling." **Warp yarns,** also called **warp**

threads or **warp ends,** are the lengthwise yarns in a fabric that run parallel to the **selvages** (self-edges, or finished edges, along the sides of a fabric). **Filling yarns,** also called **picks** or **weft yarns,** are the crosswise yarns that run across the fabric from selvage to selvage.

Generally, warp yarns are stronger and closer together than filling yarns because they are held under tension and thus are subjected to greater strain during weaving; filling yarn is under less tension.

The **count of cloth,** which tells the closeness or looseness of a weave, is indicated by listing the number of warp ends per inch followed by the number of filling picks per inch, such as 72×68. A cloth with a higher count of warp and filling yarns, for example 72×68, is more closely woven and likely to be stronger than one with a lower count, for example, 68×60.

Percale for dresses may have a count of 80×80 (or, as it is sometimes written, 80 square). This count is well balanced because it has enough yarns in both directions to make it wear well. On the other hand, some fabrics may have twice as many yarns in the warp as in the filling. A typical count for broadcloth is 144×76. In this fabric the filling yarns are fewer but heavier and balance the finer warp yarns.

Although important, the count of cloth does not tell the whole story about a fabric's construction. The type of yarn, as discussed in Chapter 5, is also a critical factor in determining fabric quality.

Customers seldom hear about counts except when buying sheets. The count for sheets is expressed by one number, which is the sum of the warp and the filling numbers. The knowledgeable customer understands that a 200 percale sheeting is better quality than a 180 percale sheeting.

The History of Weaving

Weaving has remained fundamentally the same from primitive times to today. The difference is that production today is automatic and much faster.

Primitive people used reeds and grasses, which they interlaced, or wove, into mats and baskets. Later they discovered how to suspend warp yarns from a horizontal branch of a tree and pass the filling yarns over and under them with the aid of a sharpened stick. Then they learned how to make a box frame on a small open wooden box about 9 × 6 inches and to stretch the warp yarns across its length. The hand loom of colonial times developed from this box frame. A **loom** is the frame or machine on which a cloth is woven. With the hand loom, unlike earlier weaving methods, the filling did not have to be passed over and under the individual warp yarns. Certain warp yarns could be separated from others by raising them all at once so that the filling could be passed through the separated warps, called a **shed,** in one action.

Steps in Weaving

The capital letters in the description below correspond to the labels in Figure 6-1. Before a fabric can be woven, the warp yarns (F) are wound onto the **warp beam** (G) and are strung onto the frame of the loom. The **harness** is the upright frame (A) that holds the wires, called **heddles** (B). Each heddle has an eye, like a darning needle, through which a warp yarn is threaded. Each harness controls a series of heddles that are raised

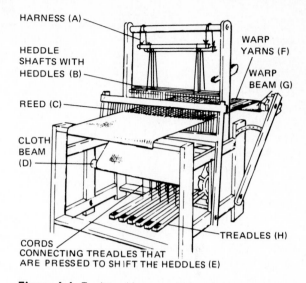

Figure 6-1. *Traditional loom on which a cloth is woven.*

or lowered to allow the filling yarns to pass through the separated warp yarns (F).

The filling yarns are carried in a **shuttle,** a boatlike device that is passed through the shed of raised warp yarns. The separation is accomplished by pressing the appropriate **treadle** (H), which raises a set of heddles (B) through which certain warps are strung. In the plain weave, only two harnesses are required. One controls the odd-numbered warps 1, 3, 5, 7, and so on, and the other controls the even-numbered warps 2, 4, 6, 8, and so on.

After a filling yarn has been passed through a shed, a rod, called a **reed,** beats down the yarn against the edge of the cloth already woven. As the work proceeds, more warp yarn is let off the warp beam and more of the woven cloth is rolled onto the **cloth beam** (D).

Although the weaving process is simple, the power loom used commercially is a complicated mechanical device that automatically raises and lowers the heddles, throws the shuttle back and forth through the shed of warp yarns, battens down the new fillings at each throw, and winds up the woven cloth. Today a great deal of weaving is done on what is called a **shuttleless loom.**

Instead of putting a very limited supply of yarn into a spindle placed in the shuttle (a supply that must be frequently replenished), yarn from a large cone is carried through the shed by a variety of means. One way uses a gripper that grasps the end of the yarn on the cone and then ejects it through the shed carrying a length of yarn with it. The gripper is carried back outside the loom to grasp the end of the next length; all this at lightning speed. Other devices to carry the yarn include a rapier that moves forward and backward rapidly carrying yarn through the shed on its forward motions. Jets of air and of water are used on some shuttleless looms; they do not require returning a carrier to pick up the next end of yarn.

The basic steps in the weaving process may be summarized as follows:

Shedding: the separating of the warp yarns into an upper and lower system of threads so that a shed may be formed through which to carry the filling yarns.

Picking: the actual passing of the filling yarn through the separated warp yarns.

Beating Up: the pushing into place of the deposited filling yarn, making it a component of the woven fabric.

Letting Off and Taking Up: the releasing of warp yarns from the roll or cylinder (warp beam) around which they have been wound and the winding or taking up of the newly woven fabric on the cloth beam.

Basic Weaves

The three basic weaves are the plain, twill, and satin weaves. Each of them has several variations. They differ in appearance because of their structural designs (designs woven into the cloth) even if they are made from identical fibers that are spun into the same type of yarn.

Plain Weave. The most common weave, the **plain weave,** consists of an even interlacing of every other warp and filling yarn. Its structural design is a checkerboard. Because it requires only a simple two-harness loom, the construction is an inexpensive one to weave. If closely woven, plain weave is firm and strong. Plain-weave fabrics are easily cleaned or laundered because of their flat surfaces. They can be made from all kinds of fibers.

Plain-weave fabrics in cotton and blends include gingham, voile, cheesecloth, batiste, nainsook, lawn, organdy, cambric, sheeting, crepe, percale, chambray, crash, chintz, cretonne, and cotton shantung. Typical plain-weave fabrics in linen are dress linen, handkerchief linen, art linen, cambric, crash, and theatrical gauze. Common plain-weave woolen fabrics include crepe, tropical worsted, challis, and homespun. Plain-weave fabrics of silk or manmade fiber are taffeta, shantung, pongee, chiffon, flat crepe, and ninon.

Because the pattern of a plain-weave fabric is not very interesting, novelty and colored yarns are often used to create different effects. Crepe yarns will produce a crinkly surface, slub yarns a bumpy surface, and yarn-dyed stripes, checks, plaids, and warp prints a more colorfully patterned surface.

Using the same two-harness loom, a weaver can further enhance the appearance or change the texture of the fabric by varying the structural design. There are two common variations of the plain weave — rib and basket.

Rib Variation. The use of heavier yarns in the warp or filling or both is called the **rib variation.** This produces a ribbed, corded, or crossbar effect in the plain weave, such as in broadcloth, striped dimity, poplin, rep, faille, and grosgrain. Care must be taken to make sure that the rib yarns are not much heavier than the other yarns. If they are, the rib yarns could rub against the finer yarns and cut them. Also, if a heavier yarn is covered by fine yarns, as in faille or bengaline, there must be a sufficient number of fine yarns to cover the rib yarn. If not, the ribs will show through, making the fabric unattractive.

Basket Variation. Instead of weaving a fabric by passing one filling yarn over and under every other warp yarn, two or more filling yarns may be passed over and under two or more warp yarns creating the **basket variation.** A basket construction cannot be woven as closely as the plain weave. As with all loosely woven fabrics, a basket weave stretches easily, may shrink when washed, and the yarns tend to slip out of place. Oxford fabric, used in men's shirting, and monk's cloth, used in draperies and bedspreads, are examples of the basket weave.

Twill Weave. Another basic weave is the **twill weave,** which is formed by passing a filling yarn over and under one, two, or three warp yarns, lapping backward one warp yarn in each successive line. The structural design looks like stairs. The surface of the fabric has diagonal ridges, called **wales,** which makes it easily recognizable.

The firm and compact twill weave produces a durable fabric. It is not as easy to keep clean as the plain weave because dirt tends to collect between the ridges. Cotton fabrics in the twill weave include gabardine and denim; wool fabrics include serge, gabardine, flannel, worsted cheviot, covert cloth, and tweed; silk fabrics include foulard, silk serge, and surah; manmade-fiber fabrics include gabardine, flannel, foulard, serge, whipcord, and surah.

The **herringbone pattern,** a variation of the twill weave, has a structural design like the backbone of a herring. Ridges run diagonally from upper left to lower right of the fabric then reverse from lower left to upper right. Herringbone can be made from 100 percent wool or blends. It is frequently used in tweeds for men's and women's coats.

Satin Weave. Although many people think of satin as the name of a shiny, smooth material, the **satin weave** produces a smooth, lustrous surface because of the way in which the yarns are interlaced. Unlike the plain and twill weaves in which the yarns are interlaced at frequent intervals, the satin weave is interlaced at less frequent intervals, thus allowing the smooth unbroken

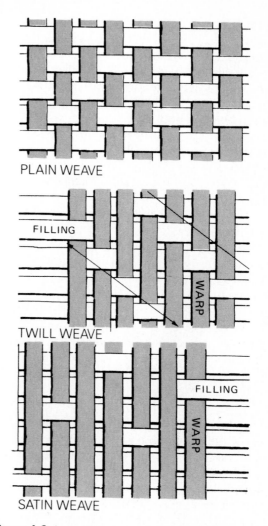

Figure 6-2. *In the plain weave, each filling yarn passes over and under each warp yarn, alternating in each row. In the twill weave, a diagonal ridge runs from upper left to lower right. In the satin weave, the warp yarns pass over many filling yarns, creating a luxurious shine.*

yarns to remain on the surface and reflect the light. The yarns that lie loose on the surface of the fabric over several other yarns are called **floats.** The longer the float, the higher the luster of the fabric. However, satins made with long floats are more likely to snag and show wear than satins made with short floats. In most cases, the warp floats over the filling. A fabric in which cotton yarn floats is commonly called **sateen.**

Satin is the weakest of the three basic weaves because the floating yarns are loose on the surface. Reeled silks, filament rayons, acetates, and nylons adapt best to the satin weave because their long fibers give luster and do not pull out with friction to make a fuzzy surface, but they may snag. Some cottons may also be used to form floats, but because its fiber is shorter, cotton must necessarily have shorter floats.

Sometimes satins are made with a rayon or silk warp and crepe yarns in the filling. The crepe filling shows on the back of the fabric. The surface is formed by the rayon or silk warp floats. A selling point for these crepe-backed satins is that both sides of the fabric can be used. Some fabrics in the satin weave are dress satin, farmer's satin, slipper satin, and sateen.

Fancy Weaves

The fancy weaves are elaborate constructions based on the three basic weaves. They include the pile weave, the leno weave, and the figured weave.

Pile Weaves. Most people like to dry themselves with a Turkish towel because they like the way it absorbs water. If you examine a Turkish towel carefully, you will see that it is made of loops that are held together by a background of a plain or twill weave. The loops are known as **pile,** and the cloth is said to be made in a **pile weave.**

In a pile fabric either two sets of warp or of filling yarns are used to form loops on the surface of the fabric. The loops may be uncut, as in Turkish towels and terry cloth bathrobes, or they may be cut, as in velvet. In terry cloth and velvet extra warp yarns are used to make the pile, and in velveteen and corduroy extra filling yarns are used to make the pile. These are cut after weaving.

Another pile fabric, **transparent velvet,** is made by weaving two layers of fabric together. Extra sets of filling yarns pass back and forth between the two fabrics and join them together to form a double fabric. A sharp blade then cuts the joining yarns between the layers, leaving two distinct fabrics each with a pile on one side.

In judging the durability of pile fabric, the background weave is very important. Several rows of filling should be used between two rows of pile so that the pile will not pull out easily. In addition, the background weave should be closely woven.

Leno Weave. The gauzy, lacelike construction made by twisting pairs of warp yarns in a figure eight and passing a filling yarn through the loops made by the twisted warp yarns is known as the **leno weave.** In addition to its lacy appearance, a selling point is its porosity, which allows air and light to penetrate. The leno weave, which is made on a special leno loom, is used in marquisette for curtains, some thermal blankets, inexpensive dishcloths, and mosquito netting.

Figured Weaves. Patterns and designs of varied intricacy that are woven into the fabric are known as **figured weaves.** Such weaves include Jacquard designs, dobby designs, and embroidered designs.

Jacquard Design. Large, intricate, woven-in designs are made on a special loom called the **Jacquard,** which is named after its inventor, Joseph Marie Jacquard. A Jacquard design combines two or more basic weaves such as plain, twill, and satin.

On the original Jacquard loom the structural design was punched into pasteboard cards similar to punched business-machine cards. The position of the holes in the Jacquard cards determined which warp yarns were to be raised. In the production of intricate designs, each warp yarn is separately controlled so that each warp can be raised according to the pattern desired. Because of the elaborate machinery and the necessary skill required to plot the Jacquard point paper designs, fabrics in this weave are more expensive than those made on ordinary looms.

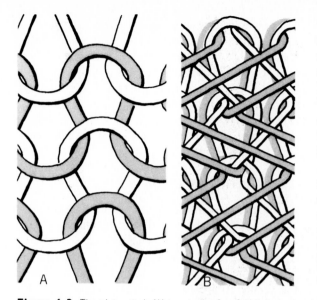

Figure 6-3. *The plain stitch (A) is a type of weft knitting; yarns run down the length of the fabric in a warp knit (B).*

Today, many of the looms that create Jacquard fabrics are controlled by computers, and electronic tape has replaced the cards. These computers are programmed to control each warp yarn separately so that great speed can be achieved in the weaving process.

Dobby Design. Small, less intricate patterns than a Jacquard are made with a special attachment to the harness loom, called a **dobby.** Dobby weaves may have geometric, diamond, or dotted designs or other small shapes woven into the fabrics. They are used in shirting and blouse fabrics, diapers, huck toweling (slack twisted face cloths usually of cotton), and some dress goods.

Embroidered Designs. There are three types of embroidered design patterns: lappet, clipped spot, and Schiffli.

Patterns are sometimes embroidered onto the fabric while it is being woven. This is done by special needles called **lappets,** which are threaded with embroidery yarn and set at right angles to the frame of the loom. With these needles simple designs such as dots, squares, stars, and floral sprays are embroidered over the regular filling yarns. Embroidered voile, organdy, and batiste can be made in this way. However, because the lappet design requires more yarn than the other dobby designs, this embroidered effect is not common.

Extra filling yarns that are larger in size than regular fillings and that may be in different colors are often used to create an embroidered effect called a **clipped spot.** The embroidery filling yarns are carried by extra shuttles that weave the yarn into the fabric at desired intervals. The yarn is cut off after each filling in the design, leaving cut fuzzy ends on one side of the fabric.

A **Schiffli machine** can embroider in any direction and make more intricate designs than lappet or clipped spot methods. Unlike the latter two designs, Schiffli designs are applied to fabric that has already been woven. Many organdies, eyelet batiste, and piques are embroidered by Schiffli machines.

Selling Points of Woven Fabrics

Woven fabrics are firm, strong, and have good dimensional stability. They are durable and withstand friction, which is especially important in men's suits. They are equally adaptable to women's wear because they drape well and can be tucked and pleated readily.

Woven fabrics can be colored by any of the major methods of dyeing and printing. Certain woven constructions are capable of showing finer pattern detail than knits. In addition, with new textured yarns and special mechanical treatments, some woven fabrics have a built-in stretching quality so that they move when the body moves, thus providing greater comfort to the wearer.

THE KNITTING PROCESS

The formation of a fabric by interlacing yarn loops is called **knitting.** Instead of two sets of yarns crossing each other, as in weaving, a single knitting yarn is looped through itself to make a chain of stitches. The **loop,** or **stitch,** is the basic unit in a knit fabric. A vertical (lengthwise) row of stitches is called a wale. A horizontal (crosswise) row of stitches is called a **course.** Knitted fabrics are broken down into two basic categories — weft knitting and warp knitting — depending on the direction in which the yarns run.

Weft Knitting

The yarns run across the width of the fabric in **weft knitting.** Weft knits have two-way stretch, modified by the types of yarn used. Spun and filament yarns and natural and manmade fibers can be used. Three basic types of stitches are used in weft knitting — the plain stitch, the purl stitch, and the rib stitch.

The **plain stitch,** which produces a smooth fabric used for all types of jersey, shows its lengthwise wales on the face of the fabric and its crosswise courses on the back. It is sometimes called the **stockinette stitch** and is the simplest knit structure.

The **purl stitch** draws alternative courses of the knit to the other side of the cloth and therefore presents the same crosswise rib appearance on both sides. Hand knitters sometimes call this **plain knitting.**

The **rib stitch** combines the plain and the purl stitches to produce a lengthwise wale on both sides of the cloth.

These stitches may be varied by combining or dropping them according to plan to produce a wide variety of surface effects. Weft-knit fabrics include single knits, double knits, jerseys, and interlocks. Hand knitting is done by the weft method.

Warp Knitting

The yarns run down the length of the fabric in **warp knitting.** Lines of yarn are arranged parallel to each other, like the warp in a woven fabric. Each yarn is controlled by a separate needle, which loops the particular yarn through itself.

Warp-knit fabrics are generally tighter, stronger, flatter, and less elastic than weft-knit fabrics. They stretch mostly in one direction.

The best-known type of warp knit is **tricot,** which is used in women's lingerie, dresses, and blouses and as a lining or backing in bonding. Another popular type of warp knit is **raschel,** which can be made in plain or more open fabrics. It is coarser than other warp knits.

The Knitting Machine

There are only two basic types of knitting machines — the flatbed needle-bar machine and the circular machine. Weft-knit fabrics are made on either type of machine; warp-knit fabrics are made almost exclusively on a flatbed machine. Computer controls are now available.

In the **flatbed needle-bar machine** the needles are arranged in a straight line and are held on a flat needle bed. The stitches move either side to side or up and down to make the fabric, which comes out flat. One type of flatbed machine is a full-fashioned knitting frame, which automatically adds or decreases stitches to widen or narrow the fabric to a desired width. Lingerie, dresses, skirts, lace, and linings (bonded) are made on this type of machine.

In the **circular knitting machine** the needles are arranged in a circle on a rotating cylinder. As the machine revolves, the needles knit the rows of loops and the fabric emerges as a circular tube. The fabric can be used for hosiery, undershirts, and dresses without any seams. More often it is slit, laid out flat, and cut up like any other fabric.

Single knits and double knits are made on a circular knitting machine. Single knits require one set of needles and do not look the same on both sides. Double knits require two sets of needles that make a cloth ribbed on both sides and double the thickness. Double knits are heavier and firmer than single knits but do not drape as well.

Gauge of Knitted Fabrics

Gauge is the term used to express the closeness of a knit. For full-fashioned hosiery it is deter-

Figure 6-4. *The circular knitting machine creates a tube of fabric that can be used for hosiery, undershirts, and seamless dresses.*

mined by the number of needles or stitches to the inch and a half, and for circular-knit hosiery, it is determined by the number per inch. As a rule, the higher the gauge number, the more closely knit, stronger, and more durable the fabric.

Selling Points of Knitted Fabrics

Knitted garments are comfortable because they give with body movement. Compared to woven fabrics they are porous and do not wrinkle easily.

Most knits are also easy to launder and do not require ironing. Knit fabrics have more surface interest and patterning than in the past and have adapted woven designs.

Garments made from many weft- and warp-knit fabrics have certain disadvantages. If one loop in the fabric breaks, it is very difficult to control the rip or run that soon occurs. Another objection is that knits snag. However, new finishing treatments and new constructions, such as using a spun yarn on the surface and a filament yarn on the back, are helping to overcome these problems. Because spun yarn is made of many short fibers, if one of these fibers is snagged, it will break and will not cause an ugly pull. Filament yarn helps to overcome the problem of bagging and sagging because it provides stability.

Care of Knitted Fabrics

Many objections to knitted fabrics can be overcome through a knowledge of their proper care. The Federal Trade Commission's (FTC) care-labeling rule has made proper care of knitted garments much easier to accomplish. Read the label to see if the article can be machine or hand washed or, in the case of some wool knits, dry-cleaned, and follow the instructions carefully.

Although most knits smooth out when worn, some articles, such as cotton-jersey polo shirts and cotton-knit dresses, are softened and smoothed by ironing.

If a run appears in a knitted article, mend it immediately. Pins should never be used as a substitute for mending because they cause loops to snag and runs to form.

LAYERED FABRICS

Either woven or knitted fabrics can be used as a base for bonding and laminating, the two types of construction that provide two layers of cloth.

Bonded Fabrics

A combination of two fabrics that have been joined together by a binding agent is called a **bonded fabric.** The technique of joining the fabrics together is called the **fabric-to-fabric** method. The purposes of the fabric-to-fabric construction are to increase the warmth of a fabric or to add strength in case one of the layers is especially weak. It is also used to mend or reinforce fabrics with a patch.

Laminated Fabrics

The **laminating** (joining) of a fabric to a plastic foam by use of an adhesive, heat, or other binding agent produces a **laminated fabric.** (See also the section on laminating in Chapter 13.) This technique is called the **fabric-to-foam method.** Consumers will recognize laminated cloth by observing that the front side is a textile fabric and the back is plastic foam. Lightweight robes, dresses, upholstery, and outer jackets are frequently constructed of laminated fabrics.

CROCHETING

Crocheting resembles knitting in some respects, but it is made with a single needle rather than two or more needles. There is, however, a machine-made knitted fabric called **knit crochet.** Crocheting involves making a continuous series of loops of yarn with a single hooked needle. The loops are hooked together to form a fabric that is used mostly for yokes, vests, and sweaters.

BRAIDING

A **braid** is made by diagonally crossing over and intertwining three or more parallel yarns over two or more other yarns. Braid is used for belting material and for trimmings for rugs and other decorative objects.

LACE

The openwork fabric made by looping, twisting, or knotting a single yarn in different ways is called **lace.** It is made by hand or machine.

Real Lace

Real lace is made by hand and is more delicate, more beautiful, and far more expensive than machine-made lace. It is generally made with linen and silk because of their strength and beauty, as proven by the many ancient lace museum pieces that are still in splendid condition.

Machine-Made Lace

Nearly all common patterns found in real laces can be made on machines. In addition, some

CROCHETING

BRAIDING

LACE

Figure 6-5. Crocheting *is making a continuous series of loops with a single hooked needle.* Braiding *is used for belting and trimmings.* Lace *is made by looping, twisting, or knotting a single yarn.*

novelty machine-made lace combines two or more designs found in real lace. In the United States machine laces are made chiefly from cotton, rayon, and nylon.

NONWOVEN FABRICS

Although weaving and knitting are the most common methods of fabric construction, there are other ways of interlocking fibers and yarns to make a textile fabric. With the exception of felting, an ancient process, all are fairly recent developments. Nonwoven fabrics are made mostly from cotton, rayon, and manmade fibers, particularly polyester and olefin. They are given a wide variety of characteristics depending on the fiber or fibers used, the method of forming a web of fibers used, and the method of binding together the fibers in the web. Some of the methods are as follows.

- Using adhesive and heat to bind the fibers together.
- Fusing manmade fibers together where they are fusible.
- Using barbed needles to entangle the fibers thoroughly, called **needle punching.**
- Using strong jets of water or air to entangle the fibers, with no adhesive or fusion, a process called **spunlaced.**
- Laying out the fibers in a trough of water evenly and then letting out the water to leave a layer of fibers that are interlocked. This wet process is similar to that of papermaking.
- Creating a film of plastic material, laying it out, embossing it, and stretching it to the point where the film separates into fibrous form, thus creating a nonwoven fabric.

A nonwoven branded fabric called Ultra-Suede (Spring Industries) has become an important fashion item for outerwear. It is a suedelike material made from 60 percent polyester fiber and 40 percent of a plastic called polyurethane. It is impregnated with synthetic resin to become a soft, pliable, smooth (and expensive) fabric that closely resembles suede cloth (discussed in Chapter 7).

More and more uses for nonwoven goods, both durable and disposable, are being uncovered. Some of the major uses are the following.

- *Disposables* such as surgical, medical, and sanitary goods; diapers; wiping cloths; and "fun" clothes.
- *Consumer durables* such as linings, tablecloths, blankets, and carpet backing.
- *Industrial goods* such as road-building material, embankment reinforcement, and filtering and packing materials.

Felts

Felts are generally made of wool or hair and are based on the fiber's natural ability to interlock because of its scaly surface. Heat, moisture, and pressure compress the fibers into a tight, compact mass. There is no adhesive or chemical action involved. Uses for felts include hats, table pads, pennants, blackboard erasers, corn plasters, phonograph record pads, and weather stripping.

Mali Fabrics

Mali fabrics are nonwoven fabrics that are made by relatively new machines. They use stitching thread to bind together (rather than interlace) warp and filling yarns. The stitching thread is also applied to webs of fiber, which is a construction somewhat similar to needle punching.

DO YOU KNOW YOUR MERCHANDISE?

1. Differentiate among weaving, knitting, and lace making.
2. Define warp and filling.
3. What are the limitations of a satin weave?
4. Name and describe two fancy weaves.
5. Define course and wale.
6. What are the two basic categories of knitted fabrics?

7. What are the advantages and the disadvantages of knits?
8. What are the differences between real lace and machine-made lace?
9. List and explain three ways of constructing a fabric other than weaving and knitting.
10. What are the major uses of nonwoven fabrics?

PUTTING YOUR MERCHANDISE KNOWLEDGE TO WORK

Select at least five fabrics worn by members of your class or group. For each fabric name the weave, knit, or other construction.

PROJECT

Put tacks or small nails evenly spaced along each end of a cigar or similar-type box. With yarn, string up the warp threads. Insert filling yarns in such a manner as to create each of the basic weaves presented in this chapter.

7

Finishing and Coloring

Finishing procedures (the fourth link in the fabric chain discussed in Chapter 5) are as important to fabric performance and aesthetic value as are fiber and yarn selection and fabric construction. Even the highest-quality fabrics can be degraded by shortcut finishing processes. The appropriate finishing treatments enhance fabrics and improve their performance.

FINISHING PROCESSES

Unless fabrics are woven or knitted from colored yarns, when they come off the loom or knitting machine they are unfinished, drab, and unattractive. At this stage they are called **grey** or **greige goods.** By means of various finishes fabrics can be changed into beautiful and useful materials. A number of finishing processes may be used to improve a fabric's appearance; to affect its stiffness, weight, or elasticity; to make it easy to care for; to prevent discomfort to the wearer; or to protect the fabric itself.

Improving the Fabric's Appearance

Finishing processes that improve the fabric's appearance include bleaching, lustering and delustering, calendering, singeing, shearing, brushing, abrading, crepeing, embossing, and moiréing.

Bleaching.   Because most fabrics are not pure white when they come from the loom or knitting

machine, they must go through a process that removes the colored matter and makes them white. This process is called **bleaching.** Bleaching is usually done with chemicals such as chlorine or peroxide. In addition to whitening the fabrics, bleaching may increase the fabric's ability to absorb dyes uniformly because natural coloring matter has been removed.

Lustering and Delustering.   A chemical treatment using a caustic soda solution will make a cotton fabric, such as sateen, shiny and lustrous. This process is called **mercerizing.** In addition, fluorescent materials, called **optical brighteners,** are sometimes used as finishes. They create the appearance of whiteness or brightness by the way the fabric reflects light.

Sometimes a lustrous fabric is not desired. To decrease the luster, special heat treatments are used on thermoplastic-fiber fabrics (polyester, nylon, and so on, discussed in Chapters 11 and 12) to change light reflection. For example, a surface coating may be applied to nylon hosiery to reduce the luster.

Calendering.   Before most fabrics can be sold, they must be pressed or calendered. **Calendering** is the process of passing the fabric between smooth, hot rollers to produce a smooth, even luster. Wool is not calendered; instead it is sponged and pressed in a manner similar to that used by a tailor when pressing a suit. Fabrics with a satiny look are usually calendered more than once.

Singeing. The process of removing the unsightly fibers projecting from the surface of smooth fabrics is known as **singeing.** The fabric is passed over hot cooper plates or through gas flames so that the fuzzy fibers are singed. This is done very quickly so that the fabric itself does not catch fire.

Shearing. The process of **shearing** accomplishes the same purpose as singeing but in a completely different manner. The shearing machine makes the pile or **nap** even and cuts off yarn imperfections.

Brushing. To raise a nap on knit or woven fabrics, the finisher uses the process of **brushing.** Brushing also removes cut, sheared fibers that have fallen into the nap or pile of a fabric.

Abrading. Fabrics may be treated by a rubbing process called **abrading.** The fabrics are stretched on rapidly revolving rollers covered with an abrasive material that polishes the cloth and provides a soft finish that resembles suede leather. This process is used for sportswear, gloves, and upholstery.

Crepeing. In Chapter 5 the process of creating crepe by varying the twist and tension in the yarn was described. Permanent crinkled effects, or crepe, can also be produced by a finishing process called **crepeing.** In this process certain parts of a fabric are printed with an alkali paste. When the fabric is washed, the printed parts shrink and the unprinted parts crinkle. Seersucker and crinkled bedspreads are often made by this method.

Embossing. Another method of producing crinkled effects is known as **embossing.** In this process the fabric is passed between hot rollers filled with indentations. Embossing is generally done on inexpensive fabrics and is not permanent. However, there is a method of embossing, called **heat setting,** that is permanent. In heat setting, plastic is applied to the fabric as it is embossed. The pressure and heat of the embossing rollers cause the embossed effect to be heat set permanently.

Moiréing. Rayon or silk may be given a watermarked appearance by means of a process called **moiréing.** The fabric, woven with heavy filling-wise ribs, is passed between heavy rollers that have raised, irregular lines. The pressing down of parts of the surface brings out their luster and thus produces the moiré.

Affecting Stiffness, Weight, and Elasticity

The finishing process commonly applied to some fabrics to give weight, crispness, or stiffness and that may hide defects is called **sizing.** Various starches, glues, and gums are used to give body, stiffness, and weight to fabrics. Generally, linens are not sized but may have some starch added to give the stiffness of new linen fabrics.

A process of adding metallic salts to silk, giving the fabric a heavy feeling and stiffness, is called **weighting.** However, weighting may come out partially or entirely in washing and dry cleaning, leaving the fabric limp. Heavily weighted silks will deteriorate in sunlight. Silk is no longer weighted in the United States, and the practice is becoming generally obsolete.

Wool can be given more weight by adding moisture and magnesium chloride, but this is not a permanent finish. A loose weave in wool may be covered up by steaming the very short waste fibers into the back of the fabric. This process is called **flocking,** but it is not permanent.

Elasticity in 100 percent woven cottons or cotton blends can be achieved in finishing by a process called **slack mercerization.** Unlike regular mercerization by which fabrics are treated with sodium hydroxide and held under tension, slack mercerization imparts stretch to fabrics by immersing them in a caustic soda bath without any tension so yarns in the fabric buckle or shrink. When the fabric is pulled to its unshrunken dimension, it is said to stretch. This method is inexpensive, but the amount of stretch is limited and its durability of the stretch is questionable.

Creating Ease in Care

One of the greatest boons to the consumer is the energy and time saved from today's ease-in-care (minimum-care) finishes. These include permanent-starchless, shrinkage-control, crease-resistant, wash-and-wear, durable or permanent-press, and soil-resistant finishes.

Permanent-Starchless Finish. A resin finish applied to cotton, linen, silk, or rayon that stiffens the fabric permanently and eliminates the need for starching after each washing because the finish does not dissolve in washing is called a **permanent-starchless finish.**

Shrinkage Control. Fabrics that are labeled preshrunk are very deceiving because the term does not mean that fabrics will not shrink any more. A Federal Trade Commission (FTC) ruling, therefore states that the term "preshrunk" on a label or advertisement must be followed by the maximum amount of further shrinkage, expressed in a percentage, called **residual shrinkage.** This residual shrinkage is controlled by the stability of the fiber, the quality of the fabric construction, and the finish applied. A salesperson should know how to interpret residual shrinkage. For example, 4 percent residual shrinkage on a 45-inch dress length actually means that the dress will shrink almost 2 inches, which is an excessive amount. Cotton and linen fabrics bearing the trademark Sanforized have been compressively shrunk and will not shrink by more than an additional 1 percent.

Wool fabrics can be finished so that only a certain amount of shrinkage remains. There are several patented processes that treat wool in fiber, yarn, or fabric form with chlorine so that it resists shrinkage by felting.

After a fabric has been finished or dyed, it is made even in width by a process called **tentering.** The fabric is laid flat, and the right and left selvages are held firmly on a frame. Then steam heat is applied to the fabric as it is pulled along the frame. After tentering, the fabric is dried and calendered. If the fabric has been stretched too much, as is sometimes done by unreliable manufacturers, it will return to its original size after laundering. This is often the cause of excessive shrinkage of fabrics.

Crease Resistance. Many fabrics made of linen, cotton, or rayon crease very readily. There are several crease-resistant finishes now used on such fabrics that add elasticity and cause them to resist creasing and to lose their wrinkles after hanging. The crease-resistant solution (usually made of a chemical resin base) may be applied to

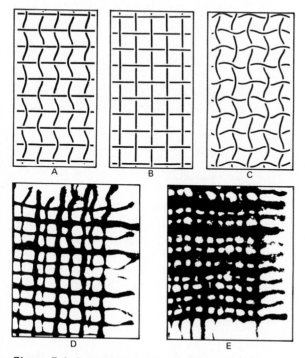

Figure 7-1. *Fabric woven on a power loom has warp threads under tension (A). Finishing processes stretch warp and filling (B); when damp, the yarns become wavy and shorten (C). The yarns of preshrunk fabric are much looser before shrinking (D) than after compressive shrinkage (E).*

the fabric during the dyeing process or to the "right" side of the fabric after it has been dyed and dried.

Wash-and-Wear. Before the development of durable-press fabrics, cotton and rayon fabrics were treated to eliminate wrinkles and reduce shrinkage. This was done chemically by changing the molecular structure of the cotton or rayon fibers and then **curing** (baking) the fabric with dry heat in a special kind of oven. It was hoped that these **wash-and-wear fabrics** would not need ironing; however, some touch-up ironing on collars, cuffs, and seams was often required.

Durable Press. The next development in eliminating ironing was to add more resin and to cure the fabric at a higher temperature than that used for wash-and-wear fabrics. This was the first process for producing **durable-press,** or **permanent-press, fabrics.** Although this treatment produced fabrics with excellent wrinkle resistance, pleat retention, and shrinkage control, it lowered the strength and abrasion resistance of the fabric. If polyester or nylon is blended with cotton, this problem is reduced.

However, even this was not the entire solution to producing durable-press fabrics. One problem that remained grew out of the fact that fabrics were cured at the mill as flat goods. When the fabric was made into garments, it "remembered" how it was when flat and tended to return to that state. This made the retention of sharp creases and pleats a problem, especially in men's slacks. The solution was to add the resin to the fabric in the mill but not to cure it until after the fabric was made into a garment. This treatment is called **postcuring.**

Soil Resistance. When fabrics are new and even after several dry cleanings, they resist or repel water and oil stains if they have been treated with a **soil repellent.** The stain stays on the surface and can be sponged off. Scotchgard and Zepel are familiar brand names of soil-repellent finishes. **Soil retardants** are various chemical compounds applied to fabrics, especially

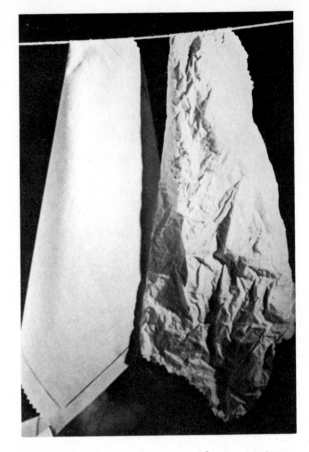

Figure 7-2. *Left: cotton fabric treated for crease resistance. Right: untreated fabric, which creases more easily.*

carpets, to provide resistance to soiling. **Soil release** is a finishing process that makes soil come out of the fabric more quickly than if it were untreated. Fabrics so treated also retain their brightness after repeated launderings and can be dry-cleaned without losing their soil-releasing properties. Visa, Soil Out, and Come Clean are brand names for this finish.

Protecting the Wearer and the Fabric

Some finishes may protect the wearer from discomforts such as cold, heat, rain, static electricity, perspiration odor, and fire. Other finishes protect the fabric itself from deterioration.

Napping. Napping raises the loose ends of the short fibers to produce a fuzz, or nap, and thus increases a fabric's warmth. Revolving cylinders covered with fine wire teeth or **teasels** (little burrlike plants) are generally used to draw up the nap. Cotton, spun rayon, and acetate can be napped to resemble wool. Many wool fabrics are napped to give them their characteristic rough finish.

Flannel is a soft, light-to-medium weight fabric that has been slightly napped on one or both sides. It was originally made of wool but is now also made of cotton or a combination of fibers. The warp yarns are usually stronger than the filling yarns in order not to sacrifice strength when napped.

Metallizing Treatment. Fabrics may be treated with an aluminum derivative whose purpose is to keep the wearer warm in winter and cool in the summer. A brand name for this finish is Milium.

Water-Repellent and Waterproofing Finishes. Water-repellent finishes should not be confused with waterproofing finishes. In **water-repellent finishes** the pores of the fabric are open for air circulation. In **waterproofing finishes** the pores of the fabric are closed.

Wax emulsions, insoluble metallic soaps, aluminum compounds, silicones, and fluorochemicals are used to make fabrics water repellent, although the treated fabrics vary in their resistance to water. These finishes can even be applied to a polyester/cotton blend that has been given a durable-press treatment.

Fabrics treated with water-repellent finishes shed water, rain, and snow; stay clean longer; resist spots and stains (spots can generally be sponged off and grease stains removed with cleaning fluid); and resist stains from perspiration. Familiar brand names of water-repellent finishes are Cravenette, Impregnole, Unixec, and Zepel. Some finishes wash out in repeated laundering, but dry cleaners can restore some of the repellent finish.

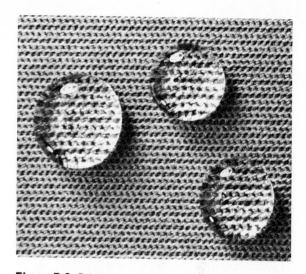

Figure 7-3. *Fabric treated with a water-repellent finish sheds water and stays clean longer.*

Air-Conditioning Finish. On a cold, windy day static electricity often causes acrylic pants to cling to your legs or nylon slips to crackle and stick to a skirt. Static may be controlled in fabrics of noncellulosic manmade fibers by increasing the humidity of the air. Also, softeners such as Sta Puf, Downy, and Negastat may be used in the wash water to counteract or carry off electrostatic charges.

Antibacterial Finish. The odor of perspiration is caused by bacterial decomposition on the skin. Chemical antiseptic finishes applied to the fabric inhibit the growth of bacteria on the fabric, as well as prevent the fabric from deteriorating.

Flame-Retardant or Fire-Resistant Finishes. In 1953 Congress passed the Flammable Fabrics Act to eliminate from the marketplace easily ignitable fabrics. In 1967 the act was amended to remove from the marketplace articles of wearing apparel and other textile produces "which are so highly flammable as to be dangerous when worn by individuals" or used for other purposes. The Consumer Product

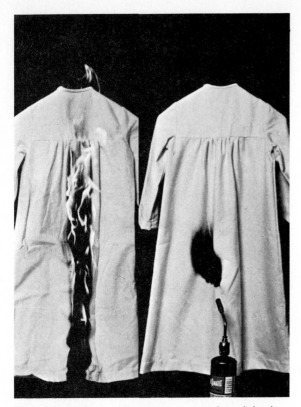

Figure 7-4. *An untreated garment, exposed to a lighted match, burns in 15 seconds, while a garment treated with a flame retardant compound and exposed to a gas flame chars but does not burn.*

Safety Commission has the responsibility for establishing the need for flammability tests, and it sets and administers standards to protect the public from fires causing personal injury, death, or significant property damage. At present there are a number of textile products that must pass government flammability standards, including carpets and children's sleepwear.

There are a number of flame-retarding chemicals on the market, such as Firegard. It is used primarily on all-cotton fabrics and withstands many washings. Another chemical, TRIS, has been banned from the market because of its link to cancer. Making a flame-retardant fabric is difficult because so many factors are involved. For example, vegetable fibers catch fire more quickly than animal fibers. Lightweight, looseweave fabrics usually burn faster than heavier fabrics.

Often the flame-retardant chemical adversely affects other properties of the fabric, such as its hand, drapability, or breathability. Even sewing thread and stitching play a role. Flammable threads cannot be used in stitching together the parts of flame-retardant children's pajamas because the flame will run right up the thread. It should be noted that some fabrics are protected not by the finish but by the flame-proof or flame-resistant qualities of certain manmade fibers (to be discussed in Chapter 12).

Abrasion-Resistant Finishes. Some natural and manmade-fiber fabrics may be damaged by frictional rubbing, called **abrasion.** One method of overcoming the problem is to blend fibers with low abrasion resistance with those with high abrasion resistance, such as nylon acrylic or polyester. In finishing, a fabric's resistance to abrasion can be increased by using resins that are hard and smooth to hold the ends of fibers in so they cannot fuzz.

Slip-Resistant Finishes. There are several chemical processes that can be used to alleviate fraying of seams and slippage (shifting) of yarns in a fabric.

Mildew- and Rot-Repellent Finishes. Fabrics made of cotton, linen, wool, and rayon are often attacked by a parasitic fungus called **mildew.** This fungus grows if fabrics are stored while wet or are not rinsed free of soap or oils in laundering. Odorless germicides or resins are used to treat fabrics to prevent mildew and rot.

Moth-Repellent Finishes. Colorless chemicals can be added to a dye bath to make a fabric mothproof. The fabric can also be sprayed with a mothproofing chemical. Simple home remedies against moth damage consist of brushing the apparel after wearing, dry-cleaning fabrics before putting them into storage, storing with moth balls or flakes, and exposing fabrics to sunlight, provided the color is fast to sunlight. Mothproofing is especially important for natural animal fibers, which are consumed as food by the moth.

COLORING PROCESSES

The following exchange might be overheard at the fashion-fabric counter. The customer asks, "Will the color run if I wash this fabric?" The salesperson answers, "No, we guarantee that it will wash satisfactorily. It has been tested and meets commercial standards. Here is the label." The customer then asks, "Will it fade if I wear it in bright sunlight?" The salesperson replies, "No. It has been tested for sunfastness, too." These are only two of the many questions that a salesperson may be asked regarding colored fabrics. All the questions of this type can be readily boiled down to one: "Is the fabric colorfast?"

Colorfastness

The beautiful appearance of a colored fabric is of little benefit to the consumer if the color does not retain its brightness during the normal life of the fabric. If a fabric shows no change of color after repeated washings, it is colorfast, or color resistant, to *washing*. **Colorfastness** means that a fabric will not change color when it is subjected to certain conditions for a given length of time. If a fabric can be exposed to bright sunlight for a certain number of hours without changing color, the fabric is colorfast to *sunlight*. Fabrics may also be colorfast to perspiration, water spotting, ironing, and crocking (rubbing off).

A label indicating "fast color" can be misleading because it does not explain to what the colors are fast. The salesperson must be careful in using the term "colorfast" because unless it is qualified, it means little.

The American Association of Textile Chemists and Colorists (Research Triangle Park, NC) has developed commercial standards for testing a fabric's colorfastness to sunlight, perspiration, laundering, dry cleaning, crocking, and fume fading. The tests are available to the entire textile industry. Many reputable manufacturers use these standards as a basis for labeling their merchandise so that retailers and consumers can judge how a fabric can be expected to perform in use.

Dyeing and Printing

Fabrics are dyed and printed in a variety of ways and with a variety of dyestuffs (coloring matter). Coloring fabrics is a complicated process. The method of dyeing, the chemical content of the dye itself, and the affinity (attraction) of the dye for the particular fibers all play a role in determining the success of the process.

Dyeing. By adding different colors and using different patterns, fabrics can be varied tremendously in appearance. Dyeing may be done during any one of several stages. Four methods of coloring fibers and yarns are discussed in Chapter 5.

Stock dyeing is used when a yarn is to be composed of a number of colors, such as for a heather mixture. The fibers are dyed before they have been blended or spun. The dyes can then deeply penetrate the fibers, producing fast colors. This method is frequently used for wool.

As explained in Chapter 5, dyeing of yarns before they are woven or knit into cloth usually produces faster colors than **piece dyeing,** in which the woven or knit fabric is immersed in a dye bath to produce a solid color. Piece dyeing, however, is widely used because it is the most economical dyeing method. It is practical to piece dye moderate amounts of fabric, whereas it is only practical to yarn dye much larger amounts. Therefore, in piece dyeing, dyers can adjust to rapid fashion changes in color.

Cross dyeing, which is one way of piece dyeing, is based on the different reactions of two or more fibers to the same dye. For example, rayon and acetate mixture can be dyed with a dyestuff that colors the rayon but is resisted by the acetate.

Dyestuffs for textiles may be divided into natural dyes and chemical, or synthetic, dyes. Natural dyes are obtained from berries, roots, flowers, and so on, of plants. The chemical dyes, which were discovered in the nineteenth century, are developed from coal tar or petroleum bases. Because natural dyes are limited in variety, quantity, and uses and they are expensive, they have been replaced largely by chemical dyes.

Vat dyes are one of the most important kinds of dyes from chemical sources. They are applied to the fabric or yarn in soluble form that is sometimes almost colorless. When oxidized they become an insoluble pigment, in bright colors, that are fast to light and washing. Indigo is the most famous color, but a wide variety of colors can be produced. The name "vat dye" comes from the fact that years ago the dyestuff was steeped in a barrel or vat.

Dyeing by Computer. Computers are now being used to determine and control color in the dyeing process. The computer calculates the proportion of each basic dye color that is mixed in the dyeing vat to achieve the desired shade. This development is leading to great savings in the cost of dyes. Also cleaning and recoloring can be performed readily with the assurance that the restored color will be correct.

Printing. The cheerful South American or Mexican designs on cotton or rayon fabrics are **printed** onto the fabrics after they have been woven. Whereas in piece dyeing the fabric is immersed in the dyebath, in printing the dyestuff, or pigments, are placed on the surface of the cloth and do not penetrate as deeply.

Printing today is done mostly by machine. There are, however, some beautiful designs still done by hand, such as hand-blocked bedspreads. Although machine-printed fabrics require a great amount of skill in the preparation of the design, the comparative speed in the printing process plus the greater quantity of fabric that can be produced from the same design makes it a less-expensive process than hand printing.

Handprinting Methods. Wooden or metal blocks with cutout portions of the design are the tools of **hand-block printing.** There is a block for each color, and dye is applied much as ink is on a rubber stamp. Each colored portion of the design is then stamped onto the fabric separately. The various color blocks together complete the pattern. Because this is done by hand, it is not as

precise as machine printing. Colors often run into one another, and the spacing between designs is not identical.

In **batik printing** the colors are placed directly onto the fabric. Parts of the fabric are brushed with wax to resist the dye. Then the whole fabric is dipped in the dye solution. Those parts that are not covered with wax take the dye. After dyeing is completed, the wax is removed either by dipping the fabric into a solvent, such as benzene, or by covering it with blotters and pressing it with a hot iron so that the blotter absorbs the melted wax.

In **stencil printing** certain portions of the fabric are made to resist the dye. A paper or metal stencil cut in the desired design is placed over the fabric. The dye takes only in the cutout spaces.

Hand-screen printing is similar to stencil printing and batik printing in that certain areas of the fabric resist the dye. The fabric is placed under a silk or nylon screen that is stretched on a frame. Portions of the screen are covered with an enamel coating that resists the dye. The dyestuff is poured onto the screen and a squeegee is passed back and forth forcing the dye through the uncoated parts of the screen. Because each color in the design requires a separate screen and because hand labor is required, hand-screen printing is expensive.

In **tie dyeing** cloth is gathered in bunches. String or rubber bands are tied around the bunches of cloth so that the tied cloth will resist the dye. The fabric is then dipped in the dye. The resulting patterns are not clearly outlined but look like sunbursts. The tying and dyeing can be repeated several times to produce varied effects.

Machine-Printing Methods. **Direct printing** is used on the majority of today's multicolored fabrics. As the name implies, the colors are printed directly onto the fabric, much the same as in the hand-block method. However, instead of individual blocks, copper rollers, each engraved with a part of the design and covered with a separate color, do the printing. After the fabrics are dry, they are passed over hot rollers and steamed to set the colors. The design may be printed on both sides of the fabric to imitate a yarn-dyed woven fabric. This is called **duplex printing.**

Photographic printing produces some delicately shaded, richly colored effects by reproducing a design on fabric. The method is similar to that used for newspaper photograph reproduction.

Screen printing has now been mechanized, making the process faster and the costs lower. The procedure is much the same as hand-screen printing, except that it is done by the machine.

Resist printing prints the desired design on the fabric with a substance that resists dye. The fabric is then piece dyed, but the printed design does not take the dye and thus appears as a white pattern against a colored background. This method differs from **resist dyeing,** in which the fabric is woven from certain yarns that are treated to resist dye and also from others that are not. The fabric so woven is then piece dyed, leaving a fabric with both colored and white yarns.

Discharge printing is frequently used on fabrics that have only two colors such as fabrics with dots. Discharge printing is the reverse of resist printing. The whole fabric is first dyed one complete color. It is then run through a roller printed with a chemical paste that removes the color from certain portions of the fabric, which may be either the design or the background portion. However, the chemical used sometimes weakens the fabric if it is not washed thoroughly. In a discharge print the colored parts of the fabric are the same color on both sides of the fabric, whereas in a direct print the colored section on the backside is often lighter than that on the front side.

Heat-Transfer Printing. In the process of **heat-transfer printing,** the design is first printed in colors on large rolls of paper. Then the printed design is pressed against the fabric and heat is applied to transfer the pattern to the fabric

and set the color. The process takes only 12 to 20 seconds, and almost any kinds of design can be printed. Sublistatic Corporation of America, which owns the process, claims that up to six colors in 2,000 color combinations are possible. Heat-transfer printing is growing more popular, especially for knits on which it is used to produce woven type effects.

Jet Printing. **Jet printing** is a new printing process that can produce a variety of patterns in many colors. Moving jets squirt streams of dye on a specified width of fabric creating the design by their movement.

Identifying Dyed and Printed Fabrics. To decide whether a fabric is dyed or printed, examine the fabric. Is it all one color or are there designs in it? If the fabric is all one color, it is probably dyed. When the fabric has a design, it is either woven in or printed. Woven-in designs are yarn dyed. If a design is printed, the fabric is usually lighter in coloring on the back than on the front. If uncertain, unravel a yarn where the design occurs. If the yarn is in different colors, the design is printed. If the yarn is all one color, the design is woven in.

VOLUNTARY STANDARDS OF QUALITY

The American National Standards Institute (ANSI), in cooperation with representatives of technical societies and national groups of manufacturers, retailers, dry cleaners, and consumers, has developed tests based on actual quality testing done by private testing agencies, especially the American Association of Textile Chemists and Colorists (AATCC) and the American Society for Testing and Materials (ASTM). The standards cover many phases of quality, including colorfastness, and may be used by any fabric or garment manufacturer. If an item meets the Institute's standards, the manufacturer may indicate this on the label.

Other good guides for judging the quality of a

fabric are the seals or certificates issued by organizations such as the Good Housekeeping Institute, the International Fabricare Institute, the Consumer Bureau of *Parents Magazine*, the Better Fabrics Testing Bureau, and the U.S. Testing Company. These seals or certificates are issued only after products have passed standard laboratory tests.

Consumers Union and Consumers' Research, both nonprofit organizations, also test all kinds of merchandise and rate the items in their monthly publications. The publication of Consumers Union is *Consumer Reports* and of Consumers' Research is *Consumers' Bulletin*.

Information on performance of textiles is reliable if it is based on standards of quality maintained by government agencies and reputable mills and garment manufacturers. Thus, it is important that a salesperson read all labels carefully to be able to interpret them for customers.

Although the care-labeling rule discussed in Chapter 5 is a step in the right direction, it is not comprehensive. For example, it may not indicate if a fabric is sufficiently colorfast to send to a commercial laundry.

scribe each of these finishes.
5. What finishes protect the fabric itself?
6. Define colorfastness. What does the word "colorfast" mean?
7. What is the difference between dyeing and printing?
8. How can a computer control the dyeing process?
9. Distinguish among the following methods: direct printing, resist printing, and discharge printing. Give examples of each method.
10. Why are government and voluntary standards of quality important to the customer, the consumer, and the salesperson?

PUTTING YOUR MERCHANDISE KNOWLEDGE TO WORK

Choose an imaginary five-piece wardrobe and write a paragraph about each article. Emphasize the types of dyeing and finishing treatments you would want each item to receive in order to meet your personal requirements.

DO YOU KNOW YOUR MERCHANDISE?

1. Explain the purposes of finishing processes.
2. List and describe the finishing processes that improve the appearance of fabrics and explain how each finishing process is applied.
3. What finishes affect the stiffness, crispness, softness, weight, and elasticity of a fabric? Describe each finish.
4. What is meant by ease-in-care finishes? De-

PROJECT

Select a garment labeled durable press or permanent press and then wash it, following the washing instructions on the fabric label or on your detergent box. When the article dries, describe its appearance and texture. Does it require any ironing? If so, is it correctly labeled durable press or permanent press?

8

Cotton, Linen, and
Other Vegetable Fibers

People have been producing cloth from vegetable fibers since prehistoric times. Linen has been found wrapped around Egyptian mummies that were entombed over 3,500 years ago. Cotton clothing was worn by people in the ancient Far and Middle East and in pre-Columbian America. Both fabrics have been used in Europe since the Middle Ages. Today we are surrounded by goods made with cotton, and although the use of linen had become rare, it is regaining its popularity for clothing.

COTTON

Formerly, cotton clothing was considered a useful staple but without fashion significance. Interest was directed toward the new manmade fibers with their own superior features as well as their novelty. Now cotton's own special features — comfort, absorbency to perspiration, durability, and dyeability — are being recognized as elements of fashion significance.

Classification of Cotton Fibers

There are different kinds of cotton, depending on the climatic conditions under which it is grown and the plant variety. Its quality, which determines its end use, varies greatly. For example, cotton used in coarse material such as unbleached muslin is not suited for use in a fine,

sheer material such as voile. Cotton is classified according to certain prescribed standards.

There are two main criteria for determining the quality of cotton: staple length and grade. Both are determined by a specialist who compares samples taken from each cotton bale with established government standards.

Staple length refers to the average length of the fibers in the **bale** (a bag originally of burlap or jute, now of a plastic). Very short staple (1/2 inch or less) is used chiefly in making materials for stuffing and padding. The extra long staple (1 3/8 inches and over) is fine in texture and is used for high-quality fabrics. Most U.S. cotton ranges from 29/32 to 1 1/8 inches long. Sea Island cotton, a very long-staple cotton, averages 1 3/4 inches in length. Egyptian, another long-staple cotton, and its U.S. offshoot, Pima, are about 1 9/16 inches in length.

The **grade** of cotton refers to its color and brightness, amount of foreign matter, and ginning preparation. There are seven degrees of whiteness, ranging from white, the highest in quality, to gray, the lowest in quality. Also, the less dirt, grit, leaves, seeds, and short and immature fibers in the cotton, the higher the quality.

Areas of Cotton Production

Cotton is produced in a great many countries, including the United States, the U.S.S.R.,

103

China, India, Pakistan, Turkey, Egypt, the Sudan, Mexico, and Brazil. The United States, which produces over one-fifth of the total output, is the largest cotton producer.

The Growing and Harvesting of Cotton

Cotton grows best in a warm, humid climate and sandy soil. The cotton seeds are planted by machine in the spring and grow into flowering plants, usually 4 to 6 feet high. When the flowers wither and die, a small green **boll** (seed pod) remains. The cotton fibers are the long strands attached to the seeds inside the boll. The boll bursts when it reaches maturity, and the cotton appears as a soft wad of fine fibers. At this point the cotton is ready for picking. After the cotton bolls are picked, they are put through the **cotton**

Figure 8-1. *Cotton comes from the soft wad of fine fibers inside the* boll, *or seed pod, of a flowering plant.*

gin, which separates the seeds from the fibers. Once separated, the cotton fibers are put through the **baling press,** which compresses them into 480-pound bales.

Because ginning does not remove all the cotton fibers from the seeds, short fibers are left adhering to them. These fibers are removed by passing the seeds through another gin just before the seeds are crushed for oil. These short fibers are called cotton linters and are used in mattress stuffing and upholstery as well as in fine paper and plastics.

Manufacture of Cotton Yarn

Cotton goes through a number of preparatory processes at the mill before it can be spun into yarn. First, the cotton is cleaned by machines that remove the heavier impurities such as seeds and dirt. The cotton fibers are then straightened and shaped into a ropelike strand by a process called **carding.** Some fibers are further straightened, called **combing,** which also removes the short fibers. Combed yarns are finer and stronger than ones that are only carded, and they are used in higher-quality fabrics.

Next, the cotton strands are combined, drawn out, and given a slight twist for added strength. Finally, each strand is drawn out more and twisted into a finished yarn by **spinning.** Some yarns are loosely twisted, others are tightly twisted. Some are spun into ply yarns. At this point yarns may be dyed.

Construction of Cotton Fabrics

Cotton yarns are usually made into fabrics by weaving, knitting, or bonding, the last being used for nonwoven fabrics. Weaving and knitting are the most common methods of constructing cotton fabric for wearing apparel.

Woven Fabrics. Because of the great versatility of cotton, most of the weaves described in Chapter 6 can be used for cotton clothing or homefurnishings. The plain weave is used in sheets and kitchen towels. The twill weave is used for some clothing such as denim jeans. The pile weave is found in plush upholstery and Turkish toweling, the leno weave in marquisette curtains, and the Jacquard weave in brocade draperies.

Knitted Fabrics. Cotton jersey made in a plain stitch is a very common knitted fabric used in T-shirts and polo shirts. Rib-knit cottons are found in the tops of men's socks, the wrists of many sweaters, and the neckbands of T-shirts and polo shirts. Cotton dresses and blouses are made in double-knit, raschel, and tricot constructions. Sometimes cotton knits, especially those used in dresses and coats, are bonded to a layer of plastic foam that helps to stabilize the knit so that it will keep its original shape and size.

Nonwoven Fabrics. Nonwoven cotton fabrics can either be all cotton or a mixture of cotton and manmade fibers. The all-cotton fibers are made from a web of fibers bonded together as explained in Chapter 6. Nonwoven cotton is used especially for disposables such as napkins, wiping cloths, tablecloths, sheets, pillowcases, and hospital gowns.

Finishing of Cotton Fabrics

With the exception of heavy cotton fabrics, such as canvas, duck, and webbing, most cottons need a number of finishing treatments to make them appealing to customers. Unless finished, cotton fabrics are rough and soiled and contain specks and other impurities. All cotton fabrics must go through the basic finishes. Special finishes may be used to give the fabric additional properties.

Basic Finishes. The processes used to produce a basic finish in cotton vary depending on the hand and texture desired. Bleaching, brushing, shearing, mercerizing, gassing, and singeing may be used to make the fabric attractive. Sizing may be used to give the fabric temporary stiffness. The fabric may be given a permanent

starchless finish. Tentering stretches the fabric to its finished width, and calendering provides a final finish to the fabric by giving it a smooth, flat surface. Napping, used to finish flannelette, increases the warmth of the fabric and makes it softer. Cotton can also be dyed and printed easily in soft or deep, vibrant shades. These finishing processes have been described in Chapter 7.

Special Finishes. In addition to the basic finishes there are other finishes that give cotton properties it does not naturally have. Many fabrics are preshrunk in order to prevent undue shrinkage when a garment is washed. Cotton fabrics can also be treated to resist flames and to provide wash-and-wear, water-repellent and antibacterial properties. In the late 1970s a treatment for cotton was found that would make a 100 percent cotton that requires no ironing.

Identification of Cotton Fabrics

The Textile Fiber Products Identification Act (TFPIA) requires that a label giving fiber content be attached to all merchandise. Sometimes, however, the label requires interpretation. For example, if the fiber content is 65 percent polyester and 35 percent cotton, the consumer should determine the advantages of each of the fibers. Polyester in a gingham dress provides strength, abrasion-resistance, and minimum-care features; the cotton provides absorption, comfort, and affinity for dyes.

Care of Cotton Fabrics

Proper care of fabrics prolongs their life and helps preserve their original appearance and texture. The Federal Trade Commission's (FTC) Trade Regulation Rule on Care Labeling requires that cotton garments carry a permanent label giving instructions on their care.

Practically all cottons are washable, and most are machine washable. For sheer fabrics or those with doubtful colorfastness, hand washing is often the best. In any case, it is wise to keep in mind a few general rules about washing fabrics.

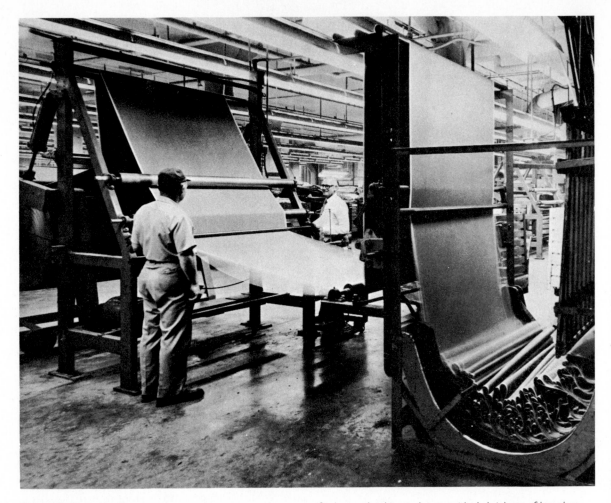

Figure 8-2. *The Sanforizing process makes cotton easier to care for by preshrinking to leave residual shrinkage of less than 1 percent.*

- Wash white and colored clothes separately. Separate delicate fabrics from heavier weights.
- Remove stains before the actual washing. It is helpful to soak the stained part in a detergent, but do not soak stains on fabrics that are not washable or colorfast. Stains may be soaked from 20 minutes to overnight. Enzyme products are good for this purpose because the enzymes break down various kinds of organic matter (protein, starch, etc.) into very small particles. See Table 8-1 for stain removal suggestions.

- Use hot water on white fabrics, warm water on colorfast colored fabrics and fabrics that have a wash-and-wear finish (synthetic resin), and lukewarm or cold water on noncolorfast fabrics. If hand washing, presoak white and light clothes for 10 to 15 minutes to remove surface dirt; do not presoak colored fabrics.
- Bleach or bluing may be added to white clothes. Do not add bleach to resin-finished cotton unless the label specifically allows it.
- Use a regular laundry detergent on most clothes. For delicate and noncolorfast gar-

Table 8-1 STAIN REMOVAL SUGGESTIONS

Type of Stain	Removal Procedure
Beverage or fruit	Place stained part over bowl and pour boiling water through it from a height. For silk, try ammonia and alcohol in equal proportions.
Blood	If possible, remove stains when fresh. Soak in cool water; then wash with soap and a little borax in warm water.
Grass	Soak in milk or in naphtha soap and warm water.
Ink	Before stain has dried, wash garment in soap and water. If stain does not come out or has dried, soak overnight in unflavored yogurt or milk if yogurt is not available. After soaking, rinse out yogurt or milk, roll in towel, and then dry. Chlorine bleach or hydrogen peroxide can be used if there is no danger of removing color. For fresh ballpoint ink stains, sponge stain repeatedly with acetone or amyl acetate. Use latter on acetate, Arnel triacetate, and Dynel and Verel modacrylics; use acetone on all other fabrics. Bleaching may be required to remove old stains.
Iodine or Mercurochrome	Wash out fresh stain with soap and water. Soak old stain in alcohol.
Iron rust	Apply salt and lemon juice. Or hold spot over boiling water and with medicine dropper apply hydrochloric (muriatic) acid diluted with equal amount of water. Be sure to follow with rinse in clear water. For silk try rubbing lightly with citric or tartaric acid and rinse thoroughly.
Mildew	Remove fresh spots on white fabrics with strong soap and water, followed by sun bleaching. For colored fabrics use paste made of powdered chalk and water, then expose to sunlight. Cottons that are not sized do not mildew easily. Starches, flour, gums, or chemicals used in certain finishing processes, plus dampness, create mildew.
Paint, varnish, or grease	Apply turpentine, benzine, or a lighter fluid.
Perspiration	Wash in soap and water. If stain does not come out, use bleach, such as mild solution of peroxide and ammonia, or one part hydrochloric acid to three or four parts water.
Scorch	For light scorch marks use few drops of hydrogen peroxide solution, then expose stain to direct sunlight, keeping it moist until stain comes out. Remove surface scorch on heavy fabrics with very fine sandpaper. Severe scorch marks cannot be removed.

ments, use a mild soap. Water softeners may be used in the last rinse to prevent fabrics from having a rough or harsh hand.

- Use a regular washing cycle for most machine-washable garments. For delicate fabrics use a gentle or delicate cycle. For resin-treated fabrics use the permanent-press cycle.
- Do not overload the washing machine.
- Most machine-washable garments can also be *machine dried*. Dry sheer fabrics at low heat, knit goods at medium heat to prevent shrinkage, and others at high heat. If tumble drying, remove clothes as soon as the machine stops. If no dryer is available, remove resin-treated fabrics from the machine before the spin cycle and drip dry them. Noncolorfast fabrics should be hung to dry so that they do not touch white or light-colored fabrics.
- When necessary, medium-weight and heavy-weight cottons should be pressed with a hot iron and sheer or thin cottons with a warm iron. When a touch-up pressing is needed on drip-dry garments, use a steam iron set at the low setting. For a fresh appearance iron cottons when they are fairly damp.

Selling Points of Cotton Fabrics

Cotton has numerous selling points. The salesperson should be aware of all of the following.

- *Comfort*. Cotton fabrics worn close to the body are very comfortable because they are soft, smooth, and feel cool. Cotton fabrics "breathe."
- *Absorbency*. Because cotton can retain many times its own weight in water, it absorbs and releases perspiration quickly, making it cool to wear in the summer. Cotton's absorbency also makes it easy to dye and bleach.
- *Versatility*. Cotton can be used for many purposes, such as a sturdy fabric for hot-air balloons and boat sails or as sheer batiste for women's and children's wear.
- *Ease in Care*. Cottons are usually machine washable, colorfast when vat dyed, and

preshrunk when Sanforized. The synthetic resin finishes on cotton provide quick drip-drying features, and the fabric requires little ironing.

- *Attractiveness*. Cotton fabric for apparel and accessories, as well as for household textiles, can be styled attractively. Some textures are shiny (polished) like silk, some are napped to resemble wool, and others are bumpy and look as if they were handmade.
- *Durability*. When cotton is spun into strong yarns and woven into close, well-balanced fabrics (warp and filling counts nearly equal), it is very durable.
- *Moth Resistance*. Cotton is not subject to attack by moths.

LINEN

Until recently, linen was so widely used for face and kitchen towels and sheets that such items came to be referred to as "linens." Today, however, cotton has replaced linen as the most widely used vegetable fiber. Linen is mostly used, either alone or in mixtures, for dresses, coordinates, place mats, wall coverings and upholstery.

Linen is the product of the fibrous stalk of the flax plant. Flax grows best in temperate climates where there is ample rainfall. Belgium, Holland, France, and the U.S.S.R. are major producers of linen, with Ireland less important than formerly. Dry weather will stunt and ripen the fiber prematurely. When harvesting time arrives, the stalks are pulled up and bundled by harvesting machines. Machines also remove the seeds from the flax.

After the flax has been harvested and the seeds removed, the fibers are loosened from the stalk by a process called **retting,** which is actually a rotting process that has several variations. After the flax fiber has been loosened by retting, it is separated from the stalk by a process called **scutching.** The stalks are run through a machine that breaks them up and removes the woody portions from the usable fiber.

Figure 8-3. *Bundles of flax are loaded into netting tanks in order to loosen the fibers.*

The scutched flax goes through a number of processes to convert it into linen yarn. First, the flax is sorted and graded. Then it is subjected to hackling and later to spinning. **Hackling,** a process similar to carding and combing cotton, separates the short, tangled fibers, called **tow,** from the longer fibers. Spinning is the process of twisting the ribbons of fibers together to form yarn. Some yarns require more twist than others. Because flax fibers are much longer and stronger than cotton fibers, however, they do not need as much twist to hold them together in the yarn.

Construction of Linen Fabrics

Most linen fabrics are woven in plain weave. They are durable, can be woven at a comparatively low cost, and can be laundered satisfactorily. Some fancy linens for sportswear and beachwear are woven in a herringbone construction. The Jacquard weave is used for damasks. Linen is also used alone or mixed with cotton for knitting sweaters.

Finishing of Linen Fabrics

Bleaching and **beetling** (beating to smooth out and add gloss) are the two major finishing treatments for linen fabrics. Other finishing processes include calendering, shearing, sizing, and tentering, which are described in Chapter 7. Linens may be treated with special finishes and may be dyed or printed during finishing.

Because customers have complained that linen wrinkles, a crease-resistant treatment has been developed and linen is often combined with a manmade fiber, especially polyester, that is naturally wrinkle resistant. On the other hand, the very fact that linen wrinkles has made it a fashion item in outer clothing.

Linen fabrics may be treated for water repellency and shrinkage control. Two of the newest finishes, permanent press and soil release, are especially important for table linens. Another special finish that can be applied to linen is flameproofing. There are two kinds — one is permanent and will withstand dry cleaning; one requires flameproofing after each cleaning.

Linens may be printed by any one of several processes. Roller printing is common for less expensive fabrics; screen printing or batik work is used for better fabrics.

Identification of Linen Fabrics

Linen can best be identified by reading the label attached to the fabric. It specifies fiber content according to the TFPIA. Pure linen fabrics must contain 100 percent linen.

Linen can also be identified by its unique feel. It is cool and leathery and is stiffer than cotton. Linen cloth is more difficult to tear than cotton cloth, and linen yarns are harder to break than cotton yarns. When broken, the ends of linen yarns are long and pointed.

Table 8-2 MINOR VEGETABLE FIBERS

Fiber	Sources	Country of Origin
Hemp	Stalks of plants, coarse fiber	Italy (best grades from U.S.S.R., other European communist countries), Near East, Korea, China, Japan (U.S. a major importer)
Manila hemp	Leaves of abaca plant	Philippines
Jute	Stalks of plants	India, especially
Ramie (rhea, China grass)	Stalks of plants	Egypt and China, especially
Sisal	Leaves of sisal plant	Indonesia, Java, West Africa, Haiti
Kapok	Seed pods of a tree	Java and tropical countries
Coir	Hairy shell of the coconut	Sri Lanka (Ceylon), especially

Care of Linen Fabrics

Linen garments contain permanent labels that give instructions for their care. Linens launder easily, although not quite as easily as cottons. Most are machine washable. Bleaches containing chlorine or hypochlorites should be diluted and used in cold water. Since sun is the best and safest bleaching agent, if desired linens may be hung in the sun to dry. The rules for stain removal given for cotton apply equally to linen. Heavy linens, especially damask, should never be heavily starched because the heavy iron needed to press the linen could break the fibers.

After linens have been washed and dried, they should be sprinkled with water and ironed damp first on the outside and then on the inside. Iron the fabric crosswise from selvage to selvage to produce luster.

Selling Points of Linen Fabrics

Although linen has been in use for thousands of years, many consumers are unaware of its special virtues. A well-informed salesperson should point out the following qualities of linen.

Durability. Flax fiber is longer and stronger than cotton fiber.

Coolness. Because flax is an excellent conductor of heat, linen makes a cool apparel fabric for spring and summer wear.

Ease in Care. Most linens are machine washable. They do not soil as quickly as cotton because flax fibers are smoother, harder, and longer than cotton fibers.

Uses	Selling Points
Cordage	Withstands water and dampness; inexpensive
Manila hats, hammocks, matting, cordage	Strong; resembles flax in appearance; inexpensive
Bags, cordage, burlap, backing for carpets	Inexpensive, good under dry conditions (weakens when wet), can't be bleached
Cordage, summer rugs, dish towels	Very durable, stronger than flax, resists mildew better
Summer rugs, coarse cordage, brushes	Very strong and durable
Stuffing for pillows, mattresses, and life preservers; not for fabrics	Moisture resistant; buoyant
Mattresses, matting, rope, brushes	Strong, stiff, elastic, brittle

Moth Resistance. Like other vegetable fibers, the flax fibers in linen are resistant to attack by moths.

Water Absorbency. The coarse pores in linen make it absorbent and thus ideal for towels.

Hygiene. Flax fiber is a poor breeding ground for germs.

MINOR VEGETABLE FIBERS

In addition to the two best-known vegetable fibers, cotton and linen, there are some other lesser-known ones used in textiles. These include hemp, jute, and ramie, which, like flax, are fibers obtained from the stalks of plants. These are collectively called bast fibers. Data on the important minor vegetable fibers are in Table 8–2.

DO YOU KNOW YOUR MERCHANDISE?

1. What does a cotton gin do to the cotton bolls?
2. How is cotton fiber manufactured into yarn?
3. List three constructions of cotton fabric.
4. What are five products of nonwoven cotton fabrics?
5. What do sizing, tentering, and napping do to cotton?
6. Give washing instructions for a colorfast red blouse.
7. Describe a general procedure to follow in any type of stain removal.
8. Name three special finishes that can be applied to linen.

9. What instructions would you give a customer for laundering a plain white linen handkerchief?
10. Name five vegetable fibers other than linen and cotton and list their major uses.

cloth and is about to buy it. Then she sees the fiber content label and looks upset. She says, "I thought it was linen. I just don't know." If you are the salesperson, how would you answer her? Report your exact words.

PUTTING YOUR MERCHANDISE KNOWLEDGE TO WORK

1. Identify a cotton fabric in a piece of clothing worn by you or a member of your class. Give at least five selling points for the item that result from the cotton content.
2. A customer is looking at tablecloths in a store. She is examining an attractive cotton

PROJECT

Obtain samples of several cotton clothing fabrics and give the following information about each: name of fabric, kind of yarns, type of construction, finishes, uses, and probable durability.

9

Silk

The history of silk dates back more than 4,000 years. According to legend, the Chinese princess Se-Ling was playing in a garden near some mulberry trees and accidentally dropped a silk cocoon into a cup of boiling hot tea. Immersed in the hot liquid, the fine silk filament separated from the cocoon. Within a short time it was discovered that the filament was strong enough to be woven into garments. For nearly 2,000 years China prospered from trading its priceless silk by jealously guarding the secrets of silk production.

Today Japan, India, China, and Brazil produce silk in quantity, and many other nations produce it in smaller amounts. In the United States, small quantities of silk were produced until the first quarter of the twentieth century. It then became no longer profitable because the costs of producing silkworms are high and a great deal of labor is needed.

PRODUCTION OF SILK

The life cycle of the silkworm is about 2 months and encompasses four stages — egg, worm, chrysalis (pupa), and moth. During the worm stage, the animal secretes a fine filament (silk) and a gummy substance that combine to form a hard cocoon about its body.

Silkworms can grow wild or can be cultivated. Wild, or **tussah,** silkworms are not cared for, and feed on uncultivated leaves such as mulberry and

scrub oak. They spin a coarse, uneven filament that is generally harsher and stiffer than the cultivated type and is about three times as thick. Wild silk is commonly used in its natural colors, which range from ecru to many shades of brown. Tussah silk can be woven into different weights of fabrics: some are used for garments, others for draperies and upholstery. When the silk is obtained from double or interlocked cocoons, the rough product is called **duoppioni silk** and is used for shantung and pongee fabrics.

Unlike tussah silkworms, **cultivated silkworms** are grown under meticulously clean conditions in which temperature, moisture, noise, and smells are carefully controlled. The silk moth lays hundreds of pin-size eggs, which are placed in an incubator and hatch into worms about the thickness of a hair and 1/8 inch long. For approximately 6 weeks these worms voraciously eat mulberry leaves night and day.

Once the food is in the worm's body it is changed into the substance that is later secreted as silk filaments. When the worm has grown to 3 or 3 1/2 inches, it stops eating and is ready to spin its cocoon. It attaches a few strands to twigs (already prepared for this purpose) and begins to secrete a fluid from two glands, one on each side of its head. When these fluids reach the air, they unite to form a single strand that is composed of **fibroin** (the silk fiber itself) and **sericin** (a protective gummy coating that is about one-fourth of the total weight). After the cocoon is completed, the worm inside goes into a dormant stage and when killed by boiling shrinks into a hard, brown, nutlike chrysalis. If the worm is allowed to live, it will emerge within 8 to 15 days as a moth and mate. The female will lay about 500 eggs and then die. In modern silkworm culture the male is destroyed because it is felt that multiple mating produces inferior silk.

Only certain cocoons are selected for breeding purposes and allowed to live. All other cocoons are subject to heat thus killing the chrysalis inside. This prevents the moth from bursting out of the cocoon and breaking the long silk filament it has spun.

MANUFACTURE OF SILK YARN

There are two kinds of silk fibers — reeled and spun. Reeled silk is obtained from unbroken cocoons, and spun silk is obtained from broken cocoons. The type of silk fiber used in making the yarn affects the appearance of the finished silk fabric.

Reeled Silk

The process of unwinding the long fibers of silk from unbroken cocoons is called **reeling**. Today reeling is done by automatic reeling machines. The long silk fibers so obtained are called **reeled silk**. These fibers range in length from 1,350 to 4,000 feet. The long length and strength of these fibers produce fabrics with high durability.

Single-reeled silk yarn is made from an average of eight cocoons reeled together. This yarn can be used for dress fabric or silk gauze. For more strength it is necessary to ply single yarn two or three times. The process of twisting the silk yarn is called **throwing**. Yarns made of reeled silk may have little twist, such as that used in a satin, or may have a tight twist, such as that used in a crepe. The tighter the twist of the yarn, the duller the luster. The luster in satin, however, is caused by the long warp float not the little twist. The denier (measure of the fineness

Figure 9-1. *Silkworms growing in an incubator eat mulberry leaves, which they digest and secrete as silk filaments when they make cocoons.*

of the yarn) can be controlled by the number of cocoons reeled together; the two filaments from a single cocoon average about 3 denier (but this varies even in the single cocoon).

Spun Silk

As the breeding moths emerge, they pierce the cocoon and break the long silk filament into short fibers. These fibers are straightened, drawn out, and spun into yarn called **spun silk**. Spun silk also comes from the tangled ends of fiber that cannot be reeled and from the fibers of defective cocoons. Spun-silk yarns go into silk broadcloth, plush, and velvet dress fabrics, as well as upholstery fabrics, hosiery, underwear, sweaters, and scarves. Because spun silk is made of short fibers, it does not have the luster, strength, or elasticity of reeled silk.

During the manufacture of spun silk, a short fiber waste, called **silk noil,** or **bourette,** is produced. It is sometimes mixed with other fibers to make fancy, nub (little balls), or novelty yarns for dress or homefurnishing fabrics.

CONSTRUCTION OF SILK FABRICS

Silk may be used in any type of weave. The satin weave is more delicate than some plain weaves but if closely woven it is quite strong. The floats should be carefully examined to determine the number of yarns over which they pass. The longer the float, the higher the luster of the fabric. However, because long floats tend to snag and show wear, the longer the float, the weaker the fabric.

When the yarn is made, the silk filaments are still covered by the gummy sericin, which makes the yarn crisp, dull, and wiry. **Raw silk** still contains sericin and can be woven that way. However, the gum is commonly removed before weaving or dyeing. In order to do this, the silk fibers must be plied and placed in boiling, soapy water.

During degumming, silk may lose from 20 to 30 percent of its original weight, but poorer grades of silk may be degummed much less. Because silk absorbs moisture readily, the lost weight was formerly replaced by immersing the silk in a solution of metallic salts from minerals such as tin, iron, or lead. Too much weighting, however, injured the silk fibers and the practice of weighting has generally been discontinued.

FINISHING OF SILK FABRICS

The end use of the silk fabric and the desired hand and appearance determine the type of finish needed. The best quality silk fabrics, however, have no finish applied. Calendering produces a polished surface on silk. **Dry decating,** often used on wool, permanently sets the luster. It is done by winding the fabric on perforated rollers through which hot water or steam is circulated. Napping, usually applied to velvets,

raises the fibers of the spun-silk yarn to the surface. Silk fabrics made into upholstery or rainwear are often treated with Scotchgard or Zepel finishes to repel water and stains. If the silk is to be used for shoe linings, germ-resistant finishes should be applied. Silk fabrics for draperies hung in public buildings are sometimes treated with a fire-retardant to comply with the Flammable Fabrics Act even though silk does not sustain flame.

IDENTIFICATION OF SILK FABRICS

A label provides the best identification of silk fabrics because by law the label must specify fiber content. A common test for silk is to apply a flame to a piece of fabric. Silk will scorch and leave a bead ash but the flame will not spread. If pure silk is burned it will leave a characteristic animal odor.

The best way to distinguish between reeled and spun silk is to unravel a yarn. If the yarn consists of long fibers that lie parallel to each other, the fabric is made of reeled silk. If the fibers are short, uneven in length, and tightly spun, the fabric is made of spun silk.

Pure silk is an all-silk fabric that contains no weighting, loading, or foreign materials except the dyes and finishes necessary to produce the desired color or finish.

According to the trade practice rules of the Federal Trade Commission (FTC), it is an unfair trade practice to use the terms "pure silk," "all silk," or "pure-dye silk" to describe silk that contains any metallic weighting.

CARE OF SILK FABRICS

All silk fabrics are classified as *fine* because they need special care for proper cleaning. However, with proper care they will wear longer than some fabrics that may seem more durable.

Silk should be cleaned as soon as it becomes soiled. Generally, it is best to dry-clean silk unless the label specifically states that it may be washed. If the label does advise laundering, silks are usually best washed by hand. Wash the item in lukewarm water with neutral soap flakes that contain no alkali (do not use detergent soap), gently squeezing the suds through the fabric. Then rinse in lukewarm water, squeezing, not wringing, the water from the fabric several times. The main problem in washing silk clothing occurs when the fabric is not all of one color. Silk dyes are sometimes not permanent and one color may blend into another. After washing, roll the silk article in a towel to absorb moisture. Iron it while it is still damp. If the silk has dried completely, cover it with a damp pressing cloth before ironing. Dry heat weakens the fibers in a silk fabric so do not hang it near a radiator or put it in a hot dryer. Ironing with a damp pressing cloth may help to remove wrinkles. Always iron silk on the back side.

Stains should be removed from silk as soon as possible. Table 8–1 gives instructions for removing various kinds of stains.

SELLING POINTS OF SILK FABRICS

Although prized for its luxuriousness, silk has many other features that make it desirable. A salesperson should point out the following features to a customer.

- *Colorfulness*. Silk dyes easily and beautifully, taking a deep, rich color.
- *Versatility*. Silk can be woven and knit into a variety of fabrics from sheer chiffons and organzas to heavier brocades and velvets.
- *Drapability*. Silk has good elasticity and will fall into graceful folds.
- *Durability*. In terms of diameter, silk is the strongest natural fiber in commercial use.
- *Warmth*. Silk is a poor conductor of both heat and electricity and is therefore comfortable to wear. It is warm in winter and cool in summer.
- *Lightweight*. Silk has a lower density (diameter of the fibers) than wool, cotton, linen, or rayon and so is lightweight and sheer.
- *Luster*. When processed, silk's smooth, translucent filaments produce a lustrous, shiny fabric.

Figure 9-2. *This Persian silk fragment, in excellent condition, dates back to the sixteenth century.*

- *Resilience.* If tightly compressed, silk will quickly spring back to its former state when released, giving it excellent wrinkle recovery.
- *Moth resistance.* Silk is not subject to attack by moths.

DO YOU KNOW YOUR MERCHANDISE?

1. Compare wild and cultivated silk.
2. Describe how the silkworm produces silk.
3. What are the characteristics of reeled silk?
4. What is spun silk? Explain three ways in which it differs from reeled silk.
5. What is silk noil? How is it used?
6. Why is silk degummed?
7. What are two ways to identify silk?
8. Describe the care of silk fabrics.
9. List three stains and describe how to remove each one from silk fabrics.
10. What are four selling points of silk?

PUTTING YOUR MERCHANDISE KNOWLEDGE TO WORK

List all the silk clothing and articles you have in your home. State their approximate age and condition.

PROJECT

Visit a home-sewing department in a store and compare the prices of silk fabrics with similar fabrics of manmade fibers.

10

Wool

Whereas for many centuries silk, discussed in Chapter 9, has been the recognized *luxury* fiber, wool, for perhaps an even longer period, has been the fiber associated with *warmth*. It still retains that reputation in spite of the newer man-made fibers that have attempted to emulate that quality.

Wool as grown serves as a protective covering for sheep. It is light cream to brown and sometimes black in color. Hair fibers are also discussed in this chapter because, like wool, they serve as the protective covering for various animals.

PRODUCTION OF WOOL

Wool quality varies considerably. It is measured by the length and diameter of the fibers, the degree of softness, the color, and the luster. The quality of wood depends on a number of factors. Some breeds of sheep product a better quality of wool than others. Merino sheep, for example, produce one of the finest highest-quality wools in the world. The part of the sheep's body from which the wool is taken affects its quality. Wool from the head, belly, and buttocks is of lower quality than wool from the shoulders and sides. If the wool is grown in cold climates and is unattended, it is heavy and coarse. If the sheep is grown primarily for meat, its wool is not as fine.

Geographic and climatic conditions also have a marked effect on wool quality. Because of Aus-

tralia's favorable climatic conditions, as well as the excellent care given its sheep, it produces wool with the finest fiber. Australia, England, New Zealand, Scotland, South Africa, the United States, and Uruguay produce good wool for clothing. Coarse wools used in carpets come from Argentina, China, U.S.S.R., New Zealand, and Turkey. The United States produces no carpet wool. The three largest wool producers in order are Australia, the U.S.S.R., and New Zealand.

Sheep are usually clipped once or twice a year. Although **fleece wool,** the best-grade wool, is shorn from living sheep, wool can also be removed from dead sheep that have been slaughtered or that have died of disease. This is called **pulled wool** because the wool fibers are pulled from the skin after it has been treated with lime paste and sweated to loosen the fibers. Pulled wool is often used in felts, flannels, blankets, and stuffing.

Sorting and Grading

One **fleece,** representing wool from one animal, contains different qualities and lengths of fibers. A **sorter** (a person who is proficient in judging the fineness and length of wool fibers) grades the fibers. The sorter spreads a fleece out, pulls it apart, and sorts the wool into about six or eight piles, according to fiber quality and length.

Scouring

The cleaning of the wool — the removal of fatty matter, dirt, and perspiration with warm water and soap — is called **scouring.** An acid solution is used to remove vegetable matter by a process called **carbonizing.** After the wool is dried, it is ready to be processed into yarn and fabric.

MANUFACTURE OF WOOL AND WORSTED YARNS

Wool is spun into two types of yarn — woolen and worsted. **Woolen yarns,** which are thick and full, are made into fabrics such as tweeds, flannels, Shetlands, and broadcloths. **Worsted yarns** are finer, smoother, and firmer and go into gabardines, sharkskins, and tropical worsteds.

In wool yarn production wool fibers are put through a process called carding, which partially straightens the fibers and lays them out in one direction. In the carding of wool, which is similar to the carding of cotton, the fibers are left fuzzy enough so that in later processing a nap (a soft, downy surface) can be raised.

In worsted yarn production the wool fibers are **combed** after carding. The carded fibers are **raked** by a machine, which removes short fibers and foreign matter and lays the fibers parallel to one another. This parallel alignment of wool fibers is a characteristic feature of worsted-wool manufacture.

Woolen yarns and fabrics are warmer than worsteds. Because of their varied fiber lengths in a nonparallel arrangement, they hold in more air preventing heat from escaping from the body. Woolens also lend themselves to napping, which increases the number of air pockets.

A salesperson can determine whether a fabric is made from woolen or worsted yarns by unraveling a yarn from the fabric. If the fibers in the yarn are of unequal length and branch out, the yarn is woolen. If the fibers are parallel and of nearly equal length, the yarn is worsted.

CONSTRUCTIONS OF WOOLEN AND WORSTED FABRICS

Wool yarns may be constructed in the various weaves and knits discussed in Chapter 6. Whenever softness and porosity are desired in a fabric, the plain weave is suitable. The men's and women's woolen suitings plain weaves include hopsacking, tropical-worsted, wool-crepe, and poplin fabrics.

The twill weave is a more durable construction than the plain weave and is frequently used for men's suits and coats in variations such as tweed, flannel, Shetland, serge, and cheviot. Lighter-weight fabrics go into women's wear.

The most common construction for wool carpets and rugs consists of pile yarns that are either woven into a backing or tufted to it. Although manmade fibers are generally used today, fine rugs often have a wool pile. Both woolen and worsted yarns may be used, but worsted yarn is preferable because it is stronger. Velvet, velour, and plush upholstery fabrics are also made in a pile weave.

Familiar knitted constructions of wool fabrics include jersey dresses, polo shirts, T-shirts, boucle dresses, socks, and sweaters.

Before finishes are applied, both woolens and worsteds are inspected for imperfections in the weave and defects in the yarn, including bumpy or knotted yarns and broken or loose threads. The fabric is thrown over a horizontal bar, and an inspector carefully examines it, marking each defect. The fabric then goes to the mender, who repairs the flaws.

Figure 10-1. *Woolen yarns (top) are thick and full, while worsted yarns (bottom) are fine, smooth, and firm.*

FINISHING OF WOOLEN AND WORSTED FABRICS

Most finishing processes for woolen and worsted fabrics differ considerably. Wool yarn is often bleached before being woven. Woolens are said to be **face finished,** which means that finishes applied to the fabric produce an attractive, soft, cushionlike surface.

Worsteds are said to be **made on the loom,** which means that the weaving process itself provides much of the final appearance — a hard and smooth surface. The beauty of worsteds lies in the weave, which is clearly visible. This is called **clear finishing.**

Sometimes customers prefer a cloth that combines the durability of a worsted with the fuzzy nap of a woolen. In order to raise a nap, the worsted is brushed. Napped worsteds are called **unfinished worsteds.**

Dyeing

Woolen and worsted fabrics absorb dye well. They may be stock dyed, yarn dyed, or piece dyed. Stock dyeing is used to produce mixtures, heathers, and fancy fabrics. Yarn dyeing is used to produce woven checks and stripes, as well as plaids. Piece dyeing, the most economical process, is used to produce solid colors. Wool fabrics are also sometimes printed, such as wool challis or printed flannel.

Fulling

Fulling, which is also known as **felting** or **milling,** is a process that compresses the fabric into a compact, thicker fabric, obscuring its weave. During fulling the fabric is pounded and twisted for 2 to 18 hours in warm, soapy water. This can shrink the fabric 10 to 25 percent, depending on the amount desired by the finisher. Fulling is used more extensively in finishing woolens than worsteds. It may be used sparingly on worsteds to soften the fabric.

Preshrinking

Both woolen and worsted fabrics must be steamed and shrunk so that there will be little further shrinkage (provided that the customer has the merchandise cleaned properly). The percentage of shrinkage to be expected after laundering should appear on the label along with the name of any patented shrinkage-control process used on the fabric.

Flocking

The process by which additional wool fibers are steamed and forced into the back of a fabric making it firmer and more compact and thus adding warmth is called **flocking.** The fibers used in flocking are obtained either by shearing a woolen fabric or from reused wool (see below). To detect flocking, brush the back of the fabric briskly with a stiff wire brush. If short fibers fall out, there has probably been some flocking. Flocking is not objectionable if good-grade fibers are used.

Napping

The process of raising fuzz on the surface of the fabric is called napping. It is used more on woolens than on worsteds. Before being napped, woolens must be fulled, washed, dried, and tentered. The fabric is passed over rapidly revolving cylinders covered with teasels or wire bristles. These pull the short fibers to the surface, forming the nap. The nap is then sheared to the desired length. Napping is used only sparingly on worsteds because the nap may wear off leaving the fabric shiny.

Other Finishes

The final finishing processes for woolens usually include steaming, tentering (framing for width adjustment), sponging, and pressing. For worsteds, tentering, brushing, sponging, and pressing are common finishes.

with certain of the features of wool and at a much lower price has attracted the mass market. Even though all-wool sweaters, scarves, and suits are much in vogue, blends of wool and manmade fibers, such as polyester, nylon, and acrylic, are enjoying a ready market.

HAIR-FIBER FABRICS

Under the Wool Products Labeling Act hair fibers are classified as **specialty fibers.** Hair fibers range from 4 to 12 inches (wool fibers, from 1 to 8 inches). Hair fibers also vary in color, fineness, and luster. They can be blended with wool in unlimited combinations, depending on the type of fabric desired.

Mohair is obtained from the hair of the Angora goat. Originating in Turkey, it is now also produced in South Africa and the United States. The fiber is long, slippery, and wiry and has no natural crimp or felting quality. It is used for coat linings and dress goods.

Cashmere, obtained from the Cashmere goat and originating in Kashmir, Asia, is also produced in China, Northern India, Iraq, Mongolia, and Tibet. It is a soft, fine, and downy fiber and is used for coats, sweaters, and blankets.

The **alpaca, llama,** and **vicuña** are all found in South America. The fibers from these animals are soft and attractive, however, the supply is scarce because these animals have not been domesticated and are rare. The vicuña provides the finest of all animal fibers. It is prized for overcoats, knitwear, scarfs, and blankets.

Camel's hair is obtained from Africa, Asia, and the U.S.S.R. It is soft and has great resistance to both heat and cold. It is used for overcoats, sweaters, blankets, and some rugs. **Horsehair** now comes primarily from South America.

DO YOU KNOW YOUR MERCHANDISE?

1. What determines the quality of wool?
2. Define fleece wool and pulled wool.
3. Explain the difference between woolen and worsted fabrics.
4. Explain why woolens are warmer than worsteds.
5. What is meant by the term "preshrunk"? Why is preshrinking important for woolen fabrics?
6. Briefly describe four regular and two special finishes for either woolens or worsteds.
7. Explain the difference between reused wool and reprocessed wool.
8. What instructions would you give a customer for laundering a wool sweater?
9. Give the selling points of a pair of woolen slacks.
10. In what ways are wool fiber similar to and different from hair fiber? How are goat, alpaca, llama, and vicuña fibers classified under the Wool Products Labeling Act?

PUTTING YOUR MERCHANDISE KNOWLEDGE TO WORK

Trace a map of the world and indicate on it the countries where wool is obtained. Also indicate the countries that produce hair fibers and give the name and the type of hair fiber produced.

PROJECT

Analyze several newspaper advertisements for woolen clothing and homefurnishings. List any terms you have learned in this chapter. Also give the selling points of the articles described in the ads.

a. Which ads did an excellent job in emphasizing the major selling points associated with wool?
b. Which did a poor job and why? Rewrite the copy for one of the ads that you feel to be unsatisfactory.

As a result of watching the silkworm spin its cocoon, an English physicist, over 300 years ago, got the idea that it might be possible to create fibers chemically. The silkworm extrudes through its glands a liquid substance that becomes a solid filament or fiber when it comes in contact with cool air. The scientist reasoned that a chemical liquid could be forced through fine holes and then hardened into fiber.

DEVELOPMENT OF RAYON

It was not until the latter half of the nineteenth century that fibers were created chemically. A French count, Hilaire de Chardonnet, learned how to do it by combining cellulose, the chief part of the cell walls of plants, with nitric acid to form a gummy substance that was pumped through tiny holes and hardened. But this nitrocellulose process proved too expensive and even dangerous. It thus gave way to the cupramonium process. Although this process is still in use today, it was soon widely replaced by the use of caustic soda to form a viscous substance that was to be forced through the tiny holes of a spineret to form filaments. This product ultimately came to be named viscose rayon. The first commercial production of viscose rayon in the United States took place in 1910. It ushered in a new era for the textile industry. Up to this time the only fibers of any commercial significance anywhere

in the world were the natural ones, primarily cotton, linen, silk, and wool.

Industry leaders agreed that the new product had its own special properties, that it must not be confused with silk, and that it must be given a generic name that all would recognize. The name "rayon" was suggested as the word that would shed a "ray of light" on the problem. This was promptly accepted as the name and was soon recognized as the generic name for the first manmade fiber. **Viscose rayon** was recognized as an outstanding variety of rayon based on the chemicals used in making the solution to be spun into filaments.

All rayons are called cellulosic because they consist of cellulose from plant life, today largely pine, hemlock, and spruce trees. The solid cellulose is converted by caustic soda into a solution that is turned back to a solid filament.

Modified rayons, or second-generation rayons, are fibers that have been altered to improve their strength, appearance, or performance. One chemical treatment used to produce high-strength rayon for automobile tires is **cross linking** in which the atoms of the fibers' molecules are specially arranged to give strength to the material.

Other rayons are made with a structure similar to the natural cellulosic fibers, cotton and linen, that have increased strength when wet. Rayon thus modified to improve its tensile strength is

Figure 11-1. *A chemical liquid is extruded through a spinneret to form filaments of manmade fiber.*

called high-wet-modulus, or high-performance, rayon. It is commonly blended with polyester to create permanent-press clothing.

More recently a third generation of rayon fibers has been created. Prima is the brand name for a high-wet-modulus rayon staple fiber with a permanent chemical crimp that was put on the market in 1977. Avril III looks and feels very much like cotton and is very durable even after repeated laundering. Fibers such as these take dye brilliantly, are very absorbent, have a nice hand, hold their shape well (called **dimensional stability**), and are readily blended with other fibers.

With these newer improvements, the rayon industry is now competing vigorously with the huge, long-established cotton industry. It was argued that rayon, based on cellulose, has the advantages of cotton plus the others mentioned above. Rayon may also be more economical to produce since it provides a more uniform fiber that needs no combing, little carding, and less

twisting. Its source, trees grown in the forests, is more reliable than the cotton boll, which is subject to the weather and disease.

ACETATE

Acetate is the generic name of a fiber derived from cellulose combined with acetate from acetic acid and acetic anhydride. The final acetate fiber has both a vegetable and chemical base and thus has some properties of cotton as well as acetate plastic.

Acetate comes in filament, tow, and staple forms, as explained below, and is used in dresses, blouses, pantsuits, sportswear, lingerie, and sleepwear and for luxury fabric such as suede and crushed velvet. It is also used for draperies and upholstery. Acetate fibers can also be modified. By being fused with heat, the fibers can be permanently crimped. Crimped acetates blend well with wool for dresses, skirts, and slacks. Acetate fibers can also be modified to produce triacetate.

TRIACETATE

Triacetate fibers contain a higher ratio of acetate to cellulose than do the acetate fibers. Triacetate fabrics come with minimum-care and wash-and-wear properties, making them ideal for traveling. Because triacetate is heat treated, it can be pressed at a much higher temperature than regular acetate. Triacetate also holds pleats well and washes well. Its abrasion resistance and tensile strength have been relatively limited but are being overcome.

PRODUCTION OF CELLULOSIC FIBERS AND YARNS

Production of cellulostic fibers and yarns starts with growing trees in the forest. About 28 years after planting, the logs are moved to a mill where a chopper reduces the logs to chips. Under pressure they are converted into pulp that is cleaned and whitened. The pulp is then pressed into sheets that look like blotting paper. After being of continuous monofilaments as-

...ngths of fibers that have been
... lengths from tow and are
...otton or wool.

Monofilament: a single filament of continuous length.

Filament Yarn: two or more continuous monofilaments assembled or held together by twist or other means.

...n

...s filament yarns are in yarn form as ...merge from the spinneret and do not have ...be spun. They are cleaned, washed, and reeled onto cones and beams ready to feed the looms and knitting machines in the fabric manufacturer's plant. They are often used in lingerie tricot, active sportswear, and industrial applications. Filament yarns are available as textured yarns and abraded yarns.

Spun Yarn

The short fibers (staple) may be twisted or spun in the same way that short lengths of natural fibers are spun for cottons, woolens, or worsteds. The texture and end product determine which method is used.

Yarns spun from staple are more irregular than filament yarns. The short ends of fibers projecting from the yarn surface produce a fuzzy or fluffy effect. Spun yarns are more bulky than filament yarns of the same weight. They are therefore more often used for porous, warm fabrics and for fabrics with rough surfaces.

Once a yarn is spun, it may be plied with another type of single yarn to make what is called **combination yarn.**

Sometimes filaments are cut into short lengths for spinning into yarn called **staple rayon.** They are carried to a cutter that chops them up into very short lengths, often a fraction of an inch. After these are washed, bleached, and baled they are ready for the yarn maufacturer to spin.

CONSTRUCTION OF CELLULOSIC FIBER YARNS INTO FABRIC

Cellulosic fiber yarns, either alone or in blends, can be used in almost any weave. The plain

Figure 11-2. Acetate fibers are tested for durability and heat resistance.

weave is found in voiles, ninons, crepes, taffetas, and challis; the rib weave in corded fabrics; the twill weave in fabrics that resemble wool. Many satin weaves are made with rayon and acetate. Yarns in Jacquard and dobby weaves produce patterned fabrics for apparel and homefurnishings.

Cellulosic fibers and yarns are also widely used in knits. The largest percentage of acetate goes into women's underwear, blouses, and dresses. Acetate tricot is commonly used as a backing in bonded fabrics.

Both rayon and acetate are used for disposable goods, including clothing, because of their absorbency and strength. Nonwoven rayon is also an important element in fabric softeners in the form of impregnated sheets, which are used in clothes dryers.

FINISHING OF THE CELLULOSIC FIBER FABRICS

Before a cloth can be dyed, printed, or treated with special finishes, it must go through a series of preliminary treatments, including removing impurities, bleaching, and tentering. Cellulosics are also singed, scoured, and sometimes embossed for textured effects. Rayon is usually preshrunk. If it is from spun yarn, it is sometimes napped to change its texture.

There is also a wide variety of functional or special finishes to give the fabrics properties they do not ordinarily have. These include permanent-press, antibacterial, flame-resistant, soil-release, and durable-press finishes.

During the past several years, the demand for acetate and triacetate filament yarns has been stimulated by the development of a variety of knitted surface finishes. By sanding, sueding, brushing and napping, knitters have introduced velours, fleeces, chenilles, and terry cloth for loungewear, sports jackets, shirts, and jump suits.

CARE OF CELLULOSIC FIBER FABRICS

As mentioned in earlier chapters, each garment made today must carry a permanent label giving

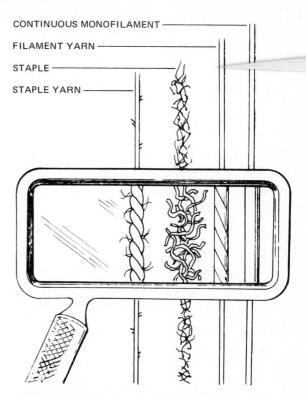

CONTINUOUS MONOFILAMENT

FILAMENT YARN

STAPLE

STAPLE YARN

Figure 11-3. *Yarns range from simple monofilament to filament yarn, made from two or more strands of continuous monofilament fibers, to staple yarn, spun from discontinuous lengths of staple fibers.*

care instructions. There are, however, certain general rules to follow in caring for fabrics made of manmade fibers.

Rayons

Most rayon fabrics wash well but fabrics of some constructions should be dry-cleaned. Washable rayons should be washed gently because they have less strength when wet than when dry. Here are a few general rules to keep in mind.

1. Mend all holes and tears before laundering.

2. Pay extra attention to soiled spots to make sure they come out.

3. Do not soak colored fabrics.

4. Use a light-duty detergent and lukewarm water. Gently squeeze suds through the fabric and rinse it in lukewarm water. Do not wring or twist the garment. If washed by machine, use the delicate setting.

5. Use bleach if necessary, but be careful because some finishes are sensitive to chlorine bleach. Starch may be added for desirable crispness.

6. Smooth or shake out garment and place it on nonrust hangers to dry. Some rayons may be machine dried at low heat.

7. Press garments while damp on the backside with the iron at a moderate setting. If front side needs ironing, use a press cloth.

Acetates

Acetate fabrics should generally be dry-cleaned. If washing is indicated, follow the same instructions given for rayons. For the sturdy, well-constructed acetate garments that can be machine washed, make sure the wash load is light and the washing time is short. Usually machine drying is not recommended.

prepared in for weaving and spinning into cloth?

5. What is rayon? How does rayon differ from acetate?

6. Describe the difference between a man-made-fiber fabric of spun yarn and one of filament yarn.

7. In what respects does triacetate differ from acetate?

8. With what natural fiber does rayon actively compete for patronage?

9. What are some general rules for washing rayon fabrics?

10. What are the chief selling points of the newer rayons? Of the acetate?

PUTTING YOUR MERCHANDISE KNOWLEDGE TO WORK

Choose two articles of clothing (one of rayon) worn by you or your classmates and outline their selling points.

DO YOU KNOW YOUR MERCHANDISE?

1. What is meant by a cellulosic fiber?
2. Write an outline of the beginnings of the rayon industry.
3. What is the basic method for making all cellulosic fibers?
4. What are the four different forms that man-made fibers extruded from the spinneret are

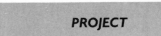

PROJECT

Ask a knowledgeable salesperson or supervisor in a yard goods department of a department or fabric store how the sales of rayon and acetate fabrics compare with those of cotton and wool and other manmade-fiber fabrics. Are the cellulose-based manmade fabrics increasing or decreasing in popularity? Why?

12

Manmade Fibers:
The Petrochemical and Natural Sources

Although rayon was first introduced in the United States in 1911 and acetate in the 1920s, it was not until 1938 that **nylon,** the first fiber synthesized purely from chemicals, appeared. Today, all manmade fibers except rayon, acetate, and triacetate are noncellulosic. These fibers account for nearly 75 percent of the fabrics manufactured in the United States and consume about 1 percent of U.S. petroleum, but the ratio may change.

THE BEGINNING OF NONCELLULOSIC FIBERS

Nylon was discovered by research chemists at E.I. du Pont de Nemours & Company. Although the public knew about its discovery on October 30, 1938, it was not until a year later that retailers in Wilmington, Delaware, had a limited supply of nylon hosiery for sale. From its successful beginning in the hosiery field, nylon's use has spread to nearly every article of wearing apparel and homefurnishings. Because of its great strength, it also has many industrial uses.

Today there are two general types of nylon that dominate world production — nylon 6.6 and nylon 6. They are used almost interchangeably. Within these two groups are hundreds of types of nylons that have different cross sections, lusters, and dyeing capabilities. Nylon is available in filament and staple forms.

GENERIC NAMES

The success of nylon led to the discovery and commercial production of some other ways of synthesizing fibers from chemicals derived largely from petroleum, natural gas, and coal. In order to avoid confusion, the Federal Trade Commission (FTC) assigns a generic name to each new fiber that differs chemically and that has significantly different properties from all other fibers on the market. As already indicated, finished goods manufactured from these fibers must be labeled with the generic name or process involved.

Nylon began as a brand name owned by du Pont, but at the expiration of the registration period it became a generic name. It may now be applied to any fiber that has the chemical composition of the original product but that may have different properties important to the consumer.

OTHER NONCELLULOSIC FIBERS DERIVED FROM PETROCHEMICALS

Experimentation has led to many manmade fibers that have chemical compositions, sources of raw materials, and properties differing from one another. Each of these has been assigned a generic name approved by the FTC and is briefly explained below.

Du Pont Announces
for the World of Tomorrow...

a new word and a new material

BETTER THINGS FOR BETTER LIVING...THROUGH CHEMISTRY

Figure 12-1. *Nylon, discovered by research chemists at E.I. du Pont de Nemours & Co., was introduced as nylon hosiery at the New York World's Fair in 1939.*

Polyester. Polyester is the generic name of fibers made from certain basic chemicals derived largely from petroleum. Like nylon, it is formed by a chemical reaction, **polymerization,** that forms the molecules into chains. Polyester is noted for its ability to impart resilience, durability, and dimensional stability to fabrics and garments. (Dimensional stability is a fabric's ability to keep its original size and shape in its intended use). Polyester fabrics are wrinkle resistant and suited for permanent-press garments. During the 1960s the use of polyester grew faster than any other fiber in the United States and it is now the leading fiber. It is often blended with cotton and rayon. Polyester comes in filament, staple, and tow forms. In filament form it has been used extensively in texturized polyester double knits.

Acrylic. Acrylic is the generic name for fibers made from a compound called acrylonitrile, which is derived from coal, air, water, petroleum, natural gas, and limestone. Acrylic fibers are noted for their soft, light, bulky, and woollike properties. They are not as strong as nylon. Acrylic fibers are used in a wide variety of products, including apparel, blankets, carpets, draperies, and hand-knitting yarns. In the United States acrylic is available in staple and tow forms only.

Modacrylic. Modacrylic, shortened form of the term "modified acrylic," is the generic name for fibers made from combinations of acrylonitrile and other materials. The chief difference between modacrylics and acrylics is that modacrylics are fire resistant. For this reason they are often used in children's sleepwear and fire-resistant curtains and draperies. They are available in staple and tow forms.

Olefin. Olefin is the generic name for fibers derived from certain petroleum products. There are two types: those produced from propylene gas, known as **polypropylene fibers,** and those produced from ethylene gas, known as **polyethylene fibers.**

Of the two, polyproplyene fiber has the more popular textile applications. It is light and strong and has a toughness and abrasion resistance exceeded only by nylon. It is not injured by rain and dampness. Its biggest market penetration so far has been indoor-outdoor carpeting, upholstery, and some industrial uses such as filter cloths, ropes, and cordage. Because it has a low melting point, polyethylene fabric has had little use in apparel. Polypropylene comes in filament, staple, and tow forms.

Spandex. Spandex is a generic term for a family of rubberlike manmade fibers that are made of a polymeric substance called **polyurethane.** Spandex has elastic properties that enable the fiber to stretch and snap back into shape like

Figure 12-2. Aramid fibers, with their high strength, toughness, and stiffness, are used in protective clothing for fire fighters, race drivers, industrial workers, and others who may be exposed to flames.

natural rubber, even though spandex fibers do not contain any rubber. Its principal uses are in foundation garments, sock tops, support hose, ski pants, and other sports apparel in which light weight and freedom of movement are essential.

Aramid. Aramid is the generic name for highly aromatic polyamide fibers with similarities to nylon. These fibers combine qualities of high strength, toughness, and stiffness never before attained in nature or by industry. The fibers retain these properties at temperatures well above 300°F. Aramid fibers are used in protective

Table 12-1 SELLING POINTS AND TRADE NAMES OF COMMON NONCELLULOSIC FIBERS

Generic Name	Selling Points	Trade Names
Nylon	Exceptionally strong Resistant to mildew, moths, tearing, and abrasion Quick drying Shape retentive; elastic and resilient Nonabsorbent, smooth, dirt does not cling, easy to wash	Actionwear Anso Antron Blue "C" Cadon Cantrece Caprolan Captiva Celanese Crepeset Cumuloft Enkaloft Enkalure Qiana Rovana Stryton Vivana Zeflon
Polyester	Resistant to shrinking, stretching, wrinkling, sunlight, abrasion, and moths Smooth, crisp looking Easy to care for; requires little or no ironing Nonallergenic; suitable for pillow stuffing Durable, light weight, strong Retains heat-set pleats and creases	Avlin Dacron Encron Fortrel Kodel Spectran Strialine Trevira
Acrylic	Comfortable; warm and lightweight, especially high-bulk yarns containing many soft air pockets Quick drying Shape retentive, resilient Resistant to sunlight, soot, smoke, and fumes; well-adapted to use in curtains, carpets, and sportswear	Acrilan Creslan Orlon Zefran

clothing for fire fighters, industrial workers, race car drivers, and military pilots; in tires; and as a reinforcing material for plastic composites.

Novoloid. Novoloid is a generic name for a fiber derived from a chemical compound called phenol, which is derived from coal. Novoloid is highly flame-resistant, lightweight, and resilient. It is also substantialy unaffected by many acids and is insoluble in organic solvents. It is being used in flame-resistant clothing linings.

Vinyon. Vinyon is the generic name for fibers composed largely of vinyl chloride. Noted for its low melting point and high resistance to chemicals, vinyon is used in industrial applications as a bonding agent for nonwoven fabrics and tea bags. Recently, a blend of 85 percent vinyon and 15 percent acrylic has been developed in England for a fiber called Thermolactyl that is used for knitted winter underwear. It is marketed in the United States by Damart of Portsmouth, New Hampshire. Laboratory tests report that it retains more body warmth per ounce of weight than any other yarn, including wool.

Generic Name	Selling Points	Trade Names
Modacrylic	Comfortable; warm, soft Nonallergenic; excellent for stuffing pillows and comforters Resilient Nonabsorbent; when used in pile fabric, pile does not weaken or flatten Resistant to ultraviolet light, fire, bacteria, and abrasion	SEF Verel Zefran
Olefin	Very light weight Resistant to abrasion, stains, and prolonged wetness Quick drying	Fibralon Herculon Marvess Vectra
Spandex	Light weight, supple Resilient, elastic Strong, durable Resistant to abrasion	Clearspan Glaspan Lycra
Saran	Sheds water Strong Easy to clean Fire-resistant	Velon
Aramid	High tensile strength (stronger than steel) Fire resistant	Kelvar Nomex
Glass	Fireproof Quick drying Strong, but has limited stretch Resistant to microorganisms, insects, and sunlight	Chemglas Fiberglas Trianti
Metallic	Luxurious looking Resistant to sunlight, abrasion, and chemicals insofar as the plastic components are resistant Durable	Chromeflex Feltmetal Lurex

Saran. Saran is a generic name for fibers produced from vinylidene chloride, which is the same compound from which Saran Wrap is made. It is a stiff, slippery plastic-type fiber used in monofilament form. It is very resistant to hard wear and sheds water. It is well suited for upholstery in automobiles and trains, garden furniture, and awnings. Although saran fibers are fire retardant, they are too heavy for wide usage as a textile material.

Anidex. Anidex is the generic name for an elastomeric acrylate fiber. It is characterized by its elasticity and may eventually be used in apparel and homefurnishings.

Vinal. Vinal is the generic name for polyvinyl alcohol fibers. Vinal fibers soften at low temperatures but have high resistance to chemicals. Their inferior ability to resist wrinkles makes them poor fibers for apparel use. Vinal is not produced in the United States.

Nytril. Nytril is the generic name for fibers composed of vinylidene dinitril from ammonia and natural gas. Nytril fibers are resilient and soft and may be in articles that do not require pressing. They are not produced in the United States.

Lastrile.   Lastrile is the generic name for a type of synthetic rubber with stretch properties. It is of minor importance and is not produced in the United States.

NONCELLULOSIC FIBERS DERIVED FROM NATURAL SOURCES

There are four kinds of noncellulosic manmade fibers that are manufactured from nonfibrous natural substances such as protein, glass, and rubber rather than from synthetic chemicals. They are glass, rubber, metallic, and azlon fibers. In general, these fibers have more specialized uses than other fibers.

Glass.   Glass is the generic name for a manufactured fiber in which the fiber-forming substance is glass. Glass fibers do not burn and have high tensile strength and density, dimensional stability, and excellent resistance to chemicals, mildew, heat, moisture, and sunlight. Although most glass is brittle, individual glass fibers are extremely fine and thus are pliable and can be woven or knitted. Glass fabrics are used in curtains and draperies, fireproof clothing, insulation, filters, and tires. They have also replaced copper wire in carrying messages with lightning speed.

Rubber.   Rubber is the generic name for a manufactured fiber in which the fiber-forming substance is composed of rubber. Rubber fibers are usually used as **core yarns** around which yarns of other fibers are wrapped or wound to protect the core from abrasion. Rubber core yarns are used where stretch and elasticity are required such as in foundation garments, surgical supports, and elastic webbing.

Metallic.   Metallic fiber is a generic name for a manufactured fiber composed of metal such as aluminum and steel (for tires). It is used in apparel for decorative purposes, and in products

such as carpets in which ability to prevent or dissipate static charges is of major importance.

Azlon.   Azlon is the generic name for manmade fibers that are produced from proteins found in nature, for example, as casein, peanuts, and corn. Azlon fibers are extremely soft and somewhat weak, especially when wet. These fibers are not produced in the United States.

MANMADE NONCELLULOSIC FIBERS WITHIN GENERIC CLASSES

Each of the generic fibers is made from materials that produce chemical reactions that conform to the standardized formula for its generic class. Many, however, are produced in a variety of types for specific end uses. This is especially true for nylon, polyester, acrylic, olefin, spandex, and aramid. The different types vary in qualities such as luster, breaking strength, stretch, and affinity for certain dye stuffs. Some are in continuous filament form and others in tow and/or staple form and are cut into various lengths.

Bicomponent Fibers.   Some fibers consist of two types from the same generic class. The chemical solutions for the two fibers are fed into the spinneret side by side, or one around the other. The process may yield a fiber that has stretch properties that provide crimping in the finished product.

Biconstituent Fibers.   The chemical solutions of two different generic manmade fibers may be fed through the spinneret to provide a fiber that has the properties of both. For example, the Monsanto Company produces Monvelle, a nylon/spandex fiber that adds stretch to the properties of nylon alone.

NEW INDUSTRIAL AND SPECIALTY FIBERS

There are some new fibers that have not yet been assigned generic names by the FTC. These include fluorcarbon, Alginate, and ceramic fibers.

Figure 12-3. *Textile yarns, made of fiberglass, being wound onto a large spool. When filled, the spool holds millions of yards of yarn.*

Fluorocarbon Fiber. E.I. du Pont originally produced fluorocarbon plastic coating named Teflon for nonstick cooking utensils. It is now produced and marketed in fiber form as filament, staple, and tow. Yarns and fabrics made of Teflon absorb *no* moisture, resist chemicals and extremely high heat, withstand friction, and remain flexible at very low temperatures. Industrially, they are used for pump packings, bearings, and filtration equipment. They are now also being used for clothing and space exploration.

Alginate Fiber. The raw material from which alginate fibers are made is algae or sea-

weed. The fibers and yarns are nonflammable but have a very low strength when wet and are thus not suited for clothing. However, wool may be blended with alginate fiber and made into cloth. The alginate is then washed out, leaving an extremely sheer woolen cloth. In addition, embroidery may be worked on a base cloth of alginate and the base then dissolved, leaving an embroidery that looks like lace.

Ceramic Fiber. Ceramic fiber has recently been developed from a base of clay. It has high resistance to heat and may become important industrially.

MANUFACTURE OF MANMADE NONCELLULOSIC YARNS AND FABRICS

The noncellulosic filaments extruded by the spinneret are made into filament and staple (including tow) to provide filament and spun yarn (including monofilament). The yarns are also made available for special purposes as textured and as abraded.

Textured Yarns

The filament of a manmade fiber is smooth and rodlike as it emerges from the spinneret. It therefore lacks the natural crimp (wave) that some natural fibers have, which limits its usage. Originally, this was the reason manmade filaments were cut up and then spun. More recently, however, methods have been developed to give chemically derived continuous filament yarns the properties of spun yarns. Filament yarns so modified are called **textured yarns.** The key to texturing is the thermoplasticity of chemical fibers. The rodlike filament is twisted or crimped along its length, and the crimp is permanently set by applying heat. The filaments then have bulk, dimension, and a soft hand. Some of these yarns also have stretch properties.

Abraded Yarns

Another way of making a filament yarn with a fuzzy surface is to run the yarn over a rough surface thus breaking or snagging the outer layer of the filaments. These yarns are called **abraded yarns.**

The general purpose noncellulosic yarns — nylon, polyester, acrylic, and modacrylic — are woven, knitted, and bonded into a wide variety of fabrics. The special purpose yarns such as olefin, spandex, aramid, and novoloid are woven for their intended use — fire resistance, weather resistance, and stretch quality.

Finishing of Manmade Noncellulosic Fabrics

A great variety of finishes are used for manmade noncellulosic fabrics, such as permanent press, durable press, soil release, and antibacterial.

CARE OF NONCELLULOSIC FIBER FABRICS

Because of their different components and properties, the various noncellulosic fiber fabrics have differing care requirements.

Nylons

Avoid washing white nylon with colored clothes because nylon picks up dye. Use a commercial bleaching powder frequently, since white nylon has a tendency to become gray after several washings. Although nylon may be washed by machine or hand, hand washing is preferable if there is any likelihood of the fabric fraying. When hand washing, squeeze out the excess moisture but do not wring.

Acrylics and Modacrylics

Firmly constructed fabrics are usually machine washable. Use medium-temperature water and avoid the spin cycle. Iron at low temperature. Napped fabrics can be brushed lightly. Steaming is not recommended for modacrylics.

Polyesters

Soak polyester collars in an enzyme presoaking product. White articles may be bleached. After machine laundering, drip dry the fabrics (omitting the spin cycle) or dry in a clothes dryer. If a dryer is used, remove the fabrics from the dryer immediately to prevent wrinkling.

Other Manmade-Fiber Fabrics

Olefins used for upholstery may be cleaned with a solvent. Because olefins are commonly used in

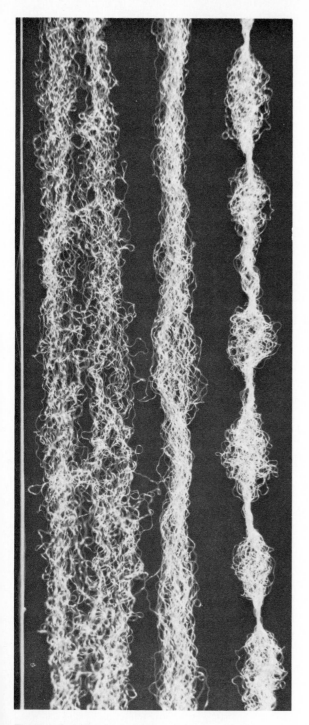

Figure 12-4. *Twisting or crimping the manmade filament creates a variety of textured yarns.*

blends, a good rule is to follow the washing instructions given for the other fibers in the blend.

Because saran sheds water, it may be used for beach chairs, seat covers, and upholstery. A damp cloth should remove dirt and soapy water will usually remove stains.

Hand wash glass-fiber fabrics in hot, sudsy water but do not scrub. Rinse in clear, warm water but do not wring. No special treatment is required for the metal yarns.

THE FUTURE FOR THE FIBERS

Experimental chemists are continually finding ways to improve the manmade fibers and are uncovering new generic fibers that will meet changing customer demand for both physical and aesthetic qualities. Although the price of petroleum products — the source of many manmade fibers — is likely to continue to rise, pound for pound the manmade fibers will perhaps continue to be less expensive than the natural fibers. Nevertheless, there will always be an established market for the natural fibers.

DO YOU KNOW YOUR MERCHANDISE?

1. How do the manmade fibers discussed in this chapter differ from rayon and the acetates?
2. What are the two outstanding petrochemical fibers that are used for nearly all clothing and homefurnishing fabrics? Explain the reason for the wide use.
3. What is a generic name? What organization gives it official recognition? About how many generic fiber names are there now?
4. Which manmade fiber has unusual stretch? For what purposes is it suitable?
5. Which fibers and fabrics are naturally fire resistant?
6. Which fibers resist rain, snow, and dampness

well? For what purposes are they well suited?

7. What special fabric constructions are frequently made from textured and abraded yarns?

8. What are the chief uses of glass fibers?

9. Give at least two selling points for each of the fabrics made from the following fibers: nylon, polyester, acrylic, olefin, saran, glass, and fluorocarbon.

10. Give care suggestions for nylon, polyester, acrylic, olefin, saran, and glass.

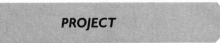

PUTTING YOUR MERCHANDISE KNOWLEDGE TO WORK

Pretend you are a salesperson. Your customer finds two dresses she likes. One is labeled rayon and the other acrylic, and she wants to know what difference the fiber will make. How will you answer her so as to help her make a choice?

PROJECT

Write to one of the large manmade fiber producers listed below or in your phonebook and ask for material on an improvement in an existing fiber or on a new generic fiber. Indicate that you want to know its outstanding features and the uses for which it is intended. Write a brief report of your findings.

Some of the leading manufacturers are as follows.

E.I. du Pont de Nemours & Co.
Textile Fibers Department
Wilmington, DE 19898

Avtex Fibers, Inc.
1185 Avenue of the Americas
New York, NY 10036

Phillips Fibers Corporation
630 Fifth Avenue
New York, NY 10020

Hoechst Fibers Industries
1515 Broadway
New York, NY 10036

Hercules, Inc.
910 Market St.
Wilmington, DE 19801

Celanese Fibers Marketing Co.
1211 Avenue of the Americas
New York, NY 10036

Monsanto Textiles Company
1114 Avenue of the Americas
New York, NY 10036

Eastman Chemical Products Inc.
1133 Avenue of the Americas
New York, NY 10036

American Enka Company
530 Fifth Avenue
New York, NY 10036

UNIT THREE

Nontextile Materials

13

Plastics:
The Ubiquitous Products

Plastics are all around you. You sit on them, sleep on them, wear them, eat from them, look through them, and hear with them. You use them in your homes, classrooms, and places of work. Although plastics have only been available for consumer use for slightly more than 100 years (with most of their growth postdating World War II), they have grown steadily in volume to become one of the major products in consumer and industrial use today.

Plastics are a whole family of products with approximately 25 distinct varieties. Each type of plastic looks, feels, and reacts in a different way when used. Therefore, plastics are chosen for the services they can provide in use. Knowing what plastics will and will not do is the job of the retailer who stocks and sells plastic products and the concern of the consumer who buys and uses them.

HISTORY OF PLASTICS

C. F. Schonbein is generally credited with the discovery of **nitrocellulose** in Basel, Switzerland, in 1845–1846. An exhibition of products made from nitrocellulose was held in London in 1860. Then in 1868 a young printer, John Wesley Hyatt, mixed nitrocellulose with camphor and alcohol. This was the first plastic, which became famous under the trade name of **Celluloid** (patented in 1870). Billiard balls, false teeth, combs,

buttons, umbrella handles, and camera film were all made from nitrocellulose.

After the development of nitrocellulose, almost 30 years passed before a chemist in Germany developed **casein.** Buttons, buckles, and glue are made from this plastic today.

In 1900, a Swiss chemist, Jacques Edwin Brandenberger, produced the first thin, clear cellulose sheeting, which he called **cellophane.** This material was used to make rayon and packaging film. Cellophane became a generic name for the product in 1930. Chemists do not consider it a true plastic.

An entirely different kind of plastic that is highly resistant to heat was developed by Dr. Leo H. Baekeland in 1909. It is **phenol-formaldehyde,** or **phenolic,** and was given the trade name Bakelite.

Since 1914 new plastics have appeared every few years. Chemists are also constantly improving those already in existence and finding new applications for them (see Table 13–1).

KINDS OF PLASTICS

Plastics have three specific characteristics. They are created mainly from chemicals; they are formed, extruded, or molded into their finished structure; and they can be made into products at relatively low cost when compared with wood, metal, and clay products.

Table 13-1 DEVELOPMENT OF PLASTICS AND SOME COMMON PRODUCT USES

Development Date	Type of Plastic	Uses
1868	Nitrocellulose (pyroxylin)	Fingernail polish, eyeglass frames
1898	Casein	Knitting needles, buttons, buckles, glue
1900	Regenerated cellulose	Cellophane for packaging
1909	Phenol-formaldehyde	Electrical appliance housings
1914	Cellulose acetate	Coatings, packaging, combs
1927	Vinyl (polyvinyl chloride—PVC)	Raincoats, shower curtains, umbrellas, handbags, shoe uppers, upholstery, floor tiles
1929	Urea-formaldehyde	Lamp fixtures, housings for small appliances
1931	Acrylic	Brush sets, dentures, edge-lighting fixtures, jewelry
1935	Ethylcellulose	Flashlight cases, screwdriver handles
1938	Nylon	Tow ropes, fishing leaders, paint brush and toothbrush bristles
1938	Polystyrene	Toys, combs, kitchen gadgets
1939	Melamine-formaldehyde	Dishes
1942	Polyethylene	Squeeze bottles, refrigerator jars, wastebaskets, packaging film
1942	Polyester	Boat hulls
1945	Cellulose propionate	Pen and pencil casings
1947	Epoxy	Glues and paints
1948	Acrylonitrile-butadiene-styrene (ABS)	Football helmets, luggage
1955	Urethane (polyurethane)	Foam cushions, sponges, toys
1956	Acetals	Automotive and plumbing parts
1957	Polypropylene	Safety helmets
1957	Polycarbonate	Appliance parts
1964	Ionomer	Packaging
1965	Polysulfone	Electrical parts and microwave ovenware
1977	Polyethylene terephthalate (PET)	Containers
1978	Polyarylates	Electrical and electronic appliance housings

Plastics are divided into two groups — thermoplastics and thermosetting. **Thermoplastics** soften or melt when heated and harden when cooled. They are thus able to be reshaped. Most of the plastics for household and personal use come under this classification.

Thermosetting plastics are shaped by the use of heat and become permanently hard. They are immune to softening or distortion when high heat is applied to the finished product. Such plastics, however, char like wood when a flame is applied to them. Bakelite was the first thermosetting plastic. Fewer home products are made from these plastics, but they are used extensively in industry.

COMPONENTS OF PLASTICS

The cellulosic plastics are made from wood pulp plus chemicals and color additives. Other plastics are made by combining resins or blends of resins, fillers and reinforcements, chemicals, and other additives. **Resins** are the main materials in a plastics mixture. The vast majority of thermoplastic resins are derived from raw materials such as benzene, ethylene, chlorine, propylene, styrene, and vinyl chloride. The mix of these raw materials is what gives each resin (polymer) family its basic characteristics.

In most instances, plastics are created by changing the structure of the molecules of the resins. **Monomers** are simple molecules. Polymerization is the linking of these molecules to form different size molecules with different properties (see Chapter 12). The prefix "poly" before a plastic indicates that polymerization has occurred. **Copolymers** are made by joining *two* different monomers together to form larger molecules with different properties. For example, ethylene, made from refinery gas or liquefied petroleum is a monomer. Through polymerization (ethylene-ethylene chains), it becomes the plastic material known as polyethylene. Linking benzene, made from crude oil, to the ethylene monomer produces the styrene monomer, which may then be linked to form polystyrene. Joining this with butadiene, made from petroleum or alcohol, forms the copolymer, styrene-butadiene. Once these new molecules are formed, they cannot be changed back to their simple molecular form.

Fillers are added to some plastics to give more body, to decrease costs, and to stretch out the amount of resin available. Common fillers include talc and wood flour.

Reinforcements serve some of the purposes of fillers as well as significantly improve tensile and impact strength. Glass fibers are the most widely used reinforcements.

Chemicals and **additives** represent a broad and important category in plastics manufacture. Depending on the type and amount of additive that is mixed into the polymer blend, subtle to substantive changes in the characteristics of the resultant material are achieved. The most important chemicals and additives for plastics are as follows.[1]

Antioxidants: When a plastic is exposed to air, antioxidants substantially slow the aging, cracking, and brittling of the material by reducing or eliminating oxidation.

Antistatic Agents: Most plastics are naturally good insulators against electricity and are nonconductors of electricity. However, they are subject to building up an electrical charge within themselves, called **static electricity.** Static electricity may result in dust attraction, handling and sticking problems, and electrical shocks, sparks, or an explosion.

Chemical antistats that are added during compounding give long-lasting protection from these faults. They act as lubricants to reduce friction or offer a conductive path that dissipates the static charge. Surface antistats applied after a plastic has been formed may be removed in handling.

Colorants: Colorants are pigments or concentrates that impart the lovely colors that characterize many plastic products. These are costly additions.

Flame Retardants: Chemical substances that reduce the speed with which something burns and its reaction to combustion are known as flame retardants. Good flame retardants incorporate several qualities such as inhibiting flames, reducing smoke, and suppressing the afterglow of materials that have burned.

Foaming or Blowing Agents: When certain chemicals or gases are heated, they create a cellular sponge structure in the plastic that makes some plastics bouncy and cushiony.

Heat Stabilizers: Polyvinyl chloride compounds are exceedingly popular plastics. They degrade, however, under modest heat rather quickly unless they are properly stabilized. Certain metal compounds are added to the plastic to reduce the chemical reactions that otherwise would occur.

Light Stabilizers: Natural sunlight has an effect on most materials including plastics. Chemical compounds can be added to certain plastics to retard the aging effect of the sun. Products such as synthetic turf, indoor-outdoor carpeting, and outdoor seating and automotive components are subject to extensive amounts of sun and thus contain light stabilizers. Acrylic plastics are surprisingly resistant to sunlight's effects. However, when used for outside signs, they also contain light stabilizers.

Plasticizers: Plasticizers make plastics, principally PVC and other vinyls, softer and more pliable. They are used in flexible products such as flooring, water hoses, textiles, and films.

MANUFACTURE OF PLASTICS

Large companies that make resins ship these plastics material in many forms, for example, as pellets, powders, or liquids or as "semifinished" tubing, sheet, or film to manufacturers. The manufacturers then form the final product by a molding, extruding, coextruding, thermoforming, casting, laminating, or foaming process.

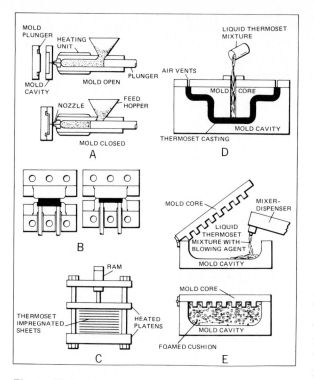

Figure 13-1. *Making plastics: (A) injection molding, (B) compression molding, (C) laminating, (D) liquid casting, and (E) foam molding.*

After being formed, plastics may be sawed, drilled, carved, sanded, or polished to finish the edges or to give a decorative effect. Plastics may also be stenciled, printed, painted, or metal plated to impart an attractive surface appearance.

Molding

Many plastic products are made by **molding,** pressing dies made from steel against the softened plastic. **Compression molding** shapes plastics through pressure, similar to making waffles in a waffle iron. This is used for many thermosetting plastics and for a few special thermoplastics.

The raw materials arrive at the factory in powder form. The molding compound, usually preheated, is poured into steel mold cavities. After the mold is closed, downward pressure is exerted and heat is applied. The heat causes the molding powder to melt into a solid mass that takes the shape of the mold into which it has been forced. When removed, the cured material is ready for sanding, polishing, hole drilling, or any other operations necessary to make an attractive and salable product. Refrigerator parts, radio cabinets, boxes, buttons, screw caps, knobs, handles, toys, camera cases, and dishes are a few of the products shaped by compression molding.

Because thermoplastics have better flow and cooling properties than thermosetting plastics, they are usually molded by high-speed injection molding or blow molding.

Injection molding is a rapid and inexpensive method of manufacturing plastic parts that are not hollow. In injection molding, plastic powder or pellets are melted by heat, and the molten mass is forced from a cylinder into a cool mold cavity, which gives the mass its desired shape. The part, or parts, can be removed in a few seconds. The list of products that can be injection molded is virtually limitless; examples are buttons, typewriter keys, combs, bowls, and parts of musical instruments.

Blow molding, like injection molding, begins with the melting of the resin. But instead of injecting the melt directly into the mold cavity, blow molding involves creating a hollow tube of the molten plastic. This tube, called a **parison,** is then fed into the mold cavity where it is forced into shape by internal air pressure (blowing). Containers that range in size from tiny vials to 55-gallon drums can be produced quickly and efficiently by this process.

Rotomolding is a variation of blow molding. Unmelted compound (pellet or powder with a plasticizer) is fed into a heated hollow mold capable of rapid rotation. The material literally fuses against the mold walls during rotation. The finished part is easily removed after chilling and opening the mold. Rotomolding is generally used for large, hollow, or deep products.

Extrusion

Just as toothpaste is forced from a tube, plastics may be shaped by continuously forcing them through a die or nozzle. In this process, which is

Figure 13-2. *Using molded plastic to form car hoods and other auto body panels is a recent manufacturing innovation.*

known as **extrusion,** the softened thermoplastic is forced through a shaped die, similar to the method of extruding rayon and acetate filaments through tiny holes in a spinneret. Thermoplastics may be extruded in the form of flat sheets, rods, tubes, or filaments of varied thicknesses and lengths. Packaging films, napkin rings, tubing, water hosing, and rigid and semirigid pipe may be made in this manner.

Coextrusion

Coextrusion is a process in which two or more dissimilar but compatible materials are fed from individual extruders to a common die on which the separate webs of film or sheet material are fused into a single-structure composite material. This is faster and lower in cost (in terms of materials consumption) than laminating (discussed below), but the purpose is similar: to achieve a uniting effect by combining the most desirable properties of two or more plastics. Thus, for example, a coextruded butter or margarine tub may have polyethylene on the interior for low cost, "clean" appearance, and chemical inertness, and impact-grade polystyrene on the outside for strength, gloss, and print reproducibility.

Thermoforming

Thermoforming is a widely used method of converting thermoplastics materials into finished products. This process, which has several variations, begins with prefabricated rolls or sheets of plastic. By a combination of vacuum, heat, and pressure, the material is softened and made to conform to a mold surface. Children's wading pools, candy and cookie tray packs, disposable containers and lids, margarine tubs, and takeout food packaging are thermoformed products.

Casting

Plastics that do not need to be very strong or to support heavy weight may be formed by pouring liquid plastic into lead-covered steel molds, which are then baked in ovens until the thermosetting plastic hardens. This process is called **casting.** Thermoplastics are melted and poured into the mold and are hardened by cooling. These molds are less expensive than those used for compression or injection molding because they do not have to withstand pressure. Clothing hangers, furniture trim, tubing, rods, sheeting, and inexpensive buttons may be made by casting.

Laminating

Sheets of thermoplastics may be pressed against similar or dissimilar materials (such as fabrics, paper, or wood) and then fused or otherwise adhered to the material, permanently bonding the various layers. This process is called **laminating.** Shower curtains, raincoat materials, artificial leather, imitation veneers for furniture, protective packaging, and safety glass are examples of articles made by laminating plastics with other plastics or with nonplastic materials.

Foaming

Almost any thermoplastic material (and, lately some thermosets) may be **foamed,** that is, filled with air bubbles. This is generally done by the use of chemicals (foaming or blowing agents) that cause the plastic to bubble. After the plastic

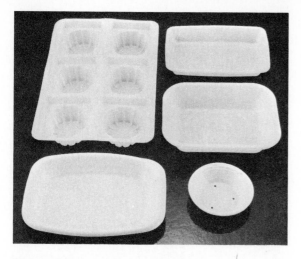

Figure 13-3. *Thermoformed plastics are used for a variety of disposable food packaging products.*

has been foamed, it is poured into a mold to set into the desired shape. Sponges, upholstery, cushioning materials, imitation leather, life jackets, life preservers, and padding for helmets are some useful products made in this manner. Foamed sheets serve as insulation and cut noise and vibration in air-conditioning units.

Metal Plating Plastics

Metallic films or flake may be deposited directly on treated plastic surfaces. Such plastics are used for car interiors and exteriors, pipes, furniture, and toys. Metallizing gives the look of metal with the lightness, durability, serviceability, and low cost of plastic.

THERMOPLASTICS

The thermoplastics, which soften when heated and permit reshaping, are by far the most familiar plastics sold through retailing firms. They are known by a wide variety of product names that are usually based on the primary resin used, as well as by trade names. To simplify this array of terms, the plastics have been grouped into families, where possible, and discussed under these groupings (by product names). See Table 13–2.

Cellulosics

All cellulose plastics use cellulose (purified cotton or wood chips) as part of the resin. Because most of the cellulosics are affected by temperatures of about 160°F, their uses are somewhat limited.

Nitrocellulose (Pyroxylin). Nitrocellulose, the oldest commercially developed plastic, is made from cellulose treated with acids (nitric and sulfuric) and mixed with softeners (camphor and alcohol). Nitrocellulose is tough and water resistant, takes clear, vivid colors, and is easily shaped and cemented. However, it is highly flammable, is easily scratched, and discolors when exposed to sunlight and heat. A liquid solution of this plastic is colored and sold as nail polish. In a rigid version, it is used as fountain pen barrels, toothbrush handles, and break-resistant watch crystals. Because of its dimensional stability (ability to retain its shape), nitrocellulose has been extensively used for eyeglass frames.

Cellulose Acetate, Cellulose Acetate Butyrate, and Cellulose Acetate Propionate. During World War I cellulose acetate was used to coat the fabrics and wooden wings of airplanes. It then emerged as a fiber for acetate fabrics. It is a syrupy material made by combining cellulose with acids (acetic acid and acetic anhydride). It is used for jewelry stones, translucent lamp shades, watch crystals, fountain pen and pencil barrels, and camera film. Nontarnishable metallic yarns are made by coating aluminum with colored acetate film.

Cellulose acetate butyrate and propionate are somewhat tougher than their parent material. They are used in blister packages to protect products on retail shelves. They do, however, have some tendency to warp and deform in the presence of moisture.

Ethylcellulose. Ethylcellulose, made from cellulose plus a caustic and ethyl (alcohol), is a slightly hazy, pale amber-colored resin that is very tough at low temperatures. It is useful as food containers, tool handles, and electrical appliance parts.

Regenerated Cellulose. Regenerated cellulose is made by treating cellulose with chemicals to turn it into a liquid. It is then extruded to make a sheet or filament form. In sheet form, it was known for many years as cellophane. In the 1920s, du Pont's moistureproof cellophane revolutionized the packaging industry. Because it is expensive to make, however, it has been increasingly replaced by other plastic films.

Acrylics

Acrylic plastics are basically made from carbon, oxygen, and hydrogen. Clear furniture, decorative ornaments, and lenses for auto and highway stop signals are some of the important uses of this clear plastic. It is also used to make fabrics water resistant and permanently stiff.

In comparison to glass, acrylic plastics have greater light transmission, weigh half as much, are warm rather than cold to the touch, and are shatterproof, making them desirable for imitation jewelry stones. The main disadvantage of acrylics is that they scratch easily, although protective coatings are available.

Acetals

Acetal plastics are made from a colorless liquid obtained by the imperfect oxidation of alcohol. When polymerized, this material has a translucent white appearance that readily takes color. It is resistant to common solvents, oils, or gasoline, has a high melting point, and is both strong and rigid. It also has inherent properties that makes it suitable for many applications that require friction, such as plumbing parts, automotive seat belt components, and aerosol bottles.

Ionomers

Both organic and inorganic materials are used to make ionomers, transparent, tough, resilient, extremely lightweight plastics. They are also highly resistant to attack by chemicals and are almost totally immune to absorbing liquids. These poly-

Acetals	Acrylic
Celcon	Korad
Cellon	Lucite
Delrin	Plexiglas
Formaldafil	Sumipex

Ionomers	Nylon (Polyamides)
Surlyn	Amidel Rilsan
	Capron Vydyne
	Minlon Xylon
	Nylafil Zytel

Polystyrene	Polysulfone
Bapolan SAN^c	Sulfil
Cosden ABS	Udel
Esbrite Absacon	
Styrafil Abson	
Bapolan	
Cycovin	
Kralastic	
Lustran	

mers bond well under heat to other materials, are highly puncture resistant, are see-through, are slow burning, and maintain their flexibility at low temperatures. Because of these properties, they are used for meat packaging and other tear-open see-through packages.

Nylon (Polyamides)

Nylon is the generic name for a family of plastics that are known as polyamides. It is so familiar to everyone in its textile form that few realize its other important uses. Nylon is used in molded form in articles such as buttons, combs, tablewear, tumblers, housing for hair blow dryers, and automobile exterior body parts. The material is also used in film applications where strength,

Table 13-2 THERMOPLASTIC TRADE NAMES[a]

Cellulosics

CELLULOSE ACETATE	ETHYLCELLULOSE	NITROCELLULOSE	REGENERATED CELLULOSE
Ampol	Ampec	Celluloid[b]	Cellophane[c]
Lumarith			
Tenite/Acetate			

Polycarbonate	Polyester		Polyethylene		Polypropylene	
Lexan	Celanex	PBT (cont.)	Ethocon	Microthene	Babolene	Procon
Merlon	PBT[c]	El Rexene	HDPE	Petrothene	El Rexene	Sumitomo
Polycarbafil	Hytrel	Kodapak	Alathon	Rumiten	Marlex	Noblen
Tuffak	Rynite	PET[c]	LDPE	Sumikathene	Moplen	Tenite
	Bapolene		Hefty	Tenite	Norchem[d]	
	Chemplex		Marlex			

Polyurethane	Polyvinyl	
Ensolite	Geon	Saran[c]
Q-Thane	Quirvil	PVC[c]
Roylar	Sumlit	PVDC[c]
	Porahyde	

[a] Unless otherwise noted, names are registered trade names.
[b] Discontinued trade name.
[c] Generic name.
[d] Trademark.

high clarity, and heat resistance are essential. In filament form, it is used for bristles in toothbrushes and paintbrushes and as strings for tennis rackets, leaders for fishing lines, and tow ropes for airplane gliders. In 1971 a flame-retardant nylon that is useful for radio and television switches and gears was perfected.

Polycarbonate

Polycarbonate plastics (made from carbolic acid, hydrogen, and oxygen) are strong, tough, and rigid. They are used in place of die-cast metals for electrical appliance housings, helmets, and boat propellors. Large returnable milk and water bottles are made from this material. Their clarity makes them useful for eyeglasses and see-through sections of business machine housings, as well as home and industrial glazing. Their impact resistance makes transparent polycarbonate sheets useful as bulletproof paneling in banks.

Polyester Thermoplastics

Polyester thermoplastics have both thermoplastic and thermosetting varieties. Three of the commonly used thermoplastic varieties are polybutylene terephthalate (PBT), polyethylene terephthalate (PET), and polyarylate.

PBT is primarily used in the automotive and electronic fields because of its high melting point ($435°F$), strength, and low moisture absorption. In consumer goods it is found in showerheads, buckles, clips, buttons, and zippers.

148   Unit Three: **Non-Textile Materials**

PET is particularly familiar in the family-size, nonreturnable carbonated beverage bottles. These are clear, lightweight, shatter resistant, and safe for all food contact. It is commonly seen in supermarkets as boil-in-bags, packaging for foods, and blister packs.

Polyarylates (aromatic polyesters) are primarily used for industrial applications as solar energy collectors and for electrical and electronic appliance housings.

Polyethylene

Polyethylene is made by a complicated process from either petroleum or natural gas. The resulting plastic, which may be either flexible or rigid, has a waxlike feel. It is the largest selling plastic in the United States.

The most common uses of low-density polyethylene (LDPE) are in film form for food packaging, garment bags, trash bags, household wraps, shrink wrapping, disposable diapers, agricultural mulch, and shopping bags.

The most recent technological innovation is linear low-density polyethylene (LLDPE), a material that permits much thinner films than conventional LDPE without sacrificing strength or other desirable properties. High-density polyethylene (HDPE) has its biggest market in blow-molded containers of up to 2-gallon capacity.

The polyethylenes are noted for their toughness, resistance to water and a wide range of chemicals, and innate flexibility that requires no chemical plasticizer. Their disadvantages are their resistance to inks and the facts that HDPE is difficult to heat seal or to bond by solvents and oils and greases tend to cling to it.

Polypropylene

Polypropylene is a petroleum-derived thermoplastic that resists heat up to about 300°F, allowing for repeated sterilization when needed. Its superb qualities include its light weight and low cost. Rigid or flexible, transparent or opaque, it is resistant to attack by chemicals and stains and has a mar-resistant surface. This plastic has been

Figure 13-4. *Large beverage bottles are often made of shatter-resistant polyethylene terephthalate, rather than being made of glass.*

used to make kitchen chairs, stools, housewares, and picnic goods. It is widely used in the bottle business for some cosmetic and food products whose color is enhanced by polypropylene's exceptional contact clarity. In 1972 a method of making polypropylene fibers flame retardant by using chemical additives was developed.

Styrene-Acrylonitrile and Acrylonitrile-Butadiene-Styrene

Polystyrene, which is made from ethyl chloride and benzene is resistant to concentrated acids and so is used as a packaging material for these substances. Because polystyrene reproduces tiny details from a mold, it is particularly useful for bottle and jar caps that require threading.

Polystyrene can be foamed before shaping. When filled with air bubbles, it makes a material that is quite rigid, strong, and lightweight and is used for molded chair frames and protective cushioning. The uncolored foamed plastic resembles snow, so it is a popular material for Christmas decorations.

Styrene-acrylonitrile resin, whose generic name is SAN, possesses gloss and clarity and is more resistant to chemicals, has higher heat tolerances, and is stronger than ordinary polystyrenes. Continuous high heat, however, may cause it to yellow over time. It is used to make pen and pencil barrels, windows, knobs, blender and mixer bowls, tumblers, and mugs.

Acrylonitrile-butadiene-styrene (ABS) is also a styrenic and is a popular synthetic rubber. Strong and tough, it resists heat almost up to the boiling point of water. It has many industrial uses and is commonly found in football helmets, battery cases, radio housings, luggage, and rigid and foamed furniture. ABS takes a high gloss, has a wide range of beautiful colors, and is resistant to breaking and scratching.

Polysulfone

Polysulfone is transparent, tough, rigid, and has high strength. It takes electroplating well and is made into electric percolators, coffee makers, and hair dryers. It does not heat up and thus can be used as microwave cookware. It is also widely used as medical instruments because it resists the high temperature of autoclave sterilization.

Urethane (Polyurethane)

Urethane is made from complicated chemicals (isocyanates and polyols) and puffs up like bread dough to as much as 25 times its original size when the liquid mixture is poured into a mold. This swelling occurs because the plastic releases carbon dioxide. The foamed plastics that result are creamy tan in color, flexible, lightweight, inexpensive, and long wearing. Depending on the formula, the material can be soft and spongy or very rigid.

In 1966 the interest in auto safety enabled flexible urethane to be used for padding in dashboards and other interior parts of automobiles. Flexible urethane is ideal for kitchen sponges and

spongelike mops because it holds nearly 20 times its weight in water. It is also used for cushiony toys and cushioning under rugs and is laminated to fabric for insulation. Its most famous use was in December 1982 as the housing for the first artificial heart to be implanted in a human. It is easily cleaned with soap and water and is not affected by dry-cleaning solvents.

If the chemical formulation of urethane is changed slightly, a rigid foamed plastic can be made. This may be used for furniture bases, mirror frames, and headboards. Home builders also use large amounts of rigid urethane as insulation in unsupported form or as the core of a structural laminated panel.

This plastic is flammable and gives off a dense acrid smoke when burned that makes it somewhat undesirable for use in furniture and bedding. It also oxidizes in air and becomes crumbly after several years of use.

Vinyls (Polyvinyls)

Vinyls are made from elements in air, natural gas, water, salt, and coal. Vinyl plastics are used in the home as table covers, refrigerator bowl covers, shower curtains, and transparent, waterproof kitchen aprons. Sturdy backyard swimming pools, beach balls, and inflatable toys and rafts are also made from vinyl. Both fabric-backed (supported film) and nonfabric-backed (unsupported film) materials that resemble leather are used for upholstery materials on livingroom furniture and seats in cars, airplanes, and boats. Another extensive use is in hard-surface floor coverings such as tiles or in place of linoleum.

Polyvinyl chloride (PVC) is by far the dominant vinyl material. The fastest-growing markets for PVC are as extruded rigid pipe and conduit and in building and construction.

Vinyl resins are tough, odorless, tasteless, and flame resistant. Many are resistant to warping, moisture, absorption, and shrinkage. Unplasticized PVC resin yields rigid products; but the more plasticizer used in a compound, the more flexible the end product. Plasticized vinyl can be stretched to as much as two and one-half times

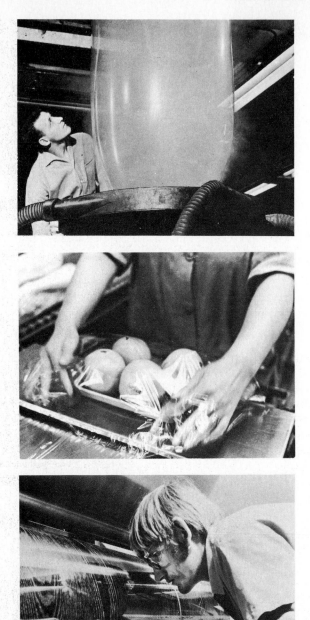

Figure 13-5. *Blowing air through a special die (top) forms a bubble that is squeezed flat to make vinyl packaging film (center). Other vinyl plastics may be decorated, as with a wood-grain pattern (bottom).*

its normal size and return to its original shape. With age, however, it loses some of its elasticity and tends to stiffen and crack. Also, the vinyl may melt if it comes in contact with heat.

Foamed vinyls, known as **expanded vinyls,** have been used for insulation in household products and for protection against cold weather in clothing. They are currently popular as imitation leather for handbags, shoes, slippers, and jackets.

Another variety of vinyl plastic, polyvinylidene chloride (PVDC), is known as **saran,** a generic (not a trade) name. In sheet form it is extensively used for meat and food wrapping and packaging because it has strong cling qualities. It also has good resistance to moisture vapor and oxygen transmission. It may also be extruded in thin strips as monofilaments. These are then woven like straw for subway and bus seats. Saran is also used in fire-resistant draperies, furniture webbing, and window shade cloth.

THERMOSETTING PLASTICS

The most important difference between thermosetting plastics and thermoplastics is in their reactions to heat. Once having been set by heat into any given form, the thermosetting plastics can never again be melted; however, open flames or high oven heat may char or burn them. The well-known thermosetting plastics are phenol-formaldehyde, urea-formaldehyde, melamine-formaldehyde, and some plastics classified as polyesters, and epoxies. For familiar trade names of products made from each of these plastics see Table 13–3.

Phenol-Formaldehyde

Phenol-formaldehyde plastics (phenolics) products are shaped mainly by two methods: compression molding or casting, although injection molding grades and some foamed products have also become available. Some phenolics are made into laminates, discussed earlier.

Molded Phenolics. Molded phenolics that go into huge presses to be shaped require filler

Table 13-3 THERMOSETTING PLASTICS TRADE NAMES

Epoxy	Melamine-Formaldehyde	Phenol-Formaldehyde			
		Molded	Cast	Laminates	Foam
Dap Duratite	Boontonware	Durez	Catalin	Formica	Esclad
Devcon	Lenoxware	Noryl	Marblette	Micarta	Esfen
Duratite	Melmac	Plenco			Isophenol
Epoxybond	Plaskon				Phenythane
Weldwood	Texasware				

Polyester	Urea-Formaldehyde
Celanar	Beetle
Dacron	Sylplast
Glad	Uformite
Melinex	Urac
Mylar	

materials to give them extra strength. These filler materials are dark in color, and the resulting plastics are therefore dark in color.

Because molded phenolics do not conduct heat or electricity, they are used as handles and bases for many products such as irons, toasters, and electric plugs, as well as housings for radios, television sets, and telephones. Because of their strength and the fact that neither water nor household chemicals affect them, molded phenolics are used as agitators for washing machines.

Cast Phenolics. Cast phenolics, which are not as strong as the molded varieties, require no dark filler and thus may have delicate to vivid colors. They may be transparent, translucent, or opaque. Like the molded phenolics, they do not absorb water or chemicals and are therefore usable for products that are washed in boiling water.

Because of the cast phenolics' color range, radio and clock cases, jewelry, and other attractive items are made from them. However, clear and white phenolics tend to yellow with age.

Phenolic Foam. In the form of foam board, phenolic foam is the newest addition to the foamed plastics. It is virtually impermeable to gases, has excellent dimensional stability, does not warp or shrink, and has good resistance to burning and low smoke density. It is used for roofing insulation and as replacement for wood panels in homes.[2]

Urea Formaldehyde

Urea formaldehyde (urea) resins are made from urea (derived from ammonia and carbon dioxide) and formaldehyde. The resulting resin is mixed with cellulose to yield a translucent plastic that may be given any desired color. Urea plastics have no noticeable odor. They have hard, durable, scratch-resistant surfaces and are not affected by boiling water. They are lightweight and resist breakage but may crack if dropped from a considerable height. They are used for bottle closures, toys, buttons, cutlery handles, cosmetic containers, lamp fixtures, and housings for electrical products. Urea resins are useful for bonding plywood and other wood joints.

Urea-formaldehyde foams, used as insulation in housing, proved to be an irritant and even toxic to some people living in the homes with such insulation; therefore they were banned for that use in 1982, but reinstated in 1983.

Melamine-Formaldehyde

Like the ureas, melamine-formaldehyde (melamine) plastics, made from calcium cyanamide mixed with formaldehyde, have unlimited color possibilities and an unusually tough surface when compared with many other plastics. They have no odor or taste and thus are used extensively for dishes. (For further discussion of melamine, see the section on plastic dishes in Chapter 25.)

Polyester

A unique plastic that can be made into film, polyester withstands roasting temperatures. It was developed in 1942, has been available since the early 1960s in film form, but only since 1971 have scientists solved the problem of how to heat seal it to make polyester bags leakproof. This clear plastic is used in cooking bags that withstand 400°F temperatures (roasts are usually cooked at 325–350°F).

Polyester film, produced under antiseptic conditions to prevent contamination by dust, is also used for magnetic recording tape and in packaging, graphic arts, and office supplies. Polyester is also available as foam for bonding to textiles and other materials. Combined with 50 percent to 80 percent glass fibers, it is used in automotive body parts, boat hulls, building panels, appliances, and business equipment housings.

Epoxy

Made from a complicated group of chemicals, epoxies may be found in liquid form as glues or paints and in solid form in outdoor insulators. They adhere particularly well to glass or to glass fibers to produce reinforced plastics with high heat resistance. Epoxies are used both as decorative coatings and protective coatings where they are tough, durable, and nonporous.

PROBLEMS WITH PLASTICS

With all their versatility, availability, and usefulness, plastics have come under criticism in a number of areas. Environmentalists are concerned with litter problems and air pollution. The government has been concerned with the flammability of plastics in some uses and with

their toxic effect under some conditions. Price-conscious customers are disturbed by the rising costs of plastics products.

Disposal of Plastics

The inability of some plastics to decompose naturally has caused a disposal problem in some areas of the United States. Materials such as tinplate, paper, and paperboard can break down and decompose when discarded, but plastics products generally do not do this. Chemists are working to make plastics **biodegradable** (able to disintegrate) when they are no longer useful. However, there is concern about the added cost of this feature and the fact that such plastics might begin to disintegrate while still on the retailer's shelves.

Plastics that are not biodegradable when discarded can be burned to get rid of them. After testing polyethylene, polystyrene, polyurethane, and polyvinyl chloride, scientists have evidence that these plastics cause no more problems than are encountered in burning other refuse. Bottles made from PVC have been criticized because when burned in incinerators, they give off a hydrogen chloride gas that, in combination with moisture, becomes highly corrosive hydrochloric acid. However, such problems can be controlled. And with the proper procedures, incineration of plastics waste can be a valuable energy resource.

Thermoplastics can be recycled. And more of this effort can be expected with the rise in resin prices (which makes reclamation economically attractive). Trash bags, for example, can be made from recycled plastic to which a filler such as carbon has been added. Using certain chemical processes, plastics can be broken down into gases and made into materials for new plastics. Some new municipal incinerators can use plastics to generate steam for conversion to electricity.

Combustibility and Toxicity

Laboratory tests have shown that plastics generally are no greater a fire hazard than other materials. In fact, many plastics are used for upholstery and stuffing materials and are flame retardant. However the Federal Trade Commission has stated that plastics used for upholstery and stuffing materials may burn and give off toxic chemicals under the actual conditions of use in homes, automobiles, and airplanes.

In 1973 the FTC singled out polyurethane and polystyrene as unsafe for use in furniture, bedding, and airplane interiors. Since then, plastics manufacturers have added inhibitors and other chemicals to control flammability and smoke evolution in such products. Also, the industry has sponsored and conducted much research aimed at minimizing the hazards of flammability and smoke.

In addition to the toxic effects that occur when some plastics are burned, two materials have been found to give off toxic substances under other conditions. In 1973, PVC bottles were withdrawn from food-contact use (including beverages) by the U.S. Food and Drug Administration on the ground that minute amounts of vinyl chloride monomer (a PVC building block identified as carcinogenic) were being leached into the liquid contents. Manufacturers withdrew these bottles from the market. But as of 1980, these problems were greatly reduced, chiefly by eliminating residual monomers. In March 1977, acrylonitrile bottles used for some soft drinks were also withdrawn from the market because of suspected leaching into contents. However, the new and presumably totally safe PET bottles have replaced them.

SELLING POINTS OF PLASTICS

Lightweight, strength, versatility, ease of use, design freedom, almost unlimited color ranges, resistance to breakage, rigidity or flexibility as needed, warmth to the touch, and the fact that a damp cloth and mild soap are all that plastics need to keep them clean and attractive make plastic articles particularly salable. Generally speaking, they may be bought and sold with confidence that they will give durable service. However, as in any business there are those who cut corners and sacrifice performance to gain a price

advantage. They perpetuate the image of plastics as a "substitute" material rather than "the real thing."

NOTES

1. See also *Modern Plastics Encyclopedia*, McGraw-Hill Book Co., New York, October 1982.
2. A. S. Wood, "Why All the Excitement About Phenolic Foam?" *Modern Plastics*, October 1981, 8860–62.

DO YOU KNOW YOUR MERCHANDISE?

1. List at least 10 different uses of plastics. Why is their use constantly expanding?
2. When was the first plastic produced? What trade name was given to that product at that time?
3. What was the first heat-resistant plastic to be developed? What was its trade name?
4. What are the main differences between thermoplastics and thermosetting plastics? Which are more commonly used? Why?
5. Name the kinds of materials that comprise or make up the majority of plastics. Why is each of those different types of components used?
6. Explain the differences between compression and injection molding; extrusion and casting; laminating and foaming.
7. What are some cautions that must be observed about plastics?
8. Why are environmentalists concerned about plastic waste?
9. What is the most widely used plastic in the United States?
10. If your firm was planning to develop its own brand of products for the following items,

what plastics would you suggest they consider for each? Dishes; jewel-look necklaces; men's and women's leatherlike jackets; floor tiles; ash trays; handles for electric toasters; mop heads and sponges; men's, women's, and children's gloves.

PUTTING YOUR MERCHANDISE KNOWLEDGE TO WORK

Assume that you are selling a sofa that is covered in a polyvinyl chloride leather-looking plastic.

Advise the customer what service it will give, how well it will wear, what precautions to take for it in the home, and how to care for it.

PROJECT

Visit a toy department, housewares department, or dinnerware department in a store. Make a list of the products on display that appear to be made from plastic. List the advantages and disadvantages of having those products made from plastic.

Leather: Nature's Insulator

In addition to leather being used for shoes, handbags, and luggage, it has emerged as a fashion material for women's blouses, dresses, shorts, pants, jackets, and coats and for men's vests, jackets, trousers, and coats. Its appeal is the soft, silky, sensuous character that can be imparted to leather.[1] In addition, leather is seasonless because it insulates from cold in the winter and from heat in the summer. As more people demand leather, it has become scarcer and more of a luxury product.

WHAT IS LEATHER?

Leather is the treated skin or part of a skin obtained from animals. Animals that are covered with feathers, wool, hair, or fur fiber have hair follicle openings that show when that covering is removed. Scales identify other animals' skins. These openings form patterns that make each animal's skin identifiable. If the hair is coarse, the holes are larger and more noticeable. Ostrich quills leave the largest hole markings and seal hair among the smallest.

The hair or scale side of the leather is the **grain side.** The side next to the **flesh** of the animal is the **flesh side.** The grain side is more durable, firmer, and smoother than the flesh side. When the grain side of the leather is intact and has not been altered in any way, the leather is known as **top grain,** considered to be the finest quality of that particular leather type. When the leather is reversed to the flesh side, neither the hair follicle openings nor the scale markings show, except in pigskin, where the openings go all the way through the leather. However, the fibers that compose the skin are visible. Raising all these fibers to a uniform height by buffing produces **suede,** a familiar form of leather.

The **shearling** is an exception to the usual leather. It comes from a short-wooled sheep or lambskin that was sheared before slaughter and processed with the wool remaining on its surface.

Leathers differ in quality for other reasons. The center back section of most animals, known as the **bend,** produces the best leather. That is where the animal develops a tough, thick hide to protect itself from snow, wind, rain, and sun, and enemies. Toward the belly section the leather becomes spongier, looser in texture, and softer. Some animals that crawl instead of walk, such as the alligator, lizard, and snake, develop fine-quality belly section leathers.

PRODUCTION OF LEATHER

Skins of animals are brought from many parts of the world to be converted into leather in U.S. tanneries. When they arrive, they are stiff, unattractive, and unusable. Skins are preserved and made useful by a process known as **tanning.**

Since only the **dermis,** or **true skin,** is

155

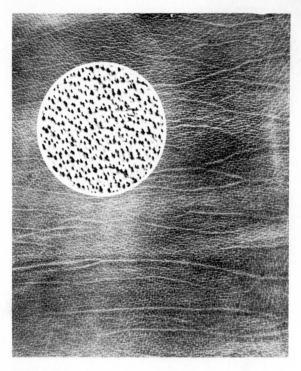

Figure 14-1. *Magnification of top leather grain shows hair follicle openings and scale markings.*

tanned, the **epidermis,** or **outer layer,** of dead skin, the hair or wool, plus all the natural liquids and oils in the skin are removed. All that is left of the dermis are the tiny short bundles of fibers, which will be converted into leather. These fibers are interlaced at various angles in groups or bundles. They give the characteristic strength to leather, and the spaces around them permit leather to breathe. Washing, soaking in chemicals, and scraping denude the skin of all but the part to be tanned. In this condition, the skin is a creamy off-white color. **Rawhide** skips the tanning process and emerges with just a surface finish to serve as a tough, enduring leather substance.

Tanning

Tanning is done by using vegetable substances (such as oak bark), oil, mineral salts (such as chrome and alum), chemicals (such as formalde-

hyde), and synthetic tanning materials made from coal tar.

Vegetable tanning, using tannic acid extracted from oak bark, hemlock, and other trees, shrubs, and nuts, produces a firm, tan-colored leather that is durable and porous yet resistant to moisture. Shoe sole, upholstery, belting, and saddle leathers and alligator and lizard are commonly vegetable tanned. This is a lengthy and costly process.

Mineral tanning uses either salts of chromium (the most used method of tanning), salts of alum (infrequently used), or salts of zirconium (a new tannage). **Chromium salts** produce a pale gray-blue leather speedily and relatively inexpensively. This leather is durable, slightly less porous than vegetable-tanned leather, and slippery when wet. It is used for shoe uppers, gloves, handbags, and clothing. **Alum** produces a soft, white, buttery-textured leather but one that stiffens in the presence of moisture. Therefore, this method of tanning has been replaced by washable tannages such as **zirconium** for items such as white shoes and baseball covers.

Oil tanning, using cod oil, leaves a soft, yellow-colored skin used for chamois skins, doeskin, and buckskin. These are exceptionally flexible and washable.

Synthetic tanning (syntans) materials, made from various chemicals, are increasingly used because the materials are readily available and the resulting products may be controlled and more speedily produced.

Combination tanning combines two or more methods listed above. Thus, chrome-tanned leathers may be retanned with vegetable substances to make **retanned leathers.** These are used especially for shoe soles, work shoes, and boots. Similarly, chrome-tanned leathers may be combined with synthetic tannages to yield softer, more flexible leathers for gloves and clothing.

FINISHING OF LEATHER

After the tanning operation the skins are wrinkled, dull, and unattractive. Processes that make

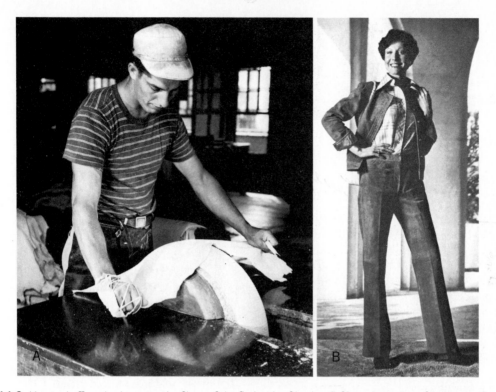

Figure 14-2. *Using a buffer wheel to raise the fibers of the flesh side of leather (left) produces the soft velvety surface of suede. Suede has become popular for a number of garments like the jacket and pants on the right.*

the skins pliable and beautiful are known as **fin-ishing processes.** These finishes are used to show the natural grain of the leather, to modify the grain, to remove the grain entirely, as well as to add color and other properties to the skins.

Splitting is a means of cutting thick skins into two, three, four, or even five layers. All these layers may subsequently be used to make leather articles. The top layer with the grain intact is top grain. If properly cared for, it will become shiny and lustrous with age and will wear well. All remaining layers are called **splits.** These lower layers may have artificial grains stamped on them, so it is not always possible to tell at a glance whether or not an article is made of top grain. Only top-grain leather may be designated as "genuine leather." Split leather usually has a rougher, coarser appearance than top-grain; it does not wear as well and costs less.

Fat liquoring is a process of rubbing animal, vegetable, or mineral oils into skins to replace the natural oils removed by the tanning process. Leather that has sufficient oil rubbed into it stays mellow and supple; without oil, leather dries out and cracks.

Coloring

Opaque **pigment** dyes that cover minor blemishes and partly obscure the grain are commonly used on leathers. **Aniline** dyes that are transparent and permit all the natural grain to show are used chiefly on top-grain leathers. Aniline dyes characteristically darken with age, giving a rich, mellow look to the leather. **Dip dyeing** is the immersing of articles in dye. The dye penetrates the skin deeply and colors all sides of the skin. Such leather articles keep their rich color well.

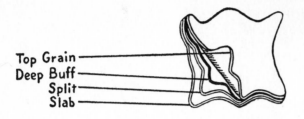

Top Grain
Deep Buff
Split
Slab

Figure 14-3. *Heavy hides may be split into as many as four layers of leather. Only the top layer has the natural grain pattern. For consumers, all lower layers are called splits.*

pigment dyes
obscures leather

Drum dyeing is a process in which aniline dyes are applied in drums during tanning. During the tumbling of the hides in the drum, the dye penetrates throughout and the color is uniform on both sides. **Spray dyeing** is a process in which the dye is sprayed on only one surface, leaving the original tanned color showing on the edges and underside of the leather. Spraying the dye only on one surface also permits two-tone or shaded effects.

Metallic Finishes

Metallic surfaces on leather may be applied by affixing a thin sheet of the desired metal to the leather and then pressing it with a machine until the metal is firmly bonded to the surface. Thin gold is used for gold finishes, and sheets of aluminum impart a silver finish. Dull-textured aluminum may resemble pewter and be so labeled.[2] Bronze and gunmetal effects are achieved through the use of metallic dyes.

Other Surface Textures and Protections

Boarding imparts a creased or bumpy texture to the surface of leather. Repeated flexing of the dampened leather by folding and creasing it in only one direction yields parallel lines. Four-way creasing raises a bumpy appearance, and eight-way boarding creates tiny pebblelike surface markings. Boarded cow, calf, pin seal, and morocco leather are examples of such surface texturing.

Glacé, or **shiny leathers,** are made either by pressing leathers with a wide, mirror-smooth flat metal plate, called **plating** or pounding them repeatedly with a glass cylinder or by coating them with a glassy spray. Smooth calf and glacé kid are examples of this type of finish.

Napping is a method of raising the fibers by using a revolving buffing wheel on the fibers of the leather, which produces a soft, velvety, fuzzy surface. When done on the flesh side this process yields suede or a coarser bucko. Some leathers that have scarred surfaces may have the grain side napped. Doeskin-finished lambskin and mocha leathers are napped on the grain side.

Embossing is a method of putting an artificial grain on leather. Popular designs embossed on grain-side leathers that have damaged surfaces and on split leathers include alligator grain, lizard grain, snake grain, and pin-seal grain. Embossing makes inexpensive leathers look expensive, split leathers look like top-grain leathers, and scarred leathers look unscarred. Such leathers must be

Figure 14-4. *Boarded leathers have a creased or bumpy texture. Left to right: morocco, calf, pin seal.*

correctly labeled such as alligator-grain calfskin, lizard-grain sheepskin, or pressed calf.

Waterproofing is the application of silicone to the leather's surface to make it waterproof without changing its breathing properties.

Patent finish is a smooth, shiny finish. It is made by putting a plastic urethane coating on any smooth-surfaced leather. Although such leather is nonporous it is not affected by cold nor does it tend to crack.

THE LEATHER INDUSTRY

Animals from every continent in the world supply the exotic and practical leathers for the goods that Americans buy and wear. Most leathers are obtained as by-products from meat and milk industries, making leathers less costly than if animals were raised just for their skins. There are approximately 500 tanneries that process countless leathers for the accessories, clothing, homefurnishings, and industrial segments of our economy.

Laws About Leather

The Endangered Species Conservation Act, passed in 1969, initially affected the alligator, crocodile, and some snakes and lizards. Most of those animals have now been removed from that endangered species list. Leather is a renewable resource. Animals may be bred repeatedly and in many cases keep an endless supply of this material available.

Other laws require that labels on leather be accurate. For example, shoes made of plastic that resembles leather must be so labeled.

Hides, Kips, and Skins

Terms such as "cowhide," "kidskin," and "kipskin" originate from the sizes and the weight of the various leathers. In the leather trade, animal skins that weight 15 pounds or less when they are shipped to the tannery are referred to as **skins.** Calves, goats, sheep, deer, and alligators fit under this category. A few animals fit under a grouping for skins that weigh 15 to 25 pounds,

known as **kips.** This term is used mainly in referring to oversize calves, whose skins are called **kipskins. Hide** refers to large animals whose skins weigh over 25 pounds; cows, oxen, buffalo, walrus, and horses come under this classification.

FASHIONABLE AND USEFUL LEATHERS

Whether you sell leather products or buy them for your own use, knowing about the animals that produce popular leathers will prove interesting and helpful. Because all leathers from one family of animals have similar qualities, the leathers below have been listed in family groups.

Cowhides and Calfskins

The great majority of leathers sold in the United States are from cows, steers, and bulls. They are obtained as by-products from the large meat-packing industries. This type of leather has a smooth, firm surface with a barely noticeable grain marking. The skin is thick, heavy, and large in size. Cowhides make durable, pliable leathers. The following are some familiar leathers from cowhide.

- *Bend leather* is the center back section of the cow used for quality products such as luggage, gun cases, tool holsters, and shoe soles.
- *Elk-finished cowhide*, sometimes called *elk-side leather*, is napped on the grain side. It is used for garment and shoe upper leather.
- *Rawhide* is cowhide that is treated with oils but not actually tanned. It is particularly tough and is used for drumheads, shoe laces for work boots, and luggage. It must be kept dry since it can mildew and rot.
- *Retanned cowhide* is made by chrome tanning and then vegetable tanning the hide to make a durable, water-resistant, porous leather desirable for thick shoe soles and uppers on work shoes.
- *Saddle grain* is fine quality vegetable-tanned aniline-dyed cowhide used for quality handbags and luggage.

- *Scotch grain* is boarded to raise a pebblelike grain used in shoe uppers.
- *Side leather* is from large cowhides that have been split down the center back for ease in handling. Each half is then known as a *side*.
- *Steerhide* is from any male cattle raised for beef.

Calfskins and *kipskins* are the young from this family of animals. Only a few days to a few weeks old, the skins have a smooth-surfaced, fine-grained look that is firm and enduring. Few of these skins are available for leather use, however. Some familiarly used terms for these leathers are as follows.

- *Alligator-grain calf* is calfskin with an alligator grain embossed on its surface.
- *Box calf* is given a boxlike effect in the grain pattern by two-way boarding the skin. It is used for shoes and handbags.
- *Crushed calfskin* is textured with a pebblelike grain achieved by boarding or embossing.
- *Ecrasé* is a calfskin with a crushed grain appearance.
- *Lizard-grain calf* is calfskin with a lizard grain embossed on its surface.
- *Patent leather* is usually a thin upper layer of cowhide or a calfskin with a urethane coating that is shiny and resistant to cracking.
- *Reversed calf* is chrome-tanned calf sueded with a coarse nap on the flesh side. It is used primarily for sport shoes.
- *Unborn calf* is skin from a prematurely born or stillborn calf. It is tanned with or without the hair left on the skin.
- *Vellum* is calfskin with a smooth surface that, like rawhide, has not been tanned but has been processed with oil. Once used as a writing surface, it is now used for lamp shades.

Sheepskins and Lambskins

The second most used leather comes from domestic and imported sheep. Domestic sheep are wool bearing. Many better quality skins come from imported haired sheep.

Leather products from these animals are generally less expensive, less durable, and less likely to hold their shape than are those made from the skins of other animals. Sheepskin leathers also tend to abrade easily. However, the leather is soft and flexible, has an attractive surface grain, takes a fine surface nap, and is comfortable when used in clothing or as accessories items. Sheepskins are often made to resemble more costly leathers. Articles made from haired-sheep leathers are better in quality than those made from domestic sheep. Some terms for these leathers are as follows.

- *Cabretta* is a leather from a species of Brazilian haired sheep. The leather resembles kidskin but is not quite as strong. This is a popular glove, garment, and slipper leather.
- *Capeskin* comes from a haired sheep and is usually glazed to resemble kidskin. It has similar uses to those of cabretta leather.
- *Castor* is a soft leather made from haired sheep and napped on the grain side. It is used mainly for slippers and gloves.
- *Chamois*, originally from a goatlike antelope, is now made from a sheepskin split that has been oil tanned and sueded.
- *Doeskin-finished lambskin* is made from selected lambskins, given a soft tannage, and napped on the grain side to resemble deerskin.
- *Electrified lambskin or sheepskin* is leather tanned with a short length of wool attached. Chemical or heat treatment is used to straighten the wool.
- *Flesher* is an undersplit of sheepskin that is napped and used as lining or for inexpensive leather articles.
- *Mocha* The grain side of this haired sheep is buffed, giving a firm, durable nap. It is usually dyed gray, black, or brown for men's gloves.
- *Morocco-grained sheepskin* is sheepskin with its grain embossed to resemble genuine morroco leather.
- *Parchment* is the skin of selected sheep, converted in the manner of rawhide to a tough, smooth material suitable for writing. It is used for diplomas, lamp shades, and drumheads.

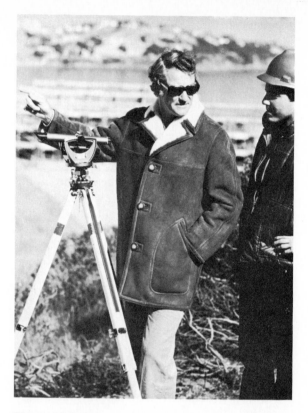

Figure 14-5. *Shearling leather, tanned with a short length of wool adhering to the sheepskin, makes comfortable and attractive coats, gloves, and footwear.*

- *Pigtex* is a trade name for pig-grained or embossed sheepskin.
- *Shearling leather* is sheep tanned with a short length of curly wool adhering to the skins. It is used for coats, jackets, slippers, boots, and gloves.
- *Skiver* (pronounced skyver) is a thin, top-grain section of sheepskin used for linings of fancy leather goods and for sweatbands for hats.
- *Suede*, a napped finish on the flesh side of sheepskins, is used for leather garments, handbags, and gloves.

Goatskins and Kidskins

Kids and goats are raised in Europe, Asia, Africa, and South America primarily for their milk and meat. The young kid or goat has a thin but strong, smooth skin with tiny holes on the grain side. As the animal grows older, these grain markings become coarser and more noticeable. The smaller the grain of the kidskin, the better the quality.

Kidskin is comfortable in gloves and shoes because this porous leather permits the hands and feet to breathe. It wrinkles easily, but textured or bumpy finishes keep the wrinkles from showing. Kidskin takes a high glaze. Such smooth, glazed leathers, because of their fineness, require care to prevent scratching or peeling. Well-known leathers from these animals include the following.

- *Bronze kid* is a glazed kidskin with a dark-colored metallic finish used for gloves, shoes, and clothing trim.
- *Crushed kid* has a creased finish achieved by boarding the leather. Shoes, handbags, boots, and slippers are made from crushed kid.
- *French kid* is fine kidskin from France.
- *Glacé kid* is glazed, chrome-tanned kidskin used for gloves, footwear, and handbags.
- *Gold kid* is leather with a thin gold leaf pressed onto the surface of the leather. The kid grain shows through the gold leaf. It is used for ornamental accessories.
- *Kid suede* is one of the strongest suede leathers. The flesh side of this leather is napped, but it retains its strength and durability. It is used for shoes, handbags, and boots.
- *Morocco* (genuine) is goatskin originally from Morocco but is now used for any fine-quality, vegetable-tanned, boarded kidskin. The term, "genuine," is often used to differentiate this leather from its sheepskin imitations. It is used for shoes, handbags, and attaché cases.
- *Silver kid* is leather with a thin sheet of aluminum, which does not tarnish, applied to the leather. It is used for ornamental accessories.

Deerskins and Elkskins

Skins from the antelope, buck, caribou, deer, elk, and gazelle make porous, smooth-textured leathers that have a good deal of stretch. Because they are wild animals, their skins are usually scarred, and the grain side must often be napped when it is used for leather articles. These leathers are known by the following names.

- *Genuine buckskin*, made from the male of the species, has a loose-fibered, wrinkled grain that is buffed or napped on the grain side. It is used for jackets, shoe uppers, men's gloves, and slippers.
- *Genuine deerskin* is the term used when the grain is left intact on any of these leathers. It is used for gloves, slippers, and garment leathers.
- *Genuine doeskin*, from the female of the species, has a soft, velvety textured skin, which, when napped on the grain side, has a silky sheen. It is used for fine-quality gloves and other leather accessories.

Pigskin

The **peccary** (a wild hog from Mexico and South America), the **carpincho** (which is actually not a pig at all but a member of the rodent family), and the **domesticated pig** are the main sources of pigskin. The peccary yields the best-quality leather; the carpincho, a heavier leather. All of these animals have bristles that, when removed, leave visible holes in groups of threes on the skins. These holes, which go right through the skin, act as beauty marks for the grain side of the skin and as ventilators. The leather is durable, but it tends to stretch in use. Most real pigskin articles will have scars that show on the surface. Familiar terms for these leathers are as follows.

- *Genuine pigskin* is the most commonly used term for these leathers. Gloves, garments, and shoes are made from this leather.
- *Pig-grained pig* is leather made from skins that have too many scars. These are covered by embossing the leather with a pig grain. Gloves, shoes, and other accessories are made from this leather.
- *Pig suede* is scarred pigskin napped on the

grain side. It usually has a texture that reveals some of the characteristic hole markings through the nap. It is used for less costly leather products than top-grain pigskin.

Horsehide

Leather from the colt, horse, pony, donkey, mule, and zebra is relatively scarce in the United States. The leather, which resembles cowhide when finished, is, with one exception, not as durable or as water repellent as cowhide. The exception is the leather made from the butt section of the animal, known as the **shell.** The shell is made from a cartilage layer under the skin. That leather is extremely durable, takes a high, glossy sheen, and is almost nonporous. Leathers from this group are familiarly known by the following names.

- *Cordovan* (genuine) leather is a hard, fine-grained, almost nonporous material from the shell section of the animal. It is sometimes called *shell*. Dyed in a deep purple-red-black color, it is used for men's long-wearing, high-quality shoes.
- *Horsehide* is the term for leather from the forepart of the animal. It was once used as the main material for baseball covers, gloves, and, occasionally, men's jackets.

Sealskins

Once used for fine-quality leather products, especially in the form of **pin seal,** which was a silky-looking, finely boarded leather, seals have now virtually disappeared from use. Since 1975 many fur-bearing and leather seals have been included on the endangered species list and by law may not be used for products for resale.

Alligator and Crocodile Skins

In 1969 alligators and crocodiles were listed as endangered species under the Conservation Act and were unavailable for leather products. An order in October 1980 easing the restriction on

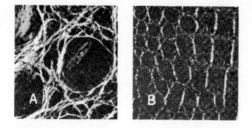

Figure 14-6. *Because alligator skins are difficult to obtain, calf leather (B) may be embossed to simulate real alligator (A).*

these animals went into effect because the population had increased significantly.[3] Some crocodile skins, however, are still restricted.[4]

It takes about 15 years for an alligator to become large enough to be commercially valuable. The almost square markings from the belly section are the most desirable. Markings from the sides and leg sections are smaller and less regular in appearance. The leather is tough and enduring but not very porous. Costly handbags, attaché cases, shoes, and other leather accessories items are made from these leathers.

Lizard Skins

Although a few lizards are also on the endangered species list, many lizards, which are found in jungles throughout the world, are still available. The leather from these animals is prized for the unique markings of the skin, which resemble small grains of uncooked rice. Some species of lizard have tiny rectangular scales that resemble miniature alligator markings. These are known as **alligator lizards** or by the trade name Lizagator. The skins make long-wearing leathers.

Snakeskins

Some snakes, such as boas and pythons, are on the endangered species list. Other snakes, such as the diamondback, cobra, and watersnake, may be used for leather products. Most snakeskins have to be backed with fabric because the skins are so thin and fragile. These leathers are used mostly for decorative leather accessories.

Table 14-1 on pages 164–167 summarizes the kinds and characteristics of leather.

CARE OF LEATHER

Quality leather articles that are well cared for can last a lifetime.[5] When purchasing a leather article, the customer should find out the best way to care for it. Part of the salesperson's responsibility is to advise the customer about the care of leather.

Leather articles that are carried or worn have durable finishes applied at the tannery. Shoes may need colored waxes applied to them. Some shiny leathers may blister slightly when spotted by rain. A good rubbing with wax before using the article will reduce this blistering.

Suede articles should be brushed with a bristle (not a wire) brush or a rubber sponge in a circular motion to remove dust, soil, and water spots. When suede becomes shiny, a fine emery board may be used to brush up the nap gently. A rubber gum eraser may be used to erase smudges on suede. There are also colored dressings that restore color to suede articles that have become grayed. Fuller's earth, a white powdery clay product, is a fine suede cleaner that removes most oils and absorbs dirt. It can be purchased under a variety of names and in several forms.

Leather articles marked "washable" may be hand washed carefully in lukewarm water in a soap mixture especially made for washing wool. After being rinsed, the articles should be carefully rolled in a towel to press out excess water and then placed away from sunlight and heat to dry slowly. When leather dries, it feels rather stiff. By pulling it gently between the fingers, you can restore the soft, supple feel. This is called **finger pressing**. Leather articles not marked "washable" and leather-trimmed apparel should be dry-cleaned by cleaners who specialize in handling leather.

Leather repair is an important part of leather care. Leather articles can be repaired by specialists who mend torn spots, replace handles or straps, reinsert linings, restitch or rebind edges, repair locks, and fix zippers.[6]

Sturdy

Table 14–1 KINDS AND CHARACTERISTICS OF LEATHER

Animal	Familiar Name	Characteristics	Uses
Cows, kips, calves	Alligator-grained calf	Embossed surface	Accessories (belts, shoes, handbags, luggage)
	Bend leather	Choice leather from center back of cowhide	Quality shoe soles, belting leathers, garments, handbags, luggage
	Box calf	Small, square-shaped design from boarding or embossing	Accessories
	Crushed calfskin	Pebbled surface made by boarding or embossing	Garments, accessories
	Ecrasé calfskin	Same as crushed calf	
	Elk-finished cowhide (erroneously called elk-side leather)	Buffed on grain side to resemble coarse suede	Garments, shoe uppers, handbags
	Lizard-grain calf	Embossed surface	Accessories
	Patent leather	Shiny, nonporous coating on grain side	Shoe uppers, handbags
	Rawhide	Untanned hide treated with oil to give off-white, tough product	Drumheads, luggage, boot laces
	Retanned cowhide	First chrome tanned then vegetable tanned for durability	Work shoes and boots
	Reversed calf	Sueded on the grain side	Sports shoes
	Saddle leather	Aniline-dyed top-grain leather	Fine-quality heavy-duty handbags and luggage
	Scotch grain	Pebble-textured surface by embossing or boarding the grain	Tailored sports shoes
	Side leather	Cowhide with any finish	Upholstered furniture, garments, shoes, accessories
	Steerhide	Top grain	Shoes, garments
	Unborn calf	Tanned with hair left on	Handbags, garments
	Vellum	Nontanned, oil-finished, off-white color calfskin	Lampshades, tambourine heads

Animal	Familiar Name	Characteristics	Uses
Sheep and lamb	Cabretta	Brazilian haired sheep top-grain leather	Gloves, garments, slippers, soft-type handbags
	Capeskin	Top-grain, South African haired sheep with glazed finish	Gloves, garments, slippers, soft-type handbags
	Castor	Haired sheep, napped on the grain side	Slippers, gloves garments
	Chamois	Oil-tanned, split sheepskin with napped surface	Cleaning materials especially for glass, shiny metal; sometimes used for linings
	Doeskin-finished lambskin	Fine napped surface on grain side	Gloves, soft-type handbags, slippers
	Electrified lambskin	Wool is left adhering to the skin — it is straightened by a chemical process	Garments, slippers, gloves, earmuffs
	Flesher	Thin undersplit of sheepskin	Inexpensive garments and accessories
	Mocha	Haired sheep originally from Mocha, Arabia; rarely available now; napped on grain side	Men's dress gloves
	Morocco-grained sheep	Embossed to resemble genuine morocco from kidskin	Bookbindings, small leather goods, handbags, small luggage items
	Parchment	Nontanned, oil-finished, off-white	Diplomas, lampshades, drumheads
	Shearling	Tanned with curly wool adhering	Garments, slippers, earmuffs, gloves
	Skiver	Thin, top-grain section	Handbag linings, sweat bands in men's hats
	Suede	Napped on flesh side	Garments, slippers, handbags, gloves
Kids, goats	Bronze kid	Metallic finish on top-grain leather	Gloves, shoes, handbags, garments, trim
	Crushed kid	Creased appearance because of boarding or embossing	Shoes, handbags, small leather goods

(continued)

Animal	Familiar Name	Characteristics	Uses
	French kid	Fine, glacé kidskin from animals raised in France	Gloves, shoes, boots, slippers, handbags
	Glacé kid	Fine, glacé kidskin from any country	Gloves, shoes, boots, slippers, handbags
	Gold kid	Thin gold leaf is pressed onto the grain side of kidskin	Gloves, handbags, shoes, small leather goods, and garments
	Kid suede	Fine quality suede, napped on flesh side of kidskin	Garments, shoes, boots, handbags, gloves
	Morocco	Boarding results in fine, pebble-grain texture that does not show scuff marks	Shoes, handbags, attaché cases
	Silver kid	Aluminum in thin sheets is pressed onto the grain side of kidskin	Shoes, handbags, garments, accessories
Deerskin, antelope, buck, elk, caribou, gazelle	Genuine buckskin	Buffed or napped on grain side of male animals' skins; soft, flexible, warm	Garment leathers, gloves, shoe uppers, slippers
	Genuine deerskin	Top grain intact; soft, flexible, warm leather	Garment leathers, gloves, slippers
	Genuine doeskin	Soft, napped on the grain side, silky leather from female of species	Fine-quality gloves, some specialty handbags
Pig, boar	Genuine pigskin	Any skin from any pig or boar; top grain skins have marks and scars in most cases, but these do not lessen the durability of the leather, which is thick, soft, and flexible	Gloves, shoes, small leather goods
	Pig-grained pig	Embossed pig grain to hide scars	Gloves, shoes, small leather goods
	Pig suede	Napped flesh side leather showing some hole markings	Gloves, shoes, small leather goods
Horse, colt	Cordovan	Hard, virtually nonporous leather from cartilage of rear section of horse; takes a glossy sheen, is very long wearing	High-quality men's shoe uppers

Animal	Familiar Name	Characteristics	Uses
	Horsehide	Flexible, porous, abrasion-resistant leather	Shoes, garment leathers, accessories; once famed as the baseball cover leather and baseball glove leather
	Shell	Same as cordovan, above	High-quality men's shoe uppers
Seals	Pin seal	Boarded, fine-textured, pebble-grained leather, shiny and flexible	Fine-quality small leather goods items, shoe uppers
	Sealskins	Slightly wrinkled apearance	Briefcases, handbags, shoe uppers
Alligator, crocodile	Alligator Crocodile	Top grain leather from the belly section of the animals; the special markings, from the removed scales, are the beauty marks of the leather; almost nonporous, long wearing, quite firm	Handbags, shoe uppers, briefcases, luggage
Lizard	Lizard	Unique skin markings in the shape of uncooked kernels of rice or tiny rectangles; firm, almost nonporous	Handbags, shoe uppers, small leather goods
Snakes	Snakeskins	Thin, flexible, scaly leathers	Handbags, shoe uppers, small leather goods, trim on articles

RECONSTITUTED LEATHER AND IMITATION LEATHER

A product known as **bonded leather** is made from fibers of waste leather that are combined with a plastic binder. This mixture is then formed into sheets, which are cut to shape for articles intended for use in place of leather.

Other plastic products may look like leather, feel like leather, and have some of the qualities of leather, but they cannot be called leather since they do not come from the skins of animals.

Imitations of leather are usually made from plastic materials. Vinyl is the material most commonly used in place of leather. It is manufactured under a variety of trade names and comes in several well-known types: stretch vinyl, which expands and contracts with movement; expanded vinyl, which has air cells that make the material soft and crushable; and nonexpanded vinyl, which may resemble calf, kid, or patent leather or may have a design embossed on its surface. Polyurethane foamed plastic products have also been used extensively as imitations of leather for shoe uppers, garments, and upholstery products. Plastic materials are also widely used for shoe soles.

NOTES

1. "When Leather Gets Silky," *The New York Times Magazine*, September 13, 1981, p. 135.
2. E. Graydon Carter, "All That Glitters Is Sold," *Time*, August 17, 1981, p. 71.
3. "Sale of Gator Products Legal Again in New York," *Women's Wear Daily*, October 21, 1980, p. 2.
4. Joseph P. Fried, "Endangered Breeds: Curbing the Market," *The New York Times*, June 26, 1982, p. 52.
5. "With Proper Care, Leather Is Forever," *The New York Times*, May 21, 1980, p. C18.
6. Angela Taylor, "High Cost of Leather Keeps Repairers Busy," *The New York Times*, May 9, 1982, p. 21.

DO YOU KNOW YOUR MERCHANDISE?

1. What are some of the unique characteristics that make leather a desirable product for apparel articles? For shoes? For gloves? For handbags and luggage?
2. Define leather, grain side, flesh side, tanning.
3. Explain the difference between top-grain and split leather. How do grained leathers and suede leathers differ?
4. Why are different tanning methods used in making leather?
5. How do finishes affect the appearance and usefulness of leather?

6. Define skin, kip, and hide.
7. Why is cowhide the most used leather?
8. Explain the advantages and disadvantages of regular sheepskin; of haired sheepskin.
9. What are some of the advantages of kidskin?
10. What important care information should customers be given about leather products?

PUTTING YOUR MERCHANDISE KNOWLEDGE TO WORK

Assume you are selling in a jacket department or specialty store that features jackets. A customer is trying to decide between a suede jacket and a plastic jacket made to look like suede. The latter is less than one-half the price of the genuine suede jacket. What sales presentation would you make to the customer about the reason to pay the higher price for the suede product?

PROJECT

To aid you in understanding and evaluating leather, make a chart of the leather articles you own. In the first column list the article; in the second column on the same line list the length of time you have owned the article; in the third column list the price of the article; and in the fourth column write your comments about the wear, comfort, appearance, and other qualities and selling points of the article.

15

Metals:
The Finite Products

Unlike wood and leather, metals are not renewable products. Metallurgists constantly search for new sources for these valuable materials. Metals are used in many ways: for weapons, utensils, transportation, buildings, bridges, tunnels, coins, and ornamentation.

Historically, metals have been mined from the earth. Gold and silver were probably the first metals used. Egyptians used lead and copper over 4,000 years ago, and around that same time, bronze (a mixture of copper and tin) was found strong enough to replace stone. Iron, first used around 1500 B.C., eventually replaced bronze. The technology of the 1970s revealed that some metals could be found in blackish, potato-sized nodules in certain parts of the ocean. With instruments that mine 14,000 to 18,000 feet down, the ocean floor is swept of these nodules that contain manganese, nickel, copper, and cobalt.[1]

CHARACTERISTICS OF METALS

An **element** is a basic substance that singly or in combination with other elements forms all other substances. A **mineral** is a crystalline element or a compound of two or more elements. A metal-bearing rock made up of one or more minerals is called **ore.** All **metals** are elements and are usually found in ores. Metals have different characteristics, which provide each one with its particular properties for certain uses. In general the following may be said of metals.

- Solid metals have a **crystalline shape** when examined closely.
- Metals are usually **opaque;** light and shadow cannot be seen through them.
- Most metals are **malleable;** they can be pounded and twisted into shape.
- Some metals are **ductile;** they can be drawn out into wirelike forms.
- Metals have **conductivity;** heat and electricity can pass through them.
- Metals have a **glossy sheen** or **luster** when new or polished.
- Except for gold that is yellow, copper that is red, and manganese that is brownish, all metals have a dark-to-pale gray **color** or a silvery color known as **white.**

OBTAINING AND USING METALS

Metal is extracted from ore either by chemical separation or by smelting. In **smelting,** the ore is placed in a blast furnace, and the metal is separated from the ore by heat. The extracted metals are then usually shaped into large, bricklike forms, called **pigs,** ready for further shaping or combining with other metals. After separation from their ores, metals may be used in their pure form, mixed with other metals to form alloys, or coated onto other metals as plating.

Pure Metals

Most metals do not have the necessary strength to be used alone. Some exceptions are wrought iron, the purest form of iron, which is used for some furniture and ornamental objects. Pure aluminum may be used as decoration on some furniture or automobiles or for jewelry.

Alloying

The word "alloy" comes from *alligare*, a Latin word that means to bind. In ancient times people learned that by melting metals and mixing them together to form alloys they could improve their characteristics, change their color, or increase or decrease their value.

Characteristics. Strength, elasticity, breaking point, hardness (resistance to scratching), workability, and melting point are characteristics of metals that may be changed by alloying them.

Color. Combining metals may cause color changes in the major metal. For example, dark steel may be made lighter gray or yellow gold may be made white or reddish.

Cost. By adding small amounts of rarer metals, a metal may be increased in value. By adding small amounts of more common metals, it may be decreased in value.

Plating

The coating of one metal with another metal is known as **plating.** This is usually done to place the more attractive or more protective metal on the surface while maintaining the strength, low cost, or other desirable qualities of the covered metal.

There are three main methods of plating: dipping, bonding, and electroplating. **Dipping** in molten metal is used in the production of some metal items. Galvanized iron or steel products, such as garbage cans, are made by dipping sheets of steel into molten zinc, which protects the steel from rusting.

Bonding was discovered in 1743 by a silversmith in Sheffield, England, who applied silver to a copper surface by heat and pressure. Such silver was known as **Sheffield silver** or **Sheffield plate,** and replicas of it are sold today. This process is used for silver and to make gold-filled and rolled-gold-plate jewelry.

Electroplating was first used in France in 1839 to coat copper with silver. Now it is also used to plate gold, rhodium, nickel, and chromium onto other metals. It is the most commonly used plating method because it binds metals securely and is relatively inexpensive. Another form of electroplating is **anodizing.** This process is used for aluminum.

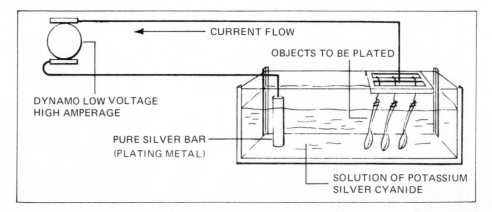

Figure 15-1. *Electroplating: Both object and plating metal are immersed in a salt solution. An electric current dissolves the plating metal, which then coats the object.*

PRECIOUS METALS

Metals that have beauty, rarity, unique qualities, and working properties that make them costly are called **precious metals.** Gold, silver, platinum and its family of metals — iridium, palladium, ruthenium, and rhodium — are the precious metals. Platinum and its family of metals are the rarest and generally most costly, gold is usually second in cost, and silver is a fraction of those costs.

Platinum, Iridium, Palladium, Ruthenium, and Rhodium

Platinum and its family of rare metals are found together in veins or nuggets and are whitish or silver in color. The main sources of platinum are the U.S.S.R., Canada, South America, and South Africa. Platinum is slightly denser than gold, and therefore fewer objects can be made from 1 ounce of platinum. Platinum can be shaped into delicate jewelry because it can be hammered into thin sheets or drawn into a fine wire.

Platinum neither tarnishes nor is affected by body acids. It is, however, a soft metal that is usually alloyed with **iridium** to make it usable for jewelry. The usual platinum alloy is 10 percent iridium, marked "10%Irid. Plat." inside a jewelry article. Sometimes 5 percent ruthenium, a less costly metal, is used in place of iridium.

Palladium is similar in appearance and jewelry characteristics but less dense and considerably less expensive than platinum. Palladium is alloyed with **ruthenium,** using 95.5 percent palladium and 4.5 percent ruthenium, to make the alloy known as **jewelry palladium.** Because this alloy darkens somewhat in use, it has never gained popularity in jewelry. Palladium is also used to make a school ring alloy whose trade name is Precium. It is composed of 25 percent palladium, 62.75 to 68.75 percent silver, and the balance in base metals. It has a silvery look and is hard and enduring.

Rhodium, a shiny white-colored metal, is used for plating platinum, white gold, and inexpensive jewelry articles. It has a bright sparkling luster, durability, and nontarnishing qualities. It is among the most costly of the platinum family of metals. As little as three 10-millionths of an inch of plating gives an enduring surface.

Gold

Gold is found in small amounts in many parts of the world. Pure gold has a beautiful pale yellow color with a bright luster. It does not tarnish and is not affected by acid. Because it is soft, however, it must be combined with another metal to give it sufficient hardness to be usable.

Karat gold is used to describe gold that is mixed with other metals. The term "karat" (K) refers to the proportion of gold, measured in twenty-fourths, in an item. Twenty-four-karat (24K) gold is 100 percent gold or **solid gold,** which is usually used only for plating. The finest quality gold alloy used in products is 22K. This means that twenty-two twenty-fourths of the alloy is gold and two twenty-fourths is another metal. Other common gold-karat proportions are 18K, 14K, 12K, and 10K. In the United States any proportion less than 10K may not be indicated in karats. The Plumb Gold Act, signed into law in 1976, became effective in 1981 for manufacturers. This act requires that karat gold assay to .003 of its stamped quality, a higher standard than was previously required. Retailers may continue to sell their stocks of karat gold indefinitely. The letter **P** is used by some manufacturers to indicate the gold is of Plumb gold standard.

The metals that are mixed with gold produce various colors. Thus, red gold is a mixture of gold with copper, green gold has some silver added to the gold and copper mixture, and white gold has some nickel added to the gold and copper mixture. Yellow gold combines gold and copper with white metals such as zinc.

Gold-filled and rolled-gold plate refer to a thin layer of karat gold alloy that is placed on top of a base metal and melted and pressed until it is firmly joined. This sandwich is then rolled to the desired thickness and articles are shaped from it.

To be called **gold-filled,** the base metal must be coated with a layer of karat gold that weighs at least one-twentieth of the weight of the entire metal used. A finer-quality gold-filled alloy's coating is twice as thick, weighing one-tenth of the entire metal used. Thus the term "1/10 14K GF" stamped inside a ring means that a layer of 14K gold has been used to cover the base metal, and the weight of this gold layer is one-tenth of the weight of the total metal in the ring.

To make **rolled-gold plate,** a thinner layer of alloy gold is used. The rolled-gold-plate layer is usually one-fortieth the total weight of the metal in the jewelry. Gold-filled jewelry gives two to four times the wear of rolled-gold-plate items. These latter are stamped "1/40 RGP" in addition to the karat quality of the gold layer.

Gold electroplate means that the base-metal article has had a layer of pure gold applied to it by an electroplating process. This coating is thinner than gold-filled or rolled-gold-plate surfaces and thus does not wear as well. The minimum thickness for such gold plating must be at least seven one-millionths of an inch of 24K gold.

Vermeil is an exception to this process. The original vermeil was made by rubbing gold with a mercury additive onto sterling silver. This was outlawed for use, however, because people were harmed by handling the mercury. Today's vermeil is a heavy gold electroplate on sterling.

Silver

Because of silver's lustrous white color and because it imparts no taste to food, it has become one of the most desired metals for flatware. Like the other precious metals, it is too soft to be used alone. Therefore copper is mixed with silver to make usable alloys. Silver comes mainly from Mexico, the U.S., Canada, and the U.S.S.R.

Sterling silver is the most commonly known alloy of silver. The name "sterling" comes from twelfth-century England, where the Germanic traders who came to ports from the east were referred to as "easterlings." The word "easterling" was eventually shortened to "sterling" and came to signify a standard of 925 parts of silver to 75 parts of copper in the silver alloy. In 1906 the United States passed a law stating that articles

marked as "sterling" had to contain that composition of metals. Great Britain and Canada have the same standard. Sterling silver is fairly hard, but the durability of the alloy depends on the thickness of the sterling used — the thicker the sterling silver, the more durable the article made from it.

Coin silver, used in the United States until 1965 for dimes, quarters, half-dollars, and silver dollars, is an alloy containing 90 percent silver and 10 percent copper. Since 1965 those coins have been made with a copper core and a nickel coating. Coin silver is harder than sterling but is neither as workable nor as beautiful.

Silver alloy has 62.75 to 68.75 percent silver, 25 percent palladium, and the rest base metals. Its trade names are Precium I (62.75 percent) and II (68.75 percent), and it is used for school rings.

Silver electroplating is used to put the attractive silver metal on the surface of base alloys or metals, such as copper, nickel silver, white metal, or ordinary steel. Silver plating varies in thickness from thin, which provides only temporary coating, to heavy, which endures for many years of constant use.

Because of silver's sensitivity to light, it is used extensively to make film for cameras. The film industry accounts for nearly half of the 160 million ounces of silver used annually in the United States.

BASE METALS

Metals that are more abundant in the earth, are not very attractive, and possess properties that make them usable for household goods and industrial purposes are called **base metals.**

Aluminum

Although there is a large amount of **aluminum** in the earth's crust, as recently as 1852 it was considered rarer than gold or silver and sold for $545 a pound. Then in 1886 aluminum was isolated from its ore inexpensively, and the metal became available for only a few cents a pound.

Aluminum is a silver-colored, lightweight, ductile, malleable, and excellent heat-conducting metal. It is readily attacked, however, by alkalies; discolors when certain foods are cooked in it; and loses its shape easily unless articles made from it are thick. Thin sheets are used as foil for packaging; thicker sheets are used for cans to hold foods and liquids; and still thicker sheets are used for cooking utensils. **Cast aluminum,** which is made by pouring aluminum into molds, is the thickest and most durable type. **Aluminum alloys** are sand cast, finished to look like pewter, and used in durable serving dishes and ornamental pieces.

Chromium

Chromium has a bluish-white color and a lustrous metallic sheen. Because it is durable and does not tarnish, it is used to plate brass, copper, and steel for jewelry, for housewares products, and for bumpers and trim on automobiles. Chromium is also the essential metal added to steel to make stainless steel.

Cobalt

Discovered in 1735, **cobalt** is a tough, lustrous, brittle, silvery-white metal that melts at a high temperature. Alloys such as stainless steel are made harder and more heat resistant by the addition of cobalt. It is also used to make the blue color in glass and ceramics and an invisible ink that turns blue under heat and then fades.

Copper

A soft, red-orange metal that is easily worked, **copper** has properties of conducting heat and electricity that make it useful for plating the bottoms of cooking utensils and for electrical wiring. Copper imparts a metallic taste to food, so copper utensils must be plated with another metal. Copper is used in many alloys such as bronze, brass, karat gold, and sterling silver. Copper takes on a green oxide coating in the presence of moisture.

Until 1982, the copper one cent coin was made of an alloy of 95 percent copper and 5 percent zinc. To save money, the U.S. mint changed to a copper-plated penny using 97.6 percent zinc and 2.4 percent copper.

Iron

Iron is one of the heaviest, strongest, and most useful of all metals. However, its dark color makes it less appealing for some uses, and its quality of rusting in the presence of moisture makes it costly to keep in good condition.

Iron obtained from iron ore by smelting is impure and not easily worked, so it is shaped by pouring the melted iron into a sand mold, known as **casting.** This **cast iron,** although thick and strong, is brittle and may crack under impact or when dropped. Iron is the main material used in making steel, the most used of all alloys.

Wrought iron has most of the impurities removed from it. This makes the iron malleable; it can thus be shaped by hammering and forging. Removal of the impurities also makes the wrought iron resistant to rusting. Decorative grills, furniture, and ornamental objects are made from wrought iron.

Magnetite is a naturally occurring magnetic material made of iron and oxygen. Known to the ancients as **lodestone,** magnetite was used in making compasses for ships.

Lead

Lead, a heavy, dark gray metal, is very soft and, unlike most metals, is a poor conductor of electricity and heat. Since it is resistant to acids, it is used in automobile storage batteries. It is also used to shield workers from x rays. For many decades lead was used in some paints. Sometimes these paints were eaten by children, causing serious lead poisoning. New laws have reduced lead content in paints. Lead also forms poisonous compounds with food. Because lead melts at a low temperature, it is used in some **solders** (alloys used to hold metal parts together) for metals with low melting points.

Magnesium

Discovered in 1808, **magnesium** is the lightest known metal. It is silvery white in color, but it corrodes rapidly in moist air leaving a dull surface. It can be alloyed with aluminum for pots and pans, with cast iron to make it malleable, and with steel to reduce rusting. As a powder, it burns hotly and can be used in signals, flares, pyrotechnics, and flash bulbs. Its oxides are also used in medicines, ceramics, and cosmetics.

Manganese

Manganese, which was isolated in 1774, is a pinkish-gray to brownish color metal. It is harder and more brittle than iron and is very important in the steel industry to toughen and harden steel. It is also used in making brass and bronze.

Nickel

Nickel is a lustrous, silvery metal that imparts a white color and hardness to karat gold, stainless steel, and nickel silver. It is also useful in plating to impart a silvery color or to add durability under a chromium plating.

Tantalum, Tin, Titanium, and Tungsten

Discovered in 1802, **tantalum** is a rare, hard, blue-gray metal that changes color by heat or electrolysis. Because it is extremely ductile, it can be drawn into a thin wire. Its resistance to corrosion makes it useful in alloys for dental, surgical, and prosthesis items.

Known since the Bronze Age, **tin** is a lustrous, silvery white metal that is very soft and easily shaped. Because it is not affected by moisture, it is plated over steel to prevent rusting. Tin is a component of many alloys and is used as an oxide in the preparation of white porcelain enamelware.

Titanium, discovered in 1791, melts at a high temperature. The metal is lustrous, has a silvery white color, and is strong, ductile, and malleable. Because it is corrosion resistant and has high ten-

sile strength, it is used in aircraft and spacecraft construction. It is also the metal that causes the star effect in star sapphires and rubies. This metal, like tantalum, changes color under heat or electrolysis.

Tungsten, a bright, steel-gray metal, is heavy, hard, and brittle. Tungsten is alloyed with steel to make some products. Tungsten carbide powder is pressed into shape, hardened at 1,450°C, and polished with diamond powder to make a scratch-proof watch case. Tungsten wire is used to create light in electric bulbs.

Zinc

A bluish-white metal that is brittle at ordinary temperatures, **zinc** can be rolled into sheets or drawn into wire when heated. When used as plating on steel, zinc helps to prevent rust from forming on the steel because even when scratched the zinc will form a film over the area. Zinc is used in small quantities in many alloys such as white gold, brass, nickel silver, German silver, and pewter. Since 1982, U.S. pennies have been made mostly of zinc.

BASE-METAL ALLOYS

The base metals may be combined to make yellow to russet or silver-colored to gray alloys.

Yellow to Russet-Colored Alloys

A yellow to yellow-white alloy, **brass** is made basically from copper and zinc with a greater proportion of copper. By adding the zinc to the copper, a soft metal that has only limited usefulness becomes a hard and enduring alloy. Brass is used in ornamental products, as a base for silver plating and gold plating, and for many industrial purposes. **Yellow brass, Dutch metal,** and **red brass** are familiar names for this alloy. Because of the copper in it, brass turns green in the presence of moisture.

Bronze, the earliest known alloy, is hard, brittle, and resonant. From 66 to 95 percent of the alloy may be copper; the balance is tin and occasionally 1 or 2 percent zinc. The properties of bronze are varied depending upon the proportion of the metals used in it. The alloy has a more russet color than brass and is used for coinage, church bells, medals, statuary, and a base material for plating. **Thailand bronze,** which is pale in color, is made from 19 to 20 percent tin, 2 to 5 percent nickel, and the balance copper.

Alloys of **imitation gold** for tableware were developed in the 1920s. Copper (88 percent) mixed with aluminum (10 percent) and nickel (2 percent) makes a gold-colored alloy (trade name Dirilyte) that is hard and durable and resists oxidation. This alloy has proven to be a popular substitute for gold.

Silver to Gray-Colored Alloys

Aluminum alloys resembling pewter are enduring and not very costly.

Britannia metal is made from copper, tin, and antimony. It is also called **white metal** because of its pale silvery color. This alloy is soft, dents and bends easily, and melts at a low temperature. Since it is soft, it has limited use except for ornamental tableware objects. Because it darkens when exposed to air for a period of time, it is usually plated with a more durable metal such as silver, chromium, or gold.

German silver is made from 50 percent copper, 25 percent nickel, and 25 percent zinc. It does not oxidize when exposed to air and is easily shaped, yet hard and durable. Many ornamental objects are made from German silver.

Monel metal, a hard, steellike alloy, is made from a half-and-half mixture of copper and nickel. It has many industrial uses such as for cylinder casings and sinks. Its stain-resisting qualities make it a particularly useful alloy.

Nickel silver, an alloy containing no silver, ranges in color from yellow tinged to silvery, depending on the amount of nickel that is mixed with the brass (copper and zinc). When 10 percent nickel is added, the slightly yellow-tinged alloy is relatively soft and easily shaped. Such

alloys are used as the bases for silver-plated holloware items. A harder, tougher, and more silver-looking alloy results when the mixture contains 18 percent nickel mixed with brass. Such alloys are used for coins and silver- or gold-plated flatware.

Pewter is an alloy that was used in colonial days for holloware and decorative home ornaments. Once made with lead, this alloy now contains from 91 to 93 percent tin, 6 to 7 percent antimony, and 1 to 2 percent copper. The standards for pewter are set by the American Pewter Guild. Pewter dents and scratches easily.

Solder is an alloy whose name is derived from *solidare,* a Latin word that means to make solid. Other metals and alloys are joined together with solder. **Soft solders** are used for alloys and metals that melt at low temperatures and, therefore, are made primarily from tin and other metals that melt at low temperatures. **Hard solders** are used for joining brass, gold, silver, and other high-temperature-melting metals. They are usually made from the metal or alloy itself combined with a metal that melts at a lower temperature.

Steel, the most used alloy, is refined iron to which varying amounts of carbon have been added. Steel may be cast, forged, rolled, or tempered and is more workable, less brittle, and more usable than iron. **Soft steels** contain only minute amounts of carbon; **hard steels** contain from 0.6 percent to over 0.8 percent carbon. High-carbon steels, used for springs and sharp cutting tools, contain over 1 percent carbon. Because steel rusts it must be protected by being kept thoroughly dry at all times; by being coated with oil or grease, paint, or porcelain; or by being plated with metals such as zinc, tin, nickel, chromium, or cadmium.

Damascus steel, a legendary metal used by the Crusaders, is remarkably hard and enduring. It has a characteristic watery or damask pattern when shaped. Its formula has been lost since the invention of firearms. However, in 1981 two researchers, using high carbon content (1 to 2 percent), developed a new version of this steel. It can be forged and hammered at a relatively low temperature then reheated and quickly quenched. This gives it a razor-sharp enduring edge that can split a hair in midair.[2]

Stainless steel, developed in 1915, has a minimum of 11.5 percent chromium (to a maximum of 20 percent) that allows it to resist both rusting and staining from the action of acids. Because stainless steel must be made in small amounts and because the addition of chromium makes it rather costly, its uses are limited to jewelry, ornamental objects, small household items, and a few industrial purposes. For finer, whiter, better quality stainless steels, nickel is added in addition to the chromium. Even finer stainless steels may include from 2 percent nickel with 12 percent chromium up to 8 percent nickel with 18 percent chromium. These latter steels are marked "18-8." They are used mainly in imported European cutlery and fine holloware products. An 18–10 steel has 10 percent nickel for added whiteness and hardness. The highest quality of stainless steel, but one that is little used commercially, is a 20–12 combination, which is 20 percent chromium and 12 percent nickel.

Table 15–1 is a summary of commonly used alloys.

SHAPING METALS AND ALLOYS

Metals and alloys are shaped in different ways, depending on their properties and the products for which they are to be used. Metals and alloys may be shaped inexpensively by casting, that is, melting them and pouring them into molds. Products made by casting are not as strong and durable as are those shaped by other methods. In 1966, metallurgists in the U.S.S.R. developed a casting method that uses an alternating magnetic field that suspends molten aluminum in midair away from the walls of the mold as it cools. This method produces a smoother, cleaner, shinier finish on the metal.[3]

Malleable metals and alloys may be **rolled** or **pressed** into sheets of metal that can later be bent, cut, or die struck to the desired shape.

Rolling is done by progressively making the metal thinner and longer until the desired gauge (thickness) of the metal has been reached. Because metals that are worked in this way become brittle, they must be heated between rollings, a process called **annealing.**

Ductile metals to be used as wires or as hollow tubes or pipes may be extended through progressively smaller and smaller holes in a die or mold until they reach the required size; this is known as **drawing.** Another method shapes cups that are drawn to size by pounding. Annealing is necessary to keep the metal or alloy from becoming brittle.

The heating and pounding into shape of metals is known as **forging.** Horseshoes were forged by the early American settlers. Today, fine cutlery and many unusually shaped iron and stainless-steel products are forged.

Metals in powder form, which were invented by William Hyde Wollaston in England in the early nineteenth century, were not used commercially until after World War II. Small items and small machine parts are made from metal

Figure 15-2. *Soldering uses an alloy to join metal parts. The joint is not as strong as a welded joint.*

Table 15–1 COMMONLY USED ALLOYS

Alloy Name	Color	Composed of
Aluminum bronze	Yellow	Copper 90%, aluminum 10%
Brass	Yellow	Copper 60–80%, zinc 20–40%
Britannia metal	Silvery white	Tin 89%, antimony 7.5%, copper 3.5%
Bronze	Yellow brown	Copper 66–95%, tin 4–33%, zinc 1–2%
Coin silver	Silver	Silver 90%, copper 10%
Damascus steel	Silvery	Iron 98–99%, carbon 1–2%
Dirilyte®	Yellow	Copper 88%, aluminum 10%, nickel 2%
Dutch metal	Yellow	Copper 60–80%, zinc 20–40%
German silver	Silver	Copper 50%, zinc 25%, nickel 25%
Gold solder (hard)	Gold	Gold, copper, zinc (varying proportions)
Jewelry palladium	Silver	Palladium 95½%, ruthenium 4½%
Karat gold: 10K to 22K	Gold	Gold 41.6–91.6%, copper, silver, zinc (varying amounts)
	Pink gold	Gold 41.6–91.6%, copper, zinc, silver, nickel
	Green gold	Gold 41.6–91.6%, silver, copper, zinc
	White gold	Gold 41.6–91.6%, copper, nickel, zinc
Monel metal	Silver	Copper 50%, nickel 50%
Nickel silver	Silver	Nickel 10–18%, zinc 17–20%, copper 62–65%
Pewter	Dark silver	Tin 91–93%, antimony 6–7%, copper 1–2%
Pinchbeck	Yellow	Copper 84%, zinc 16%
Platinum	Silver	Platinum 90%, iridium 10%
Precium I®	Silver	Silver 62.75%, palladium 25%, base metals 12.25%
Precium II®	Silver	Silver 68.75%, palladium 25%, base metals 6.25%
Silver solder (hard)	Silver	Silver, copper, zinc (varying amounts)
Slush metal	Gray	Lead, zinc (varying amounts)
Soft solder	Gray	Tin, lead (varying amounts)
Stainless steel	Silver	Iron 70–88%, chromium 12–20%, nickel 0–10%
Steel	Gray	Iron 99.2–99.4%, carbon 0.6–0.8%
White metal	Silvery white	Tin 89%, antimony 7.5%, copper 3.5%

powders effectively and efficiently with a minimum of energy and without metal waste. Metal powders are put into a die, shaped under high pressure, and passed through a furnace to set the shape permanently.

JOINING METALS AND ALLOYS

Metals and alloys that have been shaped are often joined together. **Welding** joins two pieces of metal together by heat and either hammering or pressure. Welded sections are as strong as the other parts of the metal or alloy. Aluminum cannot be welded.

Soldering unites two pieces of metal by the use of the alloy solder, which melts at a slightly lower temperature than the metal parts being joined. The joint is not as strong as welded joints.

A **rivet** is a thick pin or bolt that has a head on one side and a shank that is passed through a hole in each of the metals to be joined. Pots and pans may have handles attached by riveting.

Figure 15-3. *"Tin cans" are actually tinplated steel, made from a shallow cup (left), which is ironed, lengthened, and trimmed.*

3. Why are metals rarely used in their pure form? What are alloys?
4. What is plating? Name and describe the methods by which plating is accomplished.
5. What is meant by precious metals? Which metals are classified as precious metals?
6. What is meant by the following terms: 1/20 12K GF; 10K rolled-gold plate; and sterling silver?
7. What is pewter? What are its advantages?
8. What is steel? What is 18–8 stainless steel? What qualities does stainless steel have?
9. Explain the following: casting, rolling, drawing, and forging.
10. How are metals joined together? Explain each method used.

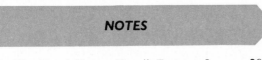

NOTES

1. "Lockheed Knows How," *Fortune*, January 28, 1980, pp. 4–5.
2. Walter Sullivan, "The Mystery of Damascus Steel Appears Solved," *The New York Times*, September 29, 1981, p. C1.
3. *Business Week*, August 7, 1978, p. 60.

DO YOU KNOW YOUR MERCHANDISE?

1. Name at least five important and familiar uses of metals.
2. Define ore, mineral, and element.

PUTTING YOUR MERCHANDISE KNOWLEDGE TO WORK

Assume you are selling a stainless steel copper-bottom pan to a customer. What features of the metals and alloys in the pan could you explain?

PROJECT

List and then analyze the markings on five metal objects that you own. Use such things as a watch, a watchband, a ring, a metal dish, flatware, or a fountain pen. What do the markings mean?

16

Lumber and Veneer:
The Universal-Use Products

Over 100,000 varieties of trees exist, but fewer than 100 types are used commercially in the United States. In addition to providing esthetic benefits, trees offer a rich source of natural materials for human needs: Lumber for houses, furniture, and home objects; wood for boats, carts, boxes, handles, and fuel for fireplace and stove. Wood is converted into paper, rayon and cellulosic plastics. Turpentine, resin, quinine, maple syrup, rubber, and tannic acid are important by-products of some trees, while others yield fruits or nuts.

HOW TREES GROW

Trees grow slowly. The **cambium layer** is the layer of wood just under the bark of the tree; it is composed of living cells that are constantly dividing and creating new bark and new wood. **Sapwood** is the new wood formed by the cambium layer; it is the living wood of the tree, which is normally lighter in color, contains more moisture, and is less compactly formed than the center portion of the tree. The **heartwood** is the darker, center portion of the tree that was once sapwood but has become inactive wood. This portion of the tree is more durable than sapwood and is more desirable for fine wooden products. The layer of wood produced by the tree's growth in a single year shows up as the **annual ring** (see Figure 16-1 on page 180).

Trees large enough for cutting into lumber are known as **saw timber.** Most trees require a minimum of 35 to 50 years to reach a useful size for harvesting. Thus, even if areas are reseeded or replanted, a great deal of time is needed before those new trees can be used. When trees are judged to be large enough to be useful, they are marked for cutting. Most trees are cut in the forests with power saws. Some very large trees are still felled by ax. The felled trees are cut into logs, most of which are sent to the lumber mill or the veneer mill, depending on their intended use. Some logs may be converted into paper, corrugated boxes, or other materials that require wood pulp; these will be sent to the pulp mill.

LUMBER

Lumber is sawed timber logs that have been cut into boards of various sizes. To be made into lumber, the cut tree must first be stripped of its bark and sawed into sections 1 inch or more in thickness. Wood can be sawed parallel to or at right angles to the annual ring. Annual rings show up as a series of irregular rings throughout the wood; the pattern of these rings in the sawed wood is known as **grain.** Thus, the method of sawing the wood affects the grain pattern. In the lumber mill the two methods of sawing are plain sawing and quarter sawing.

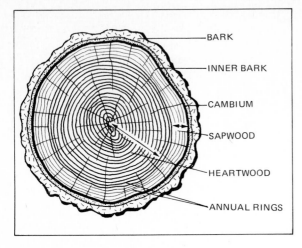

Figure 16-1. *Cross-section of a tree trunk.*

Plain-Sawed Lumber

When lumber is to be plain sawed, the wood with the bark stripped off is cut with large revolving saws that make about 25,000 revolutions per minute. As the strips of lumber are cut from the log, mechanical arms reach up and turn the log so that almost identical cuts can be made on a second, third, and fourth side. In this manner, the entire log, except for a small core section, can be cut. As there is little waste of the wood except for the sawdust from the cutting operation, this is an inexpensive method of cutting. Because the cut almost parallels the annual ring, the grain of the wood is cone shaped. Unfortunately, wood cut in this way is the most prone to warping, and therefore the wood is not very stable.

Quarter-Sawed Lumber

When lumber is to be quarter sawed, the logs must first be divided lengthwise into quarters, known as **flitches.** Each flitch is then set up on the sawing machine so that each slice of lumber is cut at right angles to the annual ring. This method produces less wood than the plain-sawing method and is therefore used less often. Quarter-

sawed wood has a straight grain that can have interesting designs, known as **flakes,** going across the face of the grain. The greatest advantage of quarter-sawed lumber is that it does not warp as readily as does plain-sawed lumber.

Seasoning

Even though quarter-sawed lumber is more resistant to warping than plain-sawed lumber, all lumber will warp and shrink to some degree. **Seasoning** is the process of slowly removing excess moisture from the lumber so that subsequent shrinking, splitting, and warping are greatly reduced. Seasoning may be accomplished by air drying or kiln drying.

Air drying of lumber is done by stacking the lumber in the lumber yard and allowing it to lose its excess moisture content over a period of time ranging from months to years, depending on the closeness of the grain of the wood, the thickness of the lumber, and the moisture present in the air. When air drying is complete, approximately

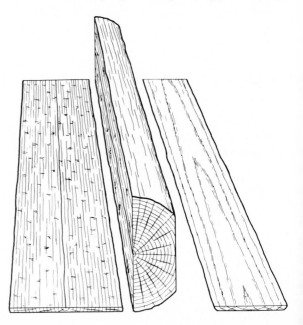

Figure 16-2. *Quarter-sawed lumber (left) is cut at right angles to the annual rings (see center). Plain-sawed lumber (right) is cut almost parallel to the annual rings.*

14 to 20 percent of the moisture content remains in the wood. Such wood is usable for products for which warping and shrinkage present few problems. Products to be used indoors or in dry climates need further drying.

Kiln drying means that the lumber has been dried in huge room-size ovens in which controlled humidity and temperature permit the excess moisture to be removed in a few days. Kiln-dried wood retains 6 to 12 percent of its moisture content and will resist warping and cracking even in centrally heated homes.

Sizes

Many methods of **sizing** lumber are used. Some familiar terms in reference to the size of lumber are as follows.

Board Foot: Lumber that is 1 inch thick, 1 foot wide, and 1 foot long, or lumber that has the equivalent volume in thicker, or wider, or longer sections.
Strips: Pieces that are less than 2 inches thick and 8 inches wide.
Boards: Sections that are less than 2 inches thick and 8 or more inches wide.
Dimension: All lumber from 2 inches up to, but not including, 5 inches thick and 4 or more inches wide.
Timbers: Lumber that is 5 inches or more in the smallest dimension.

Lumber that has been **planed** and **sanded** will be thinner and narrower than it was in its rough state. The reduction in dimension depends upon its size before planing.

Hardwoods are sold in their rough state. When referring to hardwoods, **dimension stock** refers to lumber cut to sizes to fit the finished product. By buying dimension stock, the furniture or other wood-using firm saves on shipping charges for excess lumber and waste in subsequent factory cutting.

Grading

The fewer the imperfections, the higher the grade of lumber and the more costly it will be.

The finest grades have no or only small defects. Poorer grades have increasing numbers of knots, discolorations, and spots that make the lumber less desirable, but still usable.

Standard grades of hardwood lumber are as follows.

- Top quality
  Firsts
  Seconds
- Second quality
  Selects
  No. 1 Common
- Poorer quality
  No. 2 Common
  No. 3A Common
  No. 3B Common

Standard grades of softwood lumber (see page 185) are as follows.

- Select

- Minor defects
  B
  C
  D

- Lower quality
  No. 1 Common
  No. 2 Common
  No. 3 Common
  No. 4 Common

Dimension lumber used in construction has different grade names for the higher quality material. Proper cutting of the lumber can eliminate obvious defects and make those portions usable.

VENEER

Any wood whose thickness is ³⁄₁₆ inch or thinner and whose log was cut in a veneer mill is referred to as **veneer**. Because sawing the wood into such thin sections would waste far too much of the wood, most veneers are obtained by carefully slicing sections of logs. To make the fibers of the wood pliable and soft so they can be sliced, the log with the bark removed is first soaked or steamed until it is saturated with moisture. It is

Figure 16-3. *Strips of veneer are sliced by machine, yielding adjacent sheets with similar grain patterns.*

then ready to be sliced by the rotary method, flat-cut method, or quarter-cut method.

Rotary cutting is achieved when the entire log is pressed against the sharp cutting blade as the log revolves. This results in a continuous strip of wood being cut that resembles peeling the log in one long, unbroken strip much as you would unwind a roll of tape. The grain of the wood shows up as cone-shaped figures known as **parabolas.** Such veneer is used for plywood paneling, plywood packing boxes, and hidden parts of furniture.

When a log is first cut in half and then revolved against the cutting blade, a **rotary-sliced** veneer is made. This has a similar pattern to rotary-cutting veneers except that each piece is the size of the outer half of the log from which it was cut. These are used for furniture surfaces and interior parts as well as for many industrial products.

Flat-cut veneers are also cut from half-logs. Instead of revolving the log against the knife, however, the blade moves up and down against the log, slicing it in a manner similar to slicing meat. These veneers have a center parabola with straight grain on each side of the center figure.

The most costly veneer is obtained by the **quarter-cut** method. To prepare the log for this

cutting, it must first be cut into quarters, making four wedge-shaped log sections. Each quarter of a log is separately mounted and sliced at right angles to the annual rings of the wood. This method of slicing yields a ribbonlike grain marking on the veneer that is used in costly woods for furniture and wooden articles with surface attractiveness.

Although veneer sections may be as thick as $\frac{3}{16}$ inch or as thin as $\frac{1}{200}$ inch, $\frac{1}{28}$- and $\frac{1}{36}$-inch veneers are the most frequently used for furniture surfaces. After the veneer strips are cut into easy-to-handle sizes, they are carefully dried and stacked so that matching sections are together.

Veneer Patterns

Because veneers may be sliced in a variety of directions, they reveal unique markings and grain patterns in some varieties of wood.

Butt: These swirled patterns are caused by the unusual grain structure formed by the joining of the root and the trunk of the tree. This is especially famous in walnut veneers.
Burl: Unusual growths on a tree cause these small oval and round markings. Walnut, redwood, and some rare woods exhibit these patterns.
Bird's Eye: This unusual tiny marking is believed to be caused by buds unable to break through the bark of the tree. It is peculiar to maple.
Crotch: Branches extending from the tree cause this beautiful V-shaped, featherlike pattern effect.
Fiddleback: Fine, wavy lines run crosswise at right angles to the regular grain markings. Mahogany and maple exhibit these unusual designs.
Mottle: A blurred figure is created by the grain running in various directions.
Stripe: Straight line effects in shadings of dark and light are seen in woods such as walnut, mahogany, zebrawood, and satinwood.

Matching Veneer Patterns

For unusual surface appearance of costly wooden products, attractively patterned veneers may be arranged to form unique designs. This is known as **matching.**

Figure 16-4. *Veneer slicing of American walnut. Left: rotary cut. Center: flat cut. Right: quarter-sliced.*

Book Matching: Adjacent veneers that come from the slicing machine are opened as are the pages of a book. Thus the design runs in opposite directions on the two adjacent veneers.

Slip Matching: The veneers are placed next to one another with their grain running in the same direction, thus repeating the pattern on each successive veneer.

End Matching: The top veneer is opened down, like note paper, and again, the design is reversed on the top and bottom veneer.

Four-way Matching: A combination of book and end matching is used. This gives a design that has a center motif that accentuates the angle of the veneer design.

Wedge Matching: The veneers to be used are first cut into pie-shaped pieces then fitted together.

Veneered Construction, Plywood, and Laminates

The next important step in veneering is to glue the thin veneer layer to the other layers of wood to form **plywood.** Most plywood has three, five, seven, or more layers. In three-ply wood, the two outside layers of veneer are bonded to an inner layer of veneer, called a **crossband,** or to a core of lumber in the center.

Veneered construction does not warp readily because the grains of the front and back veneers run at right angles to the grain of the crossband or core wood. As a result, the grains pull against each other and equalize tension, reducing the possibility of the wood's warping and cracking.

This is one of the salesperson's strongest selling points for veneered construction. Five-ply construction is stronger than three ply; seven ply is stronger than five ply, and so on. Five-ply veneer is the most common in plywood.

Laminated wood differs from plywood only in that the grains of the laminated wood panels, which are made from veneers or a combination with other materials, do not run at right angles to each other on the various layers. Laminates are usually bonded with plastics resins and compressed so that no warping takes place. Large structural beams of **glued-laminated wood (glu-lam)** are made up of parallel layers of bands and bonded, under pressure, with synthetic resin adhesives.

Gluing

Plywood is only as strong as the glue used to hold the various plies of wood together. If a poor-quality glue has been used, the veneer may come loose, crack, chip, or break, necessitating furniture refinishing. The difficulty of making repairs of surface damage to veneered furniture is one of its greatest disadvantages.

Furniture glues are of several types. **Animal glues** make good quality glues. They must, however, be heated when applied, and they are not waterproof. **Casein glue,** made from a milk base, is practically waterproof but more costly to use. **Plastic resin glues** for veneering, come in liquid form or in sheets that are bonded permanently to

Bird's eye maple.

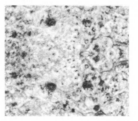

Curly maple.

Maple stumpwood.

Crotch mahogany.

Carpathian elm burl, 2-piece book matched.

Peroba fiddleback, 2-piece book matched.

❮ Book-matched mahogany.

Diamond-matched mahogany with satinwood border. ❯

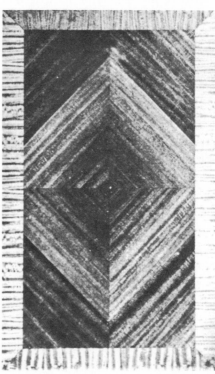

❯ ❯ Types of Veneer Patterns ❮ ❮

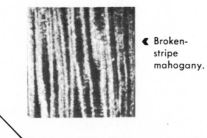

❮ Broken-stripe mahogany.

Figure 16-5. *Attractively patterned veneers may be arranged to form unique designs.*

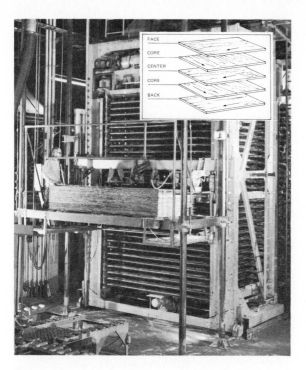

Figure 16-6. *Plywood is made by bonding veneer "sandwiches" in hot presses. To prevent warpage, the grains of the veneers run at right angles to each other.*

the various plies of wood. Some types are waterproof and will last indefinitely. Many require heat and pressure and are costly to use.

KINDS OF WOOD — HARDWOOD AND SOFTWOOD

One system of classifying trees divides them into hardwood trees and softwood trees. **Hardwoods** refer to trees with broad, flat leaves — trees that lose their leaves in the fall. The technical term for these trees is **deciduous.** The **softwoods** have pinelike needles and are known technically as **coniferous.**

Hardwoods

In comparison to softwoods, hardwoods generally have a more attractive grain pattern and a structure that permits them to hold glue, nails, or

screws more securely. Hardwoods also take a better polish and do not burn as rapidly as softwoods.

Many of the hardwoods used for furniture and other fine products are grown in the United States. Some of the more exotic hardwoods are imported. Some well-known domestic hardwoods are oak, ash, maple, and walnut; imported hardwoods are mahogany, rosewood, and ebony.

Hardwoods differ in the degrees of hardness of their woods. Table 16–1 classifies them by resistance to denting and scratching.

The following descriptions will aid you in recognizing some of the more frequently used hardwoods.

Ash.   Known as **white ash,** this famous baseball-bat wood has a straight grain, firmness, strength, moderate weight, good bending qualities and does not splinter easily. It is used for thick cutting blocks for butcher shops and for counter tops and tabletops. It is suitable wherever a clean-looking, strong white wood is needed.

Birch.   This wood is known as **yellow birch, silver birch,** and **sweet birch.** The heartwood of the tree is light yellow to reddish-brown, and the sapwood is almost white. Birch is one of the strongest, hardest woods. It polishes well, takes an attractive finish, and has a lustrous sheen. The smooth, close-grained surface of the wood gives enduring service. Because the wood tends to warp, it must be carefully seasoned. Birch is primarily used as veneer for doors and furniture. Solid wood furniture is also made from birch. Most toothpicks are made from the wood of the birch tree.

Ebony.   Often thought of as black in color, ebony actually is a very dark brown and may have lighter orange streaks. The wood is hard and heavy and takes a high polish that makes it usable for ornaments, handles, and piano keys.

Fruitwood.   Fruit-bearing trees, such as apple, cherry, olive, and pear trees, provide handsome, close-grained woods that are noted for their

Table 16-1 HARDWOODS

Type	Where Grown	Popular Uses
Harder Hardwoods		
Ash White ash	Throughout U.S. and Canada	Butcher blocks, counter and table tops
Birch Yellow, Silver, and sweet birch	U.S., especially New England, New York, Northern Michigan and Wisconsin	Solid wood furniture, veneers for doors and furniture, toothpicks
Ebony	Asia, Africa	Ornaments, handles, piano keys
Fruitwoods Apple, Cherry, Olive, Pear	Rare in U.S., Olive wood imported from France	Ornamental objects, cherry veneers
Hickory	Eastern U.S., Mexico	Hammer and ax handles, skis
Mahogany African	Central and South America	Furniture, musical instruments
mahogany	Ghana	

Philippine
  mahogany
  (luan)
	Philippines	Inexpensive flooring, cigar boxes

Northern maple	Vermont, New York, Michigan	Furniture, flooring, bobbins, spools, cue sticks, croquet balls, bowling pins, telephone cable terminals, aircraft construction, flooring, furniture
Oak	Throughout U.S.	Structural parts of frame buildings, flooring, furniture, railroad ties
White oak		Barrels, buckets
Rosewood	Brazil, India	Tools, instruments, brush backs, veneers
Softer Hardwoods		
Gumwood Red gum, black gum, tupelo	Southern U.S.	Furniture, railroad ties
Southern maple (soft, red, or silver maple)	Southern U.S.	Construction, flooring, furniture
Other softer hardwoods Aspen, basswood, yellow poplar	Throughout U.S.	Lower-priced furniture, hidden parts of better-quality furniture

beauty and coloring. Because these woods are not abundant, they are most often used for small ornamental objects, although some cherry wood veneer furniture is also produced. Olive wood has an interesting texture and streaked coloring.

Gumwood.   **Red gum, black gum,** and **tupelo,** are southern hardwoods used for furniture and railroad ties and as timber for ship building. Because of improved methods of seasoning, they are among the most widely used furniture woods. Red gum has a rosy hue and a smooth, uniformly grained surface. Black gum and tupelo are creamy in color and dent easily. Although gumwood is somewhat brittle, it is otherwise quite strong.

Hickory.   A hardwood that has toughness, strength, and resilience, hickory is used for hammer and ax handles and for skis and other sports equipment.

Mahogany.   **True mahogany** is a light brown wood with a slightly reddish cast, which is usually stained to resemble the appearance of woods that have aged for centuries. Beautiful patterns often mark the smooth surface of this rich-looking wood. Mahogany is also desirable because of its resistance to warping, its durability, and the ease with which it can be worked.

A related species of fine-quality wood from Ghana is **African mahogany.** Another wood from the Philippines that is not as good in quality but that has a similar color is sold under the name **Philippine mahogany,** or **luan.** Poorer qualities of this wood are used for floorings in Philippine huts and for cigar boxes; better qualities are used for the backs of musical instruments and for furniture.

Maple.   The wood most closely associated with the colonial period in America is **northern maple,** which colonial New Englanders used to make their furniture and floors. Because of its uniform texture and hardness, northern maple is now used for spools, bobbins, cue sticks, croquet balls, bowling pins, telephone-cable terminals,

and aircraft construction, as well as for fine maple furniture and flooring.

A second kind of maple is known as **soft, red,** or **silver maple.** It has a less close-grained appearance than the northern maple but possesses the same light color that adapts to bleaching or staining. It is used for construction, flooring, and furniture. Southern maple does not have the strength or heaviness of northern maple.

Oak.   Because oak is a rugged, sturdy-looking wood, it makes heavy, sturdy-looking objects. It is resilient and durable and can be used for structural parts of frame buildings, floorings, church pews, and railroad ties. Because it holds liquids well, **white oak** can be used for barrels and buckets. Oak is a pale-colored, coarse-grained wood that is hard and strong but splinters easily. It has a noticeable grain, which is revealed either by plain or quarter sawing.

Rosewood.   The heartwood of the rosewood tree has a magnificent grain and a dark, rich, reddish-black coloring. Because the wood is durable, it is used for tools, instruments, and brush backs. Because of its beauty, it is used for veneers for fine furniture.

Walnut and Butternut.   The walnut tree is known in the United States as the **black walnut,** in contrast to the **butternut tree,** which is known as the **white walnut.** Black walnut has rich brown shades, a smooth grain, and unusual patterns, making it suitable for veneered surfaces. Because it resists warping, carves beautifully, keeps its rich color without fading, becomes more beautiful with age and use, and is very strong, it is good for furniture construction. Because it holds its shape so well, it has been the ideal wood for gunstocks. Walnut is also one of the best-known cabinet woods. The butternut tree produces a softer, lighter wood and lacks the beauty of the black walnut's grain patterns.

Other Native Hardwoods.   Other woods that have industrial and furniture uses include

Table 16–2 SOFTWOODS

Major Types	Varieties	Popular Uses
Cedar	Western red	Paneling
	Eastern or aromatic red	Cedar chests, paneling
	Incense	Pencils, paneling
Fir	White	Home construction, railroad ties, boxes, cabinets
	Red or Douglas	Construction, marine piling, plywood
Pine	White	Boxes, crates, coffins, woodenware, matches, construction
	Northern	(Same as white pine)
	Western	Paneling and shelving
	Sugar	Industrial
	Yellow or southern	Flooring, turpentine, resin
	Ponderosa	Same as white pine
Redwood		Construction, outdoor furniture
Spruce	Red	Paper manufacture, construction, furniture, fencing, musical
	White	instruments, canoe paddles and oars
	Black	
	Sitka	

aspen, basswood, cottonwood, and yellow poplar. These may be found in lower-priced furniture for surface areas and in the hidden parts of better-quality furniture.

Softwoods

Although softwoods have fewer desirable qualities for many products than hardwoods, they are used far more extensively. Almost 80 percent of all woods used in the United States are softwoods. Their use as pulpwood for the paper mills and for various kinds of construction accounts for their greater popularity.

Cedar. Known as **western red cedar,** this is one of the most decay-resistant woods. Mature trees — from 200 to 500 years old — grow to a height of 80 to 140 feet and are as much as 5 feet in diameter. This wood is durable, holds nails well and is strong. It is attractive for paneling in rooms.

Another variety of cedar, known as **eastern** or **aromatic red cedar,** is used for closets and chests. This wood has an oil that vaporizes and destroys moth larvae, which eat hair and woolen fibers. Because the knots in the wood contain more of the oily substance, a cedar chest or cedar closet lined with knotty cedar will be more effective than one lined with plain cedar. Unless the wood is at least ¾ inch thick and the doors or drawers are kept tightly closed, the odor vapors will not be strong enough to kill the moth larvae. A light sanding once a year is also desirable to release additional oil odor.

Incense cedar is another important cedar. It is used in making pencils and paneling.

Fir. **White fir** trees grow to about 120 feet in height and 3 feet in diameter. The wood is used primarily for home and building construction, railroad ties, and boxes and crates. Better-quality woods may be used for cabinets, ironing boards, bookcases, and frames of upholstered furniture.

The wood of the white fir has moderate strength and stiffness, holds nails well, and is resistant to warping and twisting. It has a light color, which gives a clean appearance, and is lightweight, which makes it easy to handle.

Douglas fir, also known as **red fir** or **Oregon pine,** is not a true fir but has similar properties. It is hard and quite strong and is used extensively in construction and for marine piling and plywood.

Pine.   There are two main kinds of pine: white pine and yellow pine. **White pine** is also known as **northern white pine, western white pine,** and **sugar pine.** The northern variety grows in the northeastern and north-central states; the western pine comes mainly from Montana, Idaho, and Washington; and the sugar pine comes from California and southern Oregon.

The northern pine is lightweight, soft, even textured, and easily worked. It is resistant to warping and contains the least amount of resin. Western or Idaho white pine is similar to the northern variety except that it warps more. Its straight grain cuts easily. White pine is used for boxes, crates, coffins, woodenware, shade rollers, drawing boards, and matches, as well as construction. Western pine is used for paneling and shelving; while sugar pine has industrial uses.

Southern yellow pine is the name for longleaf, slash, shortleaf, and loblolly pines, which grow from Virginia to Texas. The harder ones can be used in flooring. The longleaf and slash pines produce the largest part of the world's supply of turpentine and resin. **Ponderosa pine,** although a yellow pine, resembles the white pine and is found in the Rocky Mountain states and along the Pacific Coast.

Redwood.   California redwoods are the largest trees growing in the United States. Some stumps of redwoods are large enough for dance floors, and some redwood trees have roads through them that accommodate automobiles. The redwood's unique chemical resistance to insects and decay makes it ideal for long-term use for the construction of towers, churches, farm structures, schools, and homes. The wood has a fine-grained structure and a reddish color. It also makes ideal outdoor furniture.

Spruce.   From the West come **red, white, black,** and **Sitka** spruce woods. Spruce has long fibers, which makes it desirable for paper manufacture. It has strength and stiffness, which enhance its use in construction. Spruce woods are also used for cabinet work, bleachers and grandstands, scaffolding, fencing, greenhouses, billboards and signs, ladder rails, canoe paddles, and oars. Because of its high resonant qualities, spruce is used for violin and piano sounding boards and for other structural parts of musical instruments.

WOOD COMPOSITIONS

Because of the increasing scarcity of wood, ways of using wood waste from lumber and plywood manufacture, as well as wood from diseased trees, have been developed.

Reconstituted wood is made from timber sliced into thin sheets, vat dyed to desired colors, and reassembled into "super longs" that are then cut into veneers that have no defects and that have uniformity of grain. Oak wood and trees from Africa have been reformed in this way.[1]

Particle board or **flake board** is made of wood chips and a special plastic resin that are mixed and compressed together under heat and pressure. This product is particularly useful as the core stock for veneered panels and doors, furniture, and decorative products. Particleboard is also used for drawer bottoms and backs of furniture. It has no grain and a porous appearance. Its main disadvantage is that it does not hold screws or nails well. However, it adheres well to layers of veneer and it does not warp or shrink.

Hardboard is a wood-fiber product that has no grain but that is compressed to form rigid panels of uniform density, strength, and stability. It is easily formed and shaped and is enduring. Its main uses in consumer goods are for furniture drawer bottoms and backs, panels for doors, walls, and counterfronts, and for house siding.

NOTES

1. Stanley Abercrombie, "Back to the Woods," *Interiors*, November 1979, pp. 84–85.

DO YOU KNOW YOUR MERCHANDISE?

1. In what ways are trees important to all of us?
2. What is meant by the term lumber. What is its minimum thickness?
3. What are the differences between plain-sawed and quarter-sawed lumber? Which is likely to give better service in use? Why?
4. Explain the differences between air drying and kiln drying of lumber. Which is better for use in centrally heated homes and apartments?
5. What is meant by veneer? How is it obtained? How is it used? What is veneered construction?
6. Define plywood. How is it made? What glues are successfully used to make it?
7. How do laminates differ from veneered construction?
8. Define hardwood, softwood, deciduous, coniferous.
9. Classify the following woods as hardwoods or softwoods and list one outstanding characteristic of each: oak, yellow pine, mahogany, gumwood, cedar, maple, walnut.
10. Why are some woods reconstituted? What is particleboard? How is it used?

PUTTING YOUR MERCHANDISE KNOWLEDGE TO WORK

A customer purchasing a chest of drawers in a store notices that hardboard rather than wood has been used for drawer bottoms. He questions you, as the salesperson, about its durability. What response would you give him?

PROJECT

Examine the woods in the various pieces of furniture in your home. Write a short report of the kinds of woods used and how they have performed in use.

UNIT FOUR

Apparel and Accessories

17

Children's Wear

Children today are exposed to advertising on television, on radio, and in the print media. They are often in the store at the time their clothes are purchased, know what they want, and express their wishes. However parents generally make the final selection. Many items of clothing are also purchased as gifts by grandparents, other relatives, and friends.

Parents may be especially aware of the styling and construction that are unique to children's clothing — the ways in which this clothing differs from clothing for adults. Because children often play hard, they need sturdy, well-constructed, good-quality clothes. Comfort is also important. And from an early age, children are fashion-conscious.

The needs of children change constantly as they grow from infancy to adolescence. These needs are reflected in the different kinds of clothing available in the various size ranges from infants' wear to toddlers' wear to preschoolers' wear, from girls' wear and boys' wear through subteen and prep wear.

CATEGORIES OF CHILDREN'S WEAR

Infants' clothing reflects the infant's primary clothing needs: warmth, comfort, and cleanliness. Toddlers who are learning to walk and crawl need clothes that will allow them to perform these functions without getting hurt. Preschool children are learning to dress themselves, so they need self-help features. Girls and boys between 6 and 12 years need clothes that will stand the rough wear of hard play. Children in the subteen and prep groups need school, everyday, and dress clothes that will express their increasing sense of fashion.

Infants' Wear

Clothing for infants must be warm, comfortable, and easy to keep clean. Garments should be made of fabrics that let moisture evaporate. Knitted fabrics are good choices since they provide warmth as well as ventilation.

Clothing should be roomy with plenty of room for diapers but not too bulky. Babies are most comfortable in clothes that are soft and supple. They do not usually like clothes that must be pulled over their heads, so infants' clothing often has zippered, snapped, or buttoned neck openings. Since infants grow quickly, salespeople should advise customers to purchase only what is needed for the current season.

The Layette. A collection of the articles needed by each individual baby is called a **layette**. It includes clothing and nonclothing items for an infant's wardrobe, nursery, bathing, feeding, and bedding needs (see Table 17–1).

LAYETTE ITEMS

SLEEPING GOWN

BIB

KIMONO

FRONT-CLOSING
UNDERSHIRT

ONE-PIECE SLEEPER
OR JUMPSUIT

SNAP-ON
WATERPROOF UNDERPANTS

SACQUE

BUNTING BAG

Figure 17-1. *A layette includes clothing items for an infant's wardrobe and feeding needs.*

Table 17-1 LAYETTE ITEMS

Clothing

6 slip-on or side-snap shirts

4 gowns or kimonos

2 saque sets

6 waterproof pants

4 stretch sleep 'n play sets, with room to grow

4 receiving blankets

2 blanket sleepers or sleep 'n grow bags

1 sweater set or cardigan, bonnet, and pair of booties

1 bunting suit, pair of booties, shawl

1–2 pairs of socks

Diapering

4–6 dozen cloth diapers, economical and comfortable

2 pkgs. disposable diapers, convenient

1 box diaper liners

4 sets safety pins with double locking safety heads

1 pkg. Towelettes

1 diaper pail

1 diaper stacker

1 diaper bag

3 waterproof lap pads

Bedding

2 crib blankets

4 to 5 fitted sheets

2 to 3 waterproof sheets or mattress covers

4 waterproof pads (flannelette coated)

1 crib bumper

1 comforter

Bath and Health Care Items

3 bath towels

6 washcloths

1 portable bathtub and basin
1 each soap, lotion, cream, ointment, oil, talcum powder, shampoo, cotton balls, and swabs

1 pair nail scissors

1 brush and comb

1 baby thermometer

Bottle Feeding

1 presterilized disposable nurser kit

8 8-ounce bottles plus sterilizer, standard or electrical

4 4-ounce bottles

1 electric bottle warmer

Extra nipples and caps

1 bottle brush

Breast Feeding

Breast feeding kit, bottles, bottle brush, cream, shields

2–3 bottles for water or juice

Other Feeding Items

1 feeding dish

1 warming dish

1 baby spoon

1 training cup

2–3 bibs

Furniture and Equipment

Crib

Waterproof mattress

Chest of drawers

Dressing table

Hamper

Bassinet

Scale and pad

Nursery lamp

Highchair

Playpen and pad

Exerciser

Portable swing

Toilet seat or chair

Toy box and toys

Safety gate

Outings

Carriage

Stroller

Car seat

One of the most popular items of infants' wear is the **jumpsuit.** It comes in different weights, depending on the season, and may have a hood for cool and cold weather. For comfort jumpsuits are made of a stretch yarn, often polyester or nylon. A selling point is that one size could fit a baby from birth until the baby is a few months old. Another one-piece garment that covers most of a baby's body is the **coverall.** It is styled like the coveralls worn by automotive mechanics.

Starting at 2 to 3 months of age, baby girls wear smock-type blouses or polo shirts with tights. Baby boys wear short or long sleeve polo shirts or T-shirts with tights. Older infants wear **overalls,** which are pants with attached bibs and straps over the shoulder. Overalls and other pants for infants usually have snap crotches and inseams to make changing diapers easier.

Shirts for babies are available in several styles. For newborn babies they usually have front openings and tie or snap fastenings. For babies over 6 months, they usually slip over the head and have large necklines or snap closures.

Although babies can sleep easily in most of their clothes, **nightgowns** that extend from the neck to just below the feet are sold. The gown may have mitten sleeves that flip over the hands like pockets for warmth and a drawstring hem. **Sleeping bags,** also called **blanket sleepers** or **sleep 'n grow bags,** are warmer than nightgowns. They are usually made of brushed knit, with a bag bottom, shirt top, and zipper closing.

For outdoor warmth, babies wear one-piece **snowsuits** or **buntings,** large envelopes with attached hoods. The snowsuit, which has arms and legs, may have bootee feet and extra long sleeves that may be pulled down as mittens. These garments are made of smooth nylon with quilted lining or acrylic fleece with acrylic trimming.

Between seasons babies wear **sweater sets** consisting of a cap, sweater, and booties or **sacque sets,** consisting of a jacket, snap-fastened pants with elasticized waist and legs, a bonnet or cap, and booties.

Another garment that is frequently part of an infant's wardrobe is a **kimono,** which is a loose-

CLOTHING FOR INFANTS AND CHILDREN

ETON SUIT

OVERALLS

SNOWSUIT

COVERALLS

PINAFORE

SMOCK–TYPE BLOUSE AND TIGHTS

SUNSUIT

ROMPERS

Figure 17-2. *Note the straps, large waists, elastic bands, and adjustable gathers in these items for toddlers.*

fitting garment with raglan sleeves and open down the front. A two-piece **creeper** is a short or long pant with overall top and snap crotch that is often matched to a shirt.

All infant garments must be cut full enough to go over diapers as well as all-plastic or plastic-coated nylon **baby pants.**

Diapers. Although convenient disposable diapers are preferred by most parents, cloth diapers are less expensive and can be used over again. Most cloth diapers are 100 percent cotton to ensure nonirritating comfort and softness. The diapers are available in two weaves — birdseye and gauze. Birdseye diapers are tightly woven. Gauze diapers are more absorbent and softer and cost more.

Diapers are available in flat or prefolded styles. Flat diapers allow extra folds where they are needed and can be adjusted to fit a growing baby. Prefolded diapers put extra layers where they are needed and save folding time. They are not adjustable and are more expensive.

Sizes. Those buying clothes for infants should always bear in mind that infants have large heads and big waists. When buying in advance of the season the clothing will be worn, it is necessary to project the size of the child, especially for infant gifts.

Babies generally wear **infants' sizes** from the time they are born until they start walking. There are two generally accepted methods for sizing infants' clothing. Table 17–2 shows baby sizes 3 to 36 months, with corresponding average height and weight. Remember that these heights and weights are only *averages* and individual babies will vary from them.

Table 17–3 shows baby sizes small through extra large, with corresponding height and weight.

Toddlers' Wear

When infants are 1 to $2\frac{1}{2}$ years old and begin to walk, they are **toddlers.** Their clothing is then bought in the children's department.

Table 17–2 INFANT SIZES BY AGE

Size (Months)	Height	Weight
3	24	13
6	$26\frac{1}{2}$	18
12	29	22
18	$31\frac{1}{2}$	26
24	34	29
36	$36\frac{1}{2}$	32

Table 17–3 INFANT SIZES FROM NEWBORN TO XL

Size	Height	Weight
Newborn 0–3	$25\frac{1}{2}$	14
S 0–9	$25\frac{1}{2}$–$27\frac{1}{2}$	15–19
M 12–18	28–32	20–26
L 24–30	$32\frac{1}{2}$–$36\frac{1}{2}$	27–32
XL 36	37–$38\frac{1}{2}$	33–36

Toddlers' sizes range from 1 to 4. Table 17–4 shows the relationship between these sizes and the height of the child.

Toddler clothes are for the walking child in diapers or **training pants** — thick underpants for the toilet-train period. Toddler clothes, like infant clothes, must fit over the diapers and training pants. Pants should have a snap crotch and inseam to permit easy diaper changes. Toddler shirts often have loops on the shoulders to hold the straps of overalls, creepers, and other bottoms.

Table 17–4 TODDLER SIZES

Size	Height (inches)
1T	$29\frac{1}{2}$-32
2T	$32\frac{1}{2}$-35
3T	$35\frac{1}{2}$-38
4T	$38\frac{1}{2}$-41

Toddlers have large waists and short legs. Therefore, their clothing is wider at the waist and shorter in the legs than clothing for older children, reflecting the difference in body proportions of the two age groups.

Toddlers' clothing is often made with straps or suspenders that are adjustable as the child grows. Other growth features of toddler and older children's clothing are as follows.

- Deep hems on skirts
- Raglan, kimono, or no sleeves; deep-cut armholes
- Dresses with undefined waistlines
- Long tail on shirts and blouses
- Wide seam allowances
- Elastic bands in sleeves and waists of pants, skirts, and shorts
- Stretch or knitted fabrics
- Cuffs
- Tucks that can be let out
- Pleats or gathers that can be adjusted
- Two sets of large snaps on waistlines of two-piece outfits
- Two-piece outfits and separates

Play and Everyday Clothes.   Both boy and girl toddlers wear pants or tights and tops. Pants are either long or short, depending on the season. Toddlers wear one-piece jumpsuits and overalls. Knit tops or pullovers are favorite gar-

ments for both boys and girls. Blouses for girls and shirts for boys come in many styles. T-shirts are popular for this age group, especially those imprinted with cartoon characters and other similar decorations. Jeans have become popular for toddlers, and there are even designer jeans for this age group.

In summer, **sunsuits,** short one-piece garments, are popular for boys and girls. Sometimes girls' sunsuits are modified into **rompers,** which are bloomerlike panties and elasticized leg openings.

Toddlers often wear sleepers with gripper feet in them. The fabric of the sleeper is usually heavy so that the toddler will stay warm. In cool weather, toddlers wear undershirts, sweaters, sweatshirts, or jackets. In winter, they wear **snowsuits,** which consist of matching snug jackets and pants, often with ribbing at the wrists and ankles to keep out the cold air.

Dress Clothing.   Dress clothing for girls includes short dresses, smocks, jumpers with blouses, and dresses with **pinafores,** sleeveless, apronlike covering garments, often with ruffled armholes and sashes. **Smocking,** a way of gathering cloth into regularly placed tucks with fancy stitching, is a popular decorative feature on dress-up clothing for this and other age groups. Another popular decorative feature is the **appliqué,** a cut-out piece of material laid on or fastened to a larger piece of the same or different material.

Dress clothing for boys includes long or short pants and a shirt and jacket. The **Eton suit,** which consists of a short, boxy, collarless jacket, usually of gray flannel, and matching shorts, is popular for this age group. It is generally worn with a short-sleeved, wide-collared shirt.

Moving toward Clothing Independence. As a child matures from infancy through toddlerhood to the preschool years, his or her ability to dress himself or herself increases. Newborns can do nothing for themselves, of course. Five-year-olds can dress themselves completely, although

Table 17–5 RATE OF PROGRESS CHART

Age of Child	Things Child Can Do
1 year	Shows an interest in taking off hat, shoes, and pants. Cooperates in dressing. Puts arm in armhole or extends leg for pants.
18 months	Removes mittens, hats, and socks. Unzips zipper. Cooperates in dressing.
2 years	Removes shoes, stockings, and pants. Likes to undress. Can put on some clothes; however, may put both legs in one pant leg and may get hat on backwards.
$2\frac{1}{2}$ years	Better at undressing than dressing; can take off all clothes. Can put on socks and perhaps shirt, pants, and coat, although not always accurately. May need encouragement.
3 years	Undresses rapidly and well. Can put on pants, socks, shoes, sweaters, and dress. Can unbutton front and side buttons. Cannot tell front from back or lace shoes, but may try.
4 years	Begins to distinguish front from back. Can lace shoes. May button front buttons.
5 years	Dresses self completely, lacing shoes, and buttoning front buttons. May not be able to tie shoes. Adult needs to select clothes and lay them out.

Source: Gessell, Arnold, *The First Five Years of Life*, A Guide to the Study of the Pre-School Child, New York: Harper & Row, Publishers, 1940.

they may not be able to tie their shoes. Table 17–5 shows the child's progress toward independence during the first five years of life.

Preschool Wear

Children usually pass from the toddler to preschool age group sometime after the age of $2\frac{1}{2}$. Features such as comfort, durability, and safety are important.

Sizes. Preschool sizes generally range from 2 to 6X. Table 17–6 shows the relationship of preschool sizes with five different body measurements.

The Preschool Wardrobe. Because children outgrow clothing rapidly, those purchasing their wardrobes will probably wish to minimize the expense of maintaining them. Children's wardrobes need not be large. Easy-care features permit quick and frequent laundering and rewearing.

Many of the styles worn by preschool children are similar to those worn by toddlers. Overalls, suspender pants, jumpsuits, T-shirts, and jeans are popular everyday clothes. Girls' party dresses may be trimmed with frills, ruffles, or lace. The Eton suit is a classic item for boys' dress-up wear. Other dress-up items for boys include short jackets or blazers, long or short pants, and woven or knitted shirts.

Preschool outerwear consists of ski suits, coats, water-repellent jackets, raincoats, hats, caps, and sweaters, depending on the season.

Self-Help Features. Since preschool children are learning to dress themselves, they like clothes that are easy to put on and take off. Clothes should have conveniently placed, easy-to-operate fastenings and large neck, arm, and leg openings. Slipover garments should have stretch or easy-to-open necklines. Clothes should be simply styled, with easily distinguishable fronts and backs. Stretch fabrics, elastic waistbands, suspenders, and pull-on pants and shirts are helpful features. All belts, sashes, and bows should be

Table 17–6 PRESCHOOL SIZES

	2	3	4	5	6	6X
Height	34	37	40	43	46	48
Weight	29	34	38	44	49	54
Chest	21	22	23	24	25	$25\frac{1}{2}$
Waist	$20\frac{1}{2}$	21	$21\frac{1}{2}$	22	$22\frac{1}{2}$	23
Hips	$21\frac{1}{2}$	$22\frac{1}{2}$	$23\frac{1}{2}$	$24\frac{1}{2}$	$25\frac{1}{2}$	$26\frac{1}{2}$

attached to their garments. Sleeves should be loose and buttonless. If there are buttons, they should be flat, smooth, slightly grooved, and of medium size. Buttonholes should be large.

Comfort. Children need freedom of motion almost from birth. Their clothing should reflect the fact that they crawl, walk, and perform more complex movements. Children will enjoy freedom of movement if their clothes have the following features.

- Proper fit
- Light weight
- Simple design with minimum trim
- Stretch or knit fabrics that give and are soft and absorbent
- No binding, rubbing, or pulling elements
- Correct length trousers and sleeves
- Correct fullness for bending and stooping
- Wide shoulder straps
- Loops on shoulders of shirts to keep trouser straps from slipping
- Elasticized waistbands

Durability. Clothes for active preschoolers will last longer if they are reinforced at points of wear. For example, pants can be reinforced with knee patches, and shirts can be reinforced with elbow patches. Double stitching at the crotch, pockets, buttonholes, and under the arms will make the garments more durable.

Safety Features. The most important safety features are flame-retardant fabrics, particularly for sleepwear, and light, bright colors for rainy and foggy-day clothing so children can easily be seen by motorists. Other safety features are attached hoods that turn when children turn and cannot catch on large objects to cause neck or back injuries; flat pockets that cannot catch during play; secure shoulder straps that cannot slip off a child's shoulder to restrain arm movement that would prevent a fall; long pants to protect knees; and trims and designs that will not catch or hang on door knobs, car door handles, and other protuberances.

To be avoided are large cuffs, long shoe laces or garments, large or loose sleeves, drawstring necklines, big bows, loose sashes, hood snaps that release when caught, and fasteners that can be swallowed.

Girls' and Boys' Wear

When children reach school age, their clothes are purchased in the girls' or boys' department, where sizes run from 7 to 16 for girls and 6 to 20 for boys.

School and Everyday Clothes. Boys and girls wear pants and jeans for play and school. Girls also wear dresses or jumpers and blouses.

Table 17–7 GIRLS' SIZES

		7	8	10	12	14	16
Height		51	53	55	57½	60	63
Chest	S	24½	25½	27	28½	30	31½
	R	26	27	28½	30	31½	33
	C	28½	29½	31	32½	34	35½
Waist	S	20½	21	22	23	24	25
	R	22½	23	24	25	26	27
	C	26	26½	27½	28½	29½	30½
Hip	S	25¾	26¾	28¼	32	34	34¼
	R	27½	28½	30	32¼	34¼	35¼
	C	30½	31½	33	35	37	39
Weight	S	53	59	67	77	89	103
	R	60	67	74–83	84–95	96–107	112
	C	71	79	89	102	116	132

Boys wear polo shirts, crew-neck knitted shirts, woven sport shirts, and pants.

During cold weather, school children wear jackets (often ski jackets) and pants. Lined and unlined nylon jackets, as well as sweaters, sweatshirts, and bright shiny slicker-type raincoats are popular. Many children wear quilted nylon vests in bright colors.

Activewear. The athletic look is popular with children, as it is with adults and teenagers. Warm-up and exercise suits, of knitted material, are usually brightly colored and may be decorated with stripes of contrasting colors or whimsical appliqués of fruits, vegetables, animals, or cartoon figures.

The dance look is almost as popular as the athletic look — especially among girls. Like teenagers and young adults, girls wear a wide variety of brightly colored leotards with color-coordinated tights. Over the tights they may wear knitted leg warmers, which keep legs warm in cold weather, as well as serving a decorative function. Leotards and tights may also be worn under skirts.

Dressing up. For special occasions, boys wear blazers or sport jackets and color-coordinated slacks and shirts. Girls wear party dresses, which may be trimmed with ruffles, lace, appliqué, or smocking. Girls may also wear long dresses or skirts, or long dressy pants.

Dressy coats for girls or boys are usually classic style wool coats and may have velvet accents at the neck, cuffs, and pockets.

Sizes. There are three categories of girls' sizes: regular (R), slim (S), and chubby (C). Girls' measurements (bust, waist, hips) as well as height and weight are considered. The size range is from 7 to 16, as shown in Table 17–7.

Boys' sizes are categorized as slim, regular, and husky. Height and weight as well as chest, waist, and hip measurements are considered, as shown in Table 17–8 on page 202. The **inseam** is the length from the crotch to the bottom of the trouser.

By the age of 6, a child's rate of physical growth has begun to slow down. However, all children do not develop in the same way nor at the same rate. There are great variations in body build; some youngsters are tall and slim, others

Table 17–8 BOYS' SIZES

		6	8	10	12	14	16	18	20
Height		46	50	54	58	61	64	66	68
Inseam		19	$21\frac{1}{2}$	24	$26\frac{1}{2}$	28	29	30	$31\frac{1}{2}$
Chest	S	$23\frac{1}{4}$	$25\frac{1}{2}$	$26\frac{3}{4}$	$28\frac{1}{2}$	30	$31\frac{1}{2}$	33	$34\frac{1}{2}$
	R	$24\frac{1}{2}$	$26\frac{1}{2}$	28	$29\frac{1}{2}$	$31\frac{1}{2}$	33	$34\frac{1}{2}$	36
	H	26	$27\frac{1}{2}$	29	31	33	35	$36\frac{1}{2}$	38
Waist	S	$20\frac{1}{2}$	$21\frac{1}{2}$	$22\frac{1}{2}$	$23\frac{1}{2}$	$24\frac{1}{2}$	$25\frac{1}{2}$	$26\frac{1}{2}$	$27\frac{1}{2}$
	R	$22\frac{1}{2}$	$23\frac{1}{2}$	$24\frac{1}{2}$	$25\frac{1}{2}$	$26\frac{1}{2}$	$27\frac{1}{2}$	$28\frac{1}{2}$	$29\frac{1}{2}$
	H	$24\frac{1}{2}$	$25\frac{1}{2}$	$26\frac{1}{2}$	$27\frac{1}{2}$	29	30	31	36
Weight	S	43	53	65	77	90	104	115	126
	R	49	59	73	87	100	115	126	138
	H	55	67	81	95	112	130	143	156

are tall and heavy, or short and slim, or short and stocky.

It is important to remember that children from ages 6 through 12 are quite active and participate in strenuous sports that involve the vigorous use of arms and legs. As a result, both the garment style and the fabric must be able to withstand the strain of hard wear. Garments must also fit properly and allow for muscular activities. Poor fit is the most frequent complaint of children who refuse to wear certain articles of clothing. Any child will feel uncomfortable in clothes that are too large, too small, too short, or too long.

Fashion Consciousness. By the time children reach school age, they often want to help select their own clothing. Wearing clothes they like and feel comfortable in is important to them. In addition, peer acceptance is essential, and dressing like other children in their group helps children achieve that acceptance.

Children's clothing selected to enhance a child's emotional security as well as physical comfort can contribute to the development of a healthy, self-confident personality in a number of ways:

- The child learns freedom from self-consciousness;
- The child develops a feeling of "belonging," of being part of a group without appearing different, strange, or unwanted;
- The child explores the world through touch, sight, and the other senses as the color, feel, and other attributes of clothing are experienced;
- The child develops a sense of ownership and responsibility;
- The child develops decision-making ability by learning to make wise color selections and recognizing color coordination;
- The child discovers and acts out the interior world of make-believe through dressing up in various ways.

Children's ideas about what clothing is desirable to wear are more apt to come from peers, older children, teen-agers, and young adults than from their parents. The influence by the media is also strong. Clothing and nonclothing products are imprinted with popular characters from cartoons, movies, TV, and sports. The creators of these characters usually license their use to a

Table 17–9 SUBTEEN SIZES

Size	Height (Inches)	Weight (Pounds)	Bust (Inches)	Waist (Inches)	Hips (Inches)
6	$57\frac{1}{2}$	69	27	$22\frac{1}{2}$	28
8	$58\frac{1}{2}$	79	$28\frac{1}{2}$	$23\frac{1}{2}$	30
10	$59\frac{1}{2}$	89	30	$24\frac{1}{2}$	32
12	$60\frac{1}{2}$	99	$31\frac{1}{2}$	$25\frac{1}{2}$	34
14	$61\frac{1}{2}$	109	33	$26\frac{1}{2}$	36

wide range of manufacturing firms. Characters popular in the early 1980s included Snoopy, Strawberry Shortcake, the Smurfs, and Mickey Mouse and other Walt Disney characters.

Subteens and Preps

Subteens and preps — girls and boys, respectively, between the ages of 12 and 15, care a great deal about how they look. They are conscious of labels and brands and are very much aware of the latest fads and fashions. They want to select their own clothes and often pay for purchases with money they have earned at such jobs as babysitting or delivering newspapers.

School and Everyday Clothes. Two favorites of subteens and preps are denim and twill, not only in the classic blue and khaki but in other solid colors as well. Designer and designer-look jeans are very popular. Young teenagers also wear separates and coordinates. The layered look is favored by both boys and girls. For example, a young teenage boy might wear a vest over a plaid flannel shirt over a thermal shirt or turtleneck, color coordinating all of these layers with the pants.

Work clothes or clothes derived from work clothes, such as painter's pants in bright colors coordinated with matching tops or overalls in classic blue or bright-colored denim coordinated with tops, are popular.

School clothes for this age group may be casual — jeans and corduroys — or slightly dressier. Each school has its norms and its criteria for peer acceptance. Girls may wear wool skirts with sweaters or cotton or polyester shirts or blouses, or jumpers with blouses or sweaters. Boys may wear wool-blend flannel slacks, color-coordinated sports or dress shirts, and sweaters.

Activewear. The athletic look is popular with preps and subteens. Warm-up suits, exercise suits, running shorts, leotards, tights, and leg-warmers are worn.

Outdoor Clothing. Everyday winter coats for subteens and preps include ski jackets, quilted nylon vests, duffel coats, and pea coats. Dressier coats include trench and wrap styles, reefers, and Chesterfields. Particularly popular is the all-weather coat. Subteens and preps tend to choose coats and jackets that are similar to those seen on older teenagers, peers, and young adults.

For rainwear, subteens and preps wear water-repellent trench coats, slickers, or ponchos.

Dress Clothes. Young teenage boys wear color-coordinated separates, which include a blazer, vest, and matching or coordinating pants.

Table 17–10 PREP SIZES

Waist (Inches)	25	26	27	28	29	30
Short inseam (Inches)	27	28	28	28	29	29
Medium inseam (Inches)	28	29	29	29	30	30
Long inseam (Inches)	29	30	30	30	31	31
Extra long inseam (Inches)			31	31	32	32

These can be dressed up with a shirt and tie or dressed down with a sport shirt or turtleneck. The navy blazer and the vested suit in a dark or muted color such as navy or gray and fabrics such as tweed or flannel are classics.

Young teenage girls wear simple dresses and tailored outfits. If they have jobs, they may wear shirtdresses or coordinated skirt and blouse outfits. They may want party or prom dresses of fabrics and styles similar to those of grown-up dresses but in softer colors and with girlish features such as puffed sleeves. The shiny, glittery, or glossy leotard with matching skirt or pants is popular with this age group.

Sizes. Growth is extremely uneven for people in the early teenage group. If a young teenage girl finds that subteen styles do not fit properly, she should look into the junior, petite junior, tall junior, and misses size ranges. A young teenage boy who finds that prep styles do not fit properly, should try the men's sizes. Tables 17–9 and 17–10 show the sizes available in subteen and prep clothing.

CHILDREN'S ACCESSORIES

Children's accessories departments contain fashion items such as sleepwear, underwear, hosiery, and shoes, as well as nonfashion items, such as toys, books, stuffed animals, jewelry, cosmetics, hats, and belts.

Merchandise sold in accessories departments may bear the imprints of popular characters from television shows. For example, in one year available Muppet products included telephones, children's luggage, party goods, sneakers, sheets, lunch boxes, posters, umbrellas, notebooks, and watches. These items coordinated with Muppet fashion items such as T-shirts, found in the children's clothing department.

Sleepwear

Children's sleepwear tends to be bright, colorful, and fun to wear. It may bear a licensed character such as Snoopy or may be printed with flowers, stripes, animals, or other cheerful motifs.

Toddlers wear one- or two-piece pajamas or blanket sleepers. Girls above the toddler age wear pajamas or nightgowns; the length depends on the fashion and the season. Boys usually prefer pajamas. All children's sleepwear from sizes 0 to 6X must pass a flame-retardancy test that meets a standard set by the Consumer Product Safety Commission.

Underwear

Underwear for toddlers consists of knitted T-shirts or sleeveless undershirts and knitted training pants. Knit fabrics are also used for older children because of their stretch and comfort features. Blended fabrics, for example, a 50 percent cotton, 30 percent polyester, 20 percent nylon blend, have the softness and absorbency of cotton and the strength and durability of polyester and nylon. This blend keeps its shape better than all-cotton fabrics and can be machine washed and dried easily.

Preschool children wear sleeveless shirts or short sleeve T-shirts. Girls wear banded- or ruffled-leg panties, which may be trimmed with lace, and cotton or polyester/cotton blend slips. Most slips are permanent press — an important selling point. Boys wear knitted cotton or polyester/cotton briefs and undershirts or T-shirts.

Much underwear for children is decorative. For example, some matching undershirt and pant combinations reproduce the famous costumes of cartoon-strip superheroes. Bright colors and patterns such as stripes and polka-dots and the imprint of licensed characters are popular. For warmth, children wear thermal underwear.

Subteens and preps may choose underwear that is a small version of adults' underwear. Some girls wear **training bras** at a young age. This bra has small but stretchable cups. For subteens, matching bra and panty sets are available in soft colors and fabrics; they are often trimmed with lace or ribbons or have patterns such as stripes or polka dots in sophisticated color combinations.

Hosiery

Boys and girls wear ankle, crew (calf-length), or knee socks. Girls sometimes wear nylon tights that cover the body from the waist to the toes. Socks come in a variety of blends: cotton/nylon is soft and resists shrinkage and abrasion; stretch nylon/acrylic is soft, cushiony, and can fit several foot sizes; acrylic/spandex keeps its shape and fit. Double-knit soles and heels with nylon-reinforced toes provide added duability.

Contemporary children's hosiery has a strong decorative element. Socks are color coordinated with outfits and may be striped in bright colors or have dots, circles, or checks. Some boys' socks have colored numerals.

SELLING POINTS OF INFANTS' AND CHILDREN'S WEAR

Clothing requirements of children vary with their stages and rates of growth and development. Yet certain features are desirable for all children. Clothing should provide freedom of movement, protection from severe weather, and room for growth. Also important are safety, durability, comfort, growth, and self-help features. Parents may be particularly concerned about ease of care, proper fit, and quality workmanship (discussed below). Children may be concerned about fashion.

Ease of Care

To most parents, **ease of care** means machine washable and machine or drip dryable with little or no ironing. **Durable press** is an important feature because it means clothing does not have to be ironed, will keep its shape for the wear life of the garment, and will retain sharp creases.

Much of children's clothing is made from cotton, manmade fibers, or wool. Cotton is popular because it is soft and absorbent, washable, and needs no ironing if it is knitted or marked permanent press.

Manmade fiber fabrics such as polyester, acrylic, nylon, rayon, and acetate are being used more because of their minimum-care features. These fibers are used either alone or in blends. Most are machine washable, machine dryable, and require no ironing. Wool is often blended with manmade fibers.

Proper Fit

Knowing a child's weight and measurements can help salespeople determine his or her correct size. A tape measure is the best tool for measuring the child's chest, waist, hips, and height. Length from the nape of the neck to the waist, arm length, and inseam (inner trouser leg) measurements can provide added data for proper fit. These measurements are especially important in boys' clothing.

Each manufacturer cuts differently even within the same size. Knowing these differences can enable a salesperson to aid in selecting garments that suit the child.

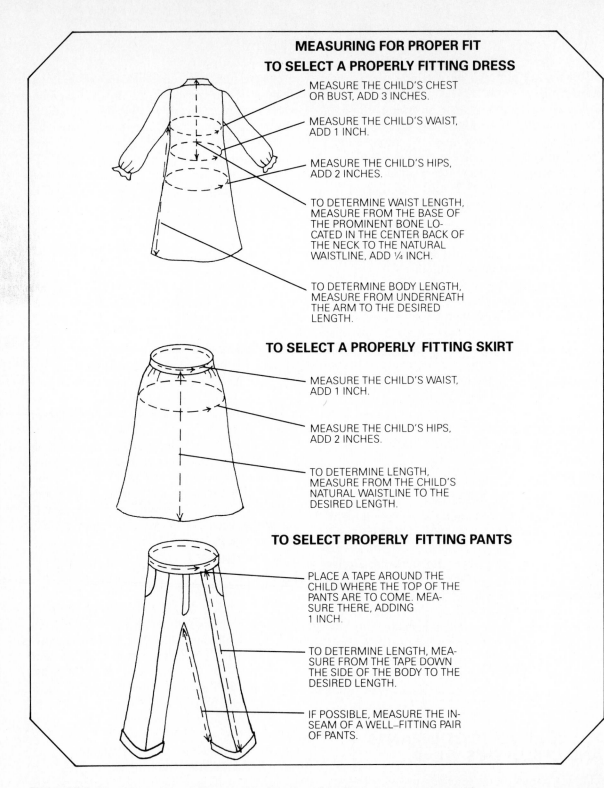

MEASURING FOR PROPER FIT

TO SELECT A PROPERLY FITTING DRESS

MEASURE THE CHILD'S CHEST OR BUST, ADD 3 INCHES.

MEASURE THE CHILD'S WAIST, ADD 1 INCH.

MEASURE THE CHILD'S HIPS, ADD 2 INCHES.

TO DETERMINE WAIST LENGTH, MEASURE FROM THE BASE OF THE PROMINENT BONE LOCATED IN THE CENTER BACK OF THE NECK TO THE NATURAL WAISTLINE, ADD ¼ INCH.

TO DETERMINE BODY LENGTH, MEASURE FROM UNDERNEATH THE ARM TO THE DESIRED LENGTH.

TO SELECT A PROPERLY FITTING SKIRT

MEASURE THE CHILD'S WAIST, ADD 1 INCH.

MEASURE THE CHILD'S HIPS, ADD 2 INCHES.

TO DETERMINE LENGTH, MEASURE FROM THE CHILD'S NATURAL WAISTLINE TO THE DESIRED LENGTH.

TO SELECT PROPERLY FITTING PANTS

PLACE A TAPE AROUND THE CHILD WHERE THE TOP OF THE PANTS ARE TO COME. MEASURE THERE, ADDING 1 INCH.

TO DETERMINE LENGTH, MEASURE FROM THE TAPE DOWN THE SIDE OF THE BODY TO THE DESIRED LENGTH.

IF POSSIBLE, MEASURE THE INSEAM OF A WELL–FITTING PAIR OF PANTS.

Figure 17-3. *The right size for a child is judged by fit and comfort. Check these points for good fit.*

Before a garment is chosen for a child, the following checks for good fit should be made:

- Examine the neckline. Is the collar low enough in the front to be comfortable and snug enough in the back so that it will neither ride up nor slip down? Look for gapping or binding that may cause irritation.
- Examine the shoulders. They should be wide and roomy enough for free arm movement, yet not so fully cut that shoulder seams will not stay in place.
- Examine the sleeves. Roomy sleeves that will not restrict movement and pull out with strain are preferred. Cuffs should be slightly loose.
- Examine the waistline. Slight looseness will allow for growth and longer wear. Elastic part of the way around will help the garment to adjust to growth. But the elastic should never be tight enough to cause red marks.
- Examine the length. Shirts and blouses should be long enough to tuck in at the waist and stay tucked in. Avoid overlong slacks and trousers that may cause the wearer to trip. Look for generous hems that will permit lengthening.
- Examine the roominess. If the garment will be worn over other clothing be sure there is adequate room.

The right size for a child is judged by fit and comfort. It is best that the child tries on a garment before it is purchased. In a properly fitting garment, a child should be able to sit, stoop, bend, reach, and stretch easily. The garment should fit smoothly, without bagging or binding.

Quality Workmanship

Even though most children outgrow their clothing rapidly, their garments receive hard wear. Quality is especially important for clothing that will be worn and laundered frequently. Customers want clothes to last even after they are outgrown because of their hand-me-down or pass-along potential. Well-made clothes have the following quality characteristics, one of which is illustrated in Figure 17–4.

REINFORCEMENT AT POINTS OF STRAIN

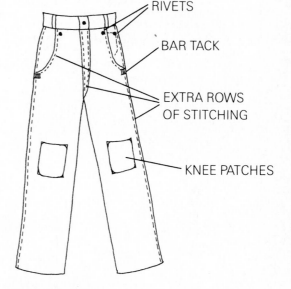

Figure 17–4. *Quality is especially important for clothing that will be worn and laundered frequently. Children's clothes receive hard wear.*

- *True grain line* can be seen in the threads of the fabric. Threads should run straight. The on-grain garments will hang straight and keep their shape better when worn.
- *Smooth, plain seams* are fine for some fabrics. They need to be at least $\frac{1}{2}$ inch wide and usually finished to keep from unraveling. Finishes include pinking, machine stitching, or overcasting.
- *Felled seams* are flat, strong seams with two rows of stitching. Raw edges may be turned under or left flat. They are especially good on play clothes and sleepwear that gets lots of pull.
- *Machine stitches* of about 12 stitches per inch gives a good seam on most fabrics.
- *Linings and interfacing* are usually made from a different fabric than the outer part of the garment. If the garment is labeled washable,

Table 17-11 GARMENTS AND THEIR FABRICS FOR TODDLER THROUGH HIGH SCHOOL AGES

Garment	Fabric
Blazers and jackets	Flannel, double knit (all wool, polyester/rayon, polyester/wool, all polyester), corduroy, denim, poplin, and tweed
Blouses and shirts	Broadcloth, gingham, percale, polyester/cotton, knitted acrylic, and knitted fleece
Coats and pantsuit coats	Melton, corduroy, pile fabrics, fleece gabardine, bonded knit, and double knit
Coats, jackets, and hat sets (toddler and preschool ages)	Tweed, flannel, wool fleece, serge, and knits
Dresses and jumpers (girls)	Broadcloth, challis, poplin, taffeta, knit or woven bonded fabrics, gingham, voile, velveteen, crepes, crash, flannel and weft and warp knits (in all fibers)
Hosiery	Nylon, cotton/nylon, nylon/acrylic, and acrylic/spandex
Jeans (all ages) and overalls (Infants through kindergarten ages)	Denim, corduroy, and dobby stripes
Pants, including pantsuits, slacks, and shorts	Tweed, corduroy, gabardine, denim, bonded knit, rib knit, stretch nylon, double knit, madras, batik, printed muslim, canvas, and velveteen
Raincoats (all ages) and all-weather coats (elementary age and up)	Oxford, canvas, denim, poplin, twill, sateen, and acrylic or modacrylic pile with zip-out lining
Robes	Quilted cotton and nylon, blanket cloth, terry cloth, flannel, and flannelette
Skirts (girls)	Poplin, flannel, gabardine, serge, double knit, and bonded knit
Sleepwear	Flannelette, cotton and man-made-fiber blends, tricot, plissé crepe, and cotton jersey
Snowsuits (toddler and preschool ages), ski jackets (elementary age and up), and ski pants (early elementary age)	Nylon in plain or rib weaves (quilted lining), stretch nylon, and twills in man-made fibers
Swimsuits	Spandex webbing, stretch nylon, and knits in various fibers
Underwear	All cotton, cotton/polyester, jersey, stretch nylon tricot, and acetate tricot

the linings and interfacings should be washable too. A good label will indicate this.

- *Trimmings* on washable garments, need to be sewn on very well and be colorfast so the colors will not run or fade.
- *Reinforcement at points of strain,* such as ends of pockets, plackets, buttonholes and button areas, knees, elbows and crotch are good features. Some types of reinforcement are **patches** — extra fabric on places such as elbows and knees; **metal rivets; extra rows of stitching** on pockets, plackets, and seams, and **bar tacks** at ends of buttonholes, pockets, and plackets.
- *Hems* in children's garments, especially dresses, need to be wide enough (at least 2 inches) to allow for growth.

Not all children's clothes will have all of these good points. But a garment can still be a good buy if the fabric, style, and fit are what the customer wants for a price he or she is willing to pay.

Fashion

Children, their parents, and the makers of children's clothes pay close attention to fashion trends. Some children's fashions — like designer jeans and other designer clothing — closely reflect adult fashions. Other children's fashions — like the craze for the "Peanuts" cartoon-strip character Snoopy — are not equally fashionable among adults.

However subject to fashion children's wear has become, it is still a fashionable, rather than a fashion, business. That is because children's manufacturers usually come out with one line for each of the year's four seasons. If a new, exciting look comes out in the middle of a season, most manufacturers cannot produce it until the following season. By then demand may have declined.

Perhaps the most enduring fashion influence on children is the freedom they enjoy in contemporary life. This freedom permits children to make their own fashion statements, to express their individuality and their membership in a peer group. "A sense of clothing develops as early as a sense of self," said actress Polly Bergen in her book, *I'd Love To, But What'll I Wear?*[1] Parents transmit to their children their own sense of values and their attitudes. As children get older, they also learn from their peers. As children's views change, their style of dressing will also change. By the time they have grown up, they will be expressing themselves through their clothing, compromising between their individuality and what is expected of them.

NOTES

1. Wideview, New York, 1977, page 58.

DO YOU KNOW YOUR MERCHANDISE?

1. What is a layette? Name and describe three types of clothing that might be included in a layette.
2. Why is the one-piece jumpsuit a popular item of infants' wear?
3. What is the difference between an infant and a toddler?
4. Why are self-help features particularly important to preschoolers? Name five self-help features of clothing.
5. What types of clothing are worn by preschool children? Which of these is similar to clothing worn by toddlers?
6. Name five safety features for children's clothing, including the two most important ones.
7. How does children's clothing reflect fashion trends?
8. How do girls' sizes differ from subteen sizes? How do boys' sizes differ from prep sizes?

9. Why is cotton a popular fabric for infants' and children's wear?
10. What are the elements of quality workmanship in children's clothing?

PUTTING YOUR MERCHANDISE KNOWLEDGE TO WORK

Select an article of infants' or children's wear. Write down all the features that might be used in selling it to a customer. Bring the garment to class and present the information about it. Consider the following features: color, fabric, current fashion, ease of care, construction.

PROJECT

Visit a children's department in two of the following kinds of stores: department store, specialty store, mass merchandiser, discount store. Examine the clothing featured in the department. Describe in writing the following elements.

- The size range of the clothing
- The styles, colors, and fabrics featured
- The manufacturers represented
- Information shown on garment tags
- Price ranges

What did you learn from examining the merchandise? How did the selections in the two stores compare on each point?

Visit and observe children in a nursery, daycare, or school setting. The children should be a target market for one or both stores you visited. Note and record the styles and colors the children are wearing and, to the extent you are able, the fabrics, manufacturers, and price ranges of their clothing.

Compare what the children are wearing to what the stores offer. Write a brief evaluation of how well the stores seem to serve their market.

18

Women's Wear: Clothing, Intimate Apparel, and Hosiery

Women want their clothing to be in fashion as well as comfortable and versatile. They mix and match with great freedom and interpret the nature of clothing occasions in a wide variety of ways.

Great variety is evident in women's apparel. There is outerwear for all kinds of activities — daytime and evening, business and social, casual and formal. Outdoor wear consists of an assortment of coats designed to make women comfortable for many different temperatures. If they are getting married or expecting babies, they can find special kinds of outerwear to suit their needs. There are also hosiery and underwear and many kinds of lounge and sleepwear available.

DAYTIME WEAR — BUSINESS, CASUAL, SOCIAL

Women's daytime apparel ranges from tailored suits and dresses for business to casual blouses or sweaters worn with skirts or pants.

Suits

Perhaps the standard article of daytime clothing — and a mainstay of the business or professional woman's wardrobe — is the suit. Suits consist of a matching skirt and jacket. Many elegant suits include matching trousers and a jacket. Some suits consist of a jacket, a skirt, and a vest or trousers, so a woman may vary the suit to the occasion.

If a woman can afford only one or two suits, she will probably be best advised to choose fabrics such as light wool gabardine or wool/synthetic blend. These will fit under coats, be wearable 8 or 9 months of the year, and be tolerable in overheated offices. Heavy wool is appropriate for out of doors in the fall and winter. Polyester, linen-look rayons, and cotton — particularly cotton seersucker — are suitable for summer suits.

Suits are available in a wide variety of styles. Three of the most important suit types are the tailored, Chanel, or cardigan, and the dressy suits. The **tailored suit** has a firm construction and crisply stitched details. The jacket collar is usually notched with discreet lapels. The skirt is either straight or flared. The **Chanel suit** has a collarless, boxy jacket, which is worn with a straight skirt. The **dressy suit** has variations that differentiate it from tailored suits or cardigans.

Separates

Many women's wardrobes are composed mainly of separates — pants, skirts, blouses, sweaters, vests, and jackets to be assembled in different ways to make different outfits.

WOMEN'S SUITS

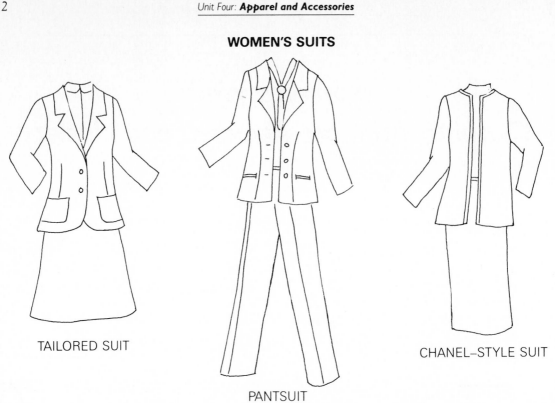

TAILORED SUIT

PANTSUIT

CHANEL–STYLE SUIT

Figure 18-1. *A mainstay of the business or professional woman's wardrobe is the suit, which may be varied to fit the occasion.*

Pants. One of the biggest changes in women's outerwear has been the general acceptance of pants or trousers and tops for almost all occasions. Because of the popularity of pants, manufacturers make them in many styles, for example, high-waisted pants or hip-huggers that ride the hips below the waistline. Some are very snug fitting; some are loose fitting. Pant legs may be tapered, straight, flared, or gathered into a band at the ankle (harem pants) or knee (knickers). A pair of midcalf long, loose, flared **culottes,** maybe seen as a divided skirt rather than pants. Shorts and Bermuda shorts are worn for summer casual wear. The more unusual styles and lengths of long pants are worn for parties and other social occasions.

Skirts. Despite the popularity of pants, skirts continue to be a staple item in most wardrobes.

In winter, many women like to wear high boots with a skirt, which is less bulky than pants when there are layers of underwear beneath. In summer, skirts are cooler than trousers or pants because they allow the air to circulate more freely.

Skirts are manufactured in a variety of lengths and styles such as sheath, pleated, dirndl, wraparound, and A-line. Business and professional women wear conservative midcalf length skirts. Longer skirts and mini skirts are worn for appropriate occasions. If it is in fashion, the floor-length skirt is generally worn in the evening.

Blouses and Sweaters. Often blouses, sweaters, and other tops are coordinated with skirts or pants — the bottoms — in color, pattern, trim, or some other way to tie the two pieces together. The tops are usually a different material from the bottoms.

Blouses may have long or short sleeves and a wide variety of necklines. They may be a cotton or cotton/polyester blend (for everyday wear) or luxurious silk (for special occasions). Most blouses button up the front, for ease of putting on, but some button up the back and others are pulled on over the head and fastened with ties at the neck or a few buttons. Jewel-necked blouses with close-fitting set-in sleeves and blouses with decorative fronts such as the tucked bib or **jabot** (a biblike ruffle) go well under suit and other jackets. A blouse that is crisply tailored is usually called a **shirt**.

A **sweater** is knit or crocheted rather than cut and sewn from yard goods like a blouse. Sweaters are generally more informal than blouses or shirts. However, many sweaters are suitable for office or business, for example, a plain sweater with a **turtle** (high round rolled) **neck**. Other sweaters, such as those with puffed shoulders, bulky yarns, or with low necklines, are suitable for social occasions. Sweaters made of thick wool are suitable for outdoor wear, such as hiking or skating. Many sweaters have **ribbing** (stretch knitting) at the neck and wrists and around the waist for snug fit.

Sweaters can be either a **pullover** or a **cardigan,** a jacketlike sweater that buttons up the front. The long-sleeved cardigan may be sold with a short-sleeved pullover to make a **sweater set.**

Some of the wide variety of neck and sleeve styles found in blouses, sweaters, and other tops are shown in Figure 18–4.

PANTS STYLES

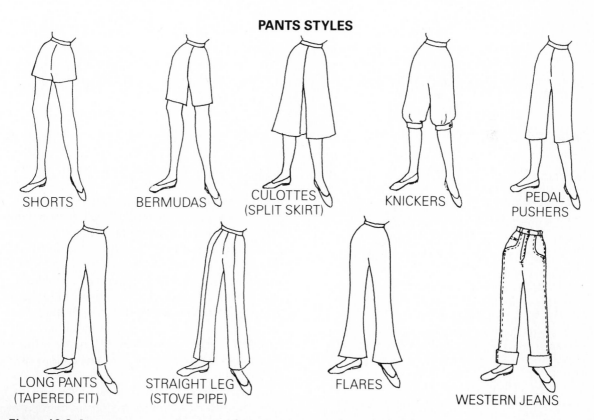

SHORTS

BERMUDAS

CULOTTES (SPLIT SKIRT)

KNICKERS

PEDAL PUSHERS

LONG PANTS (TAPERED FIT)

STRAIGHT LEG (STOVE PIPE)

FLARES

WESTERN JEANS

Figure 18-2. *Pants are now generally accepted for women to wear at almost any occasion.*

SKIRT STYLES

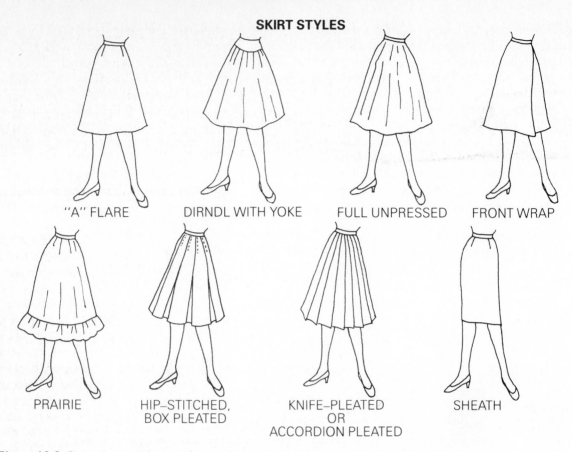

"A" FLARE   DIRNDL WITH YOKE   FULL UNPRESSED   FRONT WRAP

PRAIRIE   HIP–STITCHED,   KNIFE–PLEATED   SHEATH
                 BOX PLEATED   OR
                                    ACCORDION PLEATED

Figure 18-3. *Skirts continue to be a staple item: they are less bulky than pants and are cooler in the summer.*

Jackets. Some jackets are short coats meant to be worn outdoors for warmth and protection. Other jackets, such as blazers, are parts of outfits. **Blazers** are lightweight, loose-fitting tailored jackets. Some daytime blazers are made of leather or tweed — a thick woolen fabric often woven with strands of bumpy, uneven yarn. Many blazers are made of wool flannel or gabardine in a neutral color such as navy. Blazers can be worn with skirts, trousers, or jeans.

Other jacket types are as follows.

Vest: Waist-length sleeveless jacket
Jerkin: Hip-length sleeveless jacket
Bolero: Waist-length collarless jacket without buttons
Chinese jacket: Boxy hip-length jacket with a mandarin collar

Dresses

Dresses are included in most women's wardrobes. Some have matching jackets to make **ensembles.** A dress is a time saver for many women; it does not need to be put together as an outfit — it *is* together.

A great many dresses are cut in one of the classic styles shown in Figure 18–5. There are however, other possibilities, for example, the waist can be raised to the **empire** level or it can be lowered. Hemlines, sleeves, and necklines vary in some of the same ways discussed for skirts and tops.

Two particularly timeless dress styles are the **shirtwaist,** which combines a shirt or blouselike top with an A-line or dirndl skirt, and the

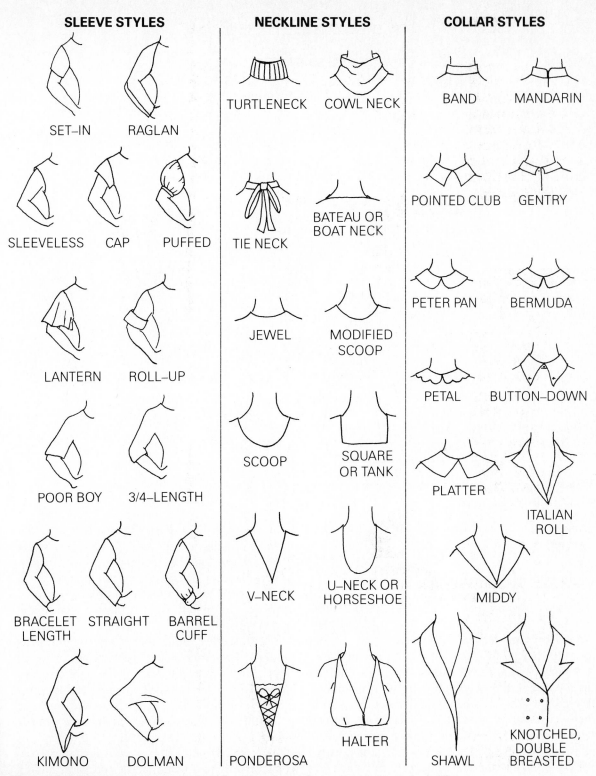

SLEEVE STYLES

SET-IN RAGLAN

SLEEVELESS CAP PUFFED

LANTERN ROLL-UP

POOR BOY 3/4-LENGTH

BRACELET LENGTH STRAIGHT BARREL CUFF

KIMONO DOLMAN

NECKLINE STYLES

TURTLENECK COWL NECK

TIE NECK BATEAU OR BOAT NECK

JEWEL MODIFIED SCOOP

SCOOP SQUARE OR TANK

V-NECK U-NECK OR HORSESHOE

PONDEROSA HALTER

COLLAR STYLES

BAND MANDARIN

POINTED CLUB GENTRY

PETER PAN BERMUDA

PETAL BUTTON-DOWN

PLATTER ITALIAN ROLL

MIDDY

SHAWL KNOTCHED, DOUBLE BREASTED

Figure 18-4. *Women may choose a variety of necklines for comfort, attractiveness, and suitability.*

DRESS STYLES

SHIRTWAIST   SMOCK DRESS   FLARE   PRINCESS   A-LINE   JUMPER

TENT   SHEATH   SUNDRESS   JACKET DRESS   DROPPED WAISTLINE   SURPLICE WRAP

Figure 18-5. *Dresses are time savers for many women — a dress is an outfit in itself.*

jumper, which is a sleeveless dress worn over sweaters or blouses.

ACTIVE SPORTSWEAR

Nowadays sportswear is a part of the ordinary wardrobe. This is especially true of leotards, tights, and leg warmers. Women wear them not only to their exercise classes but as part of their everyday clothing. **Leotards** are skin tight stretch garments covering the body from the neckline to the crotch. They can be sleeved or sleeveless and come with a great variety of necklines. Some leotards double as swimsuits; many can be worn with a matching skirt for streetwear; and nearly all can double as thermal underwear in winter.

Tights are skintight garments covering the body from the waist down. They are worn under leotards or with ordinary skirts. **Leg warmers** are heavy, warm, footless stockings worn over tights to keep dancers' muscles warm and pliable. They are also worn on the street in a number of ways, such as over pants, over or inside boots, and under skirts.

Many women find loose-thighed **jodhpurs** worn for horseback riding comfortable for casual wear. They appreciate the way the tight calves of the jodhpurs tuck into boots. A classic sport jacket for many purposes is the tweed **hacking jacket,** a riding coat with slits at the sides or back and flap pockets.

A typical ski outfit that is worn for other occasions consists of a nylon jacket and pants quilted with polyester, nylon, or down insulation. A knitted cap or nylon hood with quilted lining is worn on the head. Nylon is a suitable fabric for ski wear because it is lightweight, strong, water repellent, and quick drying. These same qualities make a nylon ski jacket an excellent choice for a short winter coat.

Like ski clothes, swim wear should be lightweight and quick drying. They should not shrink nor should their colors and finishes be affected by salt or chlorinated water. Swimmers need suits that fit the body snugly but do not constrict movement, which is why knitted materials such as stretch nylon and spandex are so popular.

For comfort and support, the bra of a swimsuit may be lined with polyurethane foam or nylon; the crotch should be lined. Generally, one-piece swimsuits are pull-on types, with stretch straps and elasticized legs. A thin, tubelike one-piece suit is called a **maillot. A tank suit** is a sturdy, well-constructed maillot. As shown in Figure 18–6, some one-piece swimsuits come with skirts, cutout sections, front panels (the sheath) or short legs.

One of the most popular styles of two-piece swimsuits is the **bikini,** consisting of a bra with adjustable straps and an abbreviated pull-on panty. Pregnant women may wear a **swimdress,** a short sleeveless dress with a separate elasticized panty.

After-swim garments include the **beach shift,** a long robe that may come with a hood that folds into a soft collar. A shortened version of the long shift is the **beach jacket.** Some swimsuits come with matching skirts or pants.

Many tennis clothes can combine with trousers or longer skirts for après-tennis wear. Although some women wear shorts on the tennis court, the classic tennis outfit for a woman is a very short skirt, often worn with a short-sleeved cotton knit shirt, or a dress. To prevent wrinkles, tennis dresses and skirts are made of crisp fabrics such as cotton pique or polyester twill. It is better if the top part of the garment is all cotton or a cotton blend so that perspiration may be absorbed. The bottom part of the outfit may be 100 percent polyester. Special short panties or briefs are worn with the tennis skirt or dress. They often have ruffles around the thigh openings, are made of a thicker material than regular underpants, and may be lined.

When people dressed more formally than they do now, white was the only acceptable color on

SWIMSUIT STYLES

BIKINI

REGULAR TWO–PIECE

MAILLOT

SHEATH

SWIMDRESS

Figure 18-6. *Swimsuits — made of lightweight, quick-drying, shrink-resistant fabrics — range from the popular bikini to the swimdress, which may be designed for pregnant women.*

the tennis court. Nowadays tennis clothes come in a variety of colors, most of them very light pastels to reflect the sun's light efficiently.

Women usually wear short, A-lined skirts on the golf course. This style allows freedom of movement but does not billow in a breeze. Golf clothes are seen for casual wear as well as on the course.

EVENING WEAR

In the early twentieth century, fashionable people who were going out for an evening invariably put on special clothes. Wealthy people even wore formal clothes to eat dinner in their own homes. This formality is no longer a rule for most people. Nowadays, people wear evening clothes for fun or special occasions such as a meal in a special restaurant, a visit to the theater, or an excursion to a discotheque.

Dinner Clothes

Elegant fabrics play an important part in establishing the sensual allure of evening clothes. For summer, sheer fabrics such as chiffon, organza, and lace are frequent choices. For fall and winter heavier fabrics such as nylon jersey, velvet, smooth satin crepe, and metallic brocade are beautiful and appropriate.

As a general rule, the dinner or theater outfit covers up more of the body than the dance outfit. At a dinner table the emphasis will be on a woman's face and hands. Consequently, the ideal dinner dress or blouse will be face framing, if not high necked. Except in summer, the arms may be covered.

The length of the skirt will depend on the formality of the occasion and social conventions. Generally, a long skirt is considered dressier than a short one, and a skirt is considered dressier than pants.

Dancing Clothes

Clothes for dancing tend to be made of soft fabrics such as nylon jersey or satin. Since the body is shown off and the dancer is in effect performing, these dance outfits show the body to best advantage. Backless or halter dresses are also appropriate.

Many of today's disco outfits derive from the classic dance costumes such as leotards and tights. They may be made of special shiny stretch materials, shot through with metallic threads, have sequins or feathers or have other elaborate decoration.

Despite the widespread popularity of disco-type evening wear, there still exist many occasions when women will feel more graceful and elegant in flowing yet clingy fabrics made into styles that float and sway with the dancer.

COATS

Coats may be classified as dressy or casual. A **dressy coat** is worn over a daytime, afternoon, or evening dress or party attire. The coat is fitted or boxy and should cover the dress. The texture of a dressy coat is generally smooth and may be shiny. **Capes** or long coats with or without hoods are suitable for formal evening wear. Winter coats are much heavier in weight than spring and fall coats are and are usually interlined.

A **casual coat** is worn over a sports outfit, such as a skirt or pantsuit, blouse or sweater with skirt, or a sporty dress. It is generally looser fitting and bulkier than a dressy coat and may come in vivid colors and patterns, for example, plaids, stripes, and bright solid colors. Casual coats come in many lengths but are often shorter than dressy coats. Casual coats include sports coats and jackets and all-weather coats (sometimes called classic) with or without zip-out linings. The classic **pea jacket** (a short, warm, double-breasted naval jacket) and quilted coat with a fiber or down filling are casual coats.

Many of the coat styles shown in Figure 18–7 can be dressy or casual depending on the fabric used. Fabric also determines the season for which a coat is suitable. Wool broadcloth, fake furlike fabrics, suede cloth, leather, vinyl, and polyurethane leather imitations are used to make dressy coats for winter. Winter coats may be

COAT STYLES

TRENCH COAT

WRAPAROUND

BALMACAAN

QUILTED COAT

POLO

CAPECOAT

PRINCESS

REEFER

BOX OR CHESTERFIELD
OR BOY COAT

CAR COAT

PEA COAT

PONCHO

CAPE

CLOAK

Figure 18-7. *Coats are the most expensive item in most people's wardrobes. Construction and styling are very important.*

made of fur or may have fur collars, cuffs, and other trimming.

Spring dress coats are often made of manmade fibers resembling silk and occasionally of real silk. However, many spring dress coats are being replaced with rain or all-weather coats (discussed below).

Casual coats for winter may be made of camel's hair, wool melton, plush, corduroy, suede, wool-blend flannel, quilted cotton, or polyester/cotton poplin with a water-repellent finish.

Because coats are the most expensive items in most people's wardrobes, it is important for customers to be guided to a wise choice. The construction and styling of a coat as well as how it fits into a woman's lifestyle, are important. Women who travel often will want a coat that packs easily and perhaps with a zip-out lining. Those who spend a lot of time in cars are best advised to choose a three-fourth length coat in a sturdy fabric. Working women who need to cultivate a businesslike appearance would do well to choose a classic cloth coat in a basic color such as tan, navy, brown, gray, wine, or black. Perhaps the most versatile of all coats are all-weather trench coats with zip-out or button-in linings.

Snow- and Rainwear

The **all-weather coat** got its name because of its zip-out lining and water-repellent finish that makes it comfortable any time of year and in rain or snow. However, *water-repellent* does not mean *waterproof*. Water-repellent coats are made of a closely woven fabric that has been chemically treated. Water tends to run off it but a heavy downpour may come through the coat. The only truly waterproof coat is made of fabric that has been treated with oil, rubber, or vinyl. These coats are called **slickers** in the United States and **mackintoshes** in Britain. They may be bright yellow (the classic slicker color) or red, which makes them easy to see in a misty downpour. Some waterproof coats are made in a short, tentlike **poncho** style, are unlined, and, if made

of nylon or another light fabric, can easily be folded and stored in a special pouch.

To keep dry and warm in wet snow, ski clothes or layers of wool are good choices. Wool is the only natural fiber that does not lose its insulating properties when it is wet. Oil-finished, heavy wool sweaters, thick jackets, or coats are among the best protections you can have from cold weather. Although people used to believe that the coats should be as thick as possible, they now believe that thinner coats with more layers underneath provide greater freedom of movement, as well as warmth. The layers trap air between them and this air has both heating and insulation properties.

Nothing is as warm and light as **down,** a soft, fluffy fur from beneath the feathers of ducks and geese. Down keeps you warm by trapping air next to your body. Generally, the fatter down coats are warmer than the thinner ones. Some coats that look like down coats are really made from quilted fiberfill, which is not as warm as down. However, if a coat will not be worn in extremely cold weather for long periods of time, a fiberfill coat may do perfectly well.

Many fillings are part feathers, which are flat and do not trap air well. The coats therefore are not really warm. Feathers also add bulk to a coat. However, coats with feathers are less expensive and more readily available than all-down coats. Twelve percent feathers is generally accepted as a reasonable mixture with 88 percent down.

SPECIAL-PURPOSE CLOTHING

The two most important types of special-purpose outerwear have their own departments in large apparel stores. These are bridal clothes and maternity clothes.

Bridal Clothes

Bridal departments carry dresses and accessories for brides and attendants. The **traditional bridal dress** has a veil and train and is all white. The **contemporary bridal dress** does not have a veil and train and is often in color. It may have a matching wreath. Most bridal dresses are floor length.

Bridesmaids and other attendants' dresses tend to be of dressy fabrics in soft colors. They are relatively covered up and conservative looking. Most stores have coordinators who will advise the customer about the appropriate clothes for an entire bridal party, including the bride's mother.

Maternity Clothes

Maternity dresses usually have full busts and provision for expansion at the waist. The skirt is longer in the front than in the back to allow for the change taking place in the mother's size. Maternity slacks have expanding elastic panels in front. Since many women work far into their pregnancies, loose chemise dresses or suits are popular items. Most customers want good-quality, long-lasting, classic-styled maternity items. Women often store their maternity clothes in case they become pregnant again. Or they may give the clothes to other pregnant women.

OUTERWEAR SIZES

For outerwear there are three basic size classifications based on build and height. These are **misses,** for the normal, mature figure; **juniors** for the shorter-waisted and shorter mature figure, and **women's** for the heavier figure. To misses and juniors have been added **talls** (over 5 feet 9 inches) and **petites** (shorter than average); and to women's have been added **half-sizes** (shorter, heavier figures) and **stouts** (very heavy figures).

The jumps in sizes range from $\frac{1}{2}$ to 2 inches for most measurements. The typical ranges are listed in Table 18–1.

Few stores carry all these sizes. Some omit the petites, most omit the talls, and few carry the stouts; many specialize in junior sizes.

SELLING POINTS OF OUTERWEAR

Virtually all women's outerwear is mass produced in factories. To determine how well a gar-

ment is made, pay attention to the following points.

- If a garment has a design, be sure the vertical lines run parallel with the warp unless the skirt or blouse is cut on the bias — (the diagonal). In the sleeve the warp should run from the shoulder seam straight to the back of the wrist bone. The filling (crosswise) yarns in the sleeves should also run straight. Both shoulder lines should be smooth. Armholes fit better if they are not cut too low.
- Make certain that side seams, waist seams, and hems have sufficient width.
- Look at the workmanship to see if the seams are stitched with strong, colorfast thread slightly darker than the fabric and finished with seam binding on the hem.
- Look to see all closings run along continuous lengthwise seams, that the underfolds of all pleats are deep, that pleats are pressed straight, that all fitted darts are straight and smooth, and that the pockets are reinforced by tape stitching at points of strain.
- Make sure that skirts and pants are cut full enough for comfort and for long garment life. The same principle applies to coats and suits, which should be cut full enough so that the arms can be raised above the head without pulling at the sleeves. (It is a good idea to try on a winter coat over a blazer or a sweater).

Table 18–1 WOMEN'S OUTERWEAR SIZES

Misses Petites Tall misses	4–20
Juniors Junior petites Tall juniors	3–15
Women's	38–52
Half-sizes	$12\frac{1}{2}$–$26\frac{1}{2}$
Stouts	$34\frac{1}{2}$–$52\frac{1}{2}$

- The fabric in the body and sleeves of a garment should be cut with the grain (the warp running vertically the length of the garment), and the garment should hang evenly at the bottom.
- Check to see that seams are even and wide enough so that they do not pull out under stress and strain. Points of strain should be reinforced, and buttonholes, buttons, and loops should be firmly sewn in place. The collar should fit neatly at the neck. The lining should be cut to fit the outer garment smoothly, without showing below the lower edge. (Scrutiny of a lining is often revealing. If the stitching is careless, the chances are the rest of the garment is badly made. A tight, solid-weave lining such as taffeta or twill wears longer than satiny linings.) The seams of garments should not pucker, although some puckering will be found on down-filled coats. Check to see that it is not excessive.

Fashion Rightness

Most women want up-to-date styles that are worn by people and groups that they admire. Many women choose clothes designed by people whose creations they have found to be well suited to themselves. A store's outergarment buyers and sales representatives should determine which styles have potential for wide acceptance, which are already growing in acceptance, which are in a period of mass selling, and which are on the decline.

Suitability and Versatility

Each garment in a woman's wardrobe should be suitable for her personal image and versatile enough to fit into her lifestyle in different ways. Knowledge of individual body types can often help a customer make the wisest choice. Table 18–2 is a guide to appropriate clothing choices for four figure types. Appropriate clothing choices can help obscure what may be considered problems in a person's figure. For example,

a dark top and a light bottom can minimize a top-heavy figure, whereas the opposite color combination can minimize a bottom-heavy figure. A V neck is flattering for a person with a short neck, whereas a high, ruffled neckline is suitable for a person with a long neck.

Versatility of clothing is especially important to women who are looking for high quality but shopping within a budget. Many women want to make sure that a blouse or sweater will go with many of the bottoms in their wardrobe. They will also want clothes that may be appropriate for evening and daytime wear or for dress-up and casual occasions. Generally, the most versatile clothing is simple and classically styled in neutral, solid colors such as black, beige, gray, or navy.

Attractiveness

The fabric and the color of the garment should be flattering to the wearer's figure and skin tone. The style of the garment should also be appropriate and thereby enhance the wearer's image. Each customer should be encouraged to find her personal style.

Comfort

Comfort is a matter of good quality, good fit, adequate warmth or coolness, and the feel of the garment against the body. It is also a matter of knowing you have dressed appropriately, since comfort in clothing is partly psychological. Some people may pick out clothing because they think they ought to have it, not because they like it or feel good in it. Some people pick the least-expensive and least-attractive clothing they can find because they feel bad spending money on themselves. The results of clothing choices can be quite significant for a person's sense of well-being, or lack of it.

Care and Durability

The care labels on many garments specify "hand wash" or "wash separately." This is especially

Table 18-2. CLOTHING FOR VARIOUS FIGURES

Tall and Thin

Wear	Avoid
Horizontal lines — tunics, two-piece outfits, wide belts, yokes, raglan shoulders	Vertical lines
Wide-panel fronts	Unbelted waistlines
Skirts — pleated, flared, draped, yoked	Narrow sheath styles
Sleeves — three-quarter length, bracelet length, full; wide cuffs	Deep V necklines
	Exaggerated shoulders
	Severely tailored suits
	Pencil-slim skirts
	Angular necklines
Coats — full, three-quarter length, and belted; capes	Long, tight-fitting sleeves
Tent silhouettes	Very high or very low heels
Full bodices, bloused tops	
Round necks, large collars	
Large accessories — big handbags and pieces of jewelry	
Shoes with medium heels	
Pants — any length and cut	
Contrasting or bold colors	
Plaids, tweeds; large or bold prints	
Crisp, bulky, or shiny fabrics	

Short and Thin

Wear	Avoid
Horizontal lines	Deep V necklines
Modified vertical lines — T, arrow, and Y lines	Exaggerated lines of any kind
Narrow- and wide-panel fronts, princess lines	Very wide shoulders, capes
Multivertical lines	Wide belts
Pleated, full flared, or draped skirts	Long jackets
Semifitted sheaths	Tunics
Bolero or short jackets	Tent silhouettes
Short V necklines, round collars and necklines	Pencil-slim skirts
Bloused bodices	Tight-fitting sleeves
Empire waistlines	Heavy trimmings
Delicate trimmings	Large handbags and accessories
Bulky, shiny, or stiff fabrics	Chunky jewelry
Bold colors	Clinging fabrics
Small prints	
Pants — any cut	

Tall and Heavy

Wear	Avoid
Vertical lines	Horizontal lines
Asymmetrical lines	Yokes, if bust is full
Diagonal lines	Princess lines
T, Y, and arrow lines	Wide-panel fronts
A-line or center-pleated skirts	Multiverticals
V necklines	Wide belts
Pointed collars	Full or pleated skirts or very straight skirts
Self-belts (less than 1½ inches wide)	Round necklines
Moderate-length jackets	Tent silhouettes
Full-length coats	Bloused bodices
Set-in sleeves	Sleeveless dresses, cap or tight sleeves
Shoes with medium heels	Boleros or short jackets
Subdued colors	Jerseys, chiffon, satin, stiff materials
Pants — straight and simple in solid colors	Plaids or large prints
	Tight-fitting styles

Short and Heavy

Wear	Avoid
Vertical lines	Horizontal lines
Assymetrical lines	Wide-panel fronts
Diagonal lines	Princess lines
Y lines	Multiverticals
V necklines	Wide belts
Set-in sleeves	Boleros and bulky tunics
Narrow, half- or self-belts, or beltless styles	Extremely long jackets
A-line skirts	Draped skirts
Center-pleated skirts	Tent silhouettes
Jackets not much below hipbone	Pencil-slim skirts
Subdued colors	Full skirts
Shoes with medium heels	Capes and three-quarter-length coats
Medium-sized handbags	Blousson tops
Pants — straight cut in solid colors	Plaids and bold prints
	Bright colors
	Clinging or stiff fabrics, bulky or crisp textures, shiny finishes
	Hip-hugger pants

true of delicate or richly colored fabrics. The salesperson must be sure to point out such care features of all garments to customers. If the garment is not cared for properly it will sag, droop, or wrinkle and the customer will be disappointed.

What is easy to care for depends on a person's situation. Whether or not a woman has easy access to a washing machine, or prefers to use a dry cleaner, or has children, or plans to travel determines the methods of care she prefers for her clothing.

In general, flat, hard weaves last longer than soft, loose ones. Twill, such as gabardine and denim, tweeds, and polyester blends are particularly long wearing. Polyester blends will outlast pure cotton. However, some cotton, such as denim, actually looks better as it gets older. Many synthetic fibers look frayed and faded as they age. Thickness for thickness, the strongest of the natural fibers is silk.

Quality and Price

A small wardrobe of good-quality, carefully chosen garments is better than a large wardrobe of garments that wear poorly and may have a short fashion life. Customers should be advised to buy the best clothes they can afford.

Many customers find they must put time and ingenuity into shopping. They take time, for example, to find a sweater that will go with more than one skirt and pair of pants. However, once the habit of careful shopping is acquired, the time required for careful selection will be reduced.

Some experienced shoppers recommend buying one expensive item to wear with items of lesser quality. If this approach is chosen, it is wise to invest the most money in the items that show the most — those that are close to the face and hands or that are worn on top, such as a blazer.

Is a designer label an assurance of quality? The answer is yes and no. Designer clothes are made in factories like other clothes and things can go wrong in the manufacturing process. However, designers' names are associated with wearable, up-to-the-minute styles and are an important selling point in some stores. Boutiques for various designers may be set up in stores to help fashion-conscious shoppers find the look they prefer. Quality-conscious customers may appreciate the strong retailing trend toward private-label merchandise that is sold under a store's own name or trademark.

INTIMATE APPAREL

Included in intimate apparel are underwear, foundation garments, bras and other garments designed to provide a firm foundation for outerwear, and loungewear and sleepwear.

Underwear

During the past few decades, technological advances have made it possible to combine fashion and function to produce soft, comfortable, colorful, lightweight underwear at affordable prices. (Thermal underwear, which keeps the wearer warm in cold weather, is discussed in Chapter 19.)

Slips. Full slips, half-slips, camisoles, and teddys function as soft lininglike layers under outerwear. A **slip** (or **full slip**) is a one-piece garment held up by shoulder straps, is slightly fitted at the waist, and has a form-fitting skirt a little shorter than the dress or skirt under which it is to be worn. Slip sizes are 32 to about 52; they run according to bust measurements. Half-size slips and strapless slips are also available.

A **half-slip** (or **petticoat**) is an underskirt that is gathered or elasticized at the waist. Some half-slips are relatively straight; others are full and circular and can be stiffened to be worn under a full skirt for a bouffant effect. Half-slips are particularly useful in the summer under a thin skirt. They are convenient for the woman who does not want slip straps to stray from the armholes of sleeveless or the necklines of open-necked dresses.

A **camisole** is like a slip top without its bottom. It usually extends slightly below the waist and may have some elastic shirring at the waist

UNDERWEAR STYLES

Figure 18-8. *Underwear and foundation garments may be lininglike layers between outerwear and skin, or they may support the figure.*

with a **peplum** (skirtlike section extending a few inches below the waist). The camisole may be worn with a half-slip or by itself, for example, under a sheer blouse with pants.

A **teddy** combines a camisole with underpants in a one-piece garment with a snap crotch. It may be worn under trousers or jumpsuits. It can be worn by itself or with a half-slip.

Underpants. There are six kinds of women's underpants. **Briefs** are very short, close-fitting, underpants with elastic or bands at the waist and thigh-top openings. A **bikini** is a brief whose top comes below the hipbone. A **hip-hugger** brief's top comes just above the hipbone.

A **panty** is an undergarment with legs cut longer than a brief. It usually has no elastic at the legs. **Tap pants** are airy and boxy panties with flared legs. **Bloomers** are panties whose legs are gathered into elastic bands. Tap pants and other panties are particularly comfortable in summer. They are best worn underskirts or dresses.

Foundation Garments

A properly fitting **foundation garment** improves the lines and fit of the outer garment by supporting and controlling the figure. Some garments are intended to give only slight support; others give a good deal more. Generally speaking, the **boned** (strips of actual bone, steel, or plastic inserted into casings in the garment to stiffen it) types give more support and control than the unboned stretch types.

Bras. A **bra**, short for **brassiere**, usually covers just the bust, but it may extend to the waistline. Most bras come with straps. Many have one-way stretch webbing on the sides to help keep the garment smooth and to ensure easy breathing. Bra sizes are indicated by the measurement around the bustline, given in inches, and the cup size, given in letters from AA to DD. Common types of bras follow.

Stretch Bra: Made of a stretch fabric and has the least support. Gives a smooth no bra look. The one-size-fits-all is for women with small-to-average firm breasts (sizes A, B, or small C).
Natural Bra: Its soft cups provide better support than the stretch bra, but it still looks natural. This is the biggest-selling bra.
Underwire Bra: Bra for large-breasted women. It is designed to provide support and lift without putting so much weight on the straps that they are uncomfortable on the wearer's shoulders.
Minimizer: Constructed to press breasts toward the sides of the bra rather than lifting them upward. This makes a large bust look about one size smaller. Minimizers come in sizes C, D, and DD.
Maximizer: Designed especially to make the most of A and AA sizes. Some have thin layers of Fiberfill in the cups. Others push the breasts up and out from underneath with a combination of miniwire and liner to make the bust measurement look larger.
Sports Bra: Especially designed to wear when running and playing tennis. They minimize tissue-destroying bounce and keep breasts comfortable. Sports bras, which are made of cotton, have wide elastic straps and no-seam cups (to prevent nipple irritation). They slip on over the head or have padded fasteners to prevent abrasion.

Strapless Bra: Designed to be worn under strapless or low-necked dresses.
Maternity or Nursing Bra: The cups of this bra may be unhooked at the top and folded down when the mother is breast-feeding her baby. These bras are generally sold in maternity departments.

In selecting a bra, a woman should be sure of these features:

- The bra lies smooth across the back.
- The bra stays in place when the arms are lifted above the head or when they are swung around.
- The straps lie flat and do not curl, although some stretch straps may do so. The straps should be adjustable for comfort.
- There are no bulges in front or under the arms. If there are, the cups are probably too small.

Girdles and Corsets. A **girdle** is a tubelike elasticized garment (sometimes with bones), designed to keep the abdomen flat and to control the hips. Most girdles close with zippers and have attached or detachable garters for stockings. They are sized according to waist measurement. A **panty girdle** is a pull-on stretch panty. Most panty girdles extend from the waist to the crotch; others extend to just above the knee or just below the knee. Control-top body warmers extend to the ankle. Sizes are determined by the wearer's waist size.

A **corselette** (also known as an **all-in-one**) combines features of the bra and girdle or panty girdle. It is sized by bust measurements and usually worn by the woman with a mature figure. A **corset**, which is heavily boned, has been designed to control the extra large figure. It is made of heavier fabrics than girdles, panty girdles, or corselettes. Special corsets for maternity wear and health purposes require professional fitting by a **corsetiere** — a corset specialist.

Loungewear and Sleepwear

The introduction of easy-care, manmade textile fibers in the 1950s brought about a lot of changes in sleepwear and loungewear. Companies began to develop styling that reflected the current fashions in outerwear. For example, when colorful prints are popular in outerwear, brightly patterned sleepwear and loungewear are also featured.

Sleepwear. The two basic categories of sleepwear are nightgowns and pajamas (sometimes spelled pyjamas). **Nightgowns** are cut on the warp (straight) or on the bias (diagonally). Some are sleeveless, with straps over the shoulders; others are made with long, puffed, or cap sleeves. Necklines may be high, often with a neck ruffle, or low in the manner of an evening dress. The gown may be floor length, midcalf length, knee length, or thigh length with matching bloomers (the **shortie**). Some gowns hang straight from a gathered yoke or neck; others are belted. All nightgowns must be roomy and soft and have no irritating seams or stiff details.

Pajamas come in coat styles (with button or zipper closings) and pullover styles. Tailored pajamas have a notched collar. Some pajamas have mandarin collars, for a Chinese look. Others have bateau necks, crew necks, or V necks. Sleeves vary as on nightgowns. Pants may be long or short. Some fit snugly; others have flared bottoms or are gathered into bands at the ankle for warmth. Some pajamas come with puffy panties — the so-called **bloomer** or **baby-doll** style.

Loungewear. The loungewear department of a store, once devoted to robes, now has many varieties of loungewear available. With the big increase in at-home entertaining, long hostess gowns and hostess pajamas have become popular. Some are even worn outside the home to parties. Hostess clothes tend to be soft and easy to wear and are made in elegant, flattering styles, some bare and some covered up. Popular styles include the tunic and the caftan. The **tunic** is a long top (covering the buttocks) that is often sold with pants of a matching fabric. The top may hang straight, be belted, or have a elasticized waist. The **caftan** is a long flared or straight gown that is cut full and loose. It has a high round neck slit in the front so the garment can be pulled over the head. The caftan often has full, flaring, wrist-length sleeves.

Recently, sportswear has been an inspiration for loungewear. Much of it imitates the warm-up suit of the runner (covered in Chapter 19).

Robes are frequently worn over a nightgown or pajamas. They can be made of warm fluffy fabrics for winter or of light airy fabrics for summer. They may be long or short, belted or loose, wraparound style or fastened in front with buttons or a zipper. Some robe styles are like outerwear coat styles, except for the fabrics.

A sheer, long, full-sleeved coatlike garment worn over a nightgown or pajamas in a similar fabric is called a **peignoir** or **negligee**. For traveling, sleep sets, consisting of a coatlike robe and nightgown or pajamas, are practical. These sets are similar to peignoir sets but are of less delicate material.

Selling Points for Underwear, Loungewear, and Sleepwear

Some of the features a salesperson should point out to a customer buying underwear, loungewear, and sleepwear are as follows.

Style and Attractiveness. Underwear and sleepwear come in tailored or highly decorated styles with ribbon, lace, and embroidery. They are available in plain colors or in prints. It is possible to coordinate an entire set of underclothing — bra, panties, and slip or slip alternative. Sleepwear and loungewear also may be coordinated, for example, the sleep and peignoir sets mentioned above.

Comfort. Almost all underwear, sleepwear, and loungewear is of manmade fibers, which makes it easy to care for. (See below.) However, some women want cotton sleepwear for summer since cotton absorbs perspiration and evaporates it rapidly. Some women also want cotton underpants. Cotton breathes and permits better air circulation. It is therefore more comfortable and healthier. Today, nearly all underpants made of nylon or other synthetics have a cotton crotch.

All underwear should be soft and lightweight, should conform to body lines, and should not show any bulkiness through outer garments. Underwear should be easy to slip on, should fit smoothly without riding up, should not restrain body movement, should not cling to the outer garment, and should not irritate the wearer's skin.

Like underwear, foundation garments should not restrain body movements, although some of these garments are necessarily confining. Foundation garments should be made of lightweight fabrics that allow the wearer to remain cool and comfortable in summer.

Loungewear and sleepwear should be easy to take on and off. They should not bind and must permit full freedom of movement. Robes should be tried on with a nightgown or pajama top (or over a blouse) to make sure they fit properly.

Care and Durability. Part of a garment's easy-care, long-life properties has to do with good workmanship. Seams and hems should be even, narrow, and smooth. The fabric and trimming should be of good quality and sewed evenly and carefully. Buttons should be sewed on securely and buttonholes should be carefully worked to cover all cut edges. There should be no loose threads hanging from any part of the garment.

Almost all underwear, sleepwear, and loungewear are made of manmade fiber or cotton blends. They are usually machine washable and quick drying and need no ironing. However, the finest and daintiest garments require hand washing in mild soap. Robes of materials like velvet may have to be dry-cleaned. If 100 percent cotton is chosen for summer, it should be borne in mind that, underpants aside, it will probably require ironing to look smooth. However, cotton like other natural fibers, wears well.

HOSIERY

Pantyhose have become so much a part of women's wardrobes, they are even sold in super-

markets. Before pantyhose, however, women wore **stockings** — usually called **nylons** because of the material from which they were most commonly made. Stockings are still sold but are worn by fewer women than pantyhose. About three-fourths of the total hosiery market is in pantyhose.

Pantyhose

Most pantyhose are made of stretch nylon. Some come in one size to fit women who range in height from 5 feet to 5 feet 10 inches and weigh from 100 to 150 pounds. Other pantyhose come in height- and weight-correlated sizes to fit very small to very large women. Also available are queen-sized and maternity pantyhose. Many pantyhose have a reinforced cotton crotch for the wearer's health.

Pantyhose come in several types suitable for different purposes.

Ultrasheer: Ultrasheer pantyhose are made from the most delicate, lightweight yarns and are therefore not as sturdy as other types of pantyhose. Because the yarn is not crimped, as it is for mesh pantyhose (see below), ultrasheers are also harder to fit. Manufacturers of top brand ultrasheer pantyhose pay more attention to knitting pantyhose proportionally, graduating the fit so the pantyhose are narrower at the ankles — the worst place for bagging.

Demisheer: Less delicate and lustrous but sturdier and less expensive than ultrasheers. Also known as sheers.

Mesh: The coarsest, strongest, and least expensive pantyhose. They are knit differently from ultrasheer or demisheer pantyhose and will not ladder or run. They are, however, subject to holes.

Opaque: Stretch nylon opaque pantyhose are heavier than the sheers and are quite durable. They are available in many colors.

Control Top: The tops of control tops pantyhose (but not the legs) have extra spandex (stretch fiber) to help hold in the wearer's stomach. They provide a smooth line under knits and other clingy fabrics.

Support Hose: Spandex is in the legs as well as the tops. The idea is that extra support will hold the leg veins in place, helping circulation and preventing varicose veins in women who are on their feet all day. Not all doctors believe the hose are actually helpful, but many women find them especially comfortable.

Sandalfoot: If the toes of pantyhose are not reinforced, they are called sandalfoot. They are intended to be worn with open-toe shoes.

Ornamental: For a decorative effect, pantyhose with overall patterns and textures and individual designs are available.

When buying pantyhose, customers should be encouraged to buy the right shade. It is usually a good idea to match hose to shoes rather than to skirts for a slender, leggy look.

Stockings

Most hosiery departments stock mid-thigh-high stockings commonly called nylons and several shorter, special-purpose versions designed to be worn with trousers and/or boots.

Like pantyhose, stockings come in ultrasheer, demisheer, and mesh varieties. They are available with a reinforced toe or sandalfoot. Support stockings are also available.

Socks

Pantyhose or stockings are the most elegant look for formal or business occasions, but socks are worn for many casual occasions, particularly with pants. Socks come in a variety of lengths for different purposes.

Knee Highs or Knee Socks: To the knee. Worn with skirts by teenagers. Some women wear them as well, especially under pants.

Crew Socks: To midcalf; the classic athletic sock. They are usually worn with athletic shoes. Some have extra layers of material under the foot to cushion it during active sports.

HOSIERY

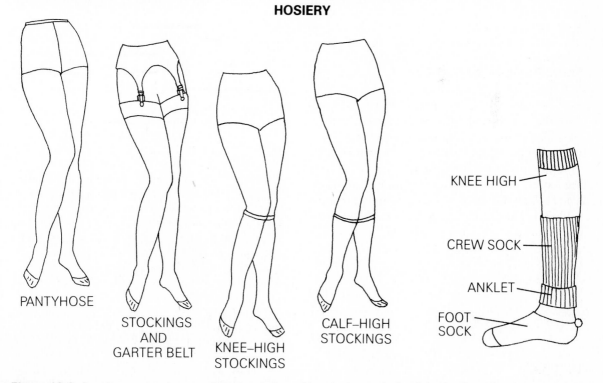

PANTYHOSE

STOCKINGS AND GARTER BELT

KNEE–HIGH STOCKINGS

CALF–HIGH STOCKINGS

KNEE HIGH

CREW SOCK

ANKLET

FOOT SOCK

Figure 18-9. *Pantyhose and socks or stockings in a variety of lengths are gradually taking the place of traditional stockings and garter belt.*

Anklets: To a little above the ankle; may have a cuff. The dainty socks children wear. Some women wear them with trousers.

Foot Socks: Below the ankle bone; covers the foot. Summer socks worn with athletic shoes. The person wearing these socks in the sun will have no tan line in the middle of her calf. Available with extra layers of soft material in the foot to cushion this part of the body during active sports.

Tights and legwarmers — often very decorative and fashionable — are also sold in the hosiery department. The tights may include dancerlike ones of opaque stretch nylon or wool or acrylic knit ones for cold weather. Legwarmers are of very heavy knit suitable for outdoor cold weather.

Selling Points of Hosiery

The following are some points salespeople should keep in mind when advising a customer in selecting hosiery.

Suitability and Versatility. The salesperson should find out where the customer intends to wear the hosiery. Ultrasheer pantyhose may be right for evening wear or for a party. Demisheer are probably better for business or everyday wear. A person planning a vacation in a hot tropical climate might be advised to purchase foot socks for tennis. A person who is planning a ski trip will need to buy the heaviest crew socks along with lighter silk or cotton socks for underneath.

Style and Attractiveness. Some people still feel that the most elegant pantyhose are the ultrasheer. They look dressy and give a completely bare leg appearance. There are, however, many exciting textures and colors to choose from in pantyhose and stockings as well as in socks, tights, and legwarmers. Salespeople should respect the personal feelings of all customers, but they can let them know that hosiery offers a variety of inexpensive fun items for them.

Comfort. Stockings and pantyhose are considered comfortable if they do not bind the leg and restrict movement, if they stay in place when worn, if they have no uncomfortable seam under the ball of the foot, if they do not pinch the toes, and if they are warm in cold weather and cool in warm weather.

Part of comfort in hosiery is fit. Sports hose should fit the leg snugly, even though they may be of bulky knit. Ultrasheers should not bag at the ankle or knee. Socks should not be so long that material bunches in the toe of the shoe or so short that the toes are cramped and cannot move. Customers cannot try on hosiery; however, they can be encouraged to develop brand preferences when they find hosiery that is especially comfortable.

The fiber from which hosiery is made greatly affects its comfort during wear. This is especially true of socks. Cotton makes a more comfortable sock than acrylic or most other synthetic fibers because of its **wicking** ability — ability to absorb moisture. Wool is probably the most comfortable sock because it can absorb moisture without becoming wet and does not lose its insulating properties when it is wet.

Care and Durability. Most customers realize that nylon stockings and pantyhose must be handled with care. Rough hands, nails, or rings can snag the yarns. Stockings and pantyhose should be washed in warm water in a mild soap solution. They should not be dried near hot steam pipes or a stove. Net bags are available for washing and drying delicate hosiery by machine. Many customers are not aware that rinsing new nylon pantyhose or stockings in lukewarm water before wearing makes them fit better.

DO YOU KNOW YOUR MERCHANDISE?

1. Why are suits and dresses still important wardrobe staples despite today's emphasis on casual clothes?

2. Why have activewear styles moved into the mainstream of U.S. fashion?
3. Describe suitable outfits for skiing, tennis, and swimming.
4. Describe suitable garments for dancing; for theater and dining.
5. Explain the difference between a dressy and a casual coat. What fabrics are commonly used for each?
6. Compare some of the advantages and disadvantages of synthetic and natural fibers for women's outerwear.
7. What is the significance of designer labels?
8. Describe five types of bra.
9. What are alternatives to the slip?
10. What are the differences among knee socks, crew socks, anklets, and foot socks?

PUTTING YOUR MERCHANDISE KNOWLEDGE TO WORK

Discuss five current trends in women's apparel. Sketch or describe five ensembles that illustrate these trends. List the fabrics you would use in the garments and discuss workmanship, styling, care, and selling points.

PROJECT

Plan a complete wardrobe for yourself or for a female member of your family. Include all outerwear, sportswear, undergarments, and sleepwear you will need. Give the styles, sizes, colors, and number of garments in each category. Determine, by shopping in stores, the approximate retail price of each item in your planned wardrobe. Also determine the retail value of the entire collection. Set an amount in advance depending on what you think you or she can afford to spend. Try to keep the value under that figure. Compare your findings with those of other members of your class. If there are major discrepancies, do they have to do with the choice of garments, with the number of garments, or with the price?

19

Men's Wear: Apparel and Furnishings

Through the ages, men have expressed themselves, their whims, and their times in their clothes. Men's fashions, like women's, derive from many sources, including social changes, new technologies, economic events, political influences, artistic attitudes, and opinion-molding forces such as motion pictures and television.

SUITS AND SEPARATES

Suits

Despite the growing popularity of casual clothes, suits are still the proper dress for business and many social occasions. There are two- and three-piece suits. Three-piece suits include a vest.

In general, **European suits** have a higher armhole and are more sharply shaped than **American suits.** Both European and American designer style suits often have the silhouette created by the French designer Pierre Cardin in the 1960s and introduced in the United States by Bonwit Teller. Designer suits influenced by European tailoring are sized on what is called the 7-inch drop. (The term **drop** has to do with the difference between the waist and chest measurement of the jacket.) For example, a suit jacket that measures 38 inches around the chest would measure 31 inches at the waist.

Traditional American suits are styled with a 6-inch drop. Because of demand, clothing makers have increased production of suits with a 7-inch differential between chest and waist measurements. A 5- or 6-inch drop continues to dominate, however.

Suit jackets may be single breasted, usually with two buttons, or double breasted, with four to six buttons. Collar and lapel widths vary according to fashion. They may be peaked or notched and with or without buttonholes. Pockets may be with or without flaps. The jacket may have a center vent, side vents, or be unvented.

There are three basic men's suit silhouettes or models: soft or natural shouldered; conventional with built-up shoulders; and shouldered or squared. These three models may be termed traditional, middle-of-the-road or contemporary, and European, respectively.

The styles of men's pants vary in a number of ways. They can fit the legs or buttocks loosely or tightly. They may be high or low **rise** (the measurement extending from the crotch to the waist or above). Waistband widths and belt loops and size, number, and style of pockets vary.

Trouser cuffs disappeared during World War II when government restrictions decreed all excess fabric be eliminated from apparel. In late sixties and early seventies wide-bottomed pants were often cuffed. Today, cuffed trousers are usually confined to traditional styles.

Some features of the traditional suit are:

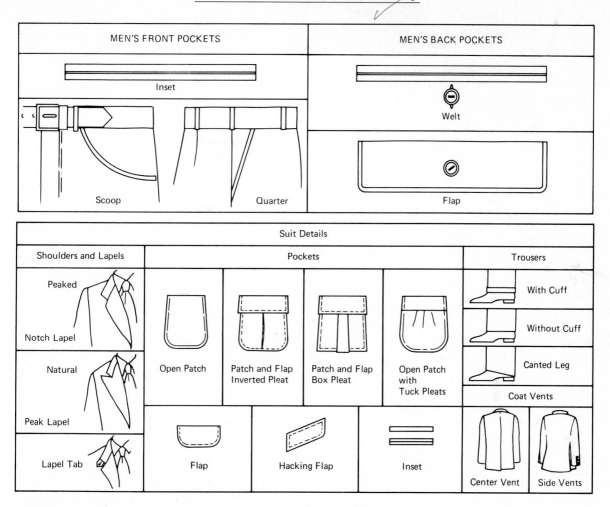

Figure 19-1. *Styles of men's pants pockets and suit details such as shoulders, lapels, pockets, trousers, and coat vents may make a great difference to a customer.*

Jacket: Natural or soft shoulders (not padded or raised); two-button or three-button closing; center vent; usually flap pockets and breast welt pocket.
Pants: Plain front; straight leg.

Some features of the European-style designer suit are as follows.

Jacket: Rope or definite shoulder; high armholes; shaped waist; one-button or two-button closing; high vents or unvented; lower patch or flap pockets; breast welt pocket.
Pants: Plain or pleated front; slant pockets.

In addition to the traditional and European suit models, a style known as **contemporary** is popular. It is essentially an in-between version of the European and traditional suits. Also popular is the updated traditional look.

Unless located in very warm or very cold climates, most retail stores carry two weights of suits — **lightweight** for spring and summer and **regular weight** for fall and winter. The lightweight suits weight 4 to 5 ounces a square yard of fabric; the regular-weight suits weigh about 7 ounces a square yard. Table 19–1 gives suiting fabrics appropriate for spring/summer and fall/winter suits.

Suit fabrics are made of natural fibers such as wool and cotton; of manmade fibers such as polyester, and (perhaps most common) of blends such as polyester/woolen and polyester/worsted. Some lightweight suitings contain silk, rayon, and linen for texture and luster.

Although handmade suits continue to be sold, even very expensive suits may be 100 percent machine made. Customers can expect good fit in today's volume-produced clothing. Here are a list of points to be considered in judging good tailoring.

- The jacket should hang smoothly with no bubble under the collar and no pulling across the shoulders.
- Collars may lie flat and smooth or roll softly.
- There should be interfacings to help garments keep their shape and hang better. Linings will help prevent wrinkles and stretching and protect against perspiration and wear.
- There should be ample material, with generous seam allowances, to allow for alterations.
- Trousers should be cut amply enough to fit comfortably.
- Vests should be cut and tailored to fit correctly.
- Pockets should be deep and made of a stout material such as cotton twill.

The size of the jacket is usually based on the girth of it measured under the arm pit and over the shoulder blades. (The customer is advised to take a deep breath during measurement.) Men's tailored suit jackets have traditionally been produced in the following proportioned sizes.

- Shorts: 36–44
- Regulars: 35–46
- Longs: 37–48
- Extra longs: 38–50
- Portlies: 39–50
- Portly shorts: 39–48
- Big and tall sizes: 46, 48, 50

Trouser size depends on the waist and inseam measurements. The latter is the length from the crotch along the inside seam to the bottom of the trousers. Trousers are available with waist sizes ranging from 32 to 40 inches, with 2-inch increments between sizes. Some trousers come in exact leg lengths, but most suit trousers come with the bottoms unfinished. A simple tailoring job, usually done in the store where the suit is purchased, provides the correct trouser length for the customer.

Sport Jackets and Dress Slacks

Many men's tailored jackets and pants have not been matched as a suit. The color or pattern of the **sport jacket** is different from that of the trousers with which it is worn. Often the texture is different too.

The so-called sport jacket, with its tailored construction, is not meant for active sports. Sport jackets such as the navy blue blazer with gold-colored buttons and the tweed jacket are acceptable in all but the most conservative business situations.

The **blazer** is a single- or double-breasted jacket in solid colors such as navy or camel. The style was created in the nineteenth century by the captain of the *HMS Blazer* as a uniform for his ship's crew. The navy blue blazer has long been a favorite. The traditional material for

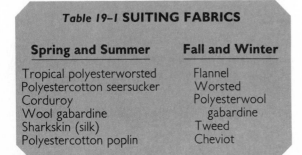

Table 19–1 SUITING FABRICS

Spring and Summer	Fall and Winter
Tropical polyesterworsted	Flannel
Polyestercotton seersucker	Worsted
Corduroy	Polyesterwool
Wool gabardine	gabardine
Sharkskin (silk)	Tweed
Polyestercotton poplin	Cheviot

blazers is wool flannel, but tropical worsted is excellent for spring and summer wear.

Blazers and other tailored sport jackets are traditionally worn with dress trousers, but many young men wear sport jackets — commonly made of a strong twilled cotton fabric — with tan chinos and jeans. This casual look is acceptable for many social occasions, particularly where the prep-school style of dress is admired.

There are also sport jackets and dress slacks in bright or pastel colors for social wear. Clothes such as a tan poplin sport jacket worn with madras plaid trousers are sometimes called **weekend wear.**

WORK AND CASUAL CLOTHES

Although originaly intended for miners and cowboys, jeans — the first were Levi's — have become a classic for casual wear around the world. Indigo blue was the first, and for a long time, only jeans color, but jeans now come in many other colors. There are also stone-dyed and prewashed types with a worn look.

Classic jeans have five pockets and straight legs. Levi's are decorated with metal studs. **Boot jeans** have flared bottoms to fit over boots.

Jeans may be worn with a sport shirt, sweatshirt, sweater, vest, or matching denim jacket. A popular collegiate look is jeans worn with a dress shirt (even a formal shirt) and a tweed or other sport jacket. In summer, cut-off jeans function as shorts.

Alternatives to jeans are the western-style twill or corduroy trousers and denim, canvas, or twill overalls. **Overalls** are cut much looser than jeans or western pants, have a bib and shoulder straps, cover most of the body in sturdy fabric, and are adaptable to changes in temperature. Because of their loose fit and adjustable shoulder straps, overalls can be worn over a light T-shirt or over many layers of warm underwear and sweaters. If they are very large and loose, they can even be worn over another pair of trousers.

Also loose in fit are the lightweight **painter's pants.** They are of less stiff material than jeans and therefore easier to bend and turn in. Painter's pants often have reinforced knees for longer wear. They are available in a rainbow of colors.

The **jump suit,** the traditional uniform of paratroopers, has been a civilian style for many years. Usually a jump suit zips up the front, is made of a wide variety of fabrics (poplin is popular), and most typically has long sleeves and a number of pockets.

Overalls, jeans, and other casual pants are measured by the size of the waist and the length of the inseam. For jumpsuits, the chest measurement must be added to those of the waist and inseam.

ACTIVE SPORTSWEAR

Men and boys take part in many active sports. This discussion will focus on four of them that have influenced men's casual clothing: golf, hiking, swimming, and running. (Skiing and tennis are covered in Chapter 18.)

Clothes for Golf

The zip-front, hip-length poplin or other lightweight jacket and short-sleeved knit pullover or polo shirt worn by golfers are staples in the wardrobes of many nongolfers. Lightweight, amply cut casual slacks, a visored cap, and shoes with cleats complete the golfer's outfit. Golfers led the way to colorful sportswear, particularly slacks, in the forties and fifties.

Hiking Clothes

The hiker's and camper's sturdy trousers, often reinforced in the seat and knees, are a part of the city-dweller's weekend look. The unlined thick wool mackinaw jacket (permitting greater freedom of movement than a lined jacket) rugged wool sweaters (which absorb water without feeling wet), heavy wool boot socks, wool cap, wool or flannel shirt, and stiff, sturdy boots have all become fashion clothing. Well-known designers make their own versions of these clothes.

Hiking and other outdoor clothes are notable for their strong construction, including reinforcement at wear points, double seaming, and durable materials. These clothes are cut generously for vigorous outdoor activity and to allow layering for changes in weather conditions.

Swimwear

Men's swimwear comes in five styles.

Racing Briefs: Jersey suits such as Speedo; some are bikini cut.
Brief-Cut Boxers: Has side vents.
Boxer Shorts: With elasticized waistbands and full cut.
Tailored, Fly-Front Shorts: Once paired with shirts as cabana sets.
Surfing Styles: Longer than usual trunks.

Competition swimmers often wear warm-up suits before, between, and after events. These suits are sometimes in the jumpsuit style but usually consist of separate trousers and top. The trousers have an elasticized waist and ample cut. The tops zip up the front and have ribbed necks and sleeves. Both tops and trousers are usually made of acrylic knit fabric and decorated with bands or stripes of brightly contrasting color at the neck, shoulders, waist, and other focal points. Often there is a band of color down each side of the trousers.

Running Clothes

In cold weather runners sometimes wear warm-up suits or running or sweat suits of fleece-backed sweatshirt material that can absorb moisture without feeling wet. **Running suits** often feature elasticized ankles, waists, and wrists. The top may be a pullover sweatshirt, with a **crew,** or round ribbed, neck and ribbed wrists or a hooded sweatshirt with pockets at the waist.

Under the running suit runners wear layers of bright-colored athletic T-shirts, usually knit of heavier material than underwear T-shirts, and thermal underwear (discussed later in the chapter).

Warm-weather running gear consists of shorts and an athletic T-shirt or tank top. Running shorts are usually made of a light, soft material such as nylon or acrylic knit. They have elasticized waists and relatively wide, short legs. They are usually bright colored, which makes the roadside dusk or early-morning runner easier to see. Some nylon running shorts have a soft lining, which makes it unnecessary for the runner to wear underwear, although he usually wears an athletic supporter.

Nylon running shorts can double as swimwear and are often paired with nylon tank tops that are perforated at small, regular intervals to make up for the fact that the lightweight nylon does not allow air to pass in and out.

The running suit has become a popular casual outfit for runners and nonrunners.

COATS AND HEAVY OUTERWEAR

Men's topcoats and overcoats may be tailored, like suits, or less structured, sturdier, and more casual. **Tailored coats** consists of overcoats, topcoats, and all-weather coats. Nontailored garments such as parkas, ski jackets and wind-breaking shells are known collectively as **heavy outerwear.**

Overcoats and Topcoats

Overcoats are heavy outer garments suitable for winter. They are made of fabrics such as cashmere, camel's hair, or tweed, often with fur or furlike trim or lining. **Topcoats,** which are made of lighter-weight fabrics, are full-length coats for fall wear. Both overcoats and topcoats are designed to be worn over suits. Their length is determined by fashion.

Two of the coats shown in Figure 19–2 have set-in sleeves; four have raglan sleeves.

Three-quarter length coats are more casual than overcoats and topcoats. A popular type of three-quarter length coat is the **duffle,** or **toggle**

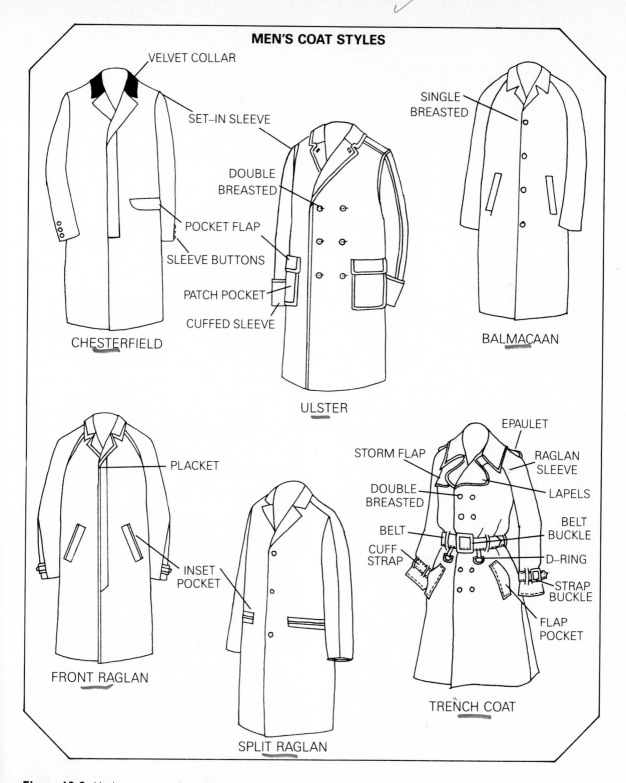

MEN'S COAT STYLES

CHESTERFIELD
- VELVET COLLAR
- SET-IN SLEEVE
- POCKET FLAP
- SLEEVE BUTTONS

ULSTER
- DOUBLE BREASTED
- PATCH POCKET
- CUFFED SLEEVE

BALMACAAN
- SINGLE BREASTED

FRONT RAGLAN
- PLACKET

SPLIT RAGLAN
- INSET POCKET

TRENCH COAT
- EPAULET
- STORM FLAP
- RAGLAN SLEEVE
- DOUBLE BREASTED
- LAPELS
- BELT
- BELT BUCKLE
- CUFF STRAP
- D-RING
- STRAP BUCKLE
- FLAP POCKET

Figure 19-2. *Men's topcoats and overcoats may be tailored, like suits, or less structured, sturdier, and more casual.*

coat. It is a heavy woolen coat, usually knee length and hooded, which is worn for protection against cold and stormy weather. Some duffle coats have real fleece linings. Tan is the most popular color, followed by navy and loden (green).

Another popular casual coat fashion for men (and women) is the pea jacket (discussed on page 218 under **Coats**).

All-Weather Coats

All-weather coats often have a water-repellent or water-resistant finish. This means they are not waterproof but will protect the wearer from mild rain. (See Chapter 18 for an explanation of why most waterproof coats are hot and uncomfortable.) All-weather coats often have a zip-out lining that makes them warm enough to be worn in cold weather. Without the lining, they can be worn in spring and fall weather.

Trench Coats.   The trench coat was designed during World War I for British officers who fought in the trenches in France. It is now a classic, all-purpose coat, often with a zip-out or button-out liner for cold weather. The outer layer of trench coats is generally of gabardine (a twill construction) or poplin, either all-cotton or a cotton/polyester blend. The famous Burberry trench coats have distinctive plaid linings.

Figure 19–2 gives the major style features to look for. The true trench coat has sleeve straps, a large collar that can be buttoned up (usually with a metal fastener) close to the neck, and a deep back vent with tab and double back yoke. The length of the trench coat should be well below the knees. The full belt is usually buckled, but some people like to have it long enough to tie. The D rings, now ornamental, were originally used to hold equipment such as canteens. Tan is the most popular color for trench coats; they are also popular in navy gabardine.

A shorter and lighter-weight relative of the trench coat is the **safari jacket.** It is a tailored casual jacket with four deep pockets. They are usually made of cotton poplin or corduroy.

Heavy Outerwear

One of the most popular and useful kinds of heavy outerwear is the **parka,** a jacket with a hood that keeps icy air from the wearer's body more efficiently than most other wraps. Parkas are short enough not to flap around the legs or tug at the neck and arms.

The **anorak** is a sport parka with raglan sleeves and a drawstring hood and waistband. A stowaway pocket at front center has handwarmer slits at either side.

The warmest, best ventilated, and lightest parka (though bulky) is stuffed with down (discussed in Chapter 18). A number of synthetic insulating materials have been developed as alternatives to down. Sontique, Hollofil, and Kodofill are the trade names of three insulations made of polyester fibers. Thinsulate combines polyester and olefin fibers. Parkas filled with these insulations have some advantages over down-filled parkas. They do not lose their warmth when they are wet and they are less bulky and less expensive than down. They are machine washable, whereas down is better maintained by dry cleaning.

A good waterproof parka material is Gore-tex, a new synthetic that breathes better than most other waterproof materials so is less hot and clammy to wear. Not waterproof, though reasonably water repellent, a 60/40 percent blend is another sensible parka material. The so-called 60/40 cloth is woven of 60 percent cotton and 40 percent nylon; it is lightweight, highly wind resistant, and well ventilated. This material works well in lightweight jackets for spring and fall and layered over warm sweaters for winter. It is also used for down-filled parkas.

A thin unlined parka or jacket is sometimes called a **shell.** A shell is a very versatile garment. With sweaters or a down-filled ski vest beneath it, the wearer will be warm in cold weather.

A shell may be considered any lightweight jacket of wind-resistant (closely woven) material. Some have ribbed or pointed collars. Many have snug-fitting, wind-resistant ribbed cuffs and a zipper all or partway up the front.

EVENING WEAR

For informal evening occasions many men wear a solid navy blue or black suit with a dress shirt and necktie. When an occasion is referred to as **black tie,** it means men are expected to wear **tuxedos.** The traditional tuxedo jacket is black with satin or faille lapels. The trousers have a stripe of the same material running from the waist to the bottom along the outer seam. The jacket has one or two buttons and may be single or double breasted. The tuxedo is worn with a pleated-front shirt with a conventional or a wing collar, a vest or a cummerbund, patent leather oxfords or pumps or plain black calf oxfords, and a black faille or satin bow tie.

Many formal shirts have French cuffs and need **cuff links.** They may require **studs** (removable shanked buttons that pass through eyelets on the shirt front to serve as fasteners) or may have fly fronts covering a row of buttons.

Some dinner jackets are in more colorful and fancier fabrics than have been traditional. These jackets come in brocades, velvets, failles, and satins in maroon, navy, green, or bright red. Other variations on traditional formal evening clothes include dressy black slip-ons with metal buckles and shirts with ruffled fronts and cuffs.

For very formal evening wear, such as weddings and state occasions, a white pique tie and a tailcoat may be worn. For daytime weddings, an **ascot** (broad neck scarf looped under the chin) may be worn with a cutaway coat and striped trousers.

SELLING POINTS OF OUTERWEAR

Keep in mind the points discussed below when buying and selling men's outerwear.

Suitability and Versatility

The garment should be appropriate for the intended use and for the wearer. It sould be wearable for as many occasions as possible and for as much of the year as possible.

Style, Attractiveness, and Fashion Rightness

The fashion consciousness of contemporary men has generated a wide range of choices for them in color, fabrics, and styles. Many men are aware of details such as widths of lapels, shoulder styling, pocket number and placement, length and cut of jackets, and cut of trousers.

Today's men have many choices. They can show individuality in dress or can conform to traditional standards. There are traditional or classic soft shoulder clothing, middle-of-the-road safe models, or designer-type styles with European flair. Above all, good taste is of prime importance.

Care and Durability

The greatest number of men's tailored suits and coats require dry-cleaning, even if they are partly or entirely of manmade fibers, so ease of care (discussed in Chapter 18) is a somewhat academic question with regard to these garments. However, coats and suits that resist wrinkling help men stay crisp looking longer. Many men take this factor into account when choosing their tailored as well as casual clothing. Some casual clothing, for example, durable-press poplin slacks and running suits, are truly wash and wear.

Quality and Price

Comparative price is important to many customers. The salesperson should be able to explain to customers how differences in price reflect differences in fabric, workmanship, and styling.

Many customers are willing to pay slightly higher prices for brand names, private- and store-labeled goods, and designer names. Many brands have a reputation for high standards of styling, appearance, quality, and construction. Designer clothes often offer a unique look.

FURNISHINGS

All these articles of clothing that accompany or are worn with men's outerwear are known collectively as **furnishings.** They include shirts, sweaters, neckties, underwear, socks, loungewear and sleepwear.

Shirts

Men's shirts may be divided into two classifications: dress shirts and sport shirts. One way of differentiating used to be that dress shirts had a collarband and sport shirts did not. This is no longer true. Today the fabrics dress and sport shirts are made of may be different, and the methods of sizing are different.

Dress Shirts.   Men's dress shirts are available in a wide range of styles, materials, sizes, and colors. There are three basic collar styles: **button-down, spread,** and **long point.** Button-down shirts are traditional and often of oxford cloth. Dress shirts have either **barrel cuffs** (single layered) or **French cuffs** (double layered, requiring cuff links). There are also a number of ways in which the body, back, and front of a shirt may be styled (see Figure 19–3). A shirt may come with no pockets or one or two pockets and with or without flaps and buttons.

The most common dress shirt fabrics are oxford cloth and broadcloth. **Oxford cloth** is a soft but sturdy basket weave fabric of cotton/polyester, usually in a 65/35 blend but also in 50/50 or 35/65 reverse blend. **Broadcloth** is a plain, tightly woven fabric with fine crosswise uneven ribs.

Dress shirts come in specific collar sizes and, if long sleeved, exact or average sleeve lengths such as 32/33 or 34/35.

Traditional shirts are full cut; designer shirts are contour cut. A salesperson should check to see if a shirt fits well as follows.

- The waist should be smooth, with no bagginess or bunching of material. It should be loose enough so the material does not pull at the buttons when the customer moves.

- Button-down collars should have a soft roll. Collars should not wrinkle; if they do, they are probably too tight.
- The shirt sleeves should stop just below the wrist bone, about $\frac{1}{2}$ inch below the edge of the jacket sleeve.
- Buttoned cuffs should fit close to the wrist and still allow movement. (Many average-length dress shirts have two buttons to permit adjustments.) Although most dress shirts are wrist length, short-sleeved shirts are available.

Sport Shirts.   Many sport shirts are woven, but many others are knitted, for example the familiar polo shirt. The **polo shirt** is a short-sleeved pullover with a three-button placket at the neck and a spread collar. These shirts are manufactured in all cotton and in cotton/polyester blends. The famous Izod polo shirt has a small alligator patch on the left breast. French tennis star Rene Lacoste, who styled the shirt with a longer shirttail in back so it would not pull out, was known as the crocodile because of the way he moved around the court. The first U.S. licensee for Lacoste was the Alligator Company, and the emblem came to be identified as an alligator. Other brands have their own distinctive patches.

A close relative of the polo shirt is the long-sleeved **rugby shirt,** which is an open-collared pullover with a three-button placket. The body of the rugby shirt is striped, and it has a plain-colored collar and placket of woven fabric (usually twill).

The rib-necked **T-shirt** is worn for sportswear as well as underwear. The art of decorating plain, short-sleeved T-shirts to advertise business enterprises or personal characteristics began in the sixties and continues.

Woven sport shirts may be long or short sleeved. Many have permanent collar stays of plastic in a pointed spread collar. Others are soft collared. Woven sport shirts often come in very bright colors, such as the **Hawaiian shirt,** a loose-fitting short-sleeved shirt usually worn out-

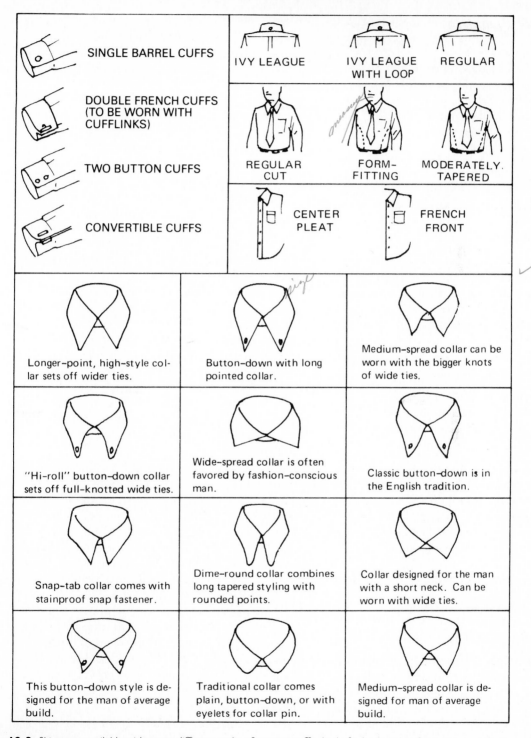

Figure 19-3. *Shirts are available with many different styling features: cuffs, body fit, back styles, front styles, and collar styles.*

side the trousers. The Hawaiian shirt has tropical designs featuring flowers, birds, palm trees, and pineapples.

Many long-sleeved wool or cotton flannel sport shirts come in plaids that originally designated Scottish clans.

Most knitted and woven sport shirts are sized by general collar measurements as follows.

- *Small*: 14 to 14½ inches
- *Medium*: 15 to 15½ inches
- *Large*: 16 to 16½ inches
- *Extra large*: 17 to 17½ inches

Sweaters

Men's sweaters come in two classic styles, pullovers and cardigans. The **pullover sweater** may have a V neck, turtleneck, or crew neck. Sleeveless V-neck sweaters are called **sweater vests. Cardigan sweaters** button down the front and may have a collar and belt.

Sweaters are sized by chest measurements as follows.

- *Small*: 34 to 36 inches
- *Medium*: 38 to 40 inches
- *Large*: 42 to 44 inches
- *Extra large*: 42 to 44 inches

Some sweaters are made of wool; the most expensive and luxurious ones are 100 percent cashmere. Also popular are lamb's wool and Shetland. Many sweaters are of manmade fibers, the most important being acrylic fibers such as Orlon. Cotton sweaters are also made.

Neckties, Scarves, and Handkerchiefs

Neckties, scarves, and handkerchiefs are popular gift items for men. They provide a decorative finishing touch to a man's outfit.

Neckties.   The two traditional forms of neckties are the four-in-hand and the bow tie. The **four-in-hand** is named after the knot once used to join the reins of two horses to be driven by one person. It is the familiar necktie cut on the bias and tied in a slip knot so the long flared ends

overlap vertically in front. The **bow tie** is short and tied in a bow knot. A very narrow tie called a **string tie** or **bolo** is sometimes worn. It is a highly regional fashion in the South and parts of the West.

Four-in-hand ties are usually 55 to 56 inches long. Their width varies with fashion and generally harmonizes with the width of the wearer's suit lapels.

Today's ties are made of silk, polyester, wool, cotton, wool challis, and blends of these fibers. Most are woven, but some are knit. Woven four-in-hand ties have pointed ends; some knit ties have square ends. Inexpensive ties may have rigid construction. Better ties will be **slip stitched,** which means that there is loose stitching in the back seam of the ties to make them more elastic. These ties also have a heavy interlining that is cut on the bias and hangs loose.

A popular variety of tie is the **regimental.** The diagonal stripes of this tie originally designated membership in an organization such as a military regiment (hence the name). Another popular tie is the **club tie,** which is studded with small embroidered emblems. The **paisley** tie is made of wool or silk imprinted or woven with a colorful design of curved, abstract shapes.

Scarves.   The most useful winter scarf is a long narrow rectangle intended to be wrapped around the neck and crossed at the front. It is worn under coats and comes in both heavy and light weights. For cold weather, woven and knitted wool, flannel, cashmere, and blends are popular. Lighter-weight scarves are made of **foulard** (silk twill), silk surah, manmade fiber fabrics, and blends. For formal wear, silks and silklike manmade fiber fabrics are popular.

A knitted wool scarf that is intended to be wrapped and rewrapped around the neck outside the coat is called a **muffler.** The muffler provides good cold-weather protection for the face and the neck.

Handkerchiefs.   Retail stores sell plain white cotton, linen, and polyester/cotton blend, as well

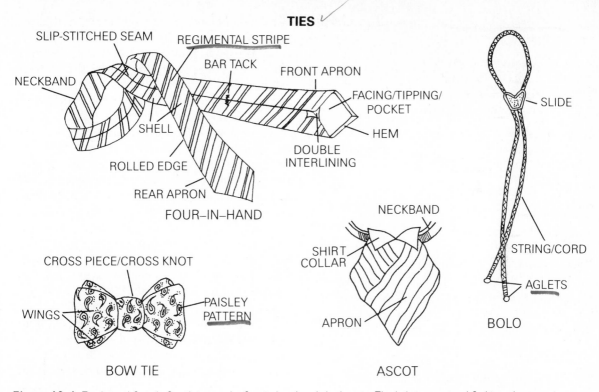

Figure 19-4. *Traditional forms of necktie are the four-in-hand and the bowtie. The bolo is a regional fashion; the ascot is a broad neck scarf.*

as monogrammed style handkerchiefs. Most stores also carry some fancy patterns and colors. A 65 percent polyester, 35 percent cotton blend is durable press and may be finished to resist bacterial growth. Some men prefer 100 percent cotton since it is more absorbent. Some handkerchiefs have hand-rolled hems (hand stitched); others have hem-stitched edges.

Manmade fibers or silk are used for decorative handkerchiefs to be worn in the breast pocket. A **pocket square** is puffed casually, never worn squared.

Underwear

Men's underwear comes in several variations, including T-shirts, athletic shirts, shorts, regular and bikini briefs, and European briefs. These garments are knitted except the shorts. They are woven and come in the **boxer style** with an elastic waist or in the **yoke style** with gripper snaps.

Shorts and Briefs. Most men's **shorts** and **briefs** (form-fitting crotch-length underpants) are of cotton/manmade fiber blends. The cotton absorbs perspiration, and the manmade fibers are easy to care for and help the shorts or briefs keep their shape.

Undershirts. Many T-shirts and athletic undershirts (sleeveless, U necked) are of cotton/polyester or cotton/nylon blends, but some men prefer all-cotton undershirts. They feel the cotton is absorbent and breathes. It does not matter if an underwear T-shirt holds its press, so the durable-press feature of blends means less than it does in some other garments.

T-shirts and athletic shirts are sized according to chest measurements as follows.

- *Small:* 30 to 34 inches
- *Medium:* 36 to 40 inches
- *Large:* 42 to 44 inches
- *Extra Large:* 46 to 52 inches.

Shorts are sized 28 to 40, according to waist size. Briefs are sized small, medium, large, and extra large according to waist size.

Brief Sizes

- *Small:* 30 to 32 inches
- *Medium:* 34 to 36 inches
- *Large:* 38 to 40 inches
- *Extra Large:* 42 to 44 inches

Thermal Underwear. For anyone planning to be exposed to cold temperatures for any length of time, thermal underwear is almost a necessity. The knit construction traps body heat between the yarns to resist cold. The union, or one-piece suit, is not as popular as the two-piece suit. Both types have wrist-length arms and ankle-length legs, usually with ribbed cuffs. Thermal underwear is commonly made of cotton and wool blends in a warp knit mesh. Some of the warmest, most comfortable, and most expensive thermal underwear is silk. Recently, a new thermal fabric has been developed in England. It has greater warmth relative to weight and greater resistance to the flow of heat than either cotton or wool. It is called Thermolactyl and is knitted from a blend of 85 percent vinyon and 15 percent acrylic fiber. Underwear made from it is available in the United States.

Hosiery

Socks come in a variety of styles and fabrics and are best classified by the types of occasions for which they are worn. There are socks for dress wear, casual wear, and work and athletic wear. Many socks are reinforced in the toe and heel to prolong their wear life. Some come with an antistatic finish to keep trouser legs from clinging to

them and lint from collecting on them. Some are treated in finishing to resist odor and bacteria.

Dress socks, which are worn with business suits and evening wear, are usually flat rib knits that come in over-the-calf and midcalf lengths. They may be knitted of 100 percent cotton (with an elasticized top) or of blends of wool and nylon or of nylon and spandex. The stretch yarns make the sock stay up. Some over-the-calf styles are 100 percent nylon, which is thought to help ease muscle strain and give support to the wearer who walks and stands for long periods of time. **Luxury socks** are knitted of lamb's wool or cashmere.

Casual socks are worn with a sports jacket and sport slacks or with a sweater and slacks. They are often made of bulky wool or acrylic yarns for softness and comfort. Sometimes nylon is added to improve fit. Frequently these socks have ribbed tops to make them stay up. Most are knit with **turned heels** — the traditional sock construction. **Tube socks** — with no defined heel — are increasingly popular. They are easier to knit and less expensive. Often tube socks and other casual socks have sporty looking stripes around the tops. Casual socks are sometimes produced in 100 percent stretch nylon for support.

Work and athletic socks are designed for long, hard wear. Typical fiber combinations are all cotton, cotton and nylon, and cotton and spandex. Winter-weight socks may be wool and nylon or 100 percent wool, which is very warm even when wet. A good layering and insulating sock (to be worn under wool socks in winter or with hiking boots) is of silk, but thin cotton is also good and is less expensive.

A terry cloth cushion sole helps a sock absorb moisture, as well as shocks, such as from running on concrete sidewalks or playing tennis on asphalt courts. Socks for sports, such as basketball or soccer, in which there is a good chance players will be injured in the legs, are usually knee high. They may be worn in conjunction with tape or padding.

Men's nonstretch hosiery come in half-size increments from $9\frac{1}{2}$ to 13. These sizes do not correspond to shoe sizes; a man who wears a size 10 shoe will find that a size 10 sock is much too small for his foot. With stretch hosiery, one or two sizes cover the range of common sizes.

Sleepwear and Loungewear

Although some men choose sleepwear and loungewear by color, design, fabric, and style, the one feature most men want is comfort.

Two basic types of pajamas are generally sold in stores. The **coat type** has front buttons or snaps, and the **pullover type** has no front closing. Most pajamas come with ankle-length trousers, but shorter lengths (above the knee) are also sold.

The coat style lends itself to woven fabrics such as broadcloth and cotton flannel for winter and crepe or percale for summer. The pullover style is often knitted and sometimes comes with a top that is a different color from the pants. Usually knits have an elastic waist and may have fitted anklets and wristlets of matching or contrasting ribbing.

Men's **robes** are usually the wraparound style and are often of flannel. Full-length robes of absorbent material such as terry cloth are called **bathrobes**. Robes of more luxurious material, such as velour, brocade, or silky fabrics, are also available; some are in **kimono** style, with full ornamental sleeves.

Men's pajamas and robe sizes are determined by chest measurements, like T-shirts (see above). Sometimes pajamas are sized A, B, C, and D.

Selling Points of Furnishings

Keep in mind the following points when buying and selling men's furnishings.

Suitability. Because there are so many colors, textures, and styles of men's furnishings (especially shirts, sweaters, ties, and scarves), those involved in its merchandising must understand the principles of wardrobe coordination. The easiest and safest way to coordinate furnisings is to use mainly solid colors, for example, a pale blue shirt and a blue-and-gray striped tie with a solid gray suit. It is also safe to match one solid color with one pattern, for example, a pink polo shirt with maroon and navy madras plaid trousers. The pink of the polo shirt is a tint of the maroon, or dark red, of the trousers. This illustrates another coordination rule. The solid color of the combination should pick up one of the colors in the patterned garment.

Combining patterns is a tricky way to coordinate clothing, although many men do wear combinations of patterns. One general rule is to select the boldest pattern first, then coordinate it with subtler patterns. Another involves separating two patterns with a solid color. For example, a solid shirt and a paisley tie may be combined with a glen plaid suit. Finally, the patterns of the various garment should be harmonious. A pattern that travels in one direction clashes with a pattern that travels in another. For example, a diagonally striped regimental tie is not quite right with a pin-striped suit. When choosing furnishings such as shirts and ties to accompany suits, avoid colors that clash and colors that fade into one another.

Appearance. The appearance of a shirt depends on the looks and quality of the fabric, on the style in which it is cut, and on the quality of the workmanship. The same is true of ties, pajamas, robes, underwear, and sweaters. However, most underwear (undershorts excepted), many sport shirts, and all sweaters are knitted rather than woven and cut. Generally the quality of machine knitting is uniform and good, but there may be many differences in the quality of yarns used and in the way the pieces of the garment are assembled and finished.

Size and Comfort. When a customer wants to buy a shirt, he must know the measurements. For dress shirts it is the size of the neck and the sleeve length. The sleeve length is measured from the nape of the neck, over the shoulders, down to the bottom of the cuff. For sport shirts it is the size of the neck or the chest size. For other furnishings it may be the chest size or waist size.

A shirt should be cut full across the chest for comfort, and it should have tails long enough to remain tucked inside the trousers. Pajamas, sweaters, underwear, and robes are more comfortable if they are cut full across the chest and do not bind the crotch and upper-thigh area. Socks should be longer than the foot but no so long they bunch up in the toe of the shoe.

Care and Durability.
The durability of shirts and other furnishings is determined by the kind of wear and care they receive, as well as by the quality of the fibers, yarns, construction, and finish.

Laboratory tests show that a 100 percent pure cotton dress shirt that is commercially washed will withstand 35 to 50 launderings. If an average of 40 commercial launderings is considered to be the life of a shirt and if that shirt is sent to the laundry every other week, then the shirt's life would be 80 weeks, or about $1\frac{1}{2}$ years. If the cotton is mercerized or the shirt is washed at home it will last longer. If polyester is blended with the cotton, the shirt will be more durable because the polyester will add strength to the material.

As discussed in Chapter 18, the notion of easy care is more complicated than was supposed when the manmade fibers, with their permanent-press features, first became popular. It should be pointed out that so-called wash-and-wear shirts do not for the most part look crisp without touch-up ironing. However, polyester-cotton blends look fresher longer.

Because polyester fibers retain oil and oil-based stains, shirts containing them must be washed frequently if they have not been given a soil-release finish.

Quality and Price.
Some customers buy primarily by price; therefore a retailer should feature price in relation to the serviceability and styling of shirts and other furnishings. As with outerwear, many men favor brand and/or designer merchandise. This merchandise commands higher prices and is generally stylish and well made.

DO YOU KNOW YOUR MERCHANDISE?

1. What is the difference between the traditional style suit and the European style suit?
2. Name some fabrics appropriate for fall/winter and spring/summer suits.
3. Differentiate among jeans, overalls, and jumpsuits.
4. Suggest the appropriate attire for two of the following sports: golf, hiking, jogging, swimming.
5. Describe both the traditional tuxedo and the new trends in formal evening wear.
6. Describe thermal underwear. With what kinds of outerwear and furnishings might it be worn to layer a warm, comfortable outfit?
7. Classify men's socks into three types and explain the differences.
8. What are the chief articles of men's underwear? How are these garments sized?
9. What are the rules that govern successful combining of patterns in men's wear?
10. How is easy care related to an individual's life-style?

PUTTING YOUR MERCHANDISE KNOWLEDGE TO WORK

Assume that you are planning to operate a men's specialty store catering to residents of your community. Make a list of all the different shirts you would carry. Consider both dress and sport shirts, and within each of these categories plan materials, sizes, colors, collar styles, and so forth. Note that you cannot carry everything someone in the community might ask for.

PROJECT

Observe and describe the usual business or work attire of 18 men in your community, with three in each of the following six groupings:

- Substantial businessmen
- Professional persons
- Blue-collar workers
- College men
- Sales representatives
- Employees in a small business establishment

(You may substitute another grouping well represented in your community if you wish.) Do there seem to be any significant differences in people's attire as related to their jobs? If so, describe the logical reasons for the differences.

20

Furs: The Exotic Products

Furs, which were first used to protect people from snow, rain, and cold, have continued to be used for their durability, warmth, beauty, and unique textures. Imitations have been developed, but none provides the glamor or feeling of luxury that real fur does.

In the late 1970s and early 1980s furs became important features in fashion showings. The demand for furs, which since 1950 had been primarily for mink and mink look-alikes, changed. Long-haired furs, short-haired furs, pieced furs, combinations of different furs, combinations of furs with fabric and leather, and an array of varied colors, textures, and elaborate designs in furs became popular. In the late 1970s men also began again to wear furs.

GOVERNMENT LAWS AND THEIR IMPACT

Consumers and fur producers are protected by an act requiring honesty in labeling furs, and fur-bearing animals are protected from extinction by a conservation requirement.

Fur Products Labeling Act ⁱⁿ

Identification of individual furs is difficult because fur may be made to look and feel different from that on the animal itself by the various dyeing, finishing, and/or construction processes used. Therefore, the U.S. government passed the

Fur Products Labeling Act, which became effective in 1952. Slight amendments were made in the law in 1961, 1967, 1969, and 1980.

Fur is defined by the Fur Products Labeling Act as any animal skin or part thereof with hair, fleece, or fur fibers attached, either in its raw or processed state. It does not include skins that are to be converted into leather. Under this law, furs must be invoiced, advertised, labeled, and sold under their accepted English names.

Waste fur, paws, heads, and belly sections, obtained from cuttings from better-quality garments, must be so labeled when sold. Furriers, disliking the term "waste fur," often refer to finished garments made from these parts as **sections.** Thus, they label a coat as a mink-section coat.

Dyes or any other color change that affects the fur's appearance must also be indicated on the label. Another animal's name, such as sable-dyed muskrat, may not be used to describe any dye or process. *long & short*

Pointing, the gluing in of hairs from other animals to make a fur look more exotic or fuller, must be so labeled. Such glued-in hairs are not as sturdy as the animal's own hair and may fall out in use.

The name of a fur may not include the name of another fur in explaining its appearance. Chinchilla rabbit, for example, may not be used to describe a gray, furry-textured rabbit skin.

248

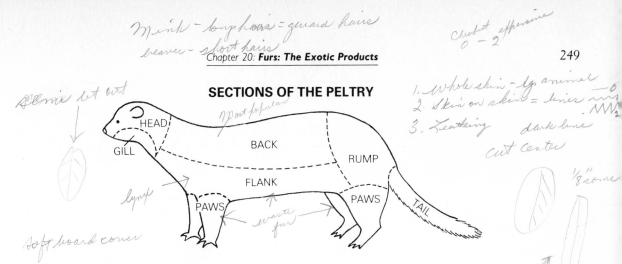

SECTIONS OF THE PELTRY

HEAD

GILL

BACK

RUMP

FLANK

PAWS

PAWS

TAIL

Figure 20-1. *Sections of the peltry: 1. Gill. 2. Head. 3. Back. 4. Rump. 5. Flank. 6. Paws. 7. Tail.*

The geographic origin of any foreign fur must be accurate and be noted on the label.

THE ENDANGERED SPECIES CONSERVATION ACT

During the 1960s, conservationists, people concerned with cruelty to animals, and people representing organizations such as the World Wildlife Fund, Friends of Animals, and the Fur Conservation Institute of America, succeeded in getting the Endangered Species Conservation Act of 1969 passed. This act prevented the importation of endangered or threatened animals that had been obtained illegally. Another act passed in 1973 and an added convention in 1977, signed by nearly 80 nations' representatives, established procedures to control and monitor the import and export of imperiled species. Animals classified as **endangered** were those species in danger of extinction. Animals classified as **threatened** were those species likely to become endangered within the foreseeable future.

Endangered fur-bearing animals include some seals, leopards, jaguars, spotted cats, tigers, ocelots, some rabbits, and some wolves. Special permits or proof that the species is neither threatened or endangered is necessary for furs from these animals to be part of intercountry or interstate commerce.[1] In 1982 the House and Senate voted a 3-year extension for this act.[2]

THE FUR INDUSTRY

North America was developed in part because of the fur industry. In fact, in the early days of American history the desire for precious furs was responsible for the establishment of a number of fur-trading posts that later became large cities such as Chicago, St. Paul, and Spokane. Other cities, including St. Louis and New Orleans, were early centers for fur collection.

Imported and Native Fur-Bearing Animals

There are about 100 different kinds of furs listed in the Fur Products Labeling Act that are available for fur garments. Although the United States imports many furs, such as beaver, fox, marten, Persian lamb, sable, and sheep, it actually has a major part of the world's fur-bearing animals either in the wild (beaver, fox, muskrat, raccoon, mink, coyote, lynx cat, skunk, and seal) or raised on ranches in North America (chinchilla, mink, nutria, and fox).

Marketing Channels for Furs

Furs pass through many hands before they reach the customer. Depending upon their origin, they may come through fur trappers or fur farmers or their cooperatives. At auction houses they may be bought by skin dealers or by large manufacturers. They then go to dressers and dyers for conversion to usable peltries. Next, large or small manufacturers will convert the skins to garments and then sell the garments to retail stores where they will be sold to customers. In between are firms that offer financial and other services to the primary channel members.

OBTAINING FURS

Russia   New York or Europe or Canada Mets

Furs are obtained from animals in the wild and from animals raised on ranches.

Markets - auction

Animals Caught in the Wild

taken wolves

Obtaining wild animals in the winter, when the skins and fur are the finest, presents a problem. This is the time when the animals are least likely to venture far from their homes. Many are caught by the use of carefully placed traps. When an animal's home is discovered, the animal may be clubbed as it emerges from its hiding place. This is more humane than shooting, since

an animal that is shot may be wounded and get away and thereby suffer. After the animals have been killed, their skins are removed. The furs are then collected at a central place and sent as raw furs to dealers or auction houses where they are sorted into bundles according to quality and size. Fur manufacturers and skin dealers then bid for the bundles of furs.

Animals Raised on Fur Farms

An important development in the fur industry occurred in 1887 when **fur farming** (the raising and breeding of animals under controlled conditions) of silver foxes was begun on Prince Edward Island off the eastern coast of Canada. Chincilla farms, mink ranches, fox farms, and nutria farms have since been developed throughout North America, Scandanavia, the U.S.S.R., Poland, Argentina, and Japan.

These fur farms made it possible to supply manufacturers with furs that were in demand. By careful breeding, fur farmers have improved the

clean - chemicals that clean w/detergent
add oil
HERE IS HOW THE NATURAL, BRED-IN COLOR MINK ARE SCIENTIFICALLY DEVELOPED:
kicker blocks → dryers w/saw dust to absorb extra oil → cold storage

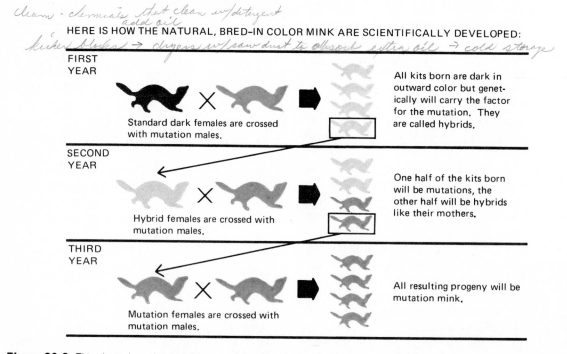

FIRST YEAR
Standard dark females are crossed with mutation males.
All kits born are dark in outward color but genetically will carry the factor for the mutation. They are called hybrids.

SECOND YEAR
Hybrid females are crossed with mutation males.
One half of the kits born will be mutations, the other half will be hybrids like their mothers.

THIRD YEAR
Mutation females are crossed with mutation males.
All resulting progeny will be mutation mink.

Figure 20-2. *This chart shows how minks are crossbred to produce hybrid and mutation minks.*

textures and colors of fur-bearing animals. The sensational mutation mink furs, for example, are the result of fur farming. When a mink was born with an odd-color fur, careful breeding of the animal to close relatives, called **inbreeding,** and to minks from nonrelated families, called **cross-breeding,** produced unique colors in the furs.

DRESSING AND DYEING FURS

Many processes are necessary to change animal skins into leather and to make the fur desirable for garments. After manufacturers purchase furs at auctions or from skin dealers, they send the furs to firms that specialize in the dressing, plucking and/or shearing, dyeing, and finishing.

Beaver hats

Dressing Furs

Dressing, the treatment of the skins so that they will not putrefy and disintegrate, is a process that resembles tanning in the leather industry. Dressing, however, does not remove the hair but may change the appearance of the hair covering. The **peltries** (raw, undressed skins) are first washed in salt water to remove dirt. Excess flesh and fat are scraped off the skin side with sharp knives. Most animals have two kinds of hair covering. The soft downlike hairs next to the skin, which provide warmth for the animal, are known as **fur fibers.** The hairs that are usually protruding beyond these and are somewhat stiffer are the **guard hairs.** They offer the animal protection against rain and other moisture. Sometimes the guard hairs may be shaved down. This process, known as **shearing,** is used on sheared, dyed muskrats and other furs to give them a rich, velvety, pile texture. In some furs, such as beaver and Alaskan fur seal, the guard hairs are plucked out completely so that only the fur fiber remains. In contrast to these sheared furs are the mink and fox furs, which depend on the length and beauty of their guard hairs for their attractiveness. (When fashion dictates, however, they too may be sheared.)

The **pelts** (undressed skins with its hair, wool, or fur) are then soaked in salt water to prepare

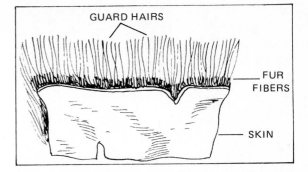

Figure 20-3. *Cross-section of fur peltry showing skin, fur fibers, and guard hairs of a long-haired fur-bearing animal.*

them for the chemical tanning solution that is applied on the skin side. These chemicals convert the skins into leather when the skins are treated, packed together, and left overnight. Grease is applied to the pelts, and huge wooden blocks, called **kickers,** beat the furs against one another to make the oil work into the fibers in the skins. This makes them pliable and soft.

The skins are then put into a huge revolving drum filled with sawdust. This process removes excess grease from the fur and makes it shiny and clean. After a prolonged drumming in fresh sawdust, the whitened skins are stretched and the fur is beaten with a rattan stick or blown with compressed air to fluff the fur and to enhance its attractiveness.

The Importance of Fur Color

The color of a finished fur garment may be natural, bleached, bleached and then dyed or just dyed. Brighteners may be added. The furs may be tip or stencil dyed or dip dyed.

Natural. When a fur is used in its **natural** coloring, only the pigments present in the animal's fur give it color. Such fur, when it is rich looking, is the most desirable of all. Many fur-bearing animals, however, do not have attractive natural colors. Chemists have therefore developed various methods of changing and improving the coloring of drab furs.

Figure 20-4. *A muslin garment is made before a fur garment is begun, in order to make any changes less expensive.*

Bleaching and Adding Brighteners.
White furs that have a yellow tinge and dark furs that are to be dyed in pale shades may first be chemically bleached. Bleached furs may become tinged with yellow or tan when they are exposed to the sun. Some furs, such as chinchillas, are lightened to make them more appealing; this is referred to as **adding brighteners.**

Dyeing. Dyeing was originally used to make less-expensive furs, such as rabbit, look like more-expensive furs. Today, however, dyeing is used to beautify furs. The Fur Products Labeling Act has specific rules about the labeling of dyed furs. When the natural color of a fur has been changed, a label or tag attached to the garment must indicate this. For example, a muskrat that has been dyed black must be labeled "dyed muskrat." The color of the dye may be mentioned also, for example, "black-dyed muskrat."

Dip Dyeing. Unless the animal's skin has been shaved after dyeing, you can tell that it has been

dip dyed (immersed in a dye bath) since the skin side will be dark. The skins of some undyed furs, however, are darkened so that they will not reveal light streaks as the fur separates while being worn. Gray Persian lamb, for example, always has a dyed leather although the fur is usually naturally gray. This skin-only dyeing process is called **leather tipping** and need not be mentioned on the label.

Tip Dyeing. Some furs have color brushed on the fur side of the garment to darken the natural color. This method, which changes the color of the fur but does not affect the skin, is known as **tip dyeing.** Often pale, off-color furs are tip dyed to resemble a more attractive color of that same fur. Tip-dyed furs will eventually fade if they are worn in sunlight.

Stencil Dyeing. When a less-expensive fur is dyed to imitate a spotted fur, such as leopard, a process called **stencil dyeing** is used to apply the spots. Dyed rabbit may be transformed in this manner.

Glazing

The final beauty treatment given to furs is known as **glazing.** It may be accomplished by spraying the furs with a chemical that imparts a sheen. In most dressing plants the skins are sprayed with water and then pressed skillfully with a specially padded iron. This makes the fur smooth and lustrous by bringing the oil from the hair to the surface. The finished fur skins are now ready to be returned to the manufacturers who will make them into salable garments.

CONSTRUCTION OF FUR GARMENTS

The construction of a fur coat or jacket is an intricate, time-consuming process that involves pattern making, cutting, and sewing.

Before a fur garment is begun, a **muslin garment** is made, fitted on a form, and analyzed. Any mistakes in the fit or any details that are not just right may thus be changed without experimenting on the costly fur. After the muslin garment is approved, the shape is transferred onto a heavyweight paper pattern, which is used as the guide for cutting and arranging the furs.

Matching Furs

Matching the furs that are to lie next to one another must be done with care. The matcher must consider the length and texture of the hair and fur, the color, any markings on the fur, and the size of the pelts. The matcher places the furs in order on the pattern and gives them to the cutter.

Cutting

The fur cutter's tools are a sharp knife that resembles a razor blade with a handle attached to it and a ruler. The cutter arranges the skins to fit the various parts of the pattern. Any markings on the fur must be matched perfectly. Then, using the fur as economically as possible, he or she cuts the skins so that each part will match the color and pattern of the fur next to it. To save costs, some manufacturers of less-expensive garments use machine cutting where possible. The skins are cut in different ways, depending on the manner in which they will be joined together.

Whole Skins. Only a few fur pelts, such as lambskins, are large enough to be made into garments without joining them together one below the other.

Skin-on-Skin Construction. The majority of fur-bearing animal skins are too short to be used for the full length of even short garments. They are joined one below the other in a method known as **skin-on-skin** construction. It is difficult to hide the seams, except with wavy- or curly-haired furs, so they are almost always visible.

Three types of skin-on-skin seams are used. For the **straight seam,** which is the easiest to cut and sew, the least expensive, and the least dura-

Figure 20-5. *A fur cutter lets out mink skins, slicing strips as narrow as $\frac{1}{8}$ inch preparatory to resewing by a machine operator.*

ble, each skin is cut straight and joined in a blocklike form to the ones above and below it. These inexpensive seams are used on some rabbit and kidskin coats. **Wavy seams** are more difficult to cut and sew and are more secure. They are used on slightly better-quality kidskins, on patterned furs such as wavy-haired lambs, and on spotted furs. The **zigzag seam** is the strongest skin-on-skin seam. The tail section of the fur is cut into a V shape, and the head section of the fur to be placed below it is cut to receive the V. These seams are popular on muskrat, squirrel, marmot, and other flat-haired fur garments.

All skin-on-skin seams produce a pattern of horizontal marks around the fur garment. Some people dislike this type of construction because the garments may make the wearer appear somewhat shorter and wider than is actually the case.

Let-Out Construction.

A costlier method of constructing garments that eliminates the horizontal markings is known as **letting out.** Some garments, especially of mink, are made of tiny strips of fur no larger than $\frac{1}{8}$ inch wide and $1\frac{1}{2}$ inches long. From the outside, however, the garment looks as if it were made of long strips of handsomely matched fur. On mink each skin is cut down the center of the dark vertical stripe running the length of the skin. Narrow strips are cut at an angle. Each tiny strip is then resewed to the strip above it and below it at a different angle. The other half of the skin is resewed in a similar manner. When the two halves are later joined, the short, broad skin has become long and narrow but still retains the darker center marking.

Variations of the letting-out process are used on muskrat, silver fox, blue fox, ermine, sable, gray Persian lamb, beaver, raccoon, and chinchilla. Because letting out takes a great deal of time, effort, and skill and uses more fur than would otherwise be necessary, it adds considerably to the cost of the garment. In advertisements, this construction is often referred to as **fully let out.**

Semi-Let-Out Construction.

When a fur garment is to be made from skins that are broad and short but a narrower, somewhat longer skin would be more attractive, a modified letting-out process, known as the **semi-let-out construction,** is used. Instead of making one skin run the length of the garment, semi-let-out construction increases each skin's length slightly. This gives more attractive lines to the garment than the skin-on-skin construction. Since only two or three cuts are made in each half-skin, the process is not very costly. It is used on squirrel skins and occasionally on chinchilla skins.

Split-Skin Construction.

The costly letting-out process used on the minks adds to the high price of the furs themselves and makes the finished garments very expensive. In 1953 some furriers introduced a new method of handling mink skins that resembled the appearance of let-out skins but was a fraction of the cost to construct. The process, known as **split-skin construction,** is used mainly on short garments such as jackets, capelets, and stoles.

Instead of cutting and restitching each skin so that the center dark mark on each mink remained in the center of each narrower strip, the skin is cut in half right through the dark stripe. The halves are then turned on end and placed side by side, with the dark stripe at the bottom of the pelt running horizontally across the back of the garment.

Plates.

Inexpensive garments are made from waste fur. Sections of the pelt, such as the neck (gills), paws, sides (flank), and parts of the belly, that are not used in good-quality garments are stitched together like pieces in a patchwork quilt. The finished oblong or square is called a **plate.** This plate is then used in the same way that cloth would be used. A pattern for a coat or jacket is laid on it, and various sections are cut for joining. The finished garment must have a label indicating that the garment was made from leftover pieces.

Leathering.

Bulky furs, such as fox, skunk, and raccoon, may have strips of leather or ribbon sewed in at intervals between strips of fur. This process, known as **leathering,** reduces the amount of fur needed. Because of the high cost of the labor involved, however, the price of the finished garment is not substantially lower. Ribbed furs are made by a combination of leathering between narrow strips of let-out fur.

Feathering.

Feathering is a process whereby let-out long-haired furs are leathered to accentuate the diagonal lines, to separate the layers of fur, and to give an overall textured effect.

Resetting.

A large, bulky skin may be made to look like two smaller skins by a process called **resetting.** First, parallel vertical cuts are made in the skin. Then every other strip is assembled to make one skin. Those remaining form the second skin.

Damaging Out. Some coats (from the inside) resemble a jigsaw puzzle with tiny jagged sections that dovetail perfectly. This joining together of small pieces of fur, known as **damaging out**, often indicates that a poorer-quality section of fur has been cut out and replaced with better-quality sections, or the damaged skin has been drawn together at that point.

Sewing and Assembling

The cut sections of fur are carefully marked and handed in groups to a sewer who stitches them together. The sewer holds the two edges of the leather sides of the furs together and stitches row after row on a machine that uses an overseam stitch. This stitch laps over and over the edges of the skins being joined. For a fitted garment several separate sections — sleeves, back, collar and lapels, and front sections — are sewn on the machine. For a swagger or box model the sections are the body, sleeves, and collar.

Nailing (Stapling) and Finishing

Fur coats cannot be pressed to make seams straight and to make the coat hang correctly. Therefore a process known as **nailing** is used to produce these effects. A large wooden board has the pattern of the sleeves, back, front pieces, collar, and lapels traced on it in chalk. As these pieces come from the sewer, they are dampened and stretched to fit the chalked pattern on the board. They are then stapled onto the board with the leather side out (in most furs) and left to dry. In let-out coats every seam for the length of the garment is stapled firmly in place to assure that the finished coat will hang and drape gracefully. Thousands of staples are used for this operation. After the fur is dry, it is removed from the board and all edges are closed and taped. The lining is sewed in and buttons, loops, and snaps are attached.

Scarves and Flings

A fur used in its original shape with a mounted head affixed and paws and tail left attached to the peltry is known as a **scarf**. Sable, mink, and fox

Figure 20-6. *Nailing. Pieces of a fur coat are stretched and stapled onto a board to fit the coat pattern.*

are some furs popularly used for scarves. Special companies mount the heads on these furs. The scarf is made of full skins unless specified otherwise for example, as a pieced-skin scarf. Flings, with no head or paws, but with tail attached, are similar in appearance to scarves.

THE FUR-BEARING ANIMALS

To help you know about the various fur-bearing animals and their characteristics, they are discussed here in their family groupings.

The Rodent Family

Rodents are well known and popularly used for some of the most desirable furs.

Beaver. In 1935, **beaver**, which is a thick-skinned fur with long, coarse guard hair, was made fashionable. The northwest U.S. to Alaska is the native habitat of the beaver. The skin was made thinner by plucking the guard hairs and shearing the remaining fur fibers to reveal a dark brown color near the center back shading to a paler gray color near the sides. Designers use beaver imaginatively, giving it dramatic colors and creating crosswise, diagonally, and lengthwise ribbed effects. Beaver is a long-wearing, warm, attractive fur. It mats slightly when wet, but reglazing makes it velvety again.

Nutria. The **nutria's** hair is not very coarse so shearing leaves a velvety appearance. A close relative of the beaver, the nutria, originally from South America and now also ranch-raised in Louisiana, is a long-wearing fur.

Muskrat. The **muskrat,** found in nearly all U.S. and Canadian regions, is a small ombre-shaded fur, is valued for its natural appearance in skin-on-skin garments and for its unique colorations. When it is dyed it resembles mink or sable. When sheared and dyed it resembles seal. Better-quality muskrats may be let out, making them quite costly. This fur is serviceable but not as durable as beaver.

Squirrel. Top-quality **squirrel** furs are a clear gray color and are made into natural squirrel coats. They come from the U.S.S.R., Scandinavia and Canada. Streaked squirrel pelts may be dyed brown to simulate more costly brown furs. Squirrel fur is suitable for jackets, capes, stoles, and scarves. It is not very durable.

Marmot. Better known as a woodchuck or groundhog, the **marmot's** fur is used to imitate costlier brown furs but is coarse and harsh in appearance and has an almost glassy luster. It is native to parts of Europe, Asia, and North America. Marmot does not wear as well as muskrat fur.

Chinchilla. Chinchilla, a native of South America, is a gray-colored, delicate, soft, perishable fur. Although there are several hundred chinchilla fur farms in the United States, it is still rare. Some brown and near-white mutations are available.

Rabbit. Because of its availability, low price, soft texture, and variety of natural colorings, rabbit is extensively used in the fun-fur and low-priced areas of the fur industry. The best fur comes from French rabbits. Ordinary yellow-brown rabbit fur can be dyed and processed to imitate almost any other fur. Attractive when new, rabbit fur tends to flatten in use and to shed rather badly. Attractive articles are made from natural white and gray rabbits.

The Weasel Family

Most of the truly exotic and expensive furs belong to the weasel family of fur-bearing animals.

Sable. One of the rarest, most luxurious, and beautiful furs comes from the Russian **sable,** a native of Siberia. It resembles dark blue-brown mink but has longer, fluffier guard hair and fur fiber. The darker the natural color, the better the quality. Costly coats, jackets, and fur accessories are made from this fur, which is usually let out.

American Sable or Marten and Fisher. A close relative of the Russian sable, is the **American sable,** or **marten,** fur. It is somewhat paler in color and slightly less dense and fluffy. **Fisher,** a larger relative, is slightly darker and longer haired. It is found in Alaska and Canada.

Baum Marten and Stone Marten. These are long-haired, fluffy-furred animals from Europe and Asia. The **Baum marten** has a yellowish coloring that is sometimes dyed to simulate sable. The **stone marten** has gray-white underfur that makes a dramatic contrast with its brown guard hair. Both of these furs are long wearing.

Ermine and American Weasel. The **ermine,** often associated with royalty, is famous for its lustrous brown coat, which turns white when the animal lives in the frozen North. Its black-tipped tail is used as trimming on various types of garments. The finest pure white ermine comes from Siberia. In some sections of North America the ermine, called the **American weasel,** retains its brown color throughout the year.

Mink and Kolinsky. American-raised **mink** is considered to be the finest mink. The **natural wild minks** have a virile look with fluffy fiber and guard hair that make a costly, long-wearing garment. **Ranch-raised minks** have a softer, more luxurious feel than wild minks. Inbred and crossbred **mutation minks** have a sumptuous feel and unique coloration ranging from black-brown through paler tans to gray blues, striped white and black, and pale pastel tones to white. Exotic trade names such as Blackglama, Lunaraine, Blue Iris, Sapphire, Autumn Haze, Pink Glo, Opal, and Jasmine are used for the mutations. **Samink,** developed in 1972, is a mutation that more nearly resembles sable and is more costly than most other minks. Most costly mink garments are let out to accentuate the beauty of the dark stripe in the center back of the animal.

A new treatment of mink is to shear the guard hair and fur fiber to make velvet-textured garments. Mink section garments are made from mink paws, necks, and sides.

Kolinsky is a fine species of Asiatic mink. The animal has a coarser texture of hair and fur fiber than American mink. Because it has a yellow-brown color, the fur is almost always dyed. The finer pelts are made into garments, and poorer quality pelts are used for trimmings.

Fitch, Wolverine, Otter, Badger, Skunk.

Fitch, more commonly known as wild ferret or polecat, from Poland and Russia, is currently being ranch raised in the United States and Scandinavia. The animal has a dramatically colored fur with yellow or white underfur and blue-brown to black moderately long guard hair. The let-out process makes garments with an exotic appearance. This is a long-wearing fur.

Wolverine, found in northern European countries, Asia, and North America, has medium-length coarse hair and a center dark area with paler brown stripes forming the animal's side fur. When let out in coats and jackets, this coloration gives a dramatic effect. Wolverine is the most durable fur and does not allow moisture to congeal on it. Therefore, it makes an ideal lining for parka hoods.

Otter fur, when plucked and sheared, resembles beaver without the ombre shading. The deep brown-colored fur is silky in texture and does not mat when wet. It is one of the most durable furs. Otter, although found on all continents except Australia, is endangered.

Badger. The Western Canadian variety is the

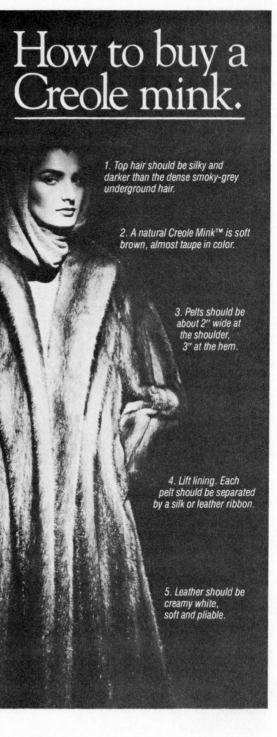

How to buy a Creole mink.

1. Top hair should be silky and darker than the dense smoky-grey underground hair.

2. A natural Creole Mink™ is soft brown, almost taupe in color.

3. Pelts should be about 2" wide at the shoulder, 3" at the hem.

4. Lift lining. Each pelt should be separated by a silk or leather ribbon.

5. Leather should be creamy white, soft and pliable.

Figure 20-7. *American-raised mink is considered to be the finest. This ad promotes a luxurious coat of ranch-raised mink.*

finest. The animal has short center-back guard hair and white-black-white striped hair effect on its sides. The fur is used for sports garments and trim on cloth coats. It is a long-wearing fur.

Skunks used in the United States are found from Canada to the Panama Canal. They have medium-length guard hair and fur fiber that are dark brown to black, with the darker color representing the better quality. The animal has a single wide stripe or a stripe that splits into two and runs from head to tail. The white stripes in the fur are coarser in texture, and are cut out when a solid-colored, let-out garment is to be constructed. In some garments the stripes are used for dramatic accents. Furs with poor color are dyed. The fur wears well, but lacks sheen, luster, and suppleness.

Little spotted skunk has a softer-textured, silkier, shorter hair and fur covering than the skunk. Its distinction comes from the white lyre-shaped marking against its dark brown to black coloration. The whiter and clearer these markings, the better the quality of the fur. Garments are made skin on skin to feature the natural fur markings. The fur is fairly durable.

The Cat Family

The animals in the cat family that are used for furs are discussed below.

Leopard. The **leopard,** from Somaliland in Africa, whose coat is considered the most beautiful of all the cat furs, is endangered. The black, rosette-shaped marks of the leopard skin are sharply contrasted with the creamy yellow background coloring of the fur.

Ocelot. The **ocelot** from South America is another endangered animal. It has slightly elongated markings on fluffy fur.

Lynx. The **lynx** obtained from Russia and Canada produces a long-haired, fluffy, light-colored fur with a few spotlike marks. Lynx is usually let out. It is a popular fur for collars on cloth coats and wears fairly well but tends to shed. **Lynx cat,** a subspecies of lynx, has a

browner coloration and more spots on its shorter fur. The **spotted cat,** a close relative of the lynx, has prominent spots and less attractive coloration. They are used in garments and for trimming on cloth coats and shed rather easily.

The Canine Family

Many fluffy, long-haired furs come from the fox, wolf, and coyote. The furs are luxurious but not noted for long wear. To make them less bulky, they may be leathered, let out, or feathered. In addition to the natural colors, many mutations have added an array of glamorous shades.

Red Fox. Red fox comes from every country north of the equator, in many colors and mutations. The richer the coloration and the thicker the guard hair, the better the fur quality. **Black fox,** an offspring of the red fox, has black fur fiber and guard hair. **Silver fox,** a famous mutation, has been ranch raised in the United States, Canada, the Scandinavian countries, and the U.S.S.R. since 1887. The quality of the silver fox depends upon the amount of silver-colored guard hairs and the thickness of the blue-black underfur. **Platina** or **platinum fox,** with a light blue, silvery hue, is a mutation of silver fox. Other mutations of red fox have amber-colored fur. The **cross fox,** with a mixture of reddish and silvery color and a cross-shaped marking on its back, is a natural offspring of the red fox.

White Fox. The **white fox** has a pure white color. Its fur is used for coats and trimming on cloth garments. The **blue fox,** actually a brown-colored fox with bluish underfur, is a color phase of the white fox. A **Norwegian blue fox** mutation has been developed that has soft-textured, luxurious-looking pale bluish-white fur.

Gray Fox. Gray fox from western United States is shorter-haired and less luxurious, with gray and brownish color. Its fur is used for sporty garments.

Wolf. Many **wolves** are on the endangered species list. The rather coarse-textured moderate length fur ranges in color from white to yellowish gray. The fur is appropriate for sporty garments. The animal is found in North America.

Coyote. **Coyote,** from the western part of North America, has a bristly, coarse guard hair on the back and a fur fiber that is short and fine in texture. The fur may be bleached or dyed to have more attractive coloration.

The Hoofed Animals

Animals having hoofs belong to the **ungulate family.**

Persian Lamb. The **Persian lamb** is one of the best-known furs in the ungulate group. Although it is not from Iran (formerly Persia), it retains its name by special permission of the Federal Trade Commission because customers have become accustomed to calling this type of fur Persian lamb. This lamb comes mainly from Central Asia, Afghanistan, South Africa, and Southwest Africa; lamb from the latter are known as **swakara.** The Persian lamb is noted for its tightly curled fur and beautiful luster. The lambs are domesticated and raised on farms. They may be naturally gray, brown, or black. Their fur is quite durable and is used for dressy coats and trimming on cloth coats. Plated garments are made from paws, heads, or other pieces.

Broadtail lamb, the moiré-designed pelt from a newborn Persian lamb, is expensive but not very durable. **Persian broadtail lamb** comes from the same kinds of lambs that are 2 or 3 days old and has slightly more curl than the broadtail lamb. **Swakara broadtail lamb** is considered to be the finest broadtail lamb bred today.

Caracul Lamb. **Caracul lamb** which comes from the U.S.S.R. and China has a beautiful, flat, wavy fur that is usually white but is occasionally brown or black.

Mouton-Processed Lamb. **Mouton-processed lamb** comes from a South American lamb that is sheared, processed to straighten the hair (called **plasticizing** or **electrifying**), and dyed. **Broadtail-processed lamb,** another variety of South American lamb, is specifically selected and sheared to resemble the more costly broadtail. Mouton-processed lamb is noted for its warmth and durability and is moderately low in price.

Kid, Goat, Pony, and Calf. **Kidskin** from China and Western India is a gray-colored, short-haired slightly wavy fur. The older **goatskin** has slightly longer fur and a heavier skin.

Pony skins from Poland and Russia resemble kidskin but are much heavier. Their short guard hair does not provide much warmth, and the fur tends to rub away as it is worn.

Calf skins have very short guard hair that is sleek and silky in appearance. Skins usually have brown coloring with white irregularly shaped spots. They are used mainly for accessory items such as vests.

Miscellaneous Fur-Bearing Animals

There are several other popularly used, fur-bearing animals.

Opossum. The **opossum,** a North American animal, is gray-white and has long guard hairs with black tips. Its fur is suitable for sportswear. The **Australian opossum** is blue-gray and has soft fur. It is also used for sportswear and as lining for cloth coats.

Raccoon. The **raccoon** has returned to popularity in recent years in a let-out version that resembles silver fox. The fur wears very well and is exceedingly warm. A fine-quality Japanese raccoon, called **tanuki,** is similar in appearance to the North American variety. When advertised, it should use the name "racoon" and the country of its source, Japan.

Seal. The *not allowed in Calif. - Endangered* **fur seal** has long been popular. Hunting of **Alaskan fur seal** is controlled by the U.S. government. Sealskins are dyed black; a rich, dark brown color known as **matara;** or a deep blue-black color known as **kitovi.** Two new fur-seal colors are silver safari and beige safari. The skins are stamped with the U.S. government label. All of the varieties not bearing the U.S. government label are obtained from South Africa, South America, Siberia, or Japan. Seal

Table 20–1 RELATIVE DURABILITY OF FURS

Excellent (Approximately 6–9 years)	Good (Approximately 4–7 years)	Fair (Approximately 3–5 years)	Poor (Approximately 1–3 years)
Otter[a]	Ranch mink	American weasel	Rabbit
Wolverine[a]	Mutation mink	American opossum	Chinchilla
Beaver	Baum marten	Fox	Mole
Alaska fur seal	Persian lamb	Pony	Broadtail lamb
Wild mink from U.S. and U.S.S.R.	Sable	Kidskin	Burunduk
Skunk	Wolf	Ermine	
Fisher	Stone marten	Lynx	
Raccoon	Muskrat	Ocelot	
Badger	Japanese mink	Squirrel	
	Kolinsky	Nutria	
	Fitch	Asiatic mink	
	Leopard	Caracul lamb	
	Australian opossum	Spotted skunk	
	Hair seal	Marmot	
	Mouton-processed lamb	Bassarisk	
		Lynx cat	
		Wild cat	
		Persian broadtail lamb	
		India lamb	
		Monkey	
		Broadtail-processed lamb	

[a] The two best-wearing furs.

furs are durable, and those of good quality are quite expensive.

DURABILITY OF FURS

As Table 20–1 shows, the fur of different animals can be expected to last different lengths of time. Durability of furs depends not only upon the animal itself, however, but also upon the following.

1. Whether the fur is sheared or not. Sheared furs move down one ranking in quality.

2. The quality of the particular fur.

3. The placement of the better pelts in the garment.

4. The amount of wear given to the fur.

5. The climate in which the fur is worn.

6. The care given the fur.

CARE OF FURS

Proper care of fur garments is essential to their serviceability as well as their beauty. Every customer should be told the following simple rules.

- Always hang a fur garment on a hanger in a cool closet. Be sure there are no hot water or heat pipes running through the closet.
- If the coat is wet, shake off the water and hang the garment to dry away from heat. The fur may mat if it is crushed with other things in a closet while it is still damp.
- When possible, avoid sitting on the fur coat. Always open the coat before sitting down so that there will be no pull on the buttons or on the hooks that hold the coat closed. Avoid rubbing a seat belt in a car or plane against fur.
- Have the fur cleaned and glazed by a furrier at least once a year. This restores beauty and luster to the fur. Furs should never be dry-

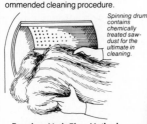
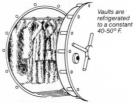
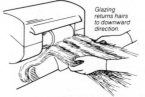

Figure 20-8. *Proper cleaning and storage is essential to maintaining furs.*

cleaned, as this removes oils from the leather and the fur and causes the skin to crack.

- If a fur is put in cold storage each summer, the customer is assured that it will not be attacked by moths or that the oils in the skins will not dry out from the hot summer weather.
- Damage should be repaired as quickly as possible to prevent its becoming worse and more difficult to fix.
- Restyling when fashion changes occur is desirable for a fur garment if such work does not cost more than one-fourth of the original cost of the garment.
- Shedding is a natural occurrence with some furs. If a fur sheds, the customer may wish to brush it gently with a soft hair brush before wearing. This will remove those hairs that were about to come out and reduce the shedding while the garment is being worn.
- The customer should shake a fur out in the air before wearing it.

NOTES

1. Joseph P. Fried, "Endangered Breeds: Curbing the Market," *New York Times*, June 26, 1982, p. 52.
2. "Senate Votes Measure on Endangered Species," *New York Times*, June 11, 1982, p. 11.

DO YOU KNOW YOUR MERCHANDISE?

1. Why was it necessary to pass the Fur Products Labeling Act?
2. What factors affect the price of furs?
3. Define the following: fur, fur fiber, guard hair, waste fur, and peltry.
4. What furs are farmed today? Why are fur-farmed animals not endangered?
5. Define the following: brighteners added, bleached fur, dyed fur, tipped fur, tip-dyed fur, stenciled fur.
6. Describe skin-on-skin construction, let-out construction, semi-let-out construction, and split-skin construction.
7. When would you suggest that a person seek let-out construction? What are its advantages and disadvantages?
8. What do leathering, feathering, and resetting mean?
9. Tell what family the following furs belong to and give as many distinguishing facts about each fur as you can: beaver, muskrat, squirrel, chinchilla, rabbit, sable, mink, platinum fox, Persian lamb, broadtail lamb, mouton-processed lamb, and fur seal.
10. Give five or more rules for the care of fur garments.

PUTTING YOUR MERCHANDISE KNOWLEDGE TO WORK

With another member of the class prepare a sales demonstration for a fur garment. Include information about the fur used; the quality of the fur; the workmanship, durability, and style of the garment; and its proper care.

PROJECT

Analyze five fur advertisements from newspapers and answer the following questions about those advertisements: What furs were mentioned? Did any of the advertisements mention mutation furs, ranch-raised furs, or that furs were "wild"? How many furs were natural? How many were dyed or otherwise color-changed? List all the construction terms that appeared in the advertisements. Write a short summary of your findings. Include in the summary your opinion of how helpful the advertisements were in aiding customers to make selections of fur garments.

21

Footwear:
The All-Occasion Necessity

Footwear is worn for fashion; for comfort; for warmth and protection; to match certain outfits; to fit special occasions; for active sports such as jogging, tennis, golf, baseball, football, ice skating, hiking, and scuba diving; for spectator sports; for school, streetwear, business, and dress occasions. It is worn by infants, children, teens, and adults.

MANUFACTURERS AND RETAILERS SERVICE THE DEMAND FOR FOOTWEAR

Shoe stores of some type exist everywhere there are retailers. Shopping malls are replete with shoe stores; department and discount stores have shoe departments. Specialty shoe stores are found in every business district.

Footwear conforms to the fashions of the times. It changes in design, materials, construction, finish, and decoration to adapt to fashion. When jogging and running came into vogue, for example, manufacturers developed shoes that would best fit the demands of these sports.

THE COST OF FOOTWEAR

Pairs of shoes vary greatly in price. Many factors enter into this wide price range, including the designer, the upper materials that vary from quality leathers to less-expensive manmade materials

or from expensive to inexpensive fabrics, and the soles that are made of leather, synthetics, rubber, or composition materials that vary in quality. Shoes are made using various constructions. They are either sewn, cemented, or injection molded, and the labor costs for these constructions vary greatly. Finishes and decoration may also add to the price of the finished shoes.

FOOT STRUCTURE, SIZING, AND FOOTWEAR FITTING

Incorrectly fitted shoes may pinch feet, make them feel as though the soles are burning, cause calluses, or deform feet with corns and bunions. Therefore getting the correct size in shoes is of the utmost importance. Since every person's foot differs from every other person's foot and since even one person's feet may vary in size, the shoe salesperson faces a difficult task in getting the right size for every customer.

A normal foot has 26 bones: 14 are toe bones, 5 are instep bones, and 7 are heel bones. These bones permit feet to be flexible. They hold the body weight of the person and absorb sudden shocks when a person runs or jumps. If these bones are crowded in a shoe, normal movement is restricted.

To handle the shocks caused by walking, running, jogging, jumping, and other such activities, the bones are joined to form arches. The arches

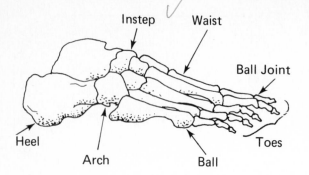

Instep Waist

Ball Joint

Heel

Arch   Ball   Toes

Figure 21-1. *A normal foot has 26 bones that permit the foot to be flexible and absorb sudden shocks.*

are suspended slightly, hold great weight, and permit elasticity and spring. Muscles, tendons, and ligaments in the foot permit proper movements; blood vessels carry nourishment to the feet; and nerves inform the brain when the foot is strained or shoes are incorrectly fitted.

Feet differ in size, shape, amount of flesh, and height of arches. Most people's feet are normal at birth. If a normal foot is correctly fitted to shoes throughout life, the person should have little or no foot discomfort. Incorrectly fitted shoes, however, can be injurious to feet.

Care of the Feet

Incorrectly fitted shoes cause temporary pain and may deform feet permanently. Painful feet may cause a person to feel tired. Proper care of feet requires that hosiery and shoes be sufficiently large and comfortable. Shoes that are too short or too tight should be discarded.

Shoes and stockings or socks should be changed daily. This allows the shoe to return to its original shape and any foot perspiration to dry out thus preventing bacterial build-up. If a shoe is making the foot tender in one spot, resting the foot by wearing a different shoe will help to allay the irritation.

For women, the height of the heel on the shoe is important to foot health. Heels over 2 inches in height throw the body off balance and necessitate a new posture to allow the woman to

stand erect. Too-high heels throw extra weight on the ball of the foot and calluses may result. Constant wearing of high heels causes the back leg muscles to shorten, which may result in pains in the back of the legs.

Size Ranges in Footwear

Shoe manufacturers make shoes in as many as 300 different sizes. Shoe sizes are measured on a scale with two size ranges. Table 21–1 shows average shoe size ranges for children through adults.

Shoe widths run from AAAA (quadruple A) to EEEEE (quintuple E). Widths are measured around the circumference of the foot at the ball. About $\frac{1}{4}$ inch exists between widths. Thus, an AAA (called triple A) shoe is about $\frac{1}{4}$ inch narrower than an AA (double A) shoe. This corresponds to a difference of about $\frac{1}{12}$ to $\frac{1}{16}$ inch across the flat sole. A given width does not correspond to a precise number of inches. Its specific size in inches is related to the length of the shoe; an AA shoe in a larger size is wider than an AA shoe in a smaller size.

Fitting Shoes

The best methods available for shoe fitting are ruler devices called **Ritz sticks,** graphs for tracing the feet called **FedoGraphs,** and the familiar steel measuring plates called **Brannock plates.** A good salesperson will measure both of the customer's feet. One foot is often larger than the other, and the larger foot should be fitted unless different size shoes can be ordered to fit each foot. The length and width of the feet should be measured in standing as well as sitting positions. Some feet may elongate and others may widen when the person is standing. Properly fitted shoes should allow for this.

The heel section of the shoe should fit snugly. Although the heel portion of the shoe gets wider as the forepart of the shoe gets wider, this additional width is almost imperceptible. Most top-quality men's shoes are made on what are called **combination lasts.** These allow for snug fit at the heel by having the heel portion at least two

Table 21–1 SHOE SIZE CLASSIFICATIONS

Category	Size Ranges	
Infants' (newborn to 2 years)	0–5	
Toddlers' (2 to 3 years)	$5\frac{1}{2}$–8	First
Children/little gents' (4 to 7 years)	$8\frac{1}{2}$–11/$8\frac{1}{2}$–$13\frac{1}{2}$	scale
Misses/youths (8 to 11 years)	$11\frac{1}{2}$–2/11–3	
Growing girls (12 to 15 years)	$2\frac{1}{2}$–9	Second
Boys (12 to 15 years)	$2\frac{1}{2}$–6	scale
Women	4–10 (or more)	
Men	5–15 (or more)	

widths narrower than the vamp portion of the shoe. Some top-quality women's shoes are also made this way.

A good salesperson will check the shoes the customer has selected to be sure that the ball of the foot fits into the widest part of the sole of the shoe and that there is at least $\frac{1}{2}$ inch of room beyond the big toe. Children should be fitted with shoes $\frac{3}{4}$ to 1 inch longer than the foot measures. The heel of the shoe should fit snugly and should not permit the foot to slip up and down. The shoe should feel comfortable on the foot. Shoes that fit properly need little or no breaking in.

Open-toe shoes should be fitted shorter than ordinary shoes because they do not restrict the movement of the toes. Conversely, shoes with extremely pointed toes should be fitted longer than square-toe shoes.

Selecting Children's Shoes

Toddlers wear shoes that are designed both for fit and to help them walk. Proper fit is essential in shoes for any age child. Care should be taken to see that shoes are comfortable and give the feet room to grow. There should be ample allowance for development of the arch.

The shape of a child's shoe is different from the shape of an adult shoe. Plenty of room is left for the toes. The heel is relatively narrow for adequate support. Big and small toe joints should be fitted to the widest measurements inside and outside the shoe. A walk test should be made to ensure a snug heel fit.

Parents or others buying children's shoes should be encouraged to get the size that fits, rather than expecting a child to grow into shoes that are too big. Important guidelines in selling and selecting children's shoes follow.

- A good-quality shoe will stand up under the rugged use a child will give it; an inexpensive shoe may not fit or wear properly.
- Shoes are not big enough because a child says they are — check the measurements.
- Be advised that the soft bone structure of a child's foot will allow it to be squeezed into a shoe several sizes too small without any particular pain or discomfort.
- It is unwise for parents to try to get their money's worth by waiting till a child complains about tight fit.
- An extra pair of shoes for school or play will guard against damp weather and perspiration.
- Children's shoe sizes change very rapidly — every 2 to 4 months from 2 to 6 years of age. New shoes need to be purchased frequently to avoid discomfort and even deformity.
- Girls' shoes with wedges or high heels, in imitation of women's styles, should be avoided. Prolonged wear shortens the achilles tendon.

Many types of shoes are worn by children. They often reflect the styles of adult shoes. Oxfords, loafers, and tennis and running shoes are popular. **Barefoot sandals** are often worn in warm weather and boots in cold or rainy weather. For dress-up occasions, young girls sometimes wear **Mary Janes,** low-heeled, broad-toed patent-leather with a single ankle or instep strap that buckles. Subteen girls may choose flat ballet-slipper-type shoes for dress-up wear.

Most children's shoes are of leather or vinyl. Some sport shoes, such as tennis shoes or Chinese slippers, are of canvas; running shoes are of nylon. Booties may be of soft knitted or woven fabrics; bootlike slippers may be of plushy or quilted fabrics. Most children's shoes have soles, but soft-sole shoes are available for infants.

CHILDREN'S SHOES

BAREFOOT SANDAL

MARY JANE

RUBBER RAINBOOT

INFANT'S SOFT–SOLED HIGHTOP SHOE

Figure 21-2. *Plenty of room is left in the toes of children's shoes, while the heels are relatively narrow.*

SHOE MATERIALS

Leather is considered to be the finest basic shoe material because of its durability and because it is a health-promoting foot-covering material. It inhibits conditions such as athlete's foot, chafing, and irritation.

Vinyls and polyurethanes resembling calf, kid, patent leather, and suede have been increasingly accepted as shoe-upper materials. Sturdy fabrics or fabrics backed with plastic to give them the needed strength make durable active sport, street, and dress shoes. Some vinyls are now produced that allow the feet to breathe.

Both leather and polyvinyl chloride plastic (PVC) are used extensively for soles. Rubber and its imitations are used for casual footwear and some active sport shoes. Manufacturers of fine footwear continue to favor leather for soles.

With the widespread use of leather substitutes for various parts of shoes came the need for proper labeling to inform consumers about the shoe materials and to avoid any misrepresentation as a result of the deceptive appearance of the shoes. Labels must be securely attached so that they remain in place until the products are actually used by the consumer. The Federal Trade Commission established the following rules, which became effective in January 1963, with minor modifications since that date.

- The word "leather" may be used in labeling and advertising shoes and slippers only when products (except for heels, inside stiffenings, and ornamentation) are entirely composed of leather. This means that shoes made of ground or shredded leather may not bear the unqualified term "leather." Also, coined names or trade names, such as Duraleather or Barkhyde, that sound as if they are a kind of leather may not be used unless the product is actually leather.
- If shoes or slippers are made of an embossed, dyed, or other type of processed leather that simulates the appearance of a different kind of leather, the label must disclose the kind of leather of which they are actually made, for

example, "simulated alligator made of cowhide."

- If the shoes or slippers appear to be made from leather but are made from nonleather material, they must be labeled and advertised in such a manner that the customer will know they are not leather, for example, "outsole and linings manmade."

- If the shoes contain visible parts of leather but the innersoles concealed from view are made from nonleather materials, the label must clearly inform the customer of this fact.

- If shoes or slippers pictured for advertising appear to be made of leather but are made from nonleather materials, the true composition of the material must be stated, as "manmade materials."

PARTS OF SHOES

A modern shoe consists of a sole, fitted with a heel and uppers. The **sole** is the part of the shoe on which the foot rests. The **heel** is a piece attached to the sole under the heel of the foot. **Uppers** are the parts of the shoe above the sole and the heel and include inside parts such as linings and outside parts such as the tongue.

The Sole

The sole is made of one or more layers of leather, cork, plastic, or rubber, depending on the quality and type of shoe and its construction. The **outsole** forms the bottom of the shoe. In quality shoes this is made of top-grain leather and is durable, flexible, water resistant, not slippery

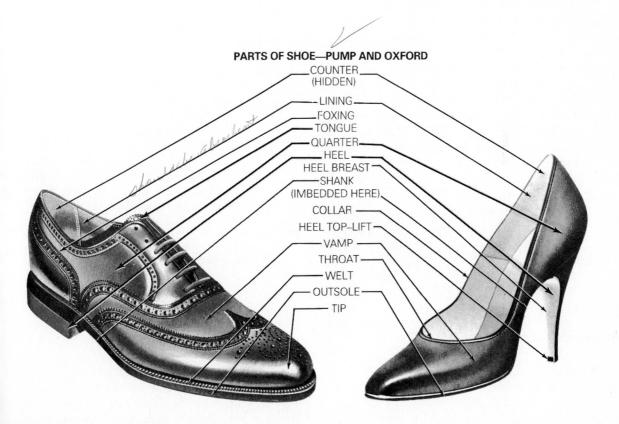

PARTS OF SHOE—PUMP AND OXFORD

COUNTER (HIDDEN)
LINING
FOXING
TONGUE
QUARTER
HEEL
HEEL BREAST
SHANK (IMBEDDED HERE)
COLLAR
HEEL TOP-LIFT
VAMP
THROAT
WELT
OUTSOLE
TIP

Figure 21-3. *This picture shows the details of shoe soles, heels, and uppers.*

when wet, and porous enough to permit the foot to breathe. Vegetable-tanned cowhide that is cut from the better parts of the hide incorporates all these qualities. Other products that resemble leather make long-wearing shoe bottoms but may lack the porosity of leather soles. The thickness of leather outsoles is measured in **irons**. Each iron is 1/48 inch thick. Outsoles of men's shoes are usually 9 to 12 irons thick; women's are usually 2 to 6 irons thick.

The **insole** is an inner part directly under the foot inside the shoe. It acts as a foundation for the shoe and enhances comfort and durability. Good-quality insoles are made of leather. Less-expensive insoles are made of plastics materials. In inexpensive shoes a specially prepared card-board (fiberboard) is sometimes used. In good-quality shoes the space between the insole and the outsole often contains a filler made of cork, felt, rubber, polyurethane, or leather. This filler adds to comfort, make the sole more water resis-tant, and eliminates squeaks. Foam rubber and polyurethane foam impart buoyancy.

The **shoe shank** is usually a tempered-steel bridge located between the heel and ball of the shoe to give added support to the arch of the foot and to help maintain the shape of the shoe. The higher the heel on the shoe, the more work the arch has to do in keeping the heel from sloping backward and ruining the shoe. Conversely, in a flat-heeled house slipper no shank is needed. In some low-heeled shoes, a wooden shank is all the support the shoe needs for the foot.

The **shoe welt** is a narrow strip of leather approximately $\frac{1}{8}$ to $\frac{1}{2}$ inch wide, used on oxford-type or heavy-duty shoes to hold the sole to the upper parts of the shoe. The welt is sometimes decorative. If it is shaped so that it rests against the upper along the seam that joins the upper and the sole, it helps make the shoe water resis-tant. The welt, when used, is visible at the joint between the upper and the sole.

A **platform** may be used on some shoes. It is a thin to very thick layer, usually of cork, felt, or foamed plastic, that is covered to match or con-trast with the upper material of the shoe. The platform cushions the walking surface of the

shoe, gives the wearer a buoyant feel, and, when thick, may make the wearer appear taller. Heel heights have to be adjusted to accommodate the extra lift given at the front of the shoe by the platform. The platform is visible on the outside of the shoe.

An **elevator** is a wedgelike device, usually made of cork, that may be built from the heel area to the toe area inside a man's shoe to give him added height.

Heels

Heels are made from wood, leather, recon-structed leather, plastic, rubber, or wood rein-forced with metal. For women's shoes, wooden or plastic heels may be covered with the same material as the shoe uppers, or they may be sprayed with an enamel paint. Such heels may chip before the shoes are ready to be discarded. **Heel lifts** are leather, nylon, polyurethane, or rubber protectors attached to the base of the heel. They are replaceable when worn down.

Parts of the Heel.   Basically, the heel has four parts. **The heel bed** or **cup** is the top of the heel that fits against the shoe. The **heel base** is the back line of the heel from the point where it meets the shoe down to the lift. The **heel breast** is the inside of the heel under the arch of the shoe. The heel lift is the replaceable part of the heel.

Types of Heels.   Separately attached heels come in two basic types, **plain** and **breasted.** Most men's and children's shoes come only in plain heels. These form an angle at the point where the heel meets the sole under the arch of the foot. Some women's heels, such as stack or built-up heels made from layers of leather glued together, are plain. For dressy or elegant shoes or shoes that are to be covered with materials used on the shoe itself, heels are often breasted. In breasted heels an extension of the heel fits under the arch of the foot to give a curved shape or arch to the shoe at that point. Breasted heels are

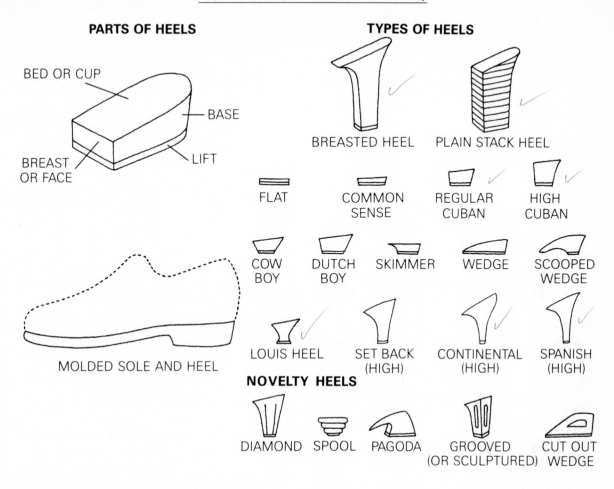

Figure 21-4. *Heels are made from wood, leather, reconstructed leather, plastic, rubber, or wood reinforced with steel.*

usually more costly to make and attach than are plain heels (see Figure 21–4).

Molded heels and soles made from rubber or plastic may appear to have a breasted or arched look. The sole and heel, however, have been made in one piece and the heel is not separately attached. This is called a **unit bottom**.

Styles of Heels. Heels on women's shoes may be referred to as **low, medium,** or **high** or by names of special shapes. Heels may be slender, medium, or thick. Following are some popular heel styles.

Plain heels

Flat Heels: Low, broad heels used on house slippers and slipperlike shoes. About $\frac{3}{8}$ to $\frac{4}{8}$ inch high.

Common-Sense Heels: Similar to flat heels but slightly higher. Approximately $\frac{5}{8}$ to $\frac{6}{8}$ inch high. Used on oxford and walking shoes.

Cuban Heels: Medium-low to medium-high heels with broad, substantial look and slightly tapered angle at the back. Ranges from $\frac{1}{8}$ to $\frac{7}{8}$ inch high.

Stacked Heels: Layers of leather or wood are glued together and the heel is cut from those layers, which show slight alternating colors. True stacked heels are costly. Imitation stacked heels are made with a layer of striped plastic used to cover the heel. Stacked heels may be any height and usually are broad.

Cowboy Heels: Medium high, broad heel with a flat breast or face and sloping back. Used on cowboy boots.

Dutchboy Heels: Slightly broader than cowboy heels, with sloping breast and back.

Breasted heels

Skimmer Heels: Medium-low heel with fairly broad support and breasted topline. About $\frac{10}{8}$ inch high.

Wedge Heels: Varying height heels built under the arch of the sole for extra support.

Scooped Wedge Heels: Similar to the wedge except for a slightly arched shape at the baseline of the heel under the arch.

Louis (Looey) Heel: Medium-high, shapely heel with a narrow walking surface.

Set Back: A high, slender heel with a straight back or baseline and an arch under the instep. $\frac{18}{8}$ inches or more high.

Continental: A high, slender heel with a shapely, arched back.

Spanish Heel: A high, slender heel with an angled back line.

Novelty Heels: Other exotic shapes such as spools, cutouts, diamond, grooved, cone, and pagoda (see Figure 21–4).

Uppers

Uppers are inside and outside sections of the shoe above the sole and the heel. Inside uppers include the following parts: The **toe box** is a stiff reinforcement under the top of some shoes to protect the toes and to help the toe retain its shape. The **counter** is the stiff reinforcement at the heel under the quarter of the shoe used to make the shoe fit snugly at the heel. The **doubler** is a cotton, felt, or foam interlining used to make the shoe look and feel richer and to add to comfort by acting as an insulating material. The **linings** are inside layers that cover the joinings and seams and make the insides of the shoes more comfortable and attractive. The best linings are made of sheepskin, nylon tricot, or good-quality cotton drill. Inexpensive linings are made of split leather, plastic made to look like leather, or heavily sized cotton.

Outside uppers include the following. The **vamp** is the front part of the shoe from the toe to the instep. The **tip** is a separate piece of material covering the toe section of the vamp and used on oxford-type shoes. The **quarter** is the section of the shoe from the instep to the center back of the heel. The **saddle** is a piece covering the instep section of some sport shoes. A **self-strap** (sometimes called a **penny**) is across the instep of a slip-on shoe. The **tongue** is the reinforcement beneath the lacings that protects the foot. The tongue may be part of the vamp or a separate, stitched-on piece. Some heavy shoes also contain a **collar,** which is a separate piece of material folded over the top of the shoe from the instep to the quarter seam.

MANUFACTURE OF SHOES

Shoes are first designed; then patterns for each part of the shoe are cut to scale and prepared for use. Shoe uppers, soles, and linings are cut by hand or machine and are stitched on sewing machines or cemented together. The completed uppers then go to the section of the factory where the lasting operation takes place.

Shoes are designed and manufactured over a special plastic form, known as a shoemaker's **last,** that is shaped like the human foot. Lasts are modified when necessary to reflect fashion characteristics such as the open toe, the pointed toe, the rounded toe, or the square toe. In 1971 the American Footwear Manufacturers Association (AFMA) standardized measurements for the heels of lasts. The association hopes eventually to standardize all measurements.

The insole is temporarily tacked onto the last. The completed upper is then pulled snugly over this form and attached to the insole. Counters and toe boxes are inserted in the correct positions. Filler is pasted on the bottom of the insole, and the outsole is then attached to the shoe. The temporary tacks are removed, and the shoe is removed from the last.

Outsoles are attached either to a welt or directly to the insole by a number of methods. These include stitching, cementing, vulcanizing,

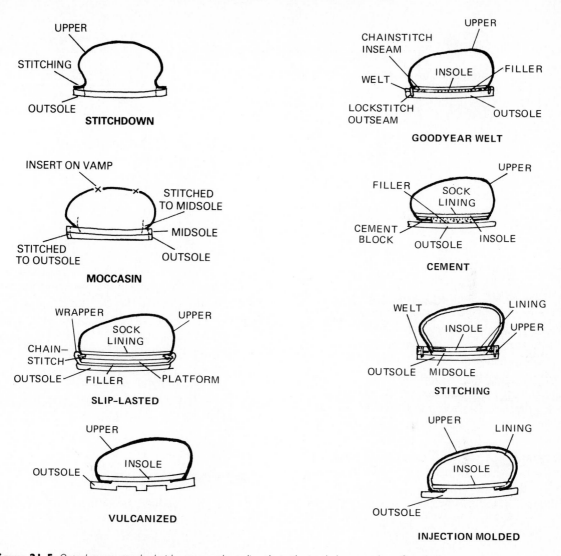

Figure 21-5. *Outsoles are attached either to a welt or directly to the insole by a number of methods.*

and molding, or the entire shoe may be made by injection molding.

Stitching

The upper may be turned outward and stitched to the outsole. This method is used for children's barefoot sandals, men's and women's casual shoes, and chukka boots. The **Goodyear welt** method is more costly, and results in a sturdier shoe. The welt is attached by a thread stitched with a curved needle to a channel cut in the bottom of the insole. The space between the insole and the outsole is filled with cork, and the outsole is stitched to the welt around the outside of the shoes.

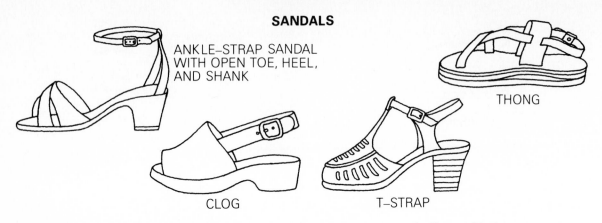

Figure 21-6. *All sandals use straps to hold the shoe onto the foot or have an upper made of strips of leather.*

Cementing

In place of stitching, **cementing,** a speedier, less-expensive method, is used on the majority of shoes made today. Slipperlike shoes that have no linings are made by cementing fabric or plastic uppers to plastic soles.

In **slip-lasted** shoes, a covering is stitched to the upper and insole before the shoe is slipped onto the last. A platform is then cemented into position, and the shank, heel, and an outsole are added.

Single-sole cementing is done by cutting the outsole in half and using one half as the insole while lasting the shoe. The other half is then cemented on to form the outsole after the shoe has been pulled over the last. This procedure is used for fine-quality women's shoes.

Vulcanizing

A method for joining rubber soles to canvas uppers, as in sneakers, is called **vulcanizing**. The canvas upper, rubber mudguards, and the rubber sole are placed over a metal last and then put into an oven and baked under pressure to cure and harden the rubber and join the parts permanently.

Molding

Since 1960, vinyl soles have been attached to uppers by a process known as injection mold-ing. Heat-softened polyvinyl chloride material is forced against the upper under pressure; the heel and sole are bonded to the upper and then shaped, cooled, and hardened in one operation. Shoes constructed in this way cannot be resoled, but the soles are tough and wear very well. The soles usually have an embossed tread. Since 1970, a polyurethane injection molding compound has been used to produce a cushioned sole in this manner.

TYPES OF FOOTWEAR

Footwear is classified according to four basic types: shoes, boots, slippers, and rubbers and overshoes. It is further classified as active sports, street, spectator sports, and dress wear. Within each type a great variety of shapes and styles are available. Fashion plays an important role in determining what styles are accepted at any one time. Footwear may harmonize or contrast with the clothing being worn. Footwear may be plain or ornamented with lacings, cutouts, stitching, overlays, or other decorations.

Shoes

Shoes come in five different categories: sandal, pump, step-in, oxford, and high top. Some of these are more commonly worn by women than men, but casual dressing and unisex fashions have made at least some items available in each category for each sex.

Sandals.   The **sandal** was originally a slab of leather held to the foot by means of narrow strips of leather. Sandals today vary in shape, but all either use straps at the instep, ankle, or leg to hold the shoe onto the foot or have an upper made of strips of leather. These straps may tie, buckle, or snap, and they may be short or wind around the leg one or more times (Figure 21-6).

Ankle Straps: Held to the foot with a strap that fits once or more around the ankle. May have open or closed toe and heel. The section that holds the strap usually extends up from the quarter of the shoe.
Barefoot Sandal: A variety of the T-strap sandal described below. Cutouts on the vamp and two straps across the instep gave this shoe its name. It has a low heel and is sturdy.
Clog: Open heel and open or closed toe shoe with sling strap to hold to the heel. Either a thick slab of

cork or a thick wooden sole is used to cushion the heel and sole part of the foot.
Thong: Held on the foot by across-the-toe straps that are attached to the sole by a projection that fits between the big and adjacent toe.
T Strap: An open- or closed-look sandal with a T-shaped strap across the instep. Heels may be any height.

Pumps.   Pumps are low-cut shoes that may have an open or closed toe and rarely use straps except for the instep or the sling strap across the back of the heel. Heels may be of any height. They may be plain or highly ornamental. The throat line on pumps is particularly important for both appearance and fit (Figure 21-7).

Classic: Closed, straight-top edge pump with no decoration; in any heel height.
D'Orsay: Similar to the classic except that the sides are low cut and may or may not be ornamented.
Flat: Any style pump with low, flat heels. Also called *skimmers* and *ballet* pumps.

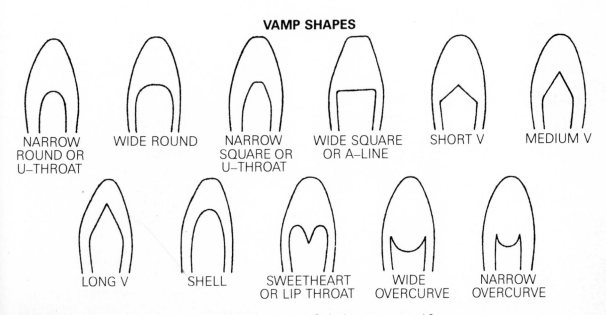

VAMP SHAPES

NARROW ROUND OR U-THROAT

WIDE ROUND

NARROW SQUARE OR U-THROAT

WIDE SQUARE OR A-LINE

SHORT V

MEDIUM V

LONG V

SHELL

SWEETHEART OR LIP THROAT

WIDE OVERCURVE

NARROW OVERCURVE

Figure 21-7. *The throat line on pumps is particularly important for both appearance and fit.*

PUMPS

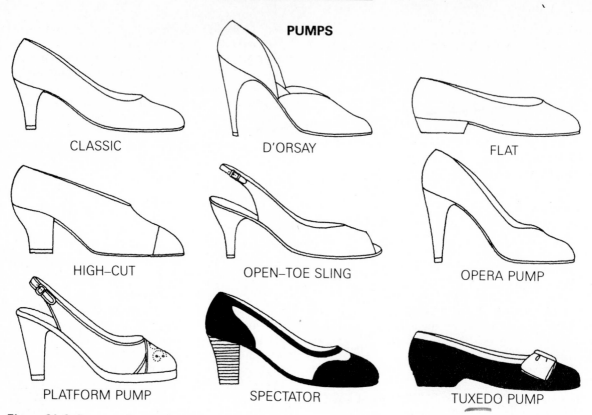

CLASSIC　　　　　D'ORSAY　　　　　FLAT

HIGH–CUT　　　　OPEN–TOE SLING　　　OPERA PUMP

PLATFORM PUMP　　　SPECTATOR　　　TUXEDO PUMP

Figure 21-8. *Pumps are low-cut shoes that may have an open or closed toe and rarely use straps, except for the sling across the back of the heel.*

High Cut: Throat line is high with narrow round or V opening.

Open-Toe: Shoe has cut-out toe section.

Open-Heel or Sling: The back part of the quarter may be kept intact, or a strap that buckles or ties may be used to hold the shoe on at the heel.

Opera Pump: Dressy shoe with closed toe and heel, similar to classic pump with high heel.

Platform Pump: Dressy or casual pump with platform added between sole and upper.

Spectator: Shoe has separate wing tip or perforated plain tip and matching decoration on the back of the shoe. The back and toe are closed; the heel is often stacked.

Tuxedo: Low-heeled, flat, closed toe and heel pump for men or women. A flat grosgrain ribbon decorates the throat line.

Step-in. Popular with men, women, and children, the step-in (Figure 21–9) is built somewhat higher than the pump but generally has no straps or laces to hold it to the foot. For men and children it always has a low heel. For women the heel may be low, medium, or high. Sometimes an elastic gore near the instep allows the shoe to spread for ease in putting it on and taking it off.

Casuals: Any soft-textured, comfortable step-in for everyday wear. Casuals usually have a high throat line over the instep, sometimes have gores on the side for easy slipping into, and have cushioned soles.

Espadrille: A summer shoe that has a rope braid wrapped platform, a cushiony sole with a wedge heel, and either a canvas, suede, or corduroy upper. The throat section is cut in a straight line across the instep.

Huaraches (also Hirache and Huaracho): Woven by hand in Mexico, usually of strips of horsehide. Stretchy, unlined, quarter-strap shoes.

Kilties: Shoes with a fringed flap over the throat. Usually used for genuine moccasin or moc-toed shoes.

Loafer: General term given to any slip-on that is soft and has a tonguelike projection over the instep with exposed elastic side gores.

Moccasins: May be unadorned, trimmed with kiltie flap or fringed tassel, beads, or chain or buckle.

Monk Strap: A man's street shoe with tonguelike projection over the instep. A wide strap fits over the instep and buckles on the side.

Penny Loafer: Moccasin-type shoe or moc-toe shoe with a stitched-on strap across the instep that has a cutout design.

Slide: Open-quarter shoe held to the foot by the high vamp. May or may not have a open toe. The woman's shoe usually has a high heel.

Tasselmoc Slip-On: Moccasin-type shoe or moc-toe shoe with tassel trim at the instep.

STEP–INS

CASUAL

ESPADRILLE

MONK STRAP

KILTIE

LOAFER

HUARACHE

JIFFIES

MOCCASIN

OPEN–TOE SLIDE

PENNY LOAFER

TASSELMOC

Figure 21-9. *The step-in, for men and women, is built somewhat higher than the pump.*

Oxford. The Oxford is worn by men, women, and children. It is a below-the-ankle shoe that usually laces in the front over the instep but may have side lacing. Oxfords give good support. Two basic types of oxfords are sold.

Bal (balmoral): A separate tongue is stitched in place by seams that hold the vamp and extensions of the quarters that lace across the instep.

Blucher: The tongue of the shoe is part of the vamp. The quarters are loose where they lace over the instep. This allows for expansion of the foot.

Toe styles further differentiate oxfords.

Moccasin or Moc-Toe: A U-shaped piece either hand stitched (in the true moccasins) or machine stitched (in the moc-toes) in the vamp of the shoe.

Novelty: Includes open-toed oxfords, cutout designs, or other nontraditional decorations.

Plain: Unadorned vamp section.

Straight Tip: Especially popular for men's shoes. A perforated, decorative toe cap of leather that fits in a straight line across the toe part of the shoe is usually found on the bal-style oxfords.

Wing Tip: Also popular for men's shoes. This perforated, decorative toe cap of leather or plastic in the shape of a 3 fits across the toe and along the sides of the vamp of a blucher or bal-style oxford.

In addition to the basic oxford styles some have special names (see Figure 21–10).

Brogue: Originally a heavy-type work shoe, the brogue now refers to any textured, durable-appearing oxford with wing-tip and blucher styling.

Ghillie: Oxford with no tongue. Used for girl's and women's street and spectator sports shoes. The cord lacing goes through specially designed eyelets and ties in a bow either at the top of the lacings or after having circled the ankle or leg.

Saddle Oxford: Low-heeled, sport-type oxford in bal style with contrasting colored and/or textured leather piece across instep and forming lace stays.

High Top. Shoes that come above the ankle and that lace are referred to as high tops. These are primarily work shoes, sports shoes, and street shoes for people who want extra ankle support. Sometimes they are referred to as **low boots.** Some infants' shoes are hightops. (See Figure 21–2 on page 266.)

OXFORDS

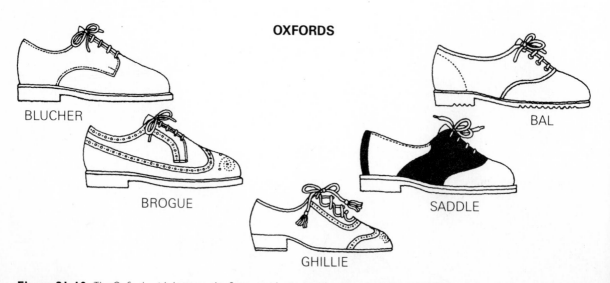

BLUCHER

BROGUE

GHILLIE

BAL

SADDLE

Figure 21-10. *The Oxford, with laces on the front or side, is worn by men, women, and children.*

Boots

Boots may be high or low, soft or stiff, ornamented or plain, cuffed or straight edge, crushed or smooth. Boots will be found that are appropriate for street, business, dress, and even formal wear. The upper part of the boot, known as the **shaft**, differentiates boots from shoes. The foot part is constructed in the manner discussed above. Boots may be pull-on style, have zippers, or have laces. They may be lined or unlined. (See Figure 21-11 on page 278).

Ankle: Low boots that cover the ankle. They may have side zippers, be pull ons, or have laces. They may or may not be cuffed.

Booty: An infant's tiny boot or a fashionable low boot for women's dress wear.

Chukka Boot: A low man's or woman's boot laced through two sets of eyelets. Sometimes called a **desert boot.** Made from suede or buck leather.

Dress Boot: Smooth leather, plastic, or fabric (including satin) boot of any height. Women's dress boots may have cuffs or straight edges. They may be zippered or pull ons and may be crushed or stiff. Men's dress boots are smooth leather, 5- to 8-inch high boots.

Engineer's Boots: End at the calf or above with stiff, sturdy zipper. Adjustable buckles at ankle and top. Gores allow the boot to fit comfortably.

Fisherman's Boots and Waders: Wide-top, waterproof boots that may cover the legs or thighs or extend up to the hips.

High Lace Boots: Also known as **lace-up** or **Granny boots.**

Jodhpur: About 5 to 8 inches high; reaches above the ankle. The smooth vamp extends up the front and is held in position by a side buckle (Figure 21-11).

Linesmen's: Sturdy, lace-up boots with blucher styling for foot ease and comfort. Shaft may be 8 to 14 inches high and have pull loops to aid in putting on the boots.

Loggers' Boots: Similar to linesmen's boots but with a higher heel to enable workers to get a good grip on the ground while cutting trees. The soles have caulks or spikes. The boot is treated to be water resistant.

Outdoor Boots: Cold-weather boots for hiking, walking, or slushing through snow and cold. They are sturdily built, lined, may zip or lace, and are either made of waterproof materials or the uppers are impregnated with silicone to help prevent moisture seepage.

Riding Boot: Tall, pull-on boots with straight shafts that are unornamented. They have low heels and are worn with riding trousers that fit inside the boot top. They may have a contrasting color band at the top shaft.

Wellington: A smooth-leather, straight-shaft boot with a vamp extension in the front above the instep. The boot is usually 10 inches or more high. It may or may not have a strap that buckles across the instep.

Western Boots: All leather pull-on boots with stacked heels that have stitched or ornamented shafts that end in an arched form about midcalf. Side pull straps allow them to be pulled on and off easily. Toes are stiff and usually curl upward. Also called **cowboy** or **cowgirl boots.**

Slippers

Slippers are built for easy on and off at-home wear, although hard-sole slippers may be used for moderate outdoor wear (Figure 21-12 on page 279). Sheepskin leather, manmade materials, and fabrics of all types, including corduroy and terry cloth, are used for slipper uppers. For better-quality slippers, kidskin, calfskin, or other fine-grained or suede leathers may be used.

Slippers may be lined or unlined. Cold-weather linings include pile linings, shearling, or fur. Trimming on slippers may include stitching, embroidery, beading, lace, fur, or maribou.

Booties: Above-ankle pull ons. For infants they may be made from knitted yarns with ball-end ties. For children and adults they may be made from any flexible material and may or may not have linings. Also called **cavaliers.**

D'Orsay: Slippers are cut to a low V on the sides. May have any height heel.

Everett: Step-in slipper with high throat that extends over the instep. May be lined or unlined.

Folding or **Pullman:** Flat-heeled or very low-heeled slippers without a shank and therefore may be folded. These are especially desirable for travel.

Hi-lo: Boot-style slipper with a lined cuff that may be worn up or down.

BOOTS

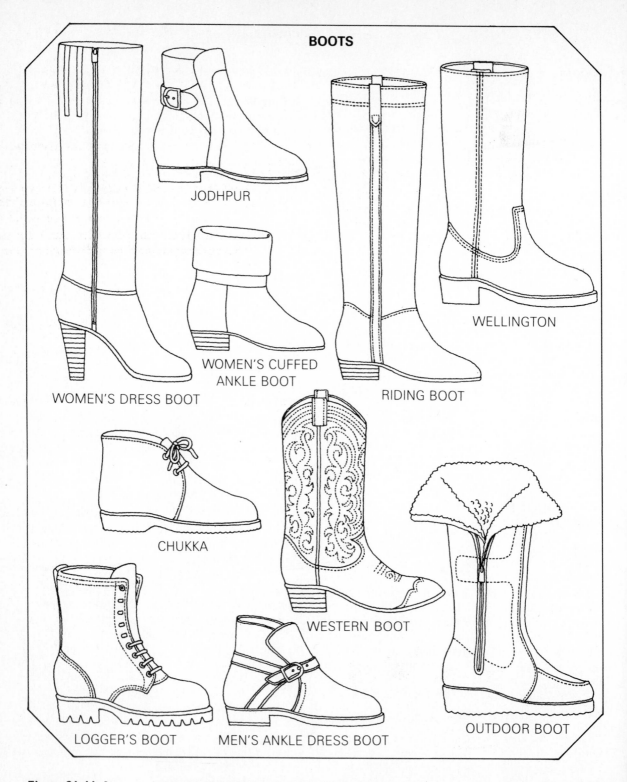

JODHPUR

WELLINGTON

WOMEN'S CUFFED
ANKLE BOOT

WOMEN'S DRESS BOOT

RIDING BOOT

CHUKKA

WESTERN BOOT

LOGGER'S BOOT

MEN'S ANKLE DRESS BOOT

OUTDOOR BOOT

Figure 21-11. *Boots are distinguished from shoes by the upper part, or shaft. They may be dressy or casual.*

SLIPPERS

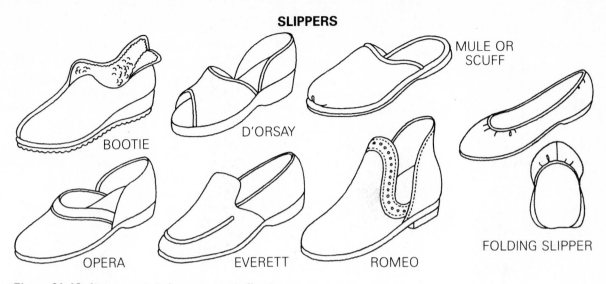

Figure 21-12. *Slippers are built for easy on and off at-home wear.*

Moccasin: True moccasin-construction slippers have soles that extend over the side of the foot and are stitched in front to the vamp.

Mule or **Scuff:** Backless slip-on; may or may not have a separate heel.

Opera: Man's or boy's slipper, low-cut on the sides, similar to the D'Orsay.

Romeo or **Juliette:** High cut, above ankle, boot-like slipper having over-the-instep shaped piece and an elastic gore in the sides.

Slip-on: General term for any slipper that is easy to slip into and out of.

Sport Shoes

Once used primarily for active sports, sport shoes have moved into a unique position. Except for business and evening wear, sport shoes may be worn everywhere. Made primarily with canvas, plastic, or leather uppers and rubber soles, many variations of these shoes are on the market. They come in above-the-ankle and below-the-ankle styles. They are often white, and many are colorfully decorated with strips of material (see Figure 21–13).

Qualities needed for active sports wearers include:

- Keeping the feet dry
- Cushioning the bottom of the foot
- Staying on the foot in use
- Reinforcing the parts of the sole most directly in contact with the roadway or court
- Protecting the foot from harm

In 1982, manufacturers introduced a new type of closure for athletic and casual oxfords that eliminated tying. The closure uses straps over the instep with buckles. When pressed down on a velcro surface, the straps hold tightly, but release easily when the tab is pulled away.

Sport shoes include the types described below.

Baseball Shoes: Leather or leatherlike oxford-type shoes with leather soles into which steel spikes are fitted for ground-gripping action. Also used for softball.

Basketball Shoes: Both above-the-ankle and below-the-ankle canvas or leather oxford-type shoes with padded, ridged rubber soles for good traction. For added comfort, some have urethane innersoles.

SPORT SHOES AND BOOTS

BOWLING SHOE

BOATING SHOE

GOLF SHOE
WITH REMOVABLE
LEATHER KILTIE

CLEATED SHOE
(FOR SOCCER, FOOTBALL,
BASEBALL, AND SOFTBALL)

BASKETBALL SHOE

RUNNING SHOE

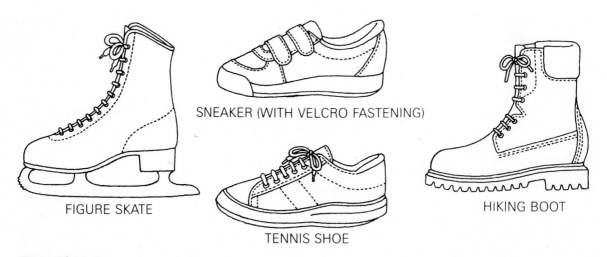

FIGURE SKATE

SNEAKER (WITH VELCRO FASTENING)

TENNIS SHOE

HIKING BOOT

Figure 21-13. *Once used primarily for active sports, sport shoes may now be worn for many occasions.*

Boat Shoes: Canvas upper and rubber soled shoes, commonly worn as boat shoes. For a dressier look, a low-cut leather oxford with a folded, laced collar and two-eyelet lacing in a moccasin style is popular.

Bowling Shoes: Snug fitting oxfords that lace from the toe to the top used for bowling. A padded lining

under the collar portion of the shoe adds to comfort.

Football and **Soccer Shoes:** Sturdy oxford shoes in leather or leatherlike plastic with lacings to hold the shoe on securely, and with leather or rubber cleats to aid in traction.

Golf Shoes: Sturdy oxfords in leather, leatherlike

plastic, or waterproof material with special steel cleats or spikes fitted into the sole and heel for firm grip.

Hikers, Survivors, Walkers: Ranging from soft, cushiony shoes for casual walking to the sturdiest of boots for climbers and mountaineers, these shoes cover a wide range of materials and styles. More enduring walkers and hikers may have canvas, leather, or plastic uppers and lace above the ankle for added protection. These usually have thick, ridged rubber soles and inner paddings. Still more rugged shoes include pacs, and survivors. The **pac** is a rubber boot that extends up to the calf of the leg. It is well insulated and waterproof. The survivor is a leather, insulated boot with a padded collar and a deeply grooved sole for sure footed climbing.

Hunting Shoes: Any shoes for walking or hiking may also be used for hunting. A waterproof hunting shoe has been designed with a rubber foot covering, a crepe rubber sole with special tread for good traction, and a padded collar.

Jogging and **Running Shoes:** Below-the-ankle, oxford type, multihued, cushioned, athletic shoes that are lightweight and durable have revolutionized the comfort and appearance of former sneakers. Most running and jogging shoes have cushioned soles, padded collars, and wrap-around soles that are upturned over the edge of the toe.

Skating Shoes: For both ice skating and roller skating, special attached-to-the-skates shoes are worn. Figure skating shoes come above the ankle for support. They are usually insulated with foam urethane, and the uppers may be leather or vinyl. The same types of shoes with higher, back-of-the-leg protection are used for ice hockey skates. Roller-skating shoes may be oxford or high-top shoe style. These shoes do not need the insulation of the ice skate, but they do need spongy innersoles and pads at the top where the oxford meets the ankle. The soles are also often wraparound to protect the toes.

Ski Boots: Unique, specially constructed boots that clamp onto skis, insulate and protect the foot and ankle, and are fitted to the wearer are an essential for ski buffs. Polyurethane shells in a wide range of colors are fitted with buckles and clamps, and padded to hug the foot, yet are lightweight and comfortable.

Sneakers: All-purpose sports shoe that may have canvas, leather, or plastic upper, ridged or smooth rubber sole, be an oxford or an over-the-ankle shoe, and have reinforcements at wear spots, such as the ankle and toe.

Swimming Shoes: All rubber, unlined step-in for protection at the beach or in the shower or pool.

Tennis shoes: Oxford type sneaker with smooth sole. May be all canvas and rubber or leather or plastic with rubber sole.

Rubbers and Galoshes

For rainy weather, ankle-high rubbers are necessary to keep shoes dry and in good condition. **Galoshes** are a high overshoe usually worn in snow and slush. Rubber, vinyl, or fabric uppers with rubber soles are used for rubbers and galoshes. Some have fancy trim, such as fur, and are lined with cotton fleece or synthetic pile fabrics for warmth; some are made to stretch to a wide range of sizes.

CARE OF SHOES

The proper care of shoes can lengthen their life as well as aid in keeping them shaped for greatest comfort and support. If possible, shoes should be changed daily to permit them to regain their shape and to allow perspiration to evaporate before wearing again. Shoes may be stored on shoe trees, which preserve their shape. Run-down heels not only make shoes unattractive but also give incorrect support for the feet. Worn heel lifts should therefore be replaced promptly. Leather shoes and boots need frequent waxing to keep the leather pliable and soft, and to lengthen their wear.

DO YOU KNOW YOUR MERCHANDISE?

1. Why is it important to purchase shoes that fit properly?
2. How are shoe sizes computed?
3. What devices are used for shoe fitting?
4. How do the Federal Trade Commission rules regarding shoes and slippers help the consumer?

5. Explain the following terms: toe box, counter, vamp, quarter, collar, insole.
6. What is a shoemaker's last and how is it used in making footwear?
7. What are the characteristics and advantages of Goodyear welt, injection molded shoes?
8. List five basic types of shoes and give an advantage for each.
9. List five different types of boots and give a special use for each.
10. List five different classifications of sport shoes and explain the important qualities needed by the wearers of each type.

PUTTING YOUR MERCHANDISE KNOWLEDGE TO WORK

Make a style analysis of the shoes or other footwear your classmates wear. Which type of footwear (shoes, boots, sneakers, other) is the most popular? Are young men's footwear styles different from young women's? What color is most frequently worn? What unusual features such as odd-shaped toes, unusual heels, trim, or materials do you notice?

PROJECT

Select from a newspaper five advertisements for either men's or women's footwear. Analyze the advertisements according to the following categories: illustration, style, materials used, construction features, fit and comfort, sizes, fashion importance. Do the advertisements describe the type of footwear being shown? Rate each advertisement based on the value of the information the customer would receive by reading it.

22

Fashion Accessories: The Dramatic Accents

Gloves, handbags, wallets, luggage, belts, umbrellas, and hats are called **accessories** because they serve useful purposes and dramatize or harmonize with apparel. Each category of merchandise is made by different manufacturers and has a language all its own.

GLOVES

Gloves are made from leathers, plastics, fabrics, furs, and combinations of these materials. The leathers used must be thin enough for comfort and sturdy enough for durability, as well as soft and supple. Vinyls and urethanes are the popular plastics materials used. They are often made to resemble leather. Glove fabrics include cotton poplin, canvas, cotton jersey, flannel, fleece, nylon, hi-bulk acrylic, wool, cashmere, and brushed rayon, as well as meshes, tricots, and crocheted lace. For waterproof gloves neoprene-coated nylon is used. Gloves may be made solely of one material or combined with palms of a different material. Linings may be added.

Parts of a Glove

If you put on a glove, stretch your fingers, and examine the glove, you can see all parts but the lining and small reinforcements. The salesperson should know the purpose of the various sections of gloves in order to be able to explain to the customer how to make the glove fit properly.

The **trank** is the general outline that forms the palm, back, and fingers of the glove. The fingers of leather, plastic, and some fabric gloves are made in four sections. The front and back sections are part of the trank. The side pieces, known as **fourchettes** or **forks,** are small, oblong pieces as long as the fingers and wide enough to provide ample space. The fourchettes may be made of the same material as the tranks or from knitted fabric or plastic. At the base of some fourchettes are tiny, triangular sections known as **quirks.** They are used for extra give between the fingers in fine quality leather gloves.

The **thumb** of the glove is made from a separate piece of material that is later stitched over the thumb hole. Thumbs differ in appearance and size. The **Bolton thumb** is bulky but provides complete freedom of movement. It is used on men's and women's sport and street gloves. The **set-in thumb** is used in stretch fabric gloves. A **keyhole thumb** is an extension from the trank that forms the inside portion of the thumb.

Linings make gloves warmer and more comfortable to wear. **Skeleton linings** cover only the trank; **full linings** provide a complete glove within a glove.

Manufacture of Gloves

Glove factories specialize in making either leather, plastic, or fabric gloves.

GLOVE DETAILS

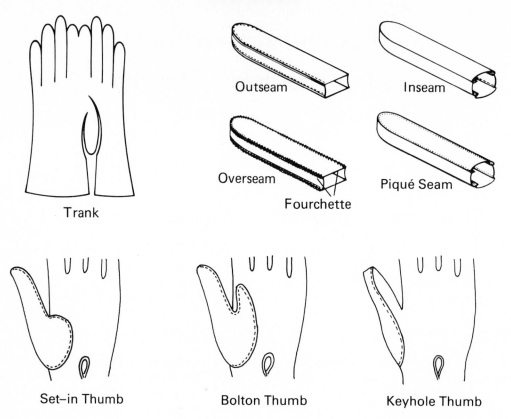

Figure 22-1. *The salesperson should know the purpose of the various sections of gloves in order to explain how to make the glove fit properly.*

Leather, Plastic, and Woven-Fabric Gloves. The first step in making gloves is to decide how many pairs of gloves should be cut from a skin or a woven fabric and to mark the individual skins or fabrics for cutting. This operation is known as **taxing.**

Cutting. **Trank cutting** refers to the cutting of the oblong form of the glove from the marked skins or fabric. The most expensive method of cutting tranks for leather gloves is known as **table cut.** The leather is dampened slightly and pulled over the edge of the table; then it is stretched and pulled until it is in the correct shape for cutting. The worker judges the feel and give of the leather and according to its nature,

measures and marks the space for the specified trank. Table-cut gloves fit well and give the hand flexibility of movement.

Less expensive leather gloves are made by a modified method of this cut, known as the **pull down cut.** No attempt is made in this method to achieve a perfect fit. Inexpensive leather gloves, plastic gloves, work gloves, bulky lined gloves, and fabric gloves are cut by a metal die that is shaped like the trank of a glove.

Finger slitting is done by steel dies that are pressed down on several layers of tranks placed face to face in pairs. In one operation they cut fingers, holes for thumbs, and, when used, the tiny triangular quirks that fit at the base between the fingers.

Stitching. **Seams** on gloves close the fingers and sides of the gloves. The closing stitch attaches the thumb, stitches the fingers together with the fourchettes, and stitches the sides of the trank together.

The seam that is least expensive and easiest to stitch is known as the **inseam.** It stitches together the edges of the glove on the inside. When the glove is turned right-side out, neither the stitches nor the edges of the material are seen.

The **outseam** is the opposite of the inseam in appearance. Both raw edges of the material and the seam used to hold them together are visible on the outside of the glove.

When the **overseam** is used, both raw edges of the leather are visible on the outside of the glove, but the stitches lap over the edges, reinforcing them and making as fine or as deep a seam as desired.

The **piqué seam** is the most finger-slimming, durable stitch for gloves. One edge of leather is lapped over the other edge so that only one raw edge shows on the outside. The glove is then stitched on the outside over a finger-shaped rod. In the **half-piqué** seam only the seams on the back are overlapped. Those on the palm side are inseam or outseam sewed. This is an inexpensive type of closing. Seams are also used for decoration. **Pointing** is used to place stitches, colored threads, braids, or beads on the back of the glove.

After gloves are closed by stitching and decorated, they are pressed from the inside by a hot metal plate that shapes and smoothes them so they are ready for shipment to stores.

Knitted Gloves. Regular knit gloves are made in wool, high-bulk acrylic yarns, or cotton string yarns. These gloves are knitted to shape either by hand or on knitting machines. The tips of the fingers are closed after knitting.

Types of Gloves

Coverings for the hand and wrist that have a separate section only for the thumb are known as **mittens.** They are made of any glove material and are lined or unlined.

The **slip-on glove** may extend to the wrist or farther up. No fasteners or openings are used.

A longer glove that has an opening inside the wrist to slip the hand in and out without remov-

GLOVE STYLES

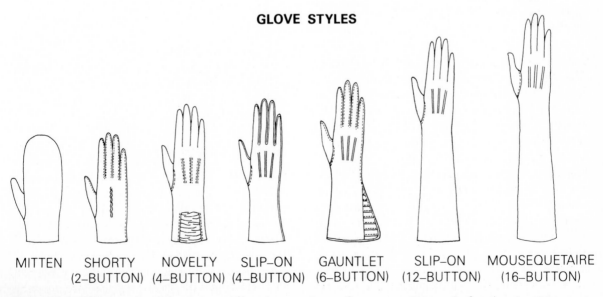

| MITTEN | SHORTY (2-BUTTON) | NOVELTY (4-BUTTON) | SLIP-ON (4-BUTTON) | GAUNTLET (6-BUTTON) | SLIP-ON (12-BUTTON) | MOUSEQUETAIRE (16-BUTTON) |

Figure 22-2. *Different styles of gloves are used for various occasions — from sporty mittens to the formal mousquetaire.*

ing the arm section of the glove is known as a **mousquetaire**. This is little used today.

Gauntlets have a wide flare above the wrist made by a separate triangular-shaped piece set into the arm section. Some ski mittens are referred to as gauntlets because they are wider above the wrist to fit over other garments.

A **shorty** is a wrist-length sports or dress glove. It may have a side or center vent for added space for inserting the hand or a center fastening with clasps, buttons, or straps. Most men's gloves are made in shorty style. **Driving gloves** are usually shorties with special palm sections, which may be knitted, to aid in gripping the steering wheel of a car.

Sports gloves range in length from shorty to midarm and in style from slim fitted to wide gauntlets. All cold-wear gloves are lined; some are interlined. Gloves are designed for each sport. Farmers, hikers, outdoor workers, and machinists need especially thick gloves.

Glove Sizes and Button Lengths

A glove that is too small will wear out at the seams and fingertips much more quickly than one that fits properly. The wrong size in a glove may also cause discomfort.

Lengths of women's gloves are measured in **buttons**. Each button corresponds to 1 inch of length, which is measured from the base of the thumb to the edge of the arm section of the glove. For example, a two-button glove is a short glove, a four-button glove is above wrist length, an eight-button glove comes to the middle of the forearm, a twelve-button glove reaches to or above the elbow, and a sixteen-button glove covers the upper forearm.

Sizes of gloves are determined when the trank is cut. The table-cut trank will give the customer the best fit in leather gloves. Fabric gloves have considerable elasticity and therefore are not sized precisely. Stretch gloves enable people with different hand sizes to wear the same size glove comfortably.

Sizes in women's leather and fabric gloves run in half-inches. Women's glove sizes range from

5 to 8. Men's sizes are S, M, L, and XL. Children's glove sizes are usually one-half the age of the child: size 0 is for the 1 year old, size 4 for the 8 year old, and so on.

Care of Gloves

Customers should be advised that gloves should be eased on gently and smoothed out immediately after removal. Perspiration is harmful to gloves unless it is permitted to evaporate before the gloves are put away.

Many leather gloves are washable, but unless they are so marked, washing may ruin them. Washable gloves should not be allowed to become too soiled before they are washed using mild soaps. Gloves not marked washable should be dry-cleaned. Leather and fabric gloves that are washable should be pulled smoothly into shape while still damp or dried over plastic hand forms. Leather gloves should be finger pressed, a gentle massage that restores their flexibility.

HANDBAGS AND SMALL LEATHER GOODS

Pouches were first used to hold coins. Coin purses that could fit into a pocket or be held in the hand were next devised. These grew in size and tiny finger or wrist straps or decorative knobs and chains were added. They became the handbag commonly used today. Men sometimes use handbags. Men and women carry attaché cases and briefcases. They also use key holders, wallets, and eyeglass cases.

Materials Used in Handbags

All leathers and suedes are used for fine-quality handbags. Bonded leathers are used for medium-priced handbags. Plastics, called "synthetics" in the handbag industry, such as vinyl and polyurethane, and a wide array of sturdy fabrics are used for volume-priced handbags. The plastics may be smooth textured, expanded, crinkled, or napped. Box-type bags with glasslike appearance are made from acrylic plastics. Little metal chain or link bags are also created. Fabrics used are pique, gingham, boucle, broadcloth, felt, taffeta, velvet, petit point, tapestry, canvas, linen crash, parachute cloth, and metallic cloth. Decorations on handbags include beading, embroidery, rhinestones, sequins, and marcasites. Straw and strawlike bags are used for summer wear. Leather, plastics, and cloth are used for small items.

Parts of a Handbag

Handbags consist of an outside material plus frame, fasteners or zippers, linings, inside coin purse, and compartments or pockets. They may have paddings and reinforcements.

Handbag frames give a distinctive shape to the bag and serve as closures. They are usually made of brass or steel and may be plated with gold, silver, or chromium or covered with leather or fabric. Bags may have frames that have been sprayed with enamel to match the material used or to simulate a leather-covered frame. **Gussets** (side gores) allow a bag to expand.

Handles that extend across the top of the bag may be short for holding in the hand, medium length to fit over the arm, or long to hang over the shoulder. There are also short handles that are attached to the back or the side of the bag. Handles may be made from the same material as the bag or from chains, bone, or rigid plastic. They may be attached by stitching on the inside or outside of the bag or be threaded through metal rings attached to posts on the bag frame.

Some bags have **coin purses** attached to the outside. Others have coin purses inside. **Zipper pockets** permit small articles to be separated from the rest of the contents of the bag.

Linings in handbags may be made from leather, leatherlike plastic, or fabric. **Interlinings,** made from cardboard, stiff plastic, cotton felt, paper, muslin, or heavy duck fabric, are glued to the bag and help to give it a firm shape.

Types of Handbags and Small Leather Items

Customers seek handbags to hold small articles and to match or accent their clothing.

Handbags may be classified into three basic groups: envelope, pouch, and box. Variations and mixing of types is very common.

Envelope: A bag with no frame. The back material forms a full flap that covers the entire face of the bag, a three-quarter flap, a half-flap, or a quarter-flap. They may have no handle, a flat back handle, a side wrist handle, or a top handle that may fit inside.

Pouch: Any bag with a zipper-top closing, a frame, and a top or side handle.

Box: Any bag with a rigid frame. Any type of handle may be used with this bag.

Popular handbags and small leather goods are described below.

Attaché Case: A box-type, hard-sided case for carrying papers. They may contain dividers or may have hinges that allow them to serve as writing desks. They have a top carrying handle and may also have a shoulder strap.

Belt Bags: Small bag with a top that fits over a belt.

Bermuda Bag: A large brightly colored fabric bag with wooden handles that often has changeable covers.

Briefs or Briefcases: To hold papers, books, and other such items. Has soft sides or accordion-pleated bottoms for expansion. Briefs may have envelope-style tops with clasps or zipper closings. They have a small top handle and may have shoulder straps. Some have outside pockets.

Camera Case: Boxlike case. Inside has many pockets. Most have a shoulder strap.

Chanel Bag: Casual pouch bag made from quilted material and a chain handle.

Clutch: A small bag without handles or with a concealed handle. Made to be held in the hand. They may have top pouchlike closure or be an envelope style.

Courier Pouch: Expandable, soft-sided bag with adjustable shoulder strap. Some resemble pouches used by couriers during the Civil War.

Drawstring: Bags that close at the top with a string or cord that pulls and shirrs the material when closed and opens easily.

Duffle Bag: A large, soft-sided bag with a handle or shoulder strap or a zip top.

Feed Bag or Bucket Bag: Large carryall with shoulder strap. Is deep and roomy and may expand.

TYPES OF HANDBAGS AND CASES

ATTACHÉ CASE

BERMUDA BAG

BRIEFCASE

CHANEL BAG

COURIER POUCH

DRAWSTRING BUCKET

ENVELOPE CLUTCH

MINAUDIÈRE

ROLL BAG

SATCHEL

PORTFOLIO

Figure 22-3. *Handbags hold articles that men or women need to carry; they may also accent a person's clothing.*

French Purse: A small, clutch-type bag with wallet-like opening and a frame with knob openers. Has pockets for coins, keys, and other small items.

Glasses Case: An open, zipper-closed, or snap-closed pouch with a smooth lining to protect eye glasses.

Hobo: A large, casual, roomy bag with a shoulder strap. Has a curved, zippered topline.

Key Case: Small envelope-shaped holder, with snap or zipper closing, to hold keys.

Minaudière: Small pouch or envelope metal bag with or without a handle for evening use. May be made from or plated with bronze, silver, or gold.

Pannier-Handled Bag: Pouch bag with a handle that extends from the center of the bag to hang over the wrist.

Portfolio: Small, flat bag with one inside pocket. It may have no handle and fit under the arm, two small center handles, or a detachable shoulder strap.

Roll Bag or Barrel Bag: Round bag with zipper or envelope-style closing and handles that curve around the bag or are attached at the side.

Satchel: Strong, double-handled pouch bag with frame and sturdy flat base.

Tote: Open at the top or with closings for security. Large two-handled carryalls.

Travel Bag: A commodious bag with securely anchored sections that may be pulled from the bag to extract the contents. Some have secret compartments; many have outside pouches. Usually have sturdy handles and shoulder straps.

Wallet Clutches: Flat wallets that may have many compartments and be held in the hand or carried in a pocket. Folding wallets are bulkier.

Care of Handbags

Handbags give better service if they are cared for properly.

- To avoid straining the seams on a bag, the customer should purchase one large enough to hold all the items that are normally carried.
- Be sure pens are closed to avoid ink stains. Cover sharp-pointed objects so they do not pierce the lining.
- Follow the care of leather rules for leather bags. Use neutral-colored creams or waxes for polishing leather bags.
- For washable leathers and synthetics, use a damp cloth with soap. Never immerse in water.

- For nonwashable fabric bags, use cleaning fluid.
- When not in use, store bags in tissue paper. Do not use plastic film since this might damage the surface finish on the bag.
- Promptly repair any tears or cuts to prevent added damage to the bag. Replace loosened handles.

Labeling Handbags and Small Leather Goods

According to the Federal Trade Commission's guidelines for the handbag industry (issued on June 27, 1969), the labeling of handbags and small leather goods must be accurate. Nonleather materials that resemble leather must be clearly labeled so that customers will know that they are not buying leather. Terms such as "scuffproof" and "scratchproof" may not be used unless the finish will neither scuff nor scratch.

LUGGAGE

Many types of luggage are needed so that manufacturers design many styles with varying amounts and sizes of carrying space. Frequently, little or no difference exists between large carryall handbags and small luggage. Luggage is usually classified as hand luggage or trunks.

Materials and Construction of Luggage

Airplane travel has created a need for lightweight materials for luggage. Lightweight carryon luggage is often made from nylon cloth or cotton canvas. Many have no frames and expand as needed. Vinyl and urethane are tough, lightweight plastics used to resemble leather or to coat over fabrics to add surface strength and resistance to abrasion. Sturdy, molded luggage is made from glass fibers bonded with vinyl plastic or from aluminum.

Leather is used for fine-quality luggage. Corduroy (trade name, Cordura) is used for some soft-sided luggage.

Canvas that has been coated with vinyl to resemble leather is popular in less-expensive lug-

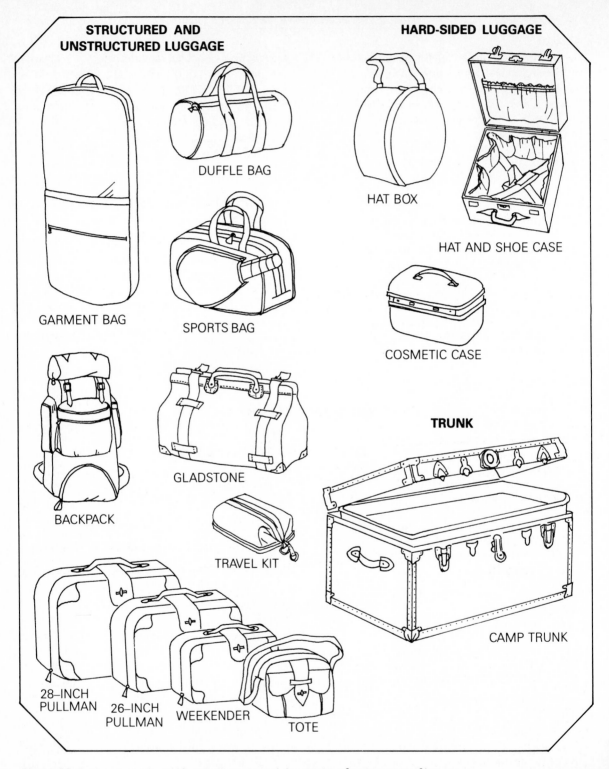

STRUCTURED AND UNSTRUCTURED LUGGAGE

DUFFLE BAG

GARMENT BAG

SPORTS BAG

BACKPACK

GLADSTONE

TRAVEL KIT

28–INCH PULLMAN

26–INCH PULLMAN

WEEKENDER

TOTE

HARD-SIDED LUGGAGE

HAT BOX

HAT AND SHOE CASE

COSMETIC CASE

TRUNK

CAMP TRUNK

Figure 22-4. *New materials and life styles have inspired the creation of various types of luggage.*

gage. The best quality of this type of luggage has a two-ply canvas base. Inexpensively constructed luggage is made of paper-covered cardboard. Leather, plastic, and metal strips are used for the reinforcements of corners and edges of luggage. Some luggage is made of aluminum.

The two most used materials for the base underneath the outside covering of hard-sided luggage are fiberboard and basswood. **Fiberboard** may vary in quality from a specially treated fiberboard with a fine rag content to a common cardboard. **Basswood,** which comes from the linden tree, is lightweight, soft, close grained, and strong. Because it is three ply, there is little danger of the wood's warping or cracking.

The lining materials inside the luggage may be made of sheepskin or other thin leather, nylon, or rayon. Less-expensive cases may have cotton or paper linings.

The **hardware** (clasps, hinges, rings to hold handles, and locks) is another important feature of luggage. Polished brass and stainless steel, which do not rust, make the best hardware. Other luggage has nickel- or brass-plated steel hardware, which may rust if scratched.

Wheels and straps have been built into some heavy-weight luggage.

Types of Luggage

New materials and life styles have inspired the creation of unstructured, semistructured, structured, and hard-sided hand luggage. As the name suggests, **hand luggage** can be carried by a traveler. Trunks, which have a larger capacity than hand luggage, are also available.

Unstructured Luggage.
Unstructured luggage has no frame or stiff sides and is therefore expandable. Nylon, vinyl, sail cloth, and canvas are the most popular materials.

Carryon or Carryall: Has secure buckle or zipper closings. Frequently has over-the-shoulder adjustable straps. Usually about 16 by 11 by 16 inches.
Club: Top-closing bag with handle and shoulder strap. Approximately 20 by $9\frac{1}{2}$ by $9\frac{1}{2}$ inches.
Drawstring Bag: Very expandable bag. Drawstring changes the bag's size as needed.

Duffle Bag: Roll-type bags with zipper closing and double-handled straps.
Garment Bags: Full-length bags with or without separate compartments. They come in various sizes for suits or dresses and either with hangers or with openings for clothes hangers. They may be folded for carrying and opened to hang up. Structured types are also made.
Roll Bag: Small bag that may be carried over the shoulder or as a backpack.
Saddle Bag: Resemble bags used for travel in the Old West.
Satchel: Resembles a doctor's bag with double hand-held handles. May have a detachable shoulder strap. Sides have gussets. Structured types are also made.
Suitcase: Any oblong-shaped bag in which articles are packed at right angles to the way they will be carried. Also available in structured, semistructured, and hard-sided models.
Tote: Top-opening carryall with or without pockets.
Tripler: Bag with sides that open as needed to triple the carrying space.

Structured Luggage.
Structured luggage has a frame and soft sides that permit some expansion.

Backpacks: Carryalls that leave the hands free.
Cosmetic Case: Small, top-lid case with mirror. Has compartments for bottles and jars. May have a tray that holds makeup and serves as a dressing table. Hard-sided models are also available.
Gladstone: Sturdy, top-opening, double-handled carryon. Reinforced with straps and corner pieces.
Pullman and Junior Pullman: Regular pullmans are suitcases approximately 26 by 17 by $7\frac{1}{2}$ inches or 28 by $18\frac{1}{2}$ by 8 inches. Junior pullmans are approximately 24 by $15\frac{1}{2}$ by 7 inches. Larger pullmans often have wheels and pull handles. Also available in unstructured and hard-sided models.
Shoulder Tote: Top-opening small carryon bag with zipper, pockets, handles, and shoulder straps.
Travel or Utility Kit: Small top-opening kit for cosmetics. Approximately 10 by 6 by $3\frac{1}{2}$ inches.
Two Suiter: Suitcase with divider that provides space for two suits, shirts or blouses, and accessories. Approximately 21 by $13\frac{3}{8}$ by $7\frac{1}{2}$ inches. Larger bags hold four suits.
Weekender: Small suitcase with pockets.

Hard-Sided Luggage. Hard-sided luggage is durable and has no give when being packed. It protects the contents well and holds its shape. In addition to types listed above, the following are made as hard-sided luggage.

Garment Carriers: Stiff-sided garment carriers fold for carrying and open to hang up. May have wheels and handle.

Hat Box: Large, round carryon that holds hats.

Hat and Shoe Case: Square or oblong deep case to carry hats and shoes.

Trunks. Traditionally trunks have been large, rigid, rectangular boxes that were too bulky and heavy to carry. However, today there are unstructured, structured, and rigid trunks for traveling.

Box or Camp Trunk: Rectangular-shaped box for traveling and storage. Approximately 40 by 22 by 22½ inches. **Dormitory trunks** are 33 by 18½ by 21 inches, and **footlockers** are 30 by 15½ by 12 inches.

Steamer Trunk: Holds clothes on hangers and in drawers.

Steamer Trunk on Wheels: Vertically or horizontally packed case with soft sides. May be wheeled when upended.

Unstructured Trunk: Large case that expands to hold entire wardrobe. Soft sides are made from durable material. Has straps and handles.

Wardrobe Trunk: Large trunk that holds an entire wardrobe on hangers with drawers for underwear and accessories.

BELTS

Belts are narrow-to-wide bands worn around the body over garments. They may be functional or decorative.

Materials Used in Belts

Any flexible material such as leather, plastic, fabric, rope, or yarn may be used for belts. Metals may be used for chain or link belts. Leather backing material is used in good-quality belts. Plastics are used in less-expensive belts and cardboard with a thin covering of a plastic or fabric is used in inexpensive belts.

Belt buckles may be made from any stiff material. Silver, solid brass, and plastic buckles are used. Steel buckles may be plated with gold or silver or covered with the material used for the belt. Some inexpensive belt buckles are sprayed with enamel paint. Buckles may have a tongue that fits into a hole in the end of the belt to hold the belt securely and to permit adjusting for size.

Construction of Belts

Belt materials are cut to the proper length and width with dies. Better-quality belts are stitched together. Lesser-quality belts are glued together.

Styles of Belts

Belts come in a wide variety of sizes and shapes. They may be as narrow as $\frac{1}{4}$ inch or as wide as 3 or 4 inches. Most belts are straight, but some are shaped or wavy. Belts may be attached by hooks, snaps, buckles, velcro, or by tieing the ends.

Braided: Western-style belts may have leather or plastic thongs plaited to form a textured surface.

Cinch or Clinch Belts: Fit snugly around the waist. May or may not have a tongue in the buckle.

Concha: Wide belt with ornamental Indian-type buckle.

Corselette: Wide belt with front lacing.

Cummerbund: Wide sash that fastens in the back.

D-ring: Ribbon belts held together with two belt buckles in the shape of D's. The ribbons fold over the buckles and may be pulled tight.

Dress: Trim, slim, and neat-looking belt. May or may not be reversible.

Fishscale: Tiny metal circlets resembling fish scales are linked together to expand and contract. A clasp buckle holds the belt on.

Money Belt: Inside fold for holding bills.

Obi: Sash with back tie and wide front.

Rope or String: Various size, specially designed cords with knotted or ornamented ends.

Sash: Belt made from wide ribbon or dress fabric. Usually ties around waist or hips or forms a bow.

Stretch Belts: Made from flexible material, of metal or fabric. Available in a wide variety of widths.

Western: Wide smooth or textured leather or imitation-leather belts.

BELTS

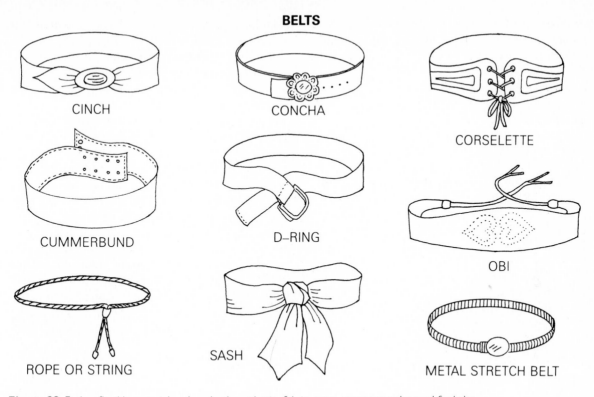

CINCH

CONCHA

CORSELETTE

CUMMERBUND

D–RING

OBI

ROPE OR STRING

SASH

METAL STRETCH BELT

Figure 22-5. *Any flexible material such as leather, plastic, fabric, rope, or yarn may be used for belts.*

Woven Fabric or Fashion Belts: Varicolored and striped woven belts made from canvas, wool, or other material. Has leather front tabs.

Wearing Belts

Men generally wear belts on trousers, slacks, and shorts. Women may or may not wear belts. Some facts about belts follow.

- Belts tend to make the wearer look shorter. Thin belts made of the same material as a dress or suit will do this less than wide belts of a contrasting color or material.
- Blousing material over a belt makes a person appear heavier.
- To elongate the waist, match the belt to the blouse or upper part of the dress.
- To elongate the skirt or pants line, match the belt to the skirt or pants.

- Bows, knots, and hanging ties add girth. Buckles add the least bulk.

UMBRELLAS

Both men's and women's umbrellas are available in a wide range of colors and designs. They are used as protection from rain or sun.

Parts of the Umbrella

Umbrellas are composed primarily of three sections: the canopy, the shank, and the handle.

The **canopy** is that part of the umbrella that spreads and protects the user from rain or sun. The material from which the canopy is made is stretched over metal ribs, which form the frame for the canopy. These ribs arch radially and impart the desired shape to the canopy. The ends of the canopy are stitched to rounded tips that slip over the ends of the ribs and hold the canopy in place. A tape attached to the canopy may be wound around it and fastened or a sheath may be slipped over the umbrella. **Spreaders** or **stretchers** are attached to the center of the ribs to enable the canopy to be opened or closed.

Between the canopy and the handle is a **shaft** (if wood) or **rod** (if metal). Over the shaft is a metal sleeve that slides up and down and enables the spreaders to which it is attached to be opened or collapsed. Two small springs, which can be depressed into the shaft by slight finger pressure, hold the sleeve in position. Some umbrellas have push-button, self-opening spreaders that operate with a hidden spring. A metal cup that fits over the tips of a closed umbrella may be affixed to the shank.

A rigid handle enables the user to hold the umbrella. Straps or cords are frequently attached to umbrellas so that they can hang over the wrist or shoulder.

Special Construction Features

The number of **ribs** in an umbrella differs, depending on the size of the umbrella, its construction, and its shape. The sturdiness of the ribs determines the quality of the umbrella. Self-opening umbrellas have 7 to 8 ribs; folding umbrellas have 8 ribs; umbrellas for young people usually have 8 ribs; slim umbrellas usually have 10 ribs; and other styles may have 16 ribs.

Materials Used for Umbrellas

The canopy is made from fabrics or plastics that are water repellent. Cotton is frequently used; it must be closely woven and may or may not have a plastic finish to increase its protective qualities. **Gloria,** originally a cotton and worsted combination but now a silk or rayon and cotton fabric, is a tightly woven, plain-weave material commonly used in men's black umbrellas. **Drill,** a twill-weave cotton, is often used for beach umbrellas. These materials are often colorfully dyed or printed.

Silk, acetate, rayon, and nylon make rain- and sun-resistant fabrics for umbrellas. Transparent umbrellas may be made from vinyl plastic. Outer sheaths may be made from the same material as the canopy or from leather or plastic.

The fabric in a **parasol,** which is used to provide protection from the sun, does not have to be water repellent and may be organdy or lace.

The ribs and spreaders are usually made of grooved metal. Steel is most commonly used for these parts. Better umbrellas have very sturdy steel ribs and spreaders. Brass plating for inexpensive umbrellas and chromium plating or enameling for more costly umbrellas keep the steel from rusting. Solid brass ribs and spreaders add to the sturdiness of the frame.

The shaft is made from wood; if made from metal, it is called a rod. The tips are made from metal or plastic. Handles are made in a wide range of materials, such as woods, plastics, bone, horn, cane, bamboo, leather, or metal. They may be carved, studded with jewels, engraved, or hand painted. The most common shapes for handles are the **crook** (shaped like a question mark), the **straight,** the **golf,** and the **opera.** Umbrellas may have braided cord, leather, or plastic straps; beads; or chains that permit easy carrying.

Types of Umbrellas

Descriptions of various types of umbrellas follow.

Ballerina or Parasol: Dainty looking with ruffled edge that resembles ballerina's skirt.
Beach: Made from waterproof materials. Has gaily colored stripes or figured patterns. Center pole is usually made of wood or aluminum and is pointed on one end to fit easily into sand or soil. Size varies from 5 to 8 feet in diameter.
Bubble Shape: Deeply domed to cover the head and shoulders. Must be made of transparent material.
Folding: Ribs fold to permit umbrella to be reduced in size for ease in carrying or packing. Men's approximately 16 inches long when folded. Women's approximately 11 inches long when folded.
Golf or Sports: Large, colorful umbrella with 8 ribs. Usually has alternating color panels in the canopy. The ribs are 27 to 35 inches long and the handle is correspondingly longer.
Japanese: Oiled-silk, bamboo-handled umbrella. Decorated with colorful Japanese characters and a wide dark band. Approximately 40 ribs.

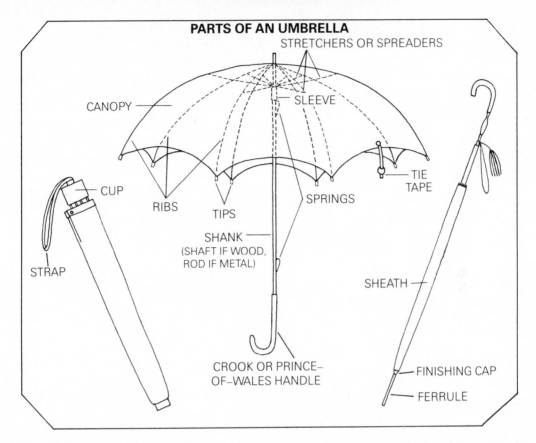

PARTS OF AN UMBRELLA

STRETCHERS OR SPREADERS

CANOPY

SLEEVE

TIE TAPE

CUP

RIBS

TIPS

SPRINGS

SHANK
(SHAFT IF WOOD,
ROD IF METAL)

SHEATH

STRAP

CROOK OR PRINCE-
OF–WALES HANDLE

FINISHING CAP

FERRULE

Figure 22-6. *Opening an umbrella in a cloudburst, few people are aware of the many parts that have been put into play.*

Regular: Men's: Approximately 23 to 24 inches in length, with 8, 10, or 16 ribs. Usually black. **Women's:** Approximately 19 inches in length, with 8 or 10 ribs. Wide variety of colors and fabrics. **Child's:** Approximately 15 inches in length, with 8 ribs. Often made in clear plastic or is colorfully decorated.
Self-Opening: Push button works hidden spring that releases sleeve, pushing ribs into place. When closed, tip ends of ribs are held in place in metal cup.
Windproof: Can be snapped back into shape if blown inside out. Regular or folding style.

Care of Umbrellas

It is desirable to open a wet umbrella after use to allow it to dry thoroughly. This keeps the fabric from spotting and from wrinkling excessively. When dry, the umbrella may be rolled neatly

and fastened shut or encased in a sheath. On a windy day the top of the umbrella should be directed into the wind to avoid its being blown inside out.

WOMEN'S HATS

Since the 1960s hats have reappeared from time to time as fashion accessories, but their main uses have been for protection and sportswear. Hats protect the head from cold and shade the eyes and skin from the hot sun. They may also harmonize with or dramatize the woman's outfit.

Materials Used for Millinery

Virtually any material may be used for millinery and its trimmings. Hats made from felt, straw,

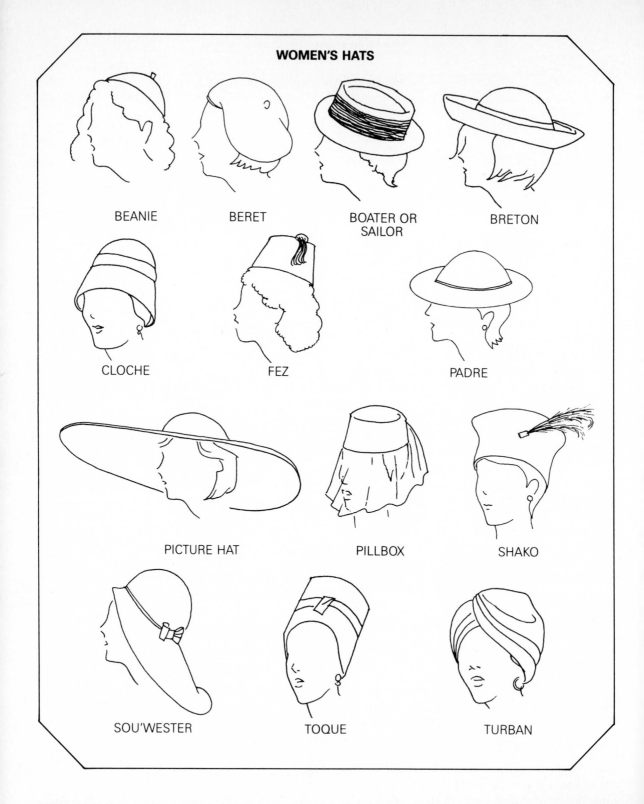

WOMEN'S HATS

BEANIE

BERET

BOATER OR SAILOR

BRETON

CLOCHE

FEZ

PADRE

PICTURE HAT

PILLBOX

SHAKO

SOU'WESTER

TOQUE

TURBAN

Figure 22-7. Hats are often used as fashion accessories, but their main function has been for protection from the sun or the cold.

fur, or sewn fabric are **structured hats.** Hats and caps made from knitted or soft fabrics are **unstructured hats.**

Wool felts are used in inexpensive millinery; **fur felts** (mostly rabbit), which are softer and more luxurious, are used in better millinery. When fur felts have a long, silky nap, they are known as **velour.** A synthetic felt made of dacron polyester fiber is used.

Felt or velour is shaped over huge, perforated cones about 3 feet high. The fibers are compressed repeatedly by steam and pressure until they have been matted to the right size for a hat and brim. Wool felt is heavily sized and may waterspot easily. Fur felts rarely have much sizing and are generally not affected by water. Steaming and brushing a felt hat will usually restore it to its original texture and appearance.

Natural and synthetic straws are used for millinery. **Natural straws** are made from palm leaves, stems, rice shoots, and grasses. Bleaching makes the straw white or cream colored. Some hats, such as the **panama, leghorn,** and **baku,** are woven into rough form. The finer the straws, the more difficult they are to weave and the more costly the finished hat. **Toyo,** made from Japanese rice paper, imitates the panama. Woven straw is **blocked** by placing the straw on a wooden form in the shape of the finished hat. This block is steamed to shape the straw. After drying, the shaped or blocked straw is removed from the form. Stiffening is then added.

Less costly straws are woven or plaited into narrow strips or braids, which are then sewed together into the desired shape. These hats may also be formed over a block.

Synthetic straws in various widths and colors are made from cellophane, rayon, and nylon.

Cotton, rayon, and nylon velvet fabrics are used for soft, drapable or stiffened hats. **Buckram frames** give the form to fabric-shaped or structured hats. Knit hats made from wool, acrylic fibers, cashmere, and mohair or fur hats are available for winter wear. Fur hats must be labeled according to the rules in the Fur Products Labeling Act (see Chapter 20). Furlike hats are made from specially constructed pile fabrics.

Many materials are used for trimmings. **Veilings** are made from fine to coarse nets, which are stiffened with glues and starches. They may be steamed to shape but may become limp if they are soaked in water. Veilings may trim a hat or form the material of the hat. Veilings that extend 9 or more inches from the crown of the hat are subject to the flammability rulings for fabrics. Ribbons, feathers, lace, artificial fruits and flowers, and metal and stone clips and pins are used in a variety of ways as decoration.

Manufacture of Women's Hats

Some designers create millinery for a custom house in which the hats are handmade and only a few are constructed from any one design. Other hats are mass produced from similar materials. Some newly designed hats are copied after a few weeks.

The actual workmanship of hats differ. All parts on better millinery are sewed into position. Less-expensive millinery may have trimmings glued on. Inexpensive hats may use machine stitching for sewed parts, and more costly hats may be completely hand sewn. Linings in expensive hats may be made from luxurious fabrics or costly laces; inexpensive hats may have a thin rayon lining or no lining.

Hat Styles

The following are hat styles with which millinery salespeople should be familiar (See Figure 22-7 for some common styles). Some men's hat styles are also adapted for women.

Beanie: Tiny, head-hugging crown made of felt, fabric, or knit materials.
Beret: A soft-crowned hat with a headband. The crown of the hat may be pulled in different directions.
Bonnet: A hat with or without a protective front brim and ribbon that ties under the chin.
Breton: A stiff hat with a rolled brim.
Cap: Fitted crown that may have a front visor or roll brim or cuff.
Cloche: A bell-shaped hat, usually with a small brim.
Derby: Stiff hat with rounded crown and small rolled brim. Commonly made from felt.

Fedora: Hat with a medium high creased crown and a snap brim that may be worn up or down.

Fez: A tall tapering felt crown with no brim and a long side tassel.

Garden Party: Very wide-brimmed floppy straw or fabric hat. May be trimmed with flowers or ribbons.

Picture: Very large floppy-brimmed hat that frames the face.

Pillbox: A small, round-shaped, stiff hat that sits on the top of the head.

Roll Cap: Unstructured knitted cap with ends rolled up to form a brim.

Sailor: Has a small to large, stiff, straight brim and a low crown with ribbon and bow trim.

Saucer: Has a small brim with low flat crown. Is worn at an angle and may have lace, flower, or ribbon trim.

Ski Cap: Knitted cap with turned-back cuff and large pom-pom on top.

Sun Helmet: Adaptation of African safari helmet.

Toque: A tall, brimless hat made from felt, straw, fur, or soft materials over a frame.

Turban: A brimless hat made from fabric draped gracefully around the head.

Watteau: Shallow-crowned, medium-wide brimmed hat with a band. May or may not be flower ornamented.

There are simple rules for choosing a suitable hat.

- *Oval Face.* Unless the wearer is very small, almost any large brim hat.
- *Round Face.* Hat with a rising crown and asymmetrical brim.
- *Square Face.* Hat with a gently irregular brim and prominent crown, worn at a softly draped angle.
- *Oblong Face.* A full brim shape that rises. Avoid narrow shapes.
- *Triangle Shape.* A shape that has emphasis and sweep at the temple and eyeline.
- *Heart Shape.* Small silhouettes worn high on the head. Avoid large, heavy shapes.

Hat Sizes

Hat sizes for girls aged 3 to 6 years are usually adjustable. Hat sizes for girls aged 6 to 12 years range from $19\frac{1}{2}$ to $21\frac{1}{2}$ inches. Hat sizes for teen-

agers range from 21 to 22 inches. Hat sizes for women are from $21\frac{3}{4}$ to $23\frac{1}{2}$ inches. Many hats, such as pillboxes and knitted caps, fit all head sizes.

In order to measure for hat size, place a tape measure around the head just over the eyebrows. A hat should never fit too snugly.

Care of Hats

Soft, unstructured hats may be folded and kept in drawers or on shelves. Felt, straw, or other shaped hats should be stored in protective boxes. These boxes should be large enough to accommodate the brim and crown without crowding. Stuffing tissue paper in the crown helps to keep the shape.

Felt, velour, velvet, and fur hats should be brushed before being worn. Occasional steaming may help to keep bows, ribbons, and veiling stiff and attractive. When soiled, hats should be cleaned by an expert unless they are unstructured and marked "washable."

MEN'S HATS

Men's and boys' head coverings come in two basic types: caps and hats. Men also wear hoods that are often part of a coat or jacket. Men's hats are made from wool or fur felt and from a wide variety of fine-to-coarse straws. Stitched hats are made from wool tweeds, canvas duck, and terry toweling materials. Caps are made from a wide range of stiff and soft fabrics. Grosgrain ribbons trim many hats, and feathers are used on the crowns of some hats. Felt hats may have brims bound with ribbon or be unbound. (See Figure 22-8.)

Styles of Men's and Boys' Caps

Caps are woven or knitted. They are usually soft and shape easily to the head. Some caps have stiffening materials to keep them in a particular shape. Most caps have visors to shade the eyes.

Beret: Soft, no-visor cap that is pulled to one side. A Scottish tam o'shanter is one type of beret.

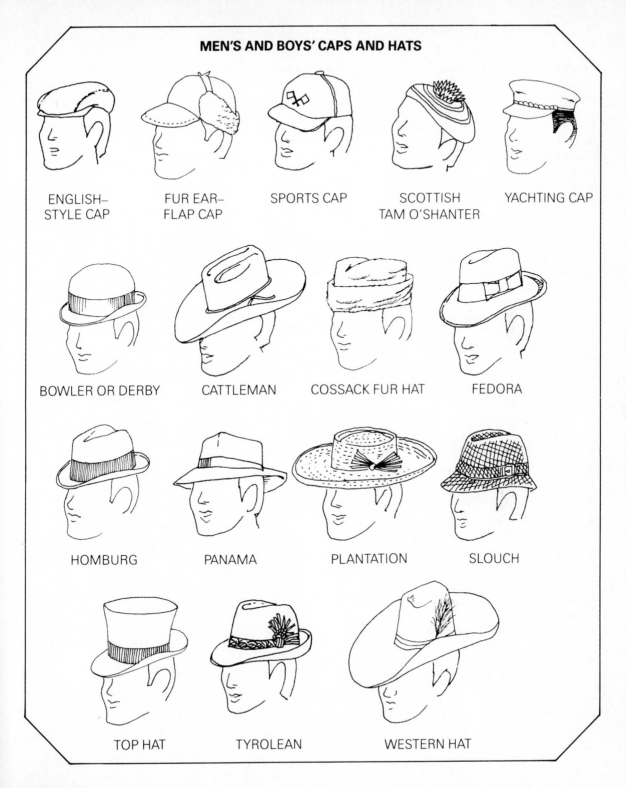

MEN'S AND BOYS' CAPS AND HATS

ENGLISH–STYLE CAP

FUR EAR–FLAP CAP

SPORTS CAP

SCOTTISH TAM O'SHANTER

YACHTING CAP

BOWLER OR DERBY

CATTLEMAN

COSSACK FUR HAT

FEDORA

HOMBURG

PANAMA

PLANTATION

SLOUCH

TOP HAT

TYROLEAN

WESTERN HAT

Figure 22-8. *Men's caps (top row) are usually softer and more closely fitted than men's hats, which have more shape, a higher crown, and a brim that encircles the crown.*

Chauffeur Cap: Twill-weave, firm fabric cap with raised front and stiff shiny visor.

Ear-Flap or Cold-Proof or Tie-Top Caps: These caps have ear flaps that can tie on top of the crown. The tie serves as a chin strap to hold the ear flaps in place when worn.

English Style Cap: Crown of cap slides forward and covers the visor. It may be made from corduroy, suede, or any stiffened material.

Knit Caps: Cold-weather caps that hug the head snugly and have deep cuffs for added warmth.

Sports Caps: Lightweight caps with high front crowns that often have insignia indicating a sport or organization. The crown may be made from a mesh with an open back and have adjustable back strap. A stiff visor protects the eyes from the sun.

Swiss Wool Helmet: Skiing or cold-weather cap that frames the face and covers the neck.

Work Cap: Sturdy material is shaped into a high-front crown and self-covered visor or bill. Usually has adjustable back strap.

Yachting Cap: Water-repellent, high-crown cap with slanted top and black shiny visor. Cap may have elaborate gold braid and ornamentation.

Styles of Men's and Boys' Hats

Hats differ from caps in that they have more shape, a higher crown, and a brim that encircles the crown. Some hats, however, are very soft and almost shapeless, and a few have the brim turned up to encircle the head. Most hats have wide or narrow stiff ribbon bands, folded fabric bands, cords, or straps that encircle the crown.

Boater, Sailor, or Skimmer: Stiff, straw hat with moderate-wide brim, straight short crown, and flat top. Has wide grosgrain band with a flat bow on the side.

Cattleman: Large western-style hat with deep center, side creases, and moderately turned-up brim.

Cossack: A fur or pile fabric hat with slanted crown, deep center crease, and wide turned-back cuff. Often made in Persian lamb, beaver, or mouton-processed lamb.

Cottage Hat: Leisure wear, crushable, water-repellent, wool tweed hat with soft crown and brim. Has self-band of tweed material.

Cowboy or Western Hat: Has a tall, center-crease

crown, fancy band with feathers or other trim, and wide brim turned up on the sides.

Derby or Bowler: A stiff felt hat with a round bowl-shaped crown and upturned small rolled brim.

Fedora: Soft felt hat with lengthwise crease on the top and (optional) front pinch of the crown. Also called a snap brim.

High Hat or Top Hat: Fur felt hat with shiny, high, stiff crown and stiffly curved side brim. Trimmed in grosgrain ribbon.

Homburg: Has a center crease in the crown with a stiffened brim turned up at the sides. The crown is trimmed with grosgrain ribbon.

Panama: Fine-quality white straw hat made from a smooth, hand-plaited straw from the choicest leaves of the jipijapa plant. The hand-blocked crown is high with a center raised crease. The small brim turns down in front. Trimmed with black grosgrain ribbon.

Pith Helmet: Lightweight hat with a stiff bowllike crown and a stiff medium-wide, turned-down brim.

Plantation Hat: Fabric or straw hat with telescope-type crown to protect the wearer from the sun.

Safari Hat: Resembles a casual-looking fedora with turned-down brim.

Slouch: Usually water repellent. The top has a center crease and may have a pinch front; the brim is usually turned down all around.

Ten-Gallon Hat: Very high-crowned and large-brimmed cowboy-style hat.

Telescope-Crown: In place of a center crease in the top of the crown, a dent is made around the circumference of the crown. The snap brim is usually worn up in the back and down in the front.

Trooper: A fabric or fur hat for cold-weather wear. Visor or bill and ear flaps are made from fur. The ear flaps are tied with a ribbon across the center top of the crown. They may be released to cover the ears. The tie is used to snap or be tied under the chin.

Tyrolean: Has a deep center crease that is spread toward the back of the crown. A braid or ornamental band usually has a colorful feather stuck in its side. The front has a snap brim that is usually worn turned down.

Sizes in Men's and Boys' Caps and Hats

Boys' cap sizes are usually given as small, medium, and large. Men's cap sizes may be similarly labeled, or they may state the size as $6\frac{7}{8}$, 7,

$7\frac{1}{8}$, $7\frac{1}{4}$, $7\frac{3}{8}$, or $7\frac{1}{2}$. To measure for size, place a tape measure around the largest part of the head above the ears. Sizes are interpreted as follows.

Table 23-1 HAT AND CAP SIZES

Boys

Head		Hat Size
$21\frac{1}{2}$ inches	S	$6\frac{7}{8}$
$21\frac{7}{8}$ inches	M	7
$22\frac{1}{4}$ inches		$7\frac{1}{8}$
$22\frac{5}{8}$ inches	L	$7\frac{1}{4}$

Men

Head (In.)	Hat Size	Head (In.)	Hat Size
$21\frac{1}{2}$	$6\frac{7}{8}$	$22\frac{5}{8}$	$7\frac{1}{4}$
$21\frac{7}{8}$	7	23	$7\frac{3}{8}$
$22\frac{1}{4}$	$7\frac{1}{8}$	$23\frac{1}{2}$	$7\frac{1}{2}$

DO YOU KNOW YOUR MERCHANDISE?

1. Explain the meaning of the following glove terms: trank, fourchette, quirk, taxing, and trank cutting.
2. Describe the following types of glove seams: inseam, overseam, piqué seam, and half-piqué.
3. Explain how to care for leather gloves that are washable and how to care for those that are not washable.
4. Name and describe five important parts of a handbag.
5. Define the following terms: envelope bag, pouch bag, box bag, and satchel.
6. What are the Federal Trade Commission's rulings about labels on handbags and small leather goods?
7. Explain the difference between hand luggage and trunks and between structured and unstructured luggage.
8. Why is polished brass or stainless steel preferable to plated steel for locks and catches on luggage?
9. What are the particular advantages of the following types of umbrellas: folding, self-opening, and windproof?
10. Name three brimless hats for women and explain the differences. Name three brimmed hats for women and explain the differences.

PUTTING YOUR MERCHANDISE KNOWLEDGE TO WORK

Select as a topic gloves, handbags, belts, small leather goods, luggage, umbrellas, women's hats, men's hats, or children's hats. Collect pictures of the merchandise. Give a 2-minute sales talk to your class using your pictures as illustrations of the various selling points.

PROJECT

Visit a store that specializes in one of the items of merchandise discussed in this chapter. What items were displayed in the window? What items were featured inside the store? What price lines did you notice within the store for these articles? What technical terms were used in displaying these goods? Define the technical terms that were used. If you were selling these items, what positive statements could you make to customers?

23

Jewelry and Watches:
The Valuable Accessories

Jewelry ranges in price from inexpensive to very costly. Usually costly jewelry is called **fine jewelry** and is expected to last for many years and, in some instances, to become an heirloom. Modestly priced jewelry, called **costume jewelry** or **fashion jewelry** is bought to match a particular outfit or to serve a specific need. Fine jewelry is made from materials that have intrinsic value. Costume jewelry usually has little intrinsic value but serves for a period of years as attractive or useful ornaments.

METALS USED IN JEWELRY

The precious metals (gold, platinum, palladium, ruthenium, iridium, rhodium, and silver), the base metals, and alloys are used in jewelry (see Chapter 15). Because of the increasing scarcity of the precious metals, they are often used with a coating or plating process or are combined with base metals. Stainless steel for watchcases and watch bands and nongold-containing alloys for class rings have been particularly popular. Metals are used alone to form all-metal jewelry items, such as chains, bracelets, rings, and watch bands, or in combination with stones or other materials.

STONES USED IN JEWELRY

Once only natural stones and paste or glass imitations were used in jewelry. Today, as demand grows and supplies of natural stones diminish, increasing numbers of **test-tube stones** have appeared on the market. Some of these are almost indistinguishable from their natural counterparts. The following is a discussion of stones according to the ways in which they are classified.

Natural Stones

Stones that are mined from the earth or obtained from the sea are known as **natural stones.** Because of their scarcity, beauty, and durability, jewelers use the term *precious* to refer to diamonds, emeralds, rubies, sapphires, and natural pearls. Other stones found in nature that are beautiful and durable are called **semiprecious** and include alexandrite, aquamarine, garnet, jade, opal, peridot, tanzanite, topaz, tourmaline, turquoise, quartz, and zircon. **Gemologists** have disliked the terms "precious" and "semiprecious" for natural stones. They argue that as stones become rarer, any natural mineral that is usable for jewelry because of its exceptional clarity, depth of color, natural attractiveness, and lasting quality should be considered precious.

Identification of Natural Stones

Natural stones may be identified in several ways as discussed below.

Shape. When stones are found in their natural state, they usually have a definite shape or form by which they may be recognized. **Crystalline stones** have angular forms. Most mined

Figure 23-1. *Diamond in its natural state (right) and after preliminary cutting (left). Final cutting will bring out the brilliance of the gem.*

stones are crystalline in form. **Amorphous stones** have no definite shape. Stones such as turquoise and opal are amorphous stones.

Hardness.   The resistance to being scratched is known as the **hardness** of the stone. The diamond is the hardest natural substance. Table 23-1 arranges natural stones from the hardest to the softest. Friedrich Mohs, a German mineralogist, developed this scale in 1822. Any stone on one line will scratch other stones on the same line and all the stones listed below it. Those with hardness of 8 or above will retain their surface attractiveness indefinitely. Those from 7.5 down need to be treated with some care.

Specific Gravity.   **Specific gravity** means the weight of a stone as compared to the weight of an equal volume of water. A stone having a specific gravity of three, for example, would be three times as heavy as water. When unmounted, you can identify stones by dropping them into liquids of known density. The specific gravity of a stone also affects its size. The more dense a stone is, the smaller it will be for a given weight.

Refractive Index.   Light entering a stone is slowed and bent away from its normal course (refraction) as it passes through the stone. Each gem mineral has its own angle of light bending, known as its **refractive index**. The degree of bending of the light can be measured to deter-

mine what the stone is. The higher the refractive index, the more light the stone will gather and reflect and the greater the sparkle of the stone. The opal has a low refractive index (1.45), whereas the diamond has a high refractive index (2.42).

Color.   Many stones are available in more than one color and similarly colored stones are not necessarily the same kind of stone.

Color in stones is caused by many factors. Tiny bits of chemical in a stone may give it a particular color. Moisture trapped in tiny cracks in the stone itself may also give it color. Stones may reflect color from other, more deeply colored stones over which they are glued or from glass pasted to them. A **doublet** is made by pasting a pale stone over a deeper-colored one; a **triplet** has a top and bottom layer of genuine stone with a layer of colored glass between them (Figure 23–2).

Color may be changed by artificially staining, bleaching, heating, or irradiating a stone. Detection of such color-added methods is often difficult.

Table 23-1 ADAPTATION OF MOHS SCALE OF HARDNESS	
10	Diamond
9	Corundum (ruby and sapphire)
8.5	Chrysoberyl (alexandrite and oriental cat's eye)
8	Topaz and spinel and beryl (emerald and aquamarine)
7.5	Garnet and zircon
7-7.5	Tourmaline
7	Quartz (amethyst, citrine, rock crystal, agate)
6-7.5	Jade (jadeite and nephrite)
6-6.5	Feldspar (moonstone), marcasite, peridot, tanzanite
5.5-6.5	Opal
5	Lapis lazuli
3.5-4	Coral
2.5-3.5	Pearl, jet, malachite
2-3	Amber
1	Talc

Figure 23-2. *Creating a doublet (left) or triplet (right) may enhance a stone's size or color.*

Synthetic Stones and Chemically Made Simulated Stones

Two categories of chemically made stones are sold in jewelry stores and departments. The stones that most closely resemble natural stones are known as **synthetics**. They are made from the identical chemical materials and have the same hardness, refractive index, and specific gravity as the natural stones. Usually only experts can distinguish these stones from the natural ones. Here is a list of the stones that have been made synthetically.

- 1902   Ruby
- 1904   Sapphire
- 1904   Spinel
- 1910   Quartz
- 1937   Emeralds
- 1954   Diamonds
- 1972   Opals and turquoise
- 1979   Ivory

A second category of chemically made stones are those stones that look like natural stones but whose chemical composition, refractive index, hardness, and specific gravity are different. These stones are sometimes erroneously called synthetics. They are listed below with their commonly used trade names in parentheses.

- 1948   Synthetic rutile (Titania); resembles diamonds
- 1955   Strontium titanate (Fabulite, Wellington Gem); diamondlike
- 1960   Yttrium-aluminum-garnet — YAG (Diamonaire); diamondlike
- 1975   Gadolinium-gallium-garnet — GGG (Diamonique II); diamondlike
- 1976   Cubic zirconia (Diamonair II, Diamonesque, Phyanite); diamondlike

The chemically constructed diamond imitations are not as hard as the diamond, but several have a higher refractive index giving them considerable sparkle. Their cost depends upon their quality.

Imitation Stones

Look-alike stones that have none of the properties of the real stones are made from ceramics, glass, and plastic. Glass can be used to imitate transparent stones. **Rhinestones** (cut glass often backed with metallic foil), for example, look like diamonds. Ceramic substances are used to imitate turquoise, lapis lazuli, and coral. Plastic substances can imitate any stones but are especially successful to make look alikes of amber, ivory, and opal.

Jewelry Stones Commonly Sold in the United States

Even though some stones may have identical characteristics in hardness and chemical composition, they may look quite different. Because such stones are made of the same substance, however, they are classified into the same grouping or family of stones. Some familiar groupings are discussed below.

Beryl: Aquamarine and Emerald. The green emerald, a precious, extremely valuable, and beautiful stone, and the pale blue-green, semiprecious aquamarine differ chemically only in the substance that gives the color to the emerald. The emerald is deep green and transparent unless badly flawed, when it is translucent. Emeralds are brittle and thus are difficult to cut and set. The synthetic emerald has a good color and is less brittle than the genuine emerald. The transparent aquamarine is the color of the seawater from which it derives its name. The deeper the color of the stone, the greater its value.

Corundum: Ruby and Sapphire. The red ruby and the blue sapphire differ from each other only in color. The red color is much rarer than the blue, making the ruby more valuable than the sapphire. The transparent sapphire comes in many different colors; the cornflower blue is rarest and most valuable. Sapphires may also be colorless, yellow, green, purple, or pink. The synthetic, colorless sapphire has been sold under the trade name Diamondite. Star rubies and star sapphires are opaque and, when deeply colored, are rare and costly. Synthetic star rubies and sapphires have also been made.

Diamond. The value of diamonds is determined by their size, color, and perfection and the quality of cutting. Diamonds advertised as **perfect** or **flawless** are stones that when magnified ten times their size show no flaws (to a trained diamond expert). The best color for a traditional stone is fine white, which shows no trace of other color in it. Occasionally diamonds are yellow, pink, red-orange, green, blue, or black. Fine-quality colored diamonds are far rarer and thus more costly than colorless stones.

Synthetic diamonds were developed in 1954. In 1970 larger ones of gem quality became available. Most synthetic diamonds are used for industrial purposes. Chemically created diamond imitations are attractive, have a great deal of sparkle, and sell for a fraction of the price of comparable size natural diamonds.

Jade: Jadeite and Nephrite. The fine-quality jadeite is translucent to opaque and varies in color from pale to rich green. Some pink, violet, and pale blue jades have also been found. Nephrite, a less expensive variety, is found in colors ranging from white to gray-green to dark green and even black.

Opal. The opal often has an intriguing play of colors caused by tiny invisible cracks within the stone that are filled with moisture. Opals may be any color of the rainbow. The darker, more fiery opals are the most valuable.

Peridot. Peridot is the jewelry stone created from the mineral **olivine**. Lava rocks are sources of this mineral also. The color of the stone ranges from light yellow-green to a brownish gray.

Quartz. Quartz comes in almost every color as well as in combinations of colors. It ranges from transparent to opaque. Its varieties include **agate**, which varies from milky white to red- or yellow-brown; **onyx**, which is black alternated with bands of white; **amethyst**, which is lilac to purple; **citrine**, which is yellow to brown in a transparent variety; and **rock crystal**, which is a colorless, glasslike stone. Quartz crystals are used in watches that need no mechanically wound parts but rely on the vibrations from the quartz itself.

Tanzanite. Tanzanite, which comes from the mineral **zoisite** was named by Tiffany and Company. It is relatively soft and cleaves easily. It is a rich blue in color and is transparent.

Topaz. Topaz, usually called *precious* topaz to differentiate it from less costly yellow to brown quartz, is hard, quite rare, and beautiful. It may be yellow, brown, colorless, pale blue (like aquamarine), green, pink, and red. The yellow colors are the most common.

Other Important Stones. Some of the more commonly used stones that derive from mineral sources are described below.

Alexandrite: A mineral form that in daylight appears to be green, but changes to red-violet under artificial light. It was named for Czar Alexander II of Russia.

Chrysoberyl: A category of stones including alexandrite and oriental cat's eye.

Cinnabar: An ore of mercury creates this inexpensive opaque red stone, which is elaborately carved by the Chinese.

Jet: Black stone made from a very hard type of coal that takes a high polish.

Lapis Lazuli: Opaque, royal blue colored stone that may have streaks of yellow or gray in less expensive types. Cabochon cut or carved.

Marcasite: Iron pyrite ore, a pale brass-yellow colored mineral, once known as *"fool's gold."*

Oriental Cat's Eye: A greenish-yellow chrysoberyl with a band of light running vertically along the stone's surface. It is of a better quality than its look-alike, the quartz cat's eye.

Spinel: A transparent stone that varies in color from ruby red to purple, sapphire blue, and orange. This stone is often mistaken in its red variety for the more costly ruby. **Synthetic spinel** resembles diamonds, amethysts, and other stones.

Tourmaline: A translucent to opaque stone that may shade in color from red at one end of the crystal to green at the other end.

Turquoise: An opaque sky-blue to apple-green stone that has a waxy luster and a soft surface that scratches rather easily. The stone is often found with ordinary rock imbedded in it, known as **matrix.** When cabochon cut, this rock may be included with the turquoise.

Zircon: Frequently used to imitate the colorless diamond, the zircon is a transparent stone that ranges from colorless to pale yellow, blue, and reddish brown. It has a bright sparkle but scratches rather easily.

Figure 23-3. *Cultured pearls become rarer and more costly as they increase in size and roundness.*

Amber. A fossil resin that was secreted from the trunks of trees buried in the earth and covered with water long ago. Amber is a transparent, translucent, or opaque substance that varies in color from honey yellow to white or brown. It is a very lightweight stone.

Coral. This stone is created by a tiny jellylike organism known as the **coral polyp,** which deposits the coral in the ocean in formations resembling the branches of a tree. Coral may be red, white, or yellow in color. The oxblood red is considered the most valuable. Coral is often carved.

Pearls. The three categories of pearls are natural, cultured, and imitation. **Natural pearls** are the product of the oyster. The oyster's shell is lined with a **nacreous solution** composed of carbonate of lime, commonly called **mother-of-pearl.** The pearl is started by a tiny irritant (such as sand) that causes the oyster to coat it with this nacreous solution in order to alleviate the irritation. If the pearl is formed next to the oyster's body, it may be round in shape, which is the most valuable type of pearl. **Baroque pearls,** which are formed against the shell, have an uneven oblong shape. Depending on the chemicals in the sea, pearls may have a rosy sheen, or they may be white, yellow, pink, red, blue, brown, green, or black. **Saltwater pearls** are also known as **oriental pearls.** They come from the Persian Gulf, and waters around Australia, Japan, Panama, and Pacific Ocean islands. **Freshwater pearls,** obtained from mussels in rivers, have a dull finish and a chalk-white color. Freshwater pearls with less luster and a wrinkled surface come from China. Black pearls come from Tahiti.

Pearls need no cutting, but they may have a hole drilled in them for use in necklaces or earrings. The matching of pearls is a tedious job that increases the cost of the pearls considerably.

Cultured pearls are made by inserting an irritant in the oyster. The oyster is then placed in a cage and is lowered into the water, where it can coat the irritant with the nacreous substance.

The longer the oyster is allowed to coat this irritant, the more valuable and attractive the pearl. When the irritant used is large and the layer of coating thin, the pearl is less attractive and brings a lower price. Only by x ray can the real pearl be differentiated from the cultured pearl.

Today few natural pearls are available, but cultured pearls are very nearly like the natural. The larger and rounder the cultured pearls, the rarer and more costly they are.

Familiar terms associated with pearls are as follows.

Keshi: Tiny, irregularly shaped natural pearls that are sometimes found in cultivated oysters along with cultured pearls.
Biwa: Smooth, irregularly shaped cultured pearls. Many come in an elongated rice-grain shape.
Chinese: Less smooth and more irregular in shape.
Akoya: Cultured saltwater pearls in sizes from 2 to 10 millimeters. The symmetrical round pearls bring the highest price.
Mobé (also spelled Mabé): Hemispherical and slightly irregular. They grow on the side of the shell instead of next to the mollusk's body.[1]
Imitation or Simulated Pearls: Manmade. Either an opaque white glass or a cellulose acetate plastic base is covered with a solution called **pearl essence,** which is made of the lustrous material from the scales of fish mixed with a plastic material to make it adhesive. Imitation pearls vary in appearance and price depending on the number of coatings of pearl essence.

MANUFACTURE OF JEWELRY

Metal in jewelry must be shaped, stones need to be cut and mounted in settings, finishing processes need to be applied, and the jewelry needs to be polished and readied for the customer.

Shaping the Metal

Jewelry made from metal may be cut from a thin sheet of the desired metal and then pounded into shape by hand. Mass-produced jewelry may be made by **embossing.** For this, the metal may be shaped by hundreds of pounds of pressure from a die that may also imprint a design onto the surface. Less durable jewelry may be **cast** by melting the metal and then pouring it or forcing it by a centrifugal system into a smooth or textured mold. After shaping, sections of metal are hand joined with metal solder.

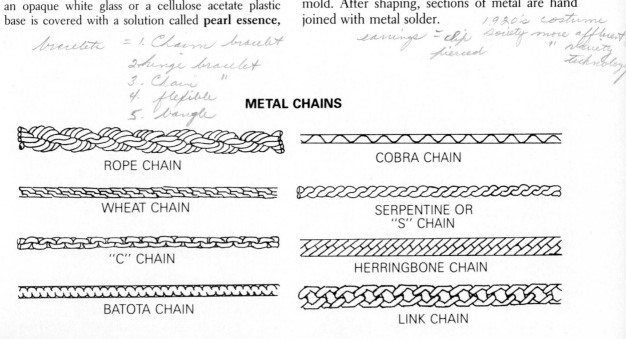

METAL CHAINS

ROPE CHAIN

WHEAT CHAIN

"C" CHAIN

BATOTA CHAIN

COBRA CHAIN

SERPENTINE OR "S" CHAIN

HERRINGBONE CHAIN

LINK CHAIN

Figure 23-4. *Chains are made by machines that cut, shape, and join the sections.*

SETTINGS

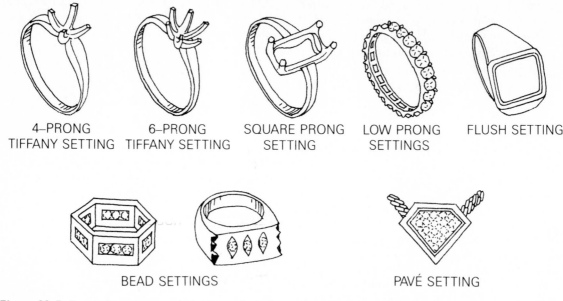

4–PRONG TIFFANY SETTING   6–PRONG TIFFANY SETTING   SQUARE PRONG SETTING   LOW PRONG SETTINGS   FLUSH SETTING

BEAD SETTINGS   PAVÉ SETTING

Figure 23-5. *Fine-quality stones must be held securely in place with a precious-metal setting.*

Finishing Metal Jewelry

When a design or initial is scratched into metal by hand or by the use of special machinery, the process is known as **engraving**. A **Florentine finish** is made by engraving the surface with a series of fine scratches. **Engine turning** involves the use of a machine to engrave geometric designs. **Chasing** is done by tapping designs into the surface of the metal item. Inexpensive jewelry may have colored enamel painted onto the surface. Better-quality jewelry has enamel baked on for permanency. **Etching** involves making designs on silver, copper, and brass articles by means of acid that eats away the metal in certain places to produce the design. Gold and silver may be **antiqued** by using chemicals that darken the surface of the metal.

Settings for Stones

Precious-metal settings must be carefully prepared to hold fine-quality stones securely and safely. For inexpensive stones less care is taken in making the settings. Some settings have long projections called **prongs** that press against the stone to hold it in place. High prong settings are known as **Tiffany settings**. **Square settings** have right-angled corner prongs that hold the stone. To hold **melees** (small diamonds) in either platinum or gold alloys, **bead settings** are made from tiny rolls of metal that are raised up from the ring metal and pressed firmly against the stone. **Pavé settings** are bead settings with a mass of stones close together. **Flush settings** hide part of the stone with a band of metal that encircles it. These settings are quite secure. Imitation stones may be held in **paste settings,** in which the stone is glued into a depression in the metal. Stones often fall out of such settings.

Shaping and Decorating Stones

A dull-looking natural or chemically created stone may be made into a sparkling gem by cutting and polishing the stone. This is done by the **lapidary** (stonecutter) who studies the shape of

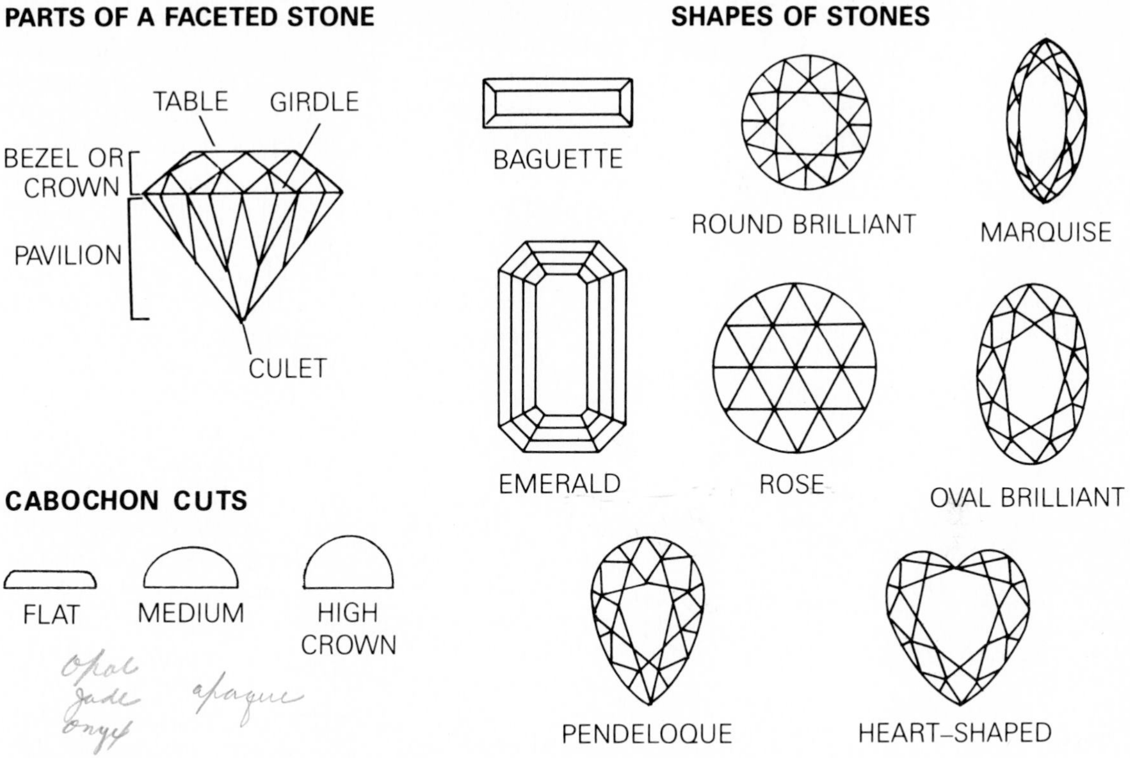

PARTS OF A FACETED STONE

TABLE   GIRDLE

BEZEL OR
CROWN

PAVILION

CULET

CABOCHON CUTS

FLAT   MEDIUM   HIGH
CROWN

Opal
Jade   *opaque*
Onyx

SHAPES OF STONES

BAGUETTE

ROUND BRILLIANT

MARQUISE

EMERALD

ROSE

OVAL BRILLIANT

PENDELOQUE

HEART–SHAPED

Figure 23-6. *Like mirrors, facets reflect light in a transparent stone, causing it to sparkle.*

the natural stone to determine how to get the largest finished stone possible with the fewest flaws.

Transparent (glasslike) stones are usually **faceted** — cut into little planes or angles, known as **facets,** that reflect like a mirror the other facets on the stone, thus causing the stone to sparkle when hit by light. Faceting is costly because it is difficult to do and wastes 40 to 50 percent of the stone that is cut. Familiar types of faceting are the **brilliant** or **full cut,** with 58 facets; the **emerald** or **step cut,** with 49 facets; and the **single cut,** with 18 facets.

Translucent and opaque stones are **cabochon cut,** which resembles a half-moon. Some cabochon-cut stones are very flat; others have a high curve. Moonstone, turquoise, star rubies, and star sapphires are stones cut in this manner.

Some stones are carved with decorative designs. **Cameos** are raised designs cut against a background that is usually darker in color. An **intaglio** is a depressed design in the stone material, which is used on some men's jewelry.

Weight and Size of Stones

The weight and size of a stone are usually measured by **carats.** This term comes from the name

Figure 23-7. *Diamonds of several different carats. The largest is the most valuable.*

WOMEN'S JEWELRY

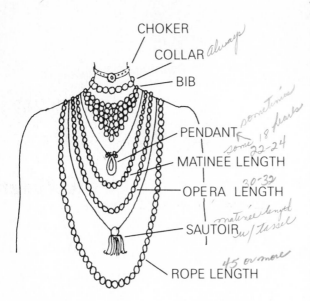

CHOKER
COLLAR *always*
BIB

PENDANT *sometimes 18 pearls*
some 22-24
MATINEE LENGTH
30-32
OPERA LENGTH
matinee length w/ tassel
SAUTOIR
45 or more
ROPE LENGTH

Figure 23-8. *Necklaces may be made of metal chains or beads of any material.*

of the tiny seeds that used to be placed on a scale to weigh the stones. The carat today is 4 grains in **avoirdupois weight** (the scale used for most consumer goods) and 3.165 grains **troy weight** (the metric scale used by jewelers and druggists). The value of a natural stone of a certain quality increases with the size. Thus, the value of a 1-carat stone is much more than twice that of the same quality ½-carat stone.

Pearls and some semiprecious stones are measured rather than weighed. The measurement is stated in **millimeters.**

TYPES OF JEWELRY

For Women

Necklaces are worn around the neck and may be made of metal chains or beads of any mate-

rial. Necklace beads may be uniform in size or graduated from large in the center front to small at the nape of the neck. When a flat necklace fits the neck atop the collarbone it is called a **collar.** A **choker** is a single-strand or multistrand necklace that fits the neck snugly. Two-to-twelve-strand necklaces that hug the base of the neck are called **bibs.** An ornament that hangs from a chain or cord is a **pendant.** A **locket** is a small case held by a chain, cord, or ribbon that holds pictures or other mementos. Longer necklaces come in lengths known as **matinee** (22 to 24 inches) and **opera** (30 to 32 inches). A **sautoir** is a matinee-length necklace with a tassel of metal links or beads. **Ropes** are 45 or more inches long.

Bracelets are decorative ornaments that encircle the arm. Round hoops of varied widths that slip over the hand are **bangle bracelets. Chain, link,** or **flexible bracelets** are made of metal links, wood, stones, glass, or plastic and metal. **Charm bracelets** have tiny curios of metal or stone that dangle from a metal chain. **Hinge bracelets** resemble bangle bracelets but have a center hinge and clasp closing to aid in putting on and removing them.

The **brooch,** which is an ornamental safety pin, may be any size or shape. An elongated brooch used to decorate suit lapels is a **lapel pin. Clips** are ornaments that clasp onto the part of the garment they are to decorate by means of a hinge and spring attachment. They may be worn singly or in pairs. **Stick pins** are long, narrow pins with ornaments on the top and a catch at the bottom.

Earrings may have screw backs or clips that grip the earlobe or may be fitted with posts and small screw heads or ear wires for people with pierced ears. Magnets have been used by some designers to hold the earring to the ear. **Button earrings** are usually round and fit against the earlobe. **Drop earrings** have a pendant or hoop that dangles. **Chandelier earrings** are extra-long drop earrings.

Rings made in fancy shapes and fitted with stones are **cocktail rings. Cluster rings** have stones set in groups. **Dinner rings** are long, narrow rings worn on the little finger. Rings containing initials or a crest are **signet rings.** **Solitaires,** often used for diamond engagement rings, are rings that contain a single stone.

Hair ornaments may be decorative or functional. **Barrettes** are clamplike devices that hold the hair in place. **Headbands** are usually worn across the forehead. **Tiaras** or **diadems** are worn like small crowns. **Pony tail rings** are circle-shaped barrettes to hold long hair at the back of the head. **Hair sticks** attach to the hair and hold ornamental flowers, stones, or animal motifs.

For Men

Men's jewelry may be both functional and ornamental. To hold ties in place, men use tie bars, tie holders, tiepins, or tie tacks. Watchbands hold wristwatches in place; fobs or fob chains are used to connect pocket watches to a garment. Key chains and key rings keep keys handy. Collar pins, cufflinks, and studs are worn with shirts.

For ornaments, men wear pins on lapels, identification or other bracelets, gold necklaces in choker and longer lengths, bead or pendant necklaces, rings, and even earrings.

For Boys and Girls

Any jewelry made for men and women may be made in appropriate sizes for boys and girls. Special **add-on-necklaces** for girls may be made with pearls, birthstones, or gold beads. To commemorate various occasions, additional beads are added until the necklace is complete.

WATCHES

During the 1970s and 1980s dramatic changes in the watch industry occurred. Additional changes are anticipated for the future. Today watches come in a variety of types, styles, and price ranges. The type of watch and the watchcase determine the price of the watch.

Types of Watches

Watches are classified into four basic types discussed below.

Mechanical Watches. Mechanical watches have been made for over 500 years. They have a familiar ticktock sound as the mechanism rotates back and forth with the unwinding of the mainspring that powers the movement. The **analog dial** has numbers or stick figures and an hour and a minute hand that move to tell the time.

Two types of mechanical watches are available. **Pin lever** watches make a loud ticking noise because metal revolves against metal causing wear and resulting in inaccuracy of timekeeping after about a year. Novelty children's watches, inexpensive pocket watches, and some sport watches are made in this manner. **Jeweled lever** are precision-made watches with each part machined to exacting measurements, assuring many years of accurate timekeeping. Moving parts revolve in **jeweled bearings** that resist friction and wear, make less noise, and assure more accurate timekeeping. Less-expensive jeweled watches may have 7 jewels or reinforcements, whereas better watches have 14, 15, 17, or 21 jewels. Special watches with calendars, timers, or other devices may have 23 or more jewels. Originally, natural rubies or sapphires were used for jeweled bearings; today synthetic jewels are used.

Watches may be hand wound, self-winding, or battery powered. When a watch is wound by hand, a coiled mainspring is tightened; as the mainspring unwinds it powers the wheels in the movement. A watch is self-wound by a weight that moves back and forth with the movement of the wearer's arm; the movement of the weight causes the mainspring to be wound. The wheels in electric watches are powered by tiny, wafer-shaped batteries.

Electronic Watches. In the 1950s a watch was developed in which the regulating mechanism is a tuning fork. This device, powered by a battery through electromagnets, transmits power to the gears that drive the watch. Tuning-fork

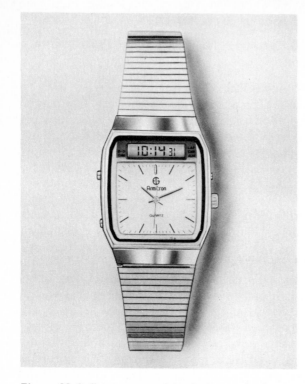

Figure 23-9. *This quartz watch has both an analog face and a digital face that can be switched to a chronograph or a date display.*

watches hum rather than tick, are more exact timekeepers than jeweled-lever watches, and have fewer moving parts to wear out.

Digital Watches. A revolution in watchmaking occurred in the early 1970s when electronics firms used their **solid state** (no moving parts) components to make watches with no sound and no minute or hour hands. These **digital watches** produce the digits on the face to tell the hours and minutes. Two types of displays are available. **Light-emitting diodes** (LED) show the time when a button is pushed. Too constant use, however, depletes the energy from the small battery. **Liquid crystal display** (LCD) seals a special liquid between two slender glass plates. This liquid displays time continuously since very little battery power is needed to make the liquid

reflect light. These numerals, however, are sometimes difficult to see at night.

Customers have been attracted by the modest price and novelty of digital watches. The LED, because it needs more frequent battery replacement and must be commanded manually to show time, has become less saleable. The LCD movements have become more in demand.

Quartz Watches. The most accurate watches are those powered by the vibrations of a **quartz crystal.** These watches have no mainspring and few cogs and gears. The quartz bar vibrates 32,769 times per second when charged by a specially produced battery that is about the size of an aspirin tablet. This vibration turns the hands of the analog watch by use of a tuning fork, balance wheel, or tiny motor. An integrated electronic chip regulates the pulses per second to move the hands accurately. Often these watches do not lose or gain time by more than 2 or 3 minutes per year. The use of a quartz crystal has permitted thinner movements to be produced, even thinner than a penny.

Variety of Timekeeping Functions

Watches may have both digital and analog faces on one watch; may tell time, day, and date; and may have chimes, alarms, and chronograph devices that record time intervals to determine speed of events. Each extra function complicates the watch mechanism and raises the cost of its manufacture.

Watchcases

Although the movement of the watch is important for timekeeping, the case may be the most costly part of the watch. Inexpensive cases may be made from stainless steel, anodized aluminum, or plated brass. Better cases may be made from karat gold, platinum, or tungsten carbide and set with precious stones. The case should be sturdy enough to protect the delicate mechanism inside it. Stainless steel, being hard and enduring, is often used for parts of a case, even with precious metals.

Watches may be made to fit wrists, finger rings, or vest pockets; to dangle from broochlike pins, to hang on neck chains, or to be inserted in pens.

CARE OF JEWELRY

Fine articles require care to keep them attractive and secure. Ring settings should be examined often to see that stones are firmly held. A soft brush used with mild soap and a little ammonia will remove film from stones. Dry rings carefully after washing.

Strings of beads or pearls should be examined frequently and restrung as needed. Knots between beads will prevent their loss if the string breaks. Pearls should be wiped with a soft damp cloth after wearing to prevent a buildup of grease and perspiration. Jewelry that is not being worn should be kept in appropriate containers in which it does not rub against other articles.

NOTE

1. Anne Marie Schiro, "The Return of Pearls: A Guide for Buyers," *The New York Times*, December 5, 1981, p. 52.

DO YOU KNOW YOUR MERCHANDISE?

1. Distinguish between costume jewelry and fine jewelry.
2. What qualities make stones precious? Name the precious stones.
3. What is meant by the hardness of a stone? Which stone is the hardest?

4. Differentiate among synthetic stones, other chemically made stones, and imitation stones.
5. Define faceting, brilliant cut, emerald cut, single cut, and cabochon cut.
6. Name stones that are available in each of the following colors: red, blue, yellow to orange, green, violet, and colorless.
7. Differentiate between saltwater and freshwater pearls and between cultured and imitation pearls.
8. Differentiate collar and choker necklaces; pendants and lockets; opera, matinee, and rope-length necklaces; and bangle and charm bracelets.
9. What are the four classifications of watches?
10. From what materials are watchcases made? How do they affect the value of the watch?

PUTTING YOUR MERCHANDISE KNOWLEDGE TO WORK

To help new and part-time salespeople, a store is planning to publish a small sales manual. They have asked you to prepare a short explanation of the following types of jewelry: collars, chokers, bibs, lockets, matinee length, and opera length. Be sure to explain them in your own words and as dramatically as you can.

PROJECT

Choose three advertisements for men's jewelry or for men's watches. Note the technical terms for the metals, finishes, and decorations. Be prepared to explain the meaning of each of the terms. If you choose watches, also be prepared to explain the types of watches advertised.

24

Cosmetics:
The Glamorizing Products

Cosmetic – kosmetikos – *Grk.*

The cosmetics industry, an $11 billion industry in the United States, has an aura of glamor and excitement. People buy cosmetics to improve their self-images and their public images, so the cosmetics industry thrives on making people look and feel good. Recognizing the importance of first impressions, consumers buy cosmetics to help them maintain an attractive appearance. The impeccable grooming of the salespeople who sell cosmetics in a store or door-to-door serves to make them models for the products they are dispensing.

WHAT ARE COSMETICS?

A fine differentiation exists between a cosmetic and a cosmetic drug. Many products considered to be cosmetics by customers and sold side-by-side with cosmetics are classified as drugs under the Food, Drug and Cosmetic Act. **Cosmetics**, as defined by this act, are intended to be "rubbed, poured, sprinkled, or sprayed on, introduced into or otherwise applied to the human body for cleansing, beautifying, promoting attractiveness, or altering the apprearance without affecting the body's structure or functions."

Products that cause physiological changes are classified as **drugs**. Antiperspirants, depilatories, bleach creams, and dandruff shampoos come under this category. Because drug testing is far more stringent than cosmetic testing, manufacturers try to avoid claims for their cosmetics that

will classify them as drugs. However, many cosmetics, because of their claims, are considered to be over-the-counter (OTC) drugs.

Dermatologists, who were once hostile to cosmetics, have changed their attitude in the past few years. They now look upon them as valuable. They know that people want cosmetics not only to make them look good but also to *do* some good. Many cosmetics perform multiple functions.

The development and testing of such multiuse products by major pharmaceutical houses has brought the era of "serious" cosmetics into being. No longer are these products considered frivolous surface makeup. They are looked on as products that protect, beautify, and improve a person's skin.[1]

A third category of materials sold in cosmetics departments includes such sundries as cosmetic brushes, toothbrushes, hairbrushes, shaving equipment, blow dryers, mirrors, and receptacles to hold cosmetic products. These are not classified either as cosmetics or as drugs.

CREATING COSMETICS

Most large cosmetics manufacturers have research and development staffs of chemists and physicians who, after hundreds of experiments, devise the formulas to be used for their products. The chemist has over 5,000 chemicals, exclusive of fragrances, to choose from in making cosmetics. Cosmetics usually contain a base or holding substance, an active ingredient that performs the desired function, a fragrance, and a color. These ingredients may be natural, synthetic, or a combination of natural and synthetic. Such natural products as water, fats, waxes, oils, talc, borax, and aloe (a gel derived from the aloe vera plant of the lily family) may be combined with more exotic-sounding chemicals such as ammonium acrylate, selenium sulphide, or paraben. In addition, solvents or thinning agents may be used.

Cosmetic Shelf Life

How long the cosmetic remains stable and usable is another question that confronts both the user and the industry. In general, cosmetics contain chemicals that help prevent oils, waxes, and other ingredients from going acrid and decomposing. However, no cosmetic product is useful indefinitely. Most cosmetics should be consumed within 3 or 4 months and no more than a year after purchase.

When using cosmetics, people should be especially careful not to allow contamination. Hands applying cosmetic should be clean, and no cosmetic, especially lipstick, should be passed around for use. Sunlight and heat both help to speed the decomposition of contents. Therefore, cosmetics kept in a cool, shady place have the best chance of retaining their freshness.

Computing Cosmetic Cost

What makes the difference in the prices of different brands of cosmetics? Often the ingredients in two different manufacturer's products are almost identical, yet one may be more costly than the other. Mystique and prestige are often the differences the customer pays for.

The cosmetic dollar must pay for all the operations needed to get the product to the ultimate consumer. These may include the research and testing needed to bring the product to market, and the packaging, advertising, and selling needed to get it to the customer.

Mass-produced products sold through supermarkets, variety stores, and discount chains can sell for less than cosmetics sold by **demonstrators,** salespeople in stores who are paid by the manufacturer to sell only that firm's product lines. Some cosmetics are sold in salons where specialists apply the cosmetics to the clients and explain their uses. Some are sold by door-to-door agents who are paid a commission up to 40 percent. Advertising also increases the price of the cosmetic. No-frill cosmetics sell for less than similar items that are extensively advertised and glamorously packaged. Exclusivity of a product also results in a higher price. Packaging is an important item. *Licensing*, using the name of a famous designer, for example, may increase the cost of a cosmetic by 5 percent or more.

The fineness of the ingredients may vary. Most cosmetic ingredients are relatively inexpensive, but a few are exotic and costly. The choice of fragrances and colors can make a difference. These components are often the most costly ingredients used.

The cosmetic dollar is spent typically in the following way.

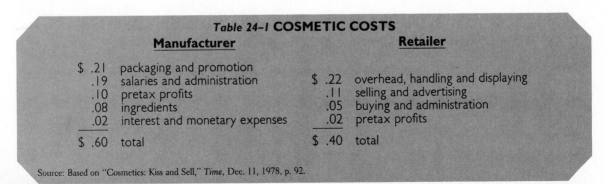

Table 24-1 COSMETIC COSTS

Manufacturer		Retailer	
$ .21	packaging and promotion	$ .22	overhead, handling and displaying
.19	salaries and administration	.11	selling and advertising
.10	pretax profits	.05	buying and administration
.08	ingredients	.02	pretax profits
.02	interest and monetary expenses		
$ .60	total	$ .40	total

Source: Based on "Cosmetics: Kiss and Sell," *Time*, Dec. 11, 1978, p. 92.

Target Markets

Today some stores are reacting to current trends by opening or expanding shops that carry natural cosmetics, whereas other retailers are basing their marketing strategy on nostalgia and are featuring products used by movie queens. Cosmetics are made to blend with every skin tone.

The use of skin care products, fragrances, shaving supplies, and hair products by men has risen dramatically in recent years. Many cosmetics companies that once made women's lines exclusively now have lines for men.

LAWS AND THEIR APPLICATION

In 1938, the Federal Food, Drug, and Cosmetic Act was promulgated in response to articles on products in the market that were dangerous to use as intended, or were impure (adulterated), or mislabeled. Since then, the Federal Trade Commission (FTC), which is empowered to oversee obedience to the law, and the Food and Drug Administration (FDA), have been amending the regulations and interpreting and enforcing the law more strictly.

Additional cosmetic rules were issued by the FTC in 1949, 1951, 1953, and 1954. (Surprisingly, only since 1962 has the federal government required drugs to be effective as well as safe.[2]) The growing influence of the consumer movement in the late 1960s and early 1970s resulted in even greater caution in the use of chemicals and more truthfulness by the cosmetic industry.

In 1969 the FTC classified wigs as cosmetics and included under its authority the advertising and labeling of these items. In 1971 synthetic wigs were placed under the jurisdiction of the Flammable Fabrics Act (see Chapter 1).

Some cosmetics may be **irritants** for some people; they cause an undesirable reaction the first time such people come in contact with a substance in the cosmetic. An **allergic** reaction to a cosmetic may develop after many uses, when a person becomes sensitized to the product.

Coal tar dyes

In 1972 cosmetic manufacturers were urged to follow a program of self-regulation. The American Medical Association endorsed the labeling of contents if products contained substances that could cause allergic reactions in users. In 1973 the FDA made the labeling of the contents of cosmetics mandatory.

Not until 1977, however, did the FDA succeed in enforcing this ruling. Even then, to protect trade secrets, manufacturers were allowed to list "fragrances" and "flavors" without stating the actual chemicals used. Many manufacturers list only the active ingredients in their products — those chemicals on which the cosmetic depends for the results claimed. Many labels appear only on the outside containers, which are often discarded before the cosmetic is used. In 1976 the FDA ruled that cautionary labels must appear on aerosol products.

In September, 1976, the FDA issued regulations that state under what circumstances a cosmetic may be labeled **hypoallergenic**, which means it is less likely than usual to cause an allergic reaction. For a product to be considered hypoallergenic, scientific studies must show it causes significantly fewer adverse reactions in human test volunteers than do competing, similar products having at least 10 percent of the market share for that product. A cosmetic claiming that it is "safe for a sensitive skin," must comply with a similar standard. The salesperson and the customer should be aware that federal law has established the following requirements.

- Cosmetics must be made of clean, fresh, non-poisonous substances that are packaged under sanitary conditions in harmless containers.
- All coloring material, except those used in hair dyes, must be certified by the U.S. Department of Agriculture.
- The labeling must be accurate, with cautions against misuse of the product. The label must not make exaggerated claims and must contain the name and address of the manufacturer and an accurate statement of the weight and content of the packaged product. Ingredients must

be listed in order of the amount used from greatest to least.

- Containers may not have false bottoms or sides that make them appear to contain more than they do.

COSMETICS AND THE SKIN

Clean, healthy skin is the first step in good grooming. The salesperson should be able to recommend skin care products appropriate for the customer's skin type. The salesperson will need a basic understanding of the skin, as well as a familiarity with the lines of products for sale.

The Skin

Because cosmetics are usually applied to the skin, a knowledge of the skin is desirable for both the salesperson and consumer. The skin is composed of the **epidermis** (the top layer) and the **dermis** (the underlying layer). Dead cells, which eventually flake off, cover the epidermis. When the flakes accumulate on the scalp, they are known as **dandruff**. The living cells of the epidermis replace the dead cells as soon as they flake away.

By keeping substances from penetrating below its surface, the epidermis protects the dermis, which contains blood vessels; nerves; hair roots; and fat, sweat, and oil glands. Although some substances can get into the body by being rubbed onto the skin's surface, most cosmetics do not penetrate underneath or affect any part of the dermis. Cosmetics applied to the skin, teeth, hair, (except for hair dyes) and nails serve only to keep them smooth, clean, and attractive. That is the

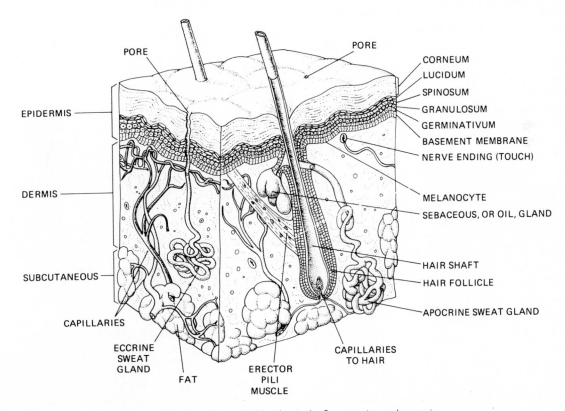

Figure 24-1. *A detailed section of the skin. Clean, healthy skin is the first step in good grooming.*

function of cosmetics, and that is how they should be presented to the customer.

The hair grows through openings in the dermis to the outside of the epidermis. When one hair is plucked out, another usually grows in its place. The skin also has **pores**, which are microscopic openings on the surface through which waste materials are exuded in the form of perspiration and through which the natural oils of the body are secreted to lubricate and nourish the surface of the skin. When bacteria and dirt clog the pores, waste cannot be released and the surface of the skin cannot be nourished by its own natural oils.

Skin may be normal, dry, oily, or a combination of these. Normal skin requires cosmetics to protect it and help keep it smooth and soft. Dry skin needs applications of lubricating creams and lotions. Oily skin needs frequent thorough cleaning and application of drying substances, such as talcum powder or mild alcoholic solutions, to obtain a more normal oil content. Combination skin is dry in some areas and oily in others, usually around the chin and nose.

The Cleanse, Tone, Moisturize (CTM) Approach

When selling skin care cosmetics to the consumer, the salesperson should be aware of the sequence of product use. Just as an artist's canvas must be clean, so the skin must be clean before cosmetics may be applied. One widely used approach to facial skin care is called the **CTM approach**. After the skin is cleaned, a toner is used, followed by a moisturizer. After this process has left the skin thoroughly clean and moist, women may apply makeup to their faces. For men, cleanse, shave, and tone (CST) is a regimen generally followed.

Soaps

Although soap is not classified as a cosmetic and is not subject to the laws pertaining to cosmetics, it is still the most universally used cleanser of the body and is often used with cosmetics.

The basic formula for soap is: Oil + Alkali = Soap + Glycerine. The differences in soaps are determined by the kinds and qualities of oil, alkalis, perfumes, and coloring agents and the processes used.

Soaps act on the skin by breaking up the greasy dirt so that it can be mixed with water and rinsed away. This action, known as **emulsifying** (mixing oil and water), is the primary function of soap. Soaps are manufactured in three ways: as floating soaps, as milled soaps, and as liquid or soft soaps.

Floating Soaps. Oils and lye (sodium hydroxide or potassium hydroxide) are mixed together in huge metal vats and cooked until all particles have been completely united and no free alkali is present. The glycerine then separates and is drawn off, leaving the soap. Soaps that are to be left in their natural color and scent may then be whipped like cream into a foaming, frothy mass. The air bubbles in such soap make it lighter than water, and so the final bar floats. Because they are so full of air, floating soaps do not last long in use.

Milled Soaps. Colored and perfumed soaps are made by a process known as **milling**. Depending on its quality, the perfume can add greatly to the cost of the soap. This soap is chipped and run between heavy metal rollers that press the ingredients tightly together. Color and perfume are added. The soap is then forced into a long tube that shapes it, and then it is cut into bars, stamped, and wrapped. Most toilet soaps are milled. Because these soap bars are compressed, they contain more soap in the same size bar than do the floating soaps.

Detergents and Soft Soaps. Detergents are products made synthetically from petroleum. They make water "wetter" causing the dirt to release easily. Some detergent cleansing bars prove to be so drying to the skin that manufacturers add cold cream to leave the surface of the skin softer. Detergents are also used in some shaving soaps and some shampoos. **Liquid or**

soft soaps contain detergent mixed with water, coloring matter and perfume. These were introduced in 1978 and for a while appeared to be so important that they were likely to overtake the floating and milled soap markets. However, consumers found that the liquid soaps did not last as long as the bar soaps, so their volume of use dwindled.

Types of Special-Purpose Soaps

Familiar types of soaps include:

Acne Soaps: These usually contain sulfur or sulfur combined with resorcinol (colorless phenol, which is carbolic acid).

Castile Soaps: These contain olive oil, considered very mild.

Cold-cream Soaps: These are usually detergent bars with cold cream added for softening the skin.

Deodorant or Germicidal Soaps: These contain antiseptic substances that deter the growth of bacteria that cause odors in perspiration. The substances used today (TBS or tribromosalcylade, and triclocarban or triclosan) all may make some people allergic to sunlight.

Glycerine Soaps: These are almost transparent and very mild.

Grit Soaps: These contain abrasives to aid in removing dirt that is embedded in the hands when people work around machinery, for example.

Hardwater Soaps: These either are made from soft detergents or contain water softeners.

Shaving Soaps: These produce a creamy, lasting lather.

Superfatted Soaps: These offset any alkaline reaction in the soap with extra oils.

Treatment Products: Creams and Lotions

Treatment lines contain related products, made by the same firm, that will cleanse, tone, moisturize and, in some cases, offer other advantages for the skin. Treatment lines have increasingly taken a larger share of the cosmetics market as the United States population ages. People may also purchase creams, lotions, toners, clay packs, eye creams, sun screens and other protecting and softening products from different manufacturers.

Lotions and creams perform a wide range of services. They may cleanse, refine, nourish, relieve acne, renew cells, bleach sun spots, or act as sun screens. Some products perform more than one function.

Cleansers. Soaps and detergent bars or soft soaps are commonly used cleansers. Some people prefer to use cleaning gels or cream cleansers. The cleaning gels and cleansers have mineral oil-based formulas, and they may also contain emulsifiers that work like soap to break down soil and wash it away. Common solvents in the cleansers are distilled water and alcohol. Other chemicals in the formula keep oil and water from separating and control mold and bacterial growth during the life of the product.

Refiners. After the skin has been thoroughly cleansed, refiners may be used to remove the skin's dead cells. These products are used less often than cleansers. **Clay packs** and **masks** are the common products in this grouping. Such products contain various oils, kaolin (a white china clay), other clays, corn starch, oatmeal, water, and glycerine. As these packs or masks dry, they pull the surface of the skin and draw out embedded soil, apparently tightening the skin. After drying for about a half hour, they are easily removed with warm water.

Nourishers. Creams and lotions that hold natural moisture in the skin help keep it smooth and radiant. Many contain such substances as mucopolysaccharides (mucous-like chemicals). They also contain oils, non-fat dry milk, water, and emulsifiers.

Special creams may also be used to soften the skin around the eyes, or to control aging. These usually contain enriching ingredients that help to promote healing, such as aloe.

Claims that creams with special ingredients will renew cells are viewed with skepticism by many doctors. The top layer of skin cells is constantly being renewed anyway, but the older a person gets, the slower this cell renewal. Any moisturizer will smooth the skin, reduce friction, and cover the skin so it looks and feels smoother and better. According to some medical doctors, products that contain petrolatum and vitamin-A acid may tend to renew cells somewhat faster than ordinary creams.[3]

Acne Creams and Lotions. Some 15 million young people between the ages of 12 and 17 are afflicted with acne. An excess of sebum (a complex of oils secreted by the body) is created by the system and remains deep in the hair follicles that are mainly concentrated on the face, chest and back. Rather than rising to the surface where this sebum could be washed away, it mixes with bacteria, blocks the hair canal, and then erupts into a lesion. Unfortunately, soaps and cleansing creams cannot reach the hair follicle areas where acne originates. The ingredients that appear to work when left on the skin are sulfur and benzoyl peroxide. The sulfur helps the existing lesions to dry out and then fall away, while the benzoyl peroxide helps to prevent new lesions from forming by releasing oxygen that kills the bacteria that cause the acne. Gels are usually more effective than lotions or creams. Scrub soaps that contain abrasive particles are not considered helpful.[4] These acne creams and lotions are classified as OTC drugs.

Bleach Creams. Products such as lemon juice and hydrogen peroxide may have a slight bleaching action on the skin when used consistently for a long period of time. However, these products lose their effectiveness quickly and work slowly.

Bleach creams (classified as OTC drugs) that promise to rid the skin of "age spots," contain **hydroquinone**, a chemical the FDA has found to be both safe and effective. The spots are basically large freckles. Hydroquinone reduces the melanin in the skin, in effect bleaching it. Any additional sun exposure, however, will encourage more spots, so users must apply more of the product. Some bleach creams incorporate sunscreens (discussed below) to reduce the creation of new spots.

Sunscreens and Sun Tan Lotions. Since the 1920s, the suntanned look has been in fashion. However, the damage the sun can do to the skin is now recognized. The parts of the sun's rays that affect the skin are the ultraviolet or UV rays. Even cloudy days may produce as much as 80 percent of UV radiation. These rays also reflect off sand and water.

The body's defense is the skin pigment, **melanin,** which acts to scatter and absorb UV radiation. The darker the skin, the more melanin to help protect the body. Freckles are little islands of melanin, but they give no protection to the skin surrounding them.

Chemicals that block the sun are used in gels, lotions, or creams. Sunscreens contain octyl dimethyl PABA (para-aminobenzoic acid), cinnamates (from oil of cinnamon), benzophenones, a light absorber, and salicylates, a salt of salicylic acid (the active ingredient in aspirin). If one of these substances irritates the skin, a product with a different sunscreen should be tried.

The amount of protection the sunscreen affords is known as the **Sun Protection Factor** or SPF. An SPF number on the tube or bottle indicates a multiple of the time it takes for the sun to produce a certain effect on the skin. A person who can tolerate 30 minutes of sun would be protected for 60 minutes with an SPF 2, and for four hours with an SPF 8. Sunscreens with ratings of SPF 15 or over almost completely block out the UV rays.

Deodorants and Antiperspirants. Perspiration is a normal process by which healthy bodies regulate their temperature. The liquid from the body is colorless and odorless, but bacteria on the skin may give perspiration an unpleasant odor. In addition to bathing, two precautions may be taken: **deodorants** mask the odor and **antiperspirants** mask the odor and locally control perspiration.

Most deodorants prevent body odor without affecting the person in any way. They come in cream, liquid, or powder form and may be patted on, sprayed on, or rolled on. They do not harm clothing.

Antiperspirants are classified as OTC drugs. The active ingredients are aluminum chloride or aluminum chlorohydrate and an antibacterial agent. Directions for the use of antiperspirants should be followed carefully. If any skin irritation results, their use should be discontinued immediately. After applying an antiperspirant, the armpits should be allowed to dry thoroughly before dressing so that clothing is not stained.

PERFUMES AND FRAGRANCE PRODUCTS

Aromatic products pervade the cosmetics industry. Almost every item from soap to hair coloration has a fragrance added to make it more appealing to the user. In addition, fragrances are sold in the form of perfumes, toilet waters, colognes, bath salts and oils, and sachets. Approximately $2 billion worth of scent is sold in the United States yearly.[5]

The Manufacture of Scents

Secrecy pervades the perfume industry. The perfumer has over 3,000 products from which to select in the blending of perfumes, and as many as 100 substances may be used to obtain one fragrance. The combination of ingredients in specific proportions is what gives a fragrance its distinctive character. Professional perfumers refer to the scents that make up a fragrance as its **notes.** Years of experience enable these experts to detect subtle differences among fragrance products. The main substances used in making perfume are essential oils, fixatives, synthetic fragrances, and alcohol.

Essential oils are the aromatic (odor-making) materials extracted from flowers, fruits, leaves, nuts, and woods. They provide the natural odors used in perfumes. When extracted, essential oils are costly and are valued up to several thousand dollars per pound. From 12 to 20 percent of a perfume consists of these oils. One pound of them, however, is enough for 10 gallons of perfume.

The odors of these natural oils or essences are not lasting if used alone, however, so either natural or synthetic **fixatives** must be added. These scarcely smell like perfume ingredients in their natural state, for fixatives are obtained from scent bags or other products from animals that exude unpleasant odors. Greatly diluted, such fixatives add a fragrant, delightful body to the scent of the perfume and make the otherwise fast-evaporating flower odors remain for hours. Synthetic fixatives (aldehydes, lactones, and esters) are commonly used today.

The synthetic fragrances are made from coal-tar substances to improve or supplant natural flower, fruit, and animal odors. Although these synthetic products make perfumes less expensive, they do not lessen the strength of the fragrance.

Fragrance Products

The combination of essential oils, fixatives, and synthetic fragrances with other ingredients creates various fragrance products. Perfume contains the greatest amount of essential oils of all perfume products, followed by eau de parfum (perfume water, "oh de par füm"), eau de toilette (toilet water, "oh de tooa let"), eau de cologne (cologne water, "oh de cōlōn"), and cologne, which has the least amount of essential oils.

Bath Oils: These may be added to bath water; they have a high concentration of perfume in an oily base.
Bath Salts: Made from sodium carbonate, perfume, and coloring agents. In addition to their delightful aroma, they soften the bath water.
Eau de Cologne: Although similar to toilet water in formulation, eau de cologne contains somewhat less essential oil and may have a spicy odor that comes from the citrus, lavender, sage, thyme, peppermint, and palm oils used in it. Eau de cologne is especially cooling and refreshing after bathing or shaving. Aftershave lotions are usually eau de colognes. Cologne is a similar but more diluted product.
Milk bath powders: These powders produce no bubbles but soften the water.
Perfumes: The natural and synthetic ingredients together with fixatives are diluted slightly with alcohol to make commercial perfumes and perfume waters, which have a lasting fragrance and may be applied behind the ears and on the neck, hair, and hands.
Sachets: Dried perfume made from aromatic petals or leaves that have been left whole, broken into smaller pieces, or powdered and packaged in a fine

mesh or net bag. These are usually placed with clothing to scent it.

Toilet Waters: Perfumes that have been diluted with a considerable amount of alcohol and distilled water. About 4 percent of essential oils are used in these products. Toilet waters are useful for spraying in a room and are refreshing on the body after bathing. The odor is not very lasting.

Today, supermarkets sell a large number of products designed to help combat substances in many water supplies that may be harmful to the skin. Bath and shower products containing "natural" essences, such as aloe from plants, algemarin from the sea, cocoa butter, and petroleum jelly, give a feeling of luxury, moisturize the skin, and impart fragrance to the user. Often coloring agents are added to these products. Further benefits can be the elimination of bathtub rings and the unpleasant smell or color of the water.

Cassettes are available that can alter room scents to create moods just as easily as audio cassettes do. Candles, sprays, and oil-treated light bulbs can all act as room perfumizers.

The Marketing of Scents

Promotion is important in the area of perfumes and related products. Over 50 percent of the top French couture designers' business is done in this area.[6] Designers in other countries are also introducing lines of perfumes.

Fragrance products are sold not only in specialty, department, and drug stores, but also by mass merchandisers. Sometimes designer lines are discounted. This serves to bring prices down, to increase selection, and to make distributors strive harder for product distinction.

To maintain prices and prestige, exclusive containers are designed for all top-line perfumes and perfume products. Limited editions of some perfumes in crystal bottles are sold for more than $100 an ounce.

Care of Perfumes, Toilet Waters, and Colognes

Perfumes, toilet waters, and colognes are available as aerosol, atomizer, or pump sprays; cream sachets; stick colognes; lotion parfums; splash-ons; potted gels; oils; and conventional perfume liquids.

Because perfumes, toilet waters, and colognes all evaporate quickly, the purchase of more than an ounce at a time is usually unwise. Stoppers should always be replaced securely in the bottles immediately after they are used; aerosol containers are airtight. Strong sunlight deteriorates the color of perfume. Also the oils in perfume may stain fabrics; therefore, it is wise to apply the perfume to the body and allow it to dry before dressing, in order to avoid staining clothing or jewelry.

MAKEUP: GLAMORIZING THE FACE AND NAILS

Cosmetics that add color to the skin and nails are called makeup. Fashions in makeup color change along with the colors popular in the apparel lines of a season. Color used on the face can change the "canvas." Colors can set a mood appropriate for business, casual, or formal social occasions. Skillful application of colors can change the contours of the face, camouflaging or highlighting features.

Powders

The base of most powders is **talc**, a soft mineral that is ground and purified. **Talcum powder** is usually pure talc with a little perfume. Boric acid or zinc stearate may be added for their antiseptic qualities. Salespeople should advise customers not to dust talc over their bodies or to cause particles to float in the air, because they may be harmful if breathed into the lungs.

In addition to talc, **face powder** may include substances such as zinc oxide, chalk, china clay, titanium dioxide, starch, and perfume. Coloring matter is added to produce different shades. Some powders such as **pressed powders** may have a cold cream base. There are also **loose powders** and **sheer covers** or **translucent powders**. Because powder looks different under electric light and daylight, people may want a different shade for evening wear.

BASIC FACE SHAPES

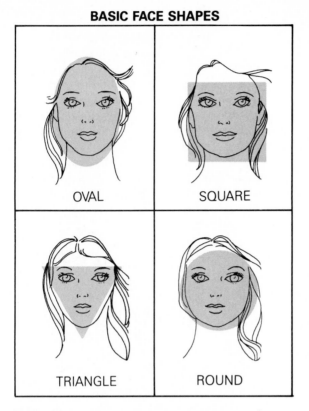

OVAL   SQUARE

TRIANGLE   ROUND

Figure 24-2. *The shape of the face is an important factor in deciding how to apply makeup.*

Makeup Bases or Foundations

The desire for smooth, satiny skin has resulted in the use of makeup bases, or foundations, which come in four types:

Cake Makeup: Consists mainly of pigmented powder in a dehydrated cream; it is good for dry skin.
Cream-base Makeup: Consists of pigmented powder in a thick cream.
Gels: Consist of sulfur in fine dispersion and are used for oily skin.
Liquid-base Makeup: An oil or water suspension of coloring matter. It is good for all skin types, although water-based liquid is best for oily skin.

Blushes

Blushes (also called rouge) come in dry cake, powder, cream, liquid, and gel forms. Dry,

brush-on blush differs from powder only in the coloring that is added. Cream blush is essentially cold cream mixed with coloring matter.

Lipstick, Lip Glosses, and Lip Blushers

It has been estimated that more than 95 percent of the women in the United States use lipstick. **Lipsticks** are basically stiff creams, gels, stains, or liquids to which coloring substances have been added. The so-called permanent lipsticks may cause allergic reactions in some people.

It is important for the salesperson to know that shades of lipstick vary and that the same shade may look different on different skins. Lipsticks are usually tested for color by marking the back of the customer's hand or the inside of the wrist with a few different shades so that their effect on the skin can be compared. **Lip glosses** impart a shine to the lips. **Lip pencils** and **liners** keep color from bleeding out of the lip line. **Lip stains** are also popular. Lipsticks come in cream formulas and frosted (pearl) formulas for shimmer effect. They can be hard or soft.

Eye Makeup

Makeup for the eyes includes mascara, eyebrow pencils, eye shadow, and eyeliners. **Mascara,** which darkens, thickens, and lengthens eyelashes, comes in cake or semiliquid form; it is applied with a brush. **Eyebrow pencils,** which can be sharpened like ordinary pencils, produce fine lines. **Eye shadow,** which comes in a wide range of tints and shades, contains coloring materials in a liquid, cream, powder, gel, or stick form. The caked powder form is most popular. **Eyeliners** are varicolored liquids similar in formula to eyeshadows and mascara.

In 1971 the *American Journal of Ophthalmology* reported that bacteria in eyeliners, mascaras, and eye shadows can cause infections. The FDA has approved a mercury additive (phenyl mercuric acetate) as a preservative in these products.

Nail Preparations

Liquid nail polish is nitrocellulose lacquer, which is dissolved in acetone or a similar solvent. Plasticizers (chemicals that impart flexibility) and coloring materials are added. When the polish is applied to the nails, the acetone evaporates, leaving a hard, colorful coating on the nails. For best results all oil should be removed from the nails before applying the polish. Two thin coats of polish are generally more lasting and attractive than a single coat.

Because the nails are merely a horny substance similar to the epidermis and to hair, they are rarely harmed by this coating. However, people may have an allergic reaction if they touch their face with nails coated with these lacquers.

Nitrocellulose lacquer is highly flammable. False nails are also available for people whose own fingernails will not grow as long as they want.

Acetone, ethyl acetate, or similar solvents, to which oil, coloring matter, and perfume may be added, are used to remove nail polish. Polish remover evaporates very quickly. It can also dry the skin. Advise customers to rub oil around their nails after using polish remover and to wash their hands and dry their nails before applying nail polish. Nail polish remover dissolves acetate fabric and is harmful to the finish on wooden furniture.

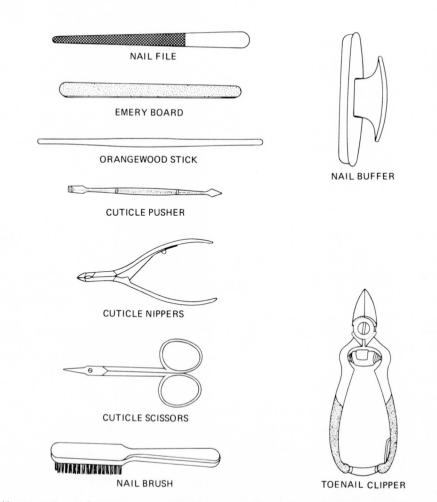

NAIL FILE

EMERY BOARD

ORANGEWOOD STICK

CUTICLE PUSHER

CUTICLE NIPPERS

CUTICLE SCISSORS

NAIL BRUSH

NAIL BUFFER

TOENAIL CLIPPER

Figure 24-3. *Various tools used for manicuring — filing, trimming, buffing, and cuticle-care implements.*

Customers should be advised to read the directions on cuticle remover bottles very carefully before using these substances. Anything strong enough to destroy the dead skin of the cuticle may be strong enough to irritate the rest of the epidermis. It is wise to wash the hands with soap and water and to apply oil after using cuticle removers.

HAIR-CARE PRODUCTS  *p.A.-5 good*

Hair frames the face and can add to a person's attractiveness. Most women maintain hair throughout their lives. Some men, however, are subject to male-pattern baldness.

The CTM (cleanse, tone, moisturize) process is also used on the hair. Treatments for hair include keeping it clean, conditioning it, curling or straightening it, modifying the color, and holding the hair style in place after setting. Most hair cosmetics are harmless; some, however, must be used with caution.

Shampoos   *alkali → more cleaning — bad*

Soaps and synthetic detergent **shampoos** are cosmetics for cleansing the hair. Lathering and non-lathering shampoos remove soil and excessive oils from hair. Special shampoos are available to aid in the removal of dandruff, condition the hair, add protein, or thicken the hair. Shampoos may contain natural products, such as herbs, skim milk, eggs, beer, and fruit extracts or they may contain special chemicals.

Dandruff removal shampoos may contain such chemicals as zinc pyrithione, which acts as a preservative, or selenium sulphide, nonmetallic elements that have helpful reactions to bacteria. The tiny amounts of chemicals used in these shampoos are not considered harmful.[7]

Hair Lotions and Conditioners

Mineral oils such as petrolatum give the highest-gloss wet look to the hair; the vegetable oils are second; and the animal oils (lanolin) give little shine, although they do nourish the hair better than the other two types of oils. Some hair lotions claim they contain no oil or grease. These usually have a high alcohol content and contain perfume ingredients. Conditioners that contain protein may temporarily help to restore protein loss.

Conditioners, once applied, remain on the hair until shampood out. Conditioners build thickness onto the hair shaft, may make the hair softer and more pliable or may help to hold the hair in place after styling.

Hair-Holding Products

The wave lotion used for setting hair is a honey-like liquid or a gel made from acacia gum, karaya gum, tragacanth gum, quinceseed, or flaxseed plus water, alcohol, and borax. Some liquid plastics substances are also used for hair setting. Lacquers to hold the hair in place after setting are available in aerosol and mechanical-pump spray form. Used to spray on hair already styled, they contain water-soluble plastic ingredients, fragrances, and alcohol. They are highly flammable and must be so labeled.

Hair-Waving Products

Permanent hair-wave kits are available for home use. The active ingredient, a strong alkaline solution, and the acid neutralizer used to "set" the curl are poisonous if taken internally. If a cut or scrape is present on the hands or head, application of these solutions may cause an unpleasant irritation.

If the alkaline solution is left on the hair too long, it may result in disintegration of some of the hair. The solution is also harmful to the nails. As a precaution, rubber or plastic gloves should be worn during application.

Hair Straighteners

For people who wish less curly hair, products are available that usually contain sodium hydroxide (lye) that straightens the hair by breaking down the cells of the hair shaft. This may weaken hair, make it brittle and even cause some loss of hair. These products must have a warning label and need to be used with care so the skin and eyes are not harmed.

Hair Removal

Hair may be removed by mechanical or chemical methods. Mechanical methods include abrasives such as sandpaper or pumice, in the form of a mitten or pad. Care must be taken not to rub so hard that the skin is harmed. Wax may be melted and applied to the area where hair is to be removed. When the wax has set, it is yanked off like adhesive tape, bringing embedded hairs with it. Frequent use of the wax may cause skin irritation.

Shaving is considered entirely safe and is especially recommended for large areas, such as men's faces and women's legs and arms. Shaving does not stimulate the growth of more hair, as some people believe. Shaving creams, soaps, powders, or lotions prevent irritation when applied before shaving.

Tweezing is somewhat painful, but for small areas, such as eyebrows, it is appropriate. Tweezing does not stop or retard the growth of hair. Tweezing is harmless when done cautiously with a clean tweezer. Care must be taken to avoid infection when hair is removed by this method.

Chemical depilatories contain chemicals such as sulfides, which are used for removal of hair from animal hides during pretanning. This was once the most common chemical for use in removing hair from arms, legs, and face. A newer chemical, known as *calcium thioglycolate*, has replaced the sulfides. Because hair is composed of substances similar to the epidermis, any preparation that is strong enough to remove unwanted hair can also remove the skin if the preparation is left on long enough. The salesperson should always caution customers about the use of chemical hair removers and should warn them to read labels and follow directions.

Hair Coloring

For many years, women have changed their hair color to look younger, more glamorous, or just different. Men have been dyeing their hair more frequently since the 1970s.

Hair color may be changed in many ways using many substances. Generally, the less permanent the change, the fewer problems the product will present to the user. Colors may be applied that wash out in one or two weeks, that fade out over a period of time, or that only depart as hair grows and the colored area is cut off.

Hair coloring materials were the one product the FDA did not require to be safe when used as intended in the original Food, Drug and Cosmetic Act of 1938. Since that time, however, the FDA has become increasingly concerned with hair coloring products and in 1978 issued a requirement that manufacturers warn customers of the danger of their product if certain dyes, known to be carcinogenic, were used. Because of that demand, manufacturers have turned to less dangerous substances in hair dyes. Even with these, however, customers should observe cautions and perform patch tests at least 24 hours before applying such coloring substances.

Types of coloring ingredients include the following.

Coal-tar Hair Dyes: Today, these are derivatives of petroleum, not coal, the source used twenty years ago. However, the chemical structure is the same. Three types are available: permanent, semipermanent, and rinses. After the 1978 ruling for warnings of danger with hair dyes, many that were named by the FDA were withdrawn from the market and replaced with other less dangerous colorations.

Henna: A leaf from an Egyptian plant known as the flower of paradise, which is used to make a dye that coats the hair. Other vegetable coloring substances are sage and camomile. These vegetable dyes tend to streak and may not color evenly.

Metal Dyes: Also known as **progressive hair dyes**. Lead acetate, the main active ingredient, reacts with the carotene of the hair and gradually forms lead sulfate. This coats the hair which goes from light amber to brown, then dark brown to black giving the illusion that the hair is returning to its original color. Some users may have an allergic reaction that results in redness and itching of the skin. According to authorities, lead acetate permeates the skin and can enter the bloodstream. However, the FDA found that the use of such hair dye would increase lead exposure by an insignificant amount. Some doctors believe that no level of lead exposure is truly safe.[8]

Permanent Hair Dyes: Coloring material absorbed by the hair shaft after it has been prepared by a hydrogen peroxide developer that bleaches some of the natural hair color. The color lasts until the hair grows out, usually about four to six weeks.

Rinses: Temporary hair dyes. These tend to coat the hair rather than to penetrate the hair shaft. They last until they are washed away by shampooing.

Semipermanent Hair Dyes: Solutions containing coal-tar chemicals that penetrate the hair shafts, but without the hydrogen peroxide, the color change tends to wear off after three or four weeks.

Vegetable Dyes: These are, on the whole, harmless.

To minimize the risks of adverse effects of hair dyes, users should apply them no more often than necessary. Permanent hair dyes should be used no oftener than once a month. Leave hair dye on during application for the minimum time allotted, and then rinse the hair and scalp thoroughly.

WIGS

Wigs and hairpieces for men and women have been in and out of fashion throughout history.

Wigs for women are complete hairpieces that cover the entire head. There are also partial hairpieces for women, such as wiglets, chignons, falls, switches, and curls. Wigs for men in various styles cover all but the sideburns and back of the head at the nape of the neck. Partial hairpieces are made to fit the areas where men often lose their hair. False mustaches, beards, and sideburns are also available.

Materials Used in Wigs

The wide differences in the prices of wigs depend on the kind and quality of material from which the hair is made, the manner in which the hair is attached to the foundation, and the quality of the foundation. Whether or not the wig is custom-made is also a factor in the price.

Hair wigs are made from human hair, which has become increasingly limited in supply. The most costly and most natural-looking wigs are from this hair. However, they require a great deal of care. According to the FTC, the designations "true hair," "natural hair," and "genuine hair" in advertising or selling can be used only to apply to human hair. **Virgin hair** refers to hair that has never been bleached, dyed, or permanented.

Synthetic hairlike materials are used to make wigs at a fraction of the cost of real-hair wigs. Acetate fiber is used for inexpensive wigs and for children's play wigs. These gleaming fibers come in a wide range of colors and can be easily washed, combed, and set. Vinyon makes a fiber with excellent curlability that may be set and reset and restyled easily. Because the color is added during the manufacture of the fiber, it withstands fading. Modacrylic fibers are considered to be the finest of the synthetics. These fibers do not frizz in heat or droop in humidity. Wigs made from modacrylic fibers look and feel like real hair. Nylon mixed with modacrylic makes a wig that maintains its hair style even while the wearer is swimming. (See chapters 11 and 12 for definitions of these terms).

Care of Wigs and Wig Products

Wigs of real hair need to be cleaned and styled every 2 to 4 weeks, depending on how often they are worn. Synthetics may be washed by hand with mild soap or mild detergent and then reset, if necessary. Most synthetics are preset and need only to be washed and combed gently. A **wig form** (head-shaped mold) keeps the wig in good condition when it is not being worn.

NOTES

1. Jane Ogle, "Entering the Age of 'Serious' Cosmetics," *The New York Times Magazine,* September 23, 1979, p. 84.
2. Janet Battaile, "The Federal Watchdog Under the Cosmetic Counter," *The New York Times,* November 16, 1980, p. 22E.

3. Jane Ogle, "Perking Up Aging Skin," *The New York Times Magazine*, February 10, 1980, p. 66.
4. "Acne: New Approaches to an Old Problem," *Consumer Reports*, August, 1981, pp. 472-7.
5. Enid Nemy, "At a Fragrance Workshop, 200 Executives are Led by the Nose," *The New York Times*, September 8, 1979, p.14.
6. "French Fashion Industry — Basse Couture — Paris," *The Economist*, July 10, 1982, p. 65.
7. Richard D. Lyons, "Cancer Is Reported in Lab Animals," *The New York Times*, May 2, 1979, p. A12.
8. Judith Vandewater, "Risk Assessment: Growing Industry Dilemma," *Women's Wear Daily*, February 27, 1981, Section II, p. 8.

DO YOU KNOW YOUR MERCHANDISE?

1. Define cosmetics. How do cosmetics and drugs differ? What are OTC products?
2. What advice would you give to the customer who said he or she had an allergic reaction to a certain product?
3. If a customer asked why a cosmetic was so costly, what explanation would you give?
4. Explain the following: epidermis, dermis, and pore. What is meant by CTM?
5. What are the four main substances used in making perfumes? How do perfume, toilet water, and cologne differ?
6. What is the difference between deodorants and antiperspirants? Which of them might be harmful to clothing?
7. What warnings would you give to the users of talcum powder, to the users of lipsticks, and to the users of nail-polish removers?
8. List and describe various methods of hair removal a customer might use.

9. What cautions should be given the customer regarding hair dyes? Describe the different results that are obtained from using vegetable hair dyes, metal hair dyes, and coal-tar hair dyes. Which products permeate the hair shaft?
10. What materials may be used to make wigs? Which is most costly? Why?

PUTTING YOUR MERCHANDISE KNOWLEDGE TO WORK

Compare and contrast two similar kinds of cosmetic products in different price lines. Consider ingredients, packaging, promotion, and any other factors that might contribute to the difference in price.

PROJECT

Compare the marketing activities of the following types of cosmetics retailers by visiting one outlet of each type:

Discounter or variety store
Department or specialty store
Small drugstore
Supermarket
Salon or cosmetics boutique
Door-to-door sales representative

Compare the product lines, customer services, and promotional activities of these retailers. For each store, sketch floor and shelf plans. What do these layouts indicate about the marketing strategies of the stores? What is the target market of each retailer?

Homefurnishings

25

Dinnerware: The Delicate Yet Sturdy Materials

Selecting dinnerware is a complicated procedure. Not only must the surface appearance, size, and shape be considered, but also the quality of the ware, the type it represents, and how it will be used.

TERMINOLOGY OF DINNERWARE PRODUCTS

Consumers will find many items for dinnerware or gift wares. Those made from a base of clay and those of plastics (made from various chemicals) will be discussed in this chapter. Glass and glasslike products will be discussed in the next chapter.

Ceramics refers to the art of making articles from baked clay. It is a generic term that may be used to refer to any types of dishes and ornaments except those made from metal, plastic, or glass. The term does not designate the type, but refers to the finest-quality to the poorest-quality baked clay products.

Pottery has two different meanings. The factory where ceramic products are made is known as a pottery. The people who make clay articles are known as **potters**. They work at a turntable called a **potter's wheel**. The products on which they work are known as **pots**.

Pottery, like ceramics, is also a generic term that applies to all articles that are made from clay and baked. However, pottery is also used to designate a specific type of product, as discussed

330

below, and this causes some confusion in the use of the term.

TYPES OF DINNERWARE

All products made from clay and baked may be divided into two major categories: nonvitrified and vitrified. The word, "vitrified," means glasslike or nonporous.

Nonvitrified Products

When clay products are **nonvitrified**, the bodies of the wares are opaque and porous. Since all dinnerware clay products have a glassy coating placed over them, this porosity does not affect the usefulness of the dishes. But it does affect their durability, resistance to breakage, ability to withstand extremes of temperature, and overall appearance. The commonly known nonvitrified products are discussed below.

Pottery. Pottery is the baked clayware that is crudest in appearance and least serviceable. The dishes are often fired in open hearths or crude ovens, and colorful glazes are added to their surfaces. They are often referred to as **peasant pottery**. These dishes, although heavy and thick, are quite fragile. They chip easily, and if exposed to temperature extremes, may get surface cracks in the glassy coating, called **crazing**. As with all nonvitrified wares, when chipped, they are no longer sanitary for food service or use. Famous types of pottery include the following.

Delft: A pottery that was first made in Holland, and later in England, with a colored clay body having an opaque white glaze.
Faience: Earthenware with a decoration of opaque colored glazes; it was originally made in Italy.
Majolica: An Italian pottery decorated with an opaque glaze.

Earthenware. Earthenware is a generic term for all nonvitrified wares as well as a term for wares that are not as crude as peasant pottery but not as fine as the better semivitreous and ironstone products. When very inexpensive "whiteware" is sold in discount stores or variety stores, it is usually earthenware. A clear glaze gives the clay dish an off-white color that makes it attractive for any type of food service. These dishes are less porous than pottery, but they will absorb water if they crack or break. The surface glaze is subject to crazing, and the dishes cannot be subjected to extremes of temperature.

Semivitreous Ware. This is finer earthenware that is made from almost white clays that have been refined to yield a better product. When fired, only very little porosity remains. Thus the glaze adheres better and is less likely to craze. The ware may be made somewhat thinner than whiteware and a great deal thinner than pottery, but it still stands up well in use. Often semivitreous wares simulate more costly vitrified products.

Ironstone. Classified as the finest earthenware, ironstone (sometimes incorrectly called **stone china**) is a durable, lighter-weight ware that may be white or colored. Manufacturers and retailers sometimes use the term in a way that causes customers to think it is stoneware or chinaware (discussed below). Ironstone is a slightly porous, well-constructed, durable ware.

Figure 25-1. *Glazed pottery is a heavy, thick type of nonvitrified product.*

Vitrified Products

When clay products are **vitrified**, the body is completely nonporous, even without the glassy coating. Most vitrified products are also translucent when a thin section is held to the light. Vitrified products may chip, crack, and break, but the sections are not porous. Therefore, even chipped plates or cups are completely sanitary to use. No crazing ever takes place with vitrified wares. Vitrified products have a bell-like tone when struck. The vitrified wares are discussed below.

Stoneware. Stoneware is a durable, heavy-looking, colorful, casual type of ware that has a vitrified body that is totally opaque. Many stoneware manufacturers put a glaze only on the inside surface of the ware. This leaves the outside dull in appearance and imparts a rough, textured look. Stoneware wears well and can withstand extremes of temperature, thus often serving as oven-to-table ware.

Felspathic Chinaware and Porcelain.
The more expensive and durable dishes, although the most fragile in appearance, are called chinaware. These dishes, which are nonporous under the glaze surface, are sanitary even when chipped. Because these dishes first came from China, the people in England referred to them as chinaware. Italians noticed the gloss of this ware, which they compared to the polished surface of a shell known as porcellana. Thus, there are two words for this fine type of dish: Americans generally call it china, and Europeans call it **porcelain**.

After the introduction of chinaware in Europe, the demand for it became great. This demand led to many attempts at imitation. In the early eighteenth century Johann Friedrich Böttger discovered kaolin clay in Germany, to which he added ground feldspar, a crystalline mineral, and suceeded in making chinaware. The feldspar fused the particles of clay, and the finished body was translucent, had a bell-like tone, and resisted extremes of temperature. Such china is referred to as **felspathic** china or porcelain. **Beleek** is a particularly translucent, thin, elegant example of this china in Ireland.

Bone China.   In the meantime the English were also experimenting. They discovered that when bone ash pulverized from the bones of oxen was added to the kaolin, they could make fine-quality chinaware. In 1800 Josiah Spode perfected this method. Some other leading English manufacturers also added the bone ash to their wares, and their dishes became known as **bone china**. The distinctively white body is strong and highly translucent. England continues to be the primary source of bone china although Japanese and U.S. potteries also make bone china.

Plastic Ware

Although dishes have been made from various types of plastics ever since plastics became popular in the early 1900s, it was not until World War II that a plastic was discovered that had the attributes needed for dishes. The U.S. Navy, seeking materials that were lightweight, resistant to breakage, sanitary in use, and attractive enough for food service, developed the first melamine plastic dishes. **Melamine**, a thermosetting (heat-resistant) plastic, makes dishes that can be used to serve hot foods and drinks and can be washed in the hottest water without damage. In 1946 manufacturers introduced melamine plastic dishes for consumers. Less desirable dishes of thermoplastics, which cannot hold hot foods and melt when placed near a hot stove, are sometimes made by manufacturers. Customers should therefore make sure that the plastic dishes they are buying are made from melamine plastic.

MATERIALS USED IN CERAMIC DISHES

Look at several different dishes or ceramic ornaments. You will notice that some of them are thicker than others, that some have entirely different shapes, that the finish on some is much shinier than the finish on others, and that some of the dishes have just a little decoration and others have a great deal. Now hold the dishes to the light. If any of the dishes are china, you can see the shadow of your fingers through the dish because china is translucent. If the dishes are opaque, they are probably earthenware or stoneware. Hold the dish carefully by the base and tap the edge gently with a pencil. Notice the difference in the tonal quality of the dishes. Those with a bell-like ring are vitrified, and those with a dull or pinglike sound are nonvitrified. If any of the dishes are chipped, put a drop of ink on the fractured section. If the ink wipes off, the dish is vitrified and is chinaware or stoneware. If the ink soaks into the fracture, the material is porous and is earthenware.

These differences in appearance, translucence, sound, and absorbency depend on the kinds of clays and other raw materials used, the way the dishes are shaped, the heat of the oven in which the dishes are baked or fired, and the method of decorating them.

Figure 25-2. *Bone china is a fine-quality chinaware with a distinctive white body. It is highly translucent.*

The basic material for all ceramic ware is clay. **Clay** is a kind of soil that is pliable when moist and can be molded. For pottery, common clay such as that suitable for modeling is used. Semivitreous ware is made from a combination of china clay and ball or blue clay, which adds moldability and strength. Stoneware uses a fire clay that is resistant to the highest heat used in food preparation. For china dishes kaolin is the finest, purest, whitest, strongest clay available.

Because clay will not melt at any termperature, feldspar, a crystalline mineral substance that melts at a rather low temperature, is ground and then added to hold the clay particles together. When combined with fine ingredients and heated at a high enough temperature, the feldspar gives translucency to the chinaware. **Flint**, a hard stone, is an ingredient commonly used for strengthening ceramic ware. It too must first be ground. Ox bones from South America are fired at a great heat and crushed into a fine powder. They are then used in place of flint in making bone china.

The coloring materials used to color clay or apply designs on ceramic products are metallic oxides. No other coloring materials can withstand the high heat used to fire clay products.

MANUFACTURE OF CERAMIC DISHES

After the clays are washed and filtered to remove stones and dirt, the powdered ingredients are stirred together with water until the mixture resembles a thick cream known as **slip**. Because all impurities must be removed for fine chinaware or earthenware, the slip is poured through a fine screen and run over magnets that attract and remove all iron particles that would otherwise make brown spots in the dishes. However, this step is omitted in making pottery, stoneware, and casual, colorful earthenware.

The slip is then pumped into filter cloths, and the water is drained off, leaving slabs of plastic clay. These slabs are stored for several weeks to permit ripening or aging, which makes the clay much easier to work. Next, a machine known as a **pugmill** is used to remove air pockets or bubbles from the clay and to blend it. The clay mixture is then ready to be shaped.

Shaping the Clay

Shaping the clay by hand on a potter's wheel is the most expensive and time-consuming method. In most factories today machines known as **jollies** or **jiggers** are used to press the inside or outside, respectively, of the clay against a mold while the clay revolves on the table, thus shaping both the inside and outside of the dish at the same time. Little chunks of clay may be shaped into handles, spouts, or knobs by being sandwiched between two parts of a mold. The object may be cast by pouring slip into a porous plaster of paris mold and left to set. After the slip sets around the edges, the center liquid is poured out to make the hollow center in the dish.

Joining Handles and Spouts

After the clay articles are shaped, molded handles, spouts, or knobs are attached with slip. Before baking, the pieces, which are still moist, are approximately one-fifth larger than they will be after they are baked. This is the amount of shrinkage that will occur during the firing process.

Making the Ware Durable

By subjecting the easily broken, unattractive-looking clay object to intense heat, it is transformed into a useful, durable, and beautiful article. The temperature at which the clay is **fired** makes a difference in the finished product. The higher the temperature, the more durable, less porous, and finer the finished ware will be. Earthenware is fired at approximately 1,000°C (approximately 1,800°F), and china and stoneware are fired at 1,250° to 1,600° (2,280° to 2,900°F). For firing, the dishes are stacked in fire-clay racks and then placed on moving belts to travel slowly through a tunnel-shaped **kiln** (oven). The ware that is removed from the cooled oven is known as **biscuit ware** or **bisque**. It has a dull, rather rough surface. Clay objects are about one-fifth larger before firing.

Applying the Glaze

It is now necessary to make the earthenware nonporous and to put a shiny finish on it and on the stoneware and the chinaware so that the dishes will be pleasant to eat from and easy to clean. This is accomplished by sanding the ware to smooth it and then covering it with a glassy coating called a **glaze**. Glaze is made by different formulas but usually contains very finely ground glass. The glaze may be sprayed or painted on,

	NONVITRIFIED	
Characteristic	**Pottery**	**Earthenware**
Body	Opaque	Opaque
Porosity	Very	Quite
Thickness	Thick	Medium
Weight	Fairly light	Light
Chips	Very easily	Easily
Body color	Very colorful	May be off-white
Crazing of glaze	Easily	Somewhat
Tone when tapped	Dull	Ping
Resistance to temperature changes	May break	May break
Cost	Fairly expensive	Inexpensive

or the article may be dipped into it. As long as the glaze remains on it, earthenware is as sanitary as chinaware.

The glazed dishes are prepared for a second, **glost firing** at a lower temperature than that of the first (biscuit or bisque) firing. This time no two pieces may be allowed to touch, as the melting glaze would weld them together. Dishes may be balanced on small clay triangles to keep the dishes from being welded to the rack on which they sit during the firing, or the glaze may be wiped off the bottom rim.

Some glazes on pottery dishes from little-known companies and on homemade ceramic products may contain free lead that combines with acid in foods, such as oranges or tomato products, and may cause lead poisoning. Estab-

lished firms constantly check their products for safety. The danger is limited to potteries fired at low temperatures, for the high temperatures used in firing products such as fine earthenware, stoneware, and chinaware burn off any lead traces and make these dishes safe for use.

Glazes adhere to the various wares in different ways. The more porous the body, the less well the glaze will hold to the ware. Since the porous body will expand and contract at a different rate from the glaze, the glaze cracks or crazes, leaving tiny marks on the surface that can fill with dirt and become unsightly and unsanitary. Vitrified bodies are fused to the glaze, which never crazes on such wares.

Table 25–1 shows the various characteristics of the wares discussed.

Table 25–1 CHARACTERISTICS OF NONVITRIFIED AND VITRIFIED PRODUCTS

| | | | VITRIFIED | |
Semivitreous	Ironstone	Stoneware	Felspathic (Porcelain)	Bone China
Opaque	Opaque	Opaque	Translucent	Translucent
Slightly	Slightly	Vitrified	Vitrified	Vitrified
Medium	Medium	Thick	Thin	Thin
Medium	Medium	Heavy	Heavy	Heavy
Somewhat easily	Somewhat easily	Resistant	Rarely	Rarely
Off-white	Off-white	Colorful	Creamy white	Pure white
May craze	May craze	None	None	None
Ping	Ping	Sharp	Bell-like	Bell-like
Fairly	Fairly	Totally	Totally	Totally
Moderate	Moderate to fairly expensive	Fairly expensive	May be very expensive	May be very expensive

MANUFACTURE OF PLASTIC DISHES

Melamine plastic dishes are named for the basic plastic compound, melamine, of which they are made. The melamine is combined with other chemicals and made into a syrup. Mixing cellulose fiber with the plastic gives it strength. When the mixture has dried, it is ground into a powder to which color may be added.

The melamine powder is next formed into large pellets. The pellets needed to form a given-size dish are placed into a press and molded into shape with heat. The heat and pressure harden the melamine permanently. Because the walls of the molds are very shiny, a glossy finish is imparted to the dishes and no added glaze is needed.

DECORATING CERAMIC AND PLASTIC WARE

In walking through a dinnerware department, you may notice that the dishes range in price from a few dollars to hundreds of dollars for the same number of pieces. These price differences are in part due to the differences in the ingredients used, the amount of care put into the making of the dishes, and the country in which the dishes are made. However, they are primarily due to the amount and kind of decoration applied. Ceramic dishes show the greatest range of prices because of differences in decoration.

When Designs Are Applied on Ceramic Ware

Decorations on ceramic dishes vary so greatly that the salesperson and customer need to know how and why they affect the price of the wares so much.

In the Clay. Designs made on the moist clay by hand, by cutting away the clay in a lacelike form, or by pressing designs on with molds are referred to as **in-the-clay decorations**. Some designs are molded separately and then pressed against the dishes, with slip being used to hold them in place. Some famous Wedgwood pieces are made this way. For color, metallic oxides may be added to the slip and painted on the wet clay. If handwork is needed, these designs may be quite costly. After the decoration is applied, the ware is fired.

Underglaze. Colors applied on the bisque after the first firing and before glazing are known as **underglaze decorations**. Colors are easier to apply, and many more details may be created than by using colored slip. Therefore, this is one of the commonly used methods of decorating dishes. Colors so applied are very durable because the designs are protected by the glaze that is applied later. The colors that can be used, however, are limited because the intense heat needed to melt the glaze over them burns out some colors. Most colors, except gold and silver (platinum), can be used in underglaze decorations. Once applied these colors become permanent when the glaze covers them.

In the Glaze. When the glazes that are applied over the clay bodies are colored, they are called **in-the-glaze decorations**. Most glazes are transparent, and the clay body shows through the glaze. However, some glazes are opaque and hide the color of the clay.

Overglaze. Decorations applied after glazing, over the glassy coating itself, are **overglaze decorations**. These decorations may rub off in time and are not as durable as underglaze decorations. All overglaze decorations must be given firings in decorating kilns to make them last longer. Each added firing raises the cost of the decoration. Because the temperature of these kilns is much lower than the heat of the glost oven, the colors retain their beauty. Gold and platinum are always applied overglaze. Delicate tints and shades may also be achieved through overglaze decoration.

Applying Designs to Ceramic Ware

Engraved lines may be scratched into the clay. **Holes** may be carved into the clay and later filled in with glaze or left open to make a pattern that has a lacy appearance. **Raised decorations** may be painted onto the clay with slip. The clay may be formed in a mold having a carved-out design that will make a raised pattern on the dish, or small molded pieces may be applied on the clay in cameo fashion. Such decoration is called **bas relief**, which means a low, raised design.

Colored designs may be made by using vari-colored clays, by coloring the glaze, or by putting colored designs on the bisque or over the glaze. They may be applied by several different methods. **Hand painting** is the oldest and one of the most expensive methods. Colors are applied by hand, or designs are touched up by hand. Lines or bands around the edges of dishes are all hand applied. **Raised enamel** may also be hand applied.

Decalcomania is a colorful transfer design that is used to imitate hand painting. The design is first printed on thin tissue paper. A sticky varnishlike material is applied to the dish, and then the tissue is pressed against the dish. After the tissue is rubbed carefully, the design adheres to the sticky substance. The tissue is then washed off, and the design that remains is fired onto the dish. This process lacks the quality of handwork but makes possible elaborately colored designs at low cost.

Transfer printing involves more handwork and so is a more expensive method of decorating ware. The design is carefully engraved onto a copper plate and then filled with the desired color and transferred to a strong piece of tissue paper. The tissue is carefully applied to the dish and rubbed until the entire design has been transferred. The tissue is then removed, and the design is fired onto the dish. Only one color may be put on at a time by this method. If more than one color is desired, each added color is usually applied by hand; the design is then called a **hand-filled print**.

Stamping is an inexpensive imitation of the transfer-print design. A pattern is cut into a rubber stamp. The stamp is then dipped into the desired color and pressed against the dish. All of these decorations must be fired for permanency.

Decorating Plastic Ware

Plastic dishes may be white or colored. For the latter special colors must be added before the dishes are shaped. Some dishes are made with a white layer inside and a colored layer outside by fusing two layers of plastic during the forming of the dish. The addition of the colored layer increases the cost of manufacturing the dishes.

In 1955 the first decorative patterns became available in plastic dishes. These are applied by means of a **foil**, a sheet of melamine with the design imprinted on it. The foil is placed in the mold, and the entire dish is fused in one operation. Thus the decoration is a permanent part of the product itself and can never be washed off or rubbed away.

GRADING OF CERAMIC WARES

In addition to the methods of manufacture, qualities of ingredients, and application of decoration, the manufacturer's standards of perfection affect the price of the products being sold. A few manufacturers who have reputations for quality merchandise have inspectors examine every finished piece. If it does not meet with the firm's standard of quality, the dish or ornament is broken to ensure that it will not be sold. This practice, of course, raises the price of the dishes that are sold. Such rigid inspection results in dishes known as **selects**. These are found only in fine-quality lines.

Other manufacturers, in order to supply the demand for less costly dishes, adopt a less critical standard. Some place designs over the dark spots or dents on the dishes to mask these imperfections. The following methods of grading are used by most manufacturers.

Run of the Kiln: Ware with no defects or with minor, not readily noticeable defects.
Second Grade: Ware with noticeable minor defects that do not affect the usefulness of the article.
Culls or Lumps: Ware with defects such as warps, chips, design errors, or cracks that may affect the article's usefulness.

Table 25-2 COMMON TYPES OF DISHES

Plates[a]	Bowls	Cups and Saucers	Serving Pieces
5 inch bread and butter	Egg cups: hour-glass-shaped double-bowled small cup	Demitasse cup and saucer: tiny, deep cup with handle	Platters or trays: large oval or round flat servers for meats
6 inch dessert	Fruit dishes: small, shallow bowl to be used at side of plate	Teacup and saucer: dainty, wide-bowled cup with handle	Vegetable dishes: round or oval deep bowls with handles or rims
8 inch tea or salad	Bouillon soup: two-handled cup	Coffee cup and saucer: larger-bowled and deeper cup	Gravy boats: oblong, lipped bowls with or without tray
9 inch luncheon	Cream soup: flatter round with or without handle	Chinese teacup: small bowl to fit in hand; no handle	Casseroles: covered serving dishes
10 inch dinner	Onion soup: cream soup with cover	Chinese teacup with cover: deep, coffee-size cup with matching lid	Covered butter dish: oblong small tray to hold a 1/4-pound butter slab
11 inch service	Eared soup: small round bowl with flat rim extensions that serve as handles		Pitcher: various-sized, deep bowl with lip and handle; serving container for liquids
	Coupe soup: large, shallow, no rim		Coffee pot: tall pot with spout that extends from the base to the upper part, with handle
	Rimmed soup: large shallow with rim		Teapot: squat pot for brewing and serving tea
	Individual casserole or ramekin: small, cream-soup size dish with cover and side-grip handle		

[a]Approximate overall sizes

CLASSIFICATION OF DISHES

Dishes may be classified by a number of different means, such as shape, size, or type.

Basic Shapes of Plates

There are only two basic shapes for plates and other flat dishes: coupe and rim. A **coupe dish** has no lip or flat edge by which it may be held while serving. Almost half of the dishes sold today are in the coupe shape. A **rim dish** has a convenient edge, which may be held while serving. The edge also provides an attractive place for decoration that will not be hidden by food.

Types of Dishes

Many varieties of dishes exist. However, for most food service, dishes may be divided into plates, bowls, cups and saucers, and serving pieces. Table 25-2 gives the most common types.

PLATES

Figure 25-3. *Plates that would be found in a complete set of dinnerware.*

Serving Pieces (cont.)

Relish dish: flat, elongated, narrow serving dish for celery, pickles, olive, and relish

Salad bowl: large, deep bowl to hold salads, fruits, or vegetables

Salt and pepper shakers: small for individual service or large for center of the table service

Sugar and creamer: sugar has cover and may have two small handles; creamer has side handle and lip; may or may not fit on matching tray

Tureen: large serving bowl for soups, stews, or other liquids; has two side handles and cover

Sizes of Dishes

The two methods of measuring flat dinnerware — plates, platters, and saucers — are overall and well to edge. **Overall measurement** is the easiest and most convenient to take. A ruler is used to measure the diameter of the dish from one edge to the other edge. This is the type of measurement a person should use in reordering dishes to match a set. **Well-to-edge measurement** is the method adopted from English manufacturers and is also known as **trade measurement.** A ruler is used to measure the dish from the inside rim across the dish to the outside of the rim. Price lists of most older firms usually carry this type of measurement.

How Dishes Are Sold

Dishes can be purchased in different combinations: sets, open stock, and place settings.

Sets. Today most people make their original purchase of dishes in **sets.** This is particularly desirable when the whole set can be purchased more inexpensively than if the items in the set were purchased individually. Sets may vary in size according to the number of persons to be served and the number of dishes desired for each serving. Sets for four, six, eight, and twelve persons are usual. In counting the number of pieces in a set, each separate part is counted. For exam-

SERVING PIECES, CUPS, AND BOWLS

RELISH DISH

CASSEROLE (SERVING)

SERVING TRAY OR PLATTER

TUREEN WITH SERVING LADLE

SALT AND PEPPER

COVERED VEGETABLE SERVING BOWL

BUTTER DISH

EARED SOUP BOWL

CREAM SOUP BOWL

GRAVY BOAT AND TRAY

SALAD BOWL

BOULLION SOUP BOWL

RIMMED SOUP BOWL

FRUIT DISH

TEAPOT

PITCHER

COFFEE POT

INDIVIDUAL CASSEROLE OR RAMEKIN

TEACUP AND SAUCER

CREAM AND SUGAR SET

COFFEE CUP AND SAUCER

EGG CUP

CHINESE TEA CUP WITH LID

CHINESE TEACUP

DEMITASSE CUP AND SAUCER

Figure 25-4. *These pieces would be found in a complete set of dinnerware.*

Table 25-3 SETS OF DISHES

	Twenty-Piece Service for Four	Forty-Piece Service for Eight	Forty-five-Piece Service for Eight
Dinner or luncheon plates	4	8	8
Cups	4	8	8
Saucers	4	8	8
Soup or cereal bowls	4	8	8
Salad plates	4	8	8
Other pieces	None	None	I covered sugar (two pieces); I creamer; I vegetable bowl; I serving platter

The 65-piece service for 12 has the same composition as the 45-piece service for 8 with 12 of each of the basic items.

ple, a gravy boat with a separate tray counts as *two* pieces but one with an attached tray (called a **fast boat**) counts as only *one* piece. The most common size sets are 20-piece (pc.) service for 4, 40-piece service for 8, 45-piece service for 8, and 65-piece service for 12. See Table 25-3.

Open Stock. If dishes are **open stock**, it is possible to purchase additional pieces to match the set. When people purchase their sets and the set is expensive or if they intend to use it for a number of years, they should make sure that individual matching dishes can be purchased in case of breakage or to enlarge the set. A dish is in open stock only as long as the manufacturer continues to make the pattern.

Place Settings. The usual way to purchase expensive chinaware is by the **place setting**. Each place setting is a complete service for one person (usually consisting of five pieces: one dinner plate, one tea or salad plate, one bread-and-butter plate, one cup, and one saucer). Some place settings have a sixth piece, a soup dish. Three-piece settings are also sold. They consist of a dinner plate, cup, and saucer. Serving dishes and additional pieces are selected from open stock as needed.

CARE OF CERAMIC AND PLASTIC DISHES

It is advisable to handle ceramic dishes carefully when washing or stacking them to avoid cracking

or chipping. Mild soapsuds and a soft dishcloth should be used; steel wool and gritty cleaners will scratch the glazed surface. Avoid drastic temperature changes that may cause the ware to crack. Dishes to be placed in the refrigerator or in very hot water should be precooled or preheated, respectively, in running water. Unless they are labeled as oven safe, dishes should not be used in the oven for heating or baking. Overglaze coloring on handles of cups will rub off if the cups are stacked one inside the other. It is advisable to hang cups by handles on hooks or to provide ample space for each cup to stand separately.

Ease in care is one of the important selling points for the plastic dishes. They are resistant to breakage but may crack or chip if they fall repeatedly on a hard surface. Melamine dishes resist extremes of temperature and can be used in the refrigerator or can be subjected to boiling water without harm. However, high heat from an oven or direct heat, such as that caused by crushing a lighted cigarette on a plate, can damage the plastic. Coffee and tea may stain plastic cups. These stains may be removed by soaking the cups in baking soda and water or by using regular commercial cleaners sold for this purpose. Gritty cleaners should never be used on plastics because they may scratch the surface. Because melamine is about 60 percent lighter in weight than other dishes, it is easy to stack and handle. The design on melamine ware cannot be worn away in use because it is part of the plastic itself.

DO YOU KNOW YOUR MERCHANDISE?

1. What are the differences between vitrified and nonvitrified wares? Classify the following as vitrified or nonvitrified wares: ironstone, stoneware, chinaware, casual earthenware, bone china, and fine earthenware.
2. What is meant by chinaware? Where did the name originate? What is meant by bone china? What country is most famous for its manufacture?
3. What are the main advantages of plastic dishes over ceramic dishes?
4. Name two ways of shaping clay objects. Explain each briefly.
5. How large is the clay object before it is fired in comparison to its size after firing?
6. Explain in-the-glaze, underglaze, and overglaze decorations.
7. Explain hand painting, decalcomania, transfer printing, and stamping.
8. Why is the decoration on plastic dishes permanent?
9. Explain the following terms: coupé dish, rim dish, overall measurement, and well-to-edge measurement.
10. Explain the following terms: sets, open stock, and place setting.

PUTTING YOUR MERCHANDISE KNOWLEDGE TO WORK

You have been asked to prepare a short explanation for new salespeople on the means of distinguishing chinaware from stoneware and how those products differ from ironstone and earthenware. Prepare to explain these differences to your classmates.

PROJECT

Visit a chinaware department or store. Analyze the displays of stock. What proportion of the stock was devoted to the display of vitrified products? What proportion was devoted to nonvitrified products? How many different patterns were shown for each grouping? Were dishes shown in sets, as open stock, or as place settings? What price ranges did you see in vitrified wares? In nonvitrified wares? Within one manufacturer's line of vitrified wares, what was the range of prices? How do you account for those price differences? Write a short report about your visit.

26

Glassware:
The Remarkable Material

Glass is a truly versatile material, and from ancient to modern times it has served people in many ways. Glass can be transparent, translucent, or opaque; it can be colorless, delicately tinted, or vibrant with color; its surface can be plain, textured, etched, or cut. Glass may shatter easily or may be highly break resistant; it may be affected by heat or may be extremely heat resistant.

GLASSMAKING

Like earthenware, glass is made from common substances found in the earth. Instead of clay, however, the basic ingredient in glass is sand. **Silica sand** is the most common mineral in the earth. The sand and other chemicals are melted in a furnace, forming **molten metal,** as the glassmakers call it, which is then shaped and cooled. When cooling is completed, the opaque sand has been transformed into transparent glass. **Glass,** then, is a molten substance shaped and cooled until it is a hard, nonporous, usually transparent material. All glass articles are vitrified and are therefore sanitary.

Formulas for Glassmaking

Thousands of different formulas exist for making glass; but for the glassware found in stores, four basic formulas are commonly used. These formulas reflect the ingredients used in the glassmaking.

Soda-Lime Glass. Because it is the least expensive and yet is durable and serviceable, **soda-lime glass** is the most widely used glass today. It was developed over 5,000 years ago. Common bottles, window panes, mirrors, inexpensive drinking glasses, glass jars, and glass dishes are usually made of soda-lime glass. Hold a bottle or an inexpensive drinking glass by the base and tap with a pencil. Notice that the glass has a rather dull tinkling sound when struck.

This glass has little luster or sparkle in comparison to more costly glasses. Because its surface is hard and brittle, soda-lime glass does not adapt well to hand-cut decorations. However, it takes designs that are pressed into its surface with sharp definition. This glass is not heat resistant, so pouring hot liquid into a cold glass is likely to cause it to break. It is fairly resistant to ordinary scratches, but will break if dropped on a hard surface.

Lead Glass. Initially called **flint glass** when it was developed in the 17th century, **lead glass** has a softer surface than lime glass, which permits it to be cut readily. It also refracts light with a brilliant display of colors. Thick cut glass became a collector's item during the eighteenth century.

Lead oxide is present in lead glass, which makes it heavy in comparison to lime glass. It also has a bell-like tone when struck lightly. Because its surface is soft, lead glass scratches easily. Because lead glass is made of costly ingredients

343

and is often hand formed, it is an expensive glass. The finest glasses have at least 24 percent lead oxide and are called **full lead glass.** They are used for fine tablewares, ornaments, optical lenses, and simulated sparkling gemstones.

Borosilicate Glass. The formula for this **heat-resistant glass** was created in 1910 in response to a demand for glass that would not expand and contract so greatly when exposed to heat or cold. The chemists found that the addition of boric oxide to the soda-lime formula would make the glass resistant to breakage when heat was applied to a cold glass. Borosilicate glass may be used in an oven or refrigerator with safety. This glass has the advantage of holding the heat longer than metal containers, of enabling you to watch foods cook, and of being easy to clean. This glass has little luster and a rather dull sound when struck. It usually has a slightly cloudy transparency.

Glass-Ceramic. Developed in the early 1950s as a material that could withstand the heat of reentry by space vehicles into the earth's atmosphere, this material has become a well-known heat-resistant product for both cooking and serving food in the home. Ceramic glass is white, extremely heat resistant, and breakage resistant. Some fine restaurants use dishes made from a special formulation of this glass in place of fine china. It has the translucence of china, a pure white body, and is highly break resistant.

Ingredients Used for Glassmaking

Sand (silica) is the main ingredient in all glass products. The finer the quality of the sand, the more nearly colorless the finished product will be. Impure sands produce less-desirable, green-tinted glass articles.

To the sand, which is about 50 to 75 percent of the formula, is added an alkali (soda or potash), which will aid the sand in melting. The third ingredient, lead oxide, lime, or boric oxide, adds the qualities of brilliance or luster, hardness or softness, and resistance to temperature

changes. Many other chemicals may be used to get further variations of color, clearness, heat resistance, and hardness. For coloring glass, mineral substances are added, such as chromium for green, cobalt for blue, copper or gold for ruby, and sulfur or selenium for yellow.

Table 26–1 summarizes the basic chemicals used and the characteristics of these various glass products; it also gives some familiar manufacturer or trade names.

Preparing and Firing the Ingredients

After being carefully cleansed of all impurities and sieved, the raw ingredients (including the coloring substances) are mixed together. This mixture is known as the **batch.** To the batch is added broken glass scrap called **cullet,** which aids in melting the batch.

The batch and cullet are put into a tank furnace where they are transformed into the molten, transparent fluid. The heat of the furnace necessary to melt the chemicals is about 2,700°F (1,482°C), a higher heat than most metals can withstand. After one day of boiling and bubbling, the mixture, now called the **metal,** is cooled slightly until it is a bright, yellow-red, thick liquid having the consistency of hot taffy.

Although many of the ingredients used in making glass are inexpensive, the firing requires a great deal of energy and is very costly. Manufacturers constantly experiment to reduce the amount of fuel needed to keep glass molten.

Shaping the Glass

After the ingredients for the glass have been prepared and melted the resulting metal is now ready to be shaped into the desired finished form. Glass (other than flat glass, which is discussed later in Chapter 29) can be shaped by free (or mouth) blowing, mold blowing, and pressing. The finished glass is identified according to the method by which it was shaped.

Free-Blown Glass. To make a glass object originally, strips of glass were wound around clay cores, and after the glass had cooled, the clay

Table 26-1 TYPES OF GLASSWARE

Factors	Soda-Lime Glass	Lead Glass	Heat-Resistant Glass	Glass-Ceramic
Main ingredients	Sand, soda, lime	Sand, soda, potash, lead oxide	Sand, soda, boric oxide	Sand, titanium dioxide, alumina, lithia, magnesia
Cost	Inexpensive	Moderate to very costly	Moderate	Moderate to costly
Luster	Soft	Brilliant, sparkling	Soft	Shiny but translucent
Tone	Pinglike	Bell-like	Pinglike	Sustained almost bell-like tone
Reaction to scratching	Resistant	Easily scratched	Resistant	Very resistant
Break resistance	Brittle, breaks quite easily	Less brittle, but thin sections break quite easily	Strong, but does break	Very strong, highly break-resistant
Takes mold design	Reproduces sharply with well-defined lines	Generally less-definitive design	Takes mold design fairly sharply	Reproduces mold marks fairly well
Ease of cutting	Difficult to cut	Takes cutting well	Difficult to cut	Very difficult to cut
Resistance to temperature changes	May break	May break	Resistant	Very resistant (can resist instantaneous drop of over 1,000°F)
Ease of cleaning	Very	Very	Very	May stain from coffee/tea; clean with solution of chlorine bleach
Common uses	Bottles, jars, windows, mirrors, plate glass, moderate priced and pressed-glass tablewares	Costly tablewares, cut glass, optical lenses, imitation jewelry stones objets d'art	Measuring cups, baby bottles, transparent bake-ware, coffee makers, signal light lenses	Opaque bakeware, white china-look dinnerware, industrial uses
Well-known manufacturer or trade names	Anchor-Hocking, Libbey, Fostoria	Baccarat, Cesca Art Glass, Kosta Boda, Lalique, Lenox Crystal, Orrefors, Steuben, Tiffin, Waterford, Val St. Lambert	Corelle,[a] Fire King, Glassbake, Pyrex	Corning Ware Cookware, Pyroceram

[a]Corelle is a special glass made to look like china. It has some of the characteristics of borosilicate ware but in other ways performs like the Pyroceram brand products.

Figure 26-1. In mold blowing, a widely used method of shaping glass, a bubble of air is blown into the viscous glass, which is later cut on a sandstone wheel.

centers were dug out. About 250 B.C. a glass-maker discovered quite accidentally that glass could be shaped by **free blowing.** This highly skilled method of shaping glass, still in use today, has changed little since its early beginning.

The glassmaker gathers a quantity of the molten glass on the end of a long metal tube, known as a **blowpipe,** through which he or she blows to expand and shape the glass. By carefully turning the blowpipe, the blower can shape the glass in any desired way. The glassblower may also use tools or a dip mold to press against the outside of the glass bubble to make a variety of forms. Any marks so impressed against the glass remain throughout any additional shaping processes.

As the glass cools, it hardens, so it is necessary to soften it again by placing it back in a small furnace, known as a **glory hole.** As soon as the glass is softened, the blower can continue shaping it. In its viscous (semiliquid) state, a mass of glass, such as a handle, can be joined permanently to the body of the article. The top of the glass article adhering to the blowpipe may then be cut off and the rim shaped and smoothed by reheating in the glory hole or by subsequent grinding and polishing. Free-blown glass is ex-

pensive, so this method is rarely used except to produce good-quality glassware.

Mold-Blown Glass. A less expensive and more widely used method of shaping glass is known as **mold blowing.** In this process the glass is gathered on the blowpipe, and a bubble of air is blown into the viscous glass. The glass is then inserted into a cast-iron mold. Blowing through the blowpipe forces the glass to expand and fill the sections of the mold. As the hot glass touches the mold, it is chilled and the outer form is shaped. The air bubble shapes the inside of the glass. The bottle is the best example of this type of craftsmansip.

The iron mold in which the glass is shaped may have designs cut into it that are reproduced as raised designs or indentations on the bottle or article being formed. Such decorative molds may fashion wares that resemble cut glass. Soda-lime glass is particularly adaptable to mold blowing.

Pressed Glass. A method of shaping glass by pushing it into molds is known as **pressing.** Hot glass will not flow readily into all the crevices of the mold. If not blown in, it must be forced into the crevices and corners by a metal plunger. At the same time, this plunger shapes and makes the inner surface smooth. The outside of the glass may have an ornamental design imprinted on its surface. Pressed glass has blunt, rounded edges, and the designs on it are often symmetrical. Heat-resistant and soda-lime glass are often made in this manner. Plates, fruit dishes, and other large, rather flat articles are shaped by pressing.

Making Glass Durable

There are two methods of making glass durable — by heat treatment and by controlled cooling. Although glass is melted at very high temperatures, glass that is given additional **heat treatment** becomes far more durable. For example, using 3,000°F temperatures to melt a smooth rim on the glass results in a bead of glass around the edge that is much tougher and more resistant to breakage than the rest of the glass. Safedge is a trade name for such an edge.

For **controlled cooling,** glass is heated and then moved through an **annealing oven,** in which the temperature is slowly reduced. The outer and inner layers of the glass are cooled simultaneously, which yields glass that is particularly durable.

Figure 26-2. *Mold-blown glass may have raised or indented designs.*

Glassware is tested for durability before it leaves the factory to make certain that it will provide satisfactory service. Each piece of glass is examined under a strong light for imperfections that will mar its beauty or affect its wearing ability. A special testing device known as a **polariscope** shows whether any stresses are present that might later cause the glass to break. Glass is also given a thermal test in which it is plunged alternately into hot and cold water or is removed from a hot oven and placed in cold water. If it withstands this test, the consumer can depend on the glassware to give good service.

DECORATING GLASSWARE

Beauty in glassware may come from the basic shape or form, the clarity or sparkle, the intensity or delicate glow of the color, or the surface additions to the glass.

Colorless Surface Designs

Glassware may be decorated in many ways without the use of color. In fact, colorless glass is such an important item that it has a special name — crystal. This name comes from the Greek word for ice. Made initially by Venetians, it was called *Cristallo*, and was the envy of other glassmakers. The name "crystal" implies no quality characteristic in the glass except that it is colorless. The methods of decorating crystal glass involve the addition of surface designs to the glassware surface, which vary greatly in method and expense. A knowledge of them will aid the customer in making appropriate selections.

Embossing. While the glass is still in its viscous state, designs may be pressed with molds onto its surface, known as embossing. Such designs may resemble cut patterns or may have a cameolike appearance. This is an inexpensive method of decorating glass.

Cutting. Small sandstone wheels are used for **cutting.** The glass with the design sketched on it is pressed against the revolving wheel. By applying just the right amount of pressure, various designs can be cut into the glass. Wheels of different sizes and shapes are used for the different parts in the design. The abrasive wheel leaves a grayed surface on the glass as it cuts the design. Inexpensive soda-lime glass may be cut by machine.

Some designs for decorative contrast are left **in the gray** (are not polished). However, if the design is to be clear and to sparkle, the glass must be polished after it is cut. **Polishing** may be accomplished by buffing with felt wheels or by dipping in acid. The buffing method is slow and costly but imparts a rich gleam to the glass. Glassware so polished is sold as **hand-polished glass.** The acid method is speedy and less expensive but does not make the glass quite as brilliant as hand polishing.

Copper-Wheel Engraving. On very select glassware pieces the designs or monograms may be engraved on the glass. Delicate-looking, intricate forms are made by holding the glass against small revolving copper disks that are covered with a wet abrasive mixture. The sections of the design that are hollowed out vary in depth, which

creates interesting effects on the outside of the glass. The design is left in the gray for contrast with the transparency of the rest of the glass.

Etching. A popular method of applying designs to glass is by means of hydrofluoric acid. This acid, which is the only acid that affects glass, decomposes the glass wherever it touches it, leaving an indented, grayed surface; this is known as **etching.** Entire sides of glass may be given a frosted appearance by dipping them in the acid for a few moments, or designs may be achieved by exposing only parts of the glass to the acid. Wax, which resists the acid, is applied to the glass. The glass is submerged in the acid for the requisite amount of time, and any spaces not covered by the wax will be attacked by the acid. The wax and acid are then washed off thoroughly. The glass emerges with a grayed, etched-out design.

Sandblasting. Sand, blown forcibly against glass by means of compressed air, will pit the surface of the glass and leave a frosted appearance. This process is called **sandblasting.** If a design or monogram is desired, a metal or rubber

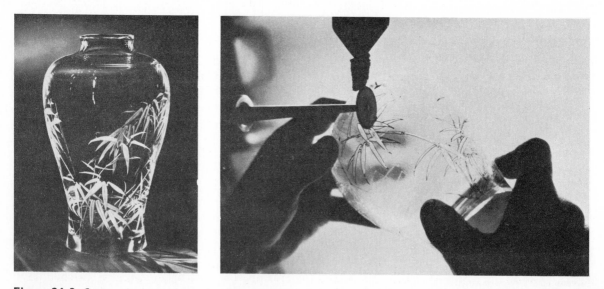

Figure 26-3. *Copper-wheel engraving makes delicate, intricate designs on select glassware.*

stencil, which protects the glass from the sand-blast except for the stencil's cutout sections, is used. Sandblasting leaves a rougher surface than etching does. When the design is deeply cut by sandblasting, the glass is known as **carved glass.**

Coloring Glassware

Cloudy or off-color glassware is the result of iron impurities that are present in the sand. Chemists have learned how to neutralize the tints caused by the impurities in the glass so even the least-expensive glassware may be crystal clear. Color-less glassware should have no color; slight green or pink tints indicate inferior ingredients or im-proper mixing.

If colored glass is desired, various minerals are added to the ingredients. Because the color is an integral part of the glass, it never wears off. Pop-ular colors are ruby red, cobalt blue, bottle green, and milky white. For special effects a layer of colored glass may be superimposed over a layer of crystal glass. Cutting through the colored layer reveals the crystal below. This fine-quality deco-rative glassware is called **cased glass.**

Colored Designs

Mineral colors in the form of various colors of enamel, gold, silver, and platinum may be ap-plied to the surface of the glass either by hand (costly) or by stencil (inexpensive). After the color has been applied, the design is fired on for permanency. Platinum and gold lines may be painted on as they are in ceramic ware and then fired and polished for permanence and brilliance. Applying gold over an etched surface is known as **encrusting;** the gold is then fired and polished.

Silver is applied to glassware by a process called **electroplating.** Glass so decorated is known as **silver deposit ware.** To make silver adhere to glass, the desired design must first be painted or stenciled on the glass with a metallic solution. After this solution has been fired onto the glass, it becomes white in color. The glass is then suspended in the electroplating bath, and the silver is deposited on the metal design. Silver

so deposited does not have to be fired. It will not rub off or wear off easily. To make it nontarnish-able, the silver may be coated with another metal, such as rhodium. Since it is costly, it is used in very thin applications, which may even-tually wear away, allowing the silver to tarnish.

CLASSIFICATIONS OF GLASSWARE

Glassware items in gift shops and stores are usually divided into groupings by manufacturer or country. These groupings are subdivided into stemware, tumblers, barware sets, and acces-sories. Other items such as ovenware and cook-ware are sold in housewares stores and departments.

Stemware

Stemware refers to drinking glasses that have a bowl, stem, and foot. These glasses are used for formal and semiformal dining occasions. The stem on the glass permits holding without warm-ing the contents by touching the bowl of the glass. Popular stemware items include the following.

Beer Goblet: Glass with wide-mouthed opening. May or may not have hollow stem. Holds 6 to 12 ounces.

Brandy Glass: Small, narrow-bowled glass for serv-ing brandy. Holds 2 ounces.

Brandy Snifter or Inhaler: Rounded bowl with nar-row opening designed to enhance the aroma of the brandy. Holds 5 to 25 ounces.

Champagne Glass: Shallow wide bowl on medium-high stem or long, hollow stem. Holds 5 to 7 ounces. Also called a **saucer champagne.** Purists reject this shape because its wide bowl permits the champagne bubbles to dissipate too quickly. Instead, connoisseurs serve champagne in a **flute,** also called a *tulip cham-pagne,* a stemmed glass with an elongated, narrow-mouth bowl.

Claret Glass: Small version of the water goblet. Has a 4 to 5 ounce capacity.

Cocktail Glass: Wide-opening glass with a deeper bowl than the champagne glass. Holds $3\frac{1}{2}$ to $4\frac{1}{2}$ ounces.

STEMMED GLASSES

Figure 26-4. *Stemware refers to drinking glasses that have a bowl, stem, and foot. Footed tumblers have bowl and foot but no stem.*

Cordial: A narrow-bowled, deep, small glass. Sometimes called a **pony.** Holds 1 or 2 ounces.

Dessert Glass: Low-stemmed, wide-bowled glass used for serving champagne. May also be used for ice cream, sherberts, or puddings. Usually holds $3\frac{1}{2}$ to 6 ounces.

Fruit Cocktail: Double-bowled glass with small bowl that fits inside larger bowl and rests on a bed of crushed ice.

Hock Wineglass: Tall-stemmed glass with narrow, elongated bowl, and usually a green stem. Used for serving white wines. Holds 5 ounces.

Hollow-stem Champagne: Wide-bowled glass with elongated hollow stem that permits bubbles to rise from base when filled with sparkling wine. Holds 5 to 6 ounces.

Liqueur Glass: Small glass for serving after-dinner liqueurs. Has $\frac{3}{4}$- to 1-ounce capacity.

On-the-Rocks Glass: Wide, deep-bowled glass with a short stem for iced cocktails. Holds 5 to 7 ounces.

Parfait Glass: Tall-bowled, narrow glass on a short stem for serving iced desserts.

Pilsner Glass: Tall-bowled glass with tapered shape on short stem. Used for serving beer. Holds 10 or more ounces.

Port Wine Glass: Round-bowled glass on medium-high stem. Holds 3 ounces.

Sherry Glass: Glass tapers from wide opening to stem. Holds 2 to 3 ounces.

Shrimp Cocktail Glass or Coupette: Broad, flat flange around a narrow, shallow bowl. Shrimp are laid on rim of glass and small glass tumbler holds sauce in bed of ice.

Water Goblet: Large bowl on medium stem. Holds 9 to $10\frac{1}{2}$ ounces.

Wine Glass: Medium-size bowl on tall stem. Holds 4 to 6 ounces.

Footed Tumblers

Footed tumblers have a bowl and foot but no stem. They are used for less-formal service. There are cocktail glasses, water goblets, and pilsners in this grouping. These glasses developed from cone-shaped ones that had no base and could not be laid down until the contents had been emptied.

Tumblers

Glasses with a flat base and no stem or foot are known as **tumblers**. They are less costly to make than the ones with separate bases and stems and are used for informal and casual service. Tumblers are the most common types of glassware sold. Popular types include the following.

Beer Mug or Tankard: Large tumbler with substantial side handle. Holds 10 or more ounces.
Cocktail Glass: Short, broad-opening glass. May also be used for serving fruit juices. Holds 4 ounces.
Collins: Tall, straight-sided glass. May or may not be frosted. Holds 10 to 10½ ounces.
Cooler: Taller than the collins. Used for iced drinks. Holds 15 to 16 ounces.

Gin Fizz or Seltzer: Short, straight-sided tumbler. Holds 6 ounces.
Highball: Tall, straight-sided tumbler. Holds 12 ounces.
Juice Glass: Small, narrow glass for fruit juices. Holds 5 to 6 ounces.
Old Fashioned: Broad, short tumbler with straight sides and usually a thick bottom (known as a **sham**). Holds 7 or 8 ounces. **Double old fashioned** is a wider, taller glass with a 15 ounce capacity.
Pilsner: Tall glass, usually with a slightly bulging top. Holds 8 to 12 ounces.
Pony: Small measuring glass for serving whiskey. Also called a **shot glass**. Usually comes in 1-, 1½-, or 2-ounce sizes. The larger glass may have markings to indicate the number of ounces being served.
Punch Cup: Small, teacup-size glass cup with side handle for serving punch. Holds about 5½ ounces.
Water Glass: Straight-sided medium-height glass for water service. Holds 8 to 10 ounces.

Barware and Other Glassware Sets

Some items of glassware sold in matching sets include the following.

TUMBLERS

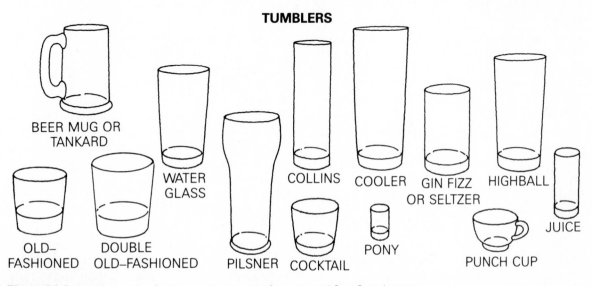

Figure 26-5. *Tumblers, with a flat base and no stem or foot, are used for informal service.*

Caster or Cruet: Oil and vinegar bottle set, usually on a tray.
Iced Tea Set: Large pitcher and matching tall tumblers. Also called a **beverage set.**
Martini Set: Tall, slender pitcher with stirrer and two to six small glasses.
Punch Set: Large, round serving bowl with six to twelve matching side-handled punch cups.
Tantalus Set: Two or three handsome liquor bottles held in a metal frame.

Accessories

Glass making lends itself to unlimited shapes and forms. Decoration may further enhance the glassware. Glass is made into many items including ashtrays, vases, cake stands, candelabra, figurines, hurricane lamps, and bottles of all types. Glass is also made into beads and pendants.

BUYING AND SELLING GLASSWARE

Glassware is sold in sets and in open stock. Some firms make complete glassware lines in matching patterns. Such lines can usually be purchased in small quantities and filled in from time to time from open stock as long as the manufacturer makes that pattern. Few people purchase entire matching sets of glass at one time. It is wise, therefore, to point out to customers the advantage of being able to fill in the glassware at a later date with other matching items.

Manufacturers have found a ready market for prepackaged glassware. Tumblers in water-glass, juice-glass, and highball sizes have been attractively packed in sets of four, six, and eight. This saves packing time and eliminates extra handing of the glasses, which might result in breakage. The cartons are attractive enough for gift wrapping.

To aid the customer in understanding and appreciating the quality of glassware the salesperson should ask the customer to feel the smooth edge, a sign of good workmansip. Hold the glass to the

light and note the brilliant luster of the lead glass or the softer glow of the soda-lime glass. In examining lead glass, tap the edge of the glass carefully with a pencil and listen to the tone. For contrast, do the same test on a soda-lime glass. When purchasing crystal glassware, note the lack of color or lack of cloudy or green tints, which means that the purest ingredients and finext mixing techniques have been used in that glass. If the glassware is colored, note the brilliance of the color.

If the glass is hand cut, hold it up so that the light is reflected by the cutting. If the glass is plate etched, examine its beauty and handwork. If the manufacturer's name is on the glass, you should be aware of the quality standards that are represented by such trademarks.

CARE OF GLASSWARE

In addition to calling attention to the beauty and durability of an article, the glassware salesperson should advise the customer on the best methods of caring for glassware.

Much of the inherent beauty of glassware depends on its sparkle. The plainest glass thoroughly cleaned and polished will reflect light attractively. Fine glassware should be washed by hand rather than in a dishwasher. Because diamonds can scratch the surface of glass, a diamond ring should not be worn while washing glassware. Mild soapsuds or commercial detergents remove grease and other dirt. For cut glass a small brush is necessary to clean all the grooves thoroughly. The glasses should then be rinsed in warm water and protected when placed on the drainboard by the use of a pad or folded towel. Wiping the glasses with a good-quality linen towel that does not shed lint will give sparkle to the items. Rubbing the glass with tissue paper will impart added sparkle.

Glasses should not be stacked one inside the other, for there is a danger of breakage. They should stand upright on the shelves. Extremes of temperature should be avoided in using glassware. If glass cups are used for serving tea or coffee, pouring the hot liquid onto a silver spoon placed inside the cup lessens the danger of breakage.

DO YOU KNOW YOUR MERCHANDISE?

1. What is glass? How old is glass manufacture? What are some of the unique features of glass?
2. Name four basic formulas for making glass and explain the characteristics of each of the glasses.
3. What ingredients are used in the making of glass? Explain how the use of different ingredients affects the finished glass.
4. Explain how the ingredients are transformed into glass.
5. What processes are used to make glass durable?
6. What is the difference between stemware and tumblers and between tumblers and footed tumblers? If a customer wanted glassware for a formal occasion, what would you suggest? Which glassware is appropriate for semiformal service and which is appropriate for informal service?
7. What are the advantages of prepackaging glassware?
8. What advice should a customer be given about cleaning, wiping, and stacking glassware and about extremes of temperature for glassware?
9. When selling glassware for table use, what are some features the salesperson should point out to the customer?
10. Explain the differences between a beer mug or tankard and a pilsner glass; a water tumbler and a cooler; a champagne glass and a hock wineglass; a parfait glass and a shrimp cocktail glass.

PUTTING YOUR MERCHANDISE KNOWLEDGE TO WORK

Prepare a sales talk on the different types of glassware sold as tableware and kitchenware. Bring samples of different kinds of glass to class for your demonstration.

PROJECT

Analyze the stock of merchandise in a store that sells glassware. How many different glassware items did you see on display? How many different sizes and shapes of each item were shown? Were the glasses sold in open stock? Was any glassware sold in prepackaged boxes? What was the price of lowest-priced box set? What were the items? How many did the box contain? What was the highest-priced boxed set? What items did it contain? How many were in the box? What were the reasons for the price differences in these two boxed sets? Make a report to the class on your findings.

27

Silver and Other Metal Flatware and Holloware

Metals are used for tablewares as flatware, holloware, and decorative objects, or gift wares. **Flatware** refers to knives, forks, spoons, and other small implements used for serving and eating food. **Holloware** made from metals (in contrast to china and glassware) refers to plates, platters, dishes, bowls, goblets, and other vessels to hold food. **Decorative objects** (or gift wares) refer to candleholders and other ornamental metal pieces used to make tables or sideboards more attractive.

FLATWARE

Flatware may be made completely of one metal or alloy, or sections that touch food may be made from one metal and handles made from another metal or other material such as wood, plastic, or bone.

Manufacture of Flatware

The manufacture of all flatware follows a basic process. Before a piece is made, however, the manufacturer must decide on the shape into which it will be formed and what design, if any, will be placed on it. Because the appearance of the flatware will affect the retail customer's desire to buy it, the manufacturer very carefully selects the shapes and designs to be used. Often consumer polls are taken to see what patterns people prefer.

The outlines of the flatware shapes and any designs to be impressed on the handles must first be cut into very hard steel dies. These dies are then forced against the metal being shaped with such pressure that they cut it to the desired shape. Other dies impress the designs in a similar fashion.

Good-quality forks and spoons are made by first cutting T-shape chunks, called **blanks,** with huge steel dies, much as cookies are stamped with a cookie cutter. These T-shape blanks are then thinned toward the handle end and across the bowl or tine end by rolling them under pressure. The T-shape blank, which is now considered to be **graded** (thick in some sections and thin in others), is cut into final form, stamped with dies that impart designs, arched for needed shaping, and trimmed to the correct size, shape, and thickness for durability and ease of handling. The tines of forks are cut to shape and in good-quality flatware are carefully finished later to make the edges smooth and round. Inexpensive forks and spoons are stamped into final shape from thin sheets of metal. All the parts of these pieces are of the same thickness. These forks and spoons bend easily under pressure and give poor service in use.

Knives may have hollow handles or flat handles. Flat-handled knives are usually less expensive; the handle and the blade are made from the same metal. Hollow handles are the most costly to make. They may be stamped in two sections and then joined together on the sides by soldering. Some hollow-handled knives are made without this soldered seam by repeatedly drawing the metal into a tubelike form, which makes a watertight handle. Knife blades, usually made from stainless steel, are then soldered into the hollow handle. Stainless steel offers a sharper, harder, more enduring cutting edge. Wooden handles are usually attached by rivets; bone and plastic handles may be attached by cement.

Quality of Flatware

Careful workmanship in flatware items may be determined by the grading, by the smooth edges of the spoons, by the polished surfaces between the tines of the forks, and by the smoothness of the joining of the two halves of knife handles (unless they are seamless handles). Knife blades for quality products are carefully shaped by being **forged** (pounded to the desired thickness). These blades have thicker sections near the handle and thinner blade sections for cutting.

Kinds of Flatware

Four basic types of flatware are made.

Sterling-Silver Flatware. Sterling-silver flatware is selected for the beauty of the article and for the weight of each piece. Different manufacturers use varying thicknesses of sterling to shape the original blanks. The heavier weights are more expensive but last much longer. The increasingly high price of silver has caused these sterling objects to be too costly for many customers who have turned to sterling substitutes. Because sterling is easily worked, elegant and elaborate designs may be used. If they require much care in hand finishing and polishing, sterling-silver pieces will cost more. Weighting with jeweler's cement is usually added to hollow-handled flatware.

Pewter, aluminum alloys, gold-colored alloy, and stainless steel flatware are formed in a similar manner except that hollow-handled knives need no weighting because the metal, being lower in cost, may be used in substantial thickness.

Figure 27-1. *Hard steel dies are pressed against metal flatware to cut outlines and designs.*

Silver-Plated Flatware. For silver-plated flatware, a nickel alloy is used for the blanks that are shaped into the finished forks, spoons, or knife handles. The nickel silver is then cleaned and polished because any oil or dust will cause the subsequent silver plating to be imperfect. The articles are then attached to a rack and placed in a silver electroplating bath until the required amount of silver has adhered to the base metal. They are then removed, polished, inspected, and wrapped. The amount of silver used on flatware determines the quality of the ware.

Some silver-plated ware is reinforced to increase its durability. Examine the backs of several teaspoons. Some better-quality silver-plated flatware has a reinforcement of silver at the points of greatest wear on the most used pieces. The reinforced parts are at the bottom of the bowl and the tip of the handle, where the article touches when it rests on the table. Because the overlay adds considerably to the durability of the silverware, it is a desirable feature to point out to the customer. Some manufacturers use a plus sign to indicate that the silver has an overlay.

Vermeil and Gold-Plated Flatware. Vermeil became popular after 1962 when Tiffany's in New York was commissioned to create replicas of old pieces for the White House. Tiffany used a heavy gold electroplate over sterling silver that reproduced the beauty of the original articles. Gold may also be plated over stainless steel, nickel silver, copper, brass, and white metal, such as Britannia metal or German silver. These, however, do not carry the name of vermeil.

Figure 27-2. *Flatware serving pieces may be sold as separate items or as part of a place setting or hostess set.*

Stainless Steel Flatware. Today's most commonly used flatware is made from stainless steel of varying qualities (see Chapter 15).

Flatware Items

To help the customers decide on their purchases, salespeople should know the names and uses of the various pieces listed in Table 27–1.

Selling Flatware

Inexpensive flatware is popularly sold in sets and open stock. Sets of silverware come in various sizes: sets for 6, 8, and 12 people are popular. All sets contain place knives and forks and teaspoons, in addition to other pieces. When people purchase a set of flatware, they may wish to add pieces later. Most patterns are available from open stock for a number of years to permit customers to fill in pieces and to replace lost pieces. People may also purchase flatware in different size place settings, such as the following.

- *Three pieces:* Knife, fork, teaspoon
- *Four pieces:* Knife, fork, teaspoon, salad fork
- *Five pieces:* Knife, fork, teaspoon, salad fork, and either a second teaspoon or a place spoon
- *Six pieces:* Knife, fork, salad fork, one or two teaspoons (or a place spoon), and a butter spreader

Sets vary in size, depending upon the number of place settings and the number of pieces in each place setting. For example, a 20-piece set for four people has the following pieces.

- 4 place knives
- 4 place forks
- 4 salad forks
- 4 place spoons
- 4 teaspoons

Some sets have double teaspoons. Other sets may substitute additional teaspoons for place spoons. Sets may also contain butter spreaders and serving pieces.

Table 27–1 FLATWARE PIECES

Piece	Description
Knives	
Place knife[a]	Regular-size knife to cut meat, fish, and vegetables.
Steak knife	Same size or slightly smaller than the place knife. Has a sharp blade made especially for cutting meat. May have fancy bone, mother-of-pearl, or wooden handles.
Fruit knife	Small knife with a sharp blade for cutting and peeling fruit.
Butter spreader	Small, dull, blunt-edged knife for spreading butter, jam, or jelly.
Butter knife	Medium-size knife with broad blade and shapely end used for cutting and serving butter.
Forks	
Place fork[a]	Regular-size fork for eating meat, fish, and vegetables.
Salad or pastry fork	Short fork with short tines for eating salads, cakes, and pies.
Ice cream fork	Cross between a fork and spoon; has small bowl with blunt half-length tines.
Cocktail or oyster fork	Short fork with thin handle and three short tines for eating shrimp, clams, and oysters.
Olive or pickle fork	Similar in appearance to the cocktail fork but has a longer handle. Used for serving olives, pickles, relishes, and lemon slices.
Cold-meat fork	Large fork for serving meats and salads. Usually has a flat surface with medium-length tines and long handle.
Spoons	
Teaspoon	Average-size oval-shaped spoon used for coffee, tea, vegetables, and pudding.
Orange, grapefruit, melon or fruit spoon	Same size as the teaspoon but with a pointed bowl for eating fruit served in the rind.
After-dinner coffee or demitasse spoon	Shorter handle and smaller bowl than the teaspoon. Suitable to use with demitasse cups.
Iced-tea spoon	Teaspoon bowl with long handle for stirring drinks served in tall glasses.
Place spoon[a]	Formerly called a dessert spoon, this is larger than a teaspoon but smaller than a tablespoon. It is used for eating soup, cereal, and puddings.
Tablespoon	A large spoon, shaped like the teaspoon but with large bowl and long handle for serving vegetables and desserts and for eating spaghetti.
Bouillon spoon	About the same size as the teaspoon, but with a round deep bowl for eating soup from bouillon cups.

(continued)

Table 27–1 **FLATWARE PIECES** (continued)

Piece	Description
Spoons	
Cream soup spoon	Slightly smaller than the place spoon. Has round bowl for eating cream, puree, or other soups.
Round bowl soup spoon	Same size as the place spoon, but with large round bowl for eating soups served in coupe or rimmed soup dishes.
Sugar spoon or shell	Teaspoon-size utensil with larger or shell-shaped bowl. Used for serving sugar.
Salt spoon	Miniature teaspoon with tiny handle and bowl for serving salt from individual, open salt dish.
Berry or serving spoon	Larger bowl than a tablespoon and usually rounder. May or may not be pierced or have a shell-like decoration. Long handle for serving vegetables, fruits, and salads. Together with the cold-meat fork, it forms a salad serving set.
Bonbon spoon	Small teaspoon-shaped spoon with flatter pierced bowl for serving nuts and candies.
Gravy ladle	Deep, round-bowl spoon with bent handle for serving gravy from gravy boat.
Jelly server	One flat edge on the side of the bowl for cutting and serving jelly.
Miscellaneous Servers	
Pie or cake server	Piece with long, blunt, triangular-shaped blade for cutting and serving pie and cake.
Tomato server	Round, flat, pierced bowl allows juice to drip through before serving sliced tomatoes and other foods.
Cheese knife or cleaver	Small flat-bladed tool for cutting and serving cheese.
Cheese plane	Flat server with sharp slot for cutting cheese.
Sugar tongs	Small pincerlike piece for serving lump sugar.

*Place knife, fork, and spoon are terms used since 1950 when the industry stopped making two different size knives and forks for dinner and luncheon use.

Service for eight is commonly sold for families. It may contain 40 pieces, that is, with or without serving pieces.

Services for twelve are triple the size of the services for four.

Sometimes firms sell **hostess sets** with the basic 20- or 40-piece sets. These hostess sets may vary, but they are commonly made up as follows.

Four-piece hostess set
- 1 butter knife
- 1 sugar shell
- 2 serving spoons or tablespoons

Five-piece hostess set
- 1 butter knife
- 1 sugar shell
- 1 pierced tablespoon

Figure 27-3. *A display of flatware should illustrate the items' proper positioning in a place setting.*

- 1 cold-meat fork
- 1 serving spoon or tablespoon

Six-piece hostess set
- 1 butter knife
- 1 sugar shell
- 1 serving spoon
- 1 cold-meat fork
- 1 gravy ladle
- 1 pie server

Displaying Flatware

Because a display of flatware items in a store helps to sell them and to illustrate their proper use in a home, the salesperson should know the general rules for placing flatware items.

1. Knives and spoons go to the right of the plate, with the spoon to the right of the knife. Forks go to the left of the plate, except the oyster fork, which is placed at the right of the knives and spoons if it is not placed on the cocktail plate.

2. All knives, forks, and spoons are placed with the handles even, one inch from the edge of the table. The cutting edge of the knife should face toward the plate.

3. All flatware items are placed in the order in which they will be used from the outside toward the plate. Thus, if soup is to be served first, the soup spoon should be at the extreme right.

4. Preferably no more than three pieces of flatware should be placed on either side of a plate. If more pieces are needed, they may be brought in at the time they are to be used.

5. When used, butter spreaders are usually placed on or near the butter dish, which is at the upper left above the dinner plate.

6. Serving pieces may be placed on or near the dishes with which they will be used.

Ten Factors to Observe When Buying or Selling Flatware

1. How does the design or shape of the pieces harmonize with other furnishings in the home?

2. How does the design or shape harmonize with the dishes and ornaments that will be used on the table?

3. How smooth and rounded are the edges of the spoons and forks? Rounded edges are more comfortable to hold than square edges.

4. How well finished are the pieces? Carefully polished edges of spoons and areas between the tines of forks indicate quality workmanship. The joints between blade of the knife and handle should be inconspicuous and smooth.

5. How well graded are the forks and spoons? If the **shanks** of the item (the part between the bowl or tines and the handle) are thicker than the rest of the piece, the item will give better service and will be more comfortable to use.

6. How well does the knife balance on the edge of the plate? Some knives slide off into the well of the plate, which is annoying.

7. Hold commonly used pieces as they will be held in use. Are they well balanced? Are they comfortable to hold?

8. On pieces with designs, the design should be on both the front and back of the piece. This raises the cost of design application but makes the set more attractive.

9. How definitive is the design? If the pieces have a pattern, it should be well outlined and definitive not flat or blurred.

10. Does the set contain the items for the right number of people?

Cutlery, Gadgets, Steak Knives

As supplements to flatware **cutlery** is used at the table or for food preparation. Knives that have the best cutting edge are made of high-content carbon steel. These knives are mostly for industrial and commercial use because they require extra care to prevent staining and rusting. Stainless-steel knives may have a sharp cutting blade and will not rust or stain. The best blades are forged and stamped; hollow-ground blades hold a keen cutting edge. Knife handles are made of wood, metal, bone, or plastic and are made in one or two pieces. If riveted, at least three rivets should be used in a handle to hold the knife tang (extension from blade) securely. Commonly used knives are listed below.

Paring Knife: Short, thin-bladed knife for peeling and sectioning vegetables and fruits; $3\frac{1}{2}$-inch blade.

Utility Knife: Slightly longer blade than the paring knife. Suitable for slicing large vegetables and cutting through large fruits; $4\frac{1}{2}$-inch blade.

Cook's or Sandwich Knife: Longer and wider blade than the utility knife. Ideal for cutting meats and for slicing tomatoes; 6-inch blade.

Cook's or Chef's Knife: Heavy, sharp, wide-bladed knife with space under handle for knuckles to fit when dicing vegetables, cutting hot meats, or slicing watermelon. The wide blade keeps hot meat from shredding; 8–10-inch blade.

Slicing or Cold-Meat Knife: Long, thin, flexible blade cuts easily through cold meats, vegetables, and fruits; 8–10-inch blade.

Boning Knife: Specially shaped, slender sharp-bladed knife used to cut around bones of meat and along veins in fruit; 6-inch blade.

Pot Fork: Long-handled two- or three-tined fork used to hold meat, fruits, and vegetables steady as they are being cut. Also used to turn and lift foods.

Cleaver: Thick, wide-bladed instrument for cutting through bones in meat and for heavy duty use in food preparation.

Steel: Long, tubular bar with tiny ridges to aid in sharpening and straightening knife edges.

Grapefruit Knife: Small version of the boning knife; to remove grapefruit and orange sections.

Bread Knife or Slicer: Serrated edge on long, thin blade cuts through hot bread without having it lose its domed form. Also permits cutting through crusty or tough skin on meats, fruits, or vegetables.

Mixing Spoon: Long-handled, large-bowled spoon to stir foods at the stove and to transfer foods from a pot or pan to a serving dish.

Spatulas: Long, rounded-end, blunt-edged tool used for turning foods while cooking and for spreading fillings and icings.

Poultry Shears: Scissorlike instrument used for cutting bone sections of chicken and other fowl.

Whisk: Curved wires with handle to beat air into mixtures as food cooks.

Steak Knives: Sharp-bladed knives often in colorful or fanciful handles that may be used in place of din-

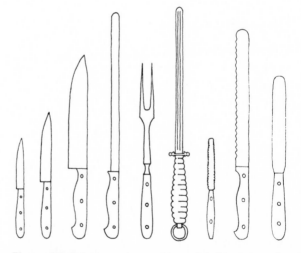

Figure 27-4. *Paring, utility, cook's, and chef's knives; pot fork, steel; grapefruit and bread knives; and spatula.*

ner knives when steak is served. Blades are approximately 5 inches long and may be sharpened.

Care of Cutlery and Gadgets

Proper care of knives will prolong their life and usefulness. The salesperson might suggest that the customer purchase a convenient wooden knife rack; this holds the knife blade in a specially provided slot and prevents blades from being dulled by hitting against other objects in a drawer. The sharpening steel should be used frequently to keep the blade ready for cutting.

HOLLOWARE AND DECORATIVE WARES

Metal bowls, cups, plates, saucers, goblets, sugar bowls, creamers, coffee and tea sets, and waiters make up the articles known as holloware. Other ornamental pieces such as candlesticks, candelabras, vases, and art objects are classified as decorative wares, gift wares, or holloware.

Manufacture of Holloware and Decorative Wares

In a few factories, holloware is made by hand. Such methods are very costly. Most holloware is mass produced by stamping, spinning, or casting. Some metals may be formed in one way, some in another.

Stamping shapes the metal (sterling silver, stainless steel, or the base metal to be plated) by squeezing it between shaped pieces of steel that keep pounding against it until the required form has been obtained. This is the most common method used for shaping holloware.

Spinning is used for small numbers of items for which dies would be too costly to construct; however, only pliable, rather soft metals can be shaped by spinning. Sterling silver and copper are usually formed by spinning. In order to shape the metal, a flat sheet of metal is placed against a wooden mold that is turning in a lathe. The worker forces a smooth steel rod against the sheet of metal, which slowly takes the form of the mold as it turns. This is a hand-guided operation, so it is rather costly.

Casting is used for complicated shapes, such as trophies, fancy borders, and handles. The metal must first be melted and then poured into a mold. Although it is possible to melt and cast sterling, this process is usually limited to metals with low melting points such as white metal that will later be silver plated.

Kinds of Holloware and Decorative Wares

As with other tableware, holloware comes in a variety of shapes, sizes, and qualities. A number of different materials may be used to make holloware, including sterling silver, plated silver, stainless steel, aluminum, and pewter. The quality of the item depends on the material used, the workmanship, the method of construction, and the type and amount of decoration.

Sterling-Silver Holloware. Some sterling-silver holloware is of a heavy gauge of silver that needs no weighting. Lightweight sterling holloware items may have a weighted base. Such a base is formed into a hollow shell that is filled with cement or pitch. This makes the article feel much heavier and gives it a sturdy base. Weighted articles must always be marked as "weighted" or "reinforced." Heavy-gauge sterling articles do not need to be weighted. The price of sterling holloware depends on the thickness of the sterling used, the size of the article, the workmanship, and the type of ornamentation.

Vermeil (heavy gold electroplate on sterling) is also used for holloware and decorative articles.

Silver-Plated Holloware and Decorative Wares. Nickel silver, copper, white metal, and brass for better-quality wares and steel for inexpensive wares are the metals and alloys used for the bases of silver-plated holloware. Because these metals are all relatively inexpensive, they may be made heavy enough to balance well and to feel sturdy; no weighting is ever used in silver-plated items.

After the base materials have been shaped and soldered together, the metal is cleaned, polished, and prepared for plating. The objects are then suspended in the silver-plating bath, and the required amount of pure silver is deposited. The more costly the piece for its size, the thicker the silver plating.

Today all true Sheffield plate is classed as antique because this method (fusing sterling to copper) has not been in use since approximately 1840. Imitations of old Sheffield are sometimes advertised as "Sheffield designs" or "Sheffield reproductions." (See Chapter 15.)

Stainless-Steel Holloware and Decorative Wares. Since stainless steel has been made more silvery in appearance and manufacturers have made more attractive bowls, cups, and bases, the demand for these items has increased. Because this metal is much more difficult to work than sterling or the base metals used for silver plate, fewer fancy designs and elaborate motifs are made. Most stainless-steel holloware is made by being stamped into rather plain shapes. No weighting is ever used in these products.

Goldlike Alloys. Materials that contain base metals but are goldlike in appearance are hard to work and are usually made in rather plain shapes. Because they are so hard, they do not scratch or bend out of shape easily.

Pewter Holloware and Decorative Wares. Pewter makes attractive decorative objects. This metal should not be made into articles that come into direct contact with stoves or high heat. Care should also be taken to avoid scratching or denting pewter.

Aluminum Holloware and Decorative Wares. Aluminum items are available in two types. **Stamped aluminum** made from sheets of polished stock that may or may not have a hammered finish. **Sand-cast aluminum** resembles pewter in appearance but is harder and more enduring and will stand up better.

Selling Holloware and Decorative Wares

Hollowares and decorative wares are usually purchased by the piece although some articles are available in sets. Some holloware articles are available in open stock so sets may be made up from individual purchases. Occasionally, a manufacturer makes holloware items to match a flatware pattern. Descriptions of some popular items and their uses follow.

Candelabra: Candlesticks with two or more branches.

Candle Snuffer: Cone shaped shell that fits over candle top. Long handle allows user to snuff candles.

Candlesticks: Medium-to-tall holders with socket for one candle each.

Casserole: Large serving bowl with lid for decorative use at the table. Usually has a glass lining in which food may be cooked and a holder in which the hot food in the glass may be served.

Centerpiece: Large bowl with deep center and wide, curved rim to hold flowers or fruit. May have an ornamental cover for the center part for use when the bowl is empty.

Chafing Dish: Large casserole on legs with one or two side handles. An alcohol burner or candle is placed in a holder under the chafing dish to keep the food warm at the table.

Coffee and Tea Services: Matching sets include coffeepot and/or teapot, sugar bowl, creamer, waste bowl (to catch the drip from the coffee or tea server), and a tray for serving.

Coffee Urn: Large coffee server with a spigot opening near the bottom of the urn.

Compotes: Short- and long-stemmed candy and nut bowls.

Console Sticks: Short, single candlesticks usually sold in pairs.

Creamers and Sugar Bowls: Sold as set with or without matching tray; most sugar bowls have lids.

Epergnes: Look like multiarmed candelabra with glass or metal bowls in place of candles to hold fruits, nuts, or candies.

Gravy Boats: Short, squat servers with elongated lips; may have separate matching tray or attached tray.

Hurricane Lamps: Console sticks with fitted glass protector that allows the candle flame to shine through.

Ice Tub or Pail: Small bucket-shaped holder for ice cubes.

Lazy Susan: Large circular tray that revolves on a stand. Food is held in compartments and selected as tray turns.

Open Bowls: Various size and shapes of uncovered bowls are used for serving breads and rolls, vegetables, and other foods.

Relish Tray: Platter with divided insert to hold various relishes.

Salt and Pepper Shakers: Matching salt and pepper shakers for individual service or for center of table are available. Because silver is adversely affected by salt, open salt cellars with glass liners and tiny spoons with matching regular pepper shakers are available.

Sherbet Dishes: Stemmed servers with or without glass liners for serving ice cream, sherbet, fruit, or seafood cocktails.

Trays: Various-sized flat metal holders with slightly raised rim; may or may not have end handles.

Trivet: Hot dish holder set on small legs.

Vegetable Dishes: Dishes with removable cover that may be used upside down as vegetable dish; some have removable insert that divides dish into two or three sections for serving more than one vegetable.

Waiters: Large serving trays with end handles.

Water Pitchers: Tall vessels for holding water, milk, or iced drinks; some have special rim across pouring spout (called ice lip) for keeping ice in pitcher while pouring.

Well and Tree Platter: Meat service platter with a series of troughs shaped like tree branches that permit meat juices to run into the well at one end of the platter.

Wine Cooler: Large, deep holder for wine bottle to be set in cracked ice ready for serving.

DECORATING METAL FLATWARE, HOLLOWARE, AND DECORATIVE WARES

Each manufacturer makes several different patterns for the same quality flatware; some may have as many as 10 to 20 patterns from which to choose. When this number is multiplied by 20 or 30 manufacturers, customers have a difficult time deciding among the vast number of flatware designs. Similarly, holloware and decorative wares have many types and styles of decoration.

Stainless-steel and gold-colored alloys are so hard that they are very resistant to scratches. This hardness also makes it difficult to put designs on the surface of these products. Therefore, the designs are usually bolder and less detailed than those used on silver.

Because the method of applying the design noticeably affects the price of the ware, it is important that the salesperson be acquainted with the methods used. Designs applied by hand require skill and many hours of tedious, exacting artistic work. Attractive and well-done machine-made designs require skill and much handwork in setting up the dies for stamping the design on the ware.

Chasing. Beautiful designs are put on the sterling-silver or copper base of plated wares by an artisan who taps sharp-pointed instruments against the surface of the metal and indents lines that outline the design. The process is known as **chasing.** The metal is not removed; it is merely pushed in to form the design. This method of decoration is reproduced by machine by stamping in the design with steel dies.

Repoussé. The most expensive method of decorating metal by hand, **repoussé decoration,** is usually applied to sterling-silver articles. The artisan works the design from the inside of the dish giving a bas-relief (raised) design on the surface of the silver. Tiny hammers are used to pound the silver and to form the raised design. Often repoussé is combined with chasing, which is known as **repoussé chasing.** Expensive coffee and tea sets, bowls, plates, and ornaments may have this type of design applied. A machine-made replica of this design is made by embossing the design on either sterling, pewter, aluminum alloys, or plated ware by means of huge steel dies.

Engraving. Skilled workers may cut a design into the metal's surface by means of sharp-pointed tools that remove the metal. This process is known as engraving. Engraved designs may be applied at the factory, or the customer may have initials, coats of arms, or other insignia engraved on the item. Familiar styles for the initials are script, which resembles handwriting; block, which is plain and appropriate for modern designs; and old English, which is ornate and suitable for period types of silver and elaborate pieces. Machine-controlled engraving, known as engine turning, puts geometric patterns on metal products. On plated items, this is done before plating and does not affect the surface metal.

Piercing.   A method of decoration popular for both sterling silver and plated ware, **piercing** may be done by hand or machine on sterling and by machine on plated ware. Workers using tiny saws and files may cut out designs, or cutting dies may stamp holes into the ware. Edges of bowls and plates and flatware items may have pierced designs.

Etching.   Silver may be coated with wax, which resists acid; then a design is cut through the wax. When the article is immersed in nitric acid, parts of the silver left unprotected by the wax are attacked by the acid, which eats out the design. This process is known as etching. The acid is then washed off and the wax removed. This method of decorating silver is used infrequently today. A similar method may be used on copper or brass products before they are plated.

Hammering.   Tiny dents that give an attractive finish may be pounded into the surface of the metal by hand or machine. This process is known as **hammering.** Plated silver and sheet aluminum holloware pieces, especially pitchers, creamers, and sugar bowls, may have hammered finishes.

Embossing.   A design is first carefully engraved on steel plates or dies. These dies are then placed in huge machines where tremendous pressure forces the pattern onto the object. This process is known as embossing. Any metal may be given a design in this manner, but the softer metals take deeper, more attractive impressions. This is the process by which most flatware designs are applied.

FINISHING METAL FLATWARE, HOLLOWARE, AND DECORATIVE WARES

Not only is the beauty of form and design important to customers, but the dull or shiny finish also affects their choice of metal products. A bright, mirrorlike finish is achieved by polishing the metal with brushes and buffing wheels. The main disadvantage of the highly polished surface of silver, pewter, or aluminum is that tiny scratches from daily use will make them dull. Stainless steel and other hard alloys maintain their finishes indefinitely.

Because silver does scratch easily, a dull finish, called a **butler** or **gray finish,** which does not show fine scratches, can be applied. (The old silver that was polished repeatedly by butlers achieved this soft luster, hence the name.) In the factory this finish is applied by means of revolving brushes that scratch the surface. Because a dull finish on stainless steel makes it resemble old silver, dull finishes have become popular on that metal. Similarly, some pewter and cast-aluminum alloys have dull finishes.

Some silver holloware items may have the interior of their bowls lined with a gold wash, which is a thin plating of pure gold that is applied by electroplating over the silver. This plating does not tarnish but will wear off in time. Colorful enamel finishes may also be baked onto silver holloware items.

Silver has always been plagued by **tarnish,** a discoloration caused by its contact with sulfur in the air, in foods, or in products such as rubber goods. To prevent silver from tarnishing, European manufacturers developed a clear enamel finish that was baked on the items. This permitted them to be used for display or food service without discoloring. Scratches, however, expose the silver, which may then tarnish. In time the finish wears away.

In 1960 a new silicone finish (made from sand and oil) for silver articles was introduced. The silicone is applied as a very thin coating. It cannot be seen, does not alter the appearance of the silver, is long lasting unless it is scratched, and keeps the silver shiny and untarnished until it wears away. Even hot coffee can be served in silicone-treated silver. The finish is used both on sterling and silver-plated holloware. Siloxi is a trade name for this finish. Epifanes is a trade name for a coating used on chromium, gold, silver, and copper. It is made from various chemicals and lasts up to 3 years.

CARE OF FLATWARE, HOLLOWARE, AND DECORATIVE WARES

Tarnish is easily rubbed off with any good silver polish and a soft cloth. Ornate designs may be cleaned by dipping a soft brush in the polish, using it on the grooved portions of the design, and then cleaning the entire article with a soft cloth. The silver should be washed and dried thoroughly after cleaning.

Tarnish may also be removed by placing the silver in an aluminum pan containing a teaspoon of baking soda and a teaspoon of table salt. The silver is then covered with water and boiled for a few minutes until the tarnish is removed. This is a quick, easy method of cleaning inexpensive items, but it leaves a dull surface and removes any oxidized coloring on the silver. This can be restored by occasionally polishing with an ordinary silver polish.

Proper care of silver items may keep tarnish at a minimum. Silver in constant use, which is washed daily in hot soapy water and dried thoroughly, is not apt to tarnish nearly as readily as silver that is only on display. Such displayed silver, when it is not to be used to hold food, may be lacquered. The colorless lacquer coating does not mar the beauty of the silver but keeps it from being attacked by chemicals in the air. However, the lacquer may peel off, and then the silver will tarnish unless relacquered. Silver that is used for special occasions should be packed away in anti-tarnish felt bags or tarnish-resistant chests. Because silver scratches easily, pieces should not be allowed to knock against each other in drawers. Common household salt will corrode silver if left in it for a long period of time; however, the salt will not harm the silver container if it is removed shortly after using. Foods, such as eggs, that contain sulfur will also darken silver.

Stainless steel owes much of its acceptance to the ease with which it maintains its attractive appearance with nothing other than occasional soap and water washings. Because it does not tarnish, stain, or rust and because there is no plating to wear away, the only care it needs is to have food particles and soil removed. Stainless steel may get water spots when washed in an automatic dishwasher. Rubbing it with a metal cleaner will remove these marks.

Gold-colored alloys rarely need any special care, but they are difficult to polish. They may be polished by hard rubbing and use of a metal polish about once a year. Pewter and aluminum alloys need only occasional polishing with a soft cloth and silver or pewter polish.

DO YOU KNOW YOUR MERCHANDISE?

1. Define flatware, holloware, decorative wares.
2. What are the problems that have made sterling silver less popular today than in previous decades? How can consumers eliminate these problems?
3. Explain how flatware is sold. What pieces are in a three-, four-, five-, and six-piece place setting? A six-piece hostess set?
4. In setting a table, on what side of the plate do the following items go: dinner knife, soup spoon, and salad fork? What is the maximum number of flatware items that should be placed at each place at the start of the meal?
5. Explain the following terms and give examples of their use: stamping, spinning, and casting.
6. What is meant by a weighted base in sterling holloware? When are weighted bases used in sterling holloware? How would a customer know a piece of holloware was weighted? Why do silver-plated holloware items not have weighted bases?

7. Why are glass liners used in some sterling-silver and silver-plated salt dishes?
8. Explain five ways of applying designs to metal flatware, holloware, and decorative wares.
9. Explain what is meant by bright finish, butler finish, and gold wash.
10. How would you advise a customer to care for silver that is used frequently? For silver that is used only rarely? What advantages do stainless steel, gold-colored alloys, pewter, and aluminum have from the standpoint of care?

PUTTING YOUR MERCHANDISE KNOWLEDGE TO WORK

A friend of yours is getting married and several members of your class have decided to pool their money for a wedding gift. You have decided that you should buy something in silver for such an important occasion. What type of item would you plan to give? What type of metal would you expect to find for a limited amount of money?

PROJECT

Visit a store that displays and sells silver and stainless-steel flatware products. Were the silverware and stainless steel displayed together or in separate areas? Were most flatware objects shown as sets, in place settings, or in some other way? How many different patterns did you see in stainless steel? In sterling silver? In plated silverware? How difficult would selection of a pattern be in the store you visited? Write a report of your visit.

28

Housewares: Food Preparation Aids

Housewares include the many kinds of cooking utensils, both with and without electricity, the variety of preparation vessels, and cutlery items (see Chapter 27). Selecting the proper utensils for cooking and serving is an important skill for the good cook. As kitchens have become smaller and more compact, kitchen utensils have become more visible — often hanging on pegboards or from dropped ceiling racks. Therefore, utensils that look handsome as kitchen decorations may also be a purchasing requirement.

COOKING UTENSILS

Traditionally, cooking utensils have been made of base metals, alloys, clay, and porcelain. In recent times plated metals and glass have been commonly used. Since the advent of microwave cooking, plastics have also been used for cooking. The major materials used in the manufacture of cooking utensils today are discussed below.

Cast Iron

Because cooks have always believed that cast-iron utensils preserve the natural flavors of foods, cast-iron baking and frying pans and Dutch ovens continue to be in demand. Cast-iron implements are made by pouring molten iron into sand molds that shape the metal. These utensils are heavy and after use become almost black in color. The advantage of using cast iron is that it heats slowly and retains heat for a relatively long period of time.

Cast-iron utensils will not rust if they are thoroughly dried after each use. However, if they are to be stored for a long period of time, each cast-iron utensil should be coated with wax or grease for protection against dampness, which causes rust.

Food tends to stick to cast iron when the utensil is new unless it is **seasoned** by slowly cooking unsalted fat into the pores of the iron for 2 or 3 hours before using it for the first time. Most cast-iron pans are preseasoned by the manufacturer and are so labeled. After preseasoning the manufacturer coats each pan with a lacquer, which serves as a protection while it is on the store shelf. This lacquer must be removed before a pan can be used for cooking. If well cared for, cast-iron utensils improve with age, becoming smoother and finer. Cast iron may also be used in utensils that are subsequently plated or coated with porcelain enamel.

Sheet Steel

Lighter-weight frying pans are made from ordinary steel, which can be rolled into thin sheets and formed by stamping. Steel pans are lighter, smoother, thinner, and conduct heat more quickly than cast iron, but they do not hold heat

367

as well and warp or bend out of shape more quickly. Sheet-steel utensils rust if not properly dried after using, but no seasoning is needed.

Plated Iron and Steel

One way to prevent cast iron and steel from rusting is to plate them with nickel or chromium. These plating metals give a silvery color to iron and steel utensils. Nickel tends to wear rather easily but is very durable if it is covered with a chromium finish. Tin (discussed below) is also commonly used to plate steel. Zinc is used only for garbage pails and items that will not be used for cooking as it combines with acids in food to form a poisonous compound.

Tin

Tinware is actually made with a thin coat of tin plated over a base of steel. Approximately 98 percent steel and 2 percent tin are used in tinware. Lids, baking pans, and cans are often made from tin-plated steel. Tinware with a heavy coating of tin is called **retinned or block tinware;** these items are a little more expensive, but they wear much better. Sometimes a gold-colored enamel lining is coated onto tin cans, which protects the color of some foods (tomatoes and red cabbage, for example) and prevents foods from discoloring the tin. Tin is also the metal used to plate the inside of copper cooking utensils.

Because tin is soft, it is easily scratched. When a tin-plated product is scratched to the base metal (steel), it is no longer rustproof. Also, tin has a tendency to stain; therefore hot foods containing acids (vinegar, tomatoes, apples, and so on) should not be cooked in tin-plated pans because the acid attacks the tin. However, when cold, these acids do not affect tin. Another disadvantage of tin is that it melts at about 450°F so tin pans should not be used for frying because frying temperatures often reach above 500°F.

Stainless Steel

Stainless steel (an alloy of steel, chromium and, occasionally, nickel) eliminates the problem of rust and reduces the staining that occurs on ordinary steel. However, it does not impart the flavor that cast iron does nor does it heat as evenly. In fact, food can easily be scorched in stainless-steel pots. To improve its heating qualities, it is necessary to combine stainless steel with other metals.

Copper is often plated onto the bottoms of stainless-steel pans to improve heat conduction. However, copper plating is never used inside a pan because copper gives food a metallic taste. The copper coating spreads heat evenly, speeds up cooking time, and prevents scorching. Because aluminum conducts heat almost as well as copper, aluminum-coated stainless-steel pots and pans are excellent for cooking. However, both copper and aluminum stain.

Another technique for improving the heating ability of stainless steel is to place a layer of carbon steel (called a **carbon core**), copper, or aluminum between two layers of stainless steel. In this construction, stainless steel is easy to care for and has important heat-diffusion properties. **Four-ply ware** is made by adding a thick aluminum-coated bottom. **Five-ply ware** has three layers of aluminum inside a top and bottom layer of stainless steel.

Copper

Because of its unique heat-conducting properties and attractive appearance, copper is an ideal metal to use on the outside of cooking utensils. However, copper reacts with many foods to impart a metallic taste. Therefore, the utensil needs to be lined with a heavy coating of tin. When the tin wears away, the utensil should be retinned or discarded. Copper also discolors easily when used for cooking, so copper polish must be used frequently on the outside of the utensil.

Aluminum

One important feature of aluminum is its attractiveness. It has a silver color, which is easily kept bright and shiny. Aluminum that has been anodized may be colored. Aluminum is also lightweight — it weighs about one-third as much as

Figure 28-1. *Stainless steel utensils begin as flat sheets (top left) that are drawn on hydraulic presses (center) to achieve the proper shape. Complete body shells are washed, inspected, and clad with copper (top right), then immersed in a plating bath (bottom left) where copper is electroplated to the bottoms. Handles are permanently welded to utensil bodies (bottom right).*

iron or copper, which means that a pan can be made as thick as cast iron while weighing only one-third as much.

Another feature of aluminum is that it spreads heat quickly and evenly; however, food cooked in aluminum pans can be scorched if the water boils away and heating is too rapid. Thus, it is wise to cook food in aluminum pans at low- or medium-heat settings. Thicker cast aluminum pans will do a better cooking job and require less water.

Thin sheet aluminum has a tendency to dent and warp, which prevents food from cooking evenly. Alkaline food substances discolor aluminum, but most discoloration can be removed by boiling a weak solution of water and vinegar or cream of tartar in the pan. Aluminum pans can also be cleaned with acid soap and stainless-steel pads. Strong soda should never be used on or with food cooked in aluminum; thus, soda should not be added to foods to be cooked in aluminum utensils. Hard water and food, if left on aluminum for any period of time, can cause pitting, so aluminum utensils should be cleaned and dried thoroughly after using.

Porcelain-Enamel and Acrylic Finishes

Porcelain-enamel coating is similar to ceramic in its composition. This coating is placed on steel, aluminum, or iron utensils by dipping them into a solution of pulverized glass and clay. The dipped piece is then baked in a hot furnace. The best-quality enamelware is dipped and baked three times; less expensive items are dipped once or twice. In less expensive items the base metal is thin and the finished product is lightweight. Better-quality items are heavier and more durable; they usually have a cast-iron or cast-aluminum base that permits excellent cooking. Enamelware comes in many colors.

Care should be used in handling enamelware because it tends to chip and crack; pans should not be stacked inside one another and care should be taken not to bang them against the sink. However, with reasonable care enamelware has many advantages: It is attractive, easy to clean, nonporous, and imparts no taste to food.

Chip- and stain-resistant acrylic finishes in colorful solid or patterned designs are bonded to the exterior of aluminum or stainless-steel utensils. These pots and pans are useful for low-temperature cooking.

Clay

Porous, unglazed clay pots shaped like casseroles and ranging in sizes that will hold $2\frac{1}{2}$ to 14 pounds of food are available for cooking chickens and tough cuts of beef. Because the pots are porous, they are soaked in water before they are used for baking. Food cooked in them is roasted quickly and becomes very tender. Browning is done by removing the top part of the casserole for the last 10 minutes of cooking. These pots are easily broken if they are dropped, and the hot pots must not be put on cool surfaces that might cause breakage. Glazed clay pots are used for baking.

Glass

Glassware used for cooking is commonly known by the trade names Pyrex and Glassbake. Glass has many advantages for cooking. First, you can see if the food is scorching or if the water is boiling away without lifting the lid. Second, being nonporous, glass does not absorb any greases or odors from the food and does not combine with any chemicals in the food itself. Third, food can be served in the same glass dish in which it has been cooked, keeping the food hot and eliminating the use of extra dishes. Fourth, glass is easy to clean by soaking food loose and then washing with soap or detergent.

Special products for baking that withstand very high heat are available. They have glazed interiors to protect food and come in a variety of colors. Notable among these products is Pyroceram, which is the trade name for **super-glass-ceramic** developed by the Corning Glass Company. It is pure white and is popular for teapots and coffeepots, casseroles, frying pans, and baking dishes.

Most glass products are easily broken and should therefore be handled with care. They can also be cracked by sudden changes in temperature; thus, they should be heated and cooled gradually. Pyroceram, which is break resistant, is very resistant to breaking from sudden temperature changes.

Nonstick Coatings for Pots and Pans

Silicone coatings are noted for their ability to keep materials from sticking to them. As coatings over metal, they make food easy to release and protect a metal such as silver from tarnishing.

Tetrafluoroethylene coatings come in two different types. Formerly dark brown to black in color, they are now also available in white. The T-Plus and Teflon trademarked wares, although somewhat scratch resistant, must not be scraped or scratched with sharp metal tools or scrapers. Food should be cooked in them at temperatures between 350 and 400°F. Foods may be cooked in such pans without oil or fat, but its addition usually adds to the food's flavor.

Silver Stone, the trade name of a du Pont tetrafluoroethylene product introduced in 1976, is a thick, three-layer surface that is fuse bonded to heavy aluminum. It is more resistant to scratching, chipping, and peeling than are the other coatings. Food may be cooked at somewhat higher temperatures with this type of coating.

Microwave Oven Ware

Containers for cooking foods in microwave ovens may be made from glass, clay, special plastics, or treated paper. In microwave ovens, the cooking is done by high-frequency radio energy that produces heat in food. These waves may be reflected, transmitted, or absorbed as they come into contact with the food container. Metal holders reflect them and are not usually desirable for microwave cooking. The other materials transmit them, allowing the food to cook quickly.

When thermoplastic substance, polysulfone, or a heat-resistant polyester resin is coated over cardboard, it makes an enduring, usable food container for microwave cooking. Some multicolored metallic foils that are coated with polysulfone are used for microwave cookware.

TYPES OF COOKING UTENSILS

Kitchen utensils may be used for food preparation as well as for cooking food on top of the stove and in regular or microwave ovens. Some bowls, pots, pans, and kettles may be used for preparation and for cooking. In other words, many utensils have several functions. For small kitchens, multipurpose, stackable utensils are particularly salable. Some ethnic foods require special utensils for preparation. Below is a list of such housewares products.

Angel Cake Pan or Baking Ring: Deep, circular baking pan with slightly tapered sides and a tubular center that may or may not lift out. Used for cooking angel food and chiffon cakes.

Broiler: Shallow, oval- or oblong-shaped pans with a wire rack that holds fish or meat near the flame and allows the fat to drip to the pan below.

Cake Pan: Various-shaped pans that are shallow for baking cake.

Canister Set: Containers with tightly fitted lids for flour, sugar, coffee, tea, and spices. Often they fit one inside the other for storage.

Casserole: Covered saucepot used for baking various foods.

Chafing Dish: Covered, usually fairly shallow pot used over a flame to cook food at the table or to keep it hot.

Chicken Fryer: Covered deep frying pan that permits food to steam as it cooks.

Coffee Pot: Usually tall, narrow vessel for cooking and/or serving coffee. Special types are dripolators, percolators, and vacuum coffee makers.

Collander: Bowl-shaped sieve or strainer made from metal or plastic that is used to drain vegetables or boiled foods such as pasta.

Condiment Set: Small shakers used to hold salt, pepper, and other spices to be used in seasoning food while cooking.

Cookie Sheet (or Tin): A flat rectangular-shaped metal utensil with one or two raised edges to be used when inserting the sheet into the oven. Used for baking cookies and biscuits.

Crepe Pan: Resembles a frying pan but is used to cook crepes on the outside of the pan. The domed bottom of the pan is dipped into the crepe mixture then turned with its bottom up to cook over the open flame. When the crepe is done, the pan is inverted to serve the finished food.

Custard Cup: Usually made from ceramics or glass. Small, deep, individual bowl-shaped containers used to bake custards in the oven.

Deep-Fat Fryer: Open saucepan with a wire-net basket insert that holds the food to be fried. When the frying is done, the wire basket is lifted from the hot fat to drain.

Double Boiler: Two pans or pots, one fitted into the top of the other. The bottom pan holds water that is heated to cook the food in the upper pot. Either part may be used alone.

Double Fry Pan: Two wells joined together with hinges. They may be used to fry two different foods simultaneously, or food, such as an omelet, may be flipped from one side to the other.

Dutch Oven: Large thick-walled saucepot that holds 5 quarts or more of food and has a close-fitting lid. It may be used to cook food on top of the stove or in the oven.

Egg Poacher: A saucepanlike utensil with an insert that holds shallow cups for eggs. The water boiling in the bottom of the pan cooks the eggs.

Fondue Pot: One- to two-quart-size squat pot used as a chafing dish to melt a special cheese mixture for use as a dip with cubes of bread.

Frying Pan or Chef Pan: Metal or ceramic wide shallow pan with a long side handle. Also known as a **skillet.**

Griddle: Very shallow, flat frying pan made from thick metal. Used in slow frying pancakes, bacon, hamburgers, and eggs.

Kettle: Large covered pot with a **bail** (arched) handle over the top. Comes in 6- to 24-quart capacity.

Measuring Cups and Spoons: Utensils with quantity markings.

Mixing Bowl: Metal, clay, glass, or plastic bowls used for mixing and preparing food. They are round with flat bottoms for ease in handling while stirring food. Mixing bowl sets may be nested for storage.

Muffin Pans or Tins: Four, six, eight, or twelve metal cups are suspended from a traylike frame. Used to bake individual muffins, rolls, cakes, or pie crusts. Cups vary in size.

Pan or Sauce Pan: Refers to a utensil with a side handle.

Pie Plate or Pan: Shallow metal utensil with flared sides for use in baking crust or crust and filling in the oven.

Pizza Pan: A round, very shallow pan with a long handle used to place the pizza in the oven for baking.

Pot or Sauce Pot: Refers to a utensil with two eared-shape handles, one on each side of the pot, or an overhead (arched) handle known as a bail handle. Pots are usually somewhat larger than pans.

Pressure Cooker: Heavy weight pots or pans with gaskets on the lids that form a tight seal when the lid is locked into position. Steam builds up from the small amount of water placed in the pot with the food. Small amounts of steam may be emitted by a steam vent activated when pressure is high. Speedy cooking is achieved by this combination of steam and pressure.

Roaster: Large open or covered oblong or oval deep-sided vessel for oven cooking and baking.

Salad Bowls: Large mixing and serving bowls of wood, glass, or metal for tossing salad greens.

Sauté Pan: Large, heavy, deep, straight-sided skillet. Used to **sauté** food in a small amount of fat or oil at high temperatures. Copper lined with tin or stainless steel clad with aluminum make the best sauté pans. A long handle on the pan is used to hold the pan while the contents are agitated over the flame.

Steamer-Cooker: A combination pan and perforated basket. Food is placed in the basket and water is boiled in the bottom chamber. A tightly fitted lid covers the cooker. The food is steamed, thereby retaining all its juices.

Tea Kettle: Vessel with a cover and spout that is used for top-of-stove boiling of water. Some whistle when the water is boiled.

Teapot: Short, squat pot with a spout and handle that is usually made from ceramic materials. Used for brewing the tea when hot water from a kettle is poured into it.

Water Pitcher: A tall vessel with a side handle and a pouring spout; used to serve water. The spout may have an **ice lip,** a piece of metal that holds the ice back as the water is being poured.

Wok: A large carbon steel flared-shape vessel with a cover that permits food to be stir fried, steamed, or stewed. A **wok set** includes a burner ring that covers the flame or electric plate on which the food is cooked, a ladle, a turner and a steaming rack.

SELLING POINTS OF COOKING UTENSILS

Wares made of finer materials and better construction are more durable and in the long run save the buyer money. Good equipment is easy to clean and can be used more economically.

For top-of-stove cooking, the pan should fit the size of the burner being used. If the pan is too small, heat escapes into the air around the pan. Also, the covers on good products fit snugly and hold in heat. Pans with flat and dull or black-colored bottoms take heat more quickly and remain heated longer. Wares made from materials that conduct heat evenly cook more satisfactorily.

Handles should be designed so that they do not cause a pan to tip when it is empty. Handles should be firmly attached to the pan, and the joining should be smooth. Rivets inside the pan are difficult to clean around. Both wooden and plastic handles remain cool when used for top-of-stove utensils. However, these handles may char or crack if the flame reaches them. Metal handles do not crack or burn, but they conduct heat readily and may be uncomfortable to handle without a pad for protection. Detachable handles for ovenware products provide cool handling of hot pots or pans.

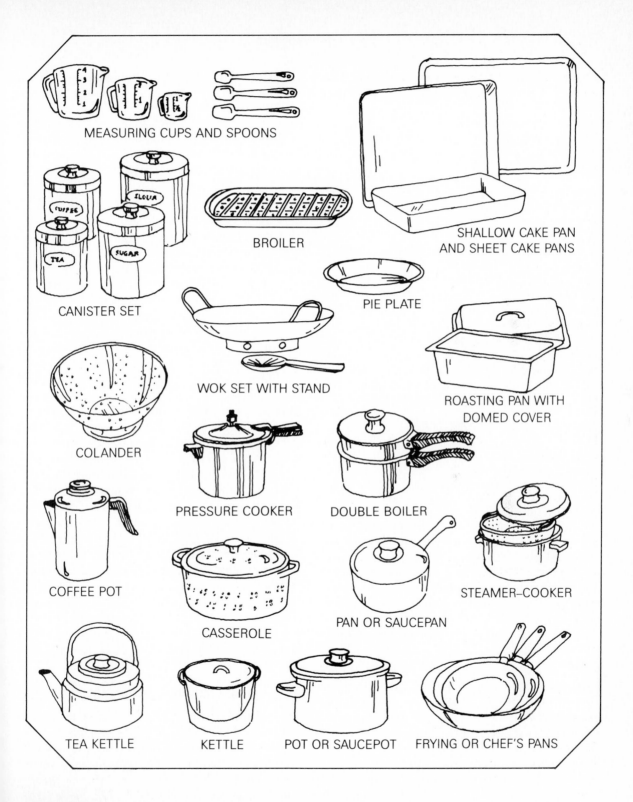

MEASURING CUPS AND SPOONS

CANISTER SET

BROILER

SHALLOW CAKE PAN
AND SHEET CAKE PANS

PIE PLATE

WOK SET WITH STAND

ROASTING PAN WITH
DOMED COVER

COLANDER

PRESSURE COOKER

DOUBLE BOILER

COFFEE POT

CASSEROLE

PAN OR SAUCEPAN

STEAMER–COOKER

TEA KETTLE

KETTLE

POT OR SAUCEPOT

FRYING OR CHEF'S PANS

Figure 28-2. *Metal utensils. Wares made of finer material are more durable and easier to clean.*

Spouts should be placed and shaped so that contents will pour easily without dripping. They should be high enough on the pot to keep contents from spilling out when the pot is full.

Lips on pots, pans, and skillets facilitate pouring out contents. If lips are placed on both sides of a pan, either hand may be used in handling the pan. Lips, of course, allow steam to escape from a covered pan unless the lid fits over the lips.

ELECTRIFIED HOUSEWARES

Electrification of products makes them easier and more convenient to use. However, the price of electricity sometimes makes such utensils costly to operate. Electric utensils can heat evenly. They have motors that allow food to be stirred, sliced, or ground with ease. To ensure that the electric appliance will perform adequately, it should carry the Underwriters' Laboratories (UL) approval. This is an independent laboratory for testing electrical wiring and devices. The appliance must also be properly handled and cared for.

Terminology

To buy and sell electrical appliances with confidence, a knowledge of key electrical terms is desirable. **Electric current** is the flowing of electricity through a wire in a manner that may be compared to water flowing through a pipe. There are two types of electric current: **direct current (DC)**, a steady current that is rarely used in this country today, and **alternating current (AC)**, a pulsating current that is most commonly used. Appliances made for one type of current will not work in a building that is wired for the other type unless an adapter is used.

Volt or voltage (V) may be thought of as the pressure behind the current. For residential wiring, 120 volts is a common voltage; 240 volts are used for some heavy appliances, such as many air conditioners and electric ranges.

Ampere or **amperage (amp)** refers to the size of the current or the actual number of electrons flowing through the wires. You may have difficulty using several appliances at the same time in a home or apartment not wired for sufficient amperes. Very old homes were wired for 30 amperes; more recently built homes are wired for 60. Modern homes are wired for 100 amperes to make it possible to run several electrical appliances at the same time.

Electric companies sell electric current by the **watt (W)**. One watt is equal to the amount of work done by 1 volt pushing 1 ampere through a circuit. The formula for determining the number of watts an appliance will use is as follows: Watts = Voltage × Amperage. A **kilowatt** is equal to 1,000 watts. A **kilowatt hour** refers to the number of kilowatts used in 1 hour. **Horsepower** is the amount of energy a motor has at normal speed. A motor using 746 watts has a rating of 1 horsepower.

Electric current flowing through a wire creates heat. The resistance of a material to the flow of current is measured by units known as **ohms.** The greater the resistance, the greater the heat that is generated and the greater the voltage that is needed to push the current through. Light or heat is created by placing resistance in the way of the current. Heating and lighting units, therefore, use more current than devices that are powered by electric motors that do not produce heat or light.

The number of volts and amperes and the kind of current to be used are indicated on most electrical appliances, which also show the number of watts the appliances will use in an hour. Thus, if this information is known, in addition to the cost of electricity per watt, the cost of running the equipment per hour can be determined.

Small Heat-Producing Housewares

The construction of electric heat-producing appliances uses wires that offer resistance to the flow of electric current. These wires are known as **heating elements** and are also called **resistance coils.** They can convert the electricity into heat as high as 1,000°F. For lightweight appliances, wires are wound around mica. Elements of this kind may be found in toasters and grills. For heavier appliances, such as irons and waffle irons, coiled wires embedded in cement are used.

Insulation is used to prevent electricity from being transmitted or spread to parts of the appliance other than the heating element; this protects the user from shocks or other harm. An example of insulation is the rubber or plastic covering on electrical wiring. An insulating material is one that does not conduct electricity. The Underwriters' Laboratories approval tag assures the customer that the proper insulation has been used.

Housings of heating appliances are usually made of chrome-plated steel. These nonrusting, nontarnishing surfaces, which are silvery in color, are easily kept clean and shiny. Handles and knobs are often made from a nonconducting thermosetting plastic.

One of the most widely used heat-producing appliances is the toaster. Another popular device is the grill, which consists of an oblong or square frame with two smooth grids that contain heating elements. Ceramic-housed slow cookers used for stews, soups, some meats, and rice are recent heating housewares.

Microwave Cooking

Noted for its speed, microwave cooking has become an important method of preparing food. Instead of heat, the microwave energy passes through appropriate utensils and into the food. "The energy causes the moisture molecules in the food to vibrate. That results in a kind of internal friction — and the friction produces heat."[1] Unfortunately, these microwaves do not penetrate the food evenly, so cooking may be uneven. Rotating-fanlike devices help to distribute the microwave energy. Some have turntables to rotate the food and keep it more evenly bombarded with the microwaves.

In microwave cooking, different power levels are available to accommodate different foods.

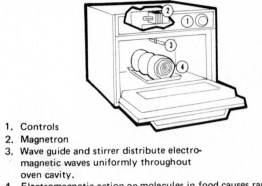

1. Controls
2. Magnetron
3. Wave guide and stirrer distribute electromagnetic waves uniformly throughout oven cavity.
4. Electromagnetic action on molecules in food causes rapid heating of food.

Figure 28-3. *Cutaway view of a microwave oven. A fast way of cooking food, microwave emits no heat.*

These range from 1,250 to 1,600 watts. The ordinary signs that food is cooked, such as brown color or crisp surfaces, do not occur in microwave cooking. The check for how well cooked the food is is done by reading the oven's gauges that record the internal temperature.

One significant advantage of the microwave oven is the fact that it emits no heat so the kitchen stays cool.

Convection Ovens

By adding a fan to blow hot air around the food, an ordinary oven may become a convection oven. This results in more even cooking. Some manufacturers claim the ovens also speed cooking somewhat.

Continuous-Cleaning Ovens

Continuous-cleaning ovens come with special oven finishes that are able to remove grease and other cooking materials from the sides of the oven during ordinary cooking. The ovens absorb and hide soil. Chemical oven cleaners cannot be used on such finishes.

A list of some heat-producing electric housewares shows the variety available.

Espresso or Cappucino Maker: Stainless-steel elaborate machine uses steam pressure to make a thick coffee that may be used in that form as espresso. If cappucino is desired, the steam is used to froth the milk that is added to the espresso. May have a separate glass carafe to hold the coffee.

Drip Coffee Maker: A reservoir heats the water and then releases it to pass through a basket containing ground coffee. This drips into a glass carafe, which is on an element that keeps it warm. There are on–off signal lights and a main heating element that switches off automatically at the end of the water-heating cycle. The glass that holds the coffee is easily cleaned, and the unit that heats the water needs to be cleaned occasionally with vinegar to counteract any build-up of minerals from hard water that might collect on the tubes and prevent the water getting to the coffee grounds.

Percolator: The warming and cooking elements are usually in the coffee pot itself. If the pot does not have a warming device, the pump and basket inside the pot must be removed to prevent continuous perking of the water through the grounds. Do not immerse the pot in water for cleaning unless the label states that it may be immersed. Tops are made to lock on in case the pot is tipped while in use. May be made of stainless steel, Pyroceram, or ceramics.

Electric Kettle: A stainless steel pot with a heating element and removable cord. After boiling, the water is kept piping hot and ready to use.

Warming Tray: Wooden and metal tray with radiant glass or Pyroceram heating areas that may be adjusted to retain heat from 160 to 265°F. May be used at a table or on a sideboard to keep foods hot while serving.

Electric Skillet: Oblong-shaped skillet with cover and detachable electric cord. Heat controls allow cooking to range from 150 to 425°F. Cool handles and bases of plastic suspend the pan from the surface on which it is placed.

Electric Omelet Pan: Steel or aluminum pan with nonstick inside surface is held on small feet that protect the surface on which it rests. The pan is set to heat to 375°F and maintain that heat for optimum cooking of omelets. By wiping the surface after use, the pan stays in perfect condition for cooking eggs. It may also be used for cooking any other fried foods where temperatures do not need to be excessive.

Electric Griddle: Flat cooking surface mounted above a heating unit allows entire meals to be cooked at the table. Usually made of steel or cast aluminum, the griddle may have a nonstick finish. Legs of thermosetting plastic protect the surface on which the griddle stands. High-speed heating units and heat controls allow a variety of foods to be cooked.

Electric Popcorn Maker or Pumper: A two-part canister allows corn to be popped with hot air that propels the corn into the upper transparent plastic holder. The lower part of the container holds the heating unit that pops the corn and then forces it with air into the upper chamber. Melted butter may be added after removal of the popped corn from the upper chamber. The entire assemblage is made of plastic and has an internal heating unit.

Slow-cooker: Large pot that fits above heating unit or that has built-in heating unit. Some accommodate steaming and deep-fat frying by the addition of separate inserts. Bodies of such pans may be made of ceramics, steel, or aluminum.

Electric Waffle Irons: Square- and round-shaped waffle irons made from stainless or chrome-plated steel with aluminum grids that have a no-stick surface are available. Some of the grids are reversible to a plain grill surface. Heating units have lights that indicate when the food should be placed on the pan and that indicate when it is ready for serving. Thermosetting plastic legs keep the pan above the surface of the table or counter for safety.

Electric Wok: Stainless-steel wok is mounted on heating unit with heat control to ensure a desired heat level for wok stir frying. Has thermosetting plastic legs.

Automatic Toaster: Oblong, boxlike holder with inserts at the top for bread or English muffins. Heating elements on each side toast the inserts. Chrome-plated steel is combined with thermosetting plastic to make an attractive, easy-to-handle unit that is safe to use. Toasters may accommodate two, four, or six slices at a time.

Toaster Oven: Small, counter-top oven. Chromed steel case has unbreakable glass front and is supported on thermosetting plastic frame. Used on counter top or at table. Removable parts make cleaning easy. Temperature settings from 200 to 500°F.

Toaster/Broiler Oven: Slightly larger than the toaster oven; permits food to be broiled as well as toasted in its interior space. Temperature controls include warm, hot, and broil.

Broiler with Rotisserie: Chromed-steel housing with thermosetting plastic frame that permits counter-

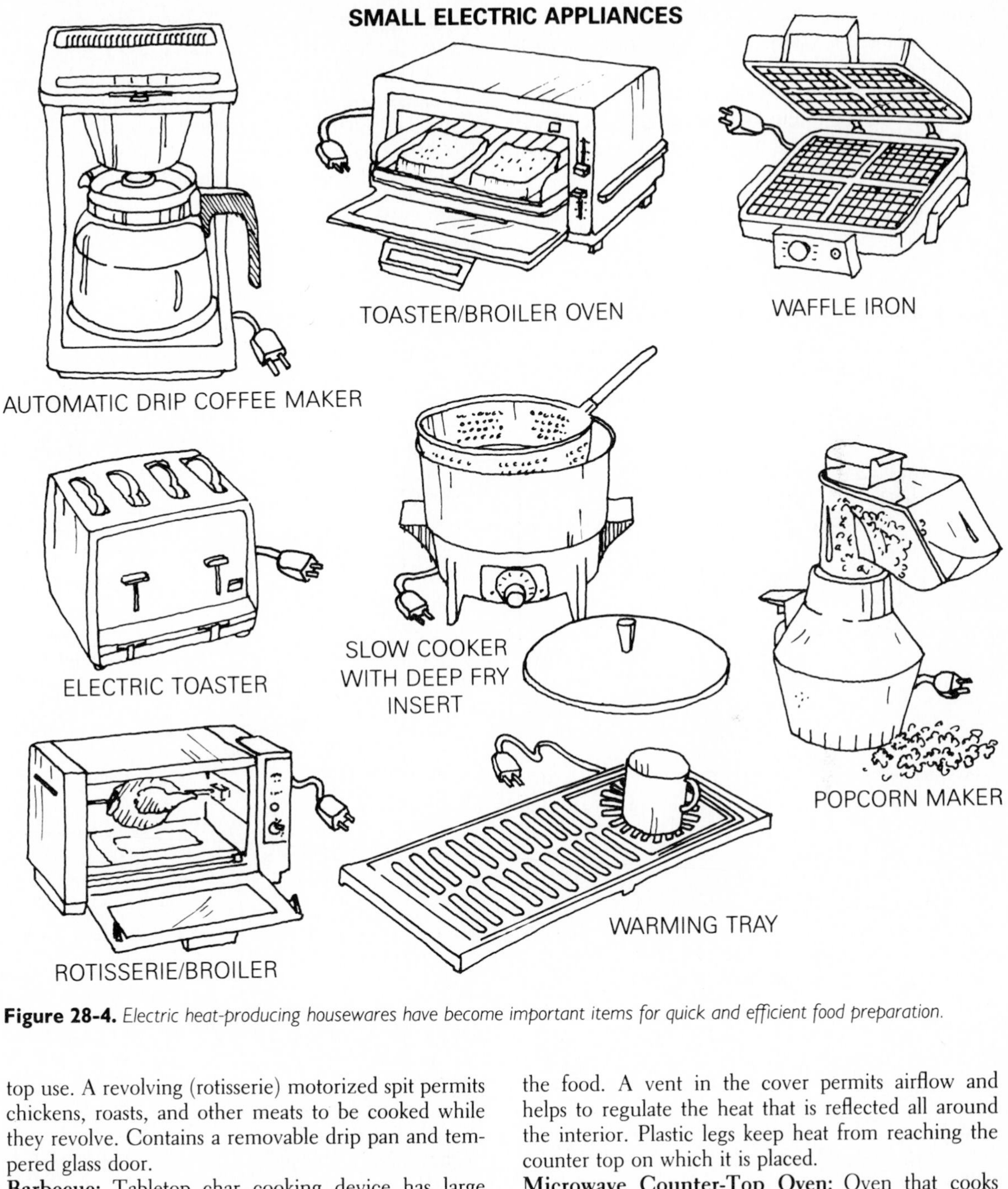

SMALL ELECTRIC APPLIANCES

AUTOMATIC DRIP COFFEE MAKER

TOASTER/BROILER OVEN

WAFFLE IRON

ELECTRIC TOASTER

SLOW COOKER WITH DEEP FRY INSERT

POPCORN MAKER

ROTISSERIE/BROILER

WARMING TRAY

Figure 28-4. *Electric heat-producing housewares have become important items for quick and efficient food preparation.*

top use. A revolving (rotisserie) motorized spit permits chickens, roasts, and other meats to be cooked while they revolve. Contains a removable drip pan and tempered glass door.

Barbecue: Tabletop char cooking device has large chromed-steel or cast-aluminum pan with domed cover. A wire rack holds the food over permanent, self-cleaning briquettes that impart a charcoal flavor to

the food. A vent in the cover permits airflow and helps to regulate the heat that is reflected all around the interior. Plastic legs keep heat from reaching the counter top on which it is placed.

Microwave Counter-Top Oven: Oven that cooks foods by shooting microwaves through them. Moisture molecules in the food vibrate, producing heat, which cooks the food.

Convection Oven: Electrically heated oven has an interior fan that keeps the heat moving evenly around the oven during cooking.

Combination Microwave and Convection Oven: Provides the dry-heat cooking desired for browning and baking and the moist-heat cooking that microwaves offer. Such an oven permits both types of cooking if desired.

Dehydrator: Boxlike device with five to nine trays to hold fruits, meats, nuts, and vegetables for dry preserving. Low heat (85° to 145°F.) slowly dehydrates (draws moisture from) the food. This heat is circulated by fan and filtered to protect the foods as they dry. The trays are removable for easy cleaning. A glass front allows the foods to be watched as they dry.

SMALL MOTOR HOUSEWARES

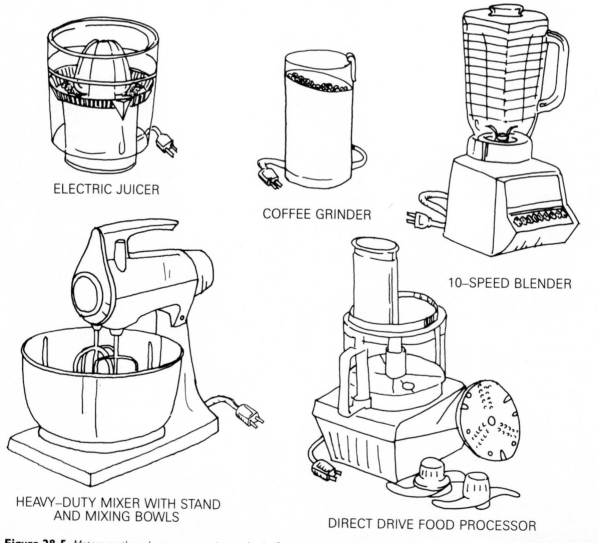

ELECTRIC JUICER

COFFEE GRINDER

10–SPEED BLENDER

HEAVY–DUTY MIXER WITH STAND AND MIXING BOWLS

DIRECT DRIVE FOOD PROCESSOR

Figure 28-5. *Motors on these housewares activate wheels, fans, churns, grinders, or blades to execute a number of operations.*

Small Motor Housewares

Instead of heating devices, electrified utensils can have motors that activate wheels, fans, churns, grinders, or blades to execute many types of operations that aid cooks. Motors may be small and have only minimum power for light duty tasks or may have more power. Speed variations are also possible. Motors are usually sealed so they need no lubricating during the life of the article. Quality motors do not overheat as long as they are used in the ways for which they were intended. Directions should be carefully followed in using all such housewares. A list of commonly used small motor housewares follows.

Electric Juicers: These range from small appliances that squeeze the juice from one-half of a lemon, orange, or grapefruit and strain it, to those that may have several fruits placed into them at once and continue to squeeze the juice until the juicer is turned off or the fruit is removed. They extract all the pulp and allow small, tender pieces to pass through the strainer while keeping seeds and larger pieces of pulp out. Plastic housings hold the motor, juicer, and strainer. A clear top allows the fruit to be watched as the juice is extracted.

Blenders: Appliances that chop, mix, and whip. They have a plastic base and a tall, lidded glass jar that fits on top of the motor housing. Various speeds allow for a variety of mixing and blending jobs. The speed of operation reduces the time needed for preparing food and makes the finished product smooth and well blended. Care must be used in handling and cleaning such appliances.

Slicers: A folding machine with table to hold meat. Stainless-steel slicers allow you to slice meats or cheese to any thickness. Safety controls make this appliance easy to use.

Coffee Grinders: To grind coffee beans just before the coffee is brewed.

Meat Grinders: Raw or cooked meat may be ground. Plastic housing holds grinders with various sized blades. Some also make sausage tubes. Stainless-steel blades do not rust. Entire machine comes apart for cleaning after each use.

Electric Mixers: They do a variety of tasks from whipping whites of eggs and creams to mixing heavy bread doughs. Motor power differs; the heavier duty motors for larger tasks are more costly to purchase and run. Mixers should lift to make it easy to remove pans, to remove beaters, and to use without the stand at the stove as needed. Some mixers have no stand and are meant to be held in the hand.

Pasta Maker: A small, counter-top machine with a high-impact plastic housing fitted with rollers that individually knead and flatten the dough and deliver it for cutting. A second roller turns out wide strips of noodles or fettuccini. A third roller has a narrower cutter that makes smaller noodles or finer fettuccini. The entire assemblage is easy to clean and to operate.

Portable Food Processors: Especially useful for slicing, grinding, and making pastry dough. Since they take up a considerable amount of space, that should be a consideration in their purchase. Two types are available: the direct drive, which is tall since the bowl sits on top of the motor housing, and the belt drive, which has the bowl next to the motor housing. Food processors carry warnings for safety in use. The blades are extremely sharp. Most machines are made so they do not operate unless properly assembled with the bowl's lid locked in place.[2]

Multipurpose Kitchen Aid: To save buying many different appliances, some manufacturers have created the all-purpose appliance that combines the activities of the others. They beat, whip, grind, slice, shred, juice, strain, grind, and make thin or thick pasta with an assortment of attachments.

CARE OF COOKING UTENSILS AND APPLIANCES

The following are some general rules to follow in caring for cooking utensils.

- Always pour water into pans after food is removed to prevent the remaining food particles from sticking.
- Do not clean utensils plated with chromium, tin, nickel, or special nonstick finishes with strong cleaning powders or metal scrapers, since these will scratch the surface plating and expose the metal underneath. Enamelware may also be scratched in this same manner.
- Avoid burning food in pans. Keep sufficient water to cover the bottom of the pan, and cook over low heat after boiling begins.
- Avoid stacking glass or enamel pans, since this may cause them to break or chip.

- Scrub nonstick finishes occasionally with special cleaners to maintain their nonstick properties.

CARE OF ELECTRIC APPLIANCES

To protect users, manufacturers have designed small appliances so they cannot be used unless they are properly assembled. Many turn off automatically when food has been cooked or processed. Some do not work unless covers are locked into position. With all those precautions, however, electric appliances can still cause problems if they are not properly handled. Blades are sharp, cords can become frayed, and machines sometimes work when they are not yet properly positioned. Therefore, they must be handled with care. Cords should be unplugged when machines are not is use. Appliances also have to be kept clean. This means dismantling them after use and washing and drying the removable parts, but motors must be kept out of water.

6. Which three metals are used as the base onto which porcelain-enamel is coated? How many layers of porcelain-enamel does a good-quality ware have?
7. Explain what is meant by a nonstick coating. What are the precautions that must be taken when using cooking nonstick utensils?
8. What are the uses of the following: double boiler, steamer, wok, broiler, pressure cooker?
9. Explain the following terms: resistance coils, insulation, microwave cooking, convection oven, continuous-cleaning oven. Why are metal pans not effective for microwave cooking?
10. What rules would you give a customer for the care of electric housewares?

1. "Microwave Ovens," *Consumer Reports*, March 1981, p. 128.
2. "Portable Food Mixers," *Consumer Reports*, July 1980, pp. 420–423.

NOTES

1. "Microwave Ovens," *Consumer Reports*, March 1981, p. 128.
2. "Portable Food Mixers," *Consumer Reports*, July 1980, pp. 420–423.

DO YOU KNOW YOUR MERCHANDISE?

1. Why are iron pans seasoned? How are iron- and steel pans protected from rusting?
2. Why are cooking utensils never plated with zinc?
3. How is tinware made? What are some disadvantages of tinware?
4. By what means are stainless-steel pans made to conduct heat evenly and quickly?
5. What are the advantages and disadvantages of aluminum cooking utensils?

PUTTING YOUR MERCHANDISE KNOWLEDGE TO WORK

Assume you are the department manager or head salesperson for a housewares store or department and that you are training new employees for saleswork. Explain the advantages and disadvantages of any one material used in utensils so that the new salespeople would be able to pass this information on to their customers.

PROJECT

Speak to five customers or friends who do some cooking and ask them what type of pots and pans (cast iron, aluminum, Silver Stone-coated, etc.) they prefer to cook with. What are their reasons for their preferences? Prepare a short report of your findings.

29

Home Accessories: Beauty With Function

Accessories are artistic aids in the home. The choice of furniture and decorative accessories in each person's home, apartment, or room reveals what that person likes and how that person lives. The accessories may be purely decorative adding color, charm, or drama to a room, or they may be both decorative and useful. Accessories such as curtains and draperies, lamps, small furniture items, and glassware may contribute both beauty and usefulness. Other items, such as clocks, mirrors, and vases may be both ornamental and useful.

CLOCKS

Clocks serve a dual purpose: to tell time and to adorn almost any room in the house. Clocks have been designed to fit into kitchens, bathrooms, bedrooms, foyers, dining rooms, living rooms, studies, TV rooms, dens, and playrooms.

Historical View of Timepieces

Sundials were the first instruments used to measure the passing of time. In the first century B.C., the Greek **water clock,** or *clepsydra,* was developed, which was operated by the flow of water through a small opening. **Candles** were then devised that could be marked to measure the passage of hours. The **hourglass,** which has sand dropping through a small orifice at a steady

rate, was another early device for time recording. In the ninth century, the first **weight-driven clock** was invented, and at the end of that century the **mechanical clock** was invented. Galileo's discovery of the principle of the pendulum led to the invention of the **pendulum clock** in 1656, which provided the first accurate timekeeping. The **balance wheel,** governed by a coiled spring, later replaced the pendulum and made small clocks and watches possible.

By 1725, clocks that were mechanically very accurate were developed, and clocks became more universally owned and used. In 1916, Henry Warren, a young inventor, perfected an **electric clock movement.** Today the **automatic electric clock,** with or without alarm, strike, or chime mechanisms, is an accurate, dependable timekeeper.

The quartz crystal clock was invented in 1929. It uses the vibrations of two crystals to drive a synchronous motor at a precise rate. The clock works with batteries. There are also unique and special clocks that use solar power or temperature changes to make them run.

Basic Clock Movements

Most clocks available today are powered in one of the following four ways.[1]

Key Wound: A knob on the back of the clock winds the mechanical mainspring that powers the clock as it unwinds. Such clocks run from 1 to 8 days before they need to be rewound. They may have separate alarms that are wound by a second knob. These clocks have a noisy to quiet ticktock sound when they are running.

Weight Driven: Heavy pulleys or weights pull chains that activate the wheels on these clocks. Most clocks with pendulums have this type of movement.

Electric: Powered by alternating current, these clocks are silent, require no winding, and keep very accurate time. If the power goes off, these clocks will stop. When the power comes back on again, the clock will function, but the time will have to be adjusted. Some electric alarm clocks have a standby battery to compensate for power failure.

Electronic: Powered by a battery, electronic impulses passing through a quartz crystal power the movement. The quartz crystal, oscillating 32,769 times per second, vibrates to turn the hands of the clock; it is controlled by an integrated electronic chip. Except when the battery runs down (it must be replaced about once a year), this clock is an excellent timekeeper.

Clock Cases

The housing for a clock will influence the value of a clock considerably. Metal cases are popular. They range from inexpensive steel with an enameled finish to cases plated with brass or chromium. More expensive metal cases are made from polished brass or bronze. Both brass and chromium are used for the trim and bezels on enameled-steel cases. The **bezel** is the grooved rim, or flange, in which a crystal is set that protects the face of the clock.

Wooden cases vary from inexpensive gumwood or tupelo through better-quality maple and birch, to rich crotch and swirl mahogany and walnut with expensive inlaid or carved decoration. Glass, plastic, and ceramic cases also vary in quality, beauty, and design. Highly polished white or colored marble also makes a dramatic case material for valuable clocks.

Clock Dial and Crystal Protectors

The **faces** or **dials** of clocks also vary in quality and attractiveness. They range from those made from paper pasted over a backing to metal dials with enameled or plated finishes. Expensive clocks may have brass dials with raised designs that are pierced or engraved by hand. Gold plating adds to the beauty and cost of some dials. Raised numerals impart a rich appearance and add to the cost of production.

Various ways of making time visible at night are used. Some dials have small lights that show the face in the dark. Others have hands and numerals coated with a phosphorescent paint.

Clock dials are protected by a clear glass or plastic, called a **crystal.** Glass is most commonly used; it resists scratching and remains clear and visible throughout the life of the clock. Plastic is increasingly used for inexpensive clocks. It gives good service as long as care is taken to prevent scratches.

Some clocks do not use protectors over the dials but have the face and hands of the clock exposed. Since crystals sometimes reflect light, these clocks are more readily visible.

Analog versus Digital Clocks

The **analog** clock is one that shows continuous time either by positioning different numbers or dots sequentially around the face. Metal hands on the clock indicate the time by pointing to the minutes and the hours. Most clocks have analog timekeeping mechanisms.

The **digital** clocks tell time by flashing the exact hour and minutes and by having an indicator show whether the time is A.M. or P.M. These digital clock faces may be numbers on a revolving plate that flash into view as the minutes change or they may be formed by light-emitting diodes (LED) (see Chapter 23).

Special Features of Clocks

Clocks may perform additional duties as timekeepers. Some have **alarms** that may be set for a predetermined wake up or alert. These alarms may be annoying buzzes, rings, or dulcet musical tones. Some clocks are combined with a radio that may waken the sleeper to music. Some alarms will work at a given hour and, if not turned off, will give the signal again 10 minutes later. Other clocks may be attached to stoves or electrical ovens to turn them on at a preset time.

Lunar Dials. Some clocks may have lunar dials that indicate the correct phase of the moon on each day. The moon dial makes one-half revolution every $29\frac{1}{2}$ days to coincide with the lunar cycle. Normally two moons are on the dial.

Talking Clocks. At the touch of a button, a talking clock, which has a voice-synthesizing system, will tell the time audibly through a built-in speaker. This clock may also work as an alarm.

Strike Clocks. Clocks that signal the hour and sometimes the quarter- and half-hour, are popular for steeples of tall buildings, as well as mantels, halls, and living and dining rooms. These clocks are equipped with a mechanism that releases a little hammer that hits against a rod or bell and gives forth a bell-like tone. Two winding spaces may be provided on the face of a wind-up clock — one for timekeeping and one for the strike mechanism. On electric clocks, a turn-off signal may be used to silence the clock at night.

Chime Clocks. Clocks that resemble strike clocks but have four or more rods against which the hammers pound and are somewhat more expensive are chime clocks. They sound a melody of four, six, eight, or more notes on the quarter-hour. This is repeated twice on the half hour, three times on the three-quarter hour, and four times on the hour. The hour is struck following the chimes. Clocks may have four-note Westminster chimes, six-note Canterbury, Winchester, or Trinity chimes, or eight-note Whitting, St. Michael, or Ave Maria chimes. Some clocks play more than one melody. Some chime clocks also contain a silencing feature for night use.[2]

Chronometer. This clock, which is used for navigation, is an extremely accurate and portable clock that carries the time of a known meridian

to use in connection with local time of the ship's position.[3]

Cuckoo Clock. The cuckoo clock is wound by means of a pulley with weights attached. Some run for 12 hours without rewinding; some run for 24 hours. When a weight comes to rest against the floor or any object, the clock no longer operates. Therefore, the clock must be placed high enough on the wall to permit the weights ample space in which to descend.

These clocks are equipped with two air chambers and bellows on either side of the case. When the quarter-hour is struck, the mechanism of the clock opens a door, a wooden bird emerges, and two coo sounds are made by the bellows expelling air. These clocks are purchased mainly as ornaments and are rarely depended upon to keep accurate time. Quality is judged by the case exterior. Expensive ones are hand carved; inexpensive cuckoo clocks may be housed in cases that are molded from composition material to simulate hand-carved cases.

Four-Hundred-Day Clock. This clock was developed in Germany around 1900. In place of an ordinary pendulum, it has a large, hollow brass balance wheel that is decorated with large knobs and is suspended on the end of a highly sensitive vertical rod. Wound only once a year, this clock's pendulumlike device rotates back and forth because of the elasticity of the metals used and the weight of the wheel. The entire clock is enclosed in a glass dome for protection and decoration. Unfortunately, these clocks are not too accurate. They tend to run fast immediately after winding and slow down considerably when the spring has partially unwound.

Perpetual Motion Clock. This clock, known as Atmos, is an accurate, jeweled-movement (see Chapter 23) timekeeper that has an automatic winding device. An inert gas, contained within a highly sensitive metal cylinder, expands with every degree of temperature change, thus putting in motion the winding mechanism. The clock is encased in a glass frame that prevents dust from getting into the delicate machinery. No oil is needed to keep the jeweled movement in good condition, so a minimum of care is required. The clock housing is made of polished brass.

TYPES OF CLOCKS

Clocks are made to accommodate many uses and needs. Some stand on the floor, some hang on the wall, and some sit on tables, desks, or other pieces of furniture.

Floor Clocks

Once an important clock for almost every large home, the **floor clock,** also called a **long clock,** lost most of its popularity as homes and apartments have shrunk in size. However, a few manufacturers still create this furniture-type clock.

Most of them house chiming or striking mechanisms and have large, easy-to-read dials and handsome pendulum and weights. They are 4 to 6 feet in height.

Contemporary Clock: A streamlined wooden case houses a contemporary-appearing dial and brass weights and pendulum.

Grandfather Clock: Traditional-appearing clock that stands 6 feet or more against a hall or living room wall. These clocks often strike the hour or have chime mechanisms. They may be powered by weight, by winding, by electricity, or by quartz movements. In addition to the mechanism, the beauty and detail on the wooden case determine the value of these clocks.

Pendulum Clock: Contemporary-appearing, mirror and brass, 4-foot-high clock reveals swinging pendulum.

Pedestal Clock: These clocks have long pendulums that extend into the hollow base that supports them.

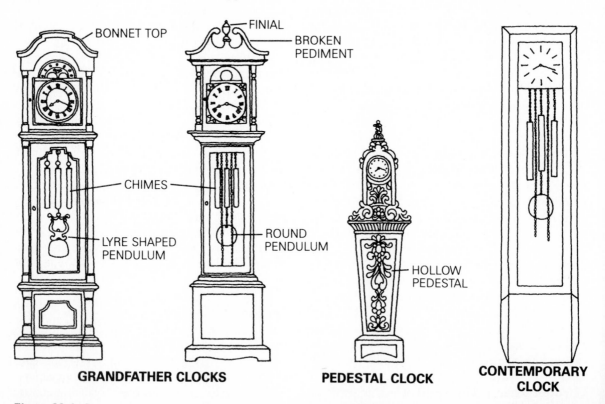

BONNET TOP

FINIAL

BROKEN PEDIMENT

CHIMES

LYRE SHAPED PENDULUM

ROUND PENDULUM

HOLLOW PEDESTAL

GRANDFATHER CLOCKS　　　**PEDESTAL CLOCK**　　　**CONTEMPORARY CLOCK**

Figure 29-1. *Once an important piece of furniture, the floor clock has lost popularity as homes have become smaller.*

WALL CLOCKS

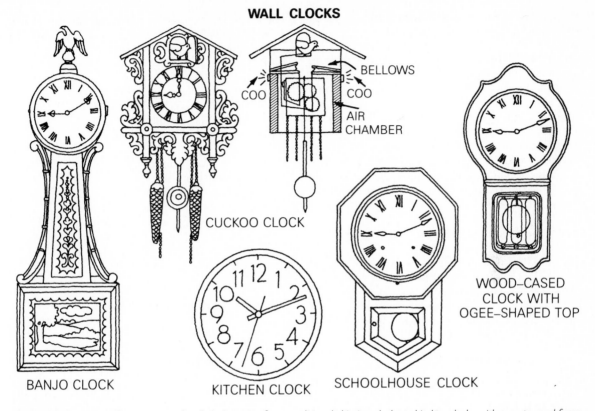

CUCKOO CLOCK

BELLOWS
COO   COO
AIR CHAMBER

WOOD–CASED CLOCK WITH OGEE–SHAPED TOP

BANJO CLOCK

KITCHEN CLOCK

SCHOOLHOUSE CLOCK

Figure 29-2. *Many different types of wall clocks exist, from traditional chiming clocks to kitchen clocks with easy-to-read faces.*

Wall Clocks

Clocks of varying size may be used to decorate walls in any room of the house. Any type of material, any shape, and any type of mechanism may be used in wall clocks. A list of popular wall clocks follows.

Banjo Clock: A wall clock shaped like a banjo and containing a pendulum. These were made in the United States from 1800 to 1850. Reproductions are made in winding, electric, and electronic models. They are suitable for the walls of living rooms, dining rooms, dens, and foyers.

Bathroom Clock: A clock that is unaffected by moisture or steam.

Calendar Clock: In 1853 the first patent for a calendar clock was issued. It had a top dial that told the hour and the minute and a bottom dial that showed the month and date. The clock was key driven and had a pendulum movement with Westminster chimes. The clock is made in reproduction today.

Cuckoo Clock: Ornamental clock from which a cuckoo emerges through a door at the top of the clock to signal the quarter-hours.

Educational Clock: Various-styled clocks allow children to learn to tell time and to develop an understanding of time in relationship to their activities. The clocks may have removable and add on parts.

Exposed Movement Clock: Plexiglas case allows the highly polished solid brass movement with nine chrome-plated chime tubes that play Westminster, Winchester, and St. Michael chimes to be viewed as the clock works.

Fob Clock: A large replica of a former railroad watch, the fob clock has Roman numerals, a sweep second hand, and a ring atop the stem winder that allows it to hang on the wall.

Girandole Clock: Today costly reproductions of the girandole clock made by Lemuel Curtis about 1815 are created for individuals. (See page 389.)

Key Wound Clock: Clocks reminiscent of those of the nineteenth century are made to be key wound. They run for 8 days and the case encloses a pendulum. Some also strike or have chimes.

Kitchen Clock: Various-shaped clocks, with or without kitchen motifs. They often have sweep second hands and may be electric or electronic.

Lantern Clock: These are shaped like the lanterns placed at the side of coaches used in the seventeenth and eighteenth centuries. The cases are usually brass with wood. Modern ones have electric or electronic movements.

Lyre-Shaped Clock: A clock housed in a case with the shape of a lyre.

Nursery Clock: Large-faced clocks with pictures and in colors that appeal to infants and toddlers.

Port-Hole Clock: Replicas of portholes on seventeenth-century ships may be created into clocks.

Schoolhouse Clock: These wooden framed clocks adorned the walls of schools in the eighteenth and early nineteenth centuries. They may be key driven with striking mechanism, electric, or electronic. A similar clock is the **depot** clock, reminiscent of the clocks traditionally found in train stations.

Ship's Bell Clock: For use on boats, ships, and in dens, clocks that strike the time according to ship's time have been designed. They are often accompanied by matching barometers that report weather conditions.

Ship's Wheel Clock: A clock that resembles the wheel of a ship but does not have the ship's bell timekeeping mode.

Sunburst-Shape Clock: Wall clocks in a gilded plaster case shaped like a sunburst.

Victorian Wall Clock: Plain, Roman numeral-dialed clock.

Wag-on-the-Wall Clock: Clock movement with a dial but no case that was popular about 1800.

Wood-Cased Pendulum Clock: Square-topped, bonnet-topped, broken-pedestal-topped, and other miscellaneous-shaped wooden cases house pendulum clocks with glass fronts that open to adjust the movement or the pendulum. They may have strike or chime mechanisms.

Mantel or Bracket Clocks

Mantels, the shelf above the fireplace, or **wall brackets** that extend out to hold a clock were popular places to rest clocks that were visible from many parts of a room. These clocks range in size from 6 to 12 inches wide and from 14 to 16 inches high. Mantel clocks may house strike or chime mechanisms. Key-wound, electric, and

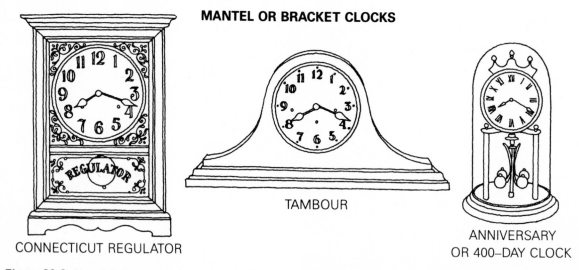

MANTEL OR BRACKET CLOCKS

CONNECTICUT REGULATOR

TAMBOUR

ANNIVERSARY OR 400–DAY CLOCK

Figure 29-3. *Mantel clocks may have key-wound, electric, or electronic movement. Traditionally placed on a shelf over the fireplace, these may also sit on tables or desks.*

electronic movements are available in these clocks. Familiar types of these clocks follow.

Acorn Clock: A shelf or mantel clock with a wooden frame in the shape of an acorn and a pendulum. They were made in Massachusetts and Connecticut in the nineteenth century and are used in homes with period furniture.

Anniversary Clock: A brass clock with a revolving pendulumlike attachment. Today's models may be electric or electronic as well as key wound. The clock movement is glass or plexiglass enclosed to reveal the entire clock. It is also called a **four-hundred-day clock.**

Bonnet-Top Clock: Elegant wooden cases designed to represent period furnishings.

Bracket Clock: Small, ornamental clock initially made to stand on a wall bracket but now used on a mantel or sideboard. The clock has a wooden case and a brass top handle. They often have chimes and may be key wound, electric, or electronic.

DESK AND TRAVEL CLOCKS

CONTEMPORARY
DESK CLOCK

TRAVEL ALARM CLOCK
WITH DIGITAL FACE

Figure 29-4. *Desk clocks are smaller than mantel clocks. Travel clocks come in a protective case.*

Cathedral Clock: Tall, stately appearing clock with wooden frame and hinged glass door, revealing a pendulum. It has strike movement and may be key wound, electric, or electronic.

Connecticut Regulator Clock: Wooden clock with pendulum and a 31-day key-wind movement and strike mechanism. It was made initially in the 1880s for schoolrooms.

Perpetual-Motion Clock: Called Atmos by Le-Coultre, the maker of this unique clock. It is powered by slight variations in air temperature. It has no winding mechanism and uses no battery or electricity.

Regulator Clock: An accurate clock that is used to set or regulate other timepieces. Today's adaptations may be key wound and have either strike or chime mechanisms. They come in a variety of cases.

Steeple Clock: A wooden mantel or table clock with pointed arches resembling church steeples.

Tambour Clock: A traditonal-design clock shaped like a camel's back. They may have strike or chime mechanisms and may be key wound, electric, or electronic.

Desk and Table Clocks and Travel Clocks

Desk and table clocks are usually smaller than mantel clocks, and the dials are less visible from other parts of the room. They usually have no chime nor strike mechanisms; some have alarms. Desk clocks may be key wound, electric, or electronic.

Travel clocks are small clocks that usually fold with the base used to protect the clock while it is being transported. Some have a leather or vinyl carrying pouch. Travel clocks are key wound or electronic.

Types of desk and travel clocks include the following.

Alarm Clock: Useful at bedside and whenever an alarm is needed. They may have buzzers, rings, or musical-chime sounds. They come in a variety of shapes and sizes and may have metal, wood, crystal, plastic, or ceramic cases. Dials may be digital or analog; some have lighted dials. Key wound, electric, and electronic clocks all are available with alarms.

Calendar Clock: Digital clocks may have the time and the date shown on the clock's face.

Clip-On Clock: The flexibility of quartz (electronic) movements allows clocks to be clipped on to bedsteads, edges of chairs, or other convenient surfaces.

Clock Radio: Clocks with digital or analog faces may be combined with radios in either electric- or electronic-type mechanisms. These also come with alarms that waken the user to radio music or sound. They are housed in wooden or plastic cases in a range of colors and shapes.

Contemporary Clock: Unusual shapes, analog faces without numbers or with dots, and sleek metal or clear plastic housings give a modern look to desk and table clocks.

Globe-Trotter's Clock: A dual-dial analog clock face that shows time in various places in the world.

Heliochronometer (Sundial): A clock with sundial-type design that is powered by a quartz movement.

Magnetic Base Clock: Quartz-powered clock is constructed to adhere to a magnetic base. This permits it to be hung upside down, sideways, or right-side up.

Tilting Clock: Clocks on flexible bases may tip at various angles for the best visibility.

Traditional Clock: Clocks reminiscent of those used in the nineteenth century have been updated with quartz movements and second sweep hands. They may also have alarms.

Travel Clock: Once limited to folding clocks in a leather or plastic case, travel clocks today have a variety of face protectors, including separate vinyl or leather cases that slip over the clock when not in use. Clocks are key wound or electronic and come with or without alarms.

CARE OF CLOCKS

Clocks need careful daily dusting with a soft cloth. If the clock has a plastic crystal, this can easily be scratched and dull the appearance of the clock. Unless motors are sealed, clock movements should be checked and cleaned by a jewelry watch repairer every few years. Clocks should be kept as free from dust and dirt as possible as these harm the inner mechanism. Since temperature changes affect the metal parts in many clocks, they should be placed where heat or cold is not excessive.

Clocks that need to be wound should be tended to regularly. Avoid overwinding the spring. Pendulum clocks run well only if the case is level and the pendulum is free to swing evenly. Clocks also need firm support if they are to be balanced and keep accurate time. Battery-powered clocks usually slow as the battery loses its power. That signals a time to replace the battery.

MIRRORS

In a home mirrors and other flat glass objects, such as table tops, desk protectors and doors in furniture, play many important roles. The clarity of glass is paramount. If the flat glass has any ripples or bends, the objects viewed through it or in it will be distorted.

Types of Flat Glass

Originally, window and mirror makers blew large bubbles of glass and then opened and flattened them, cutting out small panes of glass from the less-striated sections. This glass, known as **crown glass,** was not perfectly flat and smooth. It is used in the mullion sections of doors of some fine breakfronts and secretaries.

The making of **plate glass** was developed by the French during the reign of Louis XIV. When it was discovered that hot glass could be rolled on an iron table with iron cylinders that pressed out all the bubbles and wavy lines and that it could then be ground and polished on both sides with abrasive substances until the glass was clear and smooth, it became possible to make nondistorting glass mirrors.

For flat surfaces, such as windows and some inexpensive mirrors, **sheet glass** is used. Since 1924 smooth window glass has been made by drawing the molten glass vertically through a machine that is as high as several floors in a building. As the glass is drawn, it is flattened and smoothed and, when cool, is passed between rows of rollers. The glass continues to cool slowly as it travels through the machine. At the end of the machine the cooled flat glass is cut, examined, measured, and packed. This glass is also known as **window glass** or **shock glass.**

In 1962 the economical production of plate glass by the float process was developed. **Float** glass is formed in a continuous ribbon and then cooled on a surface of molten tin. It has an optically flat, smooth surface and fire-finished brilliance, which eliminates the need for costly grinding and polishing. Float glass is used for automobile windows and increasingly for other windows and mirrors. This glass can be made in varying thicknesses. Today plate glass produced by the float process has completely replaced the grinding-and-polishing process and has almost completely replaced sheet glass.

Turning Flat Glass into Mirrors

The first mirrors, developed around 400 B.C., were made of polished metal. Glass mirrors were first made about A.D. 1250. Because they did not give true reflections, they were not popular. After plate glass was developed, the demand for mirrors grew.

Coating Mirrors. Early mirrors were made with a coating of tin mixed with mercury that was spread on the back of the glass. In about 1840 silver was substituted for the mercury, which improved the reflective qualities of the mirror. Copper sprayed over the silver, together with a coating of mirror-backing paint, protects the silver from oxidizing.

Mirror Backings. The backing on a mirror helps to keep it in good condition and gives it different uses. Mirrors backed with fiberboard are the least expensive. The fiberboard is held to the frame either by gluing it onto the mirror or by affixing it with small clamps that fit over the edge of the glass. Better-quality backings are made from plywood. If an air space is left between the mirror and its backing, the silver is not likely to be scratched and the mirror will remain in good condition. Mirrors that are to be used for mirrored walls have adhesive backings that attach to any flat surface and hold the mirror in place.

Uses of Mirrors

Mirrors influence how a room looks in many ways. Mirrors may make a room look larger, especially if they cover an entire wall. Mirrors may make a room more attractive by focusing attention on a particular furniture item or a grouping of items and accessories. Mirrors add light by reflecting lamps or outdoor scenes. They also allow surveillance of a room. Mirrors, of course, are indispensable aids to personal grooming. In addition to their utilitarian purposes, they serve as decorative items.[4]

Kinds of Mirrors

Mirrors are made in a variety of styles, colors, and finishes to fit every need and want.

Antique Mirrors: These are made to appear mottled, to create a smoky or shadow effect, or to look veined and old. These effects are achieved by using a variety of colors and designs or by oxidizing the silver.

Beveled Mirrors: In place of a straight edge, the mirror has an edge cut at a slant to the main mirror area. The bevel gives a finished appearance to a mirror (or to plain glass), but it raises the cost.

Concave Mirrors: The glass surface is slightly bent or depressed. This results in a mirror surface that tends to magnify reflected items or images.

Convex Mirrors: The glass surface bulges in a raised center to increase the area that is reflected. These mirrors are used for safety purposes in elevators, retail stores, and factories.

Copper-Backed Mirrors: These have an electro-copper plating over the silver plating, producing a superior finish to ordinary mirrors. The copper is coated with shellac and mirror-backing paint.

Dark-Colored Mirrors: By applying a solution of lead salts before silvering, a low-reflection mirror may be used for decoration or as rearview mirrors in automobiles.

Decorated-Glass Mirrors: Small designs may be cut, etched, or sandblasted into the glass in areas of the mirror not used for viewing.

Girandole: A nineteenth-century round-shaped, convex mirror with or without an attached candle sconce. American girandoles often used an eagle as a finial over the mirror frame that was elaborately carved.

Gold-Colored Mirrors: A solution of gold salts plated on the mirror before the silver plating produces a gold-colored mirror.

One-Way Vision Mirrors: These permit people to

look through transparent glass from one side but to see only a mirror image from the other side. Used mainly as peepholes in apartment house doors leading to outer hallways.

Pier-Glass Mirrors: The glass is tall and narrow to show a person's entire figure. The frame stands on the floor and the mirror may or may not be tip tilted. Also called a **cheval glass** or a **swing glass** mirror.

Three-Way Mirrors: Mirror panels set in a frame have a center and two side sections. The side sections may be positioned so a person can see front and both sides simultaneously. These may be small enough to sit on a dressing table or tall enough to stand on the floor. The sides may be flattened out to make a three-panel mirror or folded over the center glass when not in use.

Tiles or Strips: Mirrors may be pasted or attached with studs onto a wall or other surface. If cut into sections, mirrors may tile an entire wall, or items of furniture may be made with small tiles on a flexible backing.

Venetian Mirror: Unframed wall mirror with back mounting and hangers. Available in beveled and polished edges.[5]

Installation and Care of Mirrors

Because of their weight and fragility, mirrors must be installed with care. Two or more hangers are needed with mirrors. If a mirror weighs less than 35 pounds, hooks to hold the two hangers should be placed about 4 inches apart. If a mirror weighs more than 35 pounds, the weight should be distributed by having the hangers at either side of the mirror. Adhesive-backed picture hooks are not strong enough to hold wall mirrors.

Since glass is brittle and hard, edges of glass either need to be protected by a frame or molding or the edges have to be polished so they are

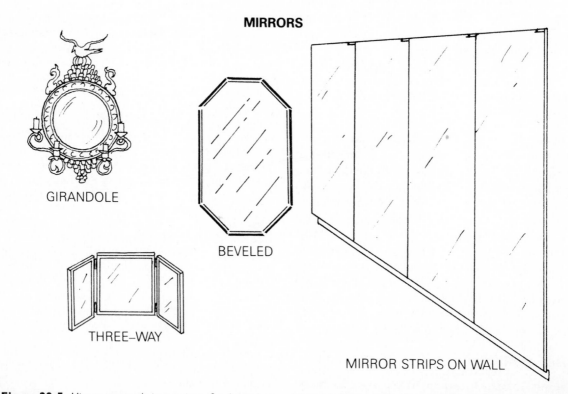

MIRRORS

GIRANDOLE

BEVELED

THREE–WAY

MIRROR STRIPS ON WALL

Figure 29-5. *Mirrors are made in a variety of styles, colors, and finishes. Clarity of glass is especially important.*

rounded to prevent damage to objects and people when they are handled. For ventilation and to keep the wall behind the mirror in good condition, felt tabs or bumpers placed at the base of the frame will allow for air space.

Mirrors should be cleaned with mild liquid cleaners and clean, soft cloths. Abrasive cleaners will scratch glass. Since grease collects on glass, special cleaners that cut grease are recommended.

VASES

Vases come in a wide variety of sizes and shapes. They range from tiny ones, known as **bud vases,** through medium-sized ones, to very large ones that may hold a bouquet of long-stemmed flowers.

Vases should be appropriate for the surroundings in which they will be used. They also should be the correct size for the flowers they are to hold. A china vase, for example, would look out of place in a rustic setting, just as a squat pottery vase would be incongruous in an elegant 18th century drawing room.

Vases should be washed carefully after use to remove all the debris from the flowers that have stood in them.

NOTES

1. Adapted from "Clocks," *Jewelers' Circular-Keystone,* September 1982, p. 170.
2. Henry B. Fried, "All about Tubular Chime Clocks," *Jewelers' Circular-Keystone,* Part I, July 1980, pp. 236–246; and Part II, August 1980, pp. 180–196.
3. Donald S. McNeil ed., *Jeweler's Dictionary,* 3rd ed. Jeweler's Circular-Keystone, 1976, Radnor, Pa., p. 143.
4. *Decorating with Mirrors,* Libbey-Owens-Ford Company, n.d., p. 11.
5. *Designing with Mirrors,* National Association of Mirror Manufacturers, n.d., p. 20.

DO YOU KNOW YOUR MERCHANDISE?

1. Briefly trace the steps in timekeeping from the sundial to the electronic clock.
2. Explain what is meant by key-wound clock; weight-driven clock; electric clock; electronic clock.
3. Explain the differences between analog and digital dials.
4. What is a lunar dial? A talking clock? A strike clock? A chime clock?
5. Explain how floor clocks, wall clocks, mantel clocks, and desk and travel clocks differ.
6. What advice about caring for a clock would you give a customer?
7. Explain the following terms: crown glass, plate glass, shock or window glass, float glass. What is the most important factor for good mirrors?
8. To what decorating uses in a home may mirrors be put?
9. What advice about installing and caring for mirrors would you give a customer?
10. What two factors should be considered when selecting a vase?

PUTTING YOUR MERCHANDISE KNOWLEDGE TO WORK

Bring a small clock to class or a picture of a clock from a newspaper or magazine. Give a short sales talk about the advantages the clock offers in use.

PROJECT

Collect three advertisements from catalogs or newspapers for clocks or for mirrors. Analyze the ads. Did they identify the type of product and its uses, the materials from which each was made, the dimensions? Was any information on care given? Rewrite one of the ads. How did you improve it?

30

Lamps and Lighting: The Indispensable Items

The visibility of the world around us depends on light, and much of our activity would not be possible if light were unavailable. Originally, people relied almost wholly on natural light. They went to bed when dark descended and arose with the first light of day. They supplemented natural light with the artificial light of **flares** or **torches** that were made by dipping wood ends in fat and then holding them near a lighted fire. **Candles** — wicks surrounded by wax — were developed next and could be more easily controlled than flares. Open flames, even from candles, were dangerous, so containers were created to hold them. The first containers were metal with holes cut into them to allow light to escape. Candles remained the main lighting mode for many decades.

In 1783, flat, woven, ribbonlike wicks were secured in a close-fitting support that held oil in a reservoir. Some lamps are designed today to represent this reservoir that held the lighter fluid. By 1816, gas distilled from coal was introduced. It produced a bright but flickering and wavering flame. By 1859, kerosene lamps, which were safer and gave a brighter light than the candle, were introduced. Glass chimneys were then created to prevent the flame from being blown out. These are recreated today in the popular hurricane lamps.

In 1879 Thomas A. Edison made the first commercially successful incandescent lamp, but gas and kerosene continued for many years to be important lamp materials. After the turn of the century, however, electric lights replaced most of the other types of lighting.

LIGHTING NEEDS

Standards have been established to help you to see without straining your eyes. Candles have long been regarded as a standard for measuring light. The luminous radiation from one candlepower source to each square foot of the inside surface of a sphere is called a **lumen,** the Latin word for light. A lumen per square foot is called a **footcandle.** Therefore, a surface 1 foot from one candlepower source is lighted to 1 footcandle. Footcandle is used as the measurement of light intensity. A light intensity 10 times as great is said to give 10 footcandles of light. Light measuring devices are used to determine the amount of light concentrated at any position in a room. The Illuminating Engineering Society of North America recommends the minimum standards of footcandles listed in Table 30–1.

Measuring Light

Translating lumens into watts, as marked on light bulbs, is difficult to do because the distance you are from the light source varies the amount of light on that place. For example, each 1 foot a person moves from the light source reduces that illumination by the square of the distance. Thus

Table 30–1 MINIMUM LIGHT STANDARDS MEASURED IN FOOTCANDLES[a]

Reading	Small print	40
	Larger print	20
	Prolonged reading	70–75
Sewing	Dark colors	100
	Medium tones	40
	Pastel colors	20
Writing	Casual	30
	Prolonged	70
Games	Cards	10
	Table tennis	40
Cooking		40
Shaving		40
Applying cosmetics		30
Movement through entryways and rooms		5

[a]Younger people adapt to light more easily than do older people. Those over 40 should increase the light by about 10 footcandles for each use.

the illumination 2 feet from the light source is one-fourth that of the amount of illumination only 1 foot from that source. If a person moves 3 feet from the light source, the light is only one-ninth the strength that it was at 1 foot. Therefore, even though the wattage may be high, if the distance is substantial the light may be relatively dim. At its source, a 15-watt bulb yields approximately 140 lumens, a 40-watt bulb yields 450 lumens, a 75-watt bulb yields 1,150 lumens, and a 100-watt bulb yields 1,700 lumens. These lumens decrease rapidly as the light source is moved away from the user.

Colors, Textures, and Finishes Affect Light

In addition to being affected by the distance from the source, light is affected by the surfaces on which it falls. Light is absorbed by dark colors and reflected by light colors. Therefore, a given amount of light in a room with white walls and ceiling will appear much brighter than the same amount of light in a room with dark red or brown walls and ceiling.

Shiny or enamel paints or surfaces cause glare that tends to intensify light and make it unpleasant to look at. Matte or dull paints or surfaces diffuse or spread light and are much more comfortable to look at. Pile textures, velvety surfaces, looped surfaces all diffuse light, whereas shiny satins tend to focus light and produce a glare. Metallic surfaces reflect the light, whereas terra cotta and dull stoneware absorb the light and diffuse it.

TYPES OF LIGHT BULBS

Two basic types of light bulbs are used for home lighting: incandescent lights and fluorescent lights.

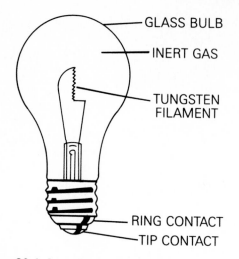

GLASS BULB

INERT GAS

TUNGSTEN
FILAMENT

RING CONTACT
TIP CONTACT

Figure 30-1. *Parts of an incandescent light bulb. These bulbs emit a brilliant, shining light.*

Incandescent Lights

Incandescent lights, initially developed by Thomas A. Edison, offer brilliant, shining light. An electrical current flows through a specially prepared, coiled tungsten filament that glows inside a sealed glass bulb filled with an inert gas. As the tungsten filament glows, molecules of the metal are moved. They are carried to the top of the bulb where they are deposited on the cooler bulb surface and this causes the bulb to darken slowly over its period of use. When a bulb finally burns out, the inside is usually quite dark with this residue.[1]

Lights are marked by watts, the units of electrical power used by electric companies. The number of watts indicates the power the bulb consumes when it burns. The higher the wattage, the more intense the light from any given bulb. Light bulbs for home use are available from 15 to 300 watts.

Bulbs may be one way or three way. **Three-way bulbs** have two filaments. Each may be operated separately, or they may be operated together. Thus, a 50-watt filament and a 100-watt filament will together yield a 150-watt bulb. Two contacts in the base of the light bulb make possi-

ble the three-way lighting effect with the proper three-way switch.

Incandescent bulbs generate a considerable amount of heat and burn out relatively quickly — 1,000 hours is about the peak life for such bulbs. The heat from these bulbs may warp or distort close-fitting lamp shades that are not made from heat-resistant materials. Some incandescent bulbs have been made that last up to 10 times as long as regular bulbs. However, their cost is higher.

Incandescent bulbs may have special finishes or use colored glass that make them more attractive for certain purposes.

Clear Glass Bulbs: Permit the highest amount of yellow-tinted light to emanate from the bulb. Glare is produced unless some shade is furnished.

Frosted Bulbs: Made by etching the inner surface of the bulb with hydrofluoric acid. The etching diffuses the light, diminishes glare, and reduces the amount of light that comes from the bulb. These bulbs give off a warm, yellow-tinted light.

Daylight Bulbs: Made from clear blue glass. They reduce the yellow tint and produce a light that more nearly resembles natural daylight.

Reflecting Bulbs: Have silvered surfaces on the lower portion of the bowl that forms reflectors to prevent light from coming out at the bottom. The light is mirrored upward in the form of indirect light.

Soft White Bulbs: Have a coating that diffuses the light.

Colored Bulbs: Have a translucent appearance. In pink, green, blue, or amber they are for everyday use. In red, green, or other bright colors they are for special use.

Fluorescent Lights

Cool, glareless, low-cost light is available from fluorescent bulbs, which were first shown at the New York and San Francisco World Fairs in 1939. These bulbs use no filaments but rather have phosphors that glow when the current flows through the mercury vapor and argon contained in the completely sealed tube.

Two types of fluorescent lighting fixtures are used: preheat and rapid start. **Preheat fixtures** have a small can-shaped metal device called a **starter** that fits into the base of the tube's socket. The starter acts only until the vapor coating inside the tube starts to glow. A ballast controls the current. **Rapid-start fixtures** have ballasts that eliminate the need for a starter. They supply the added surge needed to heat up the filament at the start.

Because the most energy is used when turning on fluorescent tubes, they should be left on when rooms are vacated for a short period of time. Except for the moment when they are turned on, they consume only minor amounts of energy.[2]

Initially, fluorescent tubes offered only a cold white light. Today, warmer glows and more flattering lights are available. However, the most flattering light is still achieved with incandescent lights or with a combination of incandescent and fluorescent lights.

Fluorescent lights come in narrow tubes that may be straight, U-shaped, or circular. The tubes are from 5 inches to 8 feet in length and from 1 to $1\frac{1}{2}$ inches in diameter. Because of their low heat radiation, materials not suitable for lamp shades used with incandescent bulbs may be used safely with fluorescent bulbs. In 1979, a fluorescent bulb that could be used in an ordinary light socket was patented.[3]

The economy of the fluorescent bulb is well known. A 40-watt fluorescent tube gives twice as much light as a 100-watt incandescent bulb, lasts 16 times as long, and runs cool enough to permit higher light levels.

CONTROLLING LIGHT

Various ways of controlling the amount of light that reaches any surface have been devised. **Tensor lamps** focus on a specific area or object, such as a book. There are bulbs that can direct light toward the ceiling, toward areas where work is to be performed, or toward areas where special effects are to be created. **Dimmers** use a **rheostat** — a device for regulating a current by means of variable resistances — and can take a room from bright to candlelight in intensity by simply turning a dial.

Light from out of doors may be controlled. Curtains and draperies, venetian blinds, and window shades may be used to control the amount of light coming in from outside. Sheer curtains may diffuse the light just slightly. Venetian blinds, shades, and heavy draperies keep most of the light from entering a room. For rooms without sufficient light from out of doors, artificial light may be needed even during the day.

FUNCTIONS OF LIGHT

Drama can be created with light, or light can be used just for daily functions. Light gives general illumination, allows you to see tasks you are performing, accents articles or areas, and creates general moods.

General Illumination

Light is usually necessary any place that people sit, walk, or talk. When no special lighting is needed, general illumination may be all that is required. Such light may be bright or dim.

Task Lighting

When a person intends to read, sew, write, type, use a computer terminal, perform a task that requires small tools, and so on, task lighting is desirable. Since general illumination is usually not strong enough for such tasks, additional lights are needed.

Accent Lighting

Sometimes people light special objects, such as sculpture or painting. Sometimes recesses in walls or cabinets are highlighted with extra lighting. Entire walls may be washed with light. Plants may be dramatized by lights that shoot upward from under the leaves.

Aesthetic or Mood Lighting

Colored lights, lights that outline certain objects, soft lights on tables, lights that accent the glow of the silver, china, and glass at the dinner table, dim lights in barrooms, or soft lights while music plays are ways of creating a special mood or atmosphere through the imaginative use of light.

DISTRIBUTION OF LIGHT

Light may be focused in many ways throughout a room.

Direct Light

Light that is focused downward so the light rays are concentrated toward the point where greatest illumination is desired is frequently found in areas where people eat, read, sew, write, or perform other manual tasks. Direct light bulbs have an opaque shade that sends the light in one direction, thus concentrating the light where it is most needed. If only this light is on, deep shadows will exist in other parts of the room.

Indirect Light

Indirect light is focused upward by means of an opaque shade so the light's rays are reflected from the ceiling or the walls. This casts a soft light that is spread fairly evenly around the room and does not create shadows.

Direct–Indirect Light

A combination light fixture that throws equal amounts of light upward and downward combines the advantages of the direct and the indirect light. The upward light eliminates sharp shadows and the downward light sheds ample light on a task area. To achieve this, the shade must be translucent rather than opaque.

Semidirect

Semidirect light is primarily concentrated on the tasks to be performed but allows some light to be spread upward. It is helpful in reducing shadows. This light can be achieved with a direct light that has openings at the top of the enclosure to allow some light to escape upward.

Semiindirect

Light from a semiindirect fixture is concentrated upward, but through openings in the shade some light is allowed to filter downward. If enough wattage is used, this type of light may achieve general lighting, as well as be sufficient for task lighting.

Diffused Light

Light that spreads evenly throughout a room, that eliminates shadows, and that gives an equal amount of light in every direction is called diffused. If the light is strong enough, even tasks may be performed easily with such light.

PROVIDING HOME LIGHTING

Light may be available in homes from three different types of fixtures: architectural or built in, attached to ceiling or walls, and portable from lamps. Except for battery-powered lights, all lights are dependent upon a source of light from wires built into the walls, ceiling, and floors in the home. Therefore, placement may be restricted somewhat by the planning done when the structure was built.

Architectural Lighting

Various types of built-in lighting arrangements are listed below.

Cove Lighting: A cove is a wooden or metal trough or groove placed near the ceiling of the room. The light, usually a fluorescent tube, is focused upward. Such a fixture is usually built along the length of the wall or over doors or windows.

Cornice Lighting: A cornice is a projection from the wall, made either of wood or metal, that reflects light downward. Cornices are enclosed at the top and usually also hold fixtures from which draperies or curtains may be hung. Cornice lighting dramatizes the curtain wall of the room and diffuses light throughout the room.

Valance Lighting: A valance may be made of wood, metal, or cloth. Since it is not enclosed at the top or bottom, light is directed both upward and downward.

Valances are superimposed over curtains or draperies.
Brackets: These are wall decorations that are usually set low on walls. They are often made to reflect light upward, downward, or both upward and downward.
Recessed Ceiling and Wall Lights: By means of a dropped ceiling, light fixtures may be built in so the light is even with the ceiling. This built-in light may come from individual spots or from luminous flat units that allow an entire area to be lighted. These luminous fixtures or **luminaries,** a term used for architectural lighting, refer to the lighting fixture and the light source. They may be mounted in the wall, within niches or recesses in the wall, or in the ceiling.
Surface Lighting on Ceilings and Walls: Luminaries that project below the ceiling or extend out from the wall may also be built in. They are covered with glass or frosted-appearing plastic or have metal or plastic **louvers** (slats that deflect the light). They give a diffused light that may be used for overall lighting or for dramatizing certain areas of the room. Some luminaries are suspended as pendants from the ceiling or walls. These also yield general illumination or may be used to focus on certain objects within a room.
Chandeliers: Lighting fixtures suspended from the ceiling may be simple or extremely elaborate.

Track Lighting

Track lighting differs from architectural lighting in that it is added after the room is otherwise complete. Track lighting is a series of lights on a wall or on a ceiling-mounted strip or track of metal. The track with wires and outlets is attached to the ceiling or wall, and the light fixtures, or cylinders are then plugged into it. They may be directed downward, upward, or sideways and may be positioned at various points along the track. These cylinders may be repositioned or removed as needs change.[4]

Lighting with Portable Lamps

Few homes rely just on architectural lighting for overall lighting and decorative effects. Some homes use little or no architectural lighting but depend almost entirely upon movable lamps for light. Lamps come in many types and sizes and offer a great deal of variety both as sources of

light and as ornaments for the home. Tall floor lamps, table lamps, desk lamps, wall and ceiling lamps, and lamps that clamp to furniture or objects are available. Movable lamps are used for mood lighting, general lighting, task lighting, and accent lighting.

MATERIALS AND MANUFACTURE OF LAMPS

There is a wide range of materials from which the exteriors of lamps may be made. The functions of lamps, however, require that parts remain fairly stable.

Parts of a Lamp

Some or all of the following parts may be found on the movable lamps used in homes.

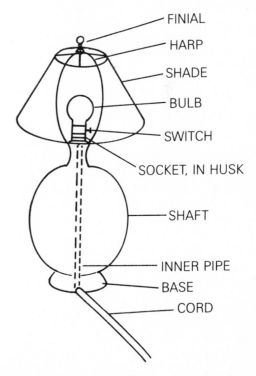

PARTS OF A PORTABLE LAMP

- FINIAL
- HARP
- SHADE
- BULB
- SWITCH
- SOCKET, IN HUSK
- SHAFT
- INNER PIPE
- BASE
- CORD

Figure 30-2. *Parts of a lamp. These may be made from a wide range of materials.*

Finial: A small, decorative knob that fits on the top of the lamp to hold the shade in place.

Harp: A brass or steel arch used to support the shade on lamps that have no diffusing bowl or no permanently attached shade.

Diffusing Bowl: A white (milk) glass, circular, dish-shaped holder that serves to soften and diffuse the light as well as support the shade.

Light Bulb: This fits into a socket that extends either from the harp or through the center of the diffusing bowl or at the top of the shaft of a lamp.

Switch: A knob that is included in the socket or is placed at some other position on the lamp. It is used to turn on the lamp.

Candle Arms: Made from the same material as the base, these extend from the socket area and hold additional light bulbs.

Husk or Holder: Supports the socket and bulb.

Shaft: The decorative outer part between the socket and the base of the lamp.

Inner Pipe: A steel rod that extends through the shaft to house the electric cord.

Base: The part on which the lamp rests.

Cord: An electric conductor made from copper wire wound with fabric or covered with rubber. It extends from the base of the lamp and is attached to the outlet.

Lamp Base and Shaft Materials

The array of materials suitable for ornamental lamp bases and shafts is almost unending.

Alabaster: A white or off-white stone that has a natural translucence. It may be made to resemble marble, coral, jade, quartz, or onyx. Alabaster is fairly soft and can chip unless it is handled with care.

Ceramic: Bases can be made from china, bone china, stoneware, earthenware, or pottery.

Glass: Lead and lime glass for lamps may be crystal clear, translucent, or opalescent. Hand cutting, etching, frosting, and enameling are a few of the decorations applied to the glass.

Leather: An outer cover of leather may be stretched over a frame to impart a richly textured appearance to a lamp. Designs may be molded in the leather, and colors may be painted onto its surface. Vinyl or polyurethane plastics may be used to imitate leather.

Marble: A close-textured stone that when polished reveals attractive graining and a rich luster.

Metal: Metals are among the most popularly used materials for shafts and bases of lamps.

Tole Lamps: Reproductions are made from brass and steel which are more durable than the originally used tin. They have painted metal bases and matching shades. Gold-colored conventional and classical motifs are stenciled onto the colored shade and base.

Plaster or Composition: Artisans have perfected a new type of plaster that is sturdy, takes a rich mellow finish, and preserves the fine detail of an original design. This plaster makes possible a wide line of beautiful lamps at low cost. Finishing touches may make the bases resemble wood, marble, jade, or china.

Semiprecious Stones: Jade, coral, quartz stones, and onyx are used for shafts and bases of collector's lamp pieces.

Wood: Wooden lamp bases may be carved, turned, or grooved to impart the desired outlines and then stained and finished to give luster and color tone to the wood.

Plastic: Plastic may imitate many other materials or be used for its own surface appeal. The edge-lighting and light-bending characteristics of the polystyrene and acrylic plastics make them unusual mediums for lamps.

Lamp Shades

Lamp shades serve both decorative and useful roles in lamps. They help to shield, direct, and diffuse light and to decorate the fixture.

Shades made of **rigid materials** have become increasingly popular. These materials should be fire proof or fire resistant, should not melt in the presence of heat, and should not discolor when used near bulbs. Metal, glass, fiberglass, and plastic are the most commonly used rigid shade materials.

Certain characteristics help **fabric or paper shades** give good service. The shade's frame should be welded at the joints since soldered joints are not as sturdy. The metal frame should be made and finished so that it will not corrode or discolor the material that will later be used to cover it. Exposed metal sections should be lacquered. The top and bottom rings of the shade should be securely attached to the covering material by sewing, riveting, or cementing with a waterproof cement. The shade material should be translucent to diffuse and soften light coming through. The inside surface of the shade should be light in color and should reflect two-thirds of the light or more. The entire shade should rest evenly and securely on the harp or reflector with which it is used. Fabric shades that are hand sewn to frames are more costly than those that are glued. The latter may come apart when washed.

Materials Used in Lamp Shades

The character of the lamp shade is largely determined by the material used for the shade.

Fabric: Virtually any fabric may be used for lamp shades. The most popular are silks, rayons, nylon, and cotton. Lace made from any type of yarn may also be used. When plain fabric is used, it may be stretched over the frame tightly to give a smooth surface or it may be pleated into tiny folds held in place on top and bottom with a binding that surrounds the lamp. Both types of surfaces have inner linings of fabric or paper to help diffuse the light and support the outer fabric.

Fiberglass: Fiberglass pressed into a mat and bonded with clear plastic yields an off-white, rigid material that makes conical-shaped lamp shades. These are fireproof, very sturdy, and long wearing. They are translucent and allow light to be diffused all around the bulb.

Glass: Glass in all its colors and forms is useful for lamp shades.

Kappa Shells: Translucent, ecru-colored shells that shed a golden light when the bulb is turned on make a dramatic, rigid shade.

Leather: Opaque shades may be made from any type of leather stretched over a frame. For translucent shades, genuine parchment, made by specially processing sheepskin, may be used.

Metal: These are rigid shades that may be shaped in a variety of ways and have dull painted to shiny enameled surfaces. Some may be pierced to allow light to come through the shade.

Mica: A translucent pale to dark amber crystalline mineral that is combined with shellac to bond the flakes for use as lamp shades.

Plastic: Plastic makes rigid lamp shades that vary from transparent to translucent to opaque. Plastics come in any color and texture and offer a variety of forms not possible in other substances. Since some plastics melt when too near heat, the user should make sure the plastic is of the thermosetting type, which does not melt, or that the shade is at a safe distance from the bulb.

Shade Attachment to the Lamp

Rigid shades may be attached directly to the shaft of the lamp, with the cord and bulb socket set inside the shade. These shades cannot be changed. **Changeable shades** come in the following varieties to fit the lamp with which they will be used.

Clip Type: A partition of metal across the top of the shade has a metal clip that spreads to hold to the bulb.

Chimney-Ring: Lamp shades that are to fit over a glass chimney require a large opening in the wires at the top of the lamp shade frame. This fits over the chimney and holds the shade in place.

Drop-Light: For lamps that hold the shade below the top of the lamp no finial is used, but a bulb socket itself holds the shade in place. This is a less expensive type of shade.

Washer-Harp Type: This shade has wires that divide the top of the shade into thirds with a ring in the center that fits atop the harp and has a screw-type finial used to hold it together.

SHAPES OF LAMP SHADES

An endless variety of lamp shades is available to suit every occasion and every taste.

Art Nouveau: Asymmetrical flower forms often in opal glass with variegated colors.

Ballerina: A shade with a wide flare that is wavy like a skirt. It is often molded in plastic or made of fabric.

Bed: Narrow, three-sided shade with two back hooks to fit over a bed's headboard.

Bell: A conical-shaped shade with a narrow top and flaring sides.

Bubble: Appears like two half spheres attached in the middle.

Candle Shade: Small shade that fits atop a single shaft small lamp.

Conical: A small shade usually not changeable.

Coolie: Short, flared shade in the shape of a Chinese coolie's work hat.

Double Conical: Useful for wall brackets; two conical shades are joined to give direct and indirect light.

Cylindrical: Narrow circular lamps shade open at top and bottom. It may be translucent or opaque.

Drum: A large, circular shade with straight sides and open top and bottom.

Ellipse: Glass or plastic shade, enclosed at the bottom, for use with overhead fixture.

Expanded Cylinder: A cylindrical-shaped shade that is slightly swelled about three-fourths way from the top.

Flared: Resembles the drum shade but the bottom of the shade is slightly wider than the top, thus allowing more downward light.

Globe: Circular glass or plastic shade that may be used on any size hanging, standing, or wall lamp.

Hexagonal: A shade that is divided into six planes. It usually has a slight flare at the bottom.

Hurricane: A tall, vase-shaped glass shade.

Oval: A slightly flared shade that is elongated rather than round.

Pagoda: Reminiscent of a Chinese pagoda, this shade has flaring, dipped sides. Usually made from rayon or silk with edge trimming.

Pleated: Paper, plastic, and some stiffened fabrics may be pleated then laced near the top to hold the pleats in place. The bottom is slightly flared.

Rectangular: A broad shade with narrow ends. The sides may be straight or slightly flared.

Shell: Shade has grooves that resemble a shell.

Shield: A shade for one side of the lamp only. It fits over the light bulb to prevent glare.

Spheroid: An oval-shaped glass or plastic bowl that may have a closed or open bottom.

Square: A four equal-sided shade.

Step Cylinder: Modern-shaped metal or plastic shade for small, direct-light lamps. The larger cylinder

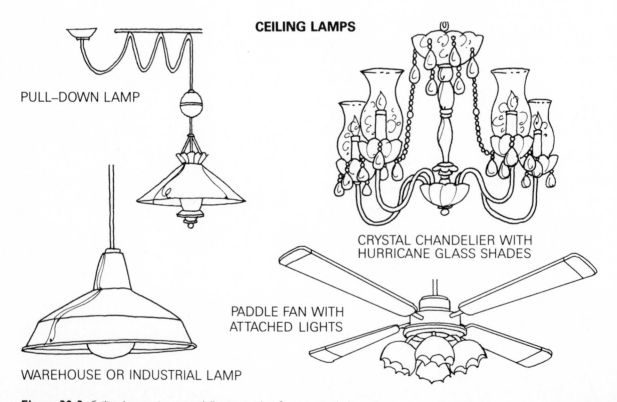

CEILING LAMPS

PULL–DOWN LAMP

CRYSTAL CHANDELIER WITH HURRICANE GLASS SHADES

PADDLE FAN WITH ATTACHED LIGHTS

WAREHOUSE OR INDUSTRIAL LAMP

Figure 30-3. *Ceiling lamps give general illumination but focus particularly on the area over which they hang.*

is attached to a smaller neck that resembles a step.

Swirl: The lamp material (usually taffeta) is twisted in a corkscrew manner around the frame to give an elaborate shape.

Tear Drop: Shaped like a drop of water; made from glass or plastic.

Tiffany: Glass in colorful shapes and designs is set into lead sections in ornate curved designs. Imitations are made from plastic.

Triangular: Metal and plastic opaque frames may be made in a triangular tent form.

TYPES OF LAMPS

Depending upon the type of decoration and the kinds of light needed, the customer has a wide selection of lamp fixtures for ceiling, wall, floor, and table use.

Ceiling Fixtures

Lamp fixtures may be hung from the ceiling or by chains. Most ceiling lamps give general illumination, but they tend to light the area over which they hang somewhat more than the other parts of the room. Popular types of ceiling lamps include the following.

Chandelier: Term for any hanging lamp that is attached to the ceiling. Chandeliers are usually rather elaborate and have many lights coming from them. They may have candlelike arms and crystal prisms that sparkle when the lights are on. Pull-down chandeliers may be adjusted for height.

Hanging Lamps: Various shaped bowls that hang from wires attached to the ceiling.

Paddle Fans with Lights: Old-fashioned paddle fans that were popular before air conditioning was available have returned to fashion. These fans may or may not have lights attached below the blades.

Swag Lights: Ceiling fixtures that are attached to a cord in a chain that is suspended from the ceiling to hold the lamp. The other end of the cord is plugged into an electric outlet.

Warehouse Lamps: Also called **industrial lamps,** these spare-looking metal pans have become fashionable for kitchens, workrooms, and dining rooms.

Wall-Mounted and Furniture-Mounted Lamps

Lamps may be affixed to walls or to individual items of furniture. Wall lights may be fixed or may have arms that extend. Such lamps give general illumination and may offer mood lighting.

Fixed Wall Lamps: Small lamps attached to the wall may have any shape shade to diffuse or direct the light.

Wall Sconces: Decorative lights that are usually used in pairs.

Furniture Clip Ons: Some lamps are made to clip onto a book or furniture. A **flex-neck clip on** lamp has a step-cylinder-shaped shade with a flexible metal attachment through which the cord is strung. This allows the shade to be tipped at any angle. A **drafting lamp** is made with clamps and metal arms with a joint that permits the lamp to swing and focus exactly as needed.

WALL–MOUNTED LAMPS

WALL SCONCES
SHOWN ON EITHER SIDE OF PICTURE

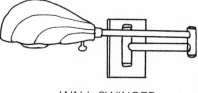

WALL SWINGER

Figure 30-4. *Wall sconces are generally mounted in pairs. The jointed arm of a wall swinger allows it to swing over a task area.*

Wall Swingers: Lamps that are attached to the wall and have jointed arms that allow them to swing out from the wall to light a task area.

Floor Lamps

Any lamp built to stand with its base on the floor is classified as a **floor lamp.** These have a base, long shaft, and a shade that may be movable and focused in an upward or downward position. Floor lamps vary in height from 48 to 70 inches. Some have adjustable heights.

Architectural: The drafting lamp may be attached to a base to stand on the floor and be positioned as needed for use.

Arc Shaped: Lamps that bend out to fit over furniture. The chrome or brass shaft swivels and turns to direct light where it is needed.

Bridge: Lamps with shafts that bend to hold a down-turned shade. The shaft may be rigid or flexible.

Downbridge: Serving the same purpose as the bridge lamp, this lamp has a separate neck attached to the shaft that holds the shade in a downward position.

Gooseneck: Lamps with shafts made of strips of metal coiled around the cord permit the shaft to be twisted and set in any direction. Many have fixed shades made from metal or plastic.

Pharmacy: Small lamps that are bent to fit over a desk or work area. They have attached shades and some have swing arms.

Rotating Shade: Lamp swivels on the upper part of the bent shaft. The opaque shade may be placed in any direction, and the entire lamp shaft may be bent to accommodate the user.

Six-Way Lamps: Three candle arm lamps with a center three-way light bulb allows six different levels of light from one lamp and gives both indirect and semidirect lighting.

Stick Lamp: Any floor lamp with a single straight thin shaft.

Swing Arm: Lamps with arms that swing out from the shaft to position the lamp for the best lighting effect.

Torchères: Tall, straight-shafted lights with upturned shades that throw light toward the ceiling or with translucent shades that allow some light to filter downward.

Tray Lamps: Stick lamps may have a glass, metal, or wooden tray about one-third the distance from the base of the lamp to hold food, ash trays and so on.

Tree Lamps: A stick lamp with branches and attached lights positioned along the shaft. May be adjusted to throw light in any direction.

Zipper Lamp: Lamp of white corrugated paper that zips together over a 60 watt bulb to give atmospheric, luminous-type light.

Table Lamps

Lamps that sit on a surface are referred to as **table lamps.** These are the most popular and versatile lamps. Sizes range from mini lamps that are $9\frac{3}{4}$ to 16 inches in height, through regular-size lamps that are up to 33 inches, to extra tall lamps that are up to 43 inches. Most use incandescent bulbs, a few use fluorescent bulbs, and some have high-intensity bulbs. Occasionally lamps are made to use old-fashioned wicks with oil reservoirs or to house candles. Designers find that almost any material may be used for the bases, shafts and shades of these lamps. The value of these lamps is determined by the quality and appearance of the shaft and shade, and ornamentation if any. Table lamps are named for their varied uses, for their base shape, for their shaft shape and for their shade shape.

Table lamps include some of the previous categories discussed and many new ones.

Architect or Drafting: Varied-sized lamps with double metal arm and a joint that permits extension or bending in several directions. An opaque shade focuses light on a specific area.

Apothecary: Metal or wooden lamp stand with metal shaft and slightly movable half-cylinder shade in metal, glass, or plastic.

Art Nouveau: A variety of lamps with straight or bent shafts that combine metal and glass in the asymmetric forms characteristic of the art nouveau decorating era.

Ball: A round, ball-shaped pot has a shaft that holds the shade.

Bean Pot: A large pot-shaped base holds a rod upward for the shade.

Boudoir or Dressing Table: Small lamps usually

FLOOR LAMPS

SIX–WAY LAMP

TREE LAMP

STICK LAMP

TORCHÈRE

DOWNBRIDGE LAMP

ARC LAMP

ZIPPER LAMP

GOOSENECK PHARMACY LAMP

Figure 30-5. *Floor lamps vary in size from 48 to 70 inches. Their shades may be movable or focused upward or downward.*

used in pairs for either side of a dressing table or vanity table. May be frilly with lace or ruffles on the shades.

Candlestick: Tall, narrow-stemmed, one-to-three stick lamps that resemble candle holders with shades attached.

Canister Shape: Tall, round holder for tea, coffee, or other condiments, made from glass, china, or plastic forms the base of the lamp. A rod through the base is used to support the shade.

Chimney: A glass globe is covered with a shade that acts as a reflector.

Cylinder: Desk-type lamp has a small cylinder of metal or plastic atop a sticklike shaft. May or may not have a flexible neck.

Desk Lamps: Most have a wooden or metal base, a rigid or flexible shaft, and a horizontal shade that bends or tilts to highlight the work area. Incandescent and fluorescent lights are used for desk lamps. Some desk lamps have rotating arms.

Egg-Shaped: An ovoid-shape shaft with a luminous translucence.

Figurine: The lamp shaft may consist of a figure of a person or an animal with superimposed shade.

Ginger Jar: The ginger jar shaft is made in metal, china, glass, or plastic, with or without decoration.

Globe: Plastic or milk-glass round globes may be fitted atop metal bases to produce a modern-appearing lamp. These give a diffused light.

Gooseneck: Metal ribbons form a flexible shaft through which the cord runs to the bulb. These gooseneck lamps may be bent in many directions for utmost service.

High-Low: The metal base on this lamp has a bolt that permits the lamp to be lowered or raised.

High Intensity: These lamps have small, special bulbs that focus light in a narrow area but that give more light, per watt, than similar regular size bulbs. The small opaque shade helps to concentrate the light.

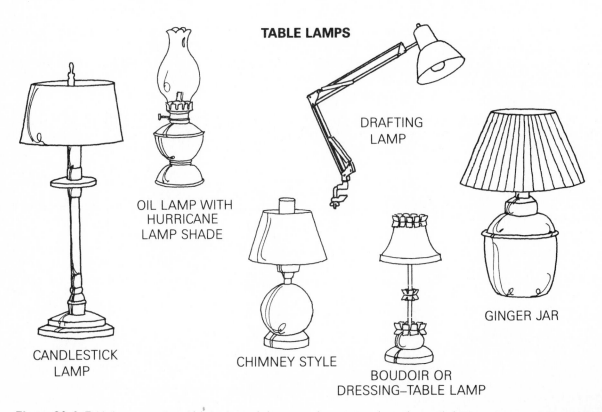

TABLE LAMPS

DRAFTING LAMP

OIL LAMP WITH HURRICANE LAMP SHADE

GINGER JAR

CANDLESTICK LAMP

CHIMNEY STYLE

BOUDOIR OR DRESSING–TABLE LAMP

Figure 30-6. *Table lamps, ranging widely in size and shape, are the most popular and versatile lamps.*

Hurricane: A glass contoured shade fits over an electric light, a candle, or an oil font to shield light.

Jug Shape: A short, squat, round shaft with or without handles. It is usually made from colorful ceramic materials. The pole extends through the jug and supports the shade.

Oil Lamps: Some still work with oil; others are electrified.

Oriental: An oriental lamp has a Chinese-appearing design. The china or metal shaft is often mounted on wood.

Pharmacy: Opaque-shaded small lamps with flexible necks are available for desks and work areas.

Piano: An elongated shade allows the entire keyboard to be lighted when this lamp is set on the piano.

Pillow Base: The hard, oblong-type pillow used by some Chinese is the inspiration for this pillow-base ceramic lamp shaft on a wooden mount.

Planter Lamps: A well where plants may be placed has a light that helps the plants to grow and casts a glow around the room.

Spice Jar: A large shaft made in the shape of a spice jar with rod that supports the shade.

Swing Arm: Lamp with an arm that swings out from the base and back in place when it is no longer needed.

Swirl: Ceramic and glass-base lamps may have a swirl design on the base that curves upward and around the neck of the lamp.

Tea Caddy: Chinese-inspired lamp shafts made from metal or ceramics with Chinese designs inscribed on them. They come in the shape of a container for tea.

Temple Jar: The shaft sits atop a wooden mount, and a Chinese design is hand painted or mechanically applied to the jar.

Temple Urn: A large lamp shaft that bulges out near the top from a narrower base.

Tilt Top: A modern-looking lamp with two shafts holds an opaque or translucent shade that tips to allow light to reach the task area.

Vienna: They use solid brass interlaced to form small checkers for light exposure. The brass is then coated with enamel to make a dramatic mood-type light.

CARE OF LAMPS

Lamps need to be cared for properly if they are to serve effectively. Lamp bases and shades may need frequent dusting. If bases are wood, they may need to have furniture polish applied peri-

odically. If the surface finishes of metal shafts and bases are removed, the metal will darken and need frequent polishing. China and glass shafts need to be washed periodically to keep them sparkling and clean. Similarly, plastic shafts need occasional washing.

Leather, mica, plastic, kappa shell, china, and glass shades may be wiped with a damp cloth to remove the surface soil. For paper parchment shades, which would be ruined with a damp cloth, wallpaper cleaner or art gum eraser used carefully will yield the best results.

Cloth-covered lamp shades may be shampooed if the bindings and edgings have been sewn to the lamp. If they have been merely glued, as is done on some inexpensive shades, the water will loosen the ornamentation and the lamp shade will lose all of its attractiveness. If the cloth-covered shade has a paper-parchment lining, it cannot be shampooed since the paper lining will buckle. If the metal lamp shade frame rusts, the lamp shade will be stained after washing unless drying is done immediately.

Cords need to be watched for any effect of wear and replaced promptly.

NOTES

1. *Home Lighting Bulb Guide*, Large Lamp Department, General Electric, n.d., p. 3.
2. Bernard Gladstone, "How to Fix Fluorescent Lights," *The New York Times*, August 3, 1978, p. C4.
3. Stacy V. Jones, "A Compact Fluorescent Lamp," *The New York Times*, October 13, 1979, p. 26.
4. "Choosing and Using Track Lighting," *Better Homes & Gardens*, October 1979, p. 54.

DO YOU KNOW YOUR MERCHANDISE?

1. Define the following terms: lumen, footcandle, incandescent light, fluorescent light.

2. Why is it difficult to translate watts into foot-candles of light?

3. Explain how daylight may be controlled. How are these terms different: general illumination, task lighting, accent lighting, and aesthetic or mood lighting.

4. Define the following terms: direct light, indirect light, direct–indirect light, semidirect light, and semi-indirect light. Tell the advantages of each.

5. How does architectural light differ from other artificial lighting?

6. Explain the following parts of a lamp: finial, harp, shaft, base.

7. What are the popularly used materials for rigid shades? For flexible shades?

8. In what ways may changeable shades be attached to lamps?

9. Explain why people may want ceiling lights, floor lamps, wall lamps, and table lamps available in one room.

10. What cautions would you give a customer about washing fabric lamp shades?

PUTTING YOUR MERCHANDISE KNOWLEDGE TO WORK

Prepare a sales presentation for the following: a fluorescent ceiling light, a drafting lamp, a torchère.

PROJECT

Visit a lamp department in a store or a lamp store. How many different kinds of lamps were on display? Did labels accompany the lamps? How much information did the labels supply? Which types of lamps were more visible in this department or store, floor lamps or table lamps? Did the lamp department or store display any ceiling or wall bracket lamps? Write a short report of your findings.

31

Floor Coverings: Beauty and Comfort Underfoot

Floor coverings can be divided into two classifications: soft-surface floor coverings, such as rugs and carpets, and hard-surface floor coverings, such as linoleum, vinyl, asphalt tile, and ceramic tile.

SOFT-SURFACE FLOOR COVERINGS

Many people cover the hard floors of their homes with various kinds of softer coverings. These softer coverings provide comfort and warmth, reduce noise, enhance the floor's beauty, and make it easier to keep the floor clean. **Rugs** are made in specific sizes and cover only a part of the floor. **Carpets** are made to be sold by the yard and to cover the entire floor. Most carpets are called **broadloom** because they are woven on looms that make carpets 4 or more yards wide. Shorter widths of carpeting can be cut in various lengths and be bound at the ends.

Fibers Used in Rugs and Carpets

Many carpets and rugs consist of a **pile front** or **face** attached to a **backing**. Some are woven flat without pile or are made of nonwoven material. The fibers chiefly used for the face of soft floor coverings are nylon, polyester, olefin, acrylic, and wool. For special purposes silk, grass, rush, cotton, sisal, jute, and even strips of paper are used.

At one time wool was the major carpet and rug fiber. However, diminishing sources of good carpet wools, resulting in high costs, and the growth of manmade fibers have led to a sharp decline in its usage. Nylon now accounts for about 80 percent of all carpet and rug fibers used in the United States, followed by polyester, olefin, and acrylic; wool is used in only 1 percent of carpet and rug fibers.

The advantages of wool carpets and rugs are their resilience, feeling of warmth, ability to take deep, rich dyes, and good resistance to abrasion. On the negative side, since wool is more scaly, it may be more difficult to keep clean and is the most expensive fiber used in machine-made rugs.

Nylon and polyester have excellent abrasion resistance and are resistant to crushing and matting. Nylon is extremely long wearing and can be dyed to bright, colorful hues. Polyester has a thick, luxurious feel and is less static prone than nylon. Acrylic resembles wool. It has fair-to-good resistance to abrasion and crushing. It is often blended with modacrylic fibers to decrease flammability. Olefin is highly resistant to mildew and fading and is used both indoors and outdoors. It has low moisture absorbency and is highly stain resistant. However, it has a low melting point and can be damaged easily, for example, by a lighted cigarette.

The material used for the back of the rug or carpet, to which the pile surface is attached, is

407

usually made of olefin or jute, or plied cotton. These fibers are strong, lightweight, and, in the case of olefin, moisture resistant.

Machine-Made Carpets and Rugs

Most carpets and rugs on the market today are made by machines. Much more emphasis is placed on the fiber content and brand name of a rug or carpet than on the type of construction. A knowledge of carpet and rug construction, however, will help the customer to make the best selection for a specific use.

Construction. There are three major methods of constructing machine-made rugs and carpets: tufting, weaving, and needle punching.

In **tufting,** a large multineedle machine inserts tufts of yarn into a prefabricated back. The needles carrying yarn are driven into the backing fabric and then are withdrawn leaving a row of loose loops of yarn on the surface. The backing fabric moves forward and the needles plunge

Figure 31-1. *A tufting machine like the one shown here can produce nine feet of 15-foot-wide broadloom in four minutes.*

back into it, leaving another row of loose loops of yarn on the surface. A heavy coating of latex is applied to the underside to hold the tufts in place. A second backing is laminated to the underside when the latex is applied, providing a better-finished product. Tufting is the fastest and most economical method of making rugs or carpets. It accounts for all but a very small percentage of the carpets made in the United States. Tufting machines can produce at least 9 feet of 15-foot wide broadloom in 4 minutes.

In **weaving,** the pile yarn is interwoven with the backing to form a fabric. The chief carpet weaves are the Wilton, Axminster, velvet, tapestry, and chenille.

In the **Wilton rug,** the wool or worsted yarns that make the pile consist of extra warp yarns. They are held securely in place by filling yarns and hooks that are manipulated by a Jacquard control. Much of the warp yarn is buried in the backing, making the Wilton rug very fine. The Wilton is made with the pile loops cut, as shown in the illustration.

In the **Axminster rug,** the pile consists of extra filling yarns. Spools of various color yarns are placed on a swinging head or arm. The ends of the yarns are inserted by means of a Jacquard control into the backing of warp and other filling yarns in a predetermined color order. The Axminster has less buried pile than the Wilton but is not as long wearing.

Machine-made rugs that look like oriental rugs in design are made on the Jacquard loom in the Wilton or Axminster weave (or a variation of them) and are called by names such as domestic orientals, American orientals, sheen-style rugs, and luster rugs. They must be clearly labeled to distinguish them from genuine oriental rugs (see Figure 31-3 on page 411).

In the **velvet rug** extra warp yarns, usually of a manmade fiber, provide the pile. There are two methods of construction. (1) In one method, the warp yarns for the filling are lifted by cutting wires that are inserted with the filling and withdrawn to cut the pile. (2) In the double-cloth method the cloth is woven with the pile warp yarns interlocking each side. A knife cuts through the double cloth to produce two fabrics with cut pile. Both are durable when closely woven and have little buried pile. If the pile is long (usually $\frac{1}{8}$ inch or longer), the rug is called **plush.**

In a **tapestry rug,** the pile consists of looped warp yarns. The colors and pattern are printed on the pile warp yarns, and the Jacquard control brings each segment of the pile to the surface at the exact point a particular color is required for the pattern.

The **chenille weave** requires two looms. One weaves a blanket, which is then cut into narrow lengthwise strips. These strips are used on the second loom as the filling pile for the rug.

In **needle punching,** a web of short staple fibers is held together by the action of barbed needles that pass through the web and entangle the fibers. This feltlike rug or carpet is usually backed with latex or a synthetic foam.

Other Machine Constructions. The carpet and rug division of Fieldcrest Mills has developed two looms that make use of construction methods other than those described above — the **Karaloc** and the **Kara-Crest.** The former combines features of the Axminster, Wilton, and velvet weaves. Needles carry colored pile yarn down into the warp where filling yarns are shot through to bind the pile into place. The Kara-Crest loom uses a fusion process of imbedding the ends of the pile yarn in each row into polyvinyl chloride spread over a jute base. The ends are cut in slices from a blanket that is first woven in the desired colored pattern. Little or no pile yarn is wasted, so the method is economical.

Design and Color. The design and texture of a rug or carpet can be created either in the construction stage by varying the colors and types of yarns used or by using a pattern attachment or in a later stage after the rug is constructed by printing the surface or carving and sculpturing it to vary the pile height. In addition, by varying

the settings on a tufting machine, a carpet can be made with both cut pile and uncut loop pile for a

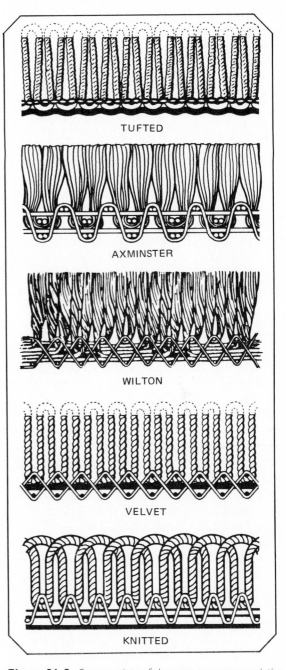

Figure 31-2. *Cross-sections of the most commmon varieties of machine-made carpets.*

wide range of design effects called **frieze.** The amount of twist and the length of the pile also affects the carpet type. For example, a frieze rug has a great deal of twist and a shag rug has extra long tufts.

Multicolor effects do not always require changing the pile yarn. Because the same dye gives different shades of color when applied to different yarns, a blend of fibers in the pile yarn can produce a heather effect in a carpet that is dyed after construction. The dyes used in modern carpets are synthetics. In carpets made by reputable manufacturers, the dyes are reasonably fast and provide spendid coloring.

In the late 1970s, new methods were developed to dye and print carpets after they were woven. One method spreads colored foam carrying dye over the surface; the foam penetrates deeply into the pile. Another method is a computer-controlled jet that transfers the pattern directly to the carpet by means of a magnetic tape.

Labeling. Federal regulations require that machine-made rugs and carpets carry labels that provide the following information: the country of origin if imported, the identifying code number or manufacturer, and the generic names of the face fibers used and the percentage of each if over 5 percent. Although not required by law, the label should also list the pattern name, color, cleaning instructions, and special treatments, such as mothproofing, soil release, and antistatic, that have been applied.

Carpets and rugs 24 square feet and over must pass a burn test. If the pile of the rug or carpet is known to have a flame-retardant finish, its label must be marked "T" to indicate that a retardant chemical has been applied. No label is required for rug fibers that are inherently flame retardant such as modacrylic. Rugs under 24 square feet that do not pass the test may be marketed but must be labeled as flammable.

Quality. The quality of a machine-made carpet may be determined by three factors: the **pile density,** the **pile height,** and the **fiber content and construction.** A tightly spaced pile is better

than a loosley spaced one. The pile height is measured from the backing to the surface of the rug. A deep pile requires more material and is thus more expensive, but this does not necessarily mean that it will outwear a densely made rug with a short pile. Yarn construction varies with the fiber used, the twist, and the number of yarns plied.

Selling Points. The quality features mentioned above are a rug's or carpet's selling points. The density and depth of the pile are easily demonstrated. The fiber or fibers used appear on the label, and each has its own features. The construction of a rug or carpet is related to price. Wilton and chenille weaves are very expensive. The Wilton weave hides much of the pile yarn, and the chenille weave may double construction costs. A good-quality tufted carpet is usually an excellent buy for the money.

Price varies with fashion, as well as quality. A type of rug that is in fashion at the moment may be in short supply and bring a higher price than a more conventional rug of higher quality. There are also fashion trends that may be important to some customers, such as wall-to-wall broadloom versus rugs that expose some of the floor. The design, color, softness of the pile, and size — all at a comparative price — are often major concerns of customers. The salesperson must discover what the customer wants in these respects and then show the appropriate carpets and rugs.

Handmade Rugs

Handmade rugs include tied, hooked, crocheted, braided, and embroidered constructions.

Construction. Rugs made on a vertical loom, on which the warp yarns are stretched vertically on the loom facing the weaver, and the yarns that form the pile are tied by hand around two warp yarns, are known as **hand-tied rugs.** Two kinds of knots used are the Senna and the Ghiordes. The pile yarns are cut with a knife by hand to the depth of pile desired. There are Chinese, Near East orientals, and Indian (Lahore) varieties of hand-tied rugs.

In **hand-hooked rugs,** the wool, cotton, or silk-rag yarns are pulled through a mesh of burlap with a metal hook. The design for the rug is drawn or printed on the burlap. The antique hooked rug may often be distinguished from the modern hooked rug by its linen backing, which generally looks rusty after some use.

Hand-crocheted rugs are made by looping strips of rags of various colors and fibers into rugs. **Hit-or-miss rugs** are made of varicolored twisted strips of rags sewed together. **Braided rugs** are made from strips that are braided before they are sewed together. Hit-or-miss rugs are generally oblong; braided rugs are usually round or oval.

Hand-embroidered rugs have a backing of woven or felted material covered in patterns and figures.

Oriental Rugs

Rugs woven by hand in the Near East, India, and China are known as **oriental rugs.** Most oriental rugs have a hand-tied pile, usually of wool but sometimes of silk. Some oriental rugs are made in a flat tapestry weave, called **kilims.**

Rugs from the Near East are usually classified according to the country or region of origin. **Persian** or **Iranian rugs** come from Iran; **Turkish rugs,** which include the **Anatolia rugs,** come from Asia Minor; **Pakistan rugs** come from Pakistan; **Caucasian rugs** come from the Caucasus Mountains area in the U.S.S.R.; **Turkoman rugs** come from the Turkmen, Uzbek, and Kazakh regions of the U.S.S.R.; and **Rumanian rugs** come from Rumania.

The rugs from these regions are further classified by the names of the towns and villages in which they are made. Each town or village has a certain characteristic weave, design, and color that makes it easily identifiable. Generally, Persian rugs are woven in floral patterns and the other rugs in bold, geometric designs.

Antique oriental rugs (generally over 100 years old) and some semiantique oriental rugs (approximately 25 to 99 years old) are highly prized because they are rare and beautiful. These

Figure 31-3. *Power-woven rugs must be clearly labeled; this one is made of polypropylene, a durable and economical material.*

rugs of closely woven, high-quality wool or silk yarn have been dyed with natural dyes in mellow colors that never fade.

Although carefully made repairs are not objectionable in an old rug, rugs with worn spots and new fringes pasted on should be avoided. A shiny spot on a rug may indicate that a worn spot has been painted over. Rubbing with a damp tissue or a handkerchief may reveal that new dye has been applied to conceal the damage.

Selecting an Oriental Rug. The following features should be considered in selecting an oriental rug.

Place of Origin. Both the country and the district are important. Persian rugs, particularly those from the Ghum, Nain, Tabriz, and Kerman districts, are of exceptionally high quality.

Since hand-tied orientals are one-of-a-kind, the labeling rules for machine-made rugs do not apply, but the salesperson should be informed about the place of origin and the fiber content.

Fiber Content. Most oriental rugs are all wool in the pile and usually in the warp. But all wools are not equal. The softest wool is generally found in the rugs woven in certain districts in Iran. The most expensive modern rugs have an all-silk pile.

Closeness of Weave. Counting the number of knots to the square inch on the back of a rug reveals the closeness of the weave. The closer the weave, the greater the amount of hand labor and usually the greater the durability. However, the backing of closely woven rugs may give way if high-quality materials have not been used. Also, some coarsely woven rugs with a high, beautiful pile, such as Oushak rugs from Turkey, give excellent wear.

Evenness of Weave. The rug should lie flat on the floor without bumps or wrinkles. If the corners curl, a rubber strip sewn underneath will solve the problem.

Evenness of Pile Length. A deep pile does not always add to the durability of a rug. A short pile, closely woven rug of fine wool may outlast a long pile loosely woven rug.

Color. Deep, mellow colors are generally preferred. Sometimes bright new rugs are treated with a chemical to tone them down, but this weakens the fibers. If a rug has been chemically treated, the backside will be brighter than the front, or the color where there are knots will be different from the color at the surface. The design should be distinct, with no running or bleeding colors and with clear, untinted white areas.

Design. An intricate design of flowers, plants, and animals artfully arranged requires more labor than one with large areas of one color without figures.

Purchasing Oriental Rugs. Oriental rugs may be purchased in leading department stores, in shops that specialize in them, or in some auction houses that are open to dealers and customers. On a square-foot basis of comparison, hand-tied oriental rugs sell for many times the price of the best-quality broadlooms and of the domestic oriental rugs woven on the Jacquard loom.

Care and Cleaning of Carpets and Rugs

Rugs and carpets, on which people walk and play constantly and on which heavy furniture rests, take more punishment than any other decorative article in the home. Therefore, the salesperson and customer should be aware of some simple procedures that will prolong the life and beauty of carpets and rugs.

Rug Cushions. A cushion or floor pad laid under a rug increases its wear life, improves the effectiveness of a vacuum cleaner in removing dirt from the rug, and makes it more pleasant to walk on. Rug cushions are made of hair felt, jute and hair mixtures, rubber, or polyurethane foam. A good-quality hair-felt cushion wears well and provides an adequate cushion for the carpet. Fibers in poor-quality hair-felt cushions tend to break off and powder after a while.

Rug cushions made of good-grade dense foam or sponge rubber give a luxurious feel underfoot and, if of good quality, wear well. For most oriental rugs, a thin cushion is preferred since the rug tends to bulge and even slip out of place on heavy cushions.

Vacuuming. Carpet manufacturers recommend that a vacuum cleaner be used twice a week in most rooms and daily in entrance halls and other areas of heavy traffic. Although a carpet sweeper will pick up surface lint, crumbs, and other soil, a good vacuum cleaner with a power-driven brush can clean down deep into the body of the rug. Never vacuum the fringes of an oriental rug. A shag carpet wih an extremely long pile should be combed frequently in one direction with a shag rake.

Figure 31-4. *Genuine oriental rugs are handmade on upright looms. Here, an Indian rugmaker follows instructions, attached to the warp yarns, for pattern and color.*

Cleaning. Spots or stains should be removed as soon as possible. If information on stain removal is not included on the label, the customer may contact the Carpet and Rug Institute in Dalton, Georgia, to obtain a copy of its booklet *How to Care for Your Carpet and Rugs*.

The salesperson should advise the customer that a carpet should be cleaned by a professional as soon as it becomes dull and vacuuming does not restore its bright appearance. If the carpet can be removed from the floor, it can be cleaned professionally at a plant. The salesperson should have a list of reliable cleaning plants. For wall-to-wall carpets and area rugs, hot water extraction cleaning is recommended.

Many consumers prefer to shampoo their carpets themselves because it is less expensive and often more convenient. A consumer can buy rug shampoo and can buy or rent a rug shampooer.

Virtually all modern, hand-tied oriental rugs are dyed with fast dyes from coal tar or petroleum, so they too can be successfully shampooed at home with a neutral soap and a shampooing device or scrubbing brush. Some oriental rugs that lack the soft coloring of the older rugs or that show worn spots are washed and then recolored with a dye pencil. This coloring may not be fast and should be rubbed to see if the colors run. If they do, the rug should be sent to a reliable dry cleaner.

Moth Prevention. The best way to prevent moths from getting into wool or hair rugs is to use the rug constantly. Sunlight and frequent spraying with insecticide are also helpful. If rugs are stored for the summer, they should either be dry-cleaned or shampooed before storing. Sometimes a dry cleaner will store a rug for the summer. If the rug is stored at home, a moth repellent should be scattered over it before it is put away. Because the aroma of cedar oil will kill any newly hatched moth larvae, cedar chests are satisfactory for storing rugs, provided they can be tightly closed.

Moving the Rug. If a certain spot in the rug is subject to extra wear from traffic or scuffing, turn the rug around or move it to prevent further wear at that point.

RESILIENT AND HARD-SURFACE FLOOR COVERINGS

Two types of noncarpeted surfaces are available for various rooms in homes — resilient coverings and hard-surface coverings. Resilient coverings have a slight give, whereas hard-surface coverings are rigid. Both types of coverings offer attractive, efficient, economical surfaces for many areas in the home, office, or public building. They are colorful, easy-to-care-for, smooth or textured surfaces that are quickly and easily installed and give many years of wear. Resilient coverings include vinyl, which has replaced the traditional linoleum, asphalt, cork, and wood. Hard-surface coverings include cement/concrete, terrazzo, ceramic tile, and bricks.

Vinyl

Vinyl is today's most popular resilient-surface floor covering. It is available in continuous rolls or in individual tiles. Nonporous vinyl is tough, durable, resilient, skidproof, and resistant to stains and mildew. Flames, however, will melt vinyl. Vinyl is available in three thicknesses: thin (about $\frac{1}{16}$ inch), average (about $\frac{1}{10}$ inch), and heavy (about $\frac{1}{5}$ inch).

Vinyl floor coverings may be bonded to vinyl foam for soft, comfortable footing and backed with asbestos for fire resistance and to help them lie flat on slightly uneven floors. The asbestos used in this way is fused into the vinyl and is in no way harmful to health.

Vinyls are made with either a dull or a shiny finish. The shiny finishes need no waxing. The dull surfaces may be made to shine with wax coatings. Vinyl surfaces may be smooth or embossed. The embossed surfaces offer more traction underfoot.

Vinyl floorings may be cut easily with shears to fit corners or around pipes. Floor tiles (usually 12 by 12 inches) that have adhesive backings will adhere to any previous flooring successfully. Vinyl that comes in roll form or without adhesive backing requires special adhesives to bond it securely to the undersurface.

Vinyl can be dry mopped to take up dust. When soiled it may be mopped with soap and water. Special cleaners may be used for the no-wax surfaces, although even soap and water leaves these shining.

Asphalt Tile

An inexpensive tile for basements or concrete flooring is made from a mixture of asbestos fibers, asphalt, adhesive materials, plus coloring. Again, the asbestos is sealed into the materials and cannot be freed, so it is harmless.

These asphalt tiles are resistant to fire and hot materials, are durable, and adjust well to uneven floor surfaces. However, grease and oil soften them and must be wiped up quickly, and only waterbase waxes should be used on them for a shiny finish.

Cork

Cork, which is a porous, excellent insulating material, may be used to cover walls or as flooring. For flooring, the cork is coated with a layer of paint or of clear varnish, which helps to protect the surface from becoming crumbly.

Wood

Thin sections of hardwood (teak and oak are the commonly used woods) are available in various sizes and thicknesses ranging from $\frac{5}{16}$ to $\frac{3}{8}$ inch. They may have butt (smooth) edges or tongue and groove (see Chapter 34 for definition of these terms) edges for firmer holding power. Parquet-looking floors can be made from narrow sections of wood forming various patterns. Random planks come in a range of widths and lengths to resemble the flooring in colonial homes. Finger-block designs have 3-to-9-inch squares set with the wood grain running at right angles to each other.

These hardwood floors come in dry-back or self-adhesive tiles. A special glue is needed to attach the dry-back tiles to the floor underneath. Wooden floors wear well and may be kept attractive looking by occasional cleaning and waxing.

Cement (Concrete)

Occasionally, low-cost concrete or cement floors are desirable in some area of a home. **Concrete** is made from **Portland cement,** water, and an **aggregate** such as sand or gravel. When poured onto a base, this mass hardens and forms an enduring floor surface that is fireproof, waterproof, and break resistant. The flooring may have color added with special paints or may be waxed.

Terrazzo

Terrazzo is composed of marble chips and coloring materials mixed with cement. It is laid over a concrete base with separations of brass strips that form a design throughout the floor. These brass strips increase the strength of the floor and act as conductors of static electricity. This is a particularly durable flooring that is not subject to harm by lighted cigarettes or matches and is impervious to effects by water and most chemicals. However, strong chemicals should be washed up if they fall onto this flooring. Terrazzo is cleaned with soap and water and may be waxed with antislip, waterproof wax.

Ceramic Tiles

Small glazed or unglazed porcelain sections, known as **tiles,** are placed side by side and cemented into place. These may be used on a floor, to make part of the wall, or to form stairs or other decorative features in a home. Ceramic tiles are waterproof when properly joined. The tiles come in squares, diamonds, hexagons, or other shapes and may be white, colored, or combined in a variety of patterns. They are very enduring but may crack if heavy, sharp articles drop on them. The only care they need is to be washed with soap and water when soiled.

Bricks

Fire clay, shaped into brick form, baked in an oven, and held together by **mortar** (a mixture of sand or ground limestone with cement) may be used as flooring. Brick floors are waterproof and fireproof.

DO YOU KNOW YOUR MERCHANDISE?

1. Distinguish between a rug and a carpet. What are the chief fibers used in soft-surface floor coverings?
2. What are the constructions suitable for making rugs by machine? What factors determine the quality of a machine-made rug? What are the most important selling points of a rug?
3. Name the various methods of constructing rugs by hand. How are oriental rugs classified?
4. What are the considerations in choosing an oriental rug?
5. What are the methods of caring for carpets and rugs in regard to vacuuming, cleaning, and protecting against moths?
6. Why do people choose resilient or hard-surface floorings in place of carpets or rugs for some areas?

7. Describe three common patterns of wood flooring.
8. Explain the differences between resilient floor coverings and hard-surface floor coverings. Which would you recommend for the kitchen, children's play rooms, bathroom, hallway?
9. Explain the basic differences between vinyl and asphalt tile; cement and ceramic tile; cork and wood flooring materials.
10. How would you recommend a customer clean a hard-surface floor?

PUTTING YOUR MERCHANDISE KNOWLEDGE TO WORK

Suggest appropriate floor coverings for the following uses: a living room with handsome hardwood parquet flooring; a kitchen in a boarding house where the owner prepares two meals daily for boarders; an entry hall in a modern apartment house where the owner wants quiet, comfort, and ease of care.

PROJECT

Visit a store in your community noted for its domestic and oriental rugs. Examine the oriental rugs and describe five of them in terms of color and design, closeness and evenness of weave, evenness in pile length, and place of origin.

Determine the price per square yard of the store's best broadloom carpeting and the prices per square foot of a fine domestic oriental rug and a fine hand-tied oriental rug. Determine the sizes of the two oriental rugs (in feet and inches). Then calculate the prices of the three rugs on a square foot basis and explain the differences in price.

32

Paints and Wall Coverings:
Background Drama
in the Home

The colors and patterns used on ceilings, walls, floors, and built-in furniture make a room bright or dark, exciting or restful, domineering or neutral as compared to other furniture and accessories. Materials that cover these spaces include paints, stains, paper, metals, wood, cork, fabric, ceramic tile, and plastics.

PAINTS, STAINS, AND ASSOCIATED PRODUCTS

Paint is a thin, opaque, protective film applied to a surface. **Stain** is a transparent coloring material used on a surface. These substances are brushed, sprayed, or dipped onto wood, paper, cement, or metal to add color. In addition, paint can protect surfaces by keeping out soil, keeping wood and paper from rotting, and preventing iron and steel from rusting and copper from turning green. Synthetic paint and stain products are now available. They have improved the ease with which these products may be applied, cared for, and cleaned up and have increased the life of the painted or stained surfaces.

Basic Materials

Opaque paints contain **pigments** (solid coloring materials; usually in powder form), which are responsible for the covering power of the paint. The more pigment used, the better the paint will

be able to mask any previous color. Most inexpensive paints require two coats to cover a surface effectively.

For white color, zinc oxide and titanium dioxide are commonly used. Since the 1950s the use of white lead has been prohibited in many states because chips of paint containing this substance, when eaten by small children, have caused lead poisoning. In 1971 interior house paints containing more than 1 percent lead were banned by the Department of Health, Education and Welfare, and in 1978 that percent was reduced to 0.06 percent.[1]

Red colors are obtained from iron oxides; yellow colors from siennas (oxides of iron and manganese) and ochres; brown from manganese; green from chromic oxide; blue from iron, cobalt, and coal-tar derivatives; and black from burned animal bones or carbon.

Oil-base paints use vegetable oils, such as linseed oil (from flax), tung oil (from seeds of a Chinese tree), soybean oil, or castor oil as **binders.** Fish oils have also been used. These oils form a hard coat when dry and help to protect the surface.

Latex-base paints use synthetic rubber, plastic (polyvinyl acetal), or acrylic (methyl methacrylate) as binders. When dry, these binders join together to form an enduring surface film. They may last as long as oil-base paints. Little drying time is needed for the latex paints.

The **thinner** in paint depends upon the binders. For oil binders, volatile liquids, such as turpentine, benzine and naphtha, and alcohol, that evaporate after the paint is applied are used. For emulsion paints (latex and acrylate types) and calcimine (essentialy chalk and glue), water is the thinning agent. With the exception of calcimine, once these paints are dry, they are unaffected by water.

Paint Primers

Primers prepare and protect the surface to be painted. They are put on after used material has been thoroughly cleaned or on new material that has never before been painted. Primers for metal surfaces **passivate** (reduce the surface tendency to rust) the metal, as well as bond the surface paint to the metal. Primers for wood seal the pores of the wood so air and water cannot get through to rot it. A layer of paint or enamel adheres to the primed surface.

Surface Finish Imparted by Paints

Paints may be smooth or textured. **Smooth paints** leave a dull-to-shiny finish, depending on the type of paint used. Smooth finishes are as follows.

Flat: Dull or matte finish with no sheen. This finish absorbs light and does not have any reflection that deters sight.
Eggshell: Slight sheen, especially when the paint is viewed from the side.
Satin: Low luster similar to the shimmer of a satin fabric.
Semigloss: Fairly lustrous shine.
High Gloss: Typical of shiny enamel paints.

Textures are achieved in paints either by running textured combs or other objects over thick paints or by adding particles of sand to the paint when it is applied. Textured paints are often used to cover disfigured walls or ceilings.

Surface Finish Imparted by Stains and Shiny Coatings

Surface coatings used particularly on wood include stains, shellac, varnish, and lacquer.

Stains. Stains are transparent materials that do not cover or protect the surface but merely change its color. The grain of wood is visible through the stain. There are water stains, oil stains, gel stains, and spirit (alcohol) stains. Water stains are usually quite resistant to fading. Oil stains accentuate ornate grains but require a covering of varnish or lacquer, necessitating a sealer coat. Gel stains are thick, do not run, have sealing qualities, and dry fast.[2] Spirit stains dry fast but penetrate only slightly and are used for touch-up work.

Stains are usually used on raw wood. The more porous the wood, the more the stain will soak into the surface and the darker it can become. When stains are applied, they should be wiped with a dry cloth shortly after application if light colors are desired. This helps to make the color uniform. Varnish, shellac, or lacquer is needed over the stain for the wood to be shiny or lustrous. A varnish stain may be applied.

Shiny Coatings. Shellac, varnish, and lacquer are available as coating finishes. **Shellac** is a durable, transparent finish once popularly used for floors and other wood surfaces. **Orange shellac** is natural in color, whereas **white shellac** has been bleached. Water, alcohol, soap, and detergents spot shellac surfaces, and shellac scratches rather easily. Shellac has never been made synthetically.

Varnish is used as a protective coating for furniture and other wood products. It is made in rich bright colors. Because varnish is thin, it is best applied to flat surfaces. **Oil varnish,** which is the best quality, uses linseed or tung oil for solvent; **spirit varnish** uses alcohol as the solvent. A **urethane varnish** can provide rich colors.

Lacquer is a fast-drying, tough, durable finish.

It is made from resins plus plasticizers for flexibility and solvents that evaporate quickly when exposed to air. Clear lacquer is often used as the final finish for furniture. Pigmented lacquers are used for metal coatings.

Types of Paints

Paints are **water based** or **oil based.** The following are types of paints that are used.

Alkyd-Lacquer Paints: Oil-based. Made from synthetic resins. Hard and tough and when silicones are added, lacquered surfaces maintain their shine permanently. Without silicones, they have a matte finish. They have excellent covering power and dry in about 1 hour. Excellent for metals; used for auto bodies.

Enamel: Smooth, shiny, hard-surfaced material made by adding a pigment to varnish and linseed oil or by the use of synthetic materials such as latex-base or polyurethane-base substances. Enamels are used for wood trim, for bathrooms, walls, kitchens and other high traffic areas. Also used for furniture. Enamels wash well and they are resistant to water stains.

Epoxy-Base Paints: Hard finish that adheres well to metals. Do not stand up well under direct sunlight. A catalyst is used to cure or dry some types of epoxy-base paint.

Latex Paints: Form an emulsion in water; that is, the pigment and binder are held in tiny droplets in water until they are spread on a surface to dry. When the water evaporates, the paint is not solvent in water and thus is waterproof. These paints are much easier to apply than traditional oil-base paints and have made painting far easier for the do-it-yourselfer. Such paints

IMPLEMENTS FOR APPLYING PAINT

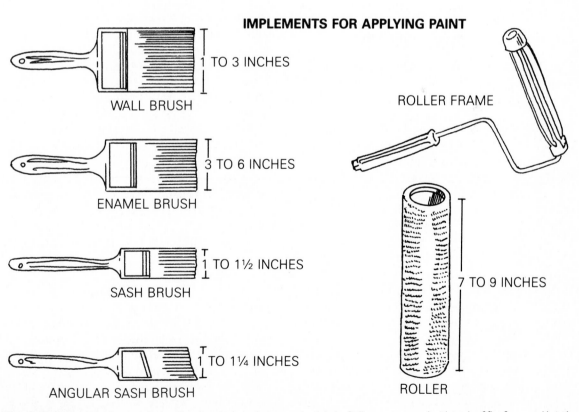

WALL BRUSH — 1 TO 3 INCHES

ENAMEL BRUSH — 3 TO 6 INCHES

SASH BRUSH — 1 TO 1½ INCHES

ANGULAR SASH BRUSH — 1 TO 1¼ INCHES

ROLLER FRAME

ROLLER — 7 TO 9 INCHES

Figure 32-1. *Paintbrushes are made of hog bristle, horsehair, or nylon bristle. Rollers are covered with pads of flat foam and bristle.*

can be applied easily without showing joining marks. They are almost odorless and dry quickly, and marks and stains may be removed with a damp cloth. The brushes and rollers used for application are cleaned simply by washing them in soap and water. When thoroughly dry, these paints have a tough, resilient finish that resists scuffs and does not separate from plaster walls or woodwork. Latex paints are available in semigloss, gloss, and matte finishes.

Luminous Paints: Made by the addition of chemicals that glow under ultraviolet light (**fluorescent paints**) or that glow in the dark (**phosphorescent paints**). Used for safety and for special effects under unusual lighting.

Metallic Paints: Use tiny flakes of the desired metal, for example, aluminum or copper, as pigment. Provide particularly protective surface coatings.

Polyurethane Paints: Come in satin, semigloss, and high-gloss enamels. They are fairly easy to apply, dry quite hard, and adhere well. They require thinners for cleanup.

Implements for Applying Paint

Several implements are available for the application of paints and lend themselves to use in different situations.

Paintbrushes. The ease of application of the paint as well as the finished appearance of the surface are affected by paintbrushes. **Hog bristles** are the traditional materials used for fine-quality natural brushes. They have elasticity and wear well. The end of each bristle is split, giving it a slightly fuzzy texture, which enables the brush to hold the paint and spread it evenly. Horsehair is also used for some natural-bristle brushes.

Nylon bristles make good brushes and are considerably less expensive than good-quality natural bristles. To give nylon bristles some of the characteristics of hog bristles, the ends are split. Nylon brushes are used with any type of paint. They are particularly good for latex paints because the fibers do not swell in contact with water, as natural bristles do. Nylon bristles last much longer and are easier to clean than natural

bristles. Oil-base paints should be applied with either natural- or nylon-bristle brushes because the solvents used in the paints may dissolve other types of bristles. Brushes should fit easily into the paint can and should be large enough to do the work with a minimum number of strokes.

The bristles of the best-quality brushes are solidly set in rubber or epoxy cement, which prevents them from shedding. The **ferrule** on a brush is the metal band that surrounds it at the base of the handle. In good-quality brushes it is made of heavy-gauge, rustproof metal securely attached to the handle. Good brushes flex easily, and the bristles are silky, soft, and springy but do not fan out excessively when pressed against a surface. Harsh, stiff brushes are less expensive and less desirable. Disposable brushes, made from polyurethane foam, may be used with oil-base, alkyd-lacquer, and latex paints.

To use a paintbrush properly, it should be dipped only to one-third of its length in the paint. To remove excess paint, tap the bristle tips lightly against the inside of the can above the surface of the liquid. If you wipe the brush across the rim of the can to remove excess paint, tiny foaming bubbles are created in the paint and these prevent getting a smooth surface. Brushes dipped into latex paint should be washed frequently to prevent hardening of the paint around the ferrule of the brush.

Brushes should be kept soft at all times. They should be thoroughly cleaned in the proper thinner immediately after use, allowed to dry, and then wrapped in paper. Never allow the bristles to dry in a bent position. If possible, hang paintbrushes to dry.

Aerosols. Aerosol paints, stains, and lacquers are packaged in airtight cans with a highly flammable propellant. In 1979, the U.S. government banned the use of aerosol with fluorocarbons as the propellant; compressed gas is now used. The contents are sprayed onto the surface. A metal ball inside the paint can acts as an agitator to mix the paint when the can is shaken.[3]

Aerosol paints leave no brush marks, get at

hard-to-reach spots, and dry fast. However, they are more expensive than paint in cans, are difficult to use, can be harmful if inhaled, and need special care to avoid open flames. Parts that are not to be painted must be masked and backgrounds should be carefully protected from overspray. Good ventilation is necessary.

Rollers and Pads. **Rollers** vary in quality and size. The come in 3-, 7-, and 9-inch widths. The best are made from a synthetic cover resembling lamb's wool. Nap lengths vary from $\frac{1}{16}$ inch to $1\frac{1}{2}$ inches. Rough surfaces require longer naps; smooth surfaces require shorter naps. When you use rollers with latex paint, the roller should be kept well covered with paint. Rollers need to be cleaned after use.

Pads are flat foam holders with a bristle facing and a handle. They vary from 5 to 9 inches in width and are useful for getting into corners.

Painting Precautions

Well-painted surfaces, for which these rules have been followed, should last from 2 to 7 years.[4]

- Check all caulking and putty inserts around windows, doors, trim areas, tubs, and sinks. If caulking is missing, water can soak in and cause swelling that later cracks the paint.
- Clean the surface with a detergent solution or paint thinner. Surfaces must be free of chalk, dust, dirt, and grease, which prevent paint from bonding securely. Sand surfaces if necessary.
- Spackle any sections that have cracks, holes or dents. **Spackle** is a premixed or powdered compound used to fill holes, cracks, and dents in walls before finishing with paint or wall coverings. A mask should be worn when mixing dry spackle and when sanding it smooth.[5]
- Remove mildew with a disinfectant that kills fungus; make sure it is thoroughly dry before painting.
- Prime any raw wood surfaces. Use paint sealer for nail and sap stains in wood.
- Stir paint thoroughly before use.

- Keep paint at the right consistency by adding thinner as needed.
- Apply even layers that are not too thick and do not drip. Do not repaint too often or paint layers will build up and cause problems.

Paint Removal

Because paint builds up over the years, it is sometimes necessary to remove the old paint. This may be done with chemicals, by scraping, or by heat.

Paint Removers: Strong chemicals that act as solvents or dissolvers of paint. These may be harmful if inhaled, so adequate ventilation is absolutely necessary. The salesperson should know that these substances are potentially dangerous, especially if not used properly.

Scrapers: Abrasives, such as sandpaper, special skins of metal with tiny punched holes that work like sandpaper, metal scrapers, rasps, and drill attachments that scratch the paint away. You may have difficulty getting into corners and around curved areas.

Heat Appliers: Blow torches may be used to remove paint, but they are an obvious fire hazard. Another heat method uses a 1,200-watt gun that delivers a blast of superheated air (480–570°F) that removes paint and varnish. The heat blisters the finish so sandpaper can scrape it off easily. Although it is very hot, it does not char the wood.[6]

Once paint has been completely removed, the surface must be coated with primers that permit coats of paint to adhere permanently.

How Paint Products Are Sold

Paint is sold in amounts varying from $\frac{1}{3}$ ounce to 5 gallons. One gallon of paint covers 400 to 450 square feet of space, or one coat on a 9-by-12-foot room. Textured surfaces use more paint than flat, even surfaces do. Enough paint should be bought at one time since different dye lots may have slightly different formulations. Some paints cover in one application; many paints require two coats.

WALL COVERINGS

For effects other than those that paint can create, various types of wall coverings are available. Also, the brick, concrete, or wood construction of some walls may offer its own attractive color and texture. The materials available for covering walls may make a room appear larger or smaller, warmer or cooler, more colorful and dramatic or more restful and relaxing. The mood of the room can be determined largely by the wall covering used.

History of Wall Coverings

Early homes used **tapestries,** large wool or silk, colorful, handmade hangings to help keep rooms cool in summer and warm in winter. By the fifteenth century, wallpaper had been introduced in Europe. Papers with a **marbleized** appearance and **flocked papers** with raised textures that resembled cut velvet were popular.[7] **Scenic papers** that made walls look like pastoral scenes were used in homes in the eighteenth century.

By 1739 the first wallpaper factory in the United States had been established in Philadelphia. All papers were hand painted or printed from wooden blocks in sections. These sections were pasted end to end to make continuous rolls. One hundred years later, inventions made possible the continuous roll printing of wallpapers in several colors. This is the process in use today. Continuous rolls are easier to hang and match and are less expensive than other wallpapers. With the advent of improved inks and plastic finishes, wallpapers have become washable. The newest development is wallpaper that can be removed from the walls easily when a change of pattern is desired.

Papermaking for Wallpaper

Paper is made from cellulose, the main substance in wood, cotton, and linen. Most paper is made from wood, which is cut up into chips that are then converted to wood pulp, either mechanically or chemically. Mechanical pulp, known as

groundwood, is made by grinding the wood into slivers. These contain impurities other than the cellulose, discolor the paper, and make it become brittle quickly. Wallpaper from this paper will not stand up for a long time. **Chemical pulp** is made by adding solutions that dissolve all the impurities, leaving the pure cellulose. Bleaching the mechanical or chemical fibers makes them a white or off-white color. They are then mixed with water and other substances that will aid color retention and strength. This slurry (mixture) is beaten to aid the fiber-to-fiber bonding necessary to convert it into paper. The slurry is then poured onto a moving wire-screen belt. The water drains through the mesh of the screen and the remaining cellulose fibers are matted to form paper. This is then smoothed and rolled onto large cylinders ready for subsequent coloring, decorating, and finishing.

Some papers are made colorfast to light and washing. Splashes of water or occasional wiping with a damp cloth will not damage the paper's surface. The weight of the paper is also a clue to quality. Generally, the lighter the weight, the poorer the quality. The weight is given on the basis of a single roll. Thus, 9-ounce paper would be lighter and thinner than 12-ounce paper.

Finishing Wall Coverings

Smooth finishes may be applied by rolling the papers through steel rollers under pressure. Textured or bumpy surfaces may be embossed with engraved rollers. Flocked textures, which resemble pile fabrics, are made by gluing shredded fibers in stencil-design formation on paper.

Vinyl and acrylic coatings, which make papers shiny or offer special protection, may be rolled on with special spreaders or laminated as sheets of vinyl film to paper or fabric backing. Adhesive backs, by which wallpaper is made ready to hang in the home by simple wetting, may be applied by special spreaders.

Printing the wallpaper with casein paints provides an endless array of designs. Each added color requires a separate operation with a roller.

Table 32–1 MEASUREMENTS FOR SINGLE STANDARD ROLLS
Number of Single Rolls Needed

Distance around room (feet)	8-foot walls	9-foot walls	10-foot walls	Ceiling
36	9	10	11	3
40	10	11	13	4
44	11	12	14	4
48	12	14	15	5
52	13	15	16	6
56	14	16	17	6
60	15	17	19	7
64	16	18	20	8
68	17	19	21	9
72	18	21	22	10

As many as 12 different colors may be printed on the paper.

Engraved designs may be applied by specially prepared copper rollers using printing inks (instead of casein paints) on paper. Because these printing inks may be superimposed over each other, many colors may be obtained with the use of just a few rollers.

Brocades, damasks, velvets, and other fabrics may be pasted onto paper backs to make exotic, costly wallpaper. Gold-leaf and other metallic finishes may be applied by hand to wallpapers. Hand-painted wallpapers in scenic designs and large murals are created by artisans. **Silk-screen printing,** a hand-operated method of stenciling a design onto grounded paper, is used when introducing a design or when only a limited quantity of wallpaper is to be produced.

Selling Wall Coverings

Although wall coverings are priced by the single roll, they come in double and triple rolls. The single roll covers about 30 square feet. Coverage also depends on pattern repeat and other features. The length of the roll depends on the width of the paper. Widths range from 20 to 28 inches.

Imported Euro-rolls contain approximately $27\frac{1}{2}$ square feet of wall covering. These are packed and sold in double Euro-rolls. A double roll measures 11 yards by 20 inches and contains approximately 55 square feet. The user should plan on approximately 25 usable square feet per single roll for estimating purposes.

Two ways of estimating the number of rolls of wall covering needed are used. (1) Multiply the length (in feet) of all the walls to be covered by the height (in feet) of the room and divide that number by the number of square feet in a roll to get the number of single rolls needed. One-half roll may be deducted for every opening (windows, doors, fireplaces, archways). Add one additional roll to ensure adequate coverage. (2) Use a measuring chart such as Table 32–1 (for standard rolls) or Table 32–2 (for Euro-rolls).

Hanging Wall Coverings

Walls must be properly prepared before you apply wall coverings. The walls must be smooth and **size,** a substance used to fill the pores of

Table 32–2 MEASUREMENTS FOR SINGLE EURO-ROLLS
Number of Single Euro-Rolls Needed

Distance around room (feet)	8-foot walls	9-foot walls	10-foot walls	Ceiling
36	12	14	16	4
40	14	16	18	6
44	16	16	20	6
48	16	20	20	8
52	18	20	22	8
56	20	22	24	8
60	20	24	28	10
64	22	24	28	10
68	24	26	28	12
72	24	28	30	14

surfaces, must be applied to prepare the walls to grip the wall covering. If the wall coverings have a **selvage,** it must be cut off. With both edges trimmed, a **butt joint** is formed when the two edges of the wall covering are brought together on the wall. The length of the covering needed for hanging should be measured, and an additional 8 inches allowed for exact fit and matching Each strip of covering should be matched to the adjacent ones as they are cut.

Many coverings are **prepasted** with the paste that is ready to be softened with water. For coverings that are not prepasted, proper wall covering adhesive must be used.

The paste is applied to the covering, and the covering is then applied to the wall. The first piece applied to a wall should be hung with the aid of a plumb line to make sure it is straight. (A **plumb line** is a weight on the end of a string that can be used to establish a true vertical line.) The covering is hung from the top line and smoothed with a brush or a cloth from the top to the bottom. If creases appear, the covering can be pulled gently from the wall and resmoothed. This operation is repeated, making sure that each strip fits snugly against the adjacent one without overlapping. Coverings must be fitted carefully around wall fixtures.

Borders, narrow strips of specially designed wall coverings to match the sections used on the walls, may be used as trim. **Railroading,** the placement of wall covering in a horizontal rather than vertical position, is done to achieve special effects. **Wall murals** are available in select wall coverings and in vinyl-coated papers. Murals come in different sizes, but are usually 13 feet 8 inches wide by 8 feet 6 inches high. They are precut into easily handled lengths and may be trimmed to fit smaller wall sections.

Figure 32-2. *Hanging wallpaper: (1) Dropping a plumb line determines the vertical position of the first strip. (2) After wallpaper has been matched and measured (3), adhesive is applied to the back with a paint roller. (4) Finally, wallpaper is positioned against the wall, leaving trim allowance, and is smoothed with a brush.*

this purpose. If there are only small marks or finger smudges to be cleaned, these may be gently erased with a gum eraser. Grease spots may be removed with regular dry-cleaning solvents, or a warm iron may be placed over a white blotter covering the spot. Washable wall coverings may be washed with mild soap or detergents and rinsed clean.

Care of Wall Coverings

Wallpapers that are affected by water are best cleaned by puttylike cleaners specially made for

Other Wall Coverings

Vinyl has become the most commonly used material for wall coverings. It is described as paper-backed, fabric-backed, or as vinyl-coated paper or fabric, depending on how the vinyl is adhered to the backing. A vinyl-acrylic substance may be coated over a lightweight cloth. This finish is strong and stain resistant and can be scrubbed. Vacuum-molded vinyls have three-dimensional designs to simulate brick, stone, or driftwood. They are available in panels from 18 by 24 inches to 24 by 48 inches. These coverings have pressure-sensitive adhesive backs that adhere when pressed to the wall.

Melamine-coated hardboard in panels or planks of 4 by 4 feet or 8 by 16 feet or in 16-inch square blocks may be permanently affixed to the wall. Wood-grain, glossy, dull, solid, marbleized, or tilelike designs are made. Polystyrene wall tiles that resemble ceramic tiles are available for bathrooms, kitchens, and laundry rooms. Heavy-gauge, 27 inches wide, vinyl is also available. It is made in a wide range of textures and colors.

Polyurethane foam may be used to make grottolike effects for hall, bath, play, or game rooms. The foam is sprayed over the wall areas to give a thick, uneven, curved form simulating the walls of a cave.

Wallpaper and Plastic Wall Coverings with Matching Fabrics

Wall coverings and matching fabrics are available. Draperies, slipcovers, bedcovers, and upholstery can be matched to the wall covering. Designs for such matched groupings are usually small and colorful.

Bricklike or Stonelike Wall Coverings

A mixture of acrylic plastic and **gypsum,** a chalklike mineral, is used for stonelike surfaces for fireplace walls. It comes in various-sized pieces to be fitted together. This material simulates the color and texture of real stone. Only its thickness (about $\frac{5}{16}$ inch thick) is different from

handling stone. It is much lighter in weight than stone.

Gypsum and fiberglass are combined to make brick look-alikes. These come in bricklike colors and pieces that are $2\frac{1}{4}$ by $7\frac{3}{4}$ by $\frac{5}{16}$ inch thick. **Cement** mixed with water can be made into blocks that look like real brick. They are $\frac{3}{8}$ inch thick. These brick-look sections may be used on walls, as the base of furniture, or on floors.

Metals

Stainless steel and aluminum in textured, relief (raised), or plain designs make costly, durable wall surfaces. For kitchen, bathroom, and elevator walls, metals may be coated with porcelain enamel for lasting beauty and economical care.

Woods

Solid-wood panels may be used for walls. Knotty pine, walnut, birch, maple, and imported woods, such as mahogany, have been used to panel entire walls or the bottom portion of walls in dens, libraries, kitchens, dining rooms, and living rooms. More commonly, veneers in thicknesses of $\frac{1}{200}$ inch or more may be backed with fabric and glued to walls to make handsome matched wood-grain surfaces. Occasional oiling is necessary to keep the wood in good condition.

Cork

Cork is thick, lightweight, and elastic. It has a porous texture that provides insulation from sound and permits nails, pins, or other sharp instruments to be imbedded in it. Cork is brown but may be painted to have a colorful, textured apearance.

Ceramic Tiles

Ceramic tiles make permanent, easily cleaned bathroom, kitchen, hallway, and den wall cover-

WALLPAPER

METAL

WOOD PANELS

CORK

CERAMIC TILE

FABRIC

Figure 32–3. *Besides wallpaper (A), one can use metal (B), wood panels (C), cork (D), ceramic tiles (E), and fabric (F) to create attractive and easy-care wall coverings that may be coordinated with other furnishings and designs.*

ings. They may be used as ornamental decoration around mantels and in dining rooms. Shiny or dull glazed tile is available in a wide range of colors, sizes, and shapes. These tiles are placed on the wall with a special cementlike adhesive that holds the tiles well. Extremes of temperature may cause the glaze to crack in time, and hitting the tiles with sharp metal objects may cause them to break; otherwise, ceramic tiles are easy to care for.

Fabrics

Fabric may be affixed to walls either by backing it with paper or by making the fabric itself stiff enough to stay smooth while it is being affixed to the wall. Fabrics may be plain or textured, rich or coarse, colorful or drab. Unless special finishes have been applied to the surface of the fabrics to make them easy to clean, they require more care than do plastics, wallpapers, tile, or metals. **Grasscloth** is made from Japanese native grasses that are hand woven and glued onto a paper backing.

Hanging Nonpaper Wall Coverings

Each substance differs in its requirements for installation. Manufacturers usually provide detailed directions for preparing the wall before affixing the surface material and in the type of adhesive to use. Many of these products come with their own adhesive. Manufacturers' instructions should be followed exactly. For expensive wallcoverings, experienced installers should be used.

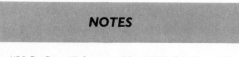

NOTES

1. "U.S. Sets February 23, 1978 for Lead Content Curb," *The Wall Street Journal*, September 2, 1977, p. 15.
2. "Interior Wood Stains," *Consumer Reports*, February 1983, p. 93.
3. "Aerosol Paints," *Consumer Reports*, September 1982, pp. 462–465.
4. Bernard Gladstone, "Home Improvement," *The New York Times*, April 1, 1982, p. C4.
5. "Spackling Compounds," *Consumer Reports*, May 1979, pp. 308–309.
6. Bernard Gladstone, "Home Improvement," *The New York Times*, November 25, 1982, p. C4.
7. Nancy McClelland, *Historic Wall-Papers*, J.B. Lippincott, Philadelphia, 1924.

DO YOU KNOW YOUR MERCHANDISE?

1. Differentiate among paint, stain, varnish, enamel, and shellac.
2. Explain the differences between latex-base and oil-base paints.
3. What are the characteristics of good brushes? Which kinds of brushes give the longest wear? What precautions should be followed for brushes for painting?
4. What are the advantages of continuous rolls of wallpapers?
5. What are the uses of plastics for wall coverings?
6. How is wallpaper priced? How is it sold?
7. How many standard rolls of wallpaper should a customer purchase for the walls of a room that is 12 feet long by 9 feet wide by 10 feet high with two windows and two doors?
8. How is wood used for wall covering? How is it kept in good condition?
9. What are the advantages of cork for use on walls?
10. What are the advantages of ceramic tiles? What precautions would you give a customer about their use?

What would you tell a customer who has asked you to explain the differences between oil-base and water-base paints? Between stains and shellacs?

Visit a store that carries wall coverings. Make a chart comparing the types of wall coverings carried. Consider textures, colors, and price ranges among the features available.

33

Curtains, Draperies, and Upholstery

Homefurnishings should harmonize with each other and with the other items in a room. They should also suit the purpose of the room. The salesperson and customer should consider textiles fabrics for windows, floors, and walls, as well as nontextiles such as blinds, furniture, lamps, and pictures.

CURTAINS

For purposes of homefurnishing, a distinction is commonly made between window curtains and draperies. **Window curtains** are sheets of lightweight, open-weave material hung on the inside of the windows. They prevent passers-by from seeing through the windows, disperse bright light from without, focus the occupants' attention indoors, and give windows a finished effect.

Draperies are heavier, decorative hangings in loose folds, generally with pinched pleats or gathers. They are used to decorate windows as well as to cover walls and doorways.

Types of Curtains

There are four basic categories of curtains: **glass** or **panel curtains** are hung next to the window pane or glass. They are often used in combination with draw draperies. They are made of thin, lacy fabric, such as ninon, organdy, or voile. One popular type is a **tambour curtain,** which is

made from heavily embroidered Swiss batiste, lawn, or net. Another type is the **casement curtain,** which is made of heavy lace, net, or casement cloth (often with a fringed edge) and is suitable for out-swinging windows or large picture windows.

Draw curtains often come with a pulley or draw cord for easy opening and closing. Some are made of opaque material to ensure privacy or to shut out bright light. When made of opaque fabrics, lined, and with tiebacks, they may be classified as draperies.

An elaborate type of draw curtain is the **Priscilla curtain,** which has ruffles across the top, two sides, and bottom. It has either a pull tape to draw up the sides or tiebacks. It may be hung in two panels to meet at the middle or crisscross with two separate rods. The fabric may be sheer, semisheer, or lacelike or printed to match a bedroom ensemble.

Sash curtains are made of thin fabrics and cover the lower half of the window.They are usually used in the kitchen or bathroom. Sheer curtains for French doors are fastened at the top and bottom. They are sold in panels about 60 inches wide, before shirring, and in various lengths.

Café or **tier curtains** are a kind of sash curtain in that one tier covers the lower half of the window. However, another tier covers the upper half. Café curtains come in sheer and semisheer

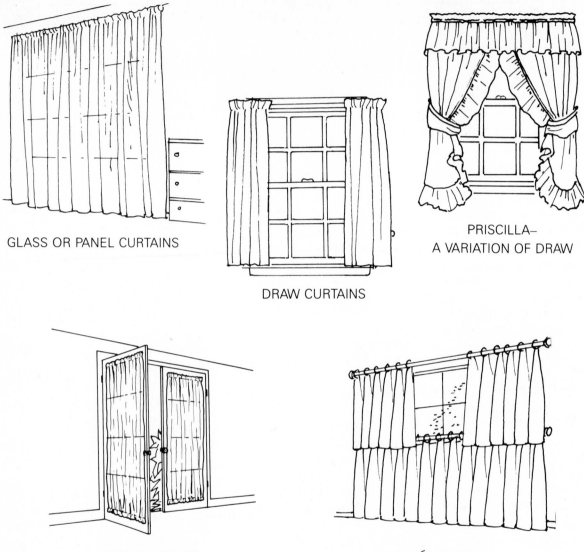

GLASS OR PANEL CURTAINS

DRAW CURTAINS

PRISCILLA—
A VARIATION OF DRAW

SASH CURTAINS

CAFÉ OR TIER

Figure 33-1. *Basic categories of window curtains, made from lightweight, open-weave material.*

fabrics, such as embroidered batiste, polyester/cotton, or rayon blends, or in heavy fabrics, such as homespun, sailcloth, or chintz.

Curtains may be used with a **valance,** which is a decorative heading of fabric across the top of the window to conceal the tops of curtains, drap-eries, or fixtures. When made of metal or wood, valances are often called **cornice boards.** Va-lances are used with sash and café curtains. When shirred, pleated, or festooned, they are used with draperies.

The two most common types of valances are

the **pinch pleated valance** in which the material is pinched every few inches 1 or 2 inches from the top, thus making pleats, and the **rod pocket valance** in which a rod is slipped through a slot at the top of the valance thereby shirring the material so that it will hang in folds.

Curtain Fibers and Fabrics

Polyester is the most popular fiber today for curtains. It is strong, durable, and unaffected by sunlight. It can be machine washed and, usually, hung right back on the window without ironing. In its untextured filament form, it is used in lace, ninon, and batiste sheer curtains. It comes in solid colors and prints. Curtains should be finished to be flame retardant.

Cotton and rayon blended with polyester or acrylic fibers are often used in curtains. Open, coarsely textured casement curtains are made by blending three or four fibers, such as acrylic, modacrylic, polyester, and rayon. Curtains are constructed by a variety of methods, including weaving, knitting, and stitch-through techniques of nonwoven goods.

Shower Curtains

There are basically two types of shower curtains — vinyl and fabric. The most popular fabric is polyester because of its washability, durability, and appearance. Cotton/polyester blends, acetates, and rayons are also used. Fabrics are usually used with a vinyl liner that keeps out the water. Some polyester curtains are treated with a water repellent, such as a solution of rubber and oil, so that a separate liner is not needed.

Shower curtains come in many designs and colors and are often coordinated with towel sets, bath mats, and toilet bowl lid and toilet tank covers.

DRAPERIES

Rich, colorful, and decorative fabrics are used in draperies today. Draperies are usually suspended from hooks on rods and have cords to pull them apart and together. Valances add to their finished look, and tiebacks of the same material are often available.

Drapery Fibers and Fabrics

A tremendous variety of fibers and fabrics are used for draperies. Cotton and blends of cotton/rayon, cotton/polyester, and rayon/polyester/acrylic are popular. A 55 percent cotton/45 percent polyester blend can be machine washed and dried and needs no ironing. This blend, which is strong and drapes well because of the polyester content, is often treated for stain resistance and permanent press. Draperies are often laminated with a foam backing or have a foam interlining to reduce the consumption of heat energy, muffle noise from without, and resist fading. Such insulated draperies may yellow and deteriorate from constant light exposure.

In the home, draperies and curtains of glass fibers and yarns have been replaced by the synthetic fibers that may have a fire-resistant finish. In public buildings, such as hotels, office buildings, and hospitals, in which the fireproof feature of glass is so important, however, curtains and other hangings of glass fibers are widely used. Fabrics of glass fiber, such as fiberglass, do not shrink, sag, or wrinkle; they are not weakened by light exposure and can be washed and dried quickly because the dirt remains on the surface.

Wool and mohair are suitable for draperies. Wool holds its shape and wrinkles hang out readily. If touched with a cigarette or lighted match, it burns slowly. It is durable and can be dyed in rich colors. Spun rayon that is made to resemble mohair has virtually replaced natural mohair. Silk can be used for formal draperies but is very expensive. Linen draperies are seldom used.

There are many types of fabrics used in draperies, including antique satin, boucle, brocade, damask, satin, and velvet.

Purchasing Draperies

A customer can buy draperies in three major forms. **Ready-made draperies** come in pairs of

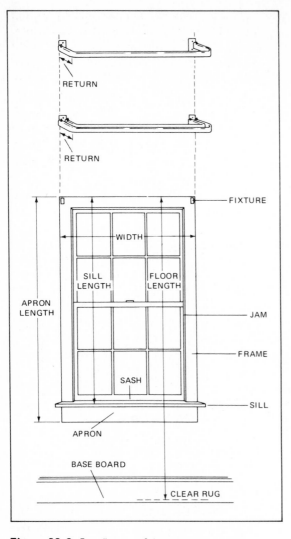

RETURN

RETURN

FIXTURE

WIDTH

SILL
LENGTH

FLOOR
LENGTH

APRON
LENGTH

JAM

FRAME

SASH

SILL

APRON

BASE BOARD

CLEAR RUG

Figure 33-2. *For all types of draperies, it is essential to take careful window measurement with a steel tape or yardstick.*

Made-to-measure draperies are made to measurements provided by the customer, who is responsible for installation. **Custom-made draperies** are usually made by hand, and measuring and installation are done by professionals. People also buy drapery material by the yard and sew their own draperies to save money.

Measuring for Draperies

Whether buying made-to-measure or custom-made draperies or buying material and making draperies, you must know how to determine the size of the draperies needed to fit the allotted space. There are four customary lengths for draperies. They are all measured from about 2 inches above the window. They may go to the sill, below the apron, to the baseboard to clear wires and heating units, or to about 1 inch from the floor. When figuring out the width of the fabric, the weight must also be considered for proper drapability. For lightweight fabrics, width of fabric should be about 3 times the width of the space to be covered; including the return of the rod (Figure 32–2). For medium-weight fabrics, $2\frac{1}{2}$ times the width of the space to be covered is adequate. For heavyweight fabrics, 2 times the width of the space is needed. Allow 12 inches more in width for overlap. If the material has a repeat pattern (a full repetition of the pattern), allow extra fabric in both width and length in order to match the pieces of material. If the repeat is less frequent, extra material may be required.

Care of Draperies and Curtains

Drapery fabrics should be preshrunk to assure that they will not shrink more than 2 or 3 percent in use. They should also be colorfast to both sunlight and atmospheric exposure. The salesperson should remind the customer to save the label and follow the instructions for cleaning.

In general, acetate curtains and rayon brocade, damask, or satin draperies are best if dry-cleaned. Most 100 percent polyesters, 100 percent cot-

panels. Each panel may be a width (about 25 inches wide each), double width, two and a half width, or triple width. Some brands come in widths of 48, 72, 96, 120, or 144 inches for each panel. Standardized lengths are 36, 45, 54, 63, 84, or 90 inches. Manufacturers are now making curtains with top hems so that adjustments in lengths must be made at the bottom rather than at the top.

tons, polyester/cotton blends, acrylics, and rayons can be machine washed; velveteen, velour, and tapestry should be dry-cleaned. Permanently glazed chintzes can be wiped like oilcloth but may lose their glazing when laundered or cleaned. Most fiberglass curtains are hand or machine washable. It is a good practice to rinse the washtub or washing machine afterward in case any loose glass fibers remain.

Linen draperies can be machine washed if the colors are fast. They will probably need pressing, which should be done while the fabric is damp. Wool or mohair-fiber draperies that have soiled spots should be cleaned immediately. If the spot has a greasy base, a dry-cleaning fluid will suffice. If not, soapy foam such as that used to clean rugs may work. When draperies need a complete cleaning, they should be sent to a dry cleaner.

Frequent brushing and vacuuming with a nozzle attachment will delay the need for com-

BLINDS AND SHADES

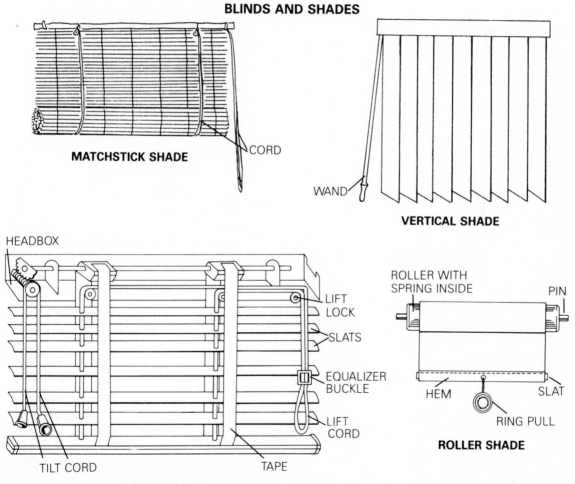

Figure 33-3. *Many people prefer roll-up shades or draw-up blinds to curtains.*

plete cleaning. Frequent cleaning and spraying with insecticides prevents moths. Before curtains and draperies are packed away, they should be thoroughly cleaned or laundered. They should be wrapped in white paper and placed in a dry place in a closet or chest. If fabrics contain wool, a spraying with insecticide or a scattering of protective crystals or mothballs will prevent moth damage.

WINDOW SHADES AND BLINDS

Instead of using curtains, many customers prefer roll-up shades or draw-up blinds. **Roller shades,** made of a stiffened opaque fabric, are controlled by a spring in the roller. When the shade is pulled down, the spring is wound tightly so that when a catch is released the shade rolls up. Shades may also be made of bamboo strips or vinyl, sometimes with contrasting horizontal yarns. **Draw-up blinds** are made of horizontal slats of steel, aluminum, or wood. They may be readily opened and closed by pulling a control cord and may be raised and lowered by means of another cord. Vertical shades may be opened or closed but not raised or lowered (see Figure 33–3).

UPHOLSTERY

The coverings for stuffed furniture and cushions that are attached (usually with nails) to the frame and sewn to the cushion are known as **upholstery** (see Chapter 34). **Slipcovers,** on the other hand, are pulled over the upholstered furniture or cushion and can be readily removed for washing or dry cleaning.

Upholstery Fibers and Fabrics

A wide variety of fabrics are available for upholstery, and a person's selection depends on the room to be furnished, the furniture style, and the life-style of the occupants. For example, if there are young children in the home, upholstery should be durable and stain resistant.

Upholstery fabrics include brocade, brocatelle, damask, frisé, rep, homespun, tweed, matelasse, cretonne, chintz, tapestry, velvet, denim, linen, and corduroy. They come in solids, plaids, stripes, floral designs, and prints. Leather, suede, and plastic-coated fabrics, such as Naugahyde, are also used.

Manmade-fiber fabrics for upholstery are usually easy to care for and therefore popular. Olefins are strong, abrasion resistant, and highly stain resistant. Nylon is abrasion resistant, strong in close weaves, and easily cleaned with soap and water or an upholstery cleaning fluid. Acrylic is a popular fiber in velvet constructions; acetate is used in satin constructions.

Cotton alone or blended with manmade fibers provides an upholstery fabric that is relatively easy to care for. There are cotton-blended chintzes and cretonnes, cotton denim and corduroy, and quilted cottons. Linen can be used satisfactorily with most furniture styles.

Because of their high price, wool and mohair are not as popular for use in the home as they once were. Since they are long wearing and resilient, however, they are still important for commercial furniture. There are many fiber blends that are popular, including nylon, cotton, and acetate; nylon and rayon; rayon and cotton; and rayon and olefin.

Many of today's upholstery fabrics come with stain-resistant finishes as a protection against spotting. In addition, spray cans of these finishes are available in stores, so the customer can apply the finish at home.

Care of Upholstery

The label is the best guide for care of upholstery. However, two general rules to keep in mind are to use a vacuum cleaner with a nozzle attachment without the brush to remove dust from upholstery and to remove stains from upholstery immediately. Soap and water can generally be used on fabrics that have been tested for colorfastness. For silk use a dry-cleaning fluid.

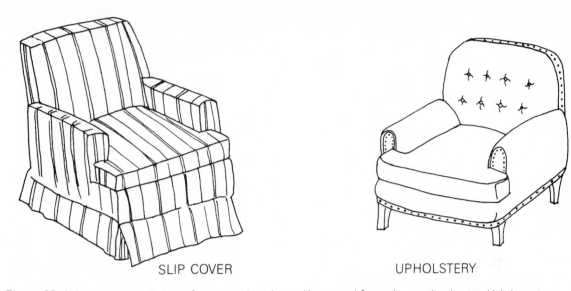

SLIP COVER   UPHOLSTERY

Figure 33-4. *Slipcovers are pulled over furniture and can be readily removed for washing or dry cleaning. Upholstery is attached to frame and cushions.*

SLIPCOVERS

Slipcovers are used to cover worn or soiled upholstery, to make upholstery more comfortable in summer and to protect it from the summer sun, and to protect fine fabrics from damage. Slipcovers may be purchased with matching draperies for a coordinated color scheme.

Types of Slipcovers

Slipcovers may be custom made for a particular sofa or chair or may be purchased ready made for a sofa or chair that is a standard style and size. Custom-made slipcovers can be purchased in a wider selection of fabrics and are more expensive than ready-made slipcovers. A knitted type of stretch cover is sold for standard styles of furniture.

An inexpensive way to cover and protect furniture is to use a **throw,** which is a knitted or woven tweedlike textured fabric, usually with a minimum-care finish. Throws are made in different sizes and can be thrown over chairs, sofas,

beds, car seats, or outdoor furniture. They can even be used as a rug for children to play or sit on.

Custom-made slipcovers should be made of good-quality fabrics. Linen or cotton crash, sailcloth, cretonne, permanent-finished chintz, bark cloth, denim, and drill are all sturdy fabrics. These fabrics are often crease resistant and shrinkage controlled and require minimum care. Luxurious-appearing fabrics and those made to resemble upholstery fabrics are often made of nubby, ribbed, slub, or tweedlike material and antique satin.

DO YOU KNOW YOUR MERCHANDISE?

1. Why is the decorative role of curtains growing in popularity?
2. Define the following terms: glass (panel) curtains, draw curtains, including Priscilla

curtains, sash curtains, and café (tier) curtains. What fabrics are suitable for each?

3. Name two fibers that are often used in curtains. Give the reasons why they are suitable for curtains.

4. How are shower curtains made to shed water?

5. Name two fibers or blends that are often used in draperies. Tell why each fiber or blend is suited for draperies.

6. In what three forms may draperies be purchased? Is it advantageous for customers to make their own draperies? Explain.

7. Differentiate between upholstery and slipcovers.

8. What are some factors about a customer's home and life-style that will affect a proper selection of upholstery?

9. Why are nylon and olefin fibers popular for upholstery?

10. What fabrics are especially suitable for slipcovers? Why?

PUTTING YOUR MERCHANDISE KNOWLEDGE TO WORK

Study the draperies and curtains in your room at school or at home, as well as in a public place such as a lounge. Decide if they are well chosen and why. In view of the information in this chapter suggest a possible better choice, giving special attention to the suitability of the fabrics chosen. Write your conclusions and the reasons for them.

PROJECT

Visit a room in a furniture store or department and make a list of all fabrics used for curtains, draperies, and upholstery. Explain the advantages, disadvantages, and proper care of each fabric in relation to the items in which it is used.

34

Furniture and Bedding: The Comfort Products

Many firms comprise the furniture industry. Many materials are used in a variety of ways by artists, designers, craftspeople, engineers, and laborers who work on the articles produced.

CLASSIFICATIONS OF FURNITURE BY TYPE

Furniture stores and departments are usually classified according to the major kinds of furniture they sell, such as occasional furniture, case goods, upholstered furniture, and bedding. More specific classifications of furniture include infants' furniture, unpainted furniture, summer furniture, and kitchen furniture.

Occasional furniture includes small furniture items such as coffee tables, magazine racks, lamp tables, small desks, and side chairs (chairs with no arms). **Case goods** primarily refer to bedroom furniture, dining room furniture, and the tables, breakfronts, and large desks used in living rooms. **Upholstered furniture,** which is furniture made with filling materials, includes couches, settees, modular units (separate sections that may be used together), club chairs, wing chairs, barrel chairs, love seats, and sofas. Most of the qualities that give upholstered furniture comfort and durability are hidden from view, so the salesperson must know the merchandise thoroughly in order to explain these qualities to the customer. **Bedding** includes mattresses and springs. Furniture

that serves as seating pieces during the day and beds at night, such as sofa beds, chair beds, day beds, and ottoman beds are also classified as bedding.

CLASSIFICATIONS OF FURNITURE BY STYLE

Customers select furniture not only by type but also by styles or periods. (These were discussed in Chapter 4.) Retailers, in addition to grouping furniture by bedroom, dining room, or living room type, group within those categories by periods and styles. Thus, large furniture stores will have one or more floors devoted to traditional styles, other sections devoted to contemporary furniture, and so on. This helps the customer make selections and helps the retail floor present an harmonious appearance.

MATERIALS USED IN FURNITURE

Wood is the traditional furniture material and continues to be the most useful for most types of furniture. The well-known hardwoods and softwoods (discussed in Chapter 16) are commonly used. In addition, redwood is often used for outdoor furniture because of its resistance to the effects of weathering. Wicker, rattan, peel, willow, fern, and bamboo, all derived from trees or bushes, are used for furniture for porches and sun rooms. However, they are not as hardy as redwood and need to be protected from the elements.

Plastics, because of their versatility, ease of use and care, and comparatively low cost, are increasingly made into small furniture items or used for coverings on furniture.

Outdoor chairs, tables, and stools may be carved from stone to make sturdy, all-weather furniture. Marble is used for table tops, end tables, lamp tables, and coffee tables.

Metals such as tubular steel, chrome- or brass-plated steel, tubular aluminum, cast iron, cast aluminum, and brass are used for casual furniture, modern chair and table bottoms, porch and garden furniture, and bedsteads.

Fiberglass, consisting of tiny fibers of glass embedded in plastic, is made into a slightly flexible material that can be molded or shaped to make lightweight, durable furniture. Paper, in the forms of ordinary cardboard, corrugated cardboard, tightly twisted strands, or Masonite (compressed wood fibers or cardboard with plastic resins), is used for the surface and for the hidden parts of furniture.

Fabrics are used in the seat and back coverings for some case goods articles and as the entire surface area of many upholstered pieces. Genuine leather or leatherlike plastics are used for upholstered furniture and seats and backs of chairs.

CASE GOODS AND OCCASIONAL FURNITURE

Although many different materials are used for case goods, wood continues to be the most-used material. It is easily worked, has the beauty of a grain pattern, is pleasant to the touch, and takes and holds attractive finishes. If damaged, it is easy to repair.

Furniture can be solid wood or veneered. The salesperson needs to know the advantages and disadvantages of each in order to advise the customer in making a selection. Most furniture today is made from a combination of plywood (veneered wood) and solid-wood (lumber) sec-

tions. For example, a desk may have large flat panels of plywood forming its top, front sections, and sides with solid-wood legs and posts. Such a piece would be labeled "veneered wood and solid wood."

Solid-Wood Furniture

Solid-wood furniture may be carved, turned, or grooved. It can be planed down if it becomes scratched or chipped and can be refinished after years of use. Very old and much-used solid-wood furniture may have the edges rounded from wear. Because it is the same piece of wood throughout, however, the appearance of the wood does not change.

A disadvantage of solid-wood furniture is its tendency to warp and crack. If the sections of the furniture are held together tightly by other pieces of wood, however, there is little chance of warping. Manufacturers often cut wood into strips $2\frac{1}{2}$ to 4 inches wide, reverse every other strip, and then glue them together. This reduces the amount any given strip may warp. Solid maple tables, chest tops, and chair seats often reveal this construction.

Veneered Furniture

A thin sheet of veneer (usually $\frac{1}{28}$ inch thick) is attached to other layers of wood or veneer to form a veneered construction. These layers are known as **plies**. Three, five, seven, or more layers of these plies are bonded at right angles to the layers above and below. This creates **cross graining**, which means that the grains of the wood pull against each other and equalize tension, reducing the possibility of warping and cracking. This is one of the strongest selling points for veneered construction. Plywood may be used for flat surfaces or may be curved by molding.

Veneer Patterns. Grain patterns in wood are meticulously put together to create attractive fronts and tops of furniture. Two apparently ordinary-looking veneers, when rearranged, often make striking symmetrical designs. Chapter 16 explains methods of veneer matching.

Plastic Veneers. For furniture that must withstand hard use, a sheet of thermosetting plastic, sometimes with a wood-like grain imprinted on its surface, is used for the top of the veneered panel. These plastic surfaces resist scratches, cuts, burns, alcohol, and food stains.

JOINING, DECORATING, AND FINISHING WOOD FURNITURE

After the plywood or solid-wood sections have been cut into the desired sizes and shapes, they are ready for joining, decorating, and finishing to make a completed piece of furniture. The methods used in each of these processes determine the strength and durability of the end product. A knowledge of them will benefit both the customer and the salesperson.

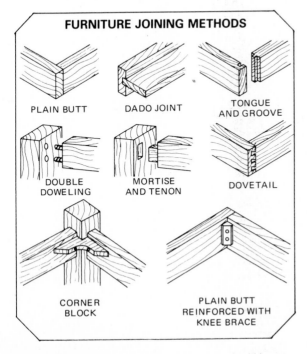

FURNITURE JOINING METHODS

PLAIN BUTT

DADO JOINT

TONGUE AND GROOVE

DOUBLE DOWELING

MORTISE AND TENON

DOVETAIL

CORNER BLOCK

PLAIN BUTT REINFORCED WITH KNEE BRACE

Figure 34-1. *Both salesperson and customer should be familiar with furniture joining methods.*

Joining

Furniture is joined using nails, screws, or glue (with or without special joints) or a combination of these. Nails are used for inexpensive furniture and for some medium-priced furniture. Screws hold pieces of wood together more securely than nails and give good support where necessary. Backs and under parts of quality furniture usually contain screws.

Almost all joints are held together by glue. Well-glued joints that will be hidden in the finished product should have the glue oozing out around the joint. Often furniture glue is stronger than the wood it bonds.

Commonly used **joints** are discussed below.

Plain Butt: One piece of wood is simply glued, nailed, or screwed to another piece of wood. It is the weakest type of joint because it does not have sufficient reinforcement and nails wiggle loose in use.

Dado Joint: There is a groove into which another piece of wood is fitted and glued. Particularly adapted for joining shelves to sides of furniture, securing drawer bottoms to sides of drawers, and holding sides of furniture to front and back panels.

Tongue and Groove: Has a rounded projection that fits into a groove of the reverse shape. Used for flooring and fitting sides of desk or bureau drawers together.

Dowel Joints: The **dowel** is a tiny peg of kiln-dried hardwood. It usually has spiral grooves cut around it that let air escape when the hole into which it is to fit is filled with glue. Dowel joints are commonly used for joining legs to the body of chairs, sofas, and tables.

Double Doweling: Use two wooden pegs spaced a short distance from each other.

Mortise and Tenon: Works on a principle similar to the dowel except that the projection (known as the tenon) is formed by cutting away the wood from one section and grooving a matching hole in the other section for an exact fit. The joint is square or rectangular. Used to hold back slats to rails on chairs and stretchers to chairlegs.

Dovetails: Triangularly shaped sections that fit together at right angles. Hold sides of drawers securely.

Reinforcements are used to strengthen furniture. Chairs may have extra blocks of wood at

Figure 34-2. *Hand-guided carving done with a spindle is an attractive method of decorating furniture.*

tool against which the wood is pressed. In **multiple-spindle carving** several spindles are attached to the main one. As one spindle is guided over a piece of wood, the others simultaneously make the same carvings on other pieces of wood that will be attached to the same or identical piece of furniture. An inexpensive imitation of carving may be obtained by molding a synthetic substance (usually styrene) and pasting it on the furniture. This pasted-on piece is known as an **applied ornament.**

Furniture legs and posts often are **turned.** The wood piece is placed on a lathe where it revolves against a moving knife blade or series of knife blades that cut out symmetrical sections, thereby shaping and rounding the leg or post.

Decoration is also done by **hand painting** or by a less expensive imitation, decalcomania, where a design painted on cellophane is glued onto the wood. When the furniture is varnished, the design is permanently affixed to the wood.

Stenciling applies color to wood or metal by painting over a cutout design. **Printed wood designs** are used on woods that have little or no natural grain. A series of inked or paint-filled rollers pass over the wood, imprinting the pattern onto it. Textured effects may be achieved with an **embossing roller,** which superimposes the design over the printed pattern on the wood.

the corners where the legs join the seat of the chair. These are known as **corner blocks** or **knee braces.** Drawers have tiny wood blocks glued at the corners and sides underneath the drawer to give added support. The **center guides** under the drawers permit the drawers to be opened and closed smoothly. Some case goods pieces may have **side guides.** Wood or metal guides for wood drawers are used. The best guides have metal runners on metal guides with ball-bearing action.

Decorating

One of the oldest and most beautiful methods of decorating furniture is by carving. A solid piece of wood may be chiseled by hand or carved by a hand-guided machine. **Hand-guided carving** is done on a **spindle,** which is a revolving cutting

Finishing

All wood furniture should be finished. Finishing makes less-expensive woods look like better-quality woods. Finishing keeps the moisture out of wood, thus helping to prevent warping. It helps to keep furniture clean by giving it a smooth, somewhat nonporous surface and protects furniture against minor scratches and scars.

If a finish changes the color but the grain of the wood is still visible, it is known as staining and is a **transparent finish.** If the finishing changes the color and covers the grain of the wood, it is an **opaque finish.** Painting with pigmented materials produces an opaque finish and may cover defects in wood.

There are many steps in finishing furniture. A typical piece might be finished as follows. First, coloring matter is applied, which is called staining. Because staining generally raises the grain, the wood is then **sanded.** For coarse-grained (oak and ash) and medium-grained woods (walnut and mahogany), a fine-sand paste known as a **filler** is next rubbed into the pores of the wood. The filler is **sealed** with a coat of shellac or lacquer, and the piece is sanded again. Then the transparent finishing coat of shellac, varnish, or lacquer is applied. Final **waxing** imparts a rich sheen to the wood. Special alcohol-resistant and fire-resistant finishes may also be applied to the furniture.

Bleaching of wood, whereby chemicals are used to remove or lighten the color, is occasionally necessary. Bleached wood tends to darken if exposed to sunlight.

Newly constructed furniture may be made to resemble antique furniture by the application of special finishes, known as **antiquing** or **distressing.** These finishes are applied after the steps outlined above. The antique appearance may be achieved by darkening the edges of the furniture, by painting small marks that resemble small

Figure 34-3. *Laminated, corrugated cardboard makes sturdy, uniquely shaped furniture with a suedelike finish.*

scratches and dents over its surface, by **specking** (spraying black paint over the entire piece in such a way as to leave small black specks all over it), by denting and scratching the furniture with the use of chains, by boring small holes that resemble worm holes, or by combinations of these methods.

Few finishing steps are used for inexpensive furniture while 18 to 21 different finishing steps give costly furniture a rich, luxurious **patina**.

Unfinished Furniture

Unfinished or unpainted wooden furniture may be purchased and then finished at home by the customer. Customers may sand and paint the furniture, or stain and varnish it, or shellac it.

PLASTIC FURNITURE

Plastics are used for furniture frames, bodies, and covering fabrics. Fillers are also made from plastics materials.

Polyurethane is a versatile plastic material that can be molded into colorful desks, chests, tables, and chairs. Polyester and polystyrene rigid plastics are used for legs and exposed frames and molded drawers with wood fronts. Wood or metal inserts that permit nails or screws to be added later can be placed in the mold and made into an integral part of the plastic form.

Chair shells of fiberglass-reinforced plastics combined with tubular metal legs make stackable, sturdy, lightweight chairs and benches. They are used in homes, schools, business, and industry.

Fire is a danger with plastic furniture, primarily because of the smoke that is emitted from many plastics when they burn. Chemicals can be used to retard burning, but smoke from smoldering plastic can still be a danger. A neoprene foam, used as cushioning in mattresses and seating has been produced that is very resistant to burning. Du Pont has made a Vonar interliner. If a flame attacks the furniture, Vonar releases a water vapor. If this does not quell the flame, chemical flame retardants are released. The material will eventually char and further protect the cushioning foam.

CARDBOARD AND FIBERBOARD FURNITURE

When **corrugated cardboard** is laminated in several layers that alternate in direction, it provides sturdy, uniquely shaped furniture with a suedelike texture. These articles absorb sound, thus reducing noise.

Recycled fiberboard made in the form of beams and tubes with a plastic surface finish is used to make tables, shelves, stools, chairs, and chair frames. These items are inexpensive and sturdy. They resist scratches, scuffs, and stains.

UPHOLSTERED FURNITURE

Upholstered furniture is available in many styles and constructions. Many stores feature upholstered furniture "in muslin," which means that the customer may select any covering material. The furniture is not actually covered in muslin but merely has a sample cover on it. The price quoted on such furniture includes the labor involved in covering it but may or may not include the cost of the fabric.

Construction of Upholstered Furniture

Quality-constructed, traditionally made upholstered furniture will give durable, comfortable service for many years. Poorly constructed furniture may sag and lump and become uncomfortable within a short period of time. The following discussion will aid the customer and salesperson in evaluating the quality of upholstered furniture.

Frame.   The best frame will be made of good-quality, kiln-dried hardwood such as as oak, birch, or maple. The use of kiln-dried hardwood prevents splitting and warping and relaxing of joints. The parts of the frame that will be seen after the furniture is finished should be of walnut, mahogany, oak, maple, or other desired wood. Sections of the frame should be reinforced with dowel or mortise and tenon joints for sturdiness.

Webbing.   The space across the seat of the

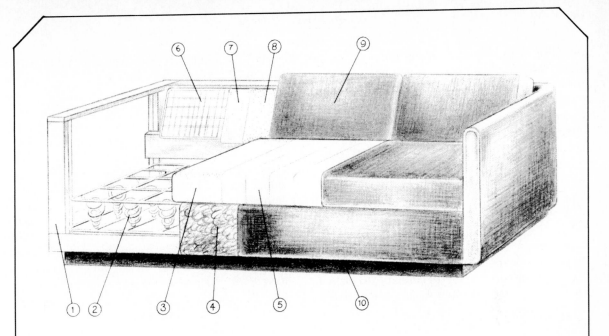

① Solid hardwood frame, double thickness at all points of stress.

② Full coil suspension on welded steel sub-frame under each seat cushion (standard model III)

③ Ultra-high resilience foam seat cushion core.

④ Hand-built resilient edge.

⑤ Sewn fiber insulator over foam core for softness.

⑥ Flex-o-lator® back spring.

⑦ Polypropylene insulator.

⑧ High density foam padding.

⑨ 100% Fortrel-7 fiberfilled back pillows sewn into strong nylon liner.

⑩ Solid oak plinth base, dowel-detailed at corners and mounted directly to frame (on model III).

Figure 34-4. *This cutaway view of an upholstered sofa shows the frame and interior padding and springs.*

furniture in the back and along the sides of the arms may have a number of different constructions. Heavy webbing material (about $2\frac{1}{2}$ to 3 inches wide) may be interlaced in a checkerboard effect and securely nailed to the frame. Heavy cotton material may be stretched across the chair bottom, back, or sides and held in place with tiny springs that keep the material taut. Steel or wooden slats are sometimes used instead of webbing or fabric. Although these are very strong, they do not always have the elasticity necessary for comfort.

Springs. Cone-shaped or barrel-shaped steel springs are secured to the webbing or the slats. In costly furniture these springs are made of thick wire (8 gauge) and are firmly interlaced. They are tied with 8 knots in high-quality and 4 knots in medium-quality constructions. The heavy cords that crisscross the coils and form these knots permit all the springs to work in unison as you sit on or lean on the furniture. Good-quality furniture uses more springs (12) in each section than does medium-quality (9) or poor-quality (6) furniture. Zigzag springs that require no tying and no interlaced webbing may be used in place of double-cone springs for lightweight but sturdy furniture. Flat bands of steel that are slightly arched offer flexibility and bounce.

Filling. Over the springs is placed a heavy burlap covering that supports the filling materials. Individual state bedding laws govern the cleanliness, sanitation, newness, and labeling of materials in this part of the furniture. Rubberized hair, cotton fibers, foam rubber, urethane foam, or polyester fibers serve as filler. The softer, more durable, and more flexible the filler, the better the quality of the finished furniture.

In good-quality furniture a muslin inner lining is placed over the filling materials to hold them securely in position. A layer of cotton batting is laid over the filling or the muslin lining as a foundation for the outer cover. It also helps to prevent filling materials from working through the outer cover. Sheets of foam rubber or polyu-rethane foam may be laid over the filling materials for added buoyancy and comfort.

Cushions. Furniture that is made with no separate cushions is said to be made of **tight seat construction.** Most upholstered furniture does have separate cushions.

The cushions may be spring filled and covered with a layer of cotton felt to make them soft and comfortable. For very soft cushions on fine-quality furniture, down and feathers may be used. **Down,** the fine covering next to the skin of ducks and geese, gives buoyance and resilience to cushions. Feathers that contain quills are mixed with the down to give body to the cushion. An excellent combination is 75 percent down and 25 percent feathers.

Foam rubber cushions keep their shape better than down, which is an important selling point for customers seeking a long-lasting neat look to their upholstered furniture. Polyurethane foam is a resilient plastic foam that is slightly less buoyant than foam rubber but is durable, holds its shape, and is noticeably lighter in weight. Polyurethane foam seat cushions are usually wrapped with a layer of a fiberfill for softness and a downlike appearance.

Polyurethane foam and foam rubber left-over sections may be shredded and used in cushions. These shredded fibers are placed in muslin inner linings to hold them in place and add comfort. They must be labeled as "shredded." Cushions may also be stuffed with acetate fibers; these lack buoyancy but help hold cushions in shape.

Some modern upholstered chairs and sofas have exposed wooden arms and legs. A foam rubber or polyurethane cushion is used on the seat.

Tufting. Tufts are used on surfaces of upholstered sofas and chairs for decoration and to hold materials securely. **Diamond tufting** is very deep, rather firm, takes great skill, and is costly. **Biscuit tufting,** a loose, block-shaped tufting, is used for modern furniture. Buttons are used on both types of tufting to hold the tufts or folds of material in shape. These buttons should be securely anchored to the background webbing so that they do not come loose.

Covering Materials. Virtually any fabric may be used to cover upholstered furniture. The tighter the weave and the stronger the yarn, the better wear the fabric will give. Fabrics that have rubber or latex backing applied will provide great tensile strength. Fabrics may have elaborate Jacquard or dobby weaves, velvet textures, or printed designs on plain or twill weave cloth. Genuine leathers and vinyl plastics and urethane, which resemble leather or fabric, are used. These materials are strong and will give many years of service if properly cared for.

All-Plastic Upholstered Furniture

There are two basic types of all-plastic upholstered furniture: **soft-type furniture** and **rigid-frame furniture.**

Soft-Type Furniture. Bean-filled vinyl furniture is made from relatively thin to heavy gauges of vinyl. The thinner types will support a moderate amount of weight adequately for a short period of use. Thick, heavy vinyl is more durable and less subject to tearing. **Bean-bag chairs** are filled with small pieces of polyester or polyvinyl. The plastic pieces shift with the weight of the person to any desired position.

Rigid-Frame Furniture. Colorful, rigid plastic frames are molded to shape and used with or without cushions, which may be attached or laid loosely against the frame. Rigid polyurethane or polyester or plastic reinforced with fiberglass may form the frame of the furniture; they may be combined with urethane foam for the back and seat sections. The shapes of such furniture are limited only by the shape of the molds.

Knock-Down Furniture

Furniture that can be shipped in flat cartons, assembled, taken apart, and reassembled is known as **knock-down** or **KD furniture.**

CARE OF CASE GOODS AND UPHOLSTERED FURNITURE

Furniture should be dusted every few days with a soft cloth that does not shed lint. Finger marks and greasy spots may be removed from wood, metal, or plastic furniture by using a soft cloth dipped in a mild soap and lukewarm water. After rubbing the area, it should be wiped with a clean, damp cloth and rubbed dry. Any moisture left on the furniture will leave marks. Water spots on wood furniture may be removed by rubbing with furniture wax or polish.

Wood furniture should be polished with a good wax polish that is rubbed in with the grain of the wood until no marks are noticeable. This gives expensive furniture a beautiful, rich luster. Such waxing should be done two or three times a year.

The special attachments on vacuum cleaners may be used to clean many pieces of upholstered furniture. These attachments should not be used on down-filled cushions, however, because the light, fluffy down might be pulled through the covering fabric by the suction. Occasional brushing keeps surface dirt from becoming embedded in the fabric covering on such cushions.

When the fabric covering on furniture is soiled, special solutions for washing upholstered furniture may be used. The salesperson should advise the customer to follow directions carefully or to have an expert do the work.

All-plastic furniture can be washed with a damp cloth. Vinyl plastic will melt in the presence of a flame, and sharp edges of metal or glass may tear it. Rigid plastics scratch easily and must be treated with care.

REGULATIONS FOR THE HOUSEHOLD FURNITURE INDUSTRY

In order to protect members of the furniture industry, the retail trade, and the public, Trade Practice Rules of the Household Furniture Industry, issued by the Federal Trade Commission, require both manufacturers and retailers to be truthful in any claims or statements made about their furniture products. In most cases labeling by hang tags is required. Any claims that are made on labels and in advertising must be accurate and must not be misleading or deceiving.

Woods. The wood used for exposed parts of furniture must be described accurately. Veneers cannot be labeled "solid wood," nor can they be described just by the accepted name of the face wood used, such as mahogany. Instead, the piece must be described as "mahogany veneer."

Nonwood Materials. Only wood materials can be labeled "wood." Hardboard, for example, which is made from wood fibers, must be called "hardboard" or "particleboard." When a surface has an imitation grain, it must be correctly labeled, such as "mahogany veneer with imitation crotch figures." Products made with plastic, metal, hardboard, or other surfaces with a wood-like finish must be accurately described, for example, "walnut-grained plastic surface."

Fillings. The materials used in upholstered or padded furniture must be accurately labeled. If other than new materials are used, this fact must be disclosed on the label. For example, a label may read, "cushions made from reused shredded foam rubber."

Geographic Origins. The place of origin of furniture must be accurate. Furniture manufac-tured in the United States, for example, may not be described as "Danish" or "Swedish modern style." Trade names must not be misleading as to the origin of the furniture. Foreign-made furniture should be identified by the country of origin. However, terms such as "French provincial" or "Chinese chippendale," because of long usage and general understanding by the public, are considered to be descriptive of the respective style rather than of the country of origin and therefore do not violate this rule.

Safety with Upholstered Furniture

In 1981, the federal Consumer Product Safety Commission reported 1,500 deaths in 39,000 upholstery furniture fires. Attempts by the commission to set mandatory fire safety standards for upholstered furniture have resulted in industry standards to protect the consumer. The Upholstered Furniture Action Council (UFAC), formed in 1977, found initially that more than 50 percent of the interior fabrics used in furniture could be ignited with a lighted cigarette. By increasing the use of fire-resistant synthetic materials and aluminum foil, heat is conducted away from the welt-cord areas where fires often begin, thus effectively reducing fire damage. Beginning in July 1983, furniture carrying the UFAC label had these safety improvements.[1]

BEDDING

Springs, mattresses, and sofa beds are known as **bedding.** Choosing the proper bedding is important to a person's sleeping comfort and general well-being.

Mattresses

A good mattress should support all parts of the body equally. It should be soft enough for the body to move normally, yet hard enough for complete relaxation. If a mattress is too hard or stiff, it will not support the small of the back; if it is too soft, it will cause muscle fatigue and lower back pain. Because comfort is a major factor in

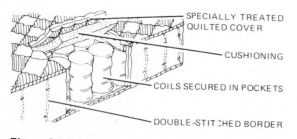

SPECIALLY TREATED QUILTED COVER

CUSHIONING

COILS SECURED IN POCKETS

DOUBLE-STITCHED BORDER

Figure 34-5. *Mattress construction: here, a cross-section of an innerspring mattress.*

selecting a mattress, the customer should lie down on it in the store before making a purchase decision.

Innerspring mattresses use springs made of tempered steel wire. These coils are usually held together by metal clips or helical wires. Some small, barrel-shaped springs are covered with fabric to assure even movement of the springs under a person's weight. Thickness of the springs, the number of springs, and the number of times each spring is coiled (5 to 7 times) determine the amount of support. An insulation layer is placed over and under the springs. This prevents the filling material from pocketing into the innerspring coil and insulates the coil from the body. Next to the insulator are filling materials, such as cotton felt or polyurethane foam, which give support and add to the comfort of the mattress. Some better-quality mattresses have quilted borders along the edges that help retain the shape.

Foam (solid) mattresses contain no innersprings and are made of thin or thick pads of foam rubber or, more commonly, polyurethane foam. Polyurethane foam mattresses are available in a regular and a newer, high-resistance urethane foam.

Air-filled mattresses are nonporous coverings that hold pumped-in air in tubelike structures. They can be quite comfortable and are easily carried when deflated. Tire pumps, vacuum cleaners, or other air pumps may be used to inflate them.

Two types of waterbeds are available. **Conventional waterbeds** have heaters that are wired to the pedestal decking or platform. A thermostat for control is on the side of the platform. The heater prevents condensation of the water and deters the formation of mildew. **Hybrid waterbeds** look like a regular mattress and foundation. They have no heater but use an insulator pad to protect the sleeper from feeling cold. Both types of beds have water mattresses that are made of strong, durable vinyl that is filled with water from a hose. The water-filled mattress is fitted into a plastic frame or safety liner that should hold

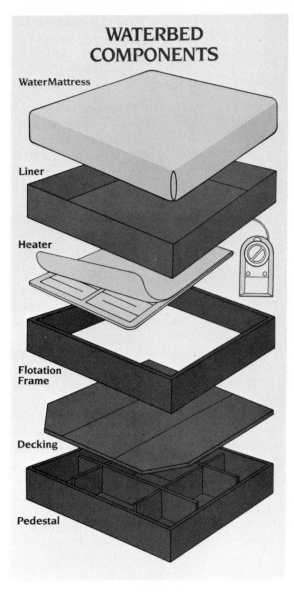

WATERBED COMPONENTS

WaterMattress

Liner

Heater

Flotation Frame

Decking

Pedestal

Figure 34-6. *A conventional waterbed has a water-filled vinyl mattress with a heater wired to the pedestal decking.*

any water that leaks out. A pedestal base supports the entire assembly. For comfortable sleeping, the water-filled mattress will exert pressure equally at all points. Most waterbeds today feature baffling systems inside the mattress to reduce the motion significantly. Special water solutions need to be used to keep the water fresh, and care must be taken not to puncture the vinyl water case.

Mattress Tickings

Both innerspring and solid mattresses are encased in fabric coverings called **tickings.** Polyester sheeting or cotton stripe tickings make good, durable cover. The outer material is quilted to a layer of filling materials. Some mattresses have tufting buttons that are attached with cords to buttons on the reverse side of the mattress. Handles on the sides facilitate turning the mattress.

Support Systems

For sleeping comfort and long life of the mattress, the support system that holds up the mattress on the bed must be carefully chosen. A **box spring** is covered in the same fabric as the mattress and is built to support the mattress correctly. The coil springs are made of resilient tempered steel and are attached with metal braces to either a wooden base or steel slats. They may be hand tied or have a steel grid with clips holding each spring to an adjacent spring to make them move in unison. The more springs used, the better the support for the mattress. In order to keep the springs from puncturing the mattress, they are covered with pads of filling material, such as cotton felt or polyurethane foam. A **foam foundation** uses a heavy built-up wood framework covered with a polyurethane foam pad. Either assemblage is encased in a ticking material, and the bottom is covered with a thin cloth tacked to the frame so that no metal is exposed.

For cots, folding cots, inexpensive sofa beds, and children's beds, **link springs,** whereby wires are interlaced in a checkerboard fashion, and **band springs,** where flat strips of metal run lengthwise and are held on the ends by helical coil springs, are the constructions used.

Mattress Sizes

Beds come in a variety of sizes, and springs and mattresses must be ordered in the correct size to fit the bed properly. Mattresses come in the following standard sizes.

- King size: 76 by 80 inches
- Queen size: 60 by 80 inches
- Full size: 53 by 75 inches
- Twin size: 39 by 75 inches

There are also a variety of special-size mattresses, including extra-long twin, full, queen, and king sizes; three-quarter size; cot size; and California King (72 by 84 inches), which is narrower and longer than a regular king size.

Care of Mattresses

Mattresses should be covered with a **pad** to keep them clean. The pads, which are made of quilted white cotton or muslin with a bonded foam rubber back, should be removed and laundered regularly. When the cover is removed for laundering, the mattress can be vacuumed to remove soil. Innerspring mattresses should be turned three or four times a year. Foam mattresses should be turned frequently from side to side and from end to end to prevent sagging in one place.

Flammability Standards for Mattresses

Flammability standards for all mattresses have existed since June 7, 1973. The government standards and tests for flammability of mattresses are established by the Consumer Product Safety Commission and are frequently revised. The customer or salesperson who desires to know the latest tests and standards may contact the Consumer Product Safety Commission, 7315 Wisconsin Avenue N.W., Washington, D.C. 20016.

Convertible Beds

Various types of upholstered furniture that convert into beds are sold. Mattresses for such convertible furniture are made in the same way as mattresses for regular beds. Their sizes, however, are modified to fit the article, and many are thinner than standard mattresses. Except for the convertible sofa, which may have a thick spring, most have flat band or zig-zag springs that lack the resilience of coiled springs. Examples of convertible beds follow.

Sofa Beds: Look like regular sofas. The back swings down and, together with the seat, forms a bed.

Convertible Sofas: Look like regular sofas with deeper bases. They hold a folded mattress that may be unfolded to make a bed. The mechanism on this should work smoothly and the mattress should be thick and comfortable.

High Risers: Contain two narrow-width mattresses, one held under the other. The lower mattress swings out and up to form one double bed or two single beds. These may have extra cushions that make them resemble sofas.

Day Beds: Cots with loose cushions that lean against a wall to form a piece of furniture that looks like a sofa. With the cushions removed, they form single beds.

Chair Beds: Large upholstered chairs with arms. They encase single-width mattresses that open, like a convertible sofa, into a single bed.

Ottoman Beds: Similar to chair beds but they have no back or arms. Can extend a chair seat for lounging comfort or convert to a single bed.

Pillows

Comfort and durability are the prime requisites in buying pillows. A twill or Jacquard ticking encases the pillow filling. The filling can be made of a variety of materials.

Down pillows are lightweight, resilient, and soft. Waterfowl feather pillows have more body and are more buoyant than down. Sometimes waterfowl feathers are combined with goose or duck down. Combinations of 80 percent down and 20 percent feathers are the best. Turkey and chicken feathers are curled artificially to make them resilient enough for fillers. They are much stiffer, heavier, and harder and consequently are seldom used in quality pillows. Crushed feathers are the poorest of these natural fillings.

Polyester fillings are nonallergenic and are not affected by insects. Foam latex and polyurethane foam cases padded with polyester fiberfill help pillows keep their shape. Foam latex fillers are resilient, mothproof, mildew proof, and nonallergenic. The density of the foam governs the pillow's softness and firmness.

Less expensive pillows may be stuffed with **kapok,** a vegetable fiber, or cotton linters, short ends of cotton fibers. However, these materials have little resilience and will become lumpy and hard in a short time.

Pillow Sizes

Pillows are made to fit different bed sizes.

- Standard size is 20 by 26 inches, for twin and double beds.
- Queen size is 20 by 30 inches; for queen-size beds.
- King size is 20 by 36 inches; for king-size beds.[2]

Pillows are also made in sizes to fit cots, cribs, and junior beds.

Care of Pillows

Pillows should be kept well aired. When feather and down pillows become soiled, they can be sent to a renovating factory where they can be resterilized. Polyester fiberfill pillows can be washed and dried quickly. If these pillows have outside fitted pillow covers that zip at one end, they may be removed and washed as often as needed. These covers protect the ticking so the rest of the pillow needs less frequent renovating or washing. Foam latex and polyurethane foam pillows are not washable.

NOTES

1. Michael de Courcy Hinds, "More Fire-Resistant Furniture," *The New York Times*, April 7, 1983, p. C13.

2. Karel Joyce Littman, "Fill, Size, Price and Other Factors in Buying Pillows," *The New York Times*, July 8, 1982, p. C10.

DO YOU KNOW YOUR MERCHANDISE?

1. What are the major classifications of furniture? Which furniture items are included in each classification?
2. Into which groups would you place the following items: chest of drawers, lamp table, coffee table, dining room set, sofa, sofa bed, dresser, innerspring mattress.
3. How are solid wood and veneered wood used in furniture construction? What are the advantages and disadvantages of each?
4. Explain the many ways plastics are used in furniture.
5. How are nails and screws used in furniture construction? Explain the various furniture joints that are used with glue. Which ones are hidden from view? Which ones may be seen by examining the furniture?
6. Why is furniture finished? Explain the differences between transparent and opaque finishes. What is meant by an antique or distressed finish?
7. Explain the differences in manufacture and in quality among the following: hand carving, spindle carving, multiple-spindle carving, and applied ornament.
8. Explain the qualities of foam rubber and of polyurethane foam for use in upholstered furniture and bedding.
9. How does a customer know what filling materials have been used in upholstered furniture?
10. Explain the following terms: waterbed, box spring, innerspring mattress.

PUTTING YOUR MERCHANDISE KNOWLEDGE TO WORK

Examine a desk, table, or chest of drawers in your home. Is the wood solid or veneered? How did you determine this? Does the surface have any decoration? If so, what type?

Make a list of the methods of reinforcing the furniture. Is the furniture solid or wobbly when in use? Do drawers slide open easily in all weather? Is the surface of the wood smooth and free from cracks? How has the furniture been joined? Have corner blocks been used for reinforcement? Write a short sales talk for the article of furniture you examined.

PROJECT

Analyze five newspaper advertisements for upholstered furniture or mattresses. Do any of the ads mention fire resistance of the product? How many tell the customer what the materials inside are? How many explain construction features? Be prepared to report to the class on your findings.

Household Linens: Bath, Bed, and Table

In the early 1800s when most textile products were imported from England, New England mills in the United States started to make sheetings and heavy cotton twill fabrics. They were called **domestics** since they were not imported. Over time, the term became limited to the textile products towels, sheets, pillow cases, blankets, comforters, bedspreads, and table coverings. These are also called **household linens**.

TOWELS

For use in the bathroom, there are bath sheets, terry or bath towels, face towels, hand or fingertip towels, and washcloths. For use in the kitchen, there are dish towels, glass and bar towels, and dishcloths.

Styles

Towels come in many patterns, including checks, stripes, plaids, tweeds, and geometrics, and in many solid colors and multicolors. Fashion designers, such as Pierre Cardin, Bill Blass, and Yves St. Laurent create novel and dramatic towel patterns. Popular cartoon characters are printed on children's towels, and monograms are embroidered onto towels. Textures vary from towels with a surface of loops on both sides to towels with a shiny surface that is sheared on one side. Towel patterns and colors may be coordinated with sheets and bedspreads.

Kitchen towels come in solid colors and prints. Designs on ceramic ware are sometimes duplicated on hand and dish towels, pot holders, and mitts.

Fabrics

Terry cloth is the most popular fabric for bathroom towels and washcloths. Terry cloth that is sheared on one side is commonly called **velour**. Terry cloth is all cotton, a rayon/cotton blend that gives a silky sheen, or 50 percent cotton, 35 percent rayon, and 15 percent polyester.

Cotton terry cloth and linen towels are often used in the kitchen. Thin towels of linen or cotton crash are commonly used for dishes. Linen and glass towelling, a fabric of smooth, hard twisted yarns, usually in the plain weave and of cotton, linen, or a mixture.

Sizes

Table 35-1 gives the sizes of towels and accessories as they appear in a large mail-order catalog.

Selling Points of Towels and Accessories

Customers want to know if a towel absorbs water quickly and easily, if it is durable, and if it is a good value. They also want to purchase towels that are attractive and that match or are coordi-

Table 35-1	
Item	**Size (Inches)**
King-size bath towel	36 by 70
Queen-size bath towel	27 by 52
Regular bath towel	24 by 44
Hand towel	16 by 26
Guest towel	11 by 18
Washcloth	12 by 12
Bath or tub mat	20 by 34
Dish towel	16 by 29
Dishcloth	12 by 12

nated with the other colors and designs in the rooms in which they will be used.

Absorbency. In pile-weave towels, such as terry cloth towels with loops on one or both sides, absorbency is determined by the number of loops per square inch. Some towels come in a honeycombed pattern in a dobby weave called **huck** or **huckaback.** They are thinner and smoother. Hand towels are often made of embroidered lightweight **crash,** a plain-weave fabric characterized by coarse, uneven yarns in linen, cotton, rayon, polyesters, or mixtures of these fibers. In the kitchen, heavy cotton, cotton terry cloth, linen, and linen/cotton crash are used for drying dishes; a lighter-weight is used for drying glasses.

Durability. The closer the weave, the more durable the towel. This is especially true in **terry towels,** in which the **ground weave** holds the loops in place. The ground weave may be determined by examining the border or the area near the hem where there are no loops. A twill weave groundwork is stronger than a basket variation. Durability is increased if polyester yarns are used in the warp.

Selvages play a role in durability. Edges should be straight, and the filling yarn should bind in the warp yarns tightly. Hems should be sewed with small, close stitches and be firmly stitched at the corners.

Attractiveness. Solid colors, colored borders, stripes, plaids, and printed patterns make towels attractive. Embroidered monograms, all-over Jacquard patterns or Jacquard borders, and hemstitching are decorations used on towels.

Value. Colored towels, colored bordered towels, or novelty towels may be more expensive than plain white towels, but this does not mean that they are better quality. Any additional decorations, such as monograms, increase the price of the towel. Usually towels with long fine loops that are sheared on one side are more expensive than unsheared towels.

Care of Towels

Most colored towels and washcloths are machine washable using a soap or detergent solution. Labels usually give instructions for the use of bleach. Pastel and high-fashion colors, such as kelly green and bright red, should be washed separately in warm water. Dark colors may be washed with similar colors. Automatic tumble drying or line drying is recommended. Towels should be removed from the dryer as soon as they are dry to avoid wrinkling. Durable-press towels, which need no ironing, should be washed using the permanent-press cycle. Terry cloth towels should never be ironed because ironing flattens the pile, thereby lessening absorbency.

BATH OR TUB MATS

Bath or tub mats or rugs are usually pile fabrics on a cotton cloth backing. For skid resistance they are sometimes backed with polyurethane foam. The pile, which may be called **shag-trimmed plush,** is often made of nylon, acrylic, or a 65 percent cotton/35 percent modacrylic blend. Nylon pile can be made to resist pilling, shedding, and matting. Wastebasket covers and toilet tank and seat covers are often made of the same fabric and in the same design as bath mats or rugs. Bath mats are machine washable in warm water and can be tumble dried. Dark colors should be washed separately.

Figure 35-1. *Kitchen linens include dish towels, glass and bar towels, and dishcloths, which are often coordinated with other accessories such as the aprons, pot holders, and mitts shown here.*

BED LINENS AND RELATED PRODUCTS

The textile articles used on a bed are sold in the linens or bedding section of a store and include mattress covers, sheets, pillowcases, blankets, comforters, quilts, and bedspreads.

Sheets and Pillowcases

Sheets and pillowcases are usually referred to as linens, which is a carryover from the past when some luxury sheets were made of linen. Today most sheets are made of cotton blends, especially with polyester. Laundry tests reveal that polyester/cotton sheets wear considerably longer than all-cotton sheets. Blends are made wrinkle free and softer by having the yarn processed in the spinning so that the cotton covers the polyester.

Blended-fabric sheets come in a wide variety of colors and patterns, which may be mixed and matched. Top sheets, bottom sheets, and pillowcases come in coordinated patterns. An all-over print top sheet can be coordinated with a solid-colored bottom sheet, and a border-printed top sheet can be matched with an all-over printed bottom sheet. Sheets also come with embroidered patterns instead of prints. Solid white sheets are still available. Most stores feature a line of sheets with popular cartoon and sports characters for children.

Pillowcases come in the same patterns and colors as sheets. Sometimes pillows are encased

Figure 35-2. *Solid colors, colored borders, stripes, Jacquard patterns, embroidered monograms, and hem-stitching make towels attractive.*

in an outer decorative case called a **pillow sham.** They are usually edged with ruffles and may be made of the same fabric as the bedspread or of a filmy organdy or lace.

Fabrics. Sheets and pillowcases are commonly classified as **percale** or **muslin.** The difference between the two fabrics is primarily the count of cloth and the carding or combing of the yarns. Percales have a count of 180 or better and muslin of 128. In general, the higher the count, the better the wearing quality. However, because of their coarser yarns, muslin sheets wear longer than percale sheets. Percales have a softer hand (feel) and are usually higher priced than muslins.

Sizes. Sheets are available in two types: flat and fitted or contour. The **flat type** is used for both top and bottom sheets; **fitted sheets** are available as bottom sheets with four contour corners and as top sheets with two contour corners.

Both flat and fitted sheets are made to fit different size mattresses. There are the four standard sizes — twin, full, queen, and king — and special-size — extralong, cot, three-quarter, and California-king size — sheets available. Special sizes are limited in the range of patterns and colors available. Pillowcases, which are sold in pairs, come in standard, queen, and king sizes.

Selling Points. Customers consider style, ease in care, size, durability, and comfort when selecting sheets and pillowcases.

Style. The salesperson should stress color and design when selling sheets and pillowcases. Some customers may be impressed by names of designers who have created special prints for sheets; some are more interested in departmental displays that show coordinated ensembles of sheets, pillowcases, bedspreads, and bathroom textiles.

Ease of Care. The no-iron or durable-press feature of many sheets and pillowcases should always be mentioned to the customer. Because most sheets are colorfast to washing, they can be machine laundered and machine dried. (Remove them promptly when the dryer stops to eliminate any wrinkling.) Another feature of no-iron sheets is that they do not wrinkle on the bed.

Although some customers complain about the stiffness and the dry, crisp hand of no-iron sheets when they are new, most consider the ease-in-care feature more important than the hand. Furthermore, no-iron sheets are softened in washing.

Soil-release finishes are applied to no-iron sheets. Oil, grease, and cosmetic stains come out during washing, eliminating the need for presoaking, cleaning fluids, or other special care.

Sheets are shrinkage controlled. The National Bureau of Standards tolerates a maximum shrinkage of only 2 percent; the Sanforized standard is 1 percent. Sheet manufacturers allow for residual shrinkage when they size sheets, so sheets of a specific size will fit the corresponding size mattress. All sizes are printed on the outside of the package.

Seconds or Irregulars. Sheets and towels that have minor imperfections in the weave or stitching are often available at reduced prices. Often the imperfections are not easy to find. This fact is an important selling point since it shows that the low price is not an indication of poor quality.

Increasing Sheet Durability.

No matter what quality of sheet is produced, the attention the customer gives it will affect its durability. Therefore, the salesperson should advise the customer to take the following steps to make sheets wear longer.

- Buy sheets in the correct size; a fitted sheet should fit properly when first used.
- Use a smooth mattress pad, especially with a tufted mattress, to reduce the wear on the sheets.
- Repair broken springs, loose nails, or projecting slivers of wood on the mattress or bed that may catch and tear the sheets.
- Mend any torn places in a sheet before it is laundered.
- Avoid strong bleaches.
- If necessary, iron the corners of pillowcases first and the hems last.
- To avoid scorching and weakening the sheets, do not use too hot an iron.
- Reverse the top and bottom sheets frequently to equalize wear, except for fitted sheets.
- When making beds, avoid forcing a fitted sheet onto the mattress.
- Rotate the household supply of sheets, if possible, so that the same sheets are never used twice in succession.

Mattress Pads

As a protection to the mattress, pads are available to place under the sheet. These are usually cotton, polyester, or a blend. They may have bands at each corner to keep them in place or cover the entire mattress.

Blankets

Blankets are bed coverings that do not have any filling. They come in winter, summer, and year-round weights, depending on the constructions and yarns used to make the blankets.

Wool fibers make the warmest blankets because of their good insulating qualities, but they are expensive, difficult to launder without shrinking and matting, and subject to damage by moths.

Acrylic fiber blankets are warm, lightweight, easy to care for, and moth resistant. Nylon and polyester blankets are also easy to care for. For summer blankets, cotton and polyester/cotton blends are used.

Nonwoven Blankets.

A recently developed process of bonding nylon fibers to a foundation of polyurethane foam, called a **flocked construction,** makes a warm yet lightweight blanket that is machine washable and dryable with a maximum shrinkage of 2 percent. Another nonwoven construction is done by punching or forcing barbed needles through a thick web of acrylic fibers. As the barbed needles are withdrawn, they entangle the fibers, forming a nonwoven fabric. This method, called the **needle-punched construction,** can produce blanket material much faster than weaving methods. Needle-punched blankets are warm and strong and shrink less and may wear longer than woven ones. They are often used as warm sheets in the winter and light blankets in the summer. They are machine washable.

Electric Blankets.

Electric blankets provide warmth from their fabric and from electric current that flows through wires embedded in the blanket. A temperature control, which you can adjust, regulates the flow of electric current through the blanket. Electric blankets for double beds may come with dual controls so that the heat in each side of the blanket can be controlled separately. When overheating occurs, safety de-

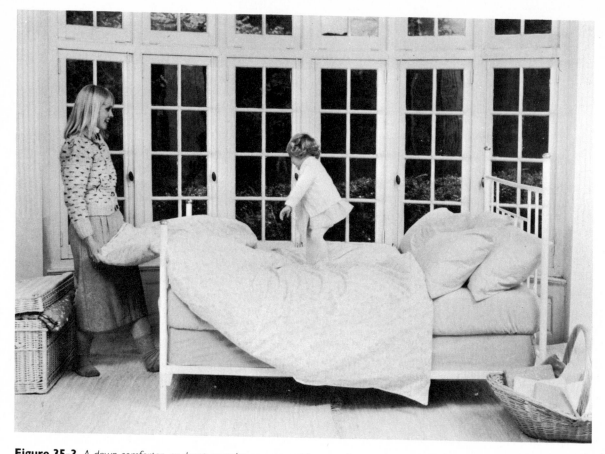

Figure 35-3. *A down comforter, or duvet, may have a removable cover that can be washed inexpensively.*

vices cut off the electric current. Customers should be sure there is an attached Underwriters' Laboratories (UL) label, which certifies that the blanket has passed certain test requirements for its electrical parts and fabric flammability.

Sizes. Blankets come in the same sizes as sheets — twin, double, queen, king, and special sizes — and are marked as such on the package. Blankets should be large enough to tuck in at the sides and foot of the bed, if desired. Some blankets come in fitted styles.

Selling Points. Blankets should have the following features.

Warmth. Blankets should provide warmth without weight.

Attractiveness. Blankets should be soft and fluffy. They are bound at top and bottom with nylon or acetate satin or taffeta. Blankets may be bought in a color and pattern that harmonize with the other colors in the bedroom.

Durability. The construction should be firm and there should be a moderately thick, strong nap. If the blanket can be lifted by its nap, the nap is strong.

Ease of Care. Many blankets are machine washable and dryable. The label should indicate if the blanket must be dry-cleaned. Bindings may need to be pressed with a warm iron.

Comforters and Quilts

Unlike blankets, comforters and quilts have stuffing. Quilts have less stuffing than comforters. They are used as a blanket that covers the bed, as a throw at the foot of the bed, or as a bedspread over a dust ruffle.

Comforters and quilts have **quilting stitches** that go through the top cover, stuffing, and backing. The stitches are decorative and functional. They make attractive designs in floral, geometric, shell, sunburst, and swirl motifs and prevent shifting and lumping of the stuffing.

The **stuffing** is commonly made of polyester fibers, although down, feathers, and other materials may be used. Sometimes the polyester-fiber filling is bonded (chemically treated) to keep the comforter extra smooth and to prevent shifting. The lightest comforters are filled with goose down.

Comforters and quilts may have solid or printed covers in cotton sateen, acetate, satin, taffeta, corduroy, or manmade fiber blends. They often come with matching pillow shams, bed ruffles, or draperies. Comforters and quilts generally come in twin, full, queen, and king sizes.

Expensive down comforters, called **duvets,** may be covered with a protective cover called a **duvet** or **comforter cover.** It is much less expensive to wash the duvet cover than to have the comforter dry-cleaned. The duvet cover can be color or design coordinated with sheets, pillow shams, and dust ruffles.

Selling Points. To help a customer decide on a comforter or quilt, a salesperson should discuss the following features.

Warmth. The stuffing should be thick enough to provide warmth. It should also be soft, lightweight, and resilient.

Attractiveness. Comforters and quilts should be attractive in color, texture, and design.

Durability. Polyester-fiber stuffing does not lump or flatten like cotton or kapok. Nylon thread for quilting is the most durable.

Ease of Care. Many quilts and comforters are made with washable covers and polyester-fiber filling and are machine washable and dryable. If they are stuffed with down, wool, or feathers or are antique patchwork quilts, they should be dry-cleaned.

Price. Down from an eider sea duck is the softest, most resilient, lightest, and most expensive stuffing. Satins and brocades are the most expensive coverings. Hand-guided machine quilting is more costly than automatic machine quilting.

Bedspreads

Bedspreads are coverings for the top, sides, and feet of the bed to make it more attractive. Bedspreads may or may not have stuffing and come in many styles.

Tufted bedspreads are made by stitching surface yarns into a backing fabric. The tufts may be cut or uncut. A **shag** is a tufted construction with very long loops; a **candlewick** has short, uncut tufts. Tufted bedspreads are made with cotton, rayon, or polyester yarns.

Chenille bedspreads are made with a caterpillarlike yarn that has a pile protruding at right angles. Plush bedspreads that look like pile are usually made of rayon that is flocked to a sturdy cotton backing. **Quilted bedspreads** have running stitches that hold the layers of fabric together and prevent shifting or stuffing. They come in two major styles. The **throw style** hangs loosely at the sides and foot or simply covers the mattress portion, with either an attached or separate dust ruffle placed between the mattress and the box spring. The **fitted style** has bell-shaped corners, inverted pleat corners, or a shirred skirt in a different material from the quilted top.

Smooth, flat bedspreads come in a variety of materials, including organdy, batiste, taffeta, seersucker, damask, matelasse, chintz, hopsacking, sateen, and tricot knit of nylon fibers. These materials may also be used in quilted bedspreads. As with other bed coverings, spreads come in sizes to fit most mattresses.

Selling Points.   The chief selling points of a bedspread are color, style, and fabric. Pile and quilted types have the extra body that many customers desire. The salesperson should stress washability or ease in cleaning, size, attractiveness, texture, and the fact that a rough or crinkled surface will not crush as readily as a smooth surface.

Sleep Covers

Beds without bedsteads may use **overlays** that reach to the floor. They are made of sturdy material, such as a cotton/polyester fabric, in solid

Figure 35-4. *Damask, a reversible Jacquard-woven fabric, can be made of linen, cotton, rayon, polyester, or a blend.*

colors, stripes, or figures. Fiber-filled (stuffed) material is also used. The standard length is 75 inches and width is 34 to 39 inches, depending on the width of the bed or the use of twin beds side by side. The height from the floor varies from 18 to 22 inches. Pillow shams of the same material, throw or tossed pillows, and floor pillows are available to cover the bed pillows.

TABLE COVERINGS

Tables are covered with cloths or place mats to protect against spills, scratches, and hot utensils and for decoration. Table coverings are frequently called "linens," even though they may be made of cotton, rayon, polyester, or blends of manmade fibers. Plastic place mats are considered textile fabrics only if they have a woven cloth or webbing as a base.

Casual Dining Cloths

For casual dining, ginghams, homespuns, dobby-woven checks, prints made to resemble crewelwork, or country plaids with hemmed or fringed edges are often used. There are also flannel-backed vinyl fabrics that can be wiped with a wet cloth. Most tablecloths and mats come with matching napkins.

Formal Dining Cloths

Linen damask, a Jacquard-woven fabric with a reversible pattern, is the most luxurious table covering; damask is also made of cotton, rayon, polyester, or blends of these fibers. Handmade crocheted lace or filet lace and embroidered linens make attractive backgrounds for china and sterling silver.

   Sizing is dressing in the form of starch. Generally, linen damasks are not sized but a little starch is put into other fabrics in finishing to give it the leathery stiffness of new linen fabrics. If two folds of a cloth are rubbed against each other and there is a noticeable change in the stiffness and body of the fabric, the cloth is oversized.

Damasks may be bleached pure white, may be slightly bleached to an oyster white, may be bleached to a deep cream color, or may be dyed in pastel shades. Damask fabric that is not fully bleached when new will wear longer than fully bleached fabric.

The current demand for frequently used tablecloths is that they be colorful, machine washable and dryable, and wrinkle free. For such purposes, polyester/cotton cloths treated for permanent press and soil release or treated texturized (surface of yarns treated by crimping and abrading) polyester cloths are satisfactory.

The largest tablecloths are called **banquet cloths;** shorter-length tablecloths are called **dinner cloths.** Napkins are sold to match tablecloths. The size of a tablecloth is determined by the shape and size of the table. The cloths are available in square, rectangular, oval, and round shapes.

Silence Cloths

It is often desirable to place a **silence cloth,** also called a **linen** or **table pad,** under a tablecloth. It deadens the noise of dishes and flatware and helps to protect the table top. Silence cloths are often made of heavy, thick cotton flannel. Sometimes the material is cut to the size of the table and attached to a stiff backing.

Care

If properly cared for, tablecloths will last a long time. Many tablecloths are durable press but damask tablecloths usually require ironing that improves the gloss. Some tablecloths have stain-repellent and soil-releasing finishes. After use, all should be washed before they are stored away.

Selling Points

In selling tablecloths, the salesperson should emphasize the suitability, fiber content, and care discussed above.

Durability depends upon the yarn count. The higher the yarn count, the more durable the fab-

ric. Hems should be evenly stitched with strong, good-quality thread in short, even, straight stitches.

COORDINATING HOUSEHOLD LINENS

Today the household linens discussed in this chapter are no longer purchased independently of one another. They have become fashion items and are coordinated from the standpoints of color, design, size, and texture. Furthermore, towels, bed coverings, and table coverings are not only coordinated with each other, but also with draperies, curtains, and floor coverings. Both the salesperson and the customer may wish to apply the principles of color and design presented in early chapters so as to create a grouping that appeals to the eye, to the sense of touch, and to the person's desire for fashion.

DO YOU KNOW YOUR MERCHANDISE?

1. What are the different kinds of towels?
2. In what sizes are towels made?
3. What materials are used for sheets and pillowcases?
4. Distinguish between muslin and percale sheets.
5. How should sheets be cared for to make them last?
6. a. What are the main fibers and constructions used in making blankets?
   b. What are the considerations in selecting an electric blanket?
7. Distinguish among blankets, comforters, quilts, and bedspreads.
8. What are the major fabrics used for bedspreads?

9. What materials and what type of table coverings are used for casual dining? For formal dining?
10. What are the selling points of tablecloths?

Make a list of all the bathroom articles of textile materials that will serve a family of four. Describe each article in terms of size, fiber, construction, color, and design. Indicate how many of each article you will require, keeping in mind washing and reserve requirements.

Make an inventory plan for a household linens department or store for the basic items in one of three major domestic lines: towels, bed coverings, or table coverings. List the types and sizes of each that should always be available. Under each type and size, list the colors you would carry (both solids and patterned). Indicate how many different qualities, as expressed in price lines, you would have in stock. Indicate whether you would carry goods of fabrics other than cotton, such as linen, manmade fibers, fabrics or blends. Indicate on your plan where the items would be stocked. Try to plan enough varieties to satisfy many different customers.

Index

461

Lotions:
  hair, 325
  skin, 319–321
Loungewear, 226–228, 245
Low-density polyethylene (LDPE), 148
Luggage, 289–292
Lumber, 179–181
Lumens of light, 392
Lunar dials, 383
Lustering process, 93
Lynx fur, 258

M

Machine-printing methods, 100–101
Mackintosh, Charles R., 68
Mackintoshes, 220
"Made on the loom" woolens, 120
Made-to-measure draperies, 432
Magnesium, 174
Magnetite, 173
Magnuson-Moss Warranty Act (1975), 11
Mahogany, 187
Maillot swimsuits, 217
Makeup products, 322–325
Mali fabrics, 92
Manganese, 174
Manmade fibers, 74, 124–138
Mantel clocks, 386–387
Maple, 187
Marmot fur, 256
Mary Janes, 266
Mascara, 323
Maternity clothes, 221
Mattresses, 446–448
Mechanical watches, 311
Melamine products, 151–152, 332, 336, 341, 425
Melanin in skin, 320
Men's apparel, 232–247, 298–301
Mercerizing process, 93
Merchandise, 1–46
  color of, 15–28
  design of, 29–46
  distribution of, 2–3
  quality of, 6–12
  types of, 47–71
  (See also specific products)
Metal plating of plastics, 145
Metal products, 169–178, 425, 426
Metallic fibers, 80, 133, 134
Metallic finishing of leather, 158
Metallizing of fabrics, 97
Metric Conversion Act (1975), 12
Metric system, 12
Microwave ovens, 371, 375
Mies van der Rohe, Ludwig, 69, 70
Mildew- and rot-repellent finishes, 98
Milled soaps, 318
Millinery, materials for, 295–297
Mineral fibers, 76

Mineral tanning, 156
Mink fur, 256–257
Mirrors, 388–391
Mission furniture, 67, 70
Mittens, 285
Modacrylic, 131, 133, 136, 327
Modified rayons, 124
Mohair fibers, 123
Moiréing process, 94
Mold-blown glass, 346
Molded heels, 269
Molded phenolics, 150–151
Molding:
  of plastics, 143
  of shoes, 271, 272
Monel metal, 175
Monochromatic color harmony, 24
Monofilament yarn, 126, 127
Monomers, 142
Moth protection, 98, 414
Motorized housewares, 378, 379
Mousquetaire gloves, 285, 286
Mouton-processed lamb fur, 259
Mufflers, 242
Multiple-spindle carving of wood, 440
Munsell, Albert H., 18
Muskrat fur, 256
Muslin garments, 252–253

N

Nail polish, 323–324
Nailing of fur, 255
Napping:
  of fabrics, 97, 105, 115, 119, 120
  of leather, 158
National Bureau of Standards (NBS), 18
National Credit Control Act (1969), 11
Natural coloring of furs, 251
Natural fibers, 74–76
Natural stones in jewelry, 302
Naturalistic designs, 30–31.
Necklaces, 309–311
Neckline styles, 215
Neckties, 242–243
Needle punching, 91, 92, 409, 455
Nephrite, 305
Neutral colors, characteristics of, 21–24
New wool, 121
Nickel, 174
Nickel plating, 368
Nickel silver, 175
Nightgowns, 193, 195, 227
Nitrocellulose, 140, 323–324
Noncellulosic fibers, 76, 77, 129–138
Nondurable goods, 12
Nontextile materials, 12, 139–190
  clay, 330–332
  furs, 248–262
  glass, 343–349
  leather, 155–168, 252, 266
  metal, 169–178, 425, 426

Nontextile materials (continued)
  plastic, 140–154, 438
  stones in jewelry, 302–307
  wood, 179–190, 415, 425, 426, 437–442, 445, 446
Nonwoven fabrics, 91–92, 105
Nourishers, skin, 319–320
Novelty yarns, 79–80
Novoloid, 132
Nutria fur, 256
Nylon products, 77, 129, 132, 146–147, 228, 327, 420
Nytril, 133–134

O

Oak, 187
Obis, 50, 292, 293
Occasional furniture, 437–439
Ocelot fur, 258
Oil-base paints, 417, 420
Oil tanning, 156
Olefin, 131, 133, 136–137
Opal, 305
Open stocks, 341, 356
Opera handles, 294
Opossum fur, 259
Optical balance, 33
Optical brighteners, 93
Orange, characteristics of, 20, 23
Ore, mineral, 169
Oriental rugs, 411–412
Ormolu mounts, 56
Ornamentation in designs, 32
Ostwald, Wilhelm, 18
Otter fur, 257
Outerwear, 203, 218–220, 236–239
Outseams of gloves, 284, 285
Outsoles of shoes, 267, 270–271
Ovens, 375
Over-the-counter (OTC) drugs, 314
Overalls, 195, 196, 235
Overglaze decorations, 336
Overlays, bed, 458
Overseams of gloves, 284, 285
Oxford cloth, 240
Oxford shoes, 276

P

Paintbrushes, 420
Painter's pants, 235
Paints, 417–421
Paisley ties, 242
Pajamas, 227, 245
Palladium, 171
Panties, 225
Pants, 212, 213, 233, 234
Pantsuits, 212
Panty girdles, 226
Pantyhose, 228–230
Parasols, 294
Parkas, 238
Particle board, 189

Pastel colors, 17
Patent finish of leather, 159
Pea jackets, 218, 219, 238
Pearls, 306–307
Peccary hogs, 162
Peltries, 249, 251
Pelts, 251
Peplums, 225
Percale, 82, 83
Perfumes, 321–322
Peridot, 305
Perkins, William, 16
Permanent-press fabrics, 96
Permanent-starchless finish, 95
Perpetual motion clocks, 383–384
Persian lamb fur, 259
Petrochemicals, fibers derived from, 129–134, 137
Petticoats, 224, 225
Pewter, 175, 362
Phenol-formaldehyde, 140, 150–151
Phenolic foam, 151
Photographic printing, 101
Phyfe, Duncan, 64–66
Picking in weaving, 84
Piece dyeing, 99, 120
Piercing of flatware, 364
Pigments, 15–17, 157, 417
Pigskins, 162
Pile in carpets, 407, 410
Pile weaves, 86,105, 119
Pillowcases, 453–454
Pillows, 449
Pin seals, 162
Pinafores, 196, 198
Pine, 189
Piqué seams of gloves, 284, 285
Place settings, 341, 356–359
Plain heels, 268, 269
Plain knitting, 88
Plain-sawed lumber, 180
Plain stitch, 88
Plain weaves, 84–85, 104, 119
Plastic-coated yarns, 80
Plastics, 140–154, 438
Plastic resin glues, 183–185
Plastic ware, 332, 336, 337, 341
Plate glass, 388
Plates of fur, 254
Platforms in shoes, 268
Plating:
  of leather, 158
  of metals, 170
Platinum, 171
Plumb Gold Act (1976), 171
Plumb lines, 424
Ply of yarn, 78
Plywood, 183, 438
Pocket square handkerchiefs, 243
Pocketbooks, (*See* Handbags)
Pointing:
  of fur, 248

Pointing: (continued)
  of gloves, 285
Poison Prevention Packaging Act (1970), 11
Polariscopes, 347
Polishing of glass, 348
Polo shirts, 240
Polyarylate, 147, 148
Polybutylene terephthalate (PBT), 147
Polycarbonate plastics, 147
Polyester products, 77, 105, 130, 132, 136, 152, 431
Polyester thermoplastics, 147–148
Polyethylene fibers, 131, 148
Polyethylene terephthalate (PET), 147, 148, 153
Polymerization, 130, 142
Polypropylene fibers, 131
Polystyrene, 148–149, 153
Polysulfone, 149
Polyurethane products, 131, 149, 153, 167, 425, 442, 444
Polyvinyl chloride (PVC), 149, 153, 266
Polyvinylidene chloride (PVDC), 150
Polyvinyls, 149–150
Pompeii (Italy) excavations, 59, 63, 64
Ponchos, 220
Pony skins, 259
Porcelain, 332
Postcuring of fabrics, 96
Powders in makeup, 322
Prang, Louis, 18
Precious metals, 171–172, 302
Precious stones, 302
Precium, 171, 172
Preheat fixtures, 394–395
Preps, clothes for, 203–204
Preschool wear, 199–200
Preshrinking of wool, 120
Pressed glass, 346–347
Pressed metals, 176
Prima, 125
Primary colors, 18
Primers, paint, 418
Printing on fabrics, 99–101
Priscilla curtains, 429, 430
Proportions in designs, 32, 33
Pugmills, 334
Pull down cutting of gloves, 284
Pulled wool, 118
Pullover pajamas, 245
Pullover sweaters, 213, 242
Pumps, 273–274
Pure colors, 19
Pure metals, 170
Pure silk, 115
Purl stitch, 88
Purses (*See* Handbags)

Q
Quadrature, 31

Quarter-cut veneers, 182
Quarter-sawed lumber, 180
Quartz, 305
Quartz watches, 312, 381
Quaternary colors, 19
Quatrefoil clovers, 53
Quilts, 457

R
Rabbit fur, 256
Raccoon fur, 259
Radial balance, 33
Radiant light, 15
Raking of wool, 119
Rapid-start fixtures, 395
Rapiers in looms, 84
Raschel warp knitting, 88
Raw silk, 115
Rawhide, 156
Rayon products, 76, 124–129
Ready-made draperies, 431–432
Real lace, 90
Receding colors, 20
Reconstituted leather, 167
Reconstituted wood, 189
Recycled wool, 121
Red, characteristics of, 20, 22
Red fox fur, 258
Redwood, 189
Reeled silk, 114, 115
Refectory tables, 55
Refiners, skin, 319
Refractive index in jewelry, 303
Regency Period, 64
Regenerated cellulose, 146
Regimental ties, 242
Regular weight suits, 234
Reinforcements in plastics, 142
Repoussé decoration, 363
Reprocessed wool, 121
Reproductions, 48
Resetting of furs, 254
Residual shrinkage, 95
Resins in plastics, 141–142
Resist dyeing, 101
Resist printing, 101
Retailers, 3
Retanned leathers, 156
Retinned ware, 368
Retting of flax, 108
Reused wool, 121
Rheostats, 395
Rhinestones, 304
Rhodium, 171
Rhythm in designs, 32, 34, 35
Rib stitch, 88
Rib variations, 84
Ribbing in sweaters, 213
Ribs of umbrellas, 294
Rigid-frame furniture, 445
Rim dishes, 338
Rings, 310